A

Philip E. Lilienthal (signature)

•   •   •

BOOK

The Philip E. Lilienthal imprint
honors special books
in commemoration of a man whose work
at the University of California Press from 1954 to 1979
was marked by dedication to young authors
and to high standards in the field of Asian Studies.
Friends, family, authors, and foundations have together
endowed the Lilienthal Fund, which enables the Press
to publish under this imprint selected books
in a way that reflects the taste and judgment
of a great and beloved editor.

D0761316

Taoist Classics

Stephen R. Bokenkamp, editor

Early Daoist Scriptures

· · · · · · · ·

Stephen R. Bokenkamp

with a contribution by Peter Nickerson

UNIVERSITY OF CALIFORNIA PRESS
Berkeley · Los Angeles · London

University of California Press
Berkeley and Los Angeles, California

University of California Press, Ltd.
London, England

© 1997 by
The Regents of the University of California

First Paperback Printing 1999

Library of Congress Cataloging-in-Publication Data

Bokenkamp, Stephen R., 1949–
    Early Daoist scriptures / Stephen R.
Bokenkamp; with a contribution by Peter
Nickerson.
        p.   cm.—(Taoist classics; 1)
    Translation of several Chinese religious texts
with extensive analysis, commentary, and
notes.
    Includes bibliographical references and
index.
    ISBN 0-520-20322-4 (alk. paper)
            0-520-21931-7 (pbk. : alk. paper)
    1. Taoism.   2. Philosophy, Taoist.
I. Nickerson, Peter.   II. Title.   III. Series.
BL 1920.B64   1997
299'.51482—dc20   96-43415
                                                CIP

Printed in the United States of America
9 8 7 6 5 4 3 2 1

The paper used in this publication meets the
minimum requirements of American National
Standard for Information Sciences—Permanence
of Paper for Printed Library Materials, ANSI
Z39.48-1984. ∞

for Lisa Berkson

Contents

Illustrations and Tables

FIGURES

TABLES

Preface

The texts translated here come from the formative years of the Daoist religion, the second through the fifth centuries C.E. During this period Daoism emerged to establish its claim as *the* religion of the Chinese people, distinguishing itself from the restricted imperial cult, the assorted practices of popular religion, and the imported religion of Buddhism. This was also a time of copious scripture production, the period during which three major scriptural traditions of Daoism—the Celestial Masters, the Shangqing (Upper Clarity), and the Lingbao (Numinous Gem)—took shape. Doctrines were codified, rituals were created, meditations and codes of practice for adherents were fashioned, and a professional priesthood with temples for communal and private worship was established.

By the time of the Tang dynasty (618–907), lines of development that began in the second century had come to fruition. Daoism was by then fully a part of Chinese life, diffused throughout the society it had helped to reunify through providing part of the ideological basis for the new regime. Tang emperors, claiming descent from Laozi himself, who had appeared in his deified form to proclaim the advent of their dynasty, were for the most part avid patrons of the religion and, early in the dynasty, gave it priority over Buddhism in their ordering of the "three teachings" (Confucianism, Daoism, and Buddhism). Scriptures were collected from throughout the kingdom and a new canon of Daoist scriptures presented to the throne. Art, literature, and philosophy all showed the vital impress of Daoist influence. Even Buddhism itself was modified by Daoist concerns, remolding itself through new schools more acceptable to Chinese concepts of spirituality, expressed most fully in Daoism.

Daoism had grown from a small sect cut off in an isolated valley to a religion with temples spread throughout the land, commanding the attention of rulers and commoners alike during one of China's most prosperous periods. This growth was a phenomenon of great consequence to the social, political, and intellectual history of China and prompts a number of questions. Since China had not before produced, and would not again produce, an indigenous religion of this scope and longevity, how did it occur in this case? Was Daoism perhaps only a native response to Buddhism? What were the sources of Daoist belief and practice, and how were these molded into what we recognize as a religion? Certainly, we cannot begin to answer such questions without a thorough analysis of the religion in all of its aspects, including particularly the written record—those texts through which Daoists at various times and from various perspectives expressed their own views on the distinctive features of their practice. This collection of translations seeks to present a portion of that written record. It is meant not as an answer to the larger questions just posed—for those are decidedly not the questions that concerned the Daoist authors we will consider—but as a contribution to our own understanding of the religion.

The impediments to our understanding are immense. None of the texts written here was composed for us—a future readership bringing wholly unpredictable cultural expectations to the task. Nor were they written even for the broader contemporary audience, that minority of the society that was more than functionally literate. The texts translated here were written for an even more select group whose predispositions and training for the task could be more accurately imagined by the writers. Much that we would like to know is taken for granted, terminology that we need explained is passed over in silence, and common words are employed in unexpected ways, while, by contrast, the authors pursue points that we might feel deserve something less than the attention lavished upon them.

Translation, stigmatized in some scholarly circles as willfully obscuring the barriers of time and culture that separate us from other worlds, is in fact one way of attempting to bridge those gaps. Translation becomes problematic only when it lulls readers with false assurances, with the glitter of glib implausibilities. One such implausibility is the notion that Chinese religious texts of the third century might be rendered into English without substantial distortion or that, once translated, even a flicker of the meaning they held for their intended audience might survive absent the kindling provided by patient explication and scholarly care. Translation, like any other work of scholarship, is really a work of interpretation. One should beware of those translators who claim to "get out of the way" so as to allow their authors to "speak for themselves," for their interpretations are hidden. The interpretations presented here will be, insofar as is humanly possible, open to view. By bearing constantly in mind that this work pretends to be no more than a work of interpretive scholarship, aiming to make available aspects of early Daoism as it was understood by those who participated in its formation, the reader will not go astray.

As with the problems of translation, the other problems mentioned earlier need to be confronted directly. We must be content to learn what these texts content themselves in revealing. With that principle in mind, I have chosen wherever possible to translate texts in their entirety rather than in judiciously selected fragments. This choice has further necessitated the long introductions that precede each text, which are meant to summarize and contextualize the information that we might today glean from them.

To many readers, the sober scholarly apparatus found here will seem at deadly odds with the fantastic and, yes, exotic face of the Daoist religion that might occasionally flash out of these pages and across the centuries to captivate us, as it assuredly did those living in early medieval China. We need to remember, though, that to the modern world, all belonging to that bygone age appears strange and exotic. If we are to understand the phenomenon of early Daoism, we must employ every means to understand it as it was understood in its time. If we are to avoid using Daoism's enticing images as mere stage props for our own fantasies, our understandable impulse to grasp intuitively the concerns of those so distant from us must be suppressed. The apparatus patiently assembled here, should it serve to remind us of this, will fulfill more than its explanatory purpose.

We might then begin to understand the exotic appeal proper to Daoist scripture, where humans spoke so self-confidently as gods.

These caveats in place, it remains to be emphasized that these translations were not produced in a vacuum. There is a context for their proper reception and understanding, one that has been carefully delineated through the work of an international group of scholars engaged in the study of the Daoist religion by reference to its literary and archaeological remains as well as to the living examples of the religion throughout Asia. The texts translated here have already figured in a number of modern studies, many of which are cited in the bibliography.

None of the scholars so cited is in any way responsible for the interpretations presented here—with the exception, that is, of Peter Nickerson, who has graciously contributed a translation with introduction to this volume. Nickerson's work on Daoist ritual petitions covers material that I would not otherwise have been able to include, and I am extremely grateful to him for his willingness to share it.

My own work on this project was supported by a one-year translations grant from the National Endowment for the Humanities. I am grateful not only for the financial support but to the Endowment's staff, particularly Dr. Martha Chomiak, and their anonymous readers for much helpful advice. Earlier, my work on some of the texts presented here was made possible by a grant from the Committee for Scholarly Communications with China, a branch of the National Science Foundation. I am further indebted to the East Asian Studies Center, the College of Arts and Sciences, and the Research and University Graduate School, all at Indiana University, which supported this work through grant supplements, travel grants, and summer fellowships. Sue Tuohy, former assistant director of the East Asian Studies Center, was an unfailing support. As ever, I am grateful to the Institute of East Asian Studies, University of California, Berkeley, for granting me the status of visiting scholar and for greeting me warmly each time I return.

The bibliographic research for this project was carried out at the Indiana University Library; the East Asian Library, University of California, Berkeley; and the Harvard–Yenching Institute Library. The staffs of these three libraries are to be thanked for their patient assistance.

It is impossible to thank appropriately all those who have aided the completion of this work. My teachers Edward H. Schafer, Anna Seidel, and, for the initial stages, Michel Strickmann have contributed more than the footnotes found here, voluminous as they are, could ever acknowledge. This is true as well of my classmates in the study of Daoism: Judith Magee Boltz, Suzanne Cahill, Donald Harper, and Terry Kleeman. Phyllis Brooks Schafer, Isabelle Robinet, Donald Harper, Terry Kleeman, Jan Nattier, Robert Campany, Franciscus Verellen, and Lisa F. Berkson all read and criticized various drafts. Phyllis Brooks Schafer, Monica Lynn North, and John Snowball North provided comfort and lodging as I trudged from computer to library. Ron Richards, Stuart and Barbara Lynn, and Lester and Phyllis Berkson provided quiet places to hide away and work. To all of these people I owe debts of gratitude that will be insufficiently repaid with copies of "the book" that has obsessed me for so long. Needless to say, none of them is responsible for any errors or lapses. Beyond me, only one person might justifiably be held responsible for the existence of this work, though not for its remaining flaws: without the forbearance of Lisa Berkson, to whom this book is dedicated, it would never have been finished.

CONVENTIONS

All of the texts translated here, with the exception of the *Xiang'er* commentary, are based on the versions found in the standard Daoist canon. Those texts will be designated by the numbers assigned to them in the *Combined Indices to the Authors and Titles of Books in Two Collections of Taoist Literature* (Harvard-Yenching Institute Sinological Index Series, no. 25), preceded by the abbreviation *HY*. For the ease of readers who want to consult the cross-references in this book or to compare the translation against the original, the page numbers of the Chinese text, followed by the letter *a* for *recto* or *b* for *verso,* are entered in the margins of the translation. The *Xiang'er* commentary, as explained more thoroughly in the introduction to that text, will be referred to by the assigned line numbers of the Dunhuang manuscript version. References to these texts in the notes will cite these page and line numbers rather than the page numbers of the translation.

This book uses a dual system of notes for the translations. The footnotes are intended for the general reader, whereas the endnotes contain information of more interest to the scholar of medieval China. Character variants, textual emendations, and defenses of translation choices are, for example, regularly assigned to the endnotes. The distinction has been a difficult one to make—perhaps because I think all of this material should be of interest to just about everyone—but I have persisted in the hope that readers with little or no previous knowledge of medieval China will thus be able to enjoy the book without too much page turning.

References to scriptures in the *Taishō shinshū daizōkyō* will include the sequential scripture number, preceded by the abbreviation *T* and followed by the volume and page numbers separated by a period. Citations from modern editions of the standard histories, reference works, and collections of Chinese texts, such as the *Shisan jing zhushu,* will be in the form "chapter: page." This procedure, will, I hope, lighten the burden of those who consult editions bound differently than those used here. In any case, the edition used is specified at first occurrence. Other abbreviations are given in the list of abbreviations, which precedes the endnotes section.

Dates are given in Chinese form, with the Western equivalent supplied in square brackets. Weights and measures have been given in approximate English equivalents. This is of little consequence except in the case of the alchemical recipe translated here (which, at any rate, I sincerely hope no one will attempt to follow, and the products of which I equally hope no one will attempt to consume).

General Introduction

The texts chosen for translation here represent three major traditions in the early development of the Daoist religion: the Celestial Masters, the Shangqing (Upper Clarity), and the Lingbao (Numinous Gem).[1] A brief account of these traditions, and of the texts chosen to represent them here, follows.

CELESTIAL MASTERS

The Way of the Celestial Masters (also known as *Zhengyi* [Correct Unity] Daoism or, often pejoratively, as the Way of the Five Pecks of Rice) is the first Daoist organization for which we have substantial documentation. The official date for the founding of Celestial Master

Daoism is 142 C.E., when Laozi, in his incarnation as a deity, appeared to the first Celestial Master, Zhang Daoling, on a mountaintop in what is now Sichuan province. By the end of the second century, Zhang's grandson, Zhang Lu, had succeeded to the title, and the community, due to the turmoil attending the fall of the Han, had taken sanctuary in the Hanzhong Valley, just north of the Sichuan Basin and over two hundred kilometers southwest of the Han capital of Chang'an. In 215 C.E., Zhang Lu surrendered to Cao Cao, the Wei general whose son was to inaugurate the Wei dynasty of the Three Kingdoms period. As a result of this act of fealty, a large portion of the Celestial Master community, perhaps a quarter of the estimated four hundred thousand who occupied the valley, was moved from Hanzhong and scattered throughout the realm, while many of its leaders were enfeoffed or otherwise ennobled.[2] Although followers from the early period doubtless remained in Sichuan, the spread of Daoism throughout China as a whole began with this diaspora of the original Celestial Master community.

The aspects of Celestial Master Daoism that most caught the attention of contemporary historians were its organization, its codes of benevolent morality, and its practice of confession and petitioning rituals—the latter being means of invoking divine powers for curing disease. The Celestial Masters introduced converts to the faith through recitations of the *Laozi*, which was interpreted in startling new ways to support the main tenets of their faith. Through such practices, the group was said to have won the allegiance of both Chinese and "barbarians" (in this case, partially sinicized members of various ethnic groups resident in Sichuan).

There is still considerable controversy over which of the surviving Celestial Master scriptures can be dated to the early years of the sect. Of the four texts chosen for inclusion here, three can be firmly dated; the fourth represents an aspect of the religion we know to have been present from the beginning.

1. The Xiang'er *commentary to the* Laozi

Although the *Laozi* text (also known as the *Daode jing*) was important to the Celestial Masters from the very beginning, this commentary most likely dates from the time when the Celestial Master community occupied the Hanzhong Valley, roughly from 190 to 215 C.E. In early sources, authorship of the commentary is ascribed to Zhang Lu, the third Celestial Master and grandson of Zhang Daoling.

The commentary provides unique insights into the beliefs and practices of the early Celestial Masters. It also attests to the uses to which they put the *Laozi* text, which was reinterpreted in ways that would inform the subsequent development of the Daoist religion. Among the more significant of these reinterpretations is that the intended audience of the *Laozi*, originally the potential sage or sage-ruler, is widened to include all humanity. Moral codes, derided as humanly contrived and counterproductive in the *Laozi*, are reinstituted, and, in fact, warrant is found for them in the text. The common people are no longer to be kept in a state of natural ignorance. Instead they are urged, under the watchful eye of the spiritual bureaucracy emanating from the Dao, to enter the ranks of the blessed through moral action. In addition, as I try to show in the introduction to my translation, the commentary contains substantial clues concerning the physiological beliefs, meditation practices, and rituals of the early Celestial Masters.

2. *Commands and Admonitions for the Families of the Great Dao*

This treatise, found in a collection of early Celestial Master documents, was composed for promulgation to a scattered Celestial Master community after the dispersal of the Hanzhong community. Dated precisely to 1 February 255 C.E., the text seems to be put into the mouth of Zhang Lu but is most likely the work of someone else (perhaps one of Zhang's sons), who received it as a spirit communication.

In this text, we get our first glimpse of the cosmology of Celestial Master religion and a specific account of how the Dao incarnated itself to aid suffering humanity throughout history. We are also introduced to the concept of "seed people," those fortunate mortals selected to survive the cataclysms brought on by the end of a world age and to populate the new era of Great Peace. Although the moral world is much the same as that revealed in the *Xiang'er* commentary,

there are further accommodations to Confucian morality, particularly the importance of hierarchies based on the family.

Written when the Wei kingdom was on the verge of collapse, the
Admonitions testifies to the further disruptions this event caused
the Celestial Master sect and to internal struggles among its leaders
brought about by official recognition. Though it pretends to address
the Celestial Master sect as a whole, we do not in fact know how
large this "saving remnant" may have been. What is clear from this
text is that the fragmentation of the sect, begun with the diaspora of
the Hanzhong community, was exacerbated not only by the collapse
of its Wei patrons, but also by internal dissension brought on by
imperial patronage itself.

3. Scripture of the Inner Explanations
of the Three Heavens

After the fall of the Wei kingdom in 266 C.E., historical documentation on the Celestial Masters is sparse for a period of some 150
years. Then, with the rise to prominence of the general Liu Yu, the
most successful of the southern generals who tried to retake northern China after its capture by the Huns in 317, and his dynastic line,
we encounter several Daoist texts written to support the throne.
These range from demonographies to more sober treatises urging a
return to ideological unity as a prerequisite for reunifying China.[3]
The *Inner Explanations,* composed between 417, when Liu Yu distinguished himself by briefly recapturing Chang'an, the old capital,
and the early 420s, after Liu had proclaimed himself emperor of the
new Song dynasty, is of the latter type.

A Celestial Master treatise announcing that it should be treated as
scripture, this text details the concern of the Dao for the Han ruling
house, now thought to be renascent in its descendant, Liu Yu.
Although the history of the Celestial Masters given in this text has
been to some extent rewritten to demonstrate this thesis, the *Inner
Explanations* still provides us with a unique account of the survival
of Celestial Master beliefs and practices during a period for which
we have little other documentation. As the title of the scripture proclaims, the text gives us full account of the "three heavens," formed
of the three pneumas that separated from the Dao at creation. It thus

presents one of the fullest surviving accounts of Celestial Master cosmology, though one subtly altered in response to the claims of two influential scriptural traditions—Shangqing and Lingbao—that had recently emerged in southern China.

The *Inner Explanations* recounts again the transformations of Laozi in aid of suffering humanity and provides an informed account of the perceived differences between Daoism and Buddhism, arguing again that the latter is fit only for barbarians and not for Chinese belief. Relative importance is given to the old Celestial Master notion, already prominent in the *Xiang'er* commentary, that deviant texts and deviant practices should be abandoned, although the new Daoist unity now clearly involves a wider variety of Daoist texts and practices than it had before.

4. *The Great Petition for Sepulchral Plaints*

Whereas this petition, translated and discussed here by Peter Nickerson, comes from a late Tang dynasty collection of documents used by priests, the text probably dates to no later than the sixth century. The general form it takes and the issues it addresses, moreover, are continuous with other surviving examples of Celestial Master petitioning ritual.

One of the primary functions of the Celestial Master priesthood, as attested in early historical accounts, was the submission of written documents to the celestial bureaucracy for the purpose of healing illness, which, as generally in the China of this period, was believed in many instances to be caused by demonic agencies. In the case of the *Great Petition,* the sources of illness among the living lie within the grave, its cause, specifically, the unhappy spirits of dead family members. Through the proper ritual submission of this petition, which was to be delivered by corporal spirits called forth from the priest's own body to the gods on high, full power of the Dao was brought to bear on a disorder emanating from one of its constituent parts, the underworld bureaucracy.

This petition thus attests to the bureaucratic prognoses and solutions that Daoism, following earlier practices that Nickerson discusses, applied as a structural framework to functions that it took over from the exorcists and shamans of earlier Chinese religion.

Beyond the exorcistic goal of ensuring that the pollution of death would not infect the living, however, Daoist interventions in such cases were directed to assuring the salvation of the troubled ancestral souls who had infected their living relations. Ancient exorcistic commands that the living and dead remain separate and not interfere in the other's affairs thus take on a new meaning in this petition.

SHANGQING

During the years 364 to 370, a number of Daoist texts were transmitted by celestial beings to a medium named Yang Xi (330–386?). These texts, entitled the Shangqing (Upper Clarity) scriptures after the name of the heaven from which the beings came, were to profoundly alter not only the history of Daoism, but that of Chinese society and letters as a whole. Written in an exalted and poetic language, the Shangqing texts revised Celestial Master ritual and incorporated much else from the religious traditions of China, all with the aim of creating a Daoist practice suitable for Yang's elite patrons and members of the gentry class who were their intimates. The Shangqing scriptures thus mark a massive infusion into Daoist practice from the grand heritage of elite literary traditions, from new terminology and insights drawn from texts such as the *Laozi,* the *Zhuangzi,* and the *Chuci* to a variety of texts and practices that were the provenance of the mystics and technicians known as *fangshi.*

These elements of the elite tradition served convincingly as the literary precursors of the astral meditations, visualizations, and drugs for personal apotheosis that Yang Xi presented as more refined than the methods of the Celestial Masters. His writings far surpassed earlier technical manuals, however, in that Yang fashioned a fully realized cosmology and pantheon, as well as enticing accounts of those—whether human or divine—who had engaged in the practices he presented. The text chosen here to represent this extensive corpus of scriptures, and to show some of the ways in which they recast previous Daoist practice into new molds, is one of the earliest that Yang received during his midnight visions.

Among the *fangshi* practices that came to be included in the Shangqing texts was alchemy, the art that sought to create the medicine of transcendence through the precisely phased baking of mineral and vegetable drugs in a closed crucible. Already attested in China in the second century B.C.E., alchemy remained a secret art, passed from master to disciple according to strict rules of transmission. Then a southern literatus, Ge Hong (283–343), penned for unrestricted distribution a passionate defense of the possibility of transcending the human state, together with the titles of a number of alchemical texts and details on the concocting of elixirs. One of the texts Ge mentions had a demonstrable influence on the Shangqing text translated here.

The Upper Scripture of Purple Texts
Inscribed by the Spirits

Like many Shangqing texts, the *Purple Texts* is a compilation of meditations leading to personal transcendence, practices that had already proved effective in the lives of the deities who made them known to Yang. This is made most clear in the third section of the text, the biography of an exalted Shangqing deity that outlines the practices by which he achieved his celestial status. Foremost among those meditations was a practice for creating the embryos of perfection within the body through the absorption of lunar and solar essences, a method meant to replace Celestial Master sexual rites, which in the Shangqing tradition were seen as vulgar.

We also find in the *Purple Texts* a fantastic account of an alchemical recipe based on an early text known to Ge Hong, the *Yellow Thearch's Scripture of the Divine Elixirs of the Nine Tripods*. As I try to show in the introduction to the *Purple Texts*, these alchemical arcana, including secret drug names, were meant primarily as metaphors for elements of the meditation practice described earlier rather than for actual production.

Finally, we are told how the deity whose biography is provided here, Li Hong, will appear at the imminent end of the world-age to rescue the seed people—chosen mortals distinguished by certain practices, virtues, and physical signs. The eschatological vision of this text reminds us forcefully of the uncertainty of the times in which it was written, some fifty years after the occupation of northern China by the Huns and a period in which the Jin dynasty, having failed to regain the northern homelands, was already showing signs of collapse.

LINGBAO

In about 400 C.E., some thirty years after Yang Xi's revelations and in the same county, just southwest of modern Nanjing, another scriptural corpus began to appear. These writings were known as the Lingbao (Numinous Gem or Spiritual Treasure) scriptures. Equally devoted to revising Celestial Master Daoism on the basis of more traditional religious practices, the Lingbao scriptures presented themselves as the antithesis of the Shangqing tradition in two major ways. First, they directly confronted Buddhism, adapting and modifying it freely on the basis of the claim that Buddhism was but a foreign version of Daoism, begun when Laozi went west to "convert the barbarians." Rather than conclude from this myth that Buddhism was meaningless for China, the author of the Lingbao texts seems to have taken the claim as license to borrow extensively from Buddhist scripture, refiguring these borrowed elements in the same way that he did the contents of other scriptures, including material from the Shangqing texts. Second, and related to this, the Lingbao scriptures concern themselves, with bodhisattva-like intensity, with the salvation of all beings. Rather than the private meditations of the Shangqing scriptures, we find in these texts communal rituals like those of the Celestial Masters. Unlike Celestial Master rites, however, the salvific efficacy of Lingbao rituals was to extend to all beings. Both of these features are much in evidence in the text chosen for translation here.

The Wondrous Scripture
of the Upper Chapters on Limitless Salvation

The *Scripture of Salvation,* although meant for private recitation in the meditation chamber rather than communal practice, was held to work in the same way as other rituals in the Lingbao corpus. Through the agency of the text and the secret celestial language it contains, the practitioner expresses knowledge of the workings of the Dao and thus activates its perfect and primordial power on behalf of souls suffering in the earth-prisons, the purgatories of Chinese belief. This feature marks the *Scripture of Salvation* as one of the "wisdom texts" of Daoism.

The constituents of this wisdom are a knowledge of the workings of the Dao from highest antiquity through a new pantheon of deities held to be more ancient and thus more exalted than those described in earlier scriptural traditions. We are given in this text an account of how the Lingbao scriptures arose from the primordial ethers and of the gods and demons, some directly inspired by Buddhism, that can be called upon to bring about salvation through recitation of the text. One of the most interesting features of the scripture is the way in which it tames the Buddhist notion of rebirth, an idea viewed as incompatible with filial piety and the ties of familial obligation that were prominent features of Chinese religion.

◆   ◆   ◆   ◆

With their synthetic concerns, the Lingbao scriptures prefigure the unifying trend that was to characterize the Daoism of the following centuries. This trend was continued by Lu Xiujing (406–477), who was responsible for collecting the original Lingbao scriptures, separating out the many scriptures written in imitation, and creating new liturgies. In 471, Lu presented to the throne the first comprehensive list of Daoist scriptures, divided, as is the canon today, into three "caverns" (*dong,* or comprehensive collections) of texts. From this point on, the traditions we have been discussing were merged, at least conceptually, and we can begin speaking of a unified Daoist religion. Sectarian distinctions and disagreements are indeed to be found in Daoist history, and its organization was never more than a loose one, but the religion proved remarkably immune to the sorts of schisms that are commonplace in the history of religions.

This unification and the texts appropriate to its study fall beyond the scope of this book. Here we must content ourselves with an initial examination of but a handful of the most important texts of the early period of the religion. Nonetheless, it is worth noting that, with the exception of the *Xiang'er* commentary, all of the texts translated here, as well as the ideas and practices they contain, continued to play a role in the development of the religion and are to be found in the Ming-period Daoist canon, the last official collection of

Daoist texts. As Isabelle Robinet has aptly put it, the history of the Daoist religion "shows us how it has ceaselessly proceeded by 'recursive loops,' taking up its past like a bundle under its arm in order to travel farther along towards new horizons, and as it goes, gleaning all sorts of treasures along the way."[4] The texts translated here, among the first stuffed into the bundle, will, once carefully unpacked, again fulfill their stated purpose, revealing traces of the Daoist Transcendent's journey across the terrain of early China.

THE WORLDVIEW OF THE DAOIST RELIGION: GENERAL PERSPECTIVES AND DEFINITIONS

Daoism

The term "Daoism" is used in writings on China to cover a wide variety of phenomena, from a bibliographic classification of philosophical texts—including the *Zhuangzi,* the *Laozi,* and other works—to vaguely defined attitudes: the love of nature, the pursuit of personal freedom, and a concomitant antipathy toward the Confucian-inspired social order, an antipathy shared by a number of recluses and disillusioned former officials throughout the course of Chinese history. In this way, Daoism and Confucianism have come to be seen as the yin and yang poles of Chinese thought. Nearly every figure in the history of Chinese society who cannot be readily identified as Confucian is apt to be portrayed as a Daoist. Those so identified include a disparate collection of practitioners, mystics, and thinkers—healers, shamans, alchemists, seekers of immortality, figures from popular religion who managed to find mention in the dynastic histories, and even a few Confucians who, toward the end of their lives, withdrew from society and found solace in one or another of the philosophical works bibliographically classed as Daoist, or even in the Daoist religion itself. In the English-speaking world in particular, the student in search of a clearer idea of just what Daoism might be has not been helped by the recent appearance of new "translations" of the *Laozi* accomplished by those whose preparation for the task has been the study of martial arts, by Western works of "oriental mysticism," or by the proliferation of self-help manuals confidently proclaiming the Dao of corporate negotiation and the like.[5]

Confusing as all this is, we need to remember that it is precisely the situation Daoism faced throughout its formative years. The Daoist Lu Xiujing might have been reading in the "Eastern Religions" section of any modern bookstore when he wrote, of some "Daoist" texts of his day, that

> it seemed as if they were written by madmen—persons lacking the inner qualities to reach the mysterious and without any desire to seek out perfection—who had written [these texts based on] what they were able to spy out [of the original scriptures], falsely taking on the name "Daoist" in their greedy search for income.[6]

And, even earlier, the Daoist author of the first text translated here confronted the same sort of debasement of what he considered the Dao when he wrote (in the indignant voice of a god): "Those mortals who commonly practice false arts proclaim them as the teachings of the Dao, but it is all fraud and may not be employed." Such plaints, in fact, appear with frequency in Daoist writings.

It is common for any religion to establish principles of orthodoxy so as to distinguish itself from rival faiths, and Daoism, as Rolf Stein has amply demonstrated, was at constant pains to distinguish itself from popular religion, but the frequency with which Daoist authors felt it necessary to write on this topic during the period under consideration here attests to a fairly high level of anxiety concerning questions of self-definition.[7] The root causes of this anxiety tell us much about the nature of the religion. In establishing their religion, Daoists borrowed extensively from the revered texts and practices of their day and thus were at constant pains to distinguish themselves from the schools of thought and the religions surrounding them—an attempt that we might regard, again thinking of our modern bookstores, as having been less than successful.

Nonetheless, we can, from the texts translated here, derive a fairly clear idea of how Daoism sought to define itself.[8] Again and again, the authors of these texts, in the face of various challenges, real and perceived, return to the assertion that what they write is authentic because it was imparted to them by the Dao itself, usually through the agency of one or more deities held to emanate directly from the Dao. How each of them sought to demonstrate this claim is of little consequence here. What does matter is that, to combat the "deviations" of Confucianism, of popular religion, or of Buddhism, or merely to correct the utterances of other Daoists, this claim is ultimately invoked. For the authors of these texts, Daoism constitutes those teachings imparted by the Dao in human time. Simply stated, then, Daoism is by its own account the higher religion of China, characterized by the doctrine that the primordial and eternal Dao acts in human history both directly, through the agency of its hypostases, particularly Laozi, and indirectly, through a pantheon of deities that include those resident in the human body.

The defining concept of the Daoist religion is thus, quite naturally, the Dao itself, but understood in a revolutionary way. The term *dao,* originally denoting a "way" or "path," came to be used in pre-Han philosophical discourse, and particularly Confucian writings, to refer to the proper course of human conduct and, by extension, to the teachings of any philosophical school, especially as those were based on the venerated ways of the sages of antiquity.[9] In the *Laozi* and the *Zhuangzi,* the foundation texts of what came to be called "philosophical Daoism," the Dao came to be seen not as human order, but as the basis of natural order itself, the way the world operates when humans leave it alone.[10] Like the *dao* of correct human conduct, the metaphysical Dao in its purest form was to be discerned not in the chaotic present, but in the distant past. Since it was precisely the paragons of Confucian order who had disturbed the workings of the Dao, this past was distant indeed, even preceding the genesis of the cosmos, when the Dao was yet undifferentiated and had not yet split into the myriad things of the sensible world. At the same time, the Dao, though inchoate, was held to be eternally present and could still be grasped in its primal fullness by those specially endowed with correct insight into the flux of existence.[11]

This *dao* of the philosophers informs religious Daoist texts as well, but in the religion based on these ideas we find an added dimension of great significance.[12] Although the philosophers allowed that the Dao was immanent, so that one with special mystical insight might comprehend the Dao in its wholeness, Daoists (a term I will hereafter reserve for adherents of the Daoist religion) held that the

Dao underwent further self-transformations, analogous to those at the creation, to incarnate itself in human history. The Dao itself was seen as partially anthropomorphic, possessed, if at first not of an image, then of likes and dislikes, desires, sentiments, and motivations—the full range of human emotions. At the same time, it might act in history through specially appointed avatars, such as Laozi, who were fully human in appearance. Finally, a whole panoply of transcendent deities, including those resident in the human body, were regarded as divine hypostases of the Dao.

There is no doubt that there were throughout history some Daoists, usually members of the literati, who held that this deification of the Dao was no more than a metaphor serving to instruct the ignorant. For the period under consideration here, though, it was the deified Dao that distinguished Daoism from other schools of thought. It is one of the features, from our perspective, that qualifies Daoism as a religion rather than a philosophy.[13]

It is important to remember that there is no single avatar of the Dao. Laozi, who from his transcendent residence on Mount Kunlun appeared to Zhang Daoling in 142 C.E. to formally inaugurate the Celestial Master religion, was not the first or only hypostasis of the Dao. As Anna Seidel, in her extensive work on the deification of Laozi during the Han dynasty, concludes, the prestigious position accorded Laozi was most likely due to the fact that he was associated with a book, the *Daode jing,* an obscure text that might be interpreted in any number of ways and that enjoyed high regard in the intellectual life of ancient China.[14] The *Laozi* text was always revered within the religion, though interpreted in new and often startling ways.[15] In a similar fashion, the figure of the deified Laozi was subjected to interpretation and elaboration. The Shangqing school held that one of their higher deities, the Great Lord of the Dao of Jade Dawn, was the "teacher of Laozi," whereas the Lingbao scriptures describe this same deity as a disciple of their own higher god, the Celestial Worthy.[16] As early as the fourth century, even Celestial Master scriptures present deities who existed prior in time and were thus more exalted than the deified Laozi.[17] Such developments were not intended to supplant Laozi, but to position the revelations in which these new figures appeared earlier in time and thus closer to the primal Dao than those of the Celestial Masters. Many of the new cosmic deities thus borrow attributes from the deified Laozi and can, like the Sage Lord Li Hong of the *Purple Texts,* translated here, be understood as having been developed from the figure of Lord Lao.

This leads us to a final aspect of our definition. Michel Strickmann, in his impressive but ultimately futile attempt to limit the term "Daoism" to the Daoist religion, defines as Daoist those who (1) "recognize the historical position of Zhang Daoling"; (2) "worship the pure emanations of the Dao rather than the vulgar gods of the people at large"; and (3) "safeguard and perpetuate their own lore and practices through esoteric rites of transmission."[18] Although almost no one has stopped speaking of pre-Han "Daoism" in connection with the *Laozi* and the *Zhuangzi,* the first part of Strickmann's definition has also been questioned. Isabelle Robinet has rightly pointed out that Zhang Daoling is not accorded reverence at all in the Shangqing scriptures, and Anna Seidel has discovered one Daoist group that worshiped Lord Lao as the embodiment of the Dao *before* the appearance of the Celestial Masters, as well as evidence of other, similar sects.[19] Thus, although our definition owes much to Strickmann's insights, we can no longer confidently state that all Daoists recognized Zhang Daoling as founder of their religion, nor can we hold that the Daoist religion has a precise beginning in 142. In fact, we cannot, with the texts that have come down to us, put a definite beginning to religious Daoism, though it now seems clear that by the Latter Han it was beginning to take shape.

Nonetheless, the Celestial Master movement marked a radical break with earlier Daoist traditions. This break came about with the recognition that, as the Dao worked everywhere in the human world through the spirits that emanated directly from it, so too should the religion reach all classes of society, including the marginally sinicized and the illiterate. A second idea, related to the first, was that the celestial bureaucracy should be replicated on earth by a hierarchy of priests who were responsible not just to one or two initiates, but to a larger body of the faithful and, through them, to the society as a whole. Earlier sects may have entertained these ideas, but the Celestial Masters were able to make them an enduring feature of the religion.[20] The social mission of Daoism, in short, begins with the Celestial Masters.

The precise mechanisms that the Celestial Masters set up to accomplish these ends—the system of twenty-four parishes with their Libationers—did not survive intact, but the social and unifying impulses of the sect did. Even the Shangqing scriptures of Yang Xi, which in many ways model themselves on the older master-disciple lineages of Han Daoism, portray salvation (albeit in lower heavens or subterrestrial study centers) as available to all Daoists while simultaneously reworking communal Celestial Master rites for individual practice. Further, through its classification of doctrines, the Shangqing movement was responsible for bringing into what was envisioned as a single Daoist system a diverse set of practices deriving from the Han period, including alchemy and certain visionary meditation techniques. The result was the creation, during the fifth century, of a tripartite categorization of Daoist scripture and practice in a single Daoist canon.[21] The Celestial Master scriptures were not one of the three, having been fully replaced in the milieu that produced this system by later revelations, but the impulse to unify diverse doctrines, classify scriptures, and grade the levels of priesthood clearly has its roots in the original vision of Celestial Master Daoism.

Furthermore, Daoist traditions of the period under consideration here without exception found it necessary to position themselves either in continuation of or in reaction to the Celestial Masters. In either case, the social history of Daoism was seen as having involved Zhang Daoling. Although we thus cannot see the Celestial Masters as the originators of religious Daoism, it is appropriate to begin with them, as they represent the telling moment when the Dao broke forth into human history.

Pneuma (qi)

The concept of *qi* as the underlying stuff of existence is common to all schools of thought in China. The notion of *qi* seems to have developed together with and to have particular relevance for concepts of the Dao. In its primordial form, before division, the Dao is

described as "nothingness," void and null. The first sign that it was
about to divide, a process that would eventuate in the creation of the
sensible world, was the appearance within this nothingness of *qi,* a
term that originally seems to have meant "breath" or "steam." All
physical objects in the universe are thus composed of relatively stable *qi,* whereas rarefied *qi* is responsible for motion and energy and
is the vital substance of life. In many respects the concept of *qi* is
comparable to the atomism of early Greek philosophy.[22] The Chinese, though, sought not for the smallest stable particle but for the
lineaments of the system as a whole, a system they recognized
immediately as being characterized first and foremost by change,
which they imagined to be regular and cyclical. As a result, they
came to represent transformations of *qi* in terms of recurring cycles,
marked off in terms of yin, yang, the five phases, or the eight trigrams. (For the eight trigrams, see figure 1; for some of the more
common associations of the eight trigrams and the five phases, see
tables 1 and 2.) In such systems, *qi* was the intervening matrix by
which things sharing the same point in the cycle might resonate and
influence one another.

Daoism, building both on such cosmological speculation and on
various practices for extending life that featured the induction into
the body of pure, cosmic *qi,* regarded *qi* as the primary medium by
which one might apprehend and eventually join with the Dao. Most
meditation practices, in one way or another, involve swallowing *qi*
and circulating it within the body, the primary difference between
Daoist meditations and similar hygiene practices being that Daoists
visualized the substance either in deified form or as the astral sustenance for *qi*-formed deities resident in the body. In fact, all of the
higher gods of Daoism were held to be concretions of *qi* from the
earliest moments of the Dao's division. *Qi* thus bridged the gulf
between the sensible and the transcendent worlds.

The term *qi* has been translated in a number of ways—"breath,"
"vapor," "energy," "pneuma." "Atom," to my knowledge, has
never been forwarded as a possible translation. It would be ideal,
had it not been co-opted by modern science. "Breath," although getting at the original meaning of the word, has too narrow a range of
connotations in English for it to function as a translation of *qi.* The
term "energy" might be accurate had early Chinese thinkers foreseen

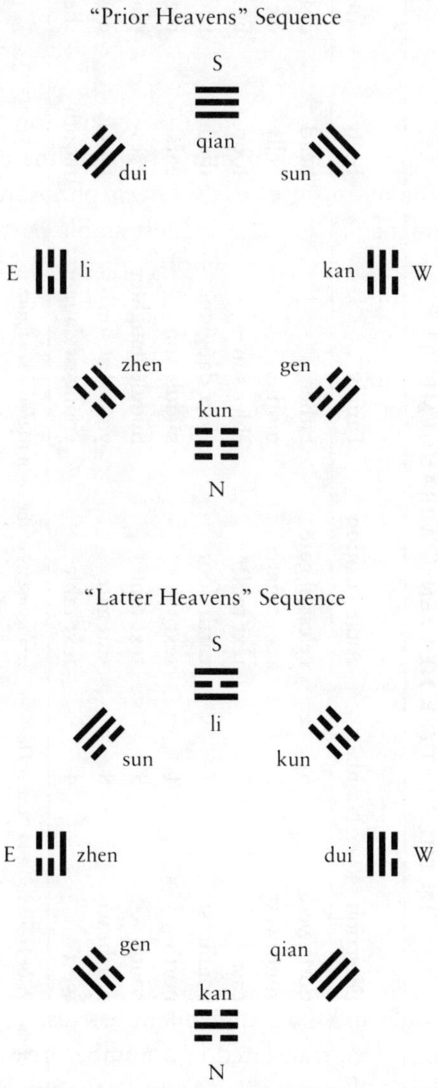

Fig. 1. The Eight Trigrams of the *Yijing*. For common associations of the eight trigrams, see table 1.

TABLE I. COMMON ASSOCIATIONS OF THE EIGHT TRIGRAMS OF THE *YIJING* (IN THE "LATTER HEAVENS" ARRANGEMENT)

	Natural Phenomena	Direction	Number	Altar Position	Family	Body	Animal
qian	heaven	northwest	6	celestial gate	father	head	dragon
kun	earth	southwest	2	moon gate	mother	belly	ox
zhen	thunder	east	3	text table[a]	elder son	foot	horse
sun	wind	southeast	7	earth door	elder daughter	thighs	hen
kan	water	north	1	text table[a]	middle son	ears	pig
li	fire	south	9	text table[a]	middle daughter	eyes	pheasant
gen	mountains	northeast	8	sun gate	youngest son	hands	dog
dui	marshes	west	4	text table[a]	youngest daughter	mouth	sheep

Note: For a representation of the "Prior Heavens" and "Latter Heavens" arrangements of the eight trigrams, see figure I.

a. According to this altar arrangement from the Lingbao scriptures, the Five-Part Script would be placed on short text tables on the four sides (north, south, east, and west) and in the center of the altar.

TABLE 2.   COMMON ASSOCIATIONS OF THE FIVE PHASES IN DAOIST TEXTS

Phase	Direction	Celestial Beast	Planet	Pneuma	Season	Number	Color	Body Part	Organ	Holy Mountain
Wood	east	Green Dragon	Jupiter	Lesser Yang	spring	9	green	eyes	liver	Tai Shan
Fire	south	Vermilion Sparrow	Mars	Greater Yang	summer	3	red	mouth	heart	Huo Shan
Earth	center	Ascending Snake	Saturn	Centrally Harmonious	Controller	12 or 1	yellow	stomach	spleen	Sung Shan
Metal	west	White Tiger	Venus	Lesser Yin	autumn	7	white	ears	lungs	Hua Shan
Water	north	Murky Warrior	Mercury	Greater Yin	winter	5	black	navel	kidneys	Heng Shan

subatomic physics, but there is no evidence that they saw matter as composed of moving *particles*. Rather, *qi* was an indivisible substance that flowed or stagnated and might, like water, be found in nature in solid, liquid, or gaseous forms. Concretions of *qi* were sometimes called *jing* (essence). "Vapor," with its connotations of evanescence, leads to confusions of a different sort, suggesting as it does that Daoists, like Buddhists, saw the world as insubstantial illusion.[23] *Pneuma,* from Greek *pnein* (to breathe) and originally meaning "spirit," is of course not quite right either, since not all forms of *qi* were regarded as spiritual. But the fact that, now that the age of pneumatic drills and pneumatic tubes is all but past, the word has few connotations for the English reader makes it, I think, preferable as a translation of *qi*.[24]

Scripture

The word translated as "scripture" is *jing,* the same word used by Confucians to designate the classics of their tradition, the master texts containing the ancient teachings on a particular subject in their fullness. The word denotes primarily the warp threads on the weaver's loom and, applied to texts, seems meant to call forth connotations of stability, thoroughness, and of providing shape to the "fabric" of society. On each of these primary texts there might be any number of commentaries or "traditions" of interpretation (*zhuan*), but the *jing* were the font of the tradition. The same word was adopted by translators to render the Sanskrit *sūtra,* the scriptures containing transcriptions of the "words of the Buddha."

Daoist conceptions of scripture are markedly different from those of Confucianism or Buddhism. The Daoist view is based on the nature of written Chinese and on the idea that the cosmic ordering of the Dao, though perverted in the present world, is still recoverable in the patterns it has laid down. Scripture is made up of *wen,* a word that means "patterns" or "markings" and, by extension, "Chinese characters," "writing," "text," and even "cultured," "civilized," or "ordered." Each Daoist text (*wen*) defines itself as a historical concretization of the eternal, divine patterns (*wen*) of the Dao inhering in the cosmos. The individual scripture is therefore regarded as part of a whole, finally unobtainable, truth—a representation of the timeless frozen in time and congealed in debased human writing (*wen*) that can, by its very nature, only point to what lies beyond. Because of this, there is the possibility of countless scriptures expressing the truths of the Dao. This is in fact the attitude we encounter in Daoism, with new scriptural tradition placing itself with respect to the others but generally regarding these earlier accounts—when there are contradictions—with civilized condescension as later or less accurate translations.

At the most rarefied level, we have actual examples of "celestial script," graphs that resemble Chinese characters but are in fact the language of heaven and require more mundane exegesis in order to be accessible to humans. Talismans—charms that could be carried or swallowed to command or empower deities or to drive off demons—also were considered to derive their efficacy from the fact that they mimicked celestial patterns (*wen*). Even those scriptures composed wholly in standard Chinese were regarded as translations into profane language of more potent divine texts. Such scriptures thus depend for their interpretation on a vast specialized vocabulary including such things as the names of deities, celestial place names, secret names for techniques and for the spirits controlling parts of the human body—all seldom encountered in other types of literature.

This conception of scripture finds full expression in the Shangqing and Lingbao revelations, with their need to position their scriptures earlier in time, and as more closely emanating from the Dao, than those of the Celestial Masters.[25] Nonetheless, the *Xiang'er* commentary presents the first scripture of Daoism, the *Daode jing*, as a direct transcript of the words of the Dao and of various transcendent beings who have already merged with the Dao. Further, the *Daode jing* requires the exegesis of the Celestial Master, for its words are apt to be misunderstood, as the commentary stridently makes clear. There is thus ample reason to believe that this Daoist conception of scripture goes back to the beginnings of the religion.

Transcendent Beings

It is common in works on China to describe Daoism as the "religion of immortality." This commonplace is not quite accurate, at least not as we in the West tend to understand immortality. The Dao itself is immortal, and the goal of Daoists was to merge with the Dao. As we have seen, however, one of the primary characteristics of the Dao is change. Specifically, the Dao moves in cycles, first dividing to form the universe in its ever-increasing complexity and then imploding back in on itself to begin all over again from its state of primal unity. This cosmic rhythm, sometimes seen as occurring in cycles of impossible magnitude—one Han source calculates the length of one cycle as 23,639,040 years—led to the concept of world-ages. Sometimes the larger world-age was said to be divided into five minor ones, each associated with one of the five phases.[26] Whatever the case, when the Dao returned to its primal unity, nothing outside of it remained and nothing continued in the state it had existed in to that point. This was as true for scriptures, deities, and powers as it was for humans who had joined with the Dao. Immortality of shape and substance was thus impossible. The best one could hope for was to "cross over" with the Dao to be formed anew in the next world-age. Many of the highest gods of Daoism were considered such precisely because they had undergone this transfiguration from the "prior heavens" to reappear in the "latter heavens."[27] That is why the texts translated here, and all others of which I am aware, tend to speak in terms of "longevity," "long life," and, more poetically, "an existence equal with that of the sun and moon" rather than of immortality.[28] As change and transformation are so central to Daoism, the details of this doctrine, though it perhaps differs only subtly from what we recognize as "immortality" in other religions, should be respected.

Beyond this distinction, about which the texts translated here tend to be quite careful, there is the additional fact that the term often translated as "immortal" (*xian*) denotes a variety of different beings, from the "earth-bound *xian*" existing on the terrestrial plane or under it in the cavern-heavens to celestial beings proper. One quality these beings share is that they have been "transferred," in the etymological gloss of the Lingbao scriptures, from the common human state to a more subtilized form of existence, closer to the nature of the Dao. There is thus not a single chasm between mortals and immortals, but a chain of being, extending from nonsentient forms of life that also experience growth and decay to the highest reaches of the empyrean.[29] The term designating those who have ascended to rungs of the ladder higher than those occupied by humans, the *xian,* will accordingly be translated as "transcendent."

In the Shangqing and Lingbao scriptures we encounter yet another type of being, the Perfected.[30] These beings, even more exalted than the transcendents, are described as having left behind all vestiges of earthly corruptibility to achieve bodies formed of stellar substance. They move effortlessly through the highest heavens and tend to be described with metaphors conveying gemlike brilliance and durability. More will be said about these beings in the introduction to the *Purple Texts.*

NOTES TO GENERAL INTRODUCTION

1. The earliest Daoist canon, compiled during the fifth century, included three groups of scriptures: the Shangqing, the Lingbao, and the Sanhuang [Three Sovereigns]. This third division seems to have comprised the *Script of the Three Sovereigns* and texts relating to it. Although there are several apparently early scriptures that have been identified (see especially Poul Anderson, "Talking to the Gods: Visionary Divination in Early Taoism (The Sanhuang Tradition)," *TR* 5.1 [1994], pp. 1–24), modern research on the Daoist canon has not clarified the nature of this corpus of scriptures to the extent that it can be confidently represented here.

2. For this estimation of the population of Hanzhong during this time and the dimensions of the diaspora, see Ōfuchi Ninji, *Shoki no dōkyō* (Tokyo: Sōbunsha, 1991), pp. 55–57.

3. For the demonographies mentioned here, see Christine Mollier, "Messianisme taoïste de la Chine médiévale: Étude du Dongyuan shenzhou jing," Ph.D. diss., Université de Paris VII. Among the texts written in the south to reunify Daoism as an ideological foundation of the state, we must certainly include several of Lu Xiujing's surviving treatises, especially *HY* 524 and *HY* 1119. This trend occurred simultaneously in northern China with the Celestial Master reforms of Kou Qianzhi (d. 448) in the northern Wei kingdom. See Richard B. Mather, "K'ou Ch'ien-chih and the Taoist Theocracy at the Northern Wei Court 425–451," in Holmes Welch and Anna Seidel, eds., *Facets of Taoism: Essays in Chinese Religion* (New Haven, Conn.: Yale University Press, 1979), pp. 103–22.

4. Isabelle Robinet, *Histoire du taoïsme: Des origines au XIVe siècle* (Paris: Cerf, 1991), p. 10, as translated by Phyllis Brooks in *The History of Taoism: Growth of a Religion from its Origins to the Fourteenth Century* (Stanford, Calif.: Stanford University Press, forthcoming). That I do not agree with Robinet on the question of whether it is possible to consider the pre-Han philosophers whose works Daoists stuffed into their "bundle" as

self-conscious parts of the Daoist tradition will become clear through the following discussion. Her history stands, however, as a magisterial study of the continuities in thought and in meditation and physiological practices that link what I still prefer to call "philosophical Daoism" to the Daoist religion.

5. In particular, see the introduction to Stephen Mitchell's "translation" of the *Daode jing,* accomplished by consulting other translations, where he claims that "the most essential preparation for my work was a fourteen-years-long course of Zen training," and Brian Walker's "translation" of the *"Huahu jing,"* apparently done from Ni Hua-ching's rather prolix English "translation" of a text that, to my knowledge, does not exist in Chinese. There are, of course, numerous other examples. A characteristic of such works is that they lay claim to "ancient mystical knowledge" for their authority, but they are best considered under the rubric of new American religions. On the susceptibility of Daoism to such exploitation, see Steve Bradbury, "The American Conquest of Philosophical Taoism," in Cornelia N. Moore and Lucy Lower, eds., *Translation East and West: A Cross-Cultural Approach* (Honolulu: University of Hawaii Press, 1992), pp. 29–41.

6. For the context of this remark, see the introduction to *The Wondrous Scripture of the Upper Chapters on Limitless Salvation* (hereafter *Scripture of Salvation*).

7. Rolf Stein, "Religious Taoism and Popular Religion from the Second to the Seventh Centuries," in Holmes Welch and Anna Seidel, eds., *Facets of Taoism: Essays in Chinese Religion* (New Haven, Conn.: Yale University Press, 1979), pp. 53–81.

8. So much wasted ink and ill will has spilled forth over the question "What is Daoism?" that precise caveats are in order. First, despite what seems to me to be the enduring nature of the principles I hope to isolate here, the definition of Daoism that I propose is not meant as a delimiting one, good for all times and places. I will not try to point out what is not Daoism—or, worse yet, what is "proto-Daoism"—but will note only the primary tenets defended in the texts translated here, so that we might use them to guide our historical researches. This "definition" is thus provisional and intended primarily to clarify aspects of the texts translated here. Second, no attempt will be made here to trace the origins of these ideas in any detail, or to confront any of the other modern efforts to set the parameters of the Daoist religion.

9. See especially the discussion in A. C. Graham, *Disputers of the Tao: Philosophical Argument in Ancient China* (La Salle, Ill.: Open Court, 1989), pp. 13–15.

10. The term "philosophical Daoism" here denotes the texts listed in the bibliographic treatise of the *Han shu* (30:1729–31), written by Ban Gu 班固 (32–92) and based on the earlier work of Liu Xin 劉歆 (d. 23 C.E.), as *Daojia* (schools of the Dao)—a total of thirty-seven different works. The customary translation of "school" (singular) for the term *jia* 家 (literally,

"family") has tended to confuse our thinking on what such classifications meant in traditional China. *Jia* might be better translated as "lineage," in that it denotes a group organized on the principles of family structure (if not in fact a family) that transmitted knowledge and skills, including the skill of textual interpretation, in a lineal fashion. As a bibliographic rubric, *Daojia* does not denote a single worldview or set of ideas—and especially not a coherent philosophical "school"—but a listing of different lineages centering on texts that discuss the Dao. Many of these texts do not survive, so it is really impossible to determine just what Ban Gu thought they all had in common. Massive amounts of scholarly effort have been expended on tracing the commonalities between those texts that do remain, but unless we have independent evidence that a single *jia* transmitted two or more of the texts, we would be better served to regard such efforts as aimed at understanding the thought processes of individual bibliographers rather than descriptions of the milieu in which the texts were transmitted and interpreted. It should be noted also that works dealing with one of the other major strands of Chinese thought, one that was to find its way into Daoism—the pursuit of transcendence—are listed separately under "recipes and techniques" and not under the *Daojia* classification (*Han shu,* 30: 1779–80).

11. For a concise overview of the Dao in pre-Han thought, see John Knoblock, *Xunzi: A Translation and Study of the Complete Works* (Stanford, Calif.: Stanford University Press, 1988), vol. 1, pp. 70–75.

12. A. C. Graham (*Disputers of the Tao,* p. 172) has pointed to one essential thought shared by both philosophical and religious Daoism, as well as by Chan (Zen) Buddhism: "that while other things move spontaneously on the course proper to them, man has separated himself from the Way by reflecting, posing alternatives, and formulating principles of action." As we will see in the *Xiang'er* commentary, that desire and willfulness serve to divorce humanity from the Dao is one of the primary messages of the text. There is, of course, much else, including the figure of the "Great Man" or "Perfected being" (Robinet, *Histoire du taoïsme,* pp. 33–41), that religious Daoism derived from the texts of philosophical Daoism.

13. By "deified" here, I do not refer to the Chinese concept *shen,* which in many cases means "holy" or "numinous" and might be applied to inanimate forces or objects, but to anthropomorphic spiritual entities that inhabited the heavens, the earth, and the human body. Anna Seidel has made the important observation that, until the advent of Daoism, commerce with celestial deities, whether divinized ancestors, nature deities, or personified abstract forces, was regarded as the prerogative of the state ("Das neue Testament des Tao—Lao tzu und die Entstehung der taoistischen Religion am Ende der Han-Zeit," *Saeculum* 29 (1978), pp. 147–72). From this perspective, it might be more accurate to state that Daoism brought the deities of the macrocosm into the system of the Dao rather than that it "deified the Dao." The *shen* that inhabited the human body, however conceived, were

already part of Han Confucianism. See Harold D. Roth, "The Early Taoist Concept of *Shen:* A Ghost in the Machine?" in Kidder Smith, Jr., ed., *Sagehood and Systematizing Thought in Warring States and Han China* (Brunswick, Maine: Bowdoin College Asian Studies Center, 1990), pp. 11–32.

14. Seidel, "Der Kaiser und sein Ratgeber—Lao Tzu und der Taoismus der Han-Zeit," *Saeculum* 29 (1978), pp. 18–50.

15. The first text translated here, the *Xiang'er* commentary, testifies to the way in which Daoists first interpreted this text as well as to the divine status of Laozi in the religion.

16. For the Lord of the Dao in the Shangqing scriptures, see *HY* 1010, 5:1b, and, for his position in the Lingbao scriptures, the *Scripture of Salvation,* translated here.

17. See the *Inner Explanations,* translated here.

18. Michel Strickmann, "On the Alchemy of T'ao Hung-ching," in Holmes Welch and Anna Seidel, eds., *Facets of Taoism: Essays in Chinese Religion* (New Haven, Conn.: Yale University Press, 1979), pp. 164–67.

19. Isabelle Robinet (*La révélation du Shangqing dans l'histoire du taoïsme,* PEFEO, no. 137 [Paris, 1984], vol. 1, pp. 72–74) takes exception to Strickmann's statement that Shangqing Daoism accorded Zhang a "high evaluation." Seidel, who still places the beginning of institutional Daoism with Zhang and the Celestial Masters, has studied the Sichuan cult, originating around 130 C.E., which produced the *Scripture of the Transformations of Laozi,* and postulates that the imperial temple to Laozi, constructed ca. 147 C.E. and far from the homeland of the Celestial Masters, was a response to popular movements that regarded Laozi as the Dao incarnate. See her *La divinisation de Lao-tseu dans le taoïsme des Han,* PEFEO, no. 71 (Paris, 1969); "Der Kaiser und sein Ratgeber"; and "Das neue Testament des Tao."

20. One such group was the Yellow Turbans, who, judging by the surviving fragments of the *Scripture of Great Peace* and historical accounts, were organized in ways quite similar to the Celestial Masters. There are, however, massive historiographical and textual problems to be solved before we can speak with confidence on this subject. See the introduction to the *Xiang'er* commentary for more on this.

21. See Ōfuchi Ninji, "The Formation of the Taoist Canon," in Holmes Welch and Anna Seidel, eds., *Facets of Taoism: Essays in Chinese Religion* (New Haven, Conn.: Yale University Press, 1979), pp. 253–68; and Robinet, *La révélation du Shangqing,* vol. 1, pp. 75–85.

22. For ways in which the Chinese conceptions of *qi* overlapped and differed from Greek atomism, see Joseph Needham, *Science and Civilisation in China* (Cambridge: Cambridge University Press), vol. 4, pt. 1 (1962), pp. 11 ff.; and Benjamin L. Schwartz, *The World of Thought in Ancient China* (Cambridge: Harvard University Press, 1985), pp. 179–84.

23. The word *vapor* has a long pedigree in this regard. The King James version of the Bible, for instance, has: "For what is your life? It is even a vapour, that appeareth for a little time, and then vanisheth away" (James 4:14).

24. The earliest use of *pneuma* to translate *qi* of which I am aware is in Edward H. Schafer, *The Vermilion Bird: T'ang Images of the South* (Berkeley: University of California Press, 1967), p. 119, where the plural form *pneumas* is also introduced. Henceforth I shall also use the common English plural form *pneumas* where necessary rather than *pneumata*.

25. See Robinet, *La révélation du Shangqing*, vol. 1, pp. 112–16; and Robert F. Campany, "Buddhist Revelation and Taoist Translation in Early Medieval China," *TR* 4.1 (1993), pp. 1–30.

26. See Stephen Bokenkamp, "Time after Time: Taoist Apocalyptic Views of History and the Founding of the T'ang Dynasty," *Asia Major*, 3d ser., 7.1 (1994), pp. 61–67.

27. See particularly the examples of Li Hong in the *Purple Texts* and the Heavenly Worthy, described in the introduction to the *Scripture of Salvation*.

28. One of the terms usually translated as "immortality," *busi* 不死, means instead "not dying"—that is, passing to a new and more exalted state of existence without first dying. There are many ways in which this was said to happen. One of the foremost was "deliverance from the corpse," during which physical and spiritual constituents of the self shed the mortal body like a cicada its chrysalis.

29. This aspect of Daoism is closely related to what has been characterized as its "bureaucratic face." See especially Stephen Bokenkamp, "Stages of Transcendence: The *Bhūmi* Concept in Taoist Scripture," in Robert E. Buswell, Jr., ed., *Chinese Buddhist Apocrypha* (Honolulu: University of Hawaii Press, 1990), pp. 119–47.

30. In some works on Daoism, the reader will find the term denoting these beings, *zhenren* 真人, translated as "true persons" or "realized persons." In fact, the opposite of *zhen* 真 is *jia* 假 ("false, fabricated, borrowed"), and the term was probably adopted to emphasize that perfection was the original state of human beings before they willfully turned from the Dao. I have chosen not to use these terms simply as a matter of convenience. The phrases "true persons" and "realized ones" are unwieldy, especially for terms that occur so often in these texts. One solution might be to abbreviate them to "the True" or "the Realized," as I have done with "Perfected," were it not for the fact that these words, standing alone, allow for understandings quite alien to the way the term *zhenren* is meant to be understood in these texts. "The True" might mean either "real people" or "the faithful," while "the Realized" carries with it inescapable connotations of mental realization, whereas Daoist perfection is always both mental and physical.

The *Xiang'er* Commentary
to the *Laozi*

INTRODUCTION

The *Xiang'er* commentary is the earliest Daoist interpretation of the *Laozi* (also known as the *Daode jing*, "Scripture of the Way and its Potencies").[1] This text was employed by the early Celestial Master organization as a catechism to be recited and learned by all the faithful. The *Xiang'er* thus represents not only a Celestial Master interpretation of the *Laozi*, but also an introduction to Celestial Master beliefs and practices. The polemical tone of much of the commentary demonstrates the missionary fervor with which the Celestial Masters strove to establish their religion. The *Xiang'er* defends its own tenets against those of Confucianism as well as against other forms of

Daoist practice and rival interpretations of the *Laozi* text, revealing
in the process the extent to which the early Celestial Masters saw
themselves as unique in practicing the teachings of a deified Laozi
and regarded the *Laozi* as his initial revelation meant especially for
them.

The fact that the *Laozi* is so widely known and studied should
simplify the task at hand. Paradoxically, the very popularity of the
text as the foremost representative of "Daoism" and the astounding
number of ways in which it has been interpreted make understanding
the *Xiang'er* commentary that much harder—and more necessary,
for the *Laozi* itself tells us nothing of the Daoist religion.

Although the Celestial Masters accorded the *Laozi* primacy over
other revealed texts as a catechism of their faith, their veneration
seems to have been directed more to the figure of Laozi (or Lord
Lao, as he was called) than to the ideas contemporaries found in the
Laozi itself, for their interpretations often run counter to the clear
intent of the text. Key words and phrases from the *Laozi* occupy
places of honor in later Daoist scripture, but they often stand for
practices and ideas of which the original text is quite innocent. Far
and away the most widely cited classical source in Daoist writings,
the *Laozi* was bestowed on new initiates with the same rituals accorded the transmission of other scriptures, but all of these activities
contradict the injunction of the *Laozi* itself that "knowledge" be
discarded.[2] Then, too, even within the Celestial Master organization, the *Laozi* did not maintain its preeminent position. Further
revelations from Lord Lao, among which we might even want to
number the *Xiang'er* commentary, at first supplemented and later
largely eclipsed it. The *Laozi* thus did not remain, as did the Torah
or the Koran, *the* canonical source of revealed wisdom, to be
returned to and reinterpreted subtly at each stage in the development
of the religion. Clearly, to understand Daoism it is the commentaries
we need to study rather than the *Laozi* itself.

Commentaries are acts of interpretation. Wittingly or unwittingly,
commentators reconfigure a text in line with their own concerns.
Because of this, yet another distorting side effect of the *Laozi*'s modern popularity needs to be directly confronted at the outset. Those
readers who already have some idea of the *Laozi*, especially if that
idea is drawn from any of the modern translations of the work, may

well feel that the *Xiang'er* commentary takes unwarranted liberties with a mystical book designed for the cultivation of individual sagehood. Before succumbing to this initial impression, however, we should recall that although the commentator is undeniably reinterpreting the *Laozi* in various ways, we ourselves, after generations of reading the text through the eyes of its medieval Chinese interpreters, are only now beginning to rediscover how that book was originally meant to be read.[3] We thus need to reserve judgment on the Daoist religion's supposed "distortions" of the *Laozi,* proposed by various "degenerescence theories" (to use Steve Bradbury's apt characterization) that portray pure Daoist philosophy as corrupted by the institutionalized and "popularizing" Daoist religion.[4]

The "real meaning" of the *Laozi* is still hotly contested terrain, as witnessed by the two or three new translations that come out each year. The introduction and translation presented here are not intended to enter into that debate or even to explore the place of the *Laozi* within Daoism, but to explicate the *Xiang'er* commentary and to learn from it as much as possible about the early Celestial Masters. I will thus not make reference to other translations or interpretations of the *Laozi,* nor will I attempt a thoroughgoing comparison of the *Xiang'er* understanding of the *Laozi* with that of other commentators and translators, a proceeding that would require another book at least as long as this one. In fact, as I will explain more fully, I have, insofar as possible, ignored other translations in the interest of attending closely to the readings of the *Xiang'er* commentary.[5]

Thus we will begin with an examination of the early history of the Celestial Master movement. This will be followed by a brief account of the evolution of the *Laozi* from a book of political gnosis to a treatise for self-cultivation, and the place of the *Xiang'er* commentary in that process. The two succeeding sections—"Meditation and Perfection of the Body" and "Morality and Governance"—constitute an introduction to the contents of the commentary itself and to the doctrines of the Celestial Masters that can be gleaned from it. I will then introduce the controversies surrounding two topics: the date of the text, and its authorship. The former, I will argue, is fairly certain—the text was written before 215 C.E.—and the second is unknowable, though the early statements that it was written by

Zhang Lu find no contradiction in the historical record. At the end of the introduction, the reader will find a brief discussion of the principles and procedures I have followed in making this translation and a "Key to Chapter Numbers" for those interested in comparing the *Xiang'er* commentary with other interpretations of the *Laozi*.

Historical Background

The history of the early Celestial Masters can be reconstructed from three types of sources: dynastic histories and official inscriptions, Daoist writings, and Buddhist polemical treatises. Each of these sources has its own bias, and each contradicts the others in fundamental ways. Historians of the period tended to lump the Celestial Masters with contemporary "rebel movements."[6] In this and other ways, they reveal their bias against the religion.[7] Little interested in doctrinal matters, contemporary historians failed to fully distinguish the teachings and practices of the Celestial Masters from those of other, similar groups. Early Daoist sources are not, properly speaking, histories of the movement at all. Their references to the early church often appear in the context of doctrinal discussion and have clearly been adjusted accordingly. Finally, Buddhist polemicists, writing in defense of a religion that was under attack as a danger to the state, uniformly attempt to turn the tables on their rival, Daoism. They report uncritically the basest allegations and exploit the inattention of the historians to associate all aspects of early Daoism with rebel ideologies.

Here, then, we shall rely on the first two types of writing—the standard histories and, to a lesser extent, the reports of Daoists themselves—to trace in broad strokes the outlines of early Celestial Master history. As is to be expected, given the nature of the sources, there remains a great deal of scholarly debate on this subject. Some alternative views will be presented in the footnotes.

Historians of the period uniformly place the Celestial Masters in some sort of relationship with the Yellow Turbans, the most prominent among the rebel groups that weakened the Han dynasty. As the exact nature of the connection between these two groups, if any, is disputed, we first need to provide some account of the Yellow Turbans.[8]

Centered in the eastern reaches of the Han empire, the Yellow Turban rebellion, led by a man named Zhang Jue, was a well-planned movement organized around a religious ideology with definite millennial aims. Zhang called his movement the "Way of Great Peace." Under the slogan that the "Yellow Heaven is about to rise," he sought to position himself and his followers as the vanguard of a new and perfect society. Though historical evidence is necessarily scant, it is almost certain that this ideology was to some extent drawn from a revealed book, the *Scripture of Great Peace,* a work that had been promulgated earlier in the dynasty by a court faction also centered in the eastern coastal region. The *Scripture of Great Peace,* which survives only in fifth- or sixth-century recensions, promotes an ideal social structure based on cosmic principles and on the notion that the moral action of each individual determines both the health of the body politic and the smooth functioning of the cosmos.[9]

The Yellow Turbans converted people to their cause through healing practices, including old methods such as incantation and doses of water infused with the ashes of talismans, and a new one—confession of sins.[10] This latter practice is significant. The *Scripture of Great Peace* relates confession to the idea that political and cosmic disease are caused by humans and must be cured on the individual level. Sin, in this text, is the failure to act in accord with one's social role, thereby blocking the circulation of the Dao's energies. Those who should labor with their bodies fail to do so, living instead in idleness; those who possess wealth keep it for their own enjoyment rather than allowing it to circulate; and those who should teach virtue only "accumulate" it, making a name for themselves.[11] These and other means of blocking the circulation of goods and life forces lead, by this account, to illness and death. We shall find a similar attitude in the *Xiang'er* commentary.

Zhang Jue organized his followers into thirty-six administrative regions. Apparently basing himself on the *Scripture of Great Peace,* with its figure of a Celestial Master (or Heavenly Teacher) who was to advise the perfect ruler, Zhang took the title "Great Sage, Excellent Teacher." He also named himself General of Heaven, bestowing on his two brothers the titles General of Earth and General of Humanity.

The new age of the Yellow Heaven was to dawn in the year 184, the beginning of a new sexagesimal cycle by the Chinese calendar. Despite well-laid plans, news of Zhang Jue's uprising reached the court, and the Yellow Turbans in the east were defeated within the year.

Like the Yellow Turbans, the Celestial Masters revered as founders three members of a Zhang family.[12] In this case, though, the three were father, son, and grandson, who led the movement in succession. The histories record that the father, Zhang Ling (Zhang Daoling in Daoist texts) was a man of Pei (in northwestern Jiangsu Province) who traveled to the kingdom of Shu (the western part of modern Sichuan) to study the Dao on Mount Crane-Call.[13] Daoist texts record that there, in the year 142 C.E., he was visited by the "newly appeared Lord Lao," the deified Laozi.[14] Laozi granted him the title "Heavenly [-appointed] Teacher" or Celestial Master. On Zhang Ling's death, the title was passed on to his son Heng and eventually to his grandson, Lu. The line of transmission, it is claimed, remains unbroken this day. These are the Celestial Masters from whom the religion takes its name.

Little is provided in the way of a history of the Celestial Master community until the events sweeping China in the latter years of the Han dynasty finally penetrated as far as the relatively isolated Sichuan Basin.[15] According to the *History of the Latter Han* (*Hou Han shu*), in the seventh month of 184 (the same year in which the Yellow Turbans rose and were defeated), another man surnamed Zhang, Zhang Xiu, led a rebellion in the southwest. His group, known as "the Way of the Five Pecks of Rice," was not suppressed. Piecing together bits of information from the histories, Ōfuchi Ninji has suggested that Zhang Xiu must have been one of the parish leaders of the Celestial Master movement.[16]

We meet Zhang Xiu again in 191. Accompanied by the third Celestial Master, Zhang Lu, he is on his way to Hanzhong, another isolated valley, though north of and not nearly so large as the Sichuan Basin. The two Zhangs have been, according to the historians, dispatched by the military governor of the province to take this region as a buffer between Sichuan and the capital. Zhang Xiu was killed and Zhang Lu subsequently established himself and his followers in the Hanzhong region.[17] The community remained in Hanzhong, according to the histories, for some thirty years.[18] At a time of extreme turbulence and warfare, Zhang Lu is reported to have fought only defensively and to have resisted the entreaties of his followers that he take the title "king" and move to establish a new dynasty.[19]

Despite his earlier connections with the branches of the Han imperial family that established themselves in Shu, during the period in Hanzhong, Zhang Lu was wholly independent.[20] It was during this time that the religious community described later on was in operation. The community was compelled to disband in 215, when Zhang Lu surrendered to the Wei general Cao Cao. After the surrender, Zhang Lu, his five sons, and his most prominent advisers were enfeoffed and the Celestial Master faithful were relocated to areas throughout the Wei kingdom.

This diaspora of the Hanzhong community was to have decisive consequences for the development of the Daoist religion, for it caused what was in effect a government based on religious doctrine to reorganize itself along entirely new principles of cohesion.[21] This metamorphosis will be explored more fully later.[22] Here we will focus on the early Celestial Master community of Hanzhong.

The histories, as we have noted, describe the religion of the Celestial Masters in ways strikingly similar to their accounts of the practices of the Yellow Turbans. The Celestial Masters also cured illness through confession. They taught honesty and loyalty and eschewed deception. When followers became ill, they were to confess their transgressions and were given "talisman water" to drink. For the purposes of confession, there were "chambers of quietness" where the ill might reflect on their faults and perform the proper ritual penances. If they were not cured thereby, the failure was said to be caused by their not keeping faith with the Dao.

There were further rites performed on behalf of the ill. Supplications were made in the form of written documents in three copies. One would be placed on a mountaintop, addressed to heaven; one buried in the earth; and one cast into the water. These were called the "hand petitions to the Three Offices."

Even the scant records of the historians indicate that everyone was regarded as "ill" in one way or another. Those newly converted to the Way of the Celestial Masters were known as "revenant forced laborers" (*guizu*). The latter part of the name was the term used in Han administration for those who owed corvée service to the state, usually military duty or the construction of roads, dikes, and so forth. And, in fact, one of the punishments exacted by the Celestial Masters for minor offenses was road-repair duty. The first part of the name seems to refer to the notion we find in the commentary that all those who do not act in accord with the Dao are no more than "mobile corpses."[23] Converts to the religion, then, may have been regarded as "revenants"—those from among the "living dead" who had returned to the true source of life and thus owed a debt of service to the Dao.

We know quite a bit more of the social organization of the Celestial Masters than we do of that of the short-lived Yellow Turbans. The faithful were divided into twenty-four "administrations" or parishes, each headed by a Libationer.[24] The Libationers instructed the people by means of the *Laozi*, which was to be memorized by chanting it in unison. In this way, even illiterate parishioners could be instructed.

From Daoist texts we know that the people were required to gather at the parishes three times each year, on the seventh day of the first month, the seventh day of the seventh month, and the fifth day of the tenth month by the lunar calendar.[25] On these occasions, their records of birth and death would be verified and communal meals would be held. Also, on these occasions, each family of the faithful would contribute five peck-measures of rice as a faith offering. It is from this practice that the Celestial Masters gained the nickname "the Way of the Five Pecks of Rice," or, in less favorable sources, "the Rice Bandits."

We even have some indication, in historical sources, of the means used to spread the religion. Along the roads leading into and through their areas of control, the Libationers set up "responsibility huts" (*yishe*), constructed something like the post-houses of the day. "Travelers"—in the days of disorder proceeding the end of the Han, more likely these were refugees—were invited to eat their fill of the rice and meat stored in these huts, but were warned that those who took excess would fall ill, in accord with the "way of the revenants." For those who broke the ordinances of the Celestial Masters, three pardons would be issued. Only then would punishment be meted out. Such leniency and concern for the sufferings of the common people had its effect. The historians recount that commoners and non-Chinese peoples alike rejoiced in the rule of the Celestial Masters.

This, then, was the community for whom the *Xiang'er* commentary was written. It was a mixed group, including both Han Chinese and sinicized members of other ethnic groups. As we will see later, the *Xiang'er* was the first commentary to the *Laozi* to be written for the common people rather than an elite readership. The text's goals are also clearly religious. One immediate conclusion to be drawn from these facts is that the *Xiang'er* commentary is less a "commentary" than a treatise that uses the *Laozi* as a point of departure. In the following section, we will see what this means.

The Body of the Dao

Any commentary on the *Laozi* will, of necessity, devote a great deal of space to the nature of the Dao, the cosmic principle underlying the order of existence. Despite this, the *Xiang'er* commentator shows little inclination toward mysticism, being much more concerned with what we might call a "practical metaphysics," a system of thought that derives moral and practical advice for a living community from a cosmology that, though alien to us, is not in itself mystical. Unconcerned with epistemology and even less with spiritual intuition, the commentary labors to provide a concrete description of how the Dao functions in the world and how humans should act to accord with it. The source of this knowledge may have lain in mystical insight or spirit possession, but the commentary does not explain how it—the commentary itself—came into being.

Just as the worldview of the text finds its basis in the shared cosmology of the period, so too the commentarial strategy of the *Xiang'er* is, in many respects, the same as that employed by any classical commentary of the period. This methodology, known as *xungu* (explanation through sound glosses), employs word-by-word exegesis that relies heavily on the assumed etymological affinity of homophonous graphs. For instance, at line 50, the commentary states, "*Gu* [valley] means desire [*yu*]," presumably suggesting that the latter graph is the correct one.[26] The tendency to focus on key words in the text appropriate to this method extends even beyond such paronomastic glosses. Commenting on the line "The gate of the mysterious feminine is the root of heaven and earth," the literal-minded commentator, having explained that the "gate of the mysterious feminine" is the vagina, goes on to assert that it is called the "root" because it is "the very crux [of existence]."

What, then, is new in the *Xiang'er*? Although it is not our purpose here to compare early commentaries to the *Laozi,* we do need to take note of one important way in which the *Xiang'er* commentary differs substantially from the influential commentaries of Heshang Gong (second century C.E.?) and Wang Bi (226–249). The *Laozi* was not written for just anyone who wanted to cultivate the Dao and become a Daoist sage, but primarily for the ruler and those members of the governing class qualified to advise him.[27] For such persons, the Dao was a cosmological system of order to which human society should conform under the governance of the sage, who alone might perfectly embody the Dao. The Heshang Gong and Wang Bi interpretations depart from this original view. These two early commentaries to the *Laozi,* through which we today tend to read it, were part of a trend that expanded the text's audience to include all of the gentry class and, in the process, altered significantly the nature of the Dao. In line with the growing interest in eremitism during the Latter Han and into the period of disunion, the figure of the sage seems to have undergone a shift. No longer was the term employed solely for the "enlightened ruler" or for those select few who, like Confucius, possessed the wondrous qualities of a heaven-appointed ruler. The Dao now might be learned, even cultivated in solitude, far from the demands of political life. Although the Heshang Gong and Wang Bi commentaries still recognized the sections of the *Laozi* most specifically concerned with governance, other sections—those dealing with the cosmological discernment and other mystical attributes of the ruler—were now seen as attainable by any member of the literati class who desired to achieve sagehood. The hermit or gentleman in retirement, who might occupy a high position under a good government but was sure to withdraw under a decadent one, could now benefit from the text.[28]

In being made available to those who strove to embody it, however, the Dao was rendered the object of mystical pursuit. Both the

Heshang Gong commentary, with its emphasis on self-cultivation, and that of Wang Bi, with its philosophical emphasis on "non-being," agree that the sage is first and foremost someone who transcends ordinary mortals in understanding and ability. In short, they hold that the *Laozi* was written for the privileged individual.

In this respect, the *Xiang'er* commentary may prove closer to pre-Han interpretations of the *Laozi*. It is concerned, first and last, with remaking society on the model of the Dao. Passages of the text show clearly that it was intended as a handbook for the enlightened ruler. At the same time, however, the Celestial Masters instructed all of the faithful by means of the *Laozi*. This is because, as the *Xiang'er* commentary explains, each person must be in complete accord with the Dao in order for society, and indeed the cosmos, to function perfectly. The pursuit of sagehood is available, indeed required, of all, not just the specially endowed (who were without exception members of the elite class). In this way, the *Xiang'er*, while preserving more fully the original focus on rulership of the *Laozi*, at the same time expands the audience of the text even more than do the other, roughly contemporary, commentaries. This aspect of the text will become apparent as we explore the nature of the Dao expressed in the *Xiang'er* commentary.

The *Xiang'er* regards a deified Laozi, or Lord Lao, as the hypostasis of the Dao and his book as the "teachings of the Dao" (*dao jiao*—the phrase that, in later texts, came to designate the religion as a whole).[29] Indeed, the two cannot be separated. Lord Lao is the Dao and the Dao is Lord Lao.[30] Through the *Laozi*, the book of the deified Lord Lao, the Dao thus speaks directly to humans.[31] Beyond Laozi's promulgation of the teachings, however, his actions in the world are not explicitly described in the commentary. Instead, the Dao itself is shown to function anthropomorphically. The Dao possesses consciousness and movement, likes and dislikes. It acts in the world not only through spreading its teachings, but also by means of its pneumas, which vivify all living things and provide the motive force behind all existence. Sometimes the pneumas of the Dao congeal to form "essences," which are the spirits that inhabit both the universe and the bodies of human beings. When allowed to flow freely, the pneumas of the Dao move through everything, providing the very stuff of life and movement.

This is especially true of human beings, who at some time in distant antiquity were fully one with the Dao, so much so that the Dao "took humanity as its name." Although the text does not expound on the nature of this primal purity, it is clear that, from their privileged position of oneness with the Dao, human beings were responsible for bringing about the end of their perfect existence through willfully perverting the pneumas of the Dao. Once deviance entered the picture, the nourishing Dao distanced itself from humanity, and people began to die.[32]

Since human and cosmic suffering and death are both traceable to mortal willfulness, the rectification of the sorry situation in which humanity finds itself must proceed on two interrelated fronts, the individual and the social. Although the commentary treats these as two sides of the same coin, we will explore them separately here, under the headings "Meditation and Perfection of the Body" and "Morality and Governance." It should be kept in mind, though, that the body of society and the body of the individual alike must, in the worldview of the *Xiang'er* commentary, be returned to harmonious unity with the body of the Dao. The two aspects are fundamentally the same, though I will here attempt to treat them individually and, insofar as is possible, without redundancy.

Meditation and Perfection of the Body

The *Xiang'er* commentary was clearly not meant as a meditation manual. But, although it does not describe in detail any method of practice, it does provide enough information for us to gain some idea of the place of physiological practices for healing and transcendence within the early Celestial Master movement. Often, these techniques are discussed in the context of distinguishing the correct methods mandated by the Dao from those employed by what the text characterizes as "those who practice false arts in the mortal world." Although we cannot always determine just who it is that the text is criticizing, such passages are valuable in that they show us what the text means to defend. The following account is based on these hints.[33] What is known of rival schools of physical cultivation will, for the most part, be relegated to the endnotes.

The basis for the practices thus alluded to in the *Xiang'er* is the

Dao itself. Just as the Dao is composed of active pneumas that coalesce into spirits, so the human body is inhabited by spirits that subsist on the pneumas of the Dao. To achieve transcendence, the individual must preserve and harmonize these internal spirits.

Desire, anger, and violent emotion represent destructive movement of the pneumas and should be avoided. Though it is true that one is injured less if, according to the movement of the five phases, the pneuma expressed is in the ascendancy, even this depletes the energies of the body. Thus, for instance, one is in less danger if one is angry on a day when the red pneumas of the heart are at their apex, though energies that might be better channeled are still wasted.

The commentary stipulates that one should eradicate these deviant tendencies of the heart in order that one may embrace "clarity and stillness." The models in this pursuit are those already well known from the *Laozi* itself—the woman, the infant, and water— together with a fourth, found only in the commentary: the Transcendent Noble. Transcendent nobility is the state or condition to which all of those to whom the commentary is addressed might aspire. Transcendent Nobles "take the Dao as their name" and are able to pass into the heavens without dying.

The term "clarity and stillness," then, refers to the stilling of emotions that is necessary to receive the life-giving pneumas of the Dao and thereby nourish and perfect the internal spirits.[34] This is achieved through meditation practice. The "pneumas of morning and evening" should be caused to descend into the human body, where they should be mixed with the body's own pneumas so that they are evenly distributed throughout—a technique described as "most essential" and as having been established by "the Master" for morning and evening practice.[35]

Although we have no specific instructions, beyond the reference to morning and evening, for the practice of "clarity and stillness," a few passages give some idea of how it might have been taught:

> Those who seek long life ... do not follow the common run of people in their shifts and turns. Instead, their thoughts are perfectly directed toward the Dao. While they are learning to be clear and still, their thoughts will temporarily be as if confused and muddy; but since they are confused and muddy, they have maintained simplicity and are about

to reach their goal. Finally, in clarity and stillness, they will be able to observe all of the subtleties. (lines 197–200)

This state of confusion and muddiness mirrors that of the undifferentiated pneumas of the Dao. Humans who lack the quality of clarity and stillness are compared to heaven and earth when they are troubled by violent storm or other natural cataclysms. That is, the pneumas of such persons are not integrated and so the pneuma of one viscera lashes forth in violent emotion.[36] Calmness and an unfocused psychophysical wholeness, modeled on the undifferentiated, "confused" state of the Dao, seem to be important for this sort of meditation. This contrasts markedly, we are told, with the visualizations practiced by others who also claim to be Daoists.[37]

Elsewhere in the text we read that "those who employ pneumas and pantingly inhale and exhale do not accord with clarity and stillness and will not long endure" (lines 367–68). This injunction, we are informed, also sets the methods of the Celestial Masters at variance with those practiced by others—here most likely the schools of hygiene.[38] For the Celestial Masters, we are to understand, pneuma is not simple "breath"—or even astral emanation—but the very exhalation of the Dao itself, the source of all life and the sustenance of celestial beings. As the commentary puts it:

> Commoners eat grain, and when the grain is gone, they die. The Transcendent nobility eat grain when they have it, and when they do not, they ingest pneumas. (lines 319–20)[39]

Once inducted into the body, these pneumas must be guided throughout, that they might nourish the body's resident spirits. We learn of this practice in passages criticizing rival Daoist groups who held that the Dao inhabited each of the five viscera in season (according to a five-phase paced cycle), where it might be discerned wearing garb of the appropriate color. No, says the commentary. "Entering into the space between heaven and earth, [the Dao] comes and goes within the human body, that's all. It is there everywhere within your skin, not just in a single spot" (lines 107–8). Clearly, it is the pneumas of the Dao and not the Dao in its entirety that might enter into the body, for elsewhere the text states:

> The heart is a regulator. It may hold fortune or misfortune, good or evil. The belly is a sack for the Dao; its pneumas constantly wish to fill it.

When the heart produces ill-omened and evil conduct, the Dao departs, leaving the sack empty. Once it is empty, deviance enters, killing the person. If one drives off the misfortune and evil in the heart, the Dao will return to it and the belly will be filled. (lines 4–6)

The reference to the heart as regulator is alluded to elsewhere in the commentary, where we find the heart's regulating action styled "the three paths of the Luminous Hall."[40] The "Luminous Hall" was a ritual building of antiquity, a model of the cosmos through which the king would move in harmony with the supposed cycling of celestial pneumas.[41] Here the concept is applied to the heart, king of the five viscera, which is to conduct the third and most vital of three pneumas—the three pneumas being yin, yang, and the "centrally harmonious," the last a blending of the previous two— through the adepts' body.[42] The text is quite specific on this point:

There are three streams in the heart. Both yang deviances and the yin harm should be shut up and not employed. The central stream is the correct one. (lines 409–10)

This is the extent of the information that can be gleaned from the *Xiang'er* commentary on the practices it proposes for "eating pneumas." Undoubtedly, oral instructions would have included methods for guiding the pneumas as they descend into the body, blend, and are apportioned by the heart to the deities resident there, but none of this finds expression here.

Another "false art" roundly savaged in the *Xiang'er* commentary is the method of sexual hygiene designed to replenish a man's store of yin essence. The substance of these critiques is made plain in the following passages:

The Dao teaches people to congeal their essences and form spirits. Today, there are in the world false practitioners who craftily proclaim the Dao, teaching by means of texts attributed to the Yellow Thearch, the Dark Maiden, Gongzi, and Rongcheng. They say that during intercourse with a woman one should not release the semen, but through meditation return its essence to the brain to fortify it. Since their [internal] spirits and their hearts are not unified, they lose that which they seek to preserve. Though they control their delight, they may not treasure it for long. (lines 86–89)

Those who practice the *Classic of the Dark Woman* and the methods of Gongzi and Rongcheng all wish to borrow. But what creditor exists who will loan? So they receive nothing. (lines 431–33)

Here, patrons of the arts of sexual hygiene, some appearing in texts dating as early as the third century B.C.E., are mentioned by name. In the context of these criticisms, the *Xiang'er* commentary advances its own methods for physiological cultivation, methods that can be identified with the ritual of "merging pneumas."[43]

The rite of "merging pneumas" has been called the Celestial Master marriage rite. In the surviving textual version of this practice, it is described as being carried out under the direction of a master and in austere ritual circumstances.[44] The act of sexual penetration itself comes only after a lengthy series of visualizations and massages of one partner by the other, accomplished with both the hands and the feet. Intercourse is also accompanied by incantation designed to conjoin the pneumas of the partners, strengthen the "five spirits" inhabiting their viscera, and join the registers of deities that the two adepts could visualize and summon.[45]

This was a practice roundly criticized in both Buddhist and Daoist circles.[46] Kou Qianzhi (d. 448) extended his animus toward the ritual of "merging pneumas" even to the early church itself, sharply criticizing the three Celestial Masters in the bargain.[47] All of this, coupled with the fact that early works on hygiene had been largely unknown up to the recent archaeological discoveries at Mawangdui and Fangmatan, has led some scholars to question whether the early Celestial Masters even employed the practice of "merging pneumas."[48] The very vehemence with which the *Xiang'er* commentary attacks the classics of sexual hygiene, coupled with other hints scattered in the text, makes it likely that they did.

Jing, the term I have been consistently translating as "essence," is regarded in the *Xiang'er* as the concretion of pneuma.[49] The pneumas of the Dao congeal to form spirits both in the macrocosm and in the microcosm of the human body. Within humans, though, this essence, like ice, is prone to melt and leak away, resulting in death.[50] Sexual intercourse is, at least for males, one of the primary ways in which the vital essence might be lost. As the commentary expresses it:

> The whitesouls are white in color. For this reason, essence [here to be understood as semen] is white, the same color as primal pneuma. The body is the vehicle of the essence, and, since essence tends to fall from it, you should carry and manage it. When the [internal] spirits are formed,

pneumas come to carry and manage the human body. If you wish to complete this task, do not depart from the One. The One is the Dao. (lines 102–5)

Essence forms spirits, and the spirits are nurtured by further influxes of pneuma. Essence tends to leak away, but the Dao, loving humanity and desiring that the species continue, has not mandated against all sexual intercourse. It does make clear, however, that any outflow of essence should be solely for the purpose of reproduction.[51] The following passage, with its additional criticism of mundane practices of sexual hygiene, elucidates these points:

> The Dao of yin and yang [i.e., sexual intercourse] is therefore similar to congealing the essences to produce life. At the age of fifty, having filled one's [productive] role, one should stop. Even when one is young, though one possesses [the capabilities for reproduction], one should rest [from intercourse] and preserve [these potencies].... If one from youth follows the path of lessening, one will endure for a long time. At present, this matter [i.e., sexual intercourse] is the cause of great injury. Why did the Dao create it? The Dao places great emphasis on the continuation of ancestral sacrifice and the survival of the species. Desiring humanity to join their essences and so produce life, the Dao teaches the youthful to preserve their essences but not to cut them off.[52] It does not teach humanity to labor [at intercourse]. This scheme of laboring [at intercourse] was thought up by the ignorant. The Dao cannot be held responsible for it. Those of higher virtue possess iron wills and are able to stop coupling for the purposes of reproducing. Thus they cut off the flow [of their essences] when they are young. Moreover, in this way they are sooner able to form beneficent [internal] spirits. These are called "essences of the Dao." (lines 55–62)

This passage makes it plain that Daoists are to preserve their essences and, optimally, refrain altogether from "coupling for purposes of reproduction." Concerned only with the preservation of essence, the passage cannot be taken as evidence that the early Celestial Masters did not practice the "merging of pneumas." In fact it does leave open the possibility that they did encourage "coupling" for purposes other than that of reproduction.

The passages immediately preceding the one just cited explain that the bodies of women are patterned after the earth and that women's sexual organs thus do not become rigid, allowing women a natural ability to preserve their essences. Men are enjoined to emulate them. It is also revealed here that both the vagina and the penis are called "the root." The significance of this appellation, and of the commentary's concern with the sexual organs, is made plain in yet another passage, which explains:

> When the pneumas of the Dao return to the root, it is even more impor-
> tant to maintain clarity and stillness.... Knowing how to treasure the
> root in clarity and stillness is the constant method of restoring one's life.
> (lines 219–20)[53]

Now, why should the pneumas of the Dao return "to the root" if the role of the male sexual organ was merely to leak away essence? We note, too, that "clarity and stillness" is vital to the meditation practice described earlier whereby the heart receives and correctly apportions the pneumas of the Dao. This passage in fact deals with "pneumas" returning to the sexual organs, and not essence. Though the two are related, essence is the more condensed and vital, in that it forms the spirits that inhabit the body. It is to be preserved at all costs. Pneuma, though it is the basic component of essence, naturally moves in and out of the body as well as circulating within it. The commentary does not say what was expected to occur when the pneumas of the Dao return to the sexual organs, but it is likely that this was regarded as the necessary precondition for the rite of "merging the pneumas."[54] Further, since the goal of all the practices involving pneuma mentioned here was to achieve the blended "centrally harmonious" pneuma, some sort of procedure designed to mix the excess yin and yang pneumas of female and male so as to avoid "deviances of yang and injuries of yin" would have been necessary. *Heqi,* the "merging of pneumas," was precisely such a method. Thus, though the term does not occur in the *Xiang'er* fragment remaining to us, the text does offer a rationale for the rite.

Finally, we need to look briefly at the goal of these practices, the *Xiang'er* concepts of transcendence. Throughout the text, the ultimate aim of those fortunate humans who are able to keep faith with the Dao is described simply as "life" or as "enduring existence" as a member of the "Transcendent nobility." The details of this postmortem existence are not made entirely clear, but, as Anna Seidel has pointed out, the *Xiang'er* contains perhaps the earliest mention of the "Palace of Greater Yin" (or "Grand Darkness," as the term is translated here), the place where the bodies of the fortunate dead are transmuted and perfected:[55]

> Grand Darkness is the palace where those who have accumulated the Dao refine their forms. When there is no place for them to stay in the world, the worthy withdraw and, feigning death, pass through Grand Darkness to have their images reborn on the other side. This is to be "obliterated without perishing." The profane are unable to accumulate good deeds, so when they die it is truly death. They are taken away in service of the Earth Offices. (lines 227–30)

As I have explained in the general introduction, Daoists do recognize the inevitable end of worldly existence. The long life they sought was not extended life in this world, but the avoidance of death, here described in terms of withdrawal, "feigned death," and continued existence in the next life. Always, as here, the "form," the physical body itself, was considered vital to such postmortem existence. There is no idea that only the spiritual constituents of the body might fly off to a continued existence in the heavens. The Palace of Grand Darkness, then, serves as the mechanism for perfecting the physical constituents of the self for such postmortem existence. Those who fail to reach it can expect to find themselves in the subterranean earth-prisons, where they will, later texts tell us, undergo an equally physical existence, but one of servitude, toil, and unremitting suffering. The *Xiang'er* commentary says no more about this destination, though it is clearly an undesirable one.

Those who do pass through the Palace of Grand Darkness are reborn "on the other side" as "images" of their former selves. Presumably this "image" will be a perfected, "refined"—the metaphor is metallurgical—simulacrum of their mundane bodies. The text does not specify where the "other side" might be; and there is no specific mention of rebirth or resurrection, ideas we now know not to have been imported with Buddhism.[56] It is not impossible that, just as Lord Lao (or "the Dao") was believed to have been successively reincarnated, so might the same have been believed of some of his more favored followers, but the *Xiang'er* provides no evidence.[57]

Whatever the ultimate destination, the conception of the Palace of Grand Darkness presented here is not divorced from the physiological practices explored earlier. The commentary develops a homology between the "greater yin" of the Palace of Grand Darkness and the lesser yin of the urogenital vesicle *shen,* where essence was thought to be stored within the human body.[58] Just as the bodies of mortals might be refined within the Palace of Grand Darkness to a more perfect, spiritual state, so within the *shen* might the essences, if they are not agitated or leaked away, be formed into spirits to inhabit the body. We shall see that the Shangqing school developed such ideas to encompass the creation within the body of a perfected embryo through absorption of solar and lunar pneumas, which were mixed in the lower abdomen. As the *shen,* the organ of reproduction, is emphasized here, similar ideas might have underlain these practices as well, but the text tells us no more about them.[59]

In later Daoist texts, similar practices designed to vivify and unify the spirits of the body are known under the name "preserving the One" or "preserving unity" (*shouyi*).[60] The *Xiang'er* commentary emphasizes that "those who keep the precepts and do not transgress them have maintained Unity. Those who do not practice the precepts will lose this Unity" (line 111). Indeed, in what the text calls the "precepts of the Dao" we read that adepts should not waste their essence and pneumas and that one should not allow the essences to "overflow." It is to these precepts and to the more conventional moral and social aspects of the *Xiang'er* commentary that we now turn.

Morality and Governance

Lines 206–7 of the commentary state in capsule form one of the central messages of the *Xiang'er* commentary:

> Whenever human beings wish to undertake some action, they should first gauge it against the precepts of the Dao, considering it calmly to determine that the principles of their action do not contravene the Dao. Only then should they gradually pursue it, so that the Dao of life does not depart from them.

As the primary and paramount teaching of Lord Lao, *the* embodiment of the Dao—in that "the One [i.e., the Dao] disperses its form as pneuma and gathers in its form as the Most High Lord Lao, whose permanent rule is on Mount Kunlun"—the *Laozi* text was regarded by the early Celestial Masters as containing the rules by which they must live so as to accord with the intentions of the Dao and gain life. Anyone who has attended to the startling variety of ways in which people have interpreted the *Laozi*—in Chan (Japanese "Zen") contexts; in modern China, Taiwan, and Singapore; even among New Age movements in the United States—will recognize that this is no simple proposition.

Unlike Wang Bi, who drew inspiration from the *Yijing,* the *Xiang'er* commentator has not interpreted the *Laozi* in light of other texts. His sources of inspiration, beyond perhaps the *Scripture of Great Peace,* remain unknown. Although we know next to nothing of his sources and methods in deriving meaning from the *Laozi,* we do have evidence of the results.

Chen Shixiang, Ōfuchi Ninji, and others have identified in the Daoist canon various scriptures that list the "*Xiang'er* precepts." These are divided into nine prescriptive precepts—the "Nine Practices"—and twenty-seven proscriptive precepts. The former are drawn from the wording of the *Laozi* itself and the latter from the *Xiang'er* commentary. Both the "Nine Practices" and the "*Xiang'er* precepts," as I will call the latter group, are further divided into three groups—upper, middle, and lower. This ordering foregrounds the numerology of the precepts—they appear in multiples of three and nine—rather than emphasizing any hierarchy of importance.[61] Though there are slight differences in wording, the various sources of the precepts are remarkably uniform and close in wording to the *Xiang'er* itself. The precepts are as follows:[62]

The Nine Practices (extracted from the *Laozi*)

1. Practice lacking falseness.
2. Practice flexibility and weakness.
3. Practice maintaining the feminine. Do not initiate actions.
4. Practice lacking fame.
5. Practice clarity and stillness.
6. Practice good deeds.
7. Practice desirelessness.
8. Practice knowing how to cease with sufficiency.
9. Practice yielding to others.

The *Xiang'er* Precepts (extracted from the Commentary)

All begin "You are admonished … ":

1. Do not delight in deviance. Delight is the same as anger.
2. Do not waste your essence and pneumas.
3. Do not injure the ascendant pneumas.
4. Do not consume beasts that contain blood, delighting in their flavor.
5. Do not envy the achievements and fame of others.
6. Do not practice false arts or point to any shape and call it the Dao.
7. Do not neglect the law [i.e., the doctrine and ritual practices] of the Dao.
8. Do not act recklessly.
9. Do not kill or speak of killing.
10. Do not study deviant texts.
11. Do not covet glory or seek it strenuously.
12. Do not seek fame.
13. Do not be deceived by your ears, eyes, or mouth.
14. Place yourself in a humble position.
15. Do not slight [the Dao] or become agitated.
16. Consider carefully all undertakings and do not be flustered.
17. Do not pamper your body with good clothes and fine foods.
18. Do not allow [your emotions and vital forces] to overflow.
19. Do not, through poverty, seek strenuously after wealth.
20. Do not commit any of the various evil acts.
21. Do not overly observe the interdictions and taboos.
22. Do not pray or sacrifice to demons and spirits.
23. Do not be obstinate.
24. Do not consider yourself inerrant.
25. Do not contend with others over right and wrong. When you meet the contentious, flee them.
26. Do not proclaim [yourself to be a] Sage or contribute to the fame of the mighty.
27. Do not delight in arms.

Even a cursory glance at these lists shows that morality is here defined in such a way as to encompass the necessity of physiological cultivation practices. Of the "Nine Practices," "clarity and stillness," as we saw earlier, refers to a specific form of pneuma ingestion. The injunction that one should "maintain the feminine" and not "initiate actions," as well as numbers 2 and 18 of the *Xiang'er* precepts, are most likely related to the practice of sexual abstinence outside of reproduction and the ritual "merging the pneumas." Even the various injunctions against anger, envy, obstinacy, desire, and delight are, as we have seen, related to the proper management of the body's pneumas and the cultivation of internal spirits. It is no wonder, then, that the accomplishment of good deeds (*shanxing*) was thought to lead to prolonged physical existence, both in this world and beyond. The commentary expresses this in a vivid parable:

> The essences might be compared to the waters of a pond and the body to the embankments along the sides of the pond. Good deeds are like the water's source. If these three things are all complete, the pond will be sturdy. If the heart does not fix itself on goodness, then the pond lacks embankments and the water will run out. If one does not accumulate good deeds, the pond is cut off at its source and the water will dry up. If one breaches the dike to irrigate fields as if it were a river or stream, then, even though the embankments hold, the original flow will leak off too and the pond will empty. When the bed of the pond becomes scorched and cracked, that is the various illnesses all emerging. If one is not cautious about these three things, the pond will become an empty ditch. (lines 329–33)

The text's emphasis on morality extends beyond self-preservation, however, to those social actions that we normally subsume under the heading of morality, but in ways that are very different from the conventional Confucian-inspired moral systems of ancient China. As an entry into this aspect of the text, let us first look at one of the key concepts of the *Laozi*, that of *wu wei*.

The very first of the "Nine Practices" enjoins one to "practice *wu wei*." William Boltz has pointed out a key passage in which the *Xiang'er* manuscript interpolates the concept of "*wu wei*" into the *Laozi* where the term does not figure in the Mawangdui manuscripts.[63] This is not yet the *wu wei* of Wang Bi, however. The *wei* of *wu wei* is in this text to be understood in terms of its close cognate *wei*, "artificial, contrived, fabricated, false." Thus, "material goods lead to artifice" (line 142), and the *wu wei* of an infant comes about because "infants are unaware of self-control" (line 113) and so cannot act willfully. Adherents are not enjoined not to act, but to still their hearts, to quiet the winds of passion, and to make the movements of the Dao their own through following its precepts. They are forbidden to act in evil ways, which for this text means "contrived" ways that originate in the human will and passions.[64] For *wu wei*, then, I have employed for this text various rather cumbersome translations such as "uncontrived," "lacking human artifice," or even "lacking willfulness" rather than the more wieldy terms "inaction" and "nonintervention" usually relied upon in translations of the *Laozi*.[65]

So defined, *wu wei* is closely connected to another important concept of the *Xiang'er* commentary, that of *xie*, "perversion, deviance."[66] The opposite of *xie* is *zheng*, "upright, morally correct," and, in fact, the way of the Celestial Masters is known in this text as the "correct law" or, in other early texts, "correct Unity"—the "Unity" or "One" being at once the Dao and the integrated state of the person who fully receives its life-giving pneumas. "Deviance" is any tendency that departs from the guiding course of the Dao. On the macrocosmic level, storms, stellar anomalies, violent wind, and other natural calamities are the result of perversion of the Dao's life-giving pneumas. Interestingly, even these are the result of human misdeed, since the Dao causes them as a warning for human beings. The primal age of "Great Peace" can be recovered only when humans return to the "correct" or "perfect" law revealed to them by Lord Lao.

Among the "deviances" are a number of physiological practices discussed earlier as well as another that will concern us here, Confucian morality. The disdain shown by the *Laozi* for the primary Confucian moral concepts is well known. The *Xiang'er* commentary intensifies this attack and places it within the all-embracing framework of its metaphysics. According to the commentary, the Dao "taught Confucius all that he knew" and his followers "have not kept faith with the writings of the Dao, but merely revere Confucius's writings, considering them the highest."[67] Contemporary Confucians are thus numbered among the "practitioners of false arts"; and, of the classics upon which they rely so heavily, "a goodly half is deviant" (line 248).

According to the *Laozi,* the reason that Confucian morality does not work is as much a linguistic (in the Saussurian mode) as a philosophical failure. Since the existence of a word not only implies but in fact bears responsibility for creating its opposite, if an enlightened ruler were to discard the Confucian virtues, the people would naturally revert to goodness, for they could then conceive of no other course.[68] The *Xiang'er* commentator follows the *Laozi* only part way in this concern. Glossing one of the key phrases in the attack of the *Laozi* on Confucianism—"When the Great Dao was discarded, humaneness and responsibility came into being"—the commentary admits:

> In high antiquity, when the Dao was employed ... all were of the same type so that the benevolent and dutiful were not distinguished from others. Today the Dao is not employed and people are all flawed. When occasionally there is a single person who is dutiful, that person is praised by all in contradistinction to others. (lines 243–46)

But, as we noticed earlier, the *Xiang'er* commentary is directed to a wider audience, not to the sage-ruler who might with impunity keep the populace in ignorance, as is advocated in the *Laozi.* At each point where the *Laozi* suggests that knowledge be discarded and the people kept in ignorance, the *Xiang'er* glosses the phrase in question to the effect that *deviant* knowledge should be discarded and that people should be kept in ignorance of *deviant* texts—Confucian texts primary among them.[69] Rather than following the *Laozi* in criticizing the Confucian solution because it is better that the populace be kept in a natural state of ignorance, the *Xiang'er* develops a truly religious alternative.

According to the *Xiang'er,* Confucian morality fails because its practitioners are not sincere. From the common people up to the highest ministers of state, morality is pursued only in hope of earthly reward and societal acclaim. Even self-proclaimed sages merely "measure themselves by chapter and verse" in pursuit of personal aggrandizement, ignoring the primary teaching duties of sagehood. Common people, seeing those who are only outwardly moral rewarded, imitate them. The result is that

> [s]ons do not care to support their fathers; people have no thought for their fields. They only pursue deviant learning, lining up outside the doors of deviant masters. They exhaust all of their energies chanting

flawed teachings, even to the end of their days. Finding that they are unable to move heaven through sincere practice of loyalty and filiality; that, though they attempt to regulate their bodies, they are unable to reach the longevity of Transcendents; and that, though they try to aid their lord, they are unable to bring about Great Peace—still the people employ these unproductive teachings unceasingly, even to the point that the capitals and cities are deserted. (lines 273–76)

The alternative to this sad state of affairs is a religious morality based not on human desire for wealth and acclaim but on fear and respect of heaven. One of the passages in which this solution is propounded, though lengthy, deserves to be cited here. Commenting on the *Laozi* passage that the ruler ought to "eliminate humaneness, discard responsibility, and the people will return to filiality and benevolence," the *Xiang'er* sets the conditions of that "return" as follows:

> When the kingdom is ruled in a manner patterned on the Dao and when those of humanity and responsibility in the world are employed, there is no need for force or reward. This is because people will become humane and responsible once their moral transformation is valued and the mind of the Dao is fully open to all. Those who are sincere by themselves will naturally be rewarded by heaven, and those who are not will naturally be punished by heaven. Heaven's scrutiny is even more thoroughgoing than any human being's. It knows fully who reveres the Dao and fears heaven. All humaneness and duty will thus be sincere.
>
> Nowadays kings rule through force and reward, so the people no longer give allegiance to Heaven.... Mortal scrutiny of good and evil deeds is just not thorough enough. But if human rewards were discontinued, all would revert to benevolence and filiality on their own. The reason for so doing runs counter to the common sense of the ordinary person, but after a long time they will come to understand and will join with the Dao. The ruler of humanity should be fully cognizant of this. (lines 277–86)

It is out of fear or awe of omniscient Heaven on the one hand and reverence for the Dao on the other that people will act morally. "Heaven," in this case, is not the supreme moral force of Confucian thought, but a celestial bureaucracy perfectly modeled on the Dao.[70] Heaven's means of oversight is through celestial officers who tally the good deeds and transgressions of humans in their books of life. According to the *Xiang'er*, the tallies of the right are reserved for those outside the Dao, who are destined for death, whereas the tallies of the left, the tallies of life, belong to those who keep the precepts of the Dao.[71] The unit by which transgressions are recorded on these tallies is the "count." A serious transgression results in the deduction of three thousand counts. According to later texts, each count equals a certain number of days, from one to ten, to be subtracted from the transgressor's life span.[72] The *Xiang'er* assures us not only that Heaven's scrutiny far surpasses that of any human ruler, but that the people will even perform good in secret, out of the fear that if their rulers and masters were to reward them, they would be deprived of Heaven's reward—the "longevity of Transcendents" (lines 257–59).

Although it excoriates contemporary, mainstream Confucian ethics, the system of religious morality proposed here is equally reliant on human desire and on its own version of "reward and punishment."[73] How then does it deal with the *Laozi*'s injunction that the people should be "without desire"? Once again, the *Xiang'er* commentator is careful to distinguish between the deviant and the correct. The *Laozi* requirement that the ruler cause the people to be without desire is glossed to the effect that people should not "covet precious goods" (lines 10–11). Number seven of the "Nine Practices" enjoins one only to "practice desirelessness," but this requirement is clearly mediated by numbers five, eleven, twelve, fourteen, seventeen, and nineteen of the *Xiang'er* precepts, which mandate against what the text considers "deviant" or human desires for wealth, position, worldly glory, and the like. As the commentary, borrowing some of the poetry of the *Laozi*, puts it:

> You should have no other concerns; only trust in the Dao should be found in the broad emptiness of your heart. Your aspiration should be like that of ice in the valley, which desires only to flow east and return to the great sea. (lines 195–97)

Despite its thoroughgoing emphasis on the moral and religious education of the populace, the *Xiang'er* commentary does present itself as a supplement to the *Laozi* in its role as a treatise on the art of governance. At points in the commentary, the ruler is addressed directly, in such phrases as "if now you wish to return to [the practice of the Dao], it is urgently important that the thearchical ruler wholeheartedly place his trust in the precepts of the Dao."[74] The ruler proves, as we should expect, key to the establishment of an era of Great Peace on the model of the Dao, for "the transformative influence of the Dao proceeds down from the top.... If the king's governance is patterned on the Dao, the officers and populace—even the lowly and the evil—will all convert to the Dao."[75]

The commentary distinguishes three sorts of rulers. First is the "lord of great sageliness," who fully makes the Dao his master and thereby brings about the auspicious omens of Great Peace. Second is the "lord of middling worthiness," who employs worthy Daoist ministers. The text warns, though, that should this lord's ministers depart one morning, the kingdom will be in danger of toppling by evening. Finally, almost beneath mention, is the ruler who transgresses the Dao, even "belittling the perfected texts in the belief that [people] will persist in following him." Such a ruler brings upon himself and his kingdom not only social disorder, but plague and demonic infestation.[76] Beyond the *Xiang'er*'s strict requirement that the ruler adopt, if not practice himself, the "correct law" of the Dao, its concept of kingship proves fully consonant with Han ideas of the thearch, especially as developed in the "weft texts," prognostic texts represented as appendices to the Confucian classics. The surviving passages that make this debt plain describe how the "essences of the Five Thearchs," each associated with one of the five phases, give birth in turn to the founder of the dynastic house that is destined to rule. When this occurs, the name of the new thearch is augured forth by the Yellow River Chart and the Luo River writings, and blazoned in the very stars of heaven.[77] All of these prodigies are described in the weft texts, which further relate that the ancient thearchs were engendered by the miraculous impregnation of their mothers by divine "essence."[78]

The *Xiang'er* recommendations for the ruler accord perfectly with the way in which Zhang Lu actually conducted himself during his regency in Hanzhong. What we know from historical sources of his benevolent rule, his avoidance of armed conflict, and his final surrender to Cao Cao all find warrant in the commentary.[79] It is likely that in Cao Cao, Zhang felt he had found a lord of at least "middling worthiness."

Beyond such suggestive details, however, there is in the *Xiang'er* commentary only indirect testimony to the practices that so impressed secular historians. As mentioned earlier, the "chamber of quietness" is likely related to the meditation practices subsumed under the designation "the practice of clarity and stillness." Confession is not specifically mentioned in the commentary, at least not under the terminology employed by the historians. We do, however, find frequent reference to the fact that illness is the result of deviance and that adepts need to contemplate all of their actions to ensure that they do not transgress the precepts of the Dao.[80] The "documents" to be addressed on behalf of transgressors to the Three Offices are not mentioned either, but a possible justification for such petitions is found in the text: the Office of Heaven records transgressions in one's book of life, and the Office of Earth is in charge of the unfortunate dead.

Secular historians further mention that, under Zhang Lu's rule, lawbreakers were forgiven three times before punishment was applied. A suggestive reference in the section on warfare that might be related to this practice urges that the Celestial Master faithful, when compelled to engage in warfare, should first "proclaim thrice the five commands, indicating to [their enemies] the precepts of the Dao and [their] willingness to receive their submission."[81] The same practice is mentioned by Lu Xiujing (406–477), who notes that, as part of the thrice yearly assemblies, the master should "correct the name rosters and make a triple announcement of the five commands so that the people know the law [of the Dao]."[82] Apparently then, the practice was not military and likely was employed for those who violated the statutes as well.

Finally, though, such "lacunae" should not bother us overly much. As the items just discussed indicate, the historians seem to have expressed Celestial Master doctrines in their own words (substituting, for instance, gui, "revenants," for what our text forthrightly calls shi, "corpses"), and at any rate, over half of the commentary is missing.

In sum, the moral universe of the Xiang'er commentary begins and ends with the concern of the Dao for its people. There is, to be sure, more than a hint of paternalism. As in Confucianism, the commoners are to be swayed by the example of their betters, whose moral influence moves them "like a wind through the slender

grasses." But in this text the status to which they might finally aspire
is the highest in the land, that of sage or even, after death, "transcendent nobility." Such a promise could not be held out by Confucianism, with its stricter models of status relationships, nor convincingly by Buddhism, in that it lacked the bureaucratic impulse.
Even Daoism, as it came to be accepted in gentry circles, moved
away from the extreme promises we find here. Recognition of this
fact renders all the more poignant the anguished exhortations of
later authors, who wrote when this ideal system was finally unravel-
ing. And it makes all the more valuable the witness of the *Xiang'er*
commentary to what was, in fact, a unique event in Chinese history.

The Authorship and Date
of the Xiang'er Commentary

The sole surviving fragment of the *Xiang'er* commentary was discovered among the documents obtained from the Buddhist grottoes
at Dunhuang and brought back to London by Sir Aurel Stein in the
early twentieth century. Numbered *S* 6825, the manuscript contains
text and commentary on only the first half of the *Laozi* text. The
opening is also torn and missing. The commentary covers part of
what is designated chapter 3 through the end of chapter 37 in standard, received editions of the *Laozi*. At the end of the manuscript, a
colophon states simply, "*Laozi, Scripture of the Dao,* upper chapter,
Xiang'er." From this it is clear that there was also a *Xiang'er* commentary to the lower, or "De," portion of the *Laozi,* a fact confirmed by bibliographic references to the text.[83]

Experts in analyzing the calligraphy and paper of Dunhuang
documents judge that the *Xiang'er* manuscript dates to roughly the
late fifth or early sixth century.[84] To date, no one has detected the
presence of "avoidance characters" that might help to ascertain with
more precision just when the manuscript was copied. The commentary is interlinear, but layed out in an archaic style. There are no
breaks between commentary and the text, and both are written in
characters of uniform size.[85] Neither is the text divided into *zhang*
or chapters, a significant fact that we shall return to in a moment.
Bibliographic references to the *Xiang'er*, where they cite an author
at all, uniformly attribute authorship either to Zhang Daoling or to
his grandson, Zhang Lu.[86]

Ōfuchi Ninji, in his thoroughgoing analysis of the text, has determined that the *Xiang'er* commentary is not to the received editions of the *Laozi,* but to the so-called Five Thousand Character version of the text, which has long been thought to have originated with the Daoist religion. He has discovered that the *Xiang'er* version of the *Laozi* is closest to that of the "Ge edition" of the text, the "Five Thousand Character" edition that appears with a preface attributed to Ge Xuan (fl. ca. 200 C.E.). Although the "Ge edition," unlike the *Xiang'er,* is normally divided into chapters, a number of manuscript copies from Dunhuang end with a colophon giving the actual number of characters as 4,999 and explaining that the text was "established by the lineally descended Master [Zhang Lu's title in Daoist texts] and divided into chapters according to the Perfected Heshang's [version of the text]."[87] Such findings on the *Laozi* text annotated in the *Xiang'er* manuscript indicate that it is authentically early, but are of little help with the question of the authorship of the commentary.

Given the paucity of information on the *Xiang'er* commentary in later texts and our lack of documentation on the early history of the Celestial Masters, it will likely remain impossible to prove with certainty that Zhang Lu was the author of the text. Nonetheless, evidence offered by Rao Zongyi and Ōfuchi Ninji lends credence to the earliest references to the commentary, which credit Zhang Lu with authorship. Lacking compelling evidence to the contrary, there is no reason to discount the witness of the early sources they have gathered.[88]

Ōfuchi's researches on the precepts based on the *Xiang'er* commentary and cited in other early works further demonstrate that, if the commentary is not in fact the work of Zhang Lu, it at any rate dates from the early Celestial Master movement.[89] Indeed, it appears from Ōfuchi's findings that the precepts came to eclipse the commentary from which they were derived. As the Heshang Gong commentary grew in importance in Daoist circles and as the doctrines expressed in the *Xiang'er* were developed in later texts, the commentary itself began to appear dated. Eventually it came to be regarded as little more than an archaic textual talisman, possessed only by Daoist "Masters of the Doctrine" of the higher order.[90]

Further, and again following the lead of Chen Shixiang, Ōfuchi points to evidence that allows us to be even more accurate in dating the commentary. The *Commands and Admonitions for the Families*

of the Great Dao, another early Celestial Master text, one written in
the voice of a Celestial Master in 255 C.E., betrays ideas very similar
to those of the *Xiang'er,* contains the words *"xiang er,"* and cites
precisely one of the *Xiang'er* precepts.[91] My own study of the
Admonitions has turned up at least six further points at which it
depends for its logic, if not its wording, on the *Xiang'er* commentary. The most compelling of these is the flurry of citations from the
Laozi, all of which rely on the understandings of the *Xiang'er* commentary, that appear at the end of the text. A brief citation from this
portion of the *Admonitions* will serve to illustrate this point:

> The Dao conceals itself and is nameless. Name is an axe that hacks at the
> body. "Good actions leave no trace." If they wish to make it so that oth-
> ers do not see their "traces," those who practice the Dao should regulate
> their bodies and nurture their lives to seek blessing. Instead of which
> you teach others to give free rein to the self. If the self is given free rein,
> people will see its traces.[92]

The locution "X is an axe that hacks away at the body" occurs
at *Xiang'er,* line 350, where it is applied to evil in general. More
telling, the *Laozi* passage cited in the *Admonitions* extract is glossed
by all other commentators of whom I am aware as meaning "one
good at traveling leaves no traces."[93] Given its parallelism with lines
such as "one good at calculations does not use counting sticks" and
"one good at tying, ties without using ropes or knots, yet it cannot
be untied," this is likely the best explanation of the *Laozi* passage.
The *Xiang'er* commentary alone takes *shan,* "good," in a moral
sense: "When one keeps faith with the Dao and practices good, there
is no trace of evil" (line 405), obviously reading the line as I have
translated it in the *Admonitions* extract.[94] This is the understanding
of the *Admonitions* author as well, since he states that "if the self is
given free rein, people will see its traces." It is almost certain, then,
that the author of the *Admonitions* is following the *Xiang'er* explanation of the line.

The remaining allusions to the *Xiang'er* commentary are mentioned in the footnotes to the translation of the *Admonitions* in this
book. Since the *Admonitions* gives the date of its circulation to all of
the Daoist faithful, we have an extremely accurate *terminus ad quem*
for the composition of the *Xiang'er* commentary—1 February 255.

As Ōfuchi notes, however, it is likely that the commentary was composed for a stable Daoist community, one (as we will see) searching
for a worthy monarch to adopt its ideas of governance. All of these
conditions best fit the Hanzhong community and point to Zhang Lu
as the most likely author.

One remaining mystery is the meaning of the title of the commentary. Several hypotheses have been offered. Chen Shixiang speculates that the name may have something to do with *cunxiang,* the
visualization of deities. Both Rao and Ōfuchi cite later scriptures
containing the two graphs *xiang* and *er* in contexts where they mean
either that celestial deities "think of you" or that adepts should
"*contemplate* them" and they will bring peace to "*you.*"[95] Indeed,
the most common meaning of the two graphs *xiang* and *er* is
"thinking of (or contemplating) you." It seems most likely that this
simple explanation is the best one. The *Admonitions* contains two
phrases that, though using only proximate wording, express this
very idea:

> If you keep your mind fixed on the Dao, the Dao will keep you in mind;
> if you do not, the Dao will not be mindful of you.

> If you cherish life and practice the Dao with your thoughts on the True
> and Correct, the Dao will cherish you. If you do not remain mindful of
> the Dao, the Dao will distance itself from you.[96]

The *Xiang'er* commentary also emphasizes this idea throughout.
Several examples follow:

> Those who keep the precepts and do not transgress them have main-
> tained Unity. Those who do not practice the precepts will lose this Unity.
> (line 111)

> Whenever human beings wish to undertake some action, they should
> first gauge it against the precepts of the Dao, considering it calmly to
> determine that the principles of their action do not contravene the Dao.
> Only then should they gradually pursue it, so that the Dao of life does
> not depart from them. (line 206)

> If people do not hold in awe the precepts of the Dao in all things and
> miss the intentions of the Dao, the Dao will depart from them. (line 365)

It seems from this that the phrase "If you think of the Dao, the
Dao will think of you" was a slogan of the early Celestial Masters.
It would make sense, then, that the commentary might be styled

"[the Dao] thinks of you," as Ōfuchi has in fact suggested. Due to the somewhat ridiculous prospect of writing throughout of the "Thinking of You" commentary as much as to the hypothetical nature of this conclusion, I have left the term untranslated here.

Structure and Conventions of the Translation

Like the Mawangdui editions of the *Laozi,* the edition presented in the *Xiang'er* manuscript is not divided into chapters. There is evidence to support the notion that the Heshang Gong edition of the text, which is known in early bibliographies as the "Heshang Gong *Laozi* [divided into] chapters and verses," was the earliest to be so divided.[97] But whether it was or not, it is clear that the division into chapters is an act of interpretation, especially given the reading conventions of classical Chinese, where, for instance, when sentence subjects are omitted one routinely assumes that the last-mentioned subject is the subject of succeeding sentences as well. In an attempt to preserve insofar as possible the structure and flow of the original text, I have thus decided not to insert, even in parentheses, any reference to the chapter divisions of other editions.

This decision has created some problems, especially in that Rao Zongyi, whose edition of the text is otherwise quite useful and readily accessible, and Mugitani Kuniō, who has produced a concordance to and accompanying transcription of the manuscript, have both decided to follow the chapter divisions of the received editions. The translation given here, then, will of necessity refer by line number to the photographic copy of S 6825 reproduced in Ōfuchi Ninji's *Tonkō dōkyō mokurokuhen.*[98] For the benefit of those who wish to compare this translation with other translations or editions of the *Laozi,* I have provided a "Key to Chapter Numbers" matching the chapter divisions of the received text to the line numbers of the *Xiang'er* text; see table 3.

In Ōfuchi's reproduction, the lines are counted off by fives. I have followed the same procedure, marking in the margins of the translation the English line in which every fifth line of Chinese text begins. Of course the line numbers of my translation will not precisely match those of the Chinese text, but the reader should be able to find the text to which I refer without too much difficulty.

TABLE 3.   KEY TO CHAPTER NUMBERS IN THE LAOZI

Laozi chap. no.	*Xiang'er* line no.	*Laozi* chap. no.	*Xiang'er* line no.
3	1–14	21	321–37
4	15–31	22	337–56
5	31–50	23	357–67
6	50–64	24	367–77
7	64–74	25	378–90
8	74–85	26	390–404
9	85–102	27	404–23
10	102–24	28	423–43
11	124–37	29	443–59
12	137–45	30	459–78
13	145–65	31	478–91
14	165–84	32	491–504
15	184–211	33	504–18
16	211–30	34	518–26
17	230–43	35	526–53
18	243–65	36	553–72
19	265–92	37	572–84
20	292–321		

There were three mistakes made by whoever originally counted the lines of the Chinese text. These are as follows:

1. The fourth line after line 90, which ends a page of the reproduction, is counted as 99 instead of 94.
2. Line 320 is counted twice, so that what should be line 325 appears as a second 320.
3. What should be line 395 is instead marked 400.

In his reproduction, Ōfuchi marks each of these mistakes with an asterisk. I have seen no reason to follow suit in this. Since my numbering serves only as a reference to the Chinese text and missing lines will obviously not be referred to in my analysis of the text, the first and third mistakes have no consequences here. I have, however, marked the second instance of line 320 with the small letter *a* and will refer to it and the following four lines as 320a, 321a, and so forth.

In translating the *Xiang'er* commentary, it was unavoidable that I also translate portions of the *Laozi,* something that had been done so many times before that it was difficult to look at the text with fresh eyes. Nonetheless, I have made every effort to remain uninfluenced by any of the numerous translations of the work and have striven to translate it as the commentary seemed to direct that I understand each line. This is an enterprise fraught with peril, I know, not only because my translation of the *Laozi* then depends entirely on my understanding of the commentary, but also because the *Xiang'er* commentator seems more interested in drawing specific lessons from the *Laozi* than in explicating its meaning. Because of this concern, he may, for instance, explicate only a single phrase from the *Laozi* and go on to discuss that, leaving the rest of the sentence alone. What he might have made of the sentence itself, in such cases, is anyone's guess. Despite such pitfalls, I have decided on this treacherous course in the conviction that my focus here is really not on the *Laozi* but on what early Daoists made of it. It therefore seemed preferable to try to fathom that understanding using all available means rather than begin with received understandings of the *Laozi* and then try to determine how the *Xiang'er* commentary differed from them.

It has accordingly not been my goal to compare any other commentary with that of the *Xiang'er.* Where the *Xiang'er* commentator is manifestly imposing meaning on the *Laozi,* as for instance when he finds the surname of Confucius in the text, I have mentioned that fact in notes.[99] References to other editions of the *Laozi* are meant in the same way: I give them only when they seem to me to throw some light on the goals of the *Xiang'er* commentator. (Readers should be aware that I have not attempted a thorough comparison of the *Xiang'er* version of the *Laozi* with other editions.)

Although I think that they were likely written at about the same time, it is likewise not my intention to engage in the debate over the relative dates of the Heshang Gong and the *Xiang'er.* Such comparisons of necessity focus on isolated passages and ideas, and I think it vital, at this stage of our researches into Daoism, that the *Xiang'er* be presented as a whole and that its ideas, and the relative weight accorded each, be presented to the reader. This introduction functions to highlight those aspects of the text that seem to me to be most important to the development of the Daoist religion, though future commentators will doubtless want to focus on other features. The translation presented here is intended to assist this next step in our understanding of the early Celestial Masters. The *Xiang'er* commentary itself has words of advice for those who would interpret it:

> The aspects of the Dao that might be separately examined are so many that there is not enough bamboo and silk to write of them all. Consequently, we go back to its reversion to the One. What would be the harm in analyzing one of its many aspects? The Dao may not be analyzed because, by doing this, we falsify its simplicity, lose its undifferentiation, and diffuse it to the extent that it is one with the deviant. (lines 170–72)

Clearly, in trying to analyze the text at all I have placed myself firmly among the deviates.

NOTES TO *XIANG'ER* COMMENTARY: INTRODUCTION

1. The sole copy of the *Xiang'er* commentary is the Dunhuang manuscript *S* 6825, which begins at the end of *zhang* 3 and continues through *zhang* 37 of the received *Laozi* text. For a fuller account of the manuscript, see the section "The Authorship and Date of the *Xiang'er* Commentary."

2. *Laozi*, 19. See lines 265–77 of the *Xiang'er* commentary for what it has made of this injunction.

3. This "rediscovery" of the *Laozi* has been fueled primarily by the Mawangdui manuscripts of the text, recovered in 1973 from an early Han tomb. The modern scholarly interpretations of the *Laozi* followed here are listed in the footnotes below.

4. Bradbury ("The American Conquest," p. 33) cites Witter Bynner's vivid characterization of Daoism as "a cult compounded of devils and derelicts, a priest-ridden clutter of superstitions founded on ignorance and fear." We can clearly see the prejudices lurking behind such bald statements of contempt, but need to guard as well against more subtle biases against "popularization" found in both ancient and modern references to Daoist uses of the *Laozi*, for these invariably tell us more about the views of the person expressing them than about the *Laozi* text itself. Among recent heritors of Bynner's jaundiced view, for instance, we must include those who attempt to distinguish the "mystical" dimension in Daoism from the "liturgical," privileging the former by tracing its descent from the *Laozi* and the *Zhuangzi* and relegating the latter to "folk religion." For one example,

see Christian Jochim, *Chinese Religions: A Cultural Perspective* (Englewood Cliffs, N.J.: Prentice-Hall, 1986), pp. 8–10.

5. See "Structure and Conventions of the Translation" at the end of this introduction.

6. The primary historical sources for the early history of the Celestial Masters are the *Sanguo zhi* [Annals of the Three Kingdoms] of Chen Shou 陳壽 (233–297) and the *Huayang guozhi* [Annals of the Kingdoms South of Mount Hua] by Chang Qu 常璩 (fl. 347), supplemented by Fan Ye's 范曄 (398–445) *Hou Han shu* [History of the Latter Han]. There also survive in the commentaries to these works citations from lost histories of the period.

7. The question of whether the early Celestial Masters should be considered a regional offshoot of the Yellow Turbans' rebel movement will be touched upon later.

8. The following account is drawn from several sources, including Werner Eichhorn, "Description of the Rebellion of Sun En and Earlier Taoist Rebellions," *Mitteilungen des Instituts für Orientforschung* 2.2 (1954), pp. 25–53, and 2.3 (1954), pp. 463–76; Werner Eichhorn, "Bemerkungen zum Aufstand des Chang Chio und zum Staate des Chang Lu," *Mitteilungen des Instituts für Orientforschung* 3 (1955), pp. 291–327; Werner Eichhorn, "T'ai-p'ing und T'ai-p'ing Religion," *Mitteilungen des Instituts für Orientforschung* 5 (1957), pp. 113–40; Howard S. Levy, "Yellow Turban Religion and Rebellion at the End of the Han," *JAOS* 76.1 (1956), pp. 214–26; Paul Michaud, "The Yellow Turbans," *MS* 17 (1958), pp. 47–127; Barbara Kandel, *Taiping Jing: The Origin and Transmission of the 'Scripture on General Welfare'—The History on an Unofficial Text* (Hamburg: Deutsche Gesellschaft für die Natur- und Völkerkunde Ostasiens, 1979); Max Kaltenmark, "The Ideology of the *T'ai-p'ing ching*," in Holmes Welch and Anna Seidel, eds., *Facets of Taoism: Essays in Chinese Religion* (New Haven, Conn.: Yale University Press, 1979), pp. 19–45; and B.J. Mansvelt-Beck, "The Date of the Taiping Jing," *TP* 66.4–5 (1980), pp. 149–82. See particularly Mansvelt-Beck for the controversies surrounding the relationship between the Yellow Turbans and the Celestial Masters.

9. Zhang Jue seems also to have been influenced by Huang-Lao doctrines. Huang-Lao was a political philosophy that gained prominence early in the Han dynasty. As the name of the school implies, its doctrines were expressed in texts associated with the Yellow Thearch (Huang Di) and with Laozi (the *Daode jing*).

10. On the use of incantation, talismans, and "talisman water" in early medicine, see Donald Harper, *Early Chinese Medical Literature: The Mawangdui Medical Manuscripts* (London: Royal Asiatic Society, 1996).

11. Kaltenmark, "Ideology of the *T'ai-p'ing ching*," pp. 33–38.

12. The following sketch of the early history of the Celestial Masters draws on Ōfuchi, *Shoki no dōkyō*, and Terry F. Kleeman, *Great Perfection: Religion and Ethnicity in a Chinese Millennial Kingdom* (Honolulu: University of Hawaii Press, forthcoming).

13. This mountain, known by various other names as well, has been identified with the modern Heming Shan 鶴鳴山, which lies some fifty kilometers to the west of the provincial capital, Chengdu.

14. According to some Daoist accounts, the *Scripture of Great Peace* was among the works bestowed on him. There is in fact evidence, some to be found in the *Xiang'er* commentary itself, that the Celestial Masters did indeed know a version of the *Scripture of Great Peace* that has come down to us. Certain of the doctrines found in that text are adopted, and others disputed, in the *Xiang'er* commentary.

15. There is, however, a fascinating stele inscription dated 173 C.E. that gives evidence of the Celestial Master transmission of texts and establishment of Libationers. See Ōfuchi, *Shoki no dōkyō*, pp. 41–44; and Ursula-Angelika Cedzich, "Das Ritual der Himmelsmeister im Spiegel früher Quellen: übersetzung und Untersuchung des liturgischen Materials im dritten chüan des Teng-chen yin-chüeh" (Ph.D. diss., Julius-Maximilians-Universität, Würzburg, 1993), pp. 32–33.

16. Ōfuchi, *Shoki no dōkyō*, pp. 46–49. On the appellation "Five Pecks of Rice" and the system of twenty-four parishes, see the discussion later in this introduction.

17. Accounts of Zhang Xiu's death differ, and none of the sources provide information on his relationship to Zhang Lu. The *Sanguo zhi* and *Hou Han shu* report that Zhang Lu murdered Zhang Xiu himself. The *Dianlüe*, though not stating that Zhang Lu killed Xiu, holds that "because of the faithfulness of Xiu's people, [Zhang Lu] carried on Xiu's enterprise and embellished [Xiu's "Way of the Five Pecks of Rice"] (cited in the *Sanguo zhi*, 8:263). The *Huayang guozhi* reports that Zhang Xiu died in battle. The lack of information on Zhang Xiu, who is not mentioned in Daoist sources, has led many scholars, beginning with the *Sanguo zhi* commentator Pei Songzhi, to propose that the graph *xiu* is an error for *heng* and that the passage must be referring to Zhang Lu's father. This assumption seems unwarranted. See Ōfuchi, *Shoki no dōkyō*, pp. 46–47.

18. This is the sort of round figure normally reported in the histories. The best estimate is that the Hanzhong community was in existence for about twenty-four years, from roughly 191 to 215. See Ōfuchi, *Shoki no dōkyō*, p. 46.

19. Ōfuchi, *Shoki no dōkyō*, pp. 50–53.

20. Zhang Lu's mother—who was favored "for her practice of the Way of the Revenants and for her youthful appearance" by the military governor of Shu, Liu Yan 劉焉—and other members of Zhang Lu's family had been kept behind in Shu as a warranty of his good faith. After Liu Yan's son succeeded Liu, he murdered Zhang Lu's mother and family members. (*Sanguo zhi*, 31:867)

21. In fact, Chinese imperial government was, throughout its history, based on principles that we today would call religious. It was a system in which, in the words of Maurice Freedman, "Caesar was the Pope and the

Pope, Caesar." There were, however, unique features in the governance Zhang Lu proposed. These will be explored in the section called "Morality and Governance."

22. See the introduction to the *Admonitions*.

23. For descriptions of those who do not keep faith with the Dao as "mobile corpses," see lines 71–74 and 248–49 of the *Xiang'er* commentary.

24. The title is derived from the Han administration, where it was granted to morally upright elders in the local community. The Celestial Masters applied the title both to men and to women. See Rolf Stein, "Remarques sur les mouvements du taoïsme politico-religieux au IIe siècle ap. J.C.," *TP* 50 (1963), pp. 42–59.

25. Stein, "Religious Taoism," pp. 69–72.

26. This is not so strange as it might sound. These two words share a phonetic element and were pronounced similarly. We know from the Mawangdui silk manuscript copy of the *Laozi* that, during the Warring States period, many homophonous words were written with the same graph and that the radicals found in received editions were added later. The *Xiang'er* commentator has here merely implied a radical where other commentators have not.

27. For expressions of this view, see Léon Vandermeersch, *La formation du Légisme*, PEFEO, no. 56 (Paris, 1965), pp. 240–70; Seidel, "Der Kaiser und sein Ratgeber," pp. 18–50; Seidel, "Das neue Testament des Tao," pp. 147–72; Graham, *Disputers of the Tao*, p. 170; and Ren Jiyu, ed., *Zhongguo daojiao shi* (Shanghai: Renmin chubanshe, 1990), pp. 37–38.

28. Seidel, "Der Kaiser und sein Ratgeber." These observations are not meant to imply that the Heshang Gong and Wang Bi commentaries to the *Laozi* were entirely apolitical in emphasis. As Alan K. L. Chan has noted in his study of the two commentaries: "Both Wang Bi and Heshang Gong are motivated by a fundamental practical concern for the well-being of the country. This, indeed, is true not only for the two commentaries, but characterizes much of traditional Chinese thought as a whole" (Alan K. L. Chan, *Two Visions of the Way: A Study of the Wang Pi and the Ho-shang-kung Commentaries on the Lao-tzu* [Albany: State University of New York Press, 1991], p. 167). We are dealing, instead, with the beginnings of the view expressed in many modern translations of the book, that the *Laozi* text is primarily concerned with *self*-cultivation. This view seems to have originated in the ardent debates of the Han over the nature of the "Sage"— the privileged being who is able to mystically comprehend the Dao and who is thus fit to advise the ruler, but might equally well withdraw into the mountains. The role of the *Zhuangzi* text in this Han-period development, which we tend from our vantage point to assume as a fact, has yet to be convincingly demonstrated. On Wang Bi's and Heshang Gong's views of the sage, see Chan, *Two Visions of the Way*, pp. 34–36 and 157, respectively.

29. Some modern scholars have made much of the fact that the "term" *daojiao* appears in the *Xiang'er* commentary. See, for instance, Rao Zongyi,

Laozi xiang'er zhu jiaojian (Shanghai: Guji chubanshe, 1991), p. 53; and Kobayashi Masayoshi, *Rikuchō dōkyōshi kenkyū* (Tokyo: Sōbunsha, 1990), pp. 314–16. Kobayashi even argues that, since the term is used to denote the Daoist religion only much later, the *Xiang'er* could not have been written in the early third century. In fact, the two words, *dao* and *jiao*, do appear in conjunction, but not as a proper noun denoting the religion as a whole. Instead, the verb *jiao*, "to teach," appears among other verbs describing actions of the Dao. In line 87 of the *Xiang'er* commentary, for example, it is stated that "[t]he Dao teaches people to ... " Thus, when the verb *jiao* appears on one occasion without an object (line 247), we should read, pace Rao and Kobayashi, "the teachings of the Dao" and not "Daoism."

30. This is apparent in the *Admonitions* as well, which speaks of a series of manifestations of the Dao in the world where other texts speak of the reappearances of Lord Lao.

31. This is literally so, for throughout the text the *Xiang'er* commentator glosses first-person pronouns in the *Laozi* with the words "'I' refers to the Dao." On only two occasions are there other speakers identified, and these are both said to be the words of a "Transcendent noble" (lines 241–43 and 305–321). But since this person or these persons are, as the context makes clear, transcended beings and thus joined with the Dao, the switch of voices is not nearly so jarring in Chinese as the English makes it sound.

32. See lines 567 ff.

33. My procedure here is more fully explained in Bokenkamp, "Traces of Early Celestial Master Physiological Practice in the *Xiang'er* Commentary," *TR* 4.2 (December 1993), pp. 37–51.

34. See line 391: "Daoists should value their essence and [internal] spirits. Clarity and stillness are the basis [for accomplishing this]."

35. Lines 203–4. The "Master" is not specified. Most likely, the term here refers to Zhang Daoling, indicating that this practice was attributed to him.

36. The attitude displayed here concerning "clarity and stillness" is closest to that found in the teaching verse of Guang Chengzi 廣成子 (*Zhuangzi*, 11:36): "You must be still; you must be clear. / Do not belabour your body. / Do not excite your seminal essences. / Thus will you live long." For a discussion and translation of the entire verse, see A. C. Graham, *Chuang-tzu: The Inner Chapters* (London: Unwin Paperbacks, 1986), pp. 176–78.

37. Such visualizations are criticized specifically at lines 106–12 and 175–80, and the "false arts" these lines condemn are discussed in endnote 26 to my translation of the *Xiang'er* commentary. See also Bokenkamp, "*Xiang'er* Commentary," pp. 44–47.

38. Harper (*Early Chinese Medical Literature,* sec. 4) discusses various early texts that contain practices for "eating vapor [i.e., pneuma]." Several of them, like the meditation described here, were to be carried out mornings

and evenings. We do not, in fact, know precisely what was different about the method that the *Xiang'er* espouses. Perhaps it was merely that the Celestial Masters insisted that these pneumas emanated from the Dao, as proposed here.

39. This idea, too, derives from early breath cultivation, as incorporated in Han cults of transcendence. Harper (*Early Chinese Medical Literature,* sec. 4) translates a passage from the Mawangdui medical texts to the effect that "[t]hose who eat grain eat what is square; those who eat vapor [pneuma] eat what is round. Round is heaven; square is earth." The avoidance of grain and ingestion of pneumas to achieve corporeal transubstantiation also figures in the *Liexian zhuan* accounts of many Transcendents and is ridiculed by Wang Chong (24:73). In such cases, the dietary prohibition is severe. Vegetable sustenance, such as pine nuts and calamus, was proposed to replace grains, which were associated with decay and death. Such a prohibition was not in effect among the early Celestial Masters, who were known as the "Way of the Five Pecks of Rice" and received faith payments in grain at the three assemblies held each year at the parishes.

40. Lines 328–29. As Rao Zongyi (*Laozi xiang'er zhu jiaojian* [Hong Kong: Tong Nam, 1956], p. 80) notes, this image appears already in the *Taiping jing,* where we read: "The triply luminous is the heart. It is in charge of ordering the Luminous Hall (*Mingtang* 明堂), which communicates with the rays of sun and moon and is named the completed paths of the three luminaries" (*Taiping jing hejiao,* ed. Wang Ming [Beijing: Zhonghua shuju, 1979], 114:596; see also 34:17–20). Other texts, including the "outer" *Scripture of the Yellow Court,* commonly describe the *Mingtang* as a palace in the head. See Kristofer M. Schipper, *Concordance du Houangt'ing King* (Paris, 1975), p. 1 lines 32–35.

41. For an analysis of the layout and significance of the *Mingtang,* which was based on the cosmic diagram known as the River-Chart, see Marc Kalinowski, "La transmission du Dispositif des Neuf Palais sous les Six Dynasties," in Michel Strickmann, ed., *Tantric and Taoist Studies in Honour of R. A. Stein,* vol. 3 (Brussels: Institut Belge des Hautes Études Chinoises, 1985), pp. 773–811.

42. This concept of the three pneumas seems to be drawn from the *Scripture of Great Peace.* See the *Taiping jing* 48:146 ff. passim; and Kaltenmark, "Ideology of the *T'ai-p'ing ching,*" pp. 26, 43.

43. This ritual was first studied by Henri Maspero (*Taoism and Chinese Religion,* trans. Frank A. Kierman, Jr. [Amherst: University of Massachusetts Press, 1981], pp. 536–41). More recently, the ritual significance of the rite has been detailed by Marc Kalinowski ("La transmission du Dispositif").

44. *HY* 1284. Although this text has yet to be subjected to a thoroughgoing study, summaries of the ritual upon which the following account is based are to be found in Kristofer M. Schipper, "The Taoist Body," *HR* 17 (1978), pp. 355–86; Kristofer M. Schipper, *The Taoist Body,* trans. Karen

C. Duval (Berkeley: University of California Press, 1993), pp. 150–52; and Douglas Wile, *Art of the Bedchamber: The Chinese Sexology Classics* (Albany: State University of New York Press, 1991), pp. 25–26.

45. On this latter point, see especially Schipper, *The Taoist Body.* The "five spirits" are deities who dwell in the brain, the lungs, the liver, the heart, and the lower abdomen. For more on the these spirits and the rite of "merging pneumas," see the *Purple Texts,* translated here.

46. In particular, see the Shangqing meditation practice meant to replace "merging pneumas," translated and discussed in the section of this book on the *Purple Texts.*

47. Mather, "Taoist Theocracy", pp. 108–11; and Yang Liansheng, "Laojun yinsong jiejing jiaoshi," *Bulletin of the Institute of History and Philology of Academia Sinica,* 28 (1956), pp. 21–24.

48. See Bokenkamp, "*Xiang'er* Commentary," for a fuller discussion of the views of Ōfuchi Ninji and Kobayashi Masayoshi on this issue.

49. This is not an idea unique to this text. See Harper, *Early Chinese Medical Literature*; and Knoblock, *Xunzi,* pp. 78–80.

50. The word used to describe the formation of spirits from pneuma in the text is, in fact, that used for the transformation of water to ice: *jie* 結, "to tie, bind, coalesce."

51. The importance of preserving "essence," in this case too described as white and thus, at least so far as its visible manifestation, equated with semen, is mentioned again at lines 427–29.

52. As Donald Harper has noticed in connection with the Mawangdui medical manuscripts, *jing,* "essence," is not equivalent to "semen," and the medical texts contain no words that do denote "semen." (Harper, *Early Chinese Medical Literature,* sec. 4.) Here, too, there is no word to express precisely what it is that the youthful may not (and that those of higher virtue are able to) "cut off" 絕. When Chinese texts do wish to denote "semen" as the agent of reproduction, they commonly employ the agricultural metaphor "seed" 種. The discussion here, like that of the texts Harper has studied, deals solely with the "essence"; thus my interpolations.

53. The ellipses represent the *Laozi* passage that the second of these phrases glosses.

54. There is, at any rate, nothing in the commentary that would indicate that the early Celestial Masters did not practice the ritual of "merging pneumas." Even if the evidence presented here is not accepted, the most that might be said is that the *Xiang'er* commentary does not mandate the practice.

55. Seidel, "Traces of Han Religion in Funeral Texts Found in Tombs," in Akizuki Kan'ei, ed., *Dōkyō to shūkyō bunka* (Tokyo: Hirakawa, 1987), p. 45; Seidel, "Post-Mortem Immortality, or: The Taoist Resurrection of the Body," *GILGUL: Essays on Transformation, Revolution and Permanence in the History of Religions* (Leiden, 1987), p. 230.

56. For a Warring States account of resurrection, see Donald Harper,

"Resurrection in Warring States Popular Religion," *TR* 5.2 (1994), pp. 13–28. Unfortunately, none of the *Xiang'er* passages that speak of things such as "transforming disintegration into renewal" specify whether they are talking about this world or the heavens.

57. For the reincarnations of the Dao itself, see the *Admonitions*, translated here.

58. Lines 427–29.

59. There is one reference to new life and the return of essence to the root, but this seems to concern only the preservation of essence to maintain the vigor one enjoyed at birth (see lines 215–19). On the Shangqing practice, see the *Purple Texts*, translated here.

60. I have argued elsewhere that the term *shouyi*, as it occurs in the *Xiang'er*, is best translated as "maintaining unity," in that it here denotes "a physico-spiritual wholeness, the state in which a human being rejoins the Dao through reintegrating its pneumas throughout the body" (Bokenkamp, "*Xiang'er* Commentary", pp. 46–49). For the term *shouyi* in the Shangqing school, see especially Isabelle Robinet, *Taoist Meditation: The Mao-Shan Tradition of Great Purity,* trans. Julian F. Pas and Norman J. Girardot (Albany: State University of New York Press, 1993), pp. 120–38.

61. For the likely significance of these numbers, see the opening pages of the *Admonitions*.

62. The translation here is based on the collated text of Ōfuchi Ninji (*Shoki no dōkyō*, pp. 251–57). Specific references to each of the precepts are noted in the footnotes to the translation.

63. The interpolated line is 無為而無不為 for 无名 of the Mawangdui manuscripts. See William G. Boltz, "The Religious and Philosophical Significance of the 'Hsiang Erh' Lao-tzu in Light of the Ma-wang-tui Silk Manuscripts," *BSOAS* 45 (1982), pp. 102–4. In fact, the *Xiang'er* gloss on this famous line says nothing of "inaction," or, to use Boltz's etymologically precise translation, "minimalizing action." It reads, in its entirety:

> The nature of the Dao is such that it does not perform evil deeds. Thus it is spiritual and is creative of all things. Daoists should take this as their model." (lines 572–73)

The same is true of other occurrences of *wu wei* throughout the *Xiang'er*. Interestingly, at chapter 10 of the received version, where we read "are you able to be aware of the four reaches of space, yet lack knowledge?" 明白四達能無知乎, the *Xiang'er* text reads instead: "As awareness reaches the four quarters, *wu wei* 明白四達而無為." The commentary to this passage says:

> Those of higher attainment have open minds and naturally increase their knowledge. Knowing evil, they discard it; knowing good, they are able to practice it. They dare not perform evil 勿敢為惡事. (lines 119–20)

This reinforces Boltz's contention that it was religious Daoist readings of the *Laozi* that imported the notion of *wu wei* into the text where it had not occurred before, but also shows that the reasons for which this was done had little to do with the way Heshang Gong and Wang Bi interpret the term.

64. Given Chinese physiological beliefs, quieting the passions is in fact the same thing as "controlling pneuma," since, as explained earlier, the emotions were thought to result from excesses of pneuma issuing from one of the five viscera.

65. Though it falls well beyond the scope of the present discussion, it is worth suggesting that the *Xiang'er* commentary here too preserves earlier understandings of the *Laozi* and that pre–Wang Bi occurrences of the term *wu wei* should perhaps all be taken in this way.

66. Both terms refer to radical departures from the true and correct, though *wei* 偽 is more often used for human actions. The opposite of *wei* in this text, as generally, is *zhen* 真, "correct, true, perfect." The implication, probably derived from the language of craft, is that the humanly produced is but a poor copy of the real thing.

67. Confucius is not, in fact, mentioned by name in the text of the *Laozi*, but the commentary finds it there by glossing the word *kong* 孔, "great," which is also Confucius's surname, as a reference to the man himself. See lines 321–22.

68. This view is most forcefully expressed in chapters 18 through 20 of the standard *Laozi*.

69. See, for instance, lines 9–12 and 117–19, passim. It is true that the *Xiang'er* commentator shows a marked disdain for anything beyond the writings of the Dao. The passage criticizing half of the five Confucian classics as "deviant" goes on to state, "Beyond the five scriptures, all of the writings, biographies, and records are the creations of corpses. These are completely deviant" (lines 248–49). The point at issue here, however, is that the commentary departs from the intent of the *Laozi* in sanctioning certain types of knowledge. To see how distinctive this interpretation of the text actually is, one need only compare lines 243–65 of the translation with the Heshang Gong commentary on chapter 18 of the *Laozi* (partially translated in Alan Chan, *Two Visions of the Way*, pp. 121–22).

70. On early Confucian conceptions of heaven, see Robert Eno, *The Confucian Creation of Heaven: Philosophy and the Defense of Ritual Mastery* (Albany: State University of New York Press, 1990).

71. Lines 519–20. According to traditional Chinese court etiquette, military officers stood to the right of the emperor, whereas civil officials stood to the left (see lines 485–87).

72. See footnote § on page 107.

73. This does not imply that the *Xiang'er* commentary simply "affirms Confucian virtues" or "absorbs Confucian thought," as Ren Jiyu (ed., *Zhongguo daojiao shi* [Shanghai: Renmin chubanshe, 1990], p. 38) claims, for it uniformly criticizes core Confucian concepts. The Celestial Master

movement, as we shall see in the *Admonitions,* did eventually adopt Confucian virtues, but only after the fall of the Hanzhong community.

74. Line 265. See also line 286 passim, where the ruler is addressed in the third person—a common form of honorific speech.

75. Lines 529 and 575–76.

76. See lines 527–41.

77. Lines 447–51 and 545–47.

78. See Bokenkamp, "Sources of the *Ling-pao* Scriptures," in Michel Strickmann, ed., *Tantric and Taoist Studies in Honour of R. A. Stein,* Mélanges chinoises et bouddhiques, no. 21 (Brussels, 1983), vol. 2, pp. 452–53; and, for a full discussion of the role of the weft texts in early Daoist notions of kingship, Anna K. Seidel, "Imperial Treasures and Taoist Sacraments: Taoist Roots in the Apocrypha," in Strickmann, *Tantric and Taoist Studies,* vol. 2, pp. 291–371.

79. The commentary's attitude toward the military follows that of the *Laozi.* Weapons are "not propitious instruments," created by the Dao only to threaten those who do not reform (lines 463–64). At the same time, the commentary does recognize the need to fight when there is no recourse. On such occasions, the enemy should be given three chances to submit, and, upon victory, the dead enemy should be mourned "as if there were a loss in your own family" (lines 489–91).

80. This point was made by Seidel (*La divinisation de Lao-tseu,* p. 77). See, for instance, lines 207–10.

81. Lines 489–91.

82. *HY* 1119, 2a9. The phrase "proclaim thrice the five commands" 三宣五令 is strikingly similar to the military practice known as "five times proclaiming the three commands" 三令五申, which was to be accomplished before the prayers for victory at the start of a campaign. See the *Kongcong zi,* attributed to Kong Fu (fl. ca. 240 B.C.E.), cited in the *DKW,* 3:814b, and the *Shiji,* 65:2161, for the militarist Sunzi's use of the commands. This military terminology may stand behind the Celestial Master term, but until the contents of the "five commands" are known, it is impossible to say.

83. Rao Zongyi (*Laozi xiang'er zhu xulun,* in *Fukui hakase shōju kinen Tōyō bunka ronshū* [Tokyo: Hirakawa, 1969]) lists fourteen references to the *Xiang'er* commentary. To these we might add the *Daojiao yishu* (*HY* 1121, 13b) and Du Guangting's 杜光庭 (850–933) *Taishang sandong chuanshou daode jing zixu lu baibiao yi* (*HY* 807, 15b). It should be noted that many of these references are to the *Xiang'er* precepts, which enjoyed an independent circulation (see later discussion), rather than to the commentary itself. Three citations of the *Xiang'er* have survived, but only one of these, the *Laozi* commentary of the Daoist Li Rong 李榮 (fl. ca. 620), cites a portion of the commentary appearing in *S* 6825. The citation is only forty-three graphs long and differs only in a three insignificant particles from the Dunhuang manuscript passage. See Rao, *Laozi xiang'er zhu xulun,* pp. 1165–68.

84. See Chen Shixiang, "*Xiang'er* Laozi daojing Dunhuang canjuan lunzheng," *Ts'ing Hua Journal of Chinese Studies*, n.s., 1.2 (1957), p. 42; and Ōfuchi, *Shoki no dōkyō*, pp. 294–96.

85. See Ōfuchi, *Shoki no dōkyō*, pp. 294–98.

86. Zhang Daoling is cited as the author of the text first in Tang works: the *Bianzheng lun*, composed by the Buddhist Falin 法琳 (*T* 2110, chap. 6, 52.531c27 ff.); the *wai zhuan* 外傳 to Li Longji's 李隆基 (r. 712–56) imperial commentary to the *Laozi* (*HY* 679, 1b); and Du Guangting's preface to the *Guang sheng yi* commentary to the *Laozi* (*HY* 725, 1:1a). The attribution to Zhang Lu occurs in somewhat earlier Daoist works: the *Dongzhen taishang taixiao langshu*, which Ōfuchi Ninji dates to the first half of the sixth century (*HY* 1341; see Ōfuchi, *Shoki no dōkyō*, pp. 281–86), and the *Chuanshou jingjie yi zhujue*, which most likely dates to the end of the Six Dynasties period (*HY* 1228, 3b; see Ōfuchi, *Shoki no dōkyō*, p. 248; and Rao, *Laozi xiang'er zhu xulun*, p. 1171 n. 9. Interestingly, Lu Deming 陸德明 (ca. 550–ca. 630), in his *Jingdian shiwen*, also reports the tradition that the commentary was from the hand of Zhang Lu. See William G. Boltz, "The 'Hsiang Erh' Lao-tzu," p. 95; and, on the error of the attribution to Liu Biao also reported by Lu, Chen Shixiang, "*Xiang'er* Laozi," pp. 43–44. From this, it seems clear that the tradition connecting the *Xiang'er* commentary to Zhang Lu is the earlier one. It also seems likely that the attribution to Zhang Daoling began in Buddhist polemics.

87. Ōfuchi, *Shoki no dōkyō*, pp. 247–52, 281–89. For an analysis of the Dunhuang manuscript copies of the "Ge edition" of the *Laozi*, see Kusuyama Haruki, "Dōtokukyōrui," *Kōza: Tonkō to Chūgoku Dōkyō* 4 (1983), pp 6–30. There is also evidence that the Shangqing founder Yang Xi 楊羲 (330–?) possessed and made his own hand copy of this "Zhang Lu" version of the *Laozi*. See Kusuyama, "Dōtokukyōrui," pp. 12–13; see also Robinet, *La révélation du Shangqing*, vol. 2, p. 415.

88. There are, to be sure, influential dissenting voices. Fukui Kōjun, Shima Kunio, Kusuyama Haruki, Naitō Motoharu, Mugitani Kunio ("Rōshi sōjichū ni tsuite," *Tōhō Gakuhō* 57 [1985], pp. 75–107), and Kobayashi Masayoshi have all argued for later dates, ranging from the fourth to the sixth century. For a discussion of the work of the first four scholars, see Kusuyama, "Dōtokukyōrui," pp. 36–38; and Chan, *Two Visions of the Way*, pp. 109–11. Kusuyama, Shima, and Naitō concern themselves primarily with the version of the *Laozi* found in the *Xiang'er* commentary and attempt to place it with respect to the Heshang Gong text and the "Ge edition." The conclusions of the other scholars are based, in large part, on their analyses of the development of early Daoist thought: they attempt to establish the primacy of some textual reference to a doctrine, idea, or term that, they assert, must have influenced the *Xiang'er*. As these arguments are complex and often dependent on the dating of other texts, it is impossible to do justice to them here. Beyond referring to a few places where the views of these scholars are discussed—Mugi-

tani's views are refuted by Ōfuchi (*Shoki no dōkyō,* pp. 310–20), Chan revisits the arguments surrounding the Heshang Gong, and I have addressed some aspects of Kobayashi's opinions in Bokenkamp, "The *Xiang'er* Commentary"—I will assert here only that I find arguments based on what little we now know of the development of Daoist thought problematical and, at any rate, not convincing enough to overturn the testimony of the early Daoist texts that mention the *Xiang'er* commentary. The most compelling witness to the early date of the *Xiang'er* commentary is the *Admonitions,* itself written in 255. (See my introduction to the translation to that text.)

89. Chen Shixiang first noticed that the nine prescriptive and twenty-seven proscriptive precepts of the *Taishang Laojun jinglü* (HY 785) were derived from the *Xiang'er.* Ōfuchi (*Shoki no dōkyō*) identifies two further copies of the same lists (HY 786, and HY 463 chap. 5), collates them, and studies the references to the precepts in other Daoist works. Ōfuchi concludes that "expounding the precepts" was one of the main goals of the *Xiang'er* commentary. I have argued against this opinion (Bokenkamp, "The *Xiang'er* Commentary"), proposing that it is more likely that the lists of precepts were derived from the commentary later, once the Celestial Master movement had come into regular contact with Buddhist communities—something that would likely not have occurred before the diaspora from Hanzhong. One piece of evidence for this is that the other early Celestial Master text, the *Admonitions,* although citing the *Xiang'er,* does not mention precepts 誡／戒 even when it is citing what later were called the *Xiang'er* precepts, but only the "prohibitions of Heaven" 天禁. It seems likely, then, that all sorts of "prohibitions" and "admonitions" were derived on an ad hoc basis from the commentary. The term I have in fact translated as "precept" throughout is written 誡 throughout the *Xiang'er* manuscript and means "admonition, remonstrance, warning." It is used both as a verb and as a noun in the *Xiang'er* and does not imply the preexistence of a list of precepts. Further indication that the precepts did not exist in listed form at the time the commentary was written is that the *Xiang'er* author, although not averse to numerical listings, nowhere mentions the precepts by number.

90. See Ōfuchi, *Shoki no dōkyō,* pp. 288–94.

91. The precept cited is number six ("Do not ... point to any shape and call it the Dao"), one that is mentioned three times in the commentary. (See Ōfuchi, *Shoki no dōkyō,* p. 270; and HY 788, 6a of the *Admonitions* translation in this book.) Ōfuchi believes that the words *xiang er* 想爾 in this text refer to the commentary. I do not think this is so, though they may be a punning reference to the title. (See endnote 3 to the *Admonitions* translation.)

92. HY 788, 19a3–7.

93. For a translation of the Heshang Gong and Wang Bi interpretations of this line, see Chan, *Two Visions of the Way,* p. 165.

94. Since the commentary also advocates that good actions be done in strict secrecy, it is easy to see why good actions should leave no trace.

95. Rao, *Laozi xiang'er zhu xulun,* p. 1169; Ōfuchi, *Shoki no dōkyō,* p. 298.

96. *HY* 788, 15a–b.

97. See Wang Ming, *Daojia he daojiao sixiang yanjiu* (Beijing: Shehui kexue yuan, 1984), p. 237, for the sensible suggestion that this division of the text occurred as a result of the popularity of the *zhangju* 章句, "chapter and verse," style of commentary that gained favor during the Latter Han.

98. Ōfuchi Ninji, *Tonkō dōkyō mokurokuhen* (Tokyo: Fukubu shoten), pp. 421–34.

99. For careful treatments of a few more of the ways in which the *Xiang'er* radically reinterpreted the *Laozi,* see William G. Boltz, "The 'Hsiang Erh' Lao-tzu"; and Ren Jiyu, ed., *Zhongguo daojiao shi* (Shanghai: Renmin chubanshe, 1990), pp. 37–41.

Translation

The Xiang'er *Commentary to the* Laozi

... then the people will not contend, nor will they steal.

Not seeing that which is desirable will make your heart unruffled.

... Not desiring to see something is like not seeing it at all. Do not allow your heart to be moved. If it is moved, restrain it. [If you do so,]¹ though the Dao departs, it will return again. But if you follow the wild promptings of your heart, the Dao will leave for good.

*The Sage regulates through emptying his heart and filling his belly,*²

The heart is a regulator.³ It may hold fortune or misfortune, good or evil. The belly is a sack for the Dao; its pneumas constantly wish to fill it. When the heart produces ill-omened and evil conduct, the Dao departs, leaving the sack empty. Once it is empty, deviance enters, killing the person. If one drives off the misfortune and evil in the heart, the Dao will return to it and the belly will be filled.

through weakening his will and strengthening his bones.

The will follows the heart in possessing both good and evil. The bones follow the belly in accommodating pneuma. When a strong will produces evil, the pneumas depart and the bones are desiccated.

If one weakens the evil will, the pneumas return and marrow fills the bones.*

He constantly causes the people to be without knowledge, without desire;

When the Dao is cut off and does not circulate, deviant writings flourish and bribery arises. Then the people contend in their avarice   10
and in their desire to study these writings. Consequently, their bodies are placed into grave danger. Such things should be prohibited. The people should not know of deviant writings; nor should they covet precious goods. Once this is accomplished, the kingdom will be easy to rule. The transformative influence of those above over those below will be like a wind through the slender grasses. If you wish this, the essential thing is that you should know to keep faith with the Dao.

and causes the knowledgeable not to dare inaction.

If his highness tirelessly keeps faith with the Dao, the knowledgeable, even though their hearts have been perverted, will still outwardly mark right and wrong. Seeing his highness acting reverently, they will dare not act otherwise.

Then all is regulated.

In this manner, the kingdom will be regulated.

Employ the Dao as it rushes in. Further, do not allow it to overflow.   15

The Dao values the centrally harmonious.† You should practice it in inner harmony. Your will should not flood over, for this is a transgression of the precepts of the Dao.‡

Be deep, resembling the primogenitor of the myriad things.

---

* In physiological practice, the bones were important as storehouses of blood and essence. The Heshang Gong commentary also makes reference to "marrow" at this point. For the importance of bones in Daoist belief, see line 271 below and p. 355 ff.

† On the "centrally harmonious" pneuma, see the section "Meditation and Perfection of the Body" in the introduction to this text.

‡ This refers to number eighteen of the *Xiang'er* precepts.

This refers to the Dao. When one practices the Dao and does not transgress the precepts, one is deep like the Dao.

Blunt its sharp edges; release its vexations.

The "sharp edge" refers to the heart as it is plotting evil. "Vexations" means anger. Both of these are things in which the Dao takes no delight. When your heart wishes to do evil, blunt and divert it; when anger is about to emerge, forgive and release it. Do not allow
20   your five viscera to harbor anger and vexation. Strictly control yourself by means of the precepts of the Dao; urge yourself on with the [hope of] long life. By these means you will reach the desired state. The stirring of vexations is like the rapid vibrations of lute strings; this is why it leads to excess.* You should strive[4] to be slow to anger, for death and injury result from these violent urges. If the five viscera are injured by anger, the Dao is not able to govern. This is why the Dao has issued such heavy injunctions against anger and why the Dao teaches about it so diligently.

The five viscera are injured when the five pneumas [which fill them]—those of metal, wood, water, fire, and earth—are rendered inharmonious.† When these are harmonious, they give birth to one another; when they clash, they attack one another. When you give vent to anger or follow your emotions, one of these pneumas will always issue forth. It issues from one of the viscera and then attacks
25   the others. The victorious pneuma will then form an illness and kill you. If you are strong in yang, a declining pneuma will emerge to attack an ascendant pneuma and there will be no injury from the anger. Even so, in this way you are only a hair's breadth from death. If you are weak, an ascendant pneuma will emerge to attack a declining pneuma and disaster will result.‡

---

* Just as the rapid vibration of one lute string causes the others to quiver, so will a violent emotion in one of the five viscera affect the others.

† The five viscera and the corresponding qualities of their pneumas are associated with the five phases as follows: lungs (metal), liver (wood), urogenital system (water), heart (fire), gall bladder (earth).

‡ The terminology used to describe the state of the pneumas here derives from a method for determining the stages in the cyclical progress of each of the five phases and their effect on the five corresponding organs of the human body. The system mentioned in the *Taiping jing* (65:232–33) titles the five stages as follows: ascendant

Harmonize your radiances; unify your dust.

When one's emotions are unmoved and one's joy and anger do not issue forth, the five viscera harmonize and are mutually productive. This is to be of one radiance and of one dust with the Dao.

Be deep and still and so perpetually present.

One who is still in this fashion endures perpetually without perishing.

Do you not yet know whose child I am? My image preceded the Thearchs.

"I" refers to the Dao, as does the phrase "preceded the The-   30
archs." The ten thousand things all alike originated in it, the nameless. It is not yet known which children from which families will be able to practice this Dao. Those who are able to practice it will pattern themselves on the Dao and will be as if they existed before the Thearchs.*

Heaven and earth are inhumane; they treat the myriad things as straw dogs.

Heaven and earth are patterned on the Dao. They are humane to all those who are good, inhumane to all those who do evil. Thus,

---

旺, adjutant 相, extended 休, captive 囚 (translated here as "declining"), and exhausted 廢. At any point in the cycle, one of the five phases will adopt each of these positions. As Rao Zongyi (*Laozi xiang'er zhu jiaojian* [Hong Kong: Tong Nam, 1956], p. 70) notes, the point here is similar to that made in the *Taiping jing*. A person's overall psychophysical health is more important than where the body's pneumas are in the cycle. Though at certain stages (particularly mentioned is when yang is approaching fullness and the heart is vivified over the other organs) one can get angry without injury to the body, it is best not to get angry at all. This accords with the first of the *Xiang'er* precepts: "Do not delight in deviance. Delight is the same as anger."

* The "Thearchs" (*Di*) were, as early as the Shang period, regarded as the ascended ancestors of the king. From 221 B.C.E. on, living emperors adopted the title. In Daoism, *Di* are the god-kings of the heavens. In this text, the Yellow Thearch occupies a special place (see below). Although these lines are commonly taken to refer to the Dao, our commentator in effect reads them in two ways simultaneously; once as a description of the Dao, and the second time as a description of those who are able to successfully emulate the Dao. This is a reading strategy used throughout the commentary.

when they destroy the myriad things, it is the evil whom they hate and whom they view as if they were grass or domestic dogs.

The Sage is inhumane; he treats the common people as if they were straw dogs.

35   The Sage models himself on heaven and earth. He is humane to good people, inhumane toward evil people. When kingly governance turns to destruction and evil, [the Sage] also views the king as a straw dog. Thus people should accumulate meritorious actions so that their essences and [internal] spirits communicate with heaven. In this way, when there are those who wish to attack and injure them, heaven will come to their aid. The common run of people are all straw dogs; their essences and spirits are unable to communicate with heaven. The reason for this is that, as robbers and thieves with evil intentions dare not be seen by government officials, their es-
40   sences and spirits are not in touch with heaven, so that when they meet with dire extremities, heaven is unaware of it.

The Yellow Thearch was a humane sage and knew the inclinations of later generations, so he plaited straw to make a dog and hung it above the gate, desiring thereby to indicate that within these gates in later generations, all would be straw dogs. But people did not understand what the Yellow Thearch meant to imply. They merely copied this practice without reforming their evil hearts.* This is certainly a great evil.

The space between heaven and earth, is it not like a bellows?

The pneumas of the Dao reside in this space—clear, subtle, and invisible. All blood-bearing beings receive them in reverence. Only
45   the ignorant do not believe this. As a result the space is here compared to a bellows. When the smelter works the bellows, air moves through the tube—that is, the hollow bamboo pipe—with a sound. [Although there is something there,] it cannot be seen. This is why it

---

* According to standard commentaries, "straw dogs" were dogs made of plaited grass used in a scapegoat ritual (see Rao, *Laozi xiang'er zhu jiaojian* [1956], p. 80). The commentary, in tracing this popular practice back to a misunderstood warning from the Yellow Thearch, indicates at the same time that all who continue this practice are marking themselves as "disciples of the straw dog" and outside of the Dao.

is here taken as a metaphor, meant to explain the matter for the ignorant.

Void, it cannot be exhausted. The more movement there is, the more it emits.

The clear pneumas are invisible, as if they were void. Yet their breathing never is exhausted. The more they move, the more it is that emerges.

Those with great learning are again and again depleted; best maintain the middle.

Those possessing great knowledge are superficial and ornate. They do not know how to hold to the Dao or to perfect the body. Once they live out their span of years, they will invariably be "depleted" [i.e., die].[5] "Again and again" means [that this has happened] more than once. It is better to study life, to maintain the centrally harmonious Dao.   50

Desiring that one's spirits do not die—this is called the mysterious feminine.

Gu [valley] means desire. Essence congeals to form [internal] spirits. If you desire to keep these spirits from perishing, you should congeal your essences and maintain them. The "feminine" is earth. The inborn nature of its body is stable. Women are patterned on it; therefore [their sexual organs] do not become rigid. If a man wishes to congeal his essence he should mentally pattern himself on earth and be like a woman. He should not work to give himself priority.[6]

The gate of the mysterious feminine is the root of heaven and earth—

The "feminine" refers to the earth. Women are patterned after it. The vagina is the "gate," the comptroller of life and death. It is the very crux [of existence] and thus is called "the root." The penis is also called "the root."

attenuated and so enduring.   55

The Dao of yin and yang is therefore similar to congealing the essences to produce life.* At the age of fifty, having filled one's [productive] role, one should stop.[7] Even when one is young, though one possesses [the capabilities for reproduction], one should rest [from intercourse] and preserve [these potencies]. "Attenuated" means slight. If one from youth follows the path of lessening, one will endure for a long time. At present, this matter [i.e., sexual intercourse] is the cause of great injury. Why did the Dao create it? The Dao places great emphasis on the continuation of ancestral sacrifice and the survival of the species. Desiring humanity to join their essences and so produce life, the Dao teaches the youthful to preserve their essences but not to cut them off. It does not teach humanity to labor [at intercourse]. This scheme of laboring [at intercourse] was thought up by the ignorant.[†] The Dao cannot be held responsible for it. Those of higher virtue possess iron wills and are able to stop coupling for the purpose of reproducing. Thus they cut off the flow [of their essences] when they are young. Moreover, in this way they are sooner able to form beneficent [internal] spirits. These are called "essences of the Dao." This is why heaven and earth lack ancestral shrines, dragons lack offspring, Transcendents lack[8] wives, and Jade Maidens lack husbands.[‡] This is the highest way of keeping faith with the Dao!

60

Employ it without belaboring it.

If one is able to practice this Dao, one ought to obtain the longevity of a Transcendent. But one should absolutely not labor [at intercourse].[9]

---

* That is to say, the joining of male (yang) and female (yin) in sexual intercourse is for the purpose of producing living beings in the same way that the "congealing of essence" in the body produces internal spirits. To understand the following discussion, it is important to remember that "essence," in its grossest form contained in the sperm of the male, was considered both a physical and a spiritual giver of life. Any squandering of the essence, then, wasted one's ability to form the spiritual embryo.

† "Laboring" at reproduction refers to the various sexual practices whose patrons are listed at lines 86–90 and 430–34.

‡ None of these spiritual entities engage in reproduction. Heaven and earth, regarded as male and female, do not, by this account, have offspring and so lack descendants to erect ancestral shrines to them.

Heaven endures and earth is longevous; they are able to last long   65
because they do not themselves give birth.

They are able to model themselves on the Dao and consequently
are able to endure for a long time by not giving birth.[10]

This is why the Sage, though he places lowest priority on his body,
finds his body given priority.

Those who seek long life do not squander their essence and
thoughts in pursuit of wealth for the maintenance of their bodies,
nor do they try to coerce their lord, seeking emoluments to glorify
themselves without merit, nor do they become gluttonous through
eating the five flavors. Clothed humbly, they do not contend with
the vulgar in fine shoes and clothes. In all of this, they place lower
priority on their own bodies and by this means[11] achieve the longevity of the Transcendents. They thus obtain good fortune greater
than that achieved by all those vulgar persons. This is what is meant   70
by "finding the body given priority."

Regarding his body as something external, he finds his body
preserved.

The meaning of this phrase is the same as that above.

Because he is without a corpse, he is able to perfect his corpse.[12]

The bodies of those who do not know the Dao of long life are but
mobile corpses. It is not the Dao that they practice, but merely the
way of the corpses.* The reason the people of the Dao are able to
achieve the longevity of Transcendents is that they do not practice
the way of the corpses. They differ from the vulgar and thus are able
to perfect their corpses, allowing them to enter the ranks of the
Transcendent nobility.

The highest goodness is like water. Water excels at benefiting the ten
thousand things and, moreover, does not contend.

---

* The word *xing*, translated in this sentence as "to practice," also means "to
move, to be mobile." Coming on the heels of the previous sentence, then, this sentence might be equally translated as "It is not the Dao that moves them, so their
movements are entirely the motions of a corpse."

75   The excellence of water is that it is able to remain supple and
weak. In this it images the Dao. Moving from high places to low, it
avoids the solid and returns to emptiness, constantly benefiting the
ten thousand things with its moisture. To the end, it does not struggle; this is why [the Dao] wishes people to take water as their
model.

Positioned in spots the masses of people detest, it is close to the Dao.

Water is able to receive defiled and impure things; in this it is
closely similar to the Dao.

For dwelling, it favors the earth; for a stopping place,[13] *it favors the
abyss.*

Water excels at seeking out nooks and hollows. Then, where it
stops, it forms depths. "Abyss" here means depths. ·

It provides through goodness and kindness.[14]

People should model themselves on water, constantly delighting
in goodness and kindness.

80   *Speak that which is good and trustworthy;*

People should constantly instruct one another in goodness and
should be trustworthy.

govern through good rule;

When the lord of the people orders his kingdom, he should
always construct his government on the model of the Dao. By this
means he will bring about order.

serve those with good abilities;

All people should desire to serve their teacher and should seek out
one with good abilities who knows the true Dao. They should not
serve the deviant, the false, or the cunning. Deviant knowledge is
proud and extravagant.

and move when the time is beneficial.

When people wish to undertake some affair, they should not

transgress the precepts of the Dao. They must not injure the ascendant pneumas.*

If one is only able to refrain from contention in these things, one will meet with nothing extraordinary.

"Only" means solely. "Extraordinary" means great. If people   85
were only able to imitate[15] water in lacking contention, they would
never meet with great harm.

Holding it and filling it is not so good as leaving it alone. Though one delights in controlling it, one may not treasure it for long.

The Dao teaches people to congeal their essences and form spirits.
Today, there are in the world false practitioners who craftily proclaim the Dao, teaching by means of texts attributed to the Yellow
Thearch, the Dark Maiden, Gongzi, and Rongcheng.† They say that
during intercourse with a woman one should not release the semen,
but through meditation return its essence to the brain to fortify it.
Since their [internal] spirits and their hearts are not unified, they lose
that which they seek to preserve.‡ Though they control their delight,
they may not treasure it for long. "As" is comparative here. "Not so
good as" means to run counter to the natural order of things.   90

Though gold and jade might fill their chamber, no one is able to preserve them.

Essence and pneuma fill the viscera. Those who do not cherish
and preserve them, who are unwilling to naturally close the heart
so that it might thereby control and harmonize [their essence and
pneumas],[16] are greatly deluded.

---

* On the "ascendant pneumas," see lines 20–26 above.
† The list of textual traditions here are those alluded to in the earlier discussion of
sexual practices. The Yellow Thearch, Rongcheng, and the Dark Maiden figure in
the *Sunü jing* (Classic of the Unadorned Woman), which was preserved in Japan in
Tamba Yasuyori's *Ishimpō*, compiled ca. 983 (see Wile, *Art of the Bedchamber*).
I have found no references to Gongzi outside of this text.
‡ "Unified" here stands for being one with the One—that is, the Dao. The sense
is that these practitioners of the sexual arts are wrong not in seeking to control ejaculation, but only in their reasons for doing so. The purpose of their practice is not to
give birth to internal spirits, but rather to "control their delight."

Those made arrogant by riches and ennoblement bring loss and injury upon themselves.

If, once one has congealed one's essences and formed spirits, there are excess yang pneumas, one should strive to cherish the self and, shutting the heart, cut off longings. It is not permissible to arrogantly deceive the yin.* Through such arrogance and deceit, injury derives. Also, the external explanation of this passage is that those who are arrogant toward the rest of the world by virtue of their power, riches, and high rank bring calamity upon themselves.†

100   *When fame and accomplishment are achieved, the body declines; this is the Dao of heaven.*[17]

Fame and accomplishment are the enemies of the body; when they are achieved, the body is obliterated. This is why the Dao prohibits them.‡ When Fan Li departed by boat, it was because he humbly trusted the intentions of the Dao. His body was not destroyed when he went into reclusion; this is the efficacy of the Dao.§

Carry and manage your whitesouls. Through embracing Unity, you will be able to keep them from separating.[18]

The whitesouls are white in color. For this reason, essence [i.e., semen] is white, the same color as primal pneuma. The body is the

---

* This would apply only to males, since they are yang in nature. "Deceiving the yin" refers to sexual practices designed to borrow feminine essence to balance excess yang in the male. Under such conditions, as the commentary states below, "who would wish to loan?"

† "External explanation" (*waishuo*) may refer to other written commentaries on the *Laozi*. The Heshang Gong commentary does in fact give a more general interpretation of this passage (*HY* 682, 1:7b).

‡ This equates to number five of the *Xiang'er* precepts.

§ The story of the recluse Fan Li is found in the earliest of Daoist hagiographies, the *Liexian zhuan*. Fan served as adviser to the king of Yue at about the time of Confucius. According to this account, he subsequently changed his name and went by sea to the kingdom of Qi, where he again gained renown as a master of drugs and alchemical arts. The brief biography concludes: "[G]eneration after generation of later people have reported seeing him." See Max Kaltenmark, *Le Lie-sien Tchouan (Biographies légendaires des immortels taoïstes de l'antiquité)* (Pékin: Université de Paris, Publications du Centre d'Études Sinologiques de Pékin. Reprint, Paris: Collège de France, 1987), pp. 102–4.

vehicle of the essence, and, since essence tends to fall from it, you should carry and manage it. When the [internal] spirits are formed, pneumas come to carry and manage the human body. If you wish to complete this task, do not depart from the One. The One is the   105
Dao.

Now, where does the Dao reside in the body of a person? How can a person hold it fast? The One does not reside within the human body. Those who say that it entrusts itself to the body are the same ones who are forever practicing false arts in the mortal world. Theirs is not the true Dao. The One exists beyond heaven and earth. Entering into the space between heaven and earth, it comes and goes within the human body; that's all. It is there everywhere within your skin, not just in a single spot. The One disperses its form as pneuma and gathers in its form as the Most High Lord Lao, whose permanent rule is on Mount Kunlun. What is sometimes called "void nothingness," sometimes the "self-actualizing," sometimes "the nameless," are all alike the One. Now that the precepts of the Dao   110
are spread abroad to instruct people, those who keep the precepts and do not transgress them have maintained Unity.[19] Those who do not practice the precepts will lose this Unity.

Those who forever practice false arts in the mortal world point to [one of the] five viscera and call it "the One."* They close their eyes and practice meditation, hoping by these means to seek good fortune. This is wrong. They depart ever further from life in so doing.

Concentrate the pneumas, achieve suppleness, and you can become as a newborn babe.

---

* The difficulty in determining a precise target for the criticisms voiced here is that any number of meditation practices were called "holding (maintaining or embracing) the One" (*shouyi, baoyi*). The same (or a similar) practice seems also to have been known as "managing the One" (*zhiyi*). For instance, Lu Yun (262–303), echoing the *Laozi*, writes in his "Rhapsody on Recluses": "Carrying and controlling, embracing the whitesouls; they embosom the primal and manage the One [*zhiyi*]," whereas his brother Lu Ji (261–303), in his "Rhapsody on the Arrayed Transcendents," describes the practice in this way: "Then they breathe in the nine yang pneumas; embracing the One [*baoyi*] and holding in the primal. They draw in the new [breath] and spit out the old." (For more versions of this practice, see lines 211–15 below and endnote 26 to this translation.)

The newborn does not act willfully [*wu wei*] and is thus joined with the Dao.* This is simply because infants are unaware of self-control. But their knowledge gradually increases and so they eventually reach old age. This passage means that if you wish to become supple and bring pneumas into your body, you should model yourself on the young child.

Cleanse and purify your mysterious and expansive gaze and you will be able to achieve flawlessness.

The human body reflects the image of heaven and earth. *Lan* means "expanse."[20] "Flaws" are evil deeds, those things in which the Dao is not pleased. You should cleanse and purify your whole body and, in your actions, ensure that you do no evil.

As you cherish the masses and regulate the kingdom, let there be no knowledge.

The lord of the people, desiring to cherish the masses so as to cause their longevity and to regulate the kingdom so as to bring about Great Peace, should earnestly plumb the intentions of the Dao. In teaching the masses, he should cause them to know the perfection of the Dao and not allow them to know of false ways or deviant doctrines.

As awareness reaches the four quarters, let there be no false action [wu wei].

Those of higher attainment have open minds and naturally increase their knowledge. Knowing evil, they discard it; knowing good, they are able to practice it. They dare not perform evil.†

As heaven and earth open and close, act the feminine.

Male and female have yang and yin orifices. Males should pattern

---

* As explained in the introduction, the term *wu wei*, frequently translated as "inaction," means in this text "lack of artifice." Here the *wu wei* of the infant is attributed to the fact that infants do not know how to exercise "self-control" and so their actions always accord with the Dao.
† Here *wu wei* is glossed as "not performing evil deeds."

themselves on earth and be like females, as I have explained in a
previous paragraph.*

*It gives birth to them and nurtures them. Giving birth, it yet does
not possess. Acting, it does not rely [on anything else]. Extending, it
does not divide [spheres of influence]. This is called the power of the
mysterious.*

The "mysterious" is heaven, which eternally patterns itself on the
Dao and moves in these ways. [The Dao] desires people to pattern
themselves on heaven.

*Thirty spokes join at a single hub, yet the utility of the cart resides
where they are not.*

In ancient times, before there were carts, [the people] were pas-   125
sive. The Dao sent Xi Zhong to create carts.† Once the ignorant
obtained the cart, they used it only to satisfy their avarice. They did
not contemplate practicing the Dao, nor were they aware of the
spirits of the Dao. When the wise saw [the cart], they understood the
beneficence of the Dao. Without uttering a sound, they were strictly
self-regulated and put great emphasis on preserving the perfection of
the Dao.‡

*Clay is molded to make vessels, yet the utility of the vessel resides
where it is lacking.*

The explanation is the same as that for carts.

---

* The male "orifice" is the urethra. For the "previous paragraph," see lines 50 ff
above.
   † Xi Zhong is the culture hero credited with the invention of the wheeled vehicle.
See Rao, *Laozi xiang'er zhu jiaojian* (1956), pp. 80–81.
   ‡ It is difficult to escape the impression that the commentator has here misunderstood, or willfully suppressed, the meaning of this and the following three lines of
the *Laozi,* which argues that the utility of such things resides as much in emptiness as
in substance. The more standard reading is: The utility of a wheel derives from the
empty spot where the spokes join; the utility of a pot, from where there is no clay;
and the utility of windows and doors, from the space within. The commentator
seems to be reading "where they are not" as "when they were not," which is equally
possible grammatically, but nonsensical in this case. The reason for the commentator's insistence on a historical explanation of these passages becomes clear once we
realize the sorts of glosses he wishes to refute. See the following passages.

*Doors and windows are hollowed out to make a room, yet the
utility of the room resides where they are not.*

The Dao caused the Yellow Thearch to invent dwellings. The explanation is the same as that for carts.

130   *Therefore, [those who] have something regard its profit; [those who]
lack it regard its utility.*

These three objects were originally difficult to create. Without the
Dao, it could not have been done. When the profane obtained these
objects, they merely coveted the profit to be gained and did not
know of the objects' origin. When the wise saw this, they returned to
and embraced [the source of the objects'] utility. This utility finds its
basis in the Dao. The hearts of the wise and the foolish are as distant
from one another as north is from south. The significance of the
above three sentences points to this.

Those who regularly practice false arts in the mortal world have
established glib and deceptive arguments, basing themselves on this
perfected text. They say that the Dao possesses a "celestial wheel-
hub" and that human beings likewise have a hub that, through concentration of breath, can be made supple. The "spokes," they claim,
135   refer to the human body for which this "hub" is the central point.
They say that nurturing the [transcendent] embryo and refining the
physical form should be like making clay into pottery. Moreover,
they say that there are doors and windows for the Dao in the human
body. All of these glosses are false deceptions and should not be
adopted. To act upon them is the height of delusion.*

The five colors are what make people blind.

They cause the dispersion of light rays from the eyes and, thus,
eventual blindness.†

---

* The Heshang Gong commentary to this passage contains traces of the "false
arts" derided here. After explaining the utility of the "hole" at the hub of a cart—
which the commentator equates with metaphysical "emptiness"—he goes on to say,
"[T]hose who regulate their bodies should root out emotion and banish desire, so
that their five viscera are vacant and spirits may come to fill them" (*HY* 682, 1:9a2–
3; Chan, *Two Visions of the Way*, p. 123).

† In ancient Chinese medical thought, eyesight was believed to be an interactive

The five tones are what make people deaf.

This does not refer to the elegant tones [of ritual music]. The sounds of Zheng and Wei clash inharmoniously and so injure people.* Listening to them too much causes one's [internal] spirits to depart and eventual deafness.

The five flavors rot peoples' mouths.

Those of the Dao do not eat them. "Rotting the mouth" refers to oral putrescence and cankers.   140

Racing about on horseback and hunting makes peoples' hearts go mad.

This is because the heart is not fixed on what is correct but concentrates only on the slaughter of innocent animals, fueled by the desire to obtain all that have not yet been caught.[21] Madness results.

Goods that are difficult to obtain cause people to practice obstruction.

This is something the Dao does not desire. One should practice the Dao to gain life, not to gain material goods. Material goods lead to artifice; thus, obtaining them will obstruct the Dao.

This is why the Sage acts for the belly, not the eyes. As a result, you should depart from that to adopt this.

In earlier paragraphs the eyes and the belly were discussed.†
One should depart from those evil actions and adopt these Daoist precepts.

Accorded favor or disgrace, be as if startled. Honor will greatly   145
injure your body.

---

process. In addition to emitting light, an object would also have to be struck by "rays" emanating from the eyes before it could be visible.

* The music of the two Warring States–period kingdoms Zheng and Wei was regarded as lascivious and indulgent. As a result, it was held to have corrupted the populace of the two kingdoms. Knoblock (*Xunzi*, p. 78) gives the Confucian sources for this belief. Here, it is likely to be a mere trope for popular music in general, since it is opposed to *yayin* (elegant tones), the music of the court.

† For the passage referred to here, see lines 1–5 above.

The Dao does not delight in those who strenuously seek after status and honor. Where there is favor, disgrace always accompanies it. The first *ruo* means "as if." When you achieve favor, you should be as if startled—less than delighted about it. The second *ruo* is the second-person pronoun.* One must depart from the Dao to seek glory. The injury thereby engendered will return to your body.

What does it mean to denigrate both favor and disgrace? One should be as if startled both in obtaining and in losing them; this is what is meant by "Accorded favor or disgrace, be as if startled."

To "denigrate" indicates that those covetous of honor are lowest in [the Dao's] estimation. They are not held in esteem by the Dao.

150   *What is meant by "honor will greatly injure your body"?*

See above.

The reason I suffer great injury is because I have a body.

The first-person pronouns here refer to the Dao. The Dao is of the highest worthiness, yet it constantly fears injury and does not dare to seek glory, since concentration on such desires injures the body. Can the bodies of those who covet honor be superior to the body of the Dao? It is wrong to transgress the precepts for the sake of one's body.

Reaching the state where I have no body, then what could harm me?

The first-person pronouns refer to the Dao. The Dao's aspiration is to be without body. It wants to nourish the spirits; that is the only
155   reason it has a "body."† Desiring that people model themselves on this, the Dao expresses it.

---

* This is not the reading of most commentators. Either they take the *ruo* to mean "like, similar to" in both cases, or they suggest alternate interpretations, as does the Heshang Gong commentary. This is yet another example of how the *Xiang'er* commentator teases moral interpretations from the *Laozi*. In this case, he derives number eleven of the *Xiang'er* precepts ("Do not covet glory or seek it strenuously") from his reading of the text.

† I have supplied the clause following the semicolon. A more literal translation would be "The Dao's aspiration is to be without body. It wants only to nourish the spirits and that's all." The final particle *erh* (and that's all) implies, I think, that the

Thus, you who are honored in body by the world—can
responsibility for the world be delegated to you?[22]

"You" here refers to those who covet honor for the sake of their persons. Such as these should not be entrusted with the title of ruler of the world. Why is this? Such persons know only to covet honor for their own sake and so will necessarily desire fine clothes, sumptuous foods, spacious palaces, lofty towers, and amassed wealth. For the sake of these things they will act willfully, causing the commoners to labor and suffer. As a result, such as these may not be made "child of heaven."* If, on the other hand, one were to accord with the intentions of the Dao, one would possess a body but not   160 cherish it, would never seek glory and favor, would not be profligate in eating and drinking, would always be frugal, and would hide good actions. Such a person, possessing the world, would certainly be without artifice and would maintain simplicity, entirely in accord with the will of the Dao.

People should only preserve their bodies, not cherish their bodies. And why is this? Keeping the precepts of the Dao, we amass good deeds, which accrue merit and assemble our essences to form [internal] spirits. Once the spirits are formed, we enjoy the longevity of the Transcendents. In this way we find our bodies treasured. Those who covet worldly glory squander their essences and mental concentration in pursuit of wealth. They place great value on food to pamper their bodies. This is how they cherish their bodies. Such actions do not accord with the Dao.

You who cherish your body as if it were the world, can the world be   165
entrusted to you?

The meaning of this line is the same as that preceding.

Dao would not have a body were it not for the necessity of providing existence to the spirits, which inhabit its body in the same way that lesser spirits inhabit the bodies of humans.

    * "Child of heaven" is the term commonly rendered "son of heaven" and refers to the ruler. The Chinese term employed is in fact the common word for "child," and, although most rulers throughout Chinese history were male, at least one woman, Wu Zhao (r. 684–705), earned for herself the sobriquet Child of Heaven.

Looking at it without seeing it, we call it "even." Listening for it without hearing it, we call it "widespread." Touching it without grasping it, we call it "subtle."

"Even" means spread evenly and widely. "Widespread" means greatly surpassing form. "Subtle" refers to the fact that the pneumas of the Dao are clear and transparent. These three things are merely ways of praising the power and beauty of the Dao.

These three aspects cannot be separately analyzed; thus they are merged in undifferentiation as the One.

170   These three things express the beauty of the Dao in simple language. The Dao is the root of the ten thousand affairs of the world. The aspects of the Dao that might be separately examined are so many that there is not enough bamboo and silk to write of them all. Consequently, we go back to its reversion to the One. What would be the harm in analyzing one of its many aspects? The Dao may not be analyzed because, by doing this, we falsify its simplicity, lose its undifferentiation, and diffuse it to the extent that it is one with the deviant.

Its ascent brings no [visible] brightness; its descent brings no [audible] whoosh.

The pneumas of the Dao constantly ascend and descend, active in heaven and on earth, within and without. The reason they are not seen is that they are clear and subtle. Ascending on high, they do not shine; descending, they do not *hu* [whoosh], which means "to move quickly with sound."

175   *Floating about, it cannot be named. Again it returns to nothing.*

The Dao is like this. It cannot be named. It is as if there were nothing there.

It is the formless form, the insubstantial image.

The Dao is of the highest worthiness. Hidden away in its subtlety, it has no shape or physical image. Since it cannot be seen or known, one can only follow its precepts. Now, those who practice false arts in the mortal world point to shapes and call them the Dao. They assign to these shapes variously colored garments, names, appearances, and heights. This is false. Such things are entirely deviant fabrications.*

This is called the vague and indistinct. In greeting it, one may not see its head; in following it, one may not see its back.

The brilliance of the Dao may not be seen, since it has neither shape nor image. 180

Grasp the Dao of the ancients in order to control the existence of [those in] the present.

How can we now know that the Dao truly exists? Observe those of ancient times who achieved transcendence and longevity. All of them practiced the Dao to achieve their station. This is how we know that the Dao has not disappeared in the present profane age.

Thereby you will know its ancient origins. This is called the thread of the Dao.

Those who are able to take the transcendent and longevous of ancient times as models in order to urge themselves along in holding to the perfection of the Dao will thereby grasp the guiding threads of the Dao.

In ancient times, those who were superior nobles were subtle and wondrous, able to communicate with the mysterious.

The "mysterious" refers to heaven. Transcendent nobles of ancient times were able to keep faith with the subtle and marvelous and were in communication with heaven.† 185

---

* This corresponds to number six of the *Xiang'er* precepts: "Do not practice false arts or point to any shape and call it the Dao." For the possible sources of such ideas, see endnote 26 to this translation.

† This passage is extremely close in wording to the Heshang Gong commentary: "[Superior noble] refers to the lord who has achieved the way. The 'mysterious' is heaven. This states that his will is in harmony with the mysterious and subtle and that his essence communicates with heaven" (*HY* 682, 1:12a8–9). The differences between the two interpretations highlight: (1) the *Xiang'er* commentator's emphasis on the need to maintain faith with the Dao; and (2) his widening of the frame of reference of the *Laozi* text so that such things are accessible to all.

Their depths were unknowable.

When people practice the Dao and honor the precepts, the subtle
pneumas return to them. These pneumas enter the innermost depths
[of their bodies] and are therefore unrecognizable.

*Precisely because they are unknowable, we are forced to fashion an
appearance for them.*

Wei [precisely] means "only, alone." "Appearance" means shape
or form. Only through practicing the Dao is this store of power
deeply implanted [in them]. Since we do not know what to call such
people, we are forced to call them "superior nobles." It is the Dao
that beautified and ennobled them.

*They were hesitant as if fording a winter river, cautious as if fearing
their neighbors.*

190   Those fording a river in winter are terrified. Those who fear
their neighbors do not dare to commit wrong for fear that it will
be known throughout the village. People who revere the Dao
and honor the precepts hesitate in their actions and should always
be fearful and reverent in this manner.

They were as self-controlled as guests.

Self-denying, they do not dare to transgress, just like a guest sitting in the hall of a host.

Dispelling [their emotions] like ice that is beginning to melt;

Passion, worry, anger, joy, and evil are all things that the Dao
does not desire. Your heart should regulate these emotions and
finally stop them, causing them to scatter as ice melts under the sun.*

195   *undifferentiated like uncarved wood; broad as a valley;*

Striving to keep faith with the perfection of the Dao, one should
discard all deviant knowledge and maintain one's original simplicity.
You should have no other concerns; only trust in the Dao should be

---

* This advice relates to number seven of the Nine Practices: "Practice desirelessness."

found in the broad emptiness of your heart. Your aspiration should be like that of ice in the valley, which desires only to flow east and return to the great sea.

they were complete and uniform, like muddy water. Muddy water will gradually clarify through stillness.

When those who seek long life are given something, they do not decline it; when something is taken from them, they have no rancor. They do not follow the common run of people in their shifts and turns. Instead, their thoughts are perfectly directed toward the Dao. While they are learning to be clear and still, their thoughts will temporarily be as if confused and muddy; but since they are confused and muddy, they have maintained simplicity and are about to reach their goal. Finally, in clarity and stillness, they will be able to   200
observe all of the subtleties.* Since inside they will be clear and luminous, they will not wish to draw near the common. These essentials of clarity and stillness are the delight of the subtle [pneumas] of the Dao.

When heaven and earth are unagitated, clouds arise and the dew emerges, providing moisture to the ten thousand things. When there is darting thunder and dashing wind, violent desiccation harms living things. [At such times,] the pneumas of the Dao hide themselves away and there is no uniform distribution. When people pattern themselves on heaven and earth, they should consequently not reach this state of desiccation. Through constantly striving after clarity and stillness, the dews of morning and evening will ascend and descend [within them] and the pneumas of the human body will consequently be uniformly distributed.[23] The Master has established these teachings concerning morning and evening [practices aimed at] clarity and stillness as the most essential. Though heaven and earth   205
might slip from their courses, these events merely serve as admonitions for the people. They will always be able to restore themselves, returning to the simplicity of the Dao. Humans lack this power. When they slip from the true course, they depart without hope of

---

* This corresponds to number five of the Nine Practices: "Practice clarity and stillness."

return.* This is why it is most important that you maintain your own integrity.

When you use stillness to move, [your actions] will gradually produce life.

Whenever human beings wish to undertake some action, they should first gauge it²⁴ against the precepts of the Dao, considering it calmly to determine that the principles of their action do not contravene the Dao. Only then should they gradually pursue it, so that the Dao of life does not depart from them.

Those who maintain this Dao do not desire fullness.

One should not allow one's will to overflow or contemplate evil actions.†

Through this lack of fullness, they are able to disintegrate and be renewed.²⁵

210

When the corpse perishes, that is disintegration; when it lives, that is "renewal." Only by holding to the Dao without allowing one's will to overflow is one able to transform disintegration into renewal.

To summon emptiness is absurd; maintain tranquillity and regulate yourself.

The perfection of the Dao contains within itself a constant measure. Unable to fully comprehend it, humans must nonetheless strive toward it. Those mortals who continually practice false arts thus promulgate their teachings, pointing at forms and calling these the Dao. They hold that it has a residence, garments of a specific color,

---

* According to Chinese ideas on the correspondence between the microcosm and the macrocosm, human "storms" of passion are precisely parallel to the thunderstorms and wind-borne droughts of the world. One apparent difference, though, is that the earth recovers from storms, but people are not often able to overcome the results of their passionate outbursts. Another possible problem with the notion of such correspondences is that it is unclear why heaven and earth, being so much closer to the Dao, are subject to storms at all. Both of these explanatory lapses are dealt with here: heaven and earth are subject to storms simply as a monitory warning to human beings. For another expression of this idea, see line 360 below.

† Once again, the *Xiang'er* commentator glosses "fullness" as "overflowing." The "overflowing" of the individual will is discussed more fully in lines 15–25 above.

and a specific height, so that one might thereby meditate upon it.[26]
In so doing, they bring intense suffering upon themselves without
propitious recompense, since it is all empty trickery. Although they
are extremely ardent in their desire that this empty deception might   215
be made real, they would be better off maintaining stillness and
[practicing] self-regulation.

The myriad things arise in concert; by this means I observe their
return. All the things in their crowded profusion—each returns to its
root.

The myriad things all contain the essences of the Dao. "Arise in
concert" refers to the moment of their birth or their first growth. "I"
refers to the Dao. When the Dao observes its essences returning,
each "returns to its root." This is why the Dao commands that people treasure and be cautious concerning their own "root."*

Returning to the root is called "stillness."

When the pneumas of the Dao return to the root, it is even more
important to maintain clarity and stillness.

Stillness is called "restoring destiny." The restoration of destiny is
called "the constant."

Knowing how to treasure the root in clarity and stillness is the   220
constant method of restoring one's life.

Knowing the constant, one is enlightened.

Knowing this constant method, one is enlightened.

Not knowing the constant, one blindly creates disaster.

Those mortals who continually practice the false arts do not
know the significance of the constant. They blindly point to their
writings, and thus all is disaster for them.

Know the constant aspect.

---

* Once again, a parallel is being drawn between the body of the Dao and that of
people. The "root" meant here is the human sexual organ.

Those who know the meaning of the constant method constantly preserve their form and aspect.

Those with the aspect are able to be impartial.

With the Dao preserving their shape and aspect, they present an aspect ennobled by heaven and earth. Positioned between heaven and earth, they do not fear death and are therefore impartial.

Impartiality is able to give life.

Able to practice the Dao and make governance impartial, they live extended lives.

225   *This life is able to make them celestial.*

Able to achieve long life, they then assist heaven.

The celestial is able to join with the Dao.

The reason heaven is able to provide enduring life is that it patterns itself on the Dao.

The Dao is able to cause them to endure.

If people are able to pattern themselves on the Dao's intentions, they will be able to endure.

Their bodies obliterated, they do not perish.

Grand Darkness is the palace where those who have accumulated the Dao refine their forms.* When there is no place for them to stay in the world, the worthy withdraw and, feigning death, pass through Grand Darkness to have their images reborn on the other side. This is to be "obliterated without perishing." The profane are unable to accumulate good deeds, so when they die it is truly death. They are
230   taken away in service of the Earth Offices.†

---

* On the Palace of Grand Darkness, where the last vestiges of dross in corruptible human bodies are refined away through a process analogous to alchemical refinement of base metals to celestial substances in the alchemist's crucible, see pp. 46 ff.
† The Earth Offices are one branch of the tripartite spiritual bureaucracy of Celestial Master Daoism, the other two being the offices of Heaven and of Water. The

Those with the highest [knowledge] possess the lowest knowledge.[27]

Knowing the Dao is the highest knowledge—true knowledge. Evil deeds represent the lowest knowledge. Even though one possesses the highest knowledge, one should also fully recognize what is evil for the purpose of reforming it so that none dare do evil.

Those with less knowledge—draw near to them and praise them.

Seeing those who pursue goodness and understand the intentions of the Dao, you may draw near to them. Seeing those who study goodness and labor diligently, you may approach them and praise them. You should further instruct them, urging them to exert themselves in service of the Dao, spreading its teachings.

Those with even less knowledge—terrify them

When you observe evil persons, admonish them concerning their willfulness and explain good actions to them. Those who listen will   235
submit. They may then be instructed and reformed. Draw near to them and explain to them the admonitions of the Dao, terrifying them with the awesome might of heaven so that they will reform themselves.

or disgrace them.

When you preach goodness to evil persons, those who are not transformed and who ridicule you are nothing but disciples of the straw dog, not humans.* You should revile and disgrace them. Do not speak with them.

Those not worth trusting are faithless.

The disciples of the straw dog lack inner trustworthiness and thus will not put faith in the words of the good.

Still, for those who value words, accomplishment will follow.

Not one of the words of the Dao may be discounted. Those who   240

---

place to which these unfortunate souls are led is not here further specified, but it is undoubtedly to be equated with the purgatories, or "earth-prisons," of later texts.
  * On the "disciples of the straw dog," see lines 40–43 above.

achieve Transcendence do so by simply honoring the words of the Dao. In all cases, accomplishment follows.

Common people say of me that I am self-actualized.

"Me" refers to the Transcendent noble. The common people do not imitate my example—that it was reverence of and keeping faith with the words of the Dao that brought this accomplishment—thinking instead that I am "self-actualized."* Those unwilling to imitate me should be instructed.

When the great Dao was discarded, humaneness and responsibility came into being.

In high antiquity, when the Dao was employed, all people were humane and responsible.† All were of the same type so that the benevolent and dutiful were not distinguished from others. Today the Dao is not employed and people are all flawed. When occasionally there is a single person who is dutiful, that person is praised by all in contradistinction to others. This is why it says, "Humaneness and responsibility came into being."

When wisdom emerged, falseness came into being.

When the true Dao is hidden away, deviant writings emerge. Those mortals who commonly practice false arts proclaim them as the teachings of the Dao, but it is all fraud and may not be employed. What are these deviant writings? Of the five scriptures,

245

---

* This is one of the passages in which the commentary slips into what is clearly the first person. Since the pronoun "I" has been introduced as referring to the "Transcendent noble," we can only assume that this is the person speaking. "Self-actualized" translates *ziran*, a word often rendered as "nature" or "naturally." Literally, it means "so of itself." The emphasis, in short, is on independence and self-sufficiency. This subtle emphasis is particularly important in the present context. It is the Dao that is the ultimate source of the accomplishment, not the inner resources of the Transcendent alone.

† Chinese philosophers divided the history of the world into three stages of decline: higher, middle, and lower antiquity. Lower antiquity tended to be identified with the recent past, whereas the golden age of higher antiquity was variously identified. For this text, higher antiquity refers to the utopian age of the Yellow Thearch. "Humanity" [*ren*] and "responsibility" [*yi*] are two of the preeminent virtues of Confucianism.

a goodly half is deviant.* Beyond the five scriptures, all of the writings, biographies, and records are the creations of corpses. These are completely deviant.

When the six sorts of relationship became inharmonious, filiality and benevolence came into being.†

When the Dao was employed, every family was filial and benevolent. All people were of the same type, so the benevolent and filial were not singled out. Today the Dao is not employed. People are not benevolent and filial, so the six relations are inharmonious. When occasionally there is a single person who is benevolent or filial, that person is praised by all in contradistinction to others. This is why it says, "Filiality and benevolence came into being." 250

When the kingdom was thrown into confusion, the loyal minister came into being.

When the Dao was employed, the Thearchs and princes personally revered and practiced it. Through constantly refining their understanding of the Dao's intentions, they made themselves subservient to the Dao. None of the officials or subjects failed to pattern themselves on their ruler. Knowing the intentions of the Dao, they considered death a trifle and valued transcendence, so that they strove with one another in loyalty and filiality. Yet they were simple and sincere in their uprightness,[28] so that those who took the title of minister were all loyal and of the same type as everyone else, without distinction. Today the Dao is not employed. The ministers all study deviant writings and practice argumentation and deception to follow the whims of the ruler. Though their faces and their words are pleasing, within they harbor evil. When occasionally there is a person who is loyal and sincere,[29] that person is praised by all in 255

---

* The term "five scriptures" refers to the five classics supposedly approved by Confucius, as designated during the Han period. These were: (1) the *Yi* [Book of Changes]; (2) the *Shu* [Book of History]; (3) the *Shi* [Book of Odes]; (4) the *Li* [Record of Rites]; and (5) the *Chunqiu* [Spring and Autumn Annals].

† The "six sorts of relationships," as defined by Confucian texts, vary somewhat, but generally refer to one's relations with father, mother, older brother, younger brother, wife, and child. Sometimes affines are included.

contradistinction to others. This is why it says, "[The loyal minister] came into being."

When the Dao was employed, ministers were loyal and children filial so that the kingdom was easily ruled. At that time ministers and children did not fear their lords or their fathers, but only the spirits of heaven. If they did not[30] act filially, they would not obtain the longevity of Transcendents. Thus they were perfectly sincere in their pursuits. When they practiced loyalty and filiality, they did not

260   want their lords and fathers to know, so they kept quiet about their actions, desiring only to receive the recompense of heaven. The reason they acted in secret was that, if the lord or their fathers knew, they would certainly reward the practitioners with high official position and recompense them with favor. In this way the merit accrued would be exhausted and heavenly favor would not fall on the practitioners. Thus, they did not wish their merit to be known. Today, though ministers and children might be loyal or filial, they all do it in order to barter their acts with the lords and fathers for merit and fame. If, having performed some deed, that deed is not particularly remarked, they become privately angry about it and say, "No one even noticed!" Such people are outwardly good, but inwardly evil, performing no deeds of true sincerity that might move heaven. Thus, the kingdom is difficult to rule.

265   If now you wish to return to [the practice of the Dao], it is urgently important that the thearchical ruler wholeheartedly place his trust in the precepts of the Dao.

If sages were no more and knowledge were discarded, the people would benefit a hundredfold.

This refers to deceptive sages with their knowledge of deviant writings. Those sages whom heaven selects are invariably accompanied by some expression of that selection. The Yellow and the Luo Rivers proclaim the Sage's name.* Moreover, [such sages] constantly expound the truth and will not transmit falsehoods. Those of

---

* This refers to two sorts of talismanic writings or charts that were believed to have been granted by heaven to confer its mandate upon a new ruler. The Yellow River produced a "River Chart"; the Luo River, the "Luo Writings." See lines 447–50 below.

the deviant ways do not place their faith in the words of enlightened sages. That is why for hundreds and thousands of years the great sages have been compelled to rehearse the truth, eradicating deviant writings.

The people of today are without accomplishment. They master the scriptures and the arts and, without having understood the truth of the Dao, proclaim themselves sages.* As they measure themselves   270 only against chapter and verse, this "sagehood" has no basis. Such as these are not able to receive the words of the Dao. They place themselves first and do not encourage people to individually strive in the practice of goodness so that, through the true Dao, the people might themselves obtain the longevity of Transcendents. On the contrary, such "sages" say that Transcendents already have their fates inscribed in their bones and that this is not something one might achieve through deeds.† Or they say that there is no Dao of life and that the books of the Dao deceive people.‡ In this way, their transgressions reach the full three thousand.§ They cause great harm to humanity, even to the extent that those who come later to the

---

* This refers once more to the Confucian scriptures. The sanctioned Confucian "arts" were ritual, music, archery, horseback riding, calligraphy, and computation.

† "Inscribed bones" derives from the belief, common among Han Confucians, that heaven has written one's fate in the shape of one's body and features. The art of physiognomy, which had many regular and part-time practitioners, found support in ancient texts that told of the strange marks found on the bodies of the sage-kings of antiquity. For instance, Wang Chong (27?–91), in the chapter of his *Lunheng* devoted to the subject of physiognomy (chap. 11, "Bones and Features"), begins by discussing the peculiar features of twelve Confucian sages. Physiognomizing thus became an art directed to the identification of the particularly worthy through observing physical marks and signs. In Daoism, too, such oddities of the body as "inscribed bones" (see pp. 349 ff.) became a sign of predestination. The belief is, in almost Lutheran fashion, criticized here because it obviates the need for moral action.

‡ Wang Chong, whose writings attempt to debunk many popular Han beliefs, including the pursuit of transcendence, may perhaps be among those meant here.

§ In Celestial Master Daoism, transgressions were believed to result in the subtraction of *suan* ("counts") from one's span of life. A certain number of counts equalled a *ji* ("mark"). We have no accounts contemporary with this text of how this system was thought to work. Ge Hong relates that one count equaled either one or three days and a mark was three hundred days (*HY* 1177, 6:5b). Another early text gives the figures one or ten days for a count and one year, or three hundred sixty days, for a mark (*HY* 615, 2:19a). Whatever the system, the maximum penalty for an infraction, mentioned in both this text and in the *Admonitions*, was three thousand. The unit was most likely the *suan* or "count."

study do not keep faith with the Dao. Thus, in myriad ways, the circle is broken. Sons do not care to support their fathers; the people have no thought for their fields. They pursue only deviant learning, lining up outside the doors of deviant masters. They exhaust all of
275   their energies chanting flawed teachings, even to the end of their days. Finding that they are unable to move heaven through sincere practice of loyalty and filiality; that, though they attempt to regulate their bodies, they are unable to reach the longevity of Transcendents; and that, though they try to aid their lord, they are unable to bring about Great Peace—still the people employ these unproductive teachings unceasingly, even to the point that the capitals and cities are deserted.* This is why we should discard deceiving sages with their deviant knowledge and allow the true sages with their knowledge of the Dao to continue uninterrupted.

Eliminate humaneness, discard responsibility, and the people will return to filiality and benevolence.

When the kingdom is ruled in a manner patterned on the Dao and when those of humanity and responsibility in the world are employed, there is no need for force or reward. This is because people will become humane and responsible once their moral transformation is valued and the mind of the Dao is fully open to all.
280   Those who are sincere by themselves will naturally be rewarded by heaven, and those who are not will naturally be punished by heaven. Heaven's scrutiny is even more thoroughgoing than any human being's. It knows fully who reveres the Dao and fears heaven. All humaneness and duty will thus be sincere.

Nowadays kings rule through force and reward, so the people no longer give allegiance to heaven. When they see an opportunity, they feign humaneness and duty in order to receive emoluments or rewards. Those observing this, though they know the actions are just outward show,[31] see how such persons obtain official position

---

* Although this description could, with justice, apply to any number of periods in Chinese history, the detail concerning deserted capitals (literally, "double-walled cities and feudatories") may well apply to the period following the Yellow Turban rebellions, when the hope for a period of "Great Peace" had been well and truly dashed.

thereby and respect them for it, practicing false humanity and duty in their turn—so that the cycle never ends. Mortal scrutiny of good and evil deeds is just not thorough enough. But if human rewards were discontinued, all would revert to benevolence and filiality on their own. The reason for their doing so runs counter to the common sense of the ordinary person, but after a long time they will come to understand and will join with the Dao. The ruler of humanity should be fully cognizant of this.

285

Eliminate skill and discard profit, and there will be no robbers or thieves.

This means deviant "skills." "Profit" refers to all treasures gained thereby. If the world does not employ deviant knowledge, robbers and thieves will cease to profit.

Texts written [on the basis of] these three sayings are still insufficient. Allow me, then, to append the following: be unadorned and embrace simplicity.

The three things mentioned above are the source of great disorder in the world. If you wish to promulgate this fact, a million texts would still not be enough. There is not enough bamboo and silk for the job.[32] As a result, this text of the Dao has been added. Its truths are not to be found in other writings. Its general explanation of these three things is sufficient to show that they are the source of disorder.

290

Lessen self-interest and decrease your desires.

What the Dao means by being without self-interest is that one should have few desires for the vulgar things of this world.

[Called to] eliminate learning without worry, what will those who assent be given? How great is the difference?

Those who do not yet know still doubt and ask: "Were I to discard deviant learning, would the Dao bestow something upon me? How great is the difference between the Dao and the deviant?" If they were to abandon deviant learning and cling only to the Dao, the Dao would certainly be given to them. The difference between

295   the Dao and the deviant ways with their perverted teachings is great.
       The Dao is life, and deviance, death. The dead belong to earth and
       the living to heaven.* This is how far apart they are.

The pleasing and the repellent†—how far apart are they?

       Those who do not yet know still doubt and question, wanting
       to know how the difference between the pleasing and the repellent
       compares with the difference between the Dao and deviant learning.
       The discrepancy is the same. "Pleasing" refers to moral goodness. It
       is a living force and thus belongs to heaven, just as the repellent is
       death and belongs to earth.

*That which human beings fear, they cannot but fear—yet vast the
number of those not yet ready.*

       The Dao established life to reward the good and death to threaten
300   the evil. Death is something all humans fear. Transcendent kings and
       nobles, like common people, know fear of death and delight in life.
       It is just that their actions differ. Ordinary people are "vast in num-
       ber" and "not yet ready" to escape death. Although they fear death,
       they still do not keep faith with the Dao, but delight in evil. Is it any
       wonder that they are not yet ready to escape death? Transcendent
       nobles fear death, but they keep faith with the Dao, maintaining its
       precepts and thus joining with life.

*The mass of people are carefree, as if enjoying a great sacrificial feast
or as if climbing a high tower in springtime.*

       The masses of common people, lacking faith in the Dao, delight in

---

       * Thanks to the researches of Anna K. Seidel ("Traces of Han Religion" and
"Post-Mortem Immortality"), we now know that this phrase echoes those commonly found in mortuary documents of the period meant to separate the realms of
the living and the dead and to protect the living from implication in the misdeeds of
their departed relatives. Its use here reiterates the remarks (see lines 71–74 above)
portraying those outside the Dao as but "mobile corpses"—doing so with a force-
fulness that would not have been lost on contemporaries.
       † The term used here, *mei,* is commonly translated "beauty." In fact, it often
denotes not merely a well-proportioned and attractive physical appearance, but
moral and psychic harmony as well. By contrast, the word translated here "repel-
lent" (*e*) connotes also "flawed, evil, inharmonious."

performing evil, like feasting [spirits] with food and drink or climbing high towers in spring.*

Our whitesouls are without sign, like [those of] an infant that has   305
not yet suckled. The demonic has nowhere to take lodging.[33]

"Our" refers to the Transcendent nobility. They rejoice only in their faithfulness to the Dao and in keeping its precepts, not in evil.†
When they find themselves in the presence of evil, their hearts are without inclination, like an infant that is not yet born.

The mass of people have excess. We alone are as if we have
abandoned everything.

The masses of common people hold evil in their breasts. They always have excess inclinations, schemes, and worries. The Transcendent nobility have released all of this from their thoughts, so that there is nothing left.

Our minds are those of dullards—so simple and straightforward.

The Transcendent nobility have a taste for the Dao and know nothing of common things. They are as simple and straightforward   310
as idiots.

The vulgar shine forth;

The vulgar do not keep faith with the Dao. Only when they see evil or the possibility of profit for themselves do they shine forth brightly.

we alone are as if beclouded.

The Transcendent nobility close their hearts so as not to be bothered by evil or [the desire for] profit. They are thus beclouded as if hidden in darkness.

---

* For more on the Daoist animus toward popular gods, the blood-eating spirits of the unhallowed dead, see line 375 below.
† This accords with number twenty of the *Xiang'er* precepts: "Do not commit any of the various evil acts."

The vulgar look into everything;

   Their knowledge of vulgar matters is exceedingly clear.

we alone are self-contained and undiscriminating,

   That is, [the Transcendent nobility] know nothing of vulgar
affairs.

*undifferentiated as if darkened, in single-mindedness that has
nothing on which it fixes.*

   The will of the Transcendent nobility is fixed on the Dao as if
they were contemplating in the darkness. Lying quietly on their
315   beds, they no longer concern themselves with vulgar matters.*
Their essential concentration fixes on the Dao, not on vulgar
matters.

*The vulgar all possess personal [reasons for their actions]. We alone
are obstinate in our impoverishment.*

   In the mortal world, common people all have their treasures and
their fame. With respect to such vulgar things, the Transcendent
nobility are unyielding in their lowly status.

*Desiring to be different from other mortals, we value drawing
sustenance from the mother.*

   The Transcendent nobility differ from the vulgar in that they do
not value glory, rank, or wealth. They value only "drawing sustenance from the mother"—that is, their own bodies. In the interior of
the body, the "mother" is the stomach, which governs the pneumas
of the five viscera. Commoners eat grain, and when the grain is
gone, they die. The Transcendent nobility eat grain when they have
320   it, and when they do not, they ingest pneumas. The pneumas return
to the stomach, which is the layered sack of the bowels. What happens when the belly is replete[34] I have already explained above.†

---

   * The "vulgar matters" referred to here are likely to include sex. See lines 62–63
above, where it is stated that "Transcendents lack wives, and Jade Maidens lack
husbands."
   † See lines 4–8 above. On practices for "eating pneumas," see pp. 42 ff..

The all-encompassing nature of Confucius's virtue came precisely from his following the Dao.*

The Dao is greater than all else. It taught Confucius all that he knew. Those of later generations have not kept faith with the writings of the Dao, but merely revere Confucius's writings, considering them the highest. This is why the Dao clarifies the situation to inform later worthies.

As an object, the Dao is obscure and indistinct.

The Dao is subtle. Since it is invisible, we can comprehend it only obscurely.

In the midst of its obscurity there are things. In the midst of its obscurity there are images.

One should not slight the Dao because it is invisible. In its midst are the great spirit pneumas; that is why it is likened to a bellows' sack.†   320a

In the midst of its dark depths are essences.

Within its vast precincts are the essences of the Dao. These are apportioned out to the ten thousand things so that the essences of the ten thousand things all have a single root.

Its essences are fully realized.

These are the officials of life and death. Since the essences are fully realized, you should treasure them.

They contain tokens of faith.

The ancient Transcendent nobles treasured[35] the essences to gain life. Today's people lose the essences and die. These are [the Dao's] eminent tokens of good faith!

Now, is it true that one can,[36] merely through congealing the essences, obtain life? No. It is essential that all of the practices be

---

* This is, of course, a misreading of the text. Confucius is not mentioned in the *Laozi.* Here the word *kong,* meaning "great" or "vast," is taken to be Confucius's surname, *Kong,* and to refer to the sage.

† On the image of the bellows, see lines 43–46 above. The phrase "great spirit pneumas" or "pneumas of the great spirits" refers to the spirits of heaven.

325   fulfilled. This is because essence is a variant form of the pneumas of the Dao. It enters into the human body as the root and the source. What happens when one holds only half of it I have already explained. Whoever desires to treasure the essences needs to practice one hundred sorts of actions and accomplish ten thousand sorts of merit. One should harmonize the five phases and banish all joy and anger. When, on the left tally of the celestial officers, one has extra counts of life, the essences will maintain them.* When evil persons treasure their essences, they trouble themselves in vain, for in the end their essence will not remain, but must certainly leak away.

    The heart corresponds to the compass. It regulates the myriad matters; thus it is called the "three paths of the Luminous Hall." While dispersing deviances of yang and injuries of yin, it holds to the center and correctly measures out the pneumas of the Dao.

330   The essences might be compared to the waters of a pond and the body to the embankments along the sides of the pond. Good deeds are like the water's source. If these three things are all complete, the pond will be sturdy. If the heart does not fix itself on goodness, then the pond lacks embankments and the water will run out. If one does not accumulate good deeds, the pond is cut off at its source and the water will dry up. If one breaches the dike to irrigate fields as if it were a river or stream, then, even though the embankments hold, the original flow will leak off too and the pond will empty.† When the bed of the pond becomes scorched and cracked, that is the various illnesses all emerging. If one is not cautious about these three things, the pond will become an empty ditch.

From ancient times to the present day, its name has abided.

---

   * According to Daoist belief, each person's fate depended on records kept by the celestial bureaucracy. These records were kept up to date by the deities that inhabited one's body, who reported to the celestial record keepers on specified days. The "right tally," kept in the celestial palace of long life, contained the record of merits contributing to longevity, and the "left tally," kept in Mount Tai, contained records of sins and the date of one's death. The dispatching of memorials to update these records was part of the thrice-yearly meetings held at the parishes. (See Ōfuchi, *Shoki no dōkyō*, pp. 334–42.) In this passage, the term "essences" connotes the deities formed of the essence and pneumas of the Dao that inhabit the body. The fact that these deities report to the deities of the macrocosm on both merits and demerits explains why it is necessary not only to "congeal the essences" to form internal spirits, but also to accumulate good merit. For "counts," see line 272 above.

   † This latter image likely alludes to the results of unbridled sexual intercourse.

Today, as in ancient times, there has been but one Dao. It does not forsake humanity.

This is how it scrutinizes ends and beginnings.[37]   335

Since the Dao came into existence, it has repeatedly scrutinized the differences between the ends and beginnings [of things].

How do I know the ends and beginnings to have been so? By means of this.

"I" here refers to the Dao. The reason it knows of both ancient and modern times, of ends and beginnings, is that it has been throughout the one Dao. This is its function.

What is bent becomes whole.

"Bent" means "humble, retiring." The moon possesses [such] humility; it is first bent and later whole and bright. Those who study the Dao run counter to the vulgar. At one point, they seem "bent" and insufficient, but they later become whole and luminous.

What is twisted will become straight.

"Twisted" also means "bent." When the bent transforms, it becomes straight. Those who study the Dao run counter to the vul-   340
gar. They alone labor assiduously. At that point they seem to be oppressive and "twisted" [in their dealings] with one another, but they later achieve correctness.

What is hollowed out will become full.

["Hollowed out"] means self-effacing and vacant. When one does no evil, in its place is emptiness. The Dao might be compared to water; it delights in filling empty places. When [the Dao] occupies the place where evil was, the pneumas of goodness return to fill you.

What is worn out will be renewed.

When living things are worn out, they are renewed.* The study of

---

* This refers to such things as plants, which die in the fall and sprout again in the spring.

the Dao exhausts one and makes one weak, but one will receive the blessings of renewal.

Through lessening, one receives. Through [hoping for] increase, one is beguiled.[38]

When one expends energy to plant grain, one will harvest a sufficiency. Heaven supplies it. There is no basis upon which one can count on obtaining good fortune, and when one hopes unrestrainedly, one will be misled. When one is so misled, the deviant fills one.

Therefore, the Sage embraces Unity and becomes a model for all-under-heaven.

The Unity is the Dao, which has established the precepts. The Sage, through practicing the precepts, embraces this unity.* The Sage constantly instructs the people of the world and acts as their model.

He does not point to himself as right and is thus made manifest.

Those who are knowledgeable delight in the Dao. Give them its precepts and instruct them. Do not speak to those who do not delight in the Dao or say to them, "I am right and you are wrong." Do not contend with them.†

He does not make himself known and is thus bright.

The Sage models himself on the Dao. He does not make much of his achievements and thus is not known for virtue or ability.

He does not hack away at his substance, and is thus possessed of merit.

Evil is the axe that hacks away at the body. The Sage patterns

---

* For the early Celestial Masters, "embracing (or maintaining) unity" meant conserving the psychophysical wholeness of the body with its apportionment of spirits emanating from the Dao. For criticisms of other practitioners' methods of "maintaining unity," see lines 110–13 and 211–15 above.

† This corresponds to number twenty-five of the *Xiang'er* precepts: "Do not contend with others over right and wrong. When you meet the contentious, flee them."

himself on the Dao and thus does not "hack away at his body," ever keeping his merits whole.*

He does not pity himself and is thus longevous.

The Sage, patterning himself on the Dao, thinks only of accumulating good deeds in order to achieve physical longevity. The practices of life are degrading and lead to poverty and depletion, but he does not feel sorry about injuries to his body or provide it with fine clothes and excellent foods.

Since he does not contend, none are able to contend with him.

The Sage does not contend with the vulgar. If there are those who wish to contend with him, he avoids them and disappears on high. How then could the vulgar contend with him?

How could the ancient saying "What is bent will become whole" be   355
false? Thus you should complete this wholeness and return to it.

That what is bent and withdrawing will later[39] be whole and bright is not a false saying. Fearing that people will not understand, [the Dao] repeats it here to instruct them.

One who speaks infrequently is self-sufficient.

That which is "self-sufficient" is the Dao. It delights in clarity and stillness. "Infrequent speech" partakes of that clarity and stillness and accords with that which is "self-sufficient"; thus it endures.

A whirlwind does not last out a morning. Rainsqualls do not last a
day.

Because they do not accord with clarity and stillness—that which is thus of itself—they do not last even a day.

Who makes these? Heaven and earth.

Heaven and earth form whirlwinds and rainsqualls as admo-   360

* As we saw above, "keeping one's merits whole" involves receiving recompense for them not on earth but from the celestial bureaucracy, which keeps detailed tallies of individual action.

nitions for humans, to demonstrate that what does not accord with the Dao will not endure.[40]

If even heaven and earth are not able to endure them, what of humanity?

Since even heaven and earth are unable to endure [such violent outbursts], when human beings through desire engage in violent action and plot various devious schemes, how can they achieve longevity?

Thus, if one acts in accord with the Dao, the Dao[41] will accept one.

Er means "in accord with." If people make their actions accord with the Dao in all things, the Dao will benevolently seek to receive them. This is called "self-actualization."

If one accords with the powers, the powers will accept one.

365   If people's actions all accord with the powers [of the Dao], the powers will wish to receive them.*

If one accords with those who miss it, one will be abandoned by the Dao.

If people do not hold in awe the precepts of the Dao in all things and miss the intentions of the Dao, the Dao will depart from them. It is automatically so.

Those whose faith is insufficient are faithless.

This has been explained in previous sections.

Those who pant do not endure.[42]

Those who employ pneumas and pantingly inhale and exhale do not accord with clarity and stillness and will not long endure.[†]

---

   * From the syntax, it appears that *de*, "virtue, power"—the active moral and suasive force of the Dao—here is anthropomorphized in the same fashion as the Dao itself. If so, the "powers" of the Dao would be the celestial spirits.
   † The term "panting" refers disparagingly to practices of breath hygiene. See Harper, *Early Chinese Medical Literature*, section 4, for a variety of breath exercises

Those who stride do not walk.

A journey of ten thousand *li* begins with a single step and is accomplished gradually through the accumulation of such steps. Now, those who take a great stride and then stand are not capable travelers. They will not long endure.

One who makes himself visible is not bright. One who considers   370
himself right is not prominent. One who spares himself garners no
merit. One who pities himself has no longevity.

This explains more fully the significance of the preceding passages.

As for their residence in the Dao . . . [43]

The crux for seeking Transcendent longevity and heaven's blessing resides in keeping faith with the Dao. One should keep the precepts in good faith and refrain from committing transgressions or contrary acts, for sins will be tallied up among the celestial officers. When the tallies of the left are depleted, you will not be granted any more chances.*

[I] say: living beings shun such activities as using excess food to offer before the spirits.

Those who practice the Dao live; those who lose the Dao die. The correct law of heaven does not reside in offering foodstuffs and praying at ancestral shrines. Thus the Dao has prohibited these   375
things and provides heavy penalties for them.† Sacrifices and food

---

to which this might refer. It is perhaps significant as well that the Heshang Gong commentary, glossing a different passage, holds that the pneumas of heaven and earth enter the human body through the nose and mouth, respectively, thereby forming the cloudsouls and whitesouls. In order to achieve the proper nourishment of these bodily spirits, "exhaling and inhaling, the successive breaths of the nose and mouth, should be continuous and subtle" (Chan, *Two Visions of the Way*, p. 140). Could this be what the *Xiang'er* commentator derides as "panting"?

* On the tally of the left, see lines 325–28 above.

† This passage has been taken to refer to the bloody sacrifices of popular religion. However, the Celestial Masters also held that heaven and earth properly lack "ancestral shrines" (see lines 62–3 above), so it is likely that the Confucian state cult, which involved the sacrifice of animals, was included as well. The prohibition

offerings are a means of commerce with deviant forces. Thus, even when there is "excess food" or implements [left over from sacrifices], Daoists will not eat or employ them.*

Therefore, those who possess the Dao will not be found there.

Those who possess the Dao will not stay where there are offerings of foodstuffs or praying at ancestral shrines.

There is a substance formed in undifferentiation, born before heaven and earth. Lone[44] and independent, it does not change. It travels in cycles without end. It can serve as the mother of all under heaven.

380   This passage sings the magnificence of the nameless Dao, in truth the mother of all below heaven.

I do not know its name, so I style it "the Dao."

"I" refers to the Dao. This again sings the perfection of the Dao. Since it is difficult to find an appropriate name for it, it is called the Dao.

Were I forced to give it a name, I would pronounce it "the great."

This means that the Dao is the greatest of all things. When it says "forced," it means that it fears there is no alternative. There is nothing to match its power.

When the Great says, "Be gone,"

"Be gone" means to drive away. When there are great spirits that nothing can control, the Dao immediately drives them off.

they are banished, and the Dao says, "To a great distance."

In a trice, it is able to drive them off to a distance.

---

accords with number twenty-two of the *Xiang'er* precepts: "Do not pray or sacrifice to demons and spirits."

* This remark seems to refer to the common Chinese practice of consuming food offerings once the steam (*qi*) has ceased rising from them and the spirits are presumed to have finished. The prohibition expressed here, though, extends even to ritual items used in such sacrifices.

When they are at a distance, the Dao says, "Return."

In a trice, it is able to bring them back.   385

The Dao is great, heaven is great, earth is great, and life is great.[45]

Among these four great things, which is greatest? The Dao is greatest.

Within the realm there are four great things, and life is one of them.

The reason that life occupies one of the four positions is that it is a separate physical manifestation of the Dao.

Humanity patterns itself on earth. Earth patterns itself on heaven. Heaven patterns itself on the Dao. The Dao is patterned on what is so of itself.

"That which is so of itself" is a variant name for the Dao. Although these things pattern themselves on one another in this fashion, they all alike are patterned on the Dao. Heaven and earth are   390
vast, yet they constantly pattern themselves on the Dao to gain life. Should not human beings then revere the Dao?

Weightiness is the root of lightness. Quiescence is the lord of agitation.

Daoists should value their essence and spirits. Clarity and stillness are the basis.*

For this reason, though the gentleman might travel all day, he does not forsake his baggage.

Value your essence and spirits in clarity and stillness, for they are the "baggage of the gentleman." Though you might travel [circulate them] all day, you cannot leave them behind.†

---

* "Weightiness" (*zhong*) is here interpreted as "to give weight to"—that is, "to value." "Lightness" seems to have reminded the commentator of the words *essence* and *clarity,* two of his key concepts, which are homophonous, or nearly so, with the word *qing* [lightness]. Other than that, it is difficult to see how this commentary fits the text.

† The syntax of this passage leads one to suspect another pun on *xing,* "to travel, put into practice, circulate."

Even though he might have a glorious and comfortable palace, transcending all others—

This refers to the child of heaven, princes, and ministers. Even though they might possess glorious palaces and be honored by others, they should strive to value clarity and stillness. They should revere and practice the precepts of the Dao.

400

how could it be that the lord of ten thousand chariots might consider his body more insignificant than [those in] his realm?

The child of heaven holds power over people, so he especially should fear heaven and revere the Dao. If he, through mistakenly considering himself to be venerable, ceases to fear the Dao of heaven, then he actually slights his own body over all others in the world.*

Through belittling it, one loses the source. Through agitation, one loses sovereignty.

Both slighting [the Dao] and agitation are extreme transgressions against the order of the Dao and earn punishment and degradation.† In this way, you will lose your original body and forfeit the motive forces that would ennoble you.

Good deeds leave no trace.

405   When one keeps faith with the Dao and practices good, there is no trace of evil.

Good words lack flaws and bring no blame.

When people go against the Dao and speak evil, heaven in each case subtracts counts of life.‡ Now, when those who keep faith with

---

* Other commentators read this passage of the *Laozi* as referring to pleasure-loving rulers who "belittle the realm for the sake of their own bodies." The *Xiang'er* commentator reads it as criticizing rulers who, paradoxically, "belittle their bodies over [those of] the realm" through imagining that they are too exalted to bow down before the Dao.

† This corresponds to number fifteen of the *Xiang'er* precepts: "Do not slight [the Dao] or become agitated."

‡ For the significance of this, see the footnote to lines 325–28 above.

the Dao speak good words and instruct others not to go against the Dao, there is no blame attached.

Right calculations do not require counting sticks.

Those who understand computation can solve problems in their minds and do not need to use counters. Those who keep faith with the Dao to the depths of their hearts do so in complete sincerity and do not require others to urge them along.

When something is well closed, though there are no locks or bars, it cannot be opened.

There are three streams in the heart. Both yang deviances and the yin harm should be shut up and not employed. The central   410
stream is the correct one. Those of perfect sincerity who are able to shut up their deviant aspirations, though they use no locks or bars, will never release them. [As for] those lacking perfect sincerity, though they use locks and bars, still [the floodgates] can be opened.*

When something is well tied, though no ropes and cords are used, it cannot be dissolved.

Fasten your will to the pursuit of life, and labor to follow the precepts of the Dao. Those who are able to do this in complete sincerity, though they use no ropes and cords, will never be dissolved. Those who lack sincerity, though they use ropes and cords, still may be dissolved.†

This is why the Sage establishes goodness to save others and does   415
not forsake them.

Ever performing good deeds, the Sage, seeing evil persons, does not forsake them but approaches to instruct them by means of the

---

* The term "three streams in the heart" refers to the "three paths of the Luminous Hall." My interpolation of the word *floodgates* is based on the metaphor of the body as a pond, found at lines 322a–31 above.

† The word *jie,* translated here as "dissolved," has the sense of "dissolution" of the physical forces of life at death. This is clearly the metaphor the commentator wishes to evoke.

precepts of the Dao. If those persons will not be converted, there is nothing more that the Sage can do.

The Sage is ever skilled at saving beings and does not forsake them.

The meaning is the same as that of the preceding passage.

This is called "putting on the luminous."

Clothe yourself in the constant brightness. Those who understand this will be illumined.

The good are masters to those who are not good.

Those who are not good learn goodness from those who are; thus these latter are masters. There has never been an evil person who learned goodness from another evil person.

The bad are a resource for the good.

420   The good have no evil in them and thus use evil persons as a resource. When an evil person appears before them, good people see that evil is intolerable and increase their efforts at self-reform.

When teachers are not valued and the resource is not cherished, although knowledge abounds, there is great confusion.

When the evil do not value the good and when the good do not use the evil to reform themselves, both are greatly mistaken.

This is the essential and wondrous teaching.

Those who fully understand this are treasured and wondrous.

Knowing the male yet preserving the female is essential for all under heaven.

You should make the male as the female.[46] If you know the
425   essential and keep still your essence and spirits, you will achieve the essential here below heaven.

Constant power does not depart; it returns again to the newborn child.

Those who concentrate their essences and do not act willfully will never be forsaken by the powers of the Dao. They will become new-born again.

Knowing the white yet preserving within the black is the model for all under heaven.

The essence is white. It is the same color as primal pneuma.*[47] Black is the color within the Palace of Grand Darkness. Within the human, this is the *shen* [i.e., urogenital organs], where the essence is stored. Leaving [the essence] unmoved and not employing it is to "preserve within the black."[48] This is the constant method for all under heaven.

Enduring power may not be borrowed. It returns again to the illimitable.

Those who know how to preserve within the black have the   430
power of the Dao ever resident within them. They do not "borrow" from others, since needing to have it given to you is not so good as keeping it by yourself. Those who practice the *Classic of the Dark Woman* and the methods of Gongzi and Rongcheng all wish to borrow.† But what creditor exists who will loan? So they receive nothing. Only those who preserve their own supply of essence and who cut off their desires are great without limit.

Those who know the possibility of glory yet preserve their debasement are the world's valleys.

If there is glory there must be disgrace. Daoists fear disgrace and

---

* In the writings of Han cosmologists, based on *Laozi* 42 ("The Dao gave birth to the one; the one gave birth to the two; the two gave birth to the three; the three gave birth to the myriad things"), "primal pneuma" was simply the first appearance of pneuma in primordial nothingness. Unfortunately, we do not possess the *Xiang'er* commentary to *Laozi* 42, but from other early texts (see "Lord Lao and the Dao" in the introduction to the *Admonitions*) we know that the Celestial Masters regarded "primal pneuma" as the third hypostasis of the Dao as it transformed itself from formless nothingness into the myriad forms of existence. Continuing to exist as an unaltered remnant of the original Dao, it represents the most subtle and creative aspect of pneuma and might be characterized as the Dao at work in the cosmos.

† "Borrowing" here refers to forms of sexual hygiene in which the male restores his personal balance of yin and yang by absorbing yin essence from a woman during sexual intercourse. For the patrons of such sexual arts, see lines 87–90 above.

435   so do not covet glory. They merely submit their aspirations to the
        Dao, desiring only long life, just like the water in valleys throughout
        the world flows eastward to return to the sea.

*If you are a valley in the world, your enduring power is sufficient
and you will revert to the state of unworked wood* [i.e., simplicity].

        Your aspiration toward the Dao should be like that of the water
        in the valleys, which flows eastward to the sea. Then the power of
        the Dao will always be sufficient. "Unworked wood" refers to the
        original pneumas of the Dao. When people practice the Dao and
        revert to this state, they join with the Dao.

*Unworked wood is broken up to make implements. The Sage
employs those with simplicity to serve as officials and elders.*

        "To make implements" one must depart from the Dao. You
        should not allow those with simplicity to be broken up [or scat-
440   tered]. The Sage is able to accomplish this. In this way, the Sage's
        officials and elders might rule over the people and bring about Great
        Peace.

This is why the greatest order does not require carving.

        The people of the Dao all know that a taste for mundane things—
        high official position, rich emoluments, good clothes, fine foods, and
        precious baubles—will not bring long life. Long life is a great bless-
        ing. To be a person of the Dao is to desire to control what is great
        and so to forebear, not allowing these mundane things to carve
        away at one's will and emotions.

Those who act from a desire to seize all of the world—

        Those who are crazed and deluded have a base desire to commit
        regicide and to seize power for themselves. Heaven will certainly
        slaughter them so that they cannot perform such deeds.

445   *I see.*

        "I" refers to the Dao. It observes alike all of those raised to high
        position by the world, so that what they should not do, they dare

not do. How then can people, in their ignorance, overcome the Dao?
If they try to, they will be injured.

They have no control over it.

The kingdom cannot be for one day without a lord. When the
essence of one of the Five Thearchs is to be born, the Yellow and the
Luo Rivers proclaim their name, the essences of the seven lodgings
appear, and the five wefts concur with them.* Such persons are
manifestly appointed by heaven and charged with rule. They have
no other choice. Those who are not appointed by heaven may not
pretend to be capable [of rule].

The spiritual implement of heaven cannot be fabricated. Those who   450
attempt to do so destroy it. Those who grasp at it lose it.

Those not appointed[49] by heaven will inevitably be destroyed.

As for beings, what is practiced leads to what ensues:

---

* These omens all originate from a type of prognosticatory literature that was
believed to represent "appendices" to the Confucian scriptures and was collectively
known as "weft texts." (The primary meaning of the word *scriptures* in the phrase
"Confucian scriptures" was "warp," the guiding threads in a piece of weaving. The
"weft" texts were thus believed to interlock with and to complete the scriptures.)
These texts held that successive dynastic houses were in fact founded by half-divine,
half-human beings, whose births were attributed to the impregnation of human
women by the "essences" of the Five Thearchs of antiquity, through the agency of
emanations from the five naked-eye planets. Primary among such writings, the
very appearance of which augured a new dynastic house, were the (Yellow) River
Chart and the Luo (River) writings, mentioned here as proclaiming the names of
each new ruler. The "seven lodgings" represent one direction (either north, south,
east, or west) of the twenty-eight lunar lodgings, those houses of Chinese astronomy
through which the sun, the moon, and the five naked-eye planets were seen to move
in orderly progression. The "five wefts" were the five naked-eye planets: Jupiter,
Venus, Mercury, Mars, and Saturn. They were seen to circle clockwise through the
firmament, whereas the lodgings circled counterclockwise, so that these asterisms
too intermeshed like the weft and warp of a weaver's loom. Through noting which
of the lodgings appeared prominently in the sky and the specific planet that seemed
to lead the others to it, the appropriate one of the five phases and its thearch could
be determined. Dynastic change was thus (at least in theory) rendered predictable,
since it followed the order of the five phases, while at the same time it was entirely
mandated by the will of heaven. See Edward Schafer, *Pacing the Void: T'ang
Approaches to the Stars* (Berkeley: University of California Press, 1977), pp. 54–84,
211–19.

This is a case of natural response. When one practices good, the Dao ensues. When one practices evil, injury results.

sometimes exhaling, sometimes blowing;

Exhalations are warm; blown breath is cold. Good and evil follow the same pattern; bad fortune and good have the same root. Though you now exhale warmly, be cautious in that you will eventually[50] blow cold. When you receive good fortune, be cautious of the bad fortune that follows.

sometimes strong, sometimes weak;

After the exertion of strength, weakness follows and weakness turns into strength again. If at first your position is strong, weakness will follow. Daoists, when they exert themselves, at first position themselves in weakness so that they will be strong afterward.

sometimes supported, sometimes falling.

Your body should constantly give birth to itself, first and foremost through calming your essence and spirits. You should not rely on others, but should support yourself. As for the lord of a threatened kingdom, if loyal officials attach themselves to him [he will succeed]; if not, he will perish. As for the ill, if physicians arrive to save them [they will live]; if not, they die.

This is why the Sage banishes excess, banishes extravagance, and banishes greatness.

[That is, the Sage] banishes extreme evil and extravagance.

460   *Those who aid the ruler of humanity by means of the Dao do not employ weapons to compel those below heaven.*

When the lord who regulates the kingdom strives to practice the virtues of the Dao, loyal officials will aid him.. They will labor to practice the Dao so that the Dao will be widespread and its powers overflowing. Then Great Peace will arrive. The lesser officers and people will cherish and respect [their rulers] and so will be easily governed. All will be like those who keep faith with the Dao; all will achieve Transcendent longevity. You should not give in[51] to arms and force. Weapons are not propitious instruments. The Dao established their forms in order to threaten those who would not reform.* You should not concentrate on weapons or delight in them. It is for this reason that the Dao has

> Separated off Storehouse and Tower;
> Placed at a distance Wolf and Bow.[52]
> Why General and the Cavalry Officers reside outside of Chamber
> And the Lance stars and *Xiuruo* are distant from the Pole.†

465

You need only trust in the Dao and then you might neglect weapons.

Such deeds easily rebound.

If one uses weapons to settle matters, the killing will not stay within bounds. The misfortune and disaster will return to your own body and to those of your children and grandchildren.‡

Where the legions encamp, brambles and nettles arise.

The army of the child of heaven is called the "legion." Since weapons do not accord with the Dao, wherever they exist only the pneumas of destruction will appear. You will not see people, only growths of brambles and nettles.

As a result, those who are good achieve it and that is all. They do not adopt force.

---

* Since the Dao is responsible for all "shapes" of everything in the world, it is necessary to explain why the Dao would have established weaponry.

† These verses demonstrate, through reference to the placement of constellations associated with war and military matters in the heavens, that the Dao holds warfare in low esteem. All of these military constellations, which were observed carefully for any anomalies that might augur warfare on earth, are distant from the center of heaven—the polestar. The constellations listed here lie outside the circle of lunar lodgings and so were visible in the northern hemisphere for only a brief time each year. Storehouse and Tower, represented by ten stars in our Centaurus, were associated with war chariots. Wolf and Bow, situated in Cancer, were important in the prediction of foreign invasions. General was the brightest among the Cavalry Officers, a group of twenty-seven stars that were situated outside the lunar-lodging Chamber. Lance, also known as "Barrier River," was formed by six stars in our Aquila. *Xiuruo* remains unidentified.

‡ The notion that a person's transgressions adversely affect the fate of his or her descendants, usually to the seventh or ninth generation, is known as the doctrine of "inherited burden." For more on the development of this idea, see p. 360.

470   To "achieve it" means to be sincere.⁵³ They perform good deeds
with utmost sincerity and that is all. They do not need to rely on
arms or base evil to make themselves strong.

Having achieved this, do not be arrogant.

Preserve goodness in utmost sincerity and do not arrogantly place
yourself above others.

Having achieved this, do not feel satisfied.

Preserve goodness in utmost sincerity and do not feel satisfied
with yourself.

Having achieved this, do not hack away at it.

Preserve goodness in utmost sincerity and do not hack away at
your own body.*

*Achieving this even when you have no say in the matter—this is to
achieve it without force.*

Preserve goodness in utmost sincerity and do not covet military
might. If, for a time, you must aid the thearchical ruler through the
lowly task of taking arms, you may do so if there is no other choice,
475   but do not delight in it. Do not adopt force as your common practice. The Wind Supervisor aided the Yellow Thearch in his attack on
Chiyou, and Lü Wang aided the Martial King in attacking Zhou,
but both did so only because there was no alternative.†

---

* This seems to relate to the phrase (line 350 above) "Evil is the axe that hacks
away at the body." Given the context, the specific evil meant here is most likely pride
and complacency.

† According to ancient legend, the Wind Supervisor (*Feng hou*), whose name was
revealed to the Yellow Thearch in a dream, lived on a remote island, whence he was
coaxed into becoming one of the thearch's three ministers. After aiding the thearch
in overthrowing the rebel Chiyou, he was said to have composed books on the military arts. (See the *Diwang shiji*, cited in the *Shiji*, 1:8.) Zhou was the dissolute final
ruler of the Shang dynasty, who was overthrown by the Martial King, founder of the
Zhou dynasty, ca. 1045 B.C.E. Lü Wang (the byname of Lü Shang) was a commoner
who was recruited by the father of the Martial King while he was fishing, as diviners
had predicted to the king (*Shiji*, 32:1477–80). Since the military exploits of both the
Wind Supervisor and Lü Wang were foretold, these men were regarded as having
been divinely selected. Thus, they had "no alternative" but to engage in warfare.
This discussion accords with the last of the *Xiang'er* precepts: "Do not delight in
arms."

After living beings reach the prime of their might, they age. This is called "not of the Dao." What is not of the Dao comes to an early end.

Having heard the Dao yet being unable to put it into practice, one ages. When this aging does not stop, one comes to an early end.

Now, excellent arms are unpropitious implements. [Living] beings are deceived by⁵⁴ them and detest them; thus those who possess the Dao do not remain there.

Weapons are not things in which the Dao delights, so those who possess the Dao do not remain by them.

The gentleman who remains at peace values the left. Those who employ weapons value the right.   480

"Left" and "right" refer to the tallies.*

Weapons are unpropitious implements; they are not the tools of the gentleman.

This further clarifies their unpropitious nature.

Employ them only when there is no choice.

This was explained previously.

Tranquillity and emotionlessness are best. Therefore, do not praise weapons.

Daoists are tranquil and emotionless. They do not praise weaponry.

Those who praise them certainly take delight in them, and this is murder. Those who delight in murder will not realize their goals in the world.

It is not permissible to understand and delight in weapons or to delight in killing.

---

* On the tallies of the left and right, the spiritual records of a person's good deeds and transgressions, see the footnote to lines 325–28.

485   *Therefore, matters of good fortune are exalted on the left; matters of mourning are exalted on the right.*[55]

"Left" and "right" refer to the tallies.

This is why the lieutenant general occupies the left; the major general occupies the right.

The lieutenant general does not specialize in the taking of life and so is patterned on the left. The major general specializes in killing and so is patterned on the right.*

Which is to say, they are positioned as at a funeral ceremony. When many are killed, mourn and weep for them. When there is victory in battle, arrange them as at a funeral ceremony.

When there is no recourse and war is unavoidable, you should always proclaim thrice the five commands, indicating to [your ene-mies] the precepts of the Dao and your willingness to receive their
490   submission.† If they do not submit, you should be compassionate toward them, mourn for them, and weep as if there were a loss in your own family. Do not rejoice [at victory].

The Dao is ever nameless.

When not taking the name of "the great," it entrusts itself to the tiny.

Though in its simplicity it is small, none under heaven dare to make it their servant.

Though the Dao be minuscule, it is the mother of all under heaven. Thus it may not be made a servant.

---

* The argument of the *Laozi* is that warfare is associated with death since the arrangement of officers in ceremonial military functions was like that of funerals in placing the highest ranks to the right. Throughout this discussion, the *Xiang'er* commentator associates the terms left and right with the tallies of life and death kept by the spirits.

† This is done to win the submission of one's enemies through the awesome power of the Dao rather than by military means. On the "five commands," see p. 57.

Were kings and lords able to maintain it, the myriad things would all serve them as guests.

Humans must not, even if they are exalted, belittle the Dao. When you are equal to this, everything in the world will submit naturally.

Heaven and earth would join in dropping sweet dew.

Heaven and earth rejoice when the king practices the Dao, and   495
life-giving moisture is produced.*

The populace would naturally make themselves equals without having been ordered to do so.

When the king reveres the Dao,
His officers and subjects will desire to emulate him.
They will not fear laws and regulations, but the spirits of heaven.
They will not dare commit wrongs but will desire only to perfect their
  bodies.
They will make themselves equals without having been commanded to
  do so.[56]

First regulate those with fame.

The people of the Dao seek life and do not covet honor and fame. Now, the kings and lords have inherited honor and fame. They have not striven for these things.† The Dao understands this and desires only that they labor to revere the Dao and practice the precepts,   500
being neither proud nor overbearing.

People who already possess fame should know when to stop.

Since kings and lords inherit fame from their ancestors, they should know how to stop when they reach sufficiency and should not seek further rank and honor.

---

* One of the facets of Chinese kingship constantly mentioned in various texts is that when heaven approves of a ruler, the rain is timely. Further, there are many records of heaven signaling its approval by dropping "sweet dew" in the courtyard of the ruler. But the focus of the *Xiang'er* is here, as elsewhere, on the populace.

† This distinction allows the message of the *Xiang'er* to appeal to the nobility, so long as they allow that their greatness was thrust upon them.

Those who know when to stop are not endangered.

All those who know to stop with sufficiency will never be threatened or harmed.*

If one were to find a comparison for the Dao here in the world, it would be like streams and valleys joining with the great rivers and the seas.

The Dao works in the world in a fashion similar to the interaction of the rivers and the seas. When people wholeheartedly aspire to the Dao they are like the water of the valleys, which desires to return to the sea.

One who knows people possesses knowledge.

505   Those who can only assess the goodness and evil of others, though knowledgeable, do not accord with the power of the Dao. The people of the Dao should reflect only upon their own persons so that they do not sink into the land of the dead. They should not judge others.

One who knows oneself possesses illumination.

Those who are like this are extremely bright.

One who overcomes others is forceful.

Those who delight in overcoming others are forceful only in name.

One who overcomes oneself is strong.

To perfect one's body through practicing good and overcoming evil is true strength.

One who recognizes sufficiency is rich.

The Dao rewards the humble and retiring.

Those who practice in strength hold to their aspirations.

---

* This matches number eight of the Nine Practices: "Practice knowing how to cease with sufficiency."

The injunctions of the Dao are extremely difficult. The Tran- 510
scendent nobility achieve the Dao only by virtue of their wills. They
do not employ clever techniques.

Those who do not lose what is theirs endure.

People, whether wealthy or poor, exalted or humble, should all
make it their business to maintain the Dao. Those who are completely sincere will have the Dao given them. The poor and lowly
should not denigrate themselves through urgently seeking to become
rich and exalted. Those who refrain from such seeking will not lose
their place and will thus endure. Yet another explanation states:
when, through emotions of joy and anger, the five phases battle and
are injured, a person dies even before the count of transgressions is
fulfilled. You should harmonize the five phases so that each peace- 515
fully occupies its place and one does not encroach upon the other.
In this way also you will endure.*

Those who die without perishing are longevous.

When a Daoist's practices are complete, the spirits of the Dao call
that person to return. Departing the world through feigned death,
the person passes through Grand Darkness to be born again and not
perish. That is longevity. Commoners have no good merits, and
when they die, they belong to the Earth Office. That is to perish.†

The great Dao floods. It may grant left or right.

"To flood" means to be widespread; the Dao is extremely widespread and great. It occupies the position of flexibility and weakness
and does not contend with the common people concerning its teachings. Those who are cautious concerning its precepts fit the tally of
the left; those who are not are placed on the tally of the right.‡57 520

---

* Although the source of this alternative explanation is not known, it does seem
to agree with the views on the emotions and their relationship to the five phases and
five viscera expressed earlier (lines 17–26 above).
    † On the palace of Grand Darkness, where the bodies of the blessed are refined,
and the Earth Office, to which the damned are consigned, see lines 227–30 above.
    ‡ Between the description of those granted the left and the right tallies there is a
subtle difference in wording that is clearly significant: those who are not cautious
concerning the precepts will be "placed" on the right; those who are cautious "fit"

The myriad things, relying upon it for life, do not decline it.

They do not decline to accept its benevolence. The Dao does not lay blame.

It accomplishes its task and is not possessed of fame. It clothes the myriad things but does not act as their ruler. It may be named "the small."

The Dao seeks no merit or fame. It is ever called "the small."

When the myriad things take refuge in it, it does not act as their ruler. It can be named "the great."

To "take refuge" means to revere. The Dao provides life indiscriminately, but still does not name itself "ruler." This is why the Dao is ever great.

525 *This is why the Sages, through never being made great, are able to complete their greatness.*

In imitation of the Dao, they first proclaim their smallness and afterward are invariably able to achieve greatness. The "great" is long life, a longevity equal to that of the Dao.*

Grasp the great image and all under heaven will proceed to you.

If the king grasps the correct law and models himself on the great Dao, all under heaven will take refuge in him. Vast territories requiring numerous post stations will arrive as if borne on the wind.† The transformative influence of the Dao proceeds down from the top. When it designates a king, it values the "one man." In its rule there are no "two lords." This is why the thearchical king
530 should constantly practice the Dao—so that it will spread to his

---

the left. Given what precedes concerning the importance of sincerity, mere caution is not quite enough to ensure that one's name appears on the tallies of life.

* The Dao is not eternal, in the sense that it withdraws into itself at the end of the cosmic cycle, to reemerge at the beginning of the next. On this concept, see particularly lines 538–40 below.

† That is to say, territories will want to join the kingdom without his even having to conquer them. That people will willingly flock to a just ruler is a notion expressed in many early Chinese texts on statecraft.

officers and to the populace. It is not the case that only Daoists can practice it and the ruler is cast aside. A lord of great sageliness who makes the Dao his master and perfects the practice, transforming all with the teaching, will find the world in order. The auspicious omens betokening Great Peace will accumulate in response to human merit.* One who achieves this is truly a Lord of the Dao.

A lord of middling worthiness, whose aspiration and faith are not pure, will find his rule supported and will be able to employ worthy officials. These ministers will aid him by means of the Dao. Though in this way the kingdom will be preserved and will remain unshaken, it will exhaust his essences and belabor his body. If his excellent adjutants depart one morning, the kingdom will be in danger of toppling by evening. This is because order came not from above but 535 from those departed ministers, and in this way the transformative influence of the Dao was subverted.

Just as water cannot flow to the west, so is it difficult to achieve lasting order even with the most excellent of ministers. How much more difficult it is when all sorts of deviant influences are mixed in governance! [How much more difficult it is] when the ruling lord transgresses the Dao, belittling the perfected texts in the belief that the human world will persist in following him and in the belief that, as king, he can continue to discard the Dao!

The Dao is both exalted and spiritual. It will never obey humans. Thus, it releases sprites and perversities and causes all sorts of transformed oddities to spread as an admonition and warning. The Dao then hides away to observe. When disorder reaches its apex, order invariably returns; the will of the Dao inevitably prevails.† This is 540 why the thearchical king and the great ministers have no choice but to earnestly and carefully investigate the Dao.

---

* The auspicious omens include such things as the River Chart (see lines 447–49).

† This describes, in simple terms, the idea that the expansion and contraction of the Dao is the source of dynastic and cosmic cycles. This concept is not fully explored in the commentary, but all of its constituents are touched upon. Particularly prominent is the idea that heaven gives signs of the arrival and departure of just rulers through various celestial signs. Just enough detail is given to convince any ruler reading this text that there was "no choice but to earnestly and carefully investigate the Dao."

When they proceed to you, there will be no harm.

When the king practices the Dao, the people[58] will proceed to him. They will all delight in the Dao. Knowing that the spirit luminaries cannot be deceived, they will fear the celestial spirits, not laws and regulations, and will not dare to commit wrong. The loyalty of ministers and the filiality of children will proceed spontaneously from their perfected hearts. The king's law will no longer cause harm to anyone. Corporal punishments—mutilations, floggings, stocks, and jails—will be no more. Thus the people will be easily ruled and the king will enjoy happiness.

545   *There will be peace and great happiness,*

When the king rules in this fashion, there will be great happiness.

and parhelia and passing comets will cease.

All harm associated with disastrous celestial transformations and anomalies—light halos around the sun and moon, encroachments of the stellar officers, and unpropitious alignments of the heavenly bodies—is brought about through human transgression. [Under the good king,] the five planets will follow their appointed courses and invading "guest stars" [i.e., comets] will not flare forth. Pestilential pneumas of all sorts will cease.[59]

When the Dao speaks, its words are insipid and lacking in flavor.

The words of the Dao run counter to the craftiness of common speech, and so the profane find them extremely flavorless. Within this flavorlessness there is the savor of life; thus the Sage savors the savor of the flavorless.

550

To look at—it is not worth seeing; to hear—it is not worth listening to; but in use it cannot be exhausted.

The Dao delights in simplicity. Its words are not excessive. Looking at the words of the Dao or hearing the precepts of the Dao, some feel that they are so hard to carry out that they are not worthy of regard. But those who are able to practice them and use them will receive blessings without end.

That which will be made to shrink must have been enlarged.

Good and evil follow the same pattern; fortune and misfortune have the same root. Where they first extend, they will later shrink.

That which will be made weak must have been strengthened.

What is at first strong is later weak. 555

That which will be destroyed must have been flourishing.

What at first flourishes will later certainly be weakened and destroyed.

That which can be taken must have been increased.

What is first gained will later be taken away.

This is called "subtle wisdom."

The four things [listed above] are the "four grievances" or the "four thieves." Those who know them are subtle and wise. Knowing them, you may aid the Dao. Daoists fear shrinking, weakness, destruction, and loss. Thus, in framing their actions, they first make themselves shrink, make themselves weak, make themselves useless, and make themselves depleted so that later they may obtain propitious results. Now, as for the destructive words of the profane, they 560 advocate the benefits of first becoming extended, strong, exalted, and well endowed,[60] so they later face the resulting inauspicious results. This is why you are admonished to know sufficiency and why humans in the world are enjoined to diminish themselves. They should concentrate on spreading benevolence, distributing their wealth, and eradicating misfortune and not dare to seek more for themselves. Those who revere the precepts of the Dao may sit in auspiciousness forever, for it is not an empty saying that those who do not know how to stop with sufficiency will reap the opposite of their excess.* Daoists do not dare to transgress this command, for, in truth, they possess this subtle wisdom.

---

* This relates to number eight of the Nine Practices: "Practice knowing how to cease with sufficiency."

The pliant and weak excel over the unbending and strong.

565   The pneumas of the Dao are subtle and weak; thus they endure and overcome everything. Water is like the Dao in its pliancy and weakness and so is able to dissolve or bore through massive rocks and cliffs. Daoists should make water their model.

Fish may not overcome the watery depths.

   The precepts might be compared to the depths, the Dao to water, and the people to fish. Once fish lose the depths and are taken from the water, they die. If people do not practice the precepts and maintain the Dao, the Dao departs from them and they die.

When the kingdom possesses an advantageous implement, it should not be shown to the people.

   Treasure your essences and do not squander them. If you allow them to move, you will experience lack. Another explanation says: the people of the Dao should rather act upon others than allow people to act upon them. They should rather avoid others and not
570 be avoided by others. They should instruct others in the good and not be taught by others. They should be angered at others, not anger others. With impartiality they should give much to others, not receive much from others. Those who act contrary to this advice are showing others the advantageous implement.*

Since the Dao never acts falsely, nothing is left undone.

   The nature of the Dao is such that it does not perform evil deeds. Thus it is spiritual and is creative of all things. Daoists should take this as their model.†

---

* Once again, the source of the alternate explanation is unknown. The first gloss takes the term *qi*, "implement, vessel," in the sense of the human body as vessel for the pneumas of the Dao. Its concern is with the vital forces (and particularly sexual essence?) that are created within the body by those pneumas. The "other explanation" places the phrase entirely in the sphere of social relations, but it differs slightly in moral emphasis from what we have read earlier. A Daoist should give to others, teach others, share with others, even avoid angering others—not to accord with the precepts of the Dao, but to avoid giving others advantage.

† This roughly coincides with number twenty of the *Xiang'er* precepts: "Do not commit any of the various evil acts."

If the king and lords are able to cling to it,

Though the king is venerated, he still should fear the Dao and keep the precepts.

then the myriad beings will transform of themselves.   575

If the king's governance is patterned on the Dao, the officers and populace—even the lowly and the evil—will all convert to the Dao.*

If this transformative influence is what you wish to put into motion, I will secure it with nameless simplicity.

When the correct [way] is lost and perverted, deviance results. When the deviant is transformed, correctness ensues. Now, if the king patterns himself on the Dao, the people will all follow the correct way. You should achieve[61] this correctness and stop, not allowing further change, since further change leads again to deviance. Seeing that change is about to occur, the Dao will secure it and control it, regulating it through nameless simplicity, which is that appearing in the precepts of the Dao. The king should [himself] imi-   580 tate the Dao in securing and controlling it, yet he is not able to do so [alone], since the common practice of the world is to revert to deviance; at least, in the age of lower antiquity this is so.†

Nameless simplicity has no desire for anything further.

The nature of the Dao in the profane world is to have no desire for anything. The king should also imitate this.

When lack of desire leads to stillness, heaven and earth set themselves right of their own accord.

The Dao is ever without desire. It delights in clarity and stillness. Thus it makes heaven and earth ever correct. Heaven and earth are

---

* This expands on the statement, made earlier, that "the Dao never acts falsely [*wu wei*]." The Dao does not coerce obedience, but acts within its nature and so serves as a model for human rulers.

† On the division of antiquity into three ages and the depravity of the latter age, see the footnote to line 245 above.

ministers of the Dao. When the king patterns himself on the Dao and keeps the precepts, his own ministers and subordinates will all correct themselves.

NOTES TO *XIANG'ER* COMMENTARY: TRANSLATION

1. This is a conjectural emendation. The beginning of the manuscript is torn, and the bottom graphs of lines 1 and 2 are missing.

2. The traditional understanding of this passage is that it refers to the political "governance" of the Sage, not self-regulation. Since the commentary discusses techniques of physical cultivation, it is clear that the author is reading the pronoun *qi* 其 ("his, her, their") in the first person rather than the third.

3. Rao Zongyi (*Laozi xiang'er zhu jiaojian* [1956], pp. 79–80), citing references to the later Daoist meditation "method of the four regulators" 四規 in which the "regulators" (*gui* 規) are bronze mirrors, proposes that the term here refers to a mirror as well. This explanation seems unnecessarily complex. The term originally denoted a compass or a circular template. The expanded meaning is anything that regulates or establishes a pattern as to size or content. For how the heart was believed to serve as a regulator, see lines 327–34.

4. The term *jisi* 積死 here is puzzling. Given the context, it appears to be a contraction of *jixi* 積習, "to become accustomed to through long practice" (*DKW* 8:625d), and *sijie* 死節, "to refrain from something even on pain of death" (*DKW* 6:737a), but I have found no occurrence of such a four-character phrase.

5. The term *qiong* 窮, translated here as "depleted," is a common trope for death.

6. The expression *wu wei shi xian* 勿為事先 is somewhat unclear in meaning. Number three of the "Nine Practices," based on this passage, reads: "Practice maintaining the feminine. Do not initiate actions [*wu xian dong* 勿先動]." Given the context here, with its implied criticisms of sexual-hygiene practice, it is likely that the phrase refers to males striving to gain balance of yin and yang through sexual congress, thus "falsely working to give themselves [literally, "serve"] priority."

7. The text has 知命, "knowing the mandate." Used to indicate the age of fifty, this phrase alludes to a passage in the *Analects* (*Lunyu* 2.4): "The master said … 'At fifty I knew the mandates of heaven.'"

8. *Wu* 無 is missing in the text and is supplied on the basis of parallelism.

9. Here I follow Rao (*Laozi xiang'er zhu jiaojian* [1956], p. 10) in reading *buke* 不可 for *buke bu* 不可不.

10. I have restored a *bu* 不 in the commentary in accord with the line it glosses. *Zi sheng* 自生 is generally reflexive ("to give life to oneself"). In the

context of sexual reproduction, we should read instead "themselves give birth." As the preceding passages indicate, heaven and earth do not engage in sexual intercourse and so "lack ancestral shrines."

11. Both Rao and Mugitani have *mu ci* 目此, but the manuscript reads *yin ci* 因此. For the copyist's way of writing the graph *yin,* see line 212, for example.

12. This is another major alteration of the *Laozi* text, which in all other versions has *si* 私, "self-interest, selfish concerns," rather than *shi* 尸, "corpse."

13. Reading *zhi* 止 for *xin* 心 in accord with the commentary. The two graphs are closely similar in the *bafang* script of our manuscript, which is presumably the same style as the manuscript from which it was copied.

14. It is difficult to see how the commentator means to read this line of text. Given the way he seems to have taken preceding lines, we would expect a reading like "in giving, it favors humanity," but the word *shan,* "to favor, to excel at, goodness," is clearly taken here, as so often in the commentary, in the latter sense.

15. Reading *fang* 仿 for *fang* 放.

16. Reading *ruo* 若 for *ku* 苦. My translation of the term *chuaiyue* 揣捝 as "control and harmonize" is conjectural. I have found only one other appearance of the term, in the *Guiguzi* (*DKW* 5:327b).

17. The received version of the *Laozi* has "once achievement is complete, fame follows and the person withdraws; this is the Dao of heaven [功成名遂身退]." The order of the elements in the first clause is here reversed. We should then read, following the gloss of the commentator: "when fame is complete and achievement follows." The commentator also takes 退 to mean "bodily decline," rather than "withdrawal" from the world of affairs.

18. This and the following five entries are, in the received version of the *Laozi,* all phrased as questions. In the *Xiang'er* manuscript, the question particle *hu* does not appear.

19. *Shouyi* 守一, the term I translate here as "maintaining Unity," is also translated as "embracing the One" or "holding the One." In other texts, the term refers to various meditation practices for visualizing and unifying the body's internal spirits. See Poul Anderson, *The Method of Holding the Three Ones: A Taoist Manual of Meditation of the Fourth Century A.D.* (London and Malm: Curzon Press, 1980), and Isabelle Robinet, "Le Ta-tung Chen-ching," in Michel Strickmann, ed., *Tantric and Taoist Studies,* vol. 2 (Brussels: Insitut Belge des Hautes Études Chinoises, 1983): 120–38. That is part of the meaning here as well, in that the *Xiang'er* precepts include injunctions concerning unifying the body's spirits and essences. But they also warn against all sorts of actions that cause the Dao to depart and the body's unity to be lost, which is why I have opted for this translation of the term. See also Bokenkamp, "*Xiang'er* Commentary," pp. 46–47.

20. *Lan* 覽 means "to survey, to gaze out across (a vast expanse)." The

gloss here does not seem to take account of the element of vision, but it should be remarked that this is totally in line with Chinese commentarial practice, which assumed that the reader would know the word and thus provided only suggestions as to the sense in which that word should be read in specific contexts.

21. Rao (*Laozi xiang'er zhu jiaojian* [1956], p. 16) interpolates the phrase *bude* 不得 at this point, reading "[They] *do not obtain* that which they should obtain."

22. The final clause of this line is missing in the manuscript but is glossed in the commentary. There is no grammatical indication that this and the following line of the *Laozi* are meant to be rhetorical questions, yet the *Xiang'er* commentator seems to read them as such. His "answer," at any rate, directly contradicts the normal understanding of the final clauses of each line: "(to such a person) you can entrust the world."

23. The Tang commentator Liangqiuzi 梁丘子 (Bai Lü-zhong 白履忠, fl. ca. 722), commenting on the line "[Transcendents] dine solely on the greatly harmonious, the yin, and the yang pneumas" of the *Scripture of the Yellow Court,* notes that those pursuing transcendence ingest yang breaths at sunrise, yin breaths at sunset, and "primal pneuma" on both occasions (*HY* 263, 60:3a). For further analysis of the practices alluded to in this passage, see the section "Meditation and Perfection of the Body" in the introduction to this text.

24. Reading, with Rao (*Laozi xiang'er zhu jiaojian* [1956], p. 20), *kao* 考 for *xiao* 孝.

25. The text here has *fu* 復 where the received edition has *bu* 不. The implications of this are discussed in William G. Boltz, "The 'Hsiang Erh' Lao-tzu," p. 116. Because I am following the commentary, my translation of the line is a bit more forceful than his, but the import is the same.

26. Ōfuchi (*Shoki no dōkyō,* p. 357 n. 2) proposes that the object of attack here might have been beliefs concerning the "spirits of the five viscera" as explicated in the *Scripture of Great Peace* (72:292, 722–23), but these spirits are expressly the "pneumas of the four seasons and the five phases" and are not to be equated with the Dao—an equation that the "false practitioners" criticized here apparently made.

The heresy is not that such meditations involve internal spirits, but that the Dao, the One, figures among them. A more likely representative is an unnamed "transcendent scripture" cited by Ge Hong 葛洪 (ca. 283–343) in his *Baopu zi neipian:*

> Lord Lao said, "Undifferentiated. Vague.—Within are images. Vague. Undifferentiated.—Within is a thing" [citing *Laozi* 21]. It is the One of which he speaks. Thus, a Transcendent Scripture states: "If you wish long life, you must be clear on maintaining the One. . . . The One has both surname and byname and clothing of a certain color. In males it is nine inches long; in females, six. Sometimes it is 2.4 inches below the navel in the lower Cinnabar Field. Sometimes it resides in the Scarlet Palace, within the Golden Porte below the heart. This is the central Cinnabar Field. Sometimes it resides between the eyebrows. Preceding within [the

head], one inch is the Luminous Hall, two inches the Cavern Chamber, and three inches the upper Cinnabar Field." All of this information is valued by Daoists, who have orally transmitted the names generation after generation, drawing blood [to seal their oath of secrecy].

Baopu zi neipian, 18:92.

For another translation, consult James R. Ware, *Alchemy, Medicine and Religion in the China of A.D. 320: The Nei P'ien of Ko Hung* (1966; reprint, New York: Dover Publications, 1981), pp. 301–2. See also Chen Shixiang, "*Xiang'er* Laozi," pp. 55–56.

27. The received commentaries all read: "(As for) the highest, those below know it exists." But the *Xiang'er* commentator finds somewhere in this phrase reference to two sorts of knowledge. I can only speculate that he is reading two preposed subjects rather than one: "[As for those with] the highest [knowledge], the lowest knowledge—they possess it." This is scarcely defensible grammatically, but something like this must have been at the back of his mind.

28. Reading, following Ōfuchi (*Shoki no dōkyō*, p. 357), *duanque* 端愨. The uncommon graph *que* is given at *DKW* 4:1137c, where it is glossed as "reverent, upright."

29. As Ōfuchi (*Shoki no dōkyō*, p. 357) has pointed out, this character is wrongly transcribed in Rao, *Laozi xiang'er zhu jiaojian* (1956), p. 24, as *jie* 誡 rather than *cheng* 誠.

30. On the basis of context, I think that a *bu* 不 has dropped out of the text at this point. If we take the text as given, another possibility might be to read: "By [merely] making their actions filial, they would not achieve the longevity of the Transcendents, [so]. . . ."

31. Reading, with Ōfuchi (*Shoki no dōkyō*, p. 367), *dujiao* 都佼 for *xie wen* 邪文.

32. Reading, with Rao (*Laozi xiang'er zhu jiaojian* [1956], p. 26), *bu sheng shou yi* 不勝受矣 for *bu sheng yi shou* 不勝矣受.

33. This line, not accounted for in the commentary, differs markedly from received versions of the *Laozi*. The translation given here is thus tentative.

34. Mugitani ("Rōshi sōjichū sakuin," p. viii, line 14) mistranscribes *shi* 實 as *bao* 寶.

35. Reading, with Ōfuchi (*Shoki no dōkyō*, p. 357), *bao* 寶 for *shi* 實.

36. Following Rao (*Laozi xiang'er zhu jiaojian* [1956], p. 29) in deleting *ke de* 可得, which appears twice at this spot and is an obvious copyist's error.

37. Concerning this line of the *Laozi* and the following, see William G. Boltz, "The 'Hsiang Erh' Lao-tzu," pp. 114–15. I have not included in the translation the gloss "*fu* 甫 means 'beginnings' [*shi* 始]."

38. Following Rao's suggestion (*Laozi xiang'er zhu jiaojian* [1956], p. 31) in reading the three occurrences of *huo* 或 in this paragraph as *huo* 惑, "beguiled, misled."

39. Reading, with Ōfuchi (*Shoki no dōkyō*, p. 357), *hou* 後 for Rao's *fu* 復 (*Laozi xiang'er zhu jiaojian* [1956], p. 32).

40. Omitted before this sentence is the phrase *shu, shui ye* 孰誰也, which defies translation beyond the nonsensical "'Who' means 'who.'"

41. On the basis of the gloss below, it seems that a second *dao* 道 has been deleted by the copyist at this point.

42. See William G. Boltz, "The 'Hsiang Erh' Lao-tzu," pp. 115–16, on the emendations to this line.

43. This is an obvious example of willful tampering with the *Laozi* text. The interpolated commentary and deletion of the topic marker *ye* 也 separates the phrase "From a standpoint within the Dao" from the following phrase, "it is called.... ," as we would otherwise translate the line, and makes room for an additional interpolated speaker—the Dao.

44. Following Rao (*Laozi xiang'er zhu jiaojian* [1956], p. 34) in removing the graph *jia* 家, and *DKW* (3:953a) in understanding the uncommon graph 冡 as *ji* 寂.

45. The received text has "the king [not life] is great." On this emendation, see William G. Boltz, "The 'Hsiang Erh' Lao-tzu," p. 113.

46. A semantic gloss, omitted in the translation, reads: "*Xi* 奚 means *he* 何. It is also close in meaning to *yao* 要 [essential]." *Xi* is a common interrogative particle, having roughly the same meaning as *he,* but the latter part of this phrase does not follow logically. Further, it is grammatically unlikely (if not impossible) for the *Laozi* to have an interrogative particle in this position. Both the received version of the *Laozi* and one Mawangdui text give the reading *xi* 溪, "mountain stream, freshet," which has traditionally been glossed in much the same way as the "mysterious valley." We might, lacking a better explanation, assume that the particle *he* here stands for its homophone *he* 垓, "kernel, nugget," but we would still be unable to account for the interrogative *xi.* If the text had been transmitted orally before being copied down, we might propose that the original version read, "*Xi* 溪 [mountain freshet] is a type of *he* 河 [river]," which was misheard as "which is a type of what." The "essential" nature of water to agriculture and transportation might explain the following line of the gloss.

47. Assuming, with Mugitani ("Rōshi sōjichū sakuin," p. xi, line 3), that the second *tong* 同 is a copyist's error. Even following Rao's punctuation (*Laozi xiang'er zhu jiaojian* [1956], p. 38), however, the meaning would be proximate: "It shares the same pneuma and is the same color as the primal." In this case, the "primal" could be nothing other than *yuanqi.*

48. The term *shen* 腎 is commonly translated as "kidneys," but, as Wile (pp. 20–21) has shown, the term denotes the entire urogenital system, including the kidneys and testes. I have thus left the term untranslated. The meditative practice of sexual abstention outlined here is modeled on the belief that the Daoist's body, after its feigned death, would hide away in the palace of Grand Darkness, where it would be transmuted to emerge as

a perfected, spiritual body (see above, lines 227–30). In analogous fashion, the seminal essence stored in the *shen* and not "utilized" in sexual intercourse would be transformed into internal deities. One cognate meditation practice, a variant of that alluded to here, is found in the Shangqing texts, where it is known by the name "maintaining the dark and the white." The meditator is told to envision a black pneuma in the Niwan Palace (a cavity in the brain), a white pneuma in the heart, and a yellow pneuma in the navel. These three pneumas are to envelop the meditator's body and then turn into a blazing fire that engulfs the body and makes it "as One." This version also warns that engaging in sexual intercourse invalidates the practice and leads to death. See Robinet, "La révélation du Shangqing," vol. 1, pp. 40–41; *HY* 1010, 10:2a-2b; *HY* 1010, 13:14b-15a; and *HY* 421, 2:20b-21b.

49. Following Ōfuchi (*Shoki no dōkyō*, p. 357) in reading *ren zhu* 任住 for *ren wang* 任往.

50. Reading, with Ōfuchi (*Shoki no dōkyō*, p. 357), *hou* 後 for *fu* 復.

51. Reading, with Rao (*Laozi xiang'er zhu jiaojian* [1956], p. 41), *fu* 服 for the graph 敗.

52. The text reads *lang hu* 狼孤, "wolf and fox," but *hu* must be a copyist's error for *hu* 弧, "bow," the nine-star constellation always associated with the star Wolf. All of these star names, with the exception of *Xiuruo* 脩柔—for which I follow Rao and Mugitani, though the first graph seems unclear in the manuscript—appear in the astronomical chapter of the *Shiji* (27:1294–1306) under the lunar stations with which they are aligned. This text also provides a general account of their significance in stellar prognostication. For the relevant passages, see Rao, *Laozi xiang'er zhu jiaojian* (1956), p. 72. On the system of lunar lodgings, see Schafer, *Pacing the Void*, pp. 79–84; and Needham, *Science and Civilisation in China*, vol. 3 (1959), pp. 231–59.

The four lines in which these names appear are rhymed and parallel in structure. They may be a citation from some other text or perhaps a passage meant for memorization. For another instances of rhyme in the commentary, see lines 495–97.

53. *Guo*, the word translated as "achieve" here and below, means "to bring to fruition." A more accurate gloss would be *cheng* 成, "to accomplish," rather than *cheng* 誠, "full-hearted sincerity," but the commentator seems intent on drawing out of the text confirmation of his moral message.

54. Reading *huo* 惑 for *huo* 或, a substitution that occurs several times in this manuscript.

55. On this line, see William G. Boltz, "The 'Hsiang Erh' Lao-tzu," p. 108.

56. This section, as Rao (*Laozi xiang'er zhu jiaojian* [1956], p. 83) has noted, is rhymed.

57. Reading "right" 右 for "left" 左 in the second phrase.

58. Emending *dao* 道 to *min* 民 on the basis of context.

59. Here the commentator has parsed the text so as to bring out and emphasize the celestial auguries that were believed to accompany heavenly appointed rulers. All other commentators break the text differently, reading this passage "[The whole world] will come to you and suffer no harm; instead, they will know safety and peace. Music and food, these are what cause passing travelers to stop...." Our commentator breaks the text right before the *and* in the sentence above and takes "passing traveler" in its derived sense of "comet." *Er* 餌, the word just translated as "food," here written with a slightly different graph (*er* 珥) that means "ring," is glossed in the commentary as meaning "light halo" or parhelion of the sun and moon. See Edward H. Schafer, *Mirages on the Sea of Time: The Taoist Poetry of Ts'ao T'ang* (Berkeley: University of California Press, 1985). Like other stellar anomalies, comets were regarded as inauspicious signs for that area of earth corresponding to the celestial domain they invaded. The terms translated as "unpropitious alignments" refer specifically to the way comets were believed to "stab" (*ce* 刺) and "string together" (*guan* 貫) the constellations and lodgings. Lunar and solar halos were also taken as inauspicious signs, as were strange "criss-crossing" alignments of the planets (Schafer, *Pacing the Void*, pp. 84–89, 109–16).

60. Following Rao (*Laozi xiang'er zhu jiaojian* [1956], p. 49) in adding *yu* 與, the fourth member of the series.

61. Reading, with Ōfuchi (*Shoki no dōkyō*, p. 357), *qi* 齊 for *zhai* 齋.

Commands and Admonitions
for the Families of the Great Dao

INTRODUCTION

When all China was divided into three parts, there was plenty to
concern historians beyond the fate of a defeated religious community. Thus we read only that, after his act of fealty to Cao Cao in
215, Zhang Lu was honored with the title "General Who Subdues
the South" and granted the income of Langzhong, a district in present-day north-central Sichuan.[1] Five of his sons and several of his
principal generals were enfeoffed as well.[2] Most surprising of all,
Zhang Lu's daughter was given in marriage to one of Cao Cao's
sons, Cao Yu, thus joining the two families into what may well have
been a continuing relationship. (We will return to this point later.)

As to the believers, we read that "several tens of thousands" of families were removed from Hanzhong to Chang'an and its surrounding areas, while elsewhere we find that another group of some eighty thousand was moved to Luoyang and Ye.[3]

Despite the lack of specific information on the fate of the Celestial Master movement once its base in Hanzhong had been taken from it, we know that the religion continued to be practiced—at least among isolated groups of believers and families. But what happened to its central organization? Did the Celestial Masters lose all cohesion after Hanzhong? And, finally, what changes were wrought by the dramatic events of 215, when the Celestial Masters relocated throughout the Wei kingdom?

The text translated here, the *Commands and Admonitions for the Families of the Great Dao* (hereafter *Admonitions*), although containing further mysteries, helps to provide answers to these questions.[4] Cast in the form of a circular addressed to members of the Celestial Master church urging them to rectify certain aspects of current practice, it gives a brief history of the religion from its inception to the years after the Hanzhong diaspora.

Historical Background

The *Admonitions* mentions three dates, one clearly the date of the document's release: the seventh day of the first month, second year of the Corrected Prime reign period—a date that corresponds to 1 February 255 C.E. Significantly, the day—the seventh of the first month—is also that reserved for the first of the three yearly assemblies of Celestial Master Daoism.[5] Presumably the text would have been read to the communities of the faithful at this time.

The *Admonitions* is written in the first person. At one point, the author writes: "After more than a hundred years, the Wei house received the mandate of Heaven.... Conforming to the celestial dispensation and the propitious times, I received the mandate to be Master [or "Teacher"] of the Kingdom." Because of this, some scholars have considered the text to have been written by Zhang Lu himself. The problem with this assumption is the date of the document, 255 C.E. We have various records of Zhang Lu's death, all unreliable in one way or another, but all placing his demise earlier than 255.[6] Since we have no information concerning Zhang's birth date or his age at the time of his submission to the Wei, we can only note that it is not impossible that he might have lived forty years after that event. We can draw no firm conclusions from the absence of subsequent historical references to him.[7]

If the *Admonitions* was in fact written by Zhang Lu, it would appear to have been something in the nature of a last will and testament to his church. Near the end of the document, we find the words "from today, I will hide from the world"—a common euphemism for death or transcendence in Daoist texts. But there are also internal indications that the text, though in the voice of Zhang Lu, was in fact a communication from an ascended Zhang Lu delivered through a medium.[8] Although the evidence is circumstantial, it is worth exploring for what it tells us of the author of the text as well as of Celestial Master practices of the time.

The *Admonitions* twice mentions messages from the spirits, using the uncommon expression *jueqi,* which I take to mean something like "breaking through the pneumas" or "distinguishing (voices emanating from) the pneumas." The passages in which this term occurs are as follows:

> The Dao has often saved your lives. Sometimes it has broken through the pneumas [*jueqi*] to speak to you; sometimes a minister or magistrate of the earlier days [in Hanzhong] has tried to reform you, but still you do not keep faith.[9]

> Ever since the fifth year of the Grand Harmony reign period [231 C.E.], each of the holders of parish positions has been self-appointed. Their selection and promotion no longer emanates from my pneumas or from the True Pneuma Controllers of Spirits. Instead you sometimes obey voices that break through the pneumas [*jueqi*], placing your faith in shadows and dreams.[10]

Although I have found no references to this term in other texts, the Celestial Masters are recorded to have had an officer specifically charged with determining the truth of mediumistic pronouncements. This was the *lingjue* 領決, whose duties are described as follows:

> [This officer] is in charge of males and females possessed by pneumas of the revenants, who cleave the pneumas [*piqi* 被氣] and transmit speech. Such officers should determine [*lingjue*] which portion [of these utterances] are to be accepted as teachings and distinguish the truth and falsity [of such utterances] among the Chinese, *Yi* 夷, *Hu* 胡, *Rong* 戎, *Di* 狄, *Di* 氐, or *Qiang* 羌 peoples.[11]

Although neither of these passages from the *Admonitions* refers to the author of the text, they indicate that the Celestial Masters were, by this time if not earlier, engaged in mediumistic practices. Further, the author describes himself in ways that might be hyperbolic but might also indicate that he is more than human. He writes, for instance, "I have circulated day and night, traveling around within the four seas and journeying beyond the eight extremities, all from the desire to cause the ruler to be humane and his ministers loyal, fathers magnanimous and sons filial." This sort of cosmic roaming is commonplace in Daoist texts but occurs most frequently in the case of either spirits or mystics and mediums.

Finally, we must ask ourselves about the significance of another date given in the *Admonitions*, 231 C.E. This date appears in the following context:

> Of all male and female officers of the various ranks granted previously, not very many are still with us. Ever since the fifth year of the Grand Harmony reign period [231], each of the holders of parish positions has been self-appointed. Their selection and promotion no longer emanates from my pneumas.[12]

Since we have no other information concerning any marked change in the fate of the Celestial Masters linked to the year 231, the explanation that comes immediately to mind is that parish positions could not emanate directly from Zhang Lu after this date because this was the date of his death.[13] Unfortunately, I am aware of no other record that gives 231 as the date of Zhang's death.

Rather than commit ourselves to any one hypothesis, then, it seems most prudent to simply state that the *Admonitions* was written in the persona of Zhang Lu and is unlikely to have come from his hand.

Consideration of the political situation in the Wei kingdom at the time the text was composed lends a certain pathos to the earnest hopes expressed by the author. After detailing the struggles of the church at the end of the Han and the high positions accorded its members after their submission to the Wei, the author continues:

> From today, I will hide from the world. I entrust you to the pure administration and the Daoist government of the Wei, [under whose rule] one

can travel alone for one thousand miles because tigers and wolves are tamed, and one can sleep without fastening one's door.[14]

This declaration of faith in the Wei kingdom was penned only eleven years before the formal end of the dynasty and well after the general whose direct descendants were to found the succeeding dynasty had seized a determinative role in the events of the time. Even the author, in passages scattered throughout the text, seems to recognize the kingdom as troubled and on the verge of collapse. But his most specific references to the troubles of the age follow directly upon the paragraph just cited:

> Yet evil ministers and their minions still do not know what it is to follow and what it is to transgress the mandate of Heaven. They compel others with trickery and lies. That which they fabricate is entirely inauspicious.[15]

Out of context, this reads as if it concerned only the Celestial Masters, but appended to the preceding concerning the "pure administration" of the Wei, these sentences more likely refer to political events that reverberated throughout the kingdom as a whole.[16] A brief survey of political events leading up to the year in which the *Admonitions* was promulgated will show this likelihood more clearly.[17]

Cao Rui, emperor of the Wei from 226 to 239, was said to have been something of a libertine and, at any rate, did not contribute to the longevity of his dynastic line. His successors all took the throne at an early age and were controlled by powerful generals and by various empresses. The first of these youthful rulers, Cao Fang, was put on the throne at the age of seven or eight. His accession was uncontested, but there was a bitter struggle over who would serve as his regents. Two men, backed by powerful factions, emerged victorious from this struggle. One was Cao Shuang, a member of the extensive imperial family, and the other was Sima Yi, whose direct descendants would establish a new dynasty, the Jin, and declare him the High Progenitor.

Although the history books make the gradual rise to power of the Sima family appear a sure thing, it was in fact a brutal and bloody process. In 249, Sima Yi put to death his fellow regent Cao Shuang, together with three generations of his family and many of his supporters. Sima Yi died in 251 and was succeeded as general by his son Sima Shi. Following this, a new faction, composed partly of surviving supporters of Cao Shuang, attempted to dislodge the Sima family. Once again the Sima clan was able to head off the plot, and in 254 the ringleaders, together with three generations of their families, were put to death. By this time the emperor, Cao Fang, had achieved his majority. At twenty-three, he no longer needed a regent. Sima Shi consequently first deposed his empress (murdering members of her family in the process), established another in her place, and then had the new empress issue an edict proclaiming Cao Fang profligate. Cao Fang was thus deposed and replaced with Cao Mao, a boy of thirteen.

However serious the family connections of Zhang Lu with the ruling house may have been, it is certain that the old Hanzhong Celestial Masters leadership found themselves invested heavily in the fate of the Cao dynasty.[18] The deposition and murder of the young emperor Cao Fang and the execution of Cao Shuang in 254 occurred only a few months before the release of the *Admonitions* to the Celestial Master faithful. The reemergence of the powerful Sima family and the perilous condition of the Wei dynasty could not but have shaken them to the bone.

Beyond the few loyalist, if somewhat disillusioned, references to the Wei, however, the overwhelming impression left by the *Admonitions* is of a Celestial Master organization scattered and in need of control. Modern scholars have frequently cited passages from the text to prove that the practices surrounding the original twenty-four parishes in Sichuan fell into desuetude once the followers had been scattered throughout northern China. With the whole text before us, though, we can read a somewhat different message as well. In harsh tones the pseudo–Zhang Lu reprimands his followers with phrases such as "You should all know this" and "Do you know the history of our Truth?" He demands a return to the former methods of choosing parish officers because, among other things, "sometimes one parish has redundant officers, while in other parishes offices remain empty." The fact that there were "redundant officers" for some parishes indicates clearly that the *Admonitions* is not simply directed at an organization that was in decline.

In fact, one of the problems the text confronts was the success of the old Hanzhong community. The fact that the Wei had enfeoffed some members of the Hanzhong community was now beginning to cause problems of dissension and struggles over control. This would be natural, given that what had once been a centralized and cohesive community was now scattered over vast distances. The *Admonitions* addresses these problems in the following terms:

> You former people [of Hanzhong] ... even go so far as to slander one another, so that lords and ministers struggle for influence, fathers and sons are not close to one another, husbands and wives envy one another, and divisions arise between brothers.[19]

There are also criticisms of those who "denigrate the Dao of the loyal minister" by shirking responsibility for mishaps that occur within their area of responsibility.[20] This is a Confucian concern, one that does not occur in the *Xiang'er* commentary. As we will see in the following section, the *Admonitions* shows a marked change in attitude toward the Confucian virtues, particularly those concerned with good government and social order. Such a shift in emphasis, as we might suspect, accompanied the appointment of Celestial Master officials to positions of governmental authority in the kingdom of Wei.

Morality and Governance

In most respects, the *Admonitions* reveals the same attitude toward ethics that we have already seen in the *Xiang'er* commentary. Whereas the term *jie*, "precepts, admonition," occurs only in the title, being replaced with the term *jin*, "prohibition, to prohibit," elsewhere in the circular, a number of the *Xiang'er* precepts are paraphrased, and one is quoted verbatim. The basis for morality is still the omniscient oversight of the spirits, who deduct counts of life for all infractions. At one point, the people of the Dao are told that they should not even harbor wild thoughts, since "spirit luminaries know all of your good and evil deeds." The fact that those who deny the Dao and its teachings commit a transgression resulting in the deduction of a "full three thousand" counts also finds mention here.[21]

What seems truly new in the *Admonitions* is the prominence given the Confucian virtues of filiality, loyalty, humaneness, and the like. To be sure, the *Xiang'er* does not attack these virtues quite so ruthlessly as does the *Laozi* itself, expressing instead the opinion that such virtues will be practiced fully "even in secret" once people do so out of fear of heaven rather from the desire to gain high station and the acclaim of other mortals. This rationale is expressed here as well, but the *Admonitions* advocates Confucian virtues in a way that the *Xiang'er* does not. We would not expect to see in the *Xiang'er*, for example, any mention of the "Dao of the loyal minister." But in the *Admonitions,* written when members of the Celestial Master hierarchy actually held office, the term does appear and the need for a loyal officialdom is greatly emphasized.

This new stress has another consequence as well. Near the end of the circular we find the following parting words:

> All of our households should transform one another through loyalty and filiality, so that fathers are magnanimous and sons filial, husbands faithful and wives chaste, elder brothers respectful and the younger obedient. Mornings and evenings you should practice "clarity and stillness." Root out all covetousness, abandon the pursuit of personal profit, and rid yourself of desire. Reform your evil cravings. Pity the poor and cherish the old. Be liberal in supplying others and in giving way to them. Drive from your heart excesses of jealousy, joy, and anger so that your emotions are constantly harmonious and your eyes and belly in accord. Aid the kingdom in strengthening its mandate.[22]

Although much of this is already familiar from the *Xiang'er* commentary—the emphasis on banishing desire; the morning and evening practice of "clarity and stillness"; the warning against excess emotion, to include even joy; and so forth—the insistence on Confucian virtues for the regulation of family life is something new. The most striking change is with respect to the status of women. Where, in the *Xiang'er,* women were mentioned only as a model for physiological practice, here they are made subject to their husbands in accord with the Confucian "five constants."[23] The same listing of intrapersonal and family hierarchies is given repeatedly in this short text. It is a striking return to the hierarchical order of what we might call "Confucian family values" and clearly represents an accommodation the nature of which we can appreciate, if not fully assess.

The goals of good governance and morality in the *Xiang'er* commentary were an age of Great Peace in this world and the oppor-

tunity to pass through the Palace of Grand Darkness for extended
life in the next. The author of the *Admonitions*, although praising
the Wei as a kingdom of "pure administration and ... Daoist government" under whose rule "one can travel alone for one thousand
miles because tigers and wolves are tamed, and one can sleep without fastening one's door," clearly does not regard it as an age of
Great Peace. The age of Great Peace is yet to come, after a period of
cataclysms that mark the end of the present period of governmental
disorder and decline. These cataclysms, and the very depravity of
contemporary humanity, indicate that the end, and with it the new
beginning, is near at hand. If the audience of the circular do not live
to see the age of Great Peace, they can be sure that their children or
their grandchildren will.

Further, those who keep faith with the Dao are promised that they
will be able to pass through the current paroxysms of war, disease,
flood, and death entirely without harm. In fact, they are to become
"seed people." The metaphor is agricultural. The "seed people" were
the elect of Daoist eschatology, those selected to survive the coming
end time to form the germ of the new populace at the beginning of a
fresh age, once all the evil had been "rooted out." It is not easy to
enter the ranks of the seed people, in that the spirits keep a close
watch on the actions of all.[24] Only if Daoists keep faith with the
Dao and avoid breaking any of its prohibitions can they be assured
of this favorable outcome.

This said, it is not clear from the *Admonitions* whether inclusion
among the "seed people" is something that the dead might hope for
as well. In that it is addressed to the living and their present social
and political situation, the *Admonitions* does not concern itself with
outlining the postmortem fates of the Daoist faithful.

Lord Lao and the Dao

Social and cosmic order depends on human deeds. War, disease,
drought, flood, and even the stellar anomalies that foretell the end of
the age are all the result of human transgression and signs that the
Dao has departed from humankind. Both the *Xiang'er* commentary
and the *Admonitions* warn, in nearly identical words, that humanity
should not cause the Dao to thus "distance itself," since "its return

would be difficult." In lines 108–9 of the *Xiang'er* we read, "The One [i.e., the Dao] disperses its form as pneuma and gathers in its form as the Most High Lord Lao." Through the brief historical account of the *Admonitions*, we learn for the first time just what was expected to occur when the Dao withdrew from human deviance and congealed its pneumas as Lord Lao. At such times, the Dao, itself "without shape or image," takes on human shape to descend as the "teacher [or Master] of the thearchical kings." In other texts, such epiphanies are described as transformations of Lord Lao; but in the *Admonitions* they are all the work of the Dao.[25] Given what we know from the *Xiang'er* commentary, this is a terminological distinction of no import whatsoever. The two are one.

The appearances of the Dao in human history are listed in the *Admonitions* as follows:

1.   To reveal to Gan Ji, toward the end of the Zhou dynasty, the "Dao of Great Peace." Gan Ji is associated with the *Scripture of Great Peace,* and the story of the Dao's appearance to him during the Zhou seems designed to provide an origin legend for the *Scripture of Great Peace* employed by the early Celestial Masters.[26]

2.   As the "historical" Laozi, to reveal the "five-thousand-character text" (the *Laozi*) to the gatekeeper Yin Xi at the western passes. This legend of the composition of the *Laozi* text in "over five thousand characters" already occurs in the *Shiji* of Sima Qian and Sima Tan.[27]

3.   As a "Perfected Person" (clearly meant to be the Buddha), to reveal the Dao in a simplified (and ultimately misunderstood) form to the barbarians of the western regions.[28]

4.   As Master Yellow Stone at the founding of the Han dynasty, to bestow a text and portents on Zhang Liang, a sage historically credited with presenting auguries of success to the first ruler.[29]

5.   On 11 June 142 C.E., to bestow on Zhang Daoling the title of Celestial Master.

Such lists of epiphanies always reveal something of the masters and teachers of the past revered by the author of the text in which they appear. The same is true here. Each of these epiphanies of the Dao in human history, with the exception of the second, involves to some extent its concern with human governance. Even the *Laozi* text itself is described in ways identical to those in which it is portrayed in the *Xiang'er:*

> In it, the prohibitions became more severe and the people were instructed in the essentials of regulating the body, nurturing life, and in the explanations of the divine Transcendents.[30]

As we have seen, the "prohibitions" or precepts derived from the *Laozi* in the *Xiang'er* commentary concern both individual practice and the regulation of society.

Interestingly, the author of the *Admonitions,* be he Zhang Lu or, as is more likely, his spirit, does not describe a further epiphany of the Dao to inaugurate the coming age of Great Peace. Lord Lao is not the savior of the apocalypse. No new order is proposed.[31] Instead, the faithful are to return to the conditions of their previous covenant with Lord Lao, as it was entered into by Zhang Daoling. Again and again, they are chided for having "forgotten" the history of their religion and for having betrayed its principles. Presumably, then, the decline of the organization had not reached the point where a completely new appearance of Lord Lao (and with it a newly appointed leader) was seen as necessary.[32]

During the course of its opening exposition on the nature of the Dao, the *Admonitions* provides us with quite a bit of information that is only hinted at in the fragmentary *Xiang'er* manuscript. For instance, quite a bit more detail is provided here on the three pneumas, which the *Xiang'er,* calling them simply yin, yang, and "the centrally harmonious," dealt with only in the context of physiological practice.[33] In the *Admonitions,* the three pneumas are associated with three colors and with the traditional triad of heaven-earth-humanity in the following way:

Mystic pneuma	azure	heaven
Inaugural pneuma	yellow	earth
Primal pneuma	white	the Dao (among humans)

These three emanations of the Dao, often described as arising sequentially as the hermetic unity of the Dao divided itself at the creation, were to be central to all Daoist cosmology. The three pneumas exist both on the macrocosmic level and within the microcosm of the human body, in ways that will be explored in the texts translated here.

The mystic pneuma, in its association with heaven, is yang, whereas the inaugural pneuma, earth, is yin. What then of the primal pneuma? It is not the cosmic Dao itself, since the Dao is said to be productive of all three. Instead, the primal pneuma needs to be understood as the medium through which the Dao is accessible to humans.

Although the *Admonitions* does not discuss physiological practice or the makeup of the human body, we know from the *Xiang'er* commentary that, of the three pneumas that enter the body—the yin, the yang, and the "centrally harmonious"—it is the latter that is to be employed in the practice of cycling pneumas through the body.[34] White primal pneuma is the same color as the essence created by the pneumas of the Dao, the preservation and nurturing of which is such a concern to the meditation practices contained in the text.[35] The importance of the third, primal pneuma as the active agent in making the Dao accessible to humanity and thus granting life is clear. The *Admonitions* warns repeatedly of the unbridled sexuality of contemporary humanity, through which humans lose their apportionment of the pneumas of the Dao:

> Delighting only in sensual pleasure, they indulge their ears and eyes in deviant practices. They are infatuated with feminine beauty, and so their essence and spirits spurt forth chaotically. They covet material things and bribes. As a result, miasmic pneumas rise up and foster all sorts of illness.[36]

The "deviant practices" are those perverse, humanly contrived solutions so often warned of in the *Xiang'er* commentary.

Finally, then, it is not to the hope of a savior, but to the standards of the old organization and to the precepts of the Dao, that the scattered remnants of the Celestial Master organization are urged to return as they confront the collapse of the Wei and the coming apocalypse. The lineage of Celestial Masters, begun with Zhang Daoling and continued in his grandson Zhang Lu, would not, we know from other sources, survive in its old form. The line of succession would have to be reconstructed by later Daoists. Even more catastrophic events, particularly the fall of northern China to the

Huns in 317, would scatter members of the Celestial Master organization even more completely. When we hear from them again, in the *Scripture of the Inner Explanations of the Three Heavens*, translated later in this book, it will be this new, southern branch of the movement that speaks. Nonetheless, despite what we might call the failure of the *Admonitions*, it does reward our attention, for it marks the beginnings of major changes in the Daoist religion that would ensure its survival to the present day.

NOTES TO ADMONITIONS: INTRODUCTION

1. Langzhong is just south of the famous Jianmen Pass, on the mountainous road into Shu. This location, and the title granted Zhang Lu, give one the impression that Zhang was intended to serve as a buffer between Cao Cao's forces and those of Liu Bei 劉備 in Sichuan. In any event, he cannot have enjoyed the income of this district for long, since the Shu-Han forces almost immediately began their attempts to retake Hanzhong, two hundred kilometers northeast of Langzhong, forcing the Wei defenders to withdraw in 219. Either as part of this campaign or as a mopping-up operation after its success, Liu Bei would certainly have retaken Langzhong.

2. One such general was Yan Pu 閻圃, who was made "Lord of the Pingle Subdistrict." The location of this appointment is not certain. One good possibility is the site of the old Pingle Guan, just west of Luoyang.

3. See Tang Changru, *Wei Jin Nanbeichao shilun shiyi* (Beijing: Zhonghua shuju, 1983), pp. 228–29.

4. The *Admonitions* appears on pp. 12a–19b of *HY* 788, a collection of Celestial Master documents. Though other of the documents collected in *HY* 788 seem to be authentically early, here we will focus only on the *Admonitions*. For an introduction to the controversies surrounding the provenance of this text, see Ōfuchi, *Shoki no dōkyō,* p. 275 n. 2, pp. 301–8. My own research, the findings of which are presented in the section "The Authorship and Date of the *Xiang'er* Commentary" and further elucidated later on, strongly suggests that the *Admonitions* was written in the persona of Zhang Lu, who had died sometime before the date of the text's composition in 255.

5. The three yearly assemblies of Celestial Master Daoism were held on the seventh day of the first month, the seventh day of the seventh month, and the fifth day of the tenth month by the Chinese calendar. See Stein, "Religious Taoism," pp. 70–71.

6. The earliest of these records is a note written by Tao Hongjing in the *Zhen'gao* (*HY* 1010, 4:14b), which states that Zhang Lu died in the year following his submission (i.e., 216) and was buried to the east of the Wei

capital, Ye (present Linzhang County, Henan). Forty-four years after his death, Tao goes on to state, Zhang's coffin was washed open in a flood and he came back to life, smeared his face with mud, laughed, and perished once more. Although Tao does not give his source for this information, it was clearly less than sympathetic toward the Celestial Masters. The detail concerning Zhang's smearing his face with mud, in particular, seems meant to deride either Zhang or the Retreat of Mud and Ashes—one of the early Celestial Master rituals—or perhaps both. The ritual was meant to rescue the participants and their ancestors from sufferings in the earth-prisons and involved the daubing of the face with "mud and ashes" in penitence. That Zhang came back to life to smear mud on his face, then, could mean only that he had ended up in the earth-prisons. More sober accounts, though their sources of information are not clear, give the date of Zhang's death as 245 (*HY* 773, 5:5b) or 252 (*HY* 1131, 7:14b).

7. Perhaps the most striking of these omissions is that discussed by Tang Changru (*Wei Jin Nanbeichao shilun shiyi*, pp. 229–30). A stele, the text of which is preserved in the *Jinshi cuipian* 金石萃編 (23:1a ff.), records one of the several memorials urging Cao Pi to adopt the title of emperor and lists the names and titles of those who presented it. Among the names are those of several of Zhang Lu's followers, but Zhang's name does not appear. Tang concludes from this that Tao Hongjing's record of Zhang's death must then be accurate. Several objections could be raised to Tang's conclusion: this memorial was only one of several presented to the throne (see the *Sanguo zhi*, 2:62–75, for the texts of some of them), and we possess none of the name lists from these other memorials. Further, if Zhang Lu had in fact gone to Langzhong after his defeat (and we cannot rely on the fragment cited by Tao attesting to his place of death), he would not have been present to sign any of these memorials. Finally, *ex nihilo, nihil fit*: the argument from silence means little when we have no other reliable evidence.

8. That this text was delivered through a medium, perhaps one of Zhang Lu's sons, was first suggested by Hu Shi in 1957 (personal communication reported by Yang Liansheng in Rao, *Laozi xiang'er zhu jiaojian* [1991], pp. 162–63).

9. *HY* 788, 14b10–15a2.

10. *HY* 788, 17a6–8.

11. *HY* 1131, 7:19a; Chen Guofu, *Daozang yuanliu kao* (Peking: Zhonghua shuju, 1963), p. 350. This passage suggests that such communications were regarded as irruptions of pneuma or voices transmitted through the pneumas. The term *lingjue* may suggest that we should take *jueqi* to mean "comprehending (voices in) the pneumas."

12. *HY* 788, 17a5–6.

13. This explanation has been suggested by Yang Liansheng (reported in Rao, *Laozi xiang'er zhu jiaojian* [1991], p. 163).

14. *HY* 788, 18a7–8.

15. *HY* 788, 18a8–18b1.

16. Note also that the passage speaks of the "mandate" of heaven, a political concept, and not the "prohibitions" of heaven, the term the *Admonitions* uses to refer to more specifically religious injunctions.

17. The following information is abstracted from the *Sanguo zhi,* chaps. 3–4, and the *Zizhi tongjian,* chaps. 70–76.

18. Tang Changru (*Wei Jin Nanbeichao shilun shiyi,* p. 230) has speculated that the Celestial Masters may have continued to enjoy imperial favor, despite several edicts issued from the throne outlawing "deviant" religious practices, due to the influence of Cao Yu, Zhang Lu's imperial "son-in-law," who managed to stay alive throughout this period. Cao Yu was especially favored of Cao Rui, who on his deathbed proposed Yu as commander in chief and regent, a position he wisely declined. Cao Yu's prudence was rewarded when his son, Cao Huan, was made emperor. Cao Huan sat on the throne for only five years, his chief contribution to history being the vehemence with which he urged Sima Zhao to take the throne, ending the Wei in 265.

19. *HY* 788, 16a1–2.

20. *HY* 788, 17b2–4.

21. *HY* 788, 17a4.

22. *HY* 788, 18b5–10.

23. *HY* 788, 16a3. To be sure, at one point the text speaks of the "men and women of the former populace [of Hanzhong] who held various offices," and we know from other texts that women Libationers continued to be appointed by the Celestial Masters throughout the fourth century.

24. *HY* 788, 17a1–3.

25. This subject, including the contributions of the *Xiang'er* and the *Admonitions,* has been fully studied by Anna K. Seidel (*La divinisation de Lao-tseu*). My remarks here are much indebted to her work. Seidel speculates that the author of the *Admonitions* wrote of the transformations of the "Dao" rather than of the deified Laozi to sharply distinguish early Celestial Master tenets from the "primitive anthropomorphism" of the Dao held by other sects. The *Scripture of the Transformations of Laozi,* a text of a mid-second-century sect of Sichuan Province, seems to have in fact proposed very different ideas concerning Laozi's actions when hidden away. The text states: "Withdrawn he nourishes life." This sect also seems to have practiced visualizations meant to find Laozi, as the Dao, resident in the human body—something the *Xiang'er* criticizes severely. For the early Celestial Masters, it was only when the pneumas of the Dao circulated freely that the One might be properly apprehended. The total withdrawal of the Dao from the world was thus not something to be desired, and its physical manifestation, whether as Lord Lao or in other forms, was a sign that humans had departed from the true path.

26. On Gan Ji, see Maeda Shigeki, "Rikuchō jidai ni okeru Kan Kichi den no hensen," *Tōhō shūkyō* 65 (1985), pp. 44–62.

27. *Shiji,* 63:2141.

28. For the story that Laozi thus "converted the barbarians," a legend meant to show that Buddhism was but a perverted form of Daoism and thus not fit for dissemination in China, see especially Erik Zürcher, *The Buddhist Conquest of China* (Leiden: E. J. Brill, 1959), vol. 2, pp. 288–320; Kusuyama Haruki, *Rōshi densetsu no kenkyū* (Tokyo: Sōbunsha, 1979), pp. 437–72; and Ōfuchi, *Shoki no dōkyō,* pp. 469–84. For another version of the story, see the translation of the *Inner Explanations of the Three Heavens* in this volume.

29. On Zhang Liang, see Wolfgang Bauer, "Der Herr vom Gelben Stein," *Oriens Extremus* 3 (1956), pp. 137–52; and Seidel, "Imperial Treasures," p. 344.

30. HY 788, 13b3–4.

31. Such a new order *was* proposed for Celestial Master Daoism by Kou Qianzhi, who, echoing many of the complaints found in this text regarding organizational decline, himself received a new revelation from Lord Lao and sought to reform the "false Dao of the three Zhangs."

32. There is evidence, though, that at least one new text had been recently revealed. This is the *Scripture of the Yellow Court,* a rhymed scripture on the gods of the body, composed by Lord Lao himself. The text is mentioned twice in the *Admonitions,* on one occasion in such a way that it appears that the *Scripture of the Yellow Court* was revealed to Zhang Lu (or the pseudo–Zhang Lu) himself. On this text, see *HY* 788, 14b8 and 16a7, and, on the possibility that other texts are mentioned as well, endnote 4 to the translation.

33. It is likely that a more detailed description of the three pneumas of the macrocosm would have appeared in the commentary to *Laozi* 42. The only surviving manuscript of the *Xiang'er* commentary ends with *Laozi* 37. For the "three pneumas" in the *Xiang'er,* see the section "Meditation and Perfection of the Body" in the introduction to that text. The term "primal pneuma" is also mentioned at lines 427–29, and implicitly at line 103—again in the context of physiological practice.

34. See the discussion on pp. 43 ff.

35. See especially the *Xiang'er,* lines 102–4 and 427–29.

36. HY 788, 12b10–13a2.

Translation

Commands and Admonitions
for the Families of the Great Dao

The great Dao is that which encompasses heaven and earth, is joined
with and nourishes all forms of life, and controls the myriad initiatory mechanisms.* Without shape or image, it is undifferentiated
and yet spontaneously gives birth to the million species. Though it
is something to which humans cannot put a name, from heaven and
earth on down everything is born and dies through the Dao.

The Dao bestows itself by means of subtle pneumas. There are
three colors, associated with the mystic, the primal, and the inaugural pneumas. The mystic is azure and formed heaven. The inaugural is yellow and formed earth. The primal is white and formed
the Dao.† Within the three pneumas, the Dao controls all above and

---

* "Initiatory mechanisms" translates *ji*. A word that originally designated a
crossbow trigger, in philosophical writing it came to denote any initiatory or moti-
vating force.

† This system of three pneumas is part of a tradition of cosmological speculation
that began during the Han and is based ultimately on the enigmatic proclamation of
Laozi 42: "The Dao gave birth to the one. The one gave birth to the two. The two
gave birth to the three. The three gave birth to the myriad things." The system of
three pneumas portrayed here seems to owe something to the formulation of the
Taiping jing (34: 17–20), in which the third of the three pneumas, the "centrally
merged" pneuma, is portrayed as a harmonious stasis that, if properly cultivated,
leads to Great Peace in governance and longevity for the individual. Such a notion
may underlie our text's claim that the third pneuma, here called primal pneuma, is
again productive of the Dao, presumably as it is active in the mundane world.

below and is the father and mother of the myriad things. Thus it is
most revered and most holy. From heaven and earth on down, there
is nothing that is not born through receiving these pneumas. All
longevous creatures are able to preserve the Dao, holding in its
pneumas. Thus possessed of essence and [internal] spirits, they
breathe in and out and have yin and yang natures.

12b

The Dao gave birth to heaven. Heaven gave birth to earth. The
earth gave birth to humans.* All were born of the three pneumas.
Three threes are nine. Thus people have nine orifices and nine pneumas.† When these nine pneumas flow without obstruction, the five
viscera are untroubled. When the five viscera are untroubled, the six
storehouses are settled.‡ When the six storehouses are settled, the
corporeal spirits are luminous. When the corporeal spirits are luminous, one approaches the Dao. So, humans who practice good and
maintain the Dao are cautious not to lose the Dao of life. Not losing
it, they receive the triple [pneumas]. Since they are not separated
from the triple pneumas, they are able to change together with
heaven and earth.

The *Yijing* says: "After heaven and earth came into existence,
there were the myriad things. After the myriad things, there were
male and female. After male and female, there were husband and
wife. After husband and wife, there were father and son."[1] Now, the
mention of "father and son" indicates the desire to continue through

---

* This passage, like almost all Daoist cosmogonies, echoes *Laozi* 42: "The Dao
gave birth to the one. The one gave birth to the two. The two gave birth to the three.
The three gave birth to the myriad things." Unfortunately, we do not have the corresponding section of the *Xiang'er* commentary, for it would be interesting to see
if it also relates this idea to the three pneumas, which do appear in the surviving
manuscript.

† I have no evidence on the nine pneumas of the human body. The *Taiping
jing* speaks of nine categories of human beings, each representative of a specific
"pneuma," which it is their duty to harmonize (Kaltenmark, "Ideology of the *T'ai-
p'ing ching*," pp. 31–32). Later Daoist texts tell of the articulation of the three
pneumas into nine, but from a cosmological perspective. Neither of these ideas seems
to apply here. Possibly what is meant is the reticulation of the pneuma in the body,
an idea presented in such early medical texts as the *Su wen*, where we find listed
anger, joy, sorrow, fear, cold, heat, surprise, fatigue, and thought as the "nine pneumas" (*DKW* 1:361a).

‡ The five viscera are the heart, lungs, liver, spleen, and urogenital organs. The
"six storehouses" are the throat, stomach, large intestine, small intestine, gallbladder,
and bladder.

a hundred generations, so one's seed and family name can continue. But in lower antiquity, lineages are short-lived and the people are largely ignorant and shallow.* Delighting only in sensual pleasure, they indulge their ears and eyes in deviant practices. They are infat-   13a uated with feminine beauty and so their essence and spirits spurt forth chaotically. They covet material things and bribes. As a result, miasmic pneumas rise up and foster all sorts of illness.

Ever since the time of the Yellow Thearch, the people have been crafty.† They make oxen serve them and they ride horses.‡ They pass bribes to become officials. During the time of the Five Thearchs, there was a gradual decrease in longevity. The three eras—Xia, Shang, and Zhou—saw a turn to desire for worldly profit.§ Then the Inaugural Thearch of the Qin and the Five Hegemons attacked and injured one another and banditry arose.‖ Millions died—more than can be counted. All of this occurred through loss of faith with the Dao.

---

* The division of antiquity into three ages is common, though the demarcation points differ. Confucian texts, for example, begin lower antiquity with Confucius. In Daoist texts, lower antiquity generally seems to have begun with the mythical Five Thearchs: the Yellow Thearch, Zhuanxu, Ku, Yao, and Yu. This is the case here and with the *Xiang'er,* in that both begin the decline with the Yellow Thearch. In the *Scripture of Great Peace,* too, the age of "high antiquity" was the age of Great Peace, while morals became progressively more depraved during the ages of middle and lower antiquity. See Kaltenmark, "Ideology of the *T'ai-p'ing ching,*" pp. 22–23. In all of these texts, lower antiquity includes the age in which the texts' authors were writing.

† On the Yellow Thearch and his foreknowledge of the fall of humanity, see the *Xiang'er,* lines 40–43.

‡ This observation seems bizarrely inappropriate until we recall the *Xiang'er* gloss at lines 125–29: "In ancient times, before there were carts, [the people] were passive. The Dao sent Xi Zhong to create carts. Once the ignorant obtained the cart, they used it only to satisfy their avarice. They did not contemplate practicing the Dao, nor were they aware of the spirits of the Dao. When the wise saw [the cart], they understood the beneficence of the Dao. Without uttering a sound, they were strictly self-regulated and put great emphasis on preserving the perfection of the Dao." The riding of horses is, on the other hand, related to hunting and warfare, equally excoriated in the *Xiang'er* (lines 140–41 and 460–65). We do not, unfortunately, have the commentary to *Laozi* 46, which states: "In a world possessing the Dao, chargers are let out to pasture for their dung; in a world without the Dao, warhorses are raised outside the city walls."

§ The Shang (c. 1766–1045 B.C.E.) and Zhou (c. 1045–221 B.C.E.) are historical dynasties. The Xia, traditionally assigned the dates 2205–1766 B.C.E. and founded by the sage-king Yu, is not.

‖ The Inaugural Thearch of the Qin, unifier of the Central Kingdom and first to take the name "high god" (translated here as "Thearch" in view of the fact that the

Generation after generation, the Dao acted as the teacher of the thearchical kings, but they were unable to revere and serve it. As a result, when there were troubles such as social upheaval or the fall of dynasties, though the Dao was there to aid in the crisis, not one in ten thousand survived.

The Dao values human life. At the end of the Zhou, one emerged to uphold the Dao in Langye. Thereupon the Dao bestowed upon that man, Gan Ji, the "Dao of Great Peace."* The revival began in the east. In the east he began to save the populace from mud and ashes.† Although there were those who inclined to belief in the Dao,

---

word thereafter might refer either to the emperors of humans or the emperors of heaven), was Ying Zheng (r. 246–210 B.C.E.). The "Five Hegemons" were the rulers of the five strongest kingdoms, who sought power during the Spring and Autumn period of the Zhou dynasty by taking the title of hegemon under the nominal authority of the Zhou ruling house. (These are variously enumerated; see the DKW, 1:505a). By extension, the term refers to the powerful kingdoms that were defeated by the Qin when it unified China in 221.

* Gan Ji is also known as Yu Ji. (The graph yu differs from the graph gan only in a slight hook on the bottom stroke, much like the difference between the letters g and q.) The issue of Gan Ji's association with the Scripture of Great Peace appears in two main early traditions. The History of the Latter Han and the Chronicles of the Three Kingdoms tell of a Taiping qingling shu that was presented to the throne by Gong Chong during the reign of the Han Shundi emperor (r. 126–145). This book is described as a "spirit writing" that Gong received from his master, Yu Ji, in Langye (roughly modern Shandong Province, in northeastern China), and indeed the same account appears in some Daoist texts. Early Celestial Master scriptures, though, are consistent in placing Gan Ji's receipt of the Scripture of Great Peace in the late Zhou and make no mention of Gong Chong's role in the transmission of the text. The preface to the One-hundred-eighty Precepts of the Most High Lord Lao (HY 785, 2a9 ff.; HY 1026, 39:1a5 ff.) dates the event to the reign of King Nan (r. 314–256 B.C.E.). The Inner Explanations of the Three Heavens also clearly places Gan Ji during the same time period. Since the historical texts concerning Gong Chong's receipt of the Taiping book tell us nothing about Yu Ji, it is possible that he was believed to be a Transcendent who had received the text earlier and "reappeared" to Gong at a later date. Lacking textual confirmation, this solution must remain conjectural.

† The multivalence of the Chinese particle used here would also permit the reading "to save the people through mud and ashes," and in fact there was an early Daoist ritual of repentance, probably originating with the Celestial Masters, known as the "Retreat of Mud and Ashes." (See endnote 6 to the introduction to this translation.) This ritual is not, however, elsewhere claimed to have originated with the Taiping jing or with Gan Ji. Further, the term "mud and ashes" is common in texts of this period not only as a metaphor for suffering and degradation, but as synecdoche for the twin dangers of flood and fire, which attended periods of misrule. It is this latter usage, originating in the Shangshu (8:161b), rather than the technical Daoist one, that seems most appropriate in this context. In five-phases cosmology, the east is symbolic of wood, spring, and new growth, while fire (south, summer) and water (north, winter) are, respectively, the phases of excess yang and excess yin.

the first transformative influence was slight. The people obeyed only when it came to matters of dietary regimen and sexual practice. Gradually, this [influence] widened to include their parents, siblings, and the spirits to whom they performed sacrifice.* Eventually, the pneumas of the Dao would spread to cover the entire land within the four seas.

13b

The Dao was then born again through transformation [and came to] the western pass. This came about because the teachings of Great Peace were not complete. There was need of an enlightened master's verbal instructions and of rectification through talismanic orders. The Dao further created the five-thousand-character text, which emanated from the essentials of the divine Transcendents.† In it, the prohibitions became more severe and the people were instructed in the essentials of regulating the body, nurturing life, and in the explanations of the divine Transcendents. It was entrusted to the commander of the pass, Yin Xi.‡ These transmissions were fairly complete, but most of the people of that generation were ignorant and their hearts were moreover closed. Masses of people died, and of ten thousand, not one was preserved.

The Dao then went westward into the land of the barbarians to transmit the practices of the Dao.§ In this case, the prohibitions were

---

* This seems a little strange. It is likely that a reformation of the sorts of spirits to whom people performed sacrifice is meant. Number twenty-three of the *Xiang'er* precepts is "Do not pray or sacrifice to demons and spirits," and the *Xiang'er* (lines 364–66) gives the reason as being that "sacrifices and food offerings are a means of commerce with deviant forces." For Daoist proscriptions against the "blood-eating" gods of the profane, see Stein, "Religious Taoism."

† This characterization of the *Laozi* as containing the words of Transcendents as well as of Laozi himself echoes the *Xiang'er* commentary (see especially lines 241 and 305–21).

‡ This is the early legend that the *Daode jing,* or "five-thousand-character text," was composed by Laozi during the latter days of the Zhou dynasty at the request of Yin Xi, guardian of the western pass, who was loath to let the great sage leave the kingdom without some record of his knowledge. Interestingly, whereas the instructions for regulating the body and for nurturing life are, at least arguably, in the *Laozi,* this early text contains no "prohibitions" and certainly no "explanations of the divine Transcendents." We do, however, find these things attributed to the *Laozi* in the *Xiang'er* commentary. What is being discussed here is the true understanding of the *Laozi* as elucidated in the *Xiang'er* commentary.

§ This is an early account of the legend that Laozi, after departing from the Zhou kingdom, went west to become the Buddha. When this legend had gained enough currency, Buddhist polemicists were quick to point out that it was wildly anachronistic. (See endnote 28 to the introduction to this translation.)

extremely severe. There were no provisions for yin and yang. They were neither to take life, nor to eat living things. The barbarians were unable to place their faith in the Dao, and so the Dao transformed into a perfected Transcendent. This Transcendent intermingled with the people of Heaven.* They floated in the air, disporting themselves among the clouds. When they came to soar along the banks of the Weak Waters, the barbarians bowed down to them, knocking their heads millions of times, [so that the crowns of their heads were like] real mirrors reflecting into Heaven.† Since then, the barbarians have shaved their heads and cut off their sidelocks to seal their determination to keep faith with that Perfected Person. Thus the Way of Perfection flourished there. It was not the case that the Dao acted only for the barbarians and not for the people of the Qin dynasty. The people of the Qin just did not accept the perfect Dao.‡

14a

When the generations of the Five Hegemons became weak, the red Han house received the mandate of Heaven.§ The Dao aided them in restoring order from chaos. It revealed the writings of Master Yellow Stone and bestowed them upon Zhang Liang.‖

But the Dao also transforms its shape. Who is there that is able to perceive its perfection? Though the Han house was thus established, its last generations moved at cross-purposes to the will of the Dao. Its citizens pursued profit, and the strong fought bitterly with the

---

* This seems to be an explanation for the marvelous devas and Apsaras that appear in early Chinese translations of Buddhist scripture. At the same time, we need to remember that India was known in Chinese texts as Tianzhu, "heavenly *zhu*." It is only natural that the place should abound in such spirits.

† "Weak Waters" is the name of a mythical river believed to be in the western regions near the abode of the Queen Mother of the West. This is a fanciful explanation for the tonsures Buddhist monks receive on ordination.

‡ As Ōfuchi has pointed out in *Shoki no dōkyō*, p. 302, the name Qin here refers to the pre–Han dynasty and not, as Yang Liansheng holds, to the northern Qin of the Six Dynasties period.

§ The "Five Hegemons" usually refers to the five dominant states and rulers during the Spring and Autumn period of the Zhou dynasty. Here, though, the term seems to be a general one meaning the contending kingdoms of the late Zhou.

‖ Zhang Liang (d. 189 B.C.E.) was, as early as the Former Han, regarded as the "Master," or teacher, of the Han ruling house. His confirmation of the Han mandate was a military text and seal he had supposedly received from his master, Lord Yellow Stone. In the apocrypha of the Latter Han, Lord Yellow Stone is identified with Laozi. In later Celestial Master texts, Zhang is said to be a direct ancestor of Zhang Daoling.

weak. The Dao mourned the fate of the people, for were it once to depart, its return would be difficult.* Thus did the Dao cause Heaven to bestow its pneuma, called the "newly emerged Lord Lao," to rule the people, saying, "What are demons that the people should only fear them and not place faith in the Dao?" Then Lord Lao made his bestowal on Zhang Daoling, making him Celestial Master. He was most venerable and most spiritual and so was made the master of the people.

You should all know this. He was ennobled above heaven and earth, and yet your hearts are closed. Each day, each month, each year, you increasingly desire to please your mouths and bellies and give free rein to your ears and eyes. You do not keep faith with the Dao. Those who have died are numbered in the tens of thousands. Is this not lamentable?

On the first day of the fifth month in the first year of the Han Peace reign period [11 June 142 C.E.], the Dao created the Way of the Covenantal Authority of Correct Unity at Red-Stone Wall at Quting of Lin'ang County, the Commandery of Shu.² Binding tallies were formed with heaven and earth, and the twenty-four parishes were established to promulgate the primal, original, and inaugural pneumas to rule the people.†

14b

You do not know even the basics of the Dao, nor can you distinguish its true revelations from the false. You only strive with one another for high status in the world and worry about assigning one another a social standing. In so doing, you turn your backs on the Dao and rebel against its powers. You wish to follow human understanding, but the human understanding delights in chaos!

---

* On the notion that the Dao withdraws and "hides itself away" when deviance flourishes, taking shape as Lord Lao on Mount Kunlun to await a new chance to reveal itself in the world, see the *Xiang'er,* lines 109–10 and 538–41. When the Dao withdraws itself, people's lives are shortened, as we have seen.

† The "twenty-four parishes" were the administrative centers of the Celestial Master movement. Located in the Sichuan Basin and southern Shaanxi, they were held to be aligned with the twenty-four pneumas of earth, which marked the seasons in fifteen-day periods. Parishioners and parish officials were associated with one or another of the twenty-four sites, where they were required to gather each year in assembly on the seventh day of the first month, the seventh day of the seventh month, and the fifth day of the tenth month. These assemblies included ritual practice as well as such duties as reporting births and deaths.

It was precisely this that caused Zhang Jue with his Yellow Turbans to foment insurrection. Do you know who Zhang Jue was?*
From his time the dead have been numbered in the tens of millions.
His deviant Dao caused the pneumas [of the correct Dao] to be
divided during the last generations [of the Han].

The parish people remained in Hanzhong for over forty years.†
The prohibitions of the Dao, the origins of the True and Correct, the
explanations of the divine Transcendents—all were promulgated to
you by the Dao. This is the extent to which the Dao thinks of you!³

How regrettable, how injurious it is to consider the *Seven-
Character Verses of the Wondrous Perfected on the Three Numina*
to be not True and not Correct, and on this basis to proclaim that
the Dao deceives its people.‡⁴

Coming to the time when the kingdom of the righteous toppled,
those who fled into exile and those killed were numbered by the tens
of thousands.§ This injured the will of the people. Since the exile,
we have been scattered over the entire kingdom. The Dao has often
saved your lives. Sometimes it has broken through the pneumas to
speak to you; sometimes a minister or magistrate of the earlier days
[in Hanzhong] has tried to reform you, but still you do not keep
faith. This is extremely regrettable.

If you wish morning, you must first have evening. If you desire

15a

---

* The question is clearly ironical in tone. On Zhang Jue, leader of the Yellow
Turbans, see the section "Historical Background" in the introduction to the
Xiang'er.
† Historical sources set the duration of the Hanzhong community at thirty years.
‡ The *Seven-Character Verses of the Wondrous Perfected on the Three Numina*
refers to the *Huangting jing* [Scripture of the Yellow Court], a text on the gods
inhabiting the human body written in seven-character verse. There is evidence that
Yang Xi received a new and improved version of this text, so that the scripture
referred to here might be that now designated *The Outer-Phosphor Scripture of the
Yellow Court*. See Schipper, *The Taoist Body*, pp. 105–8. Robinet (*Taoist Meditation*, pp. 55–60) disputes this opinion on the relative dates of the two texts and
provides a very fine analysis of both the inner and outer scriptures. In the "outer"
scripture as we have it today, the "Three Weird Numina" refers to the three cloudsouls of the human body. The text begins: "Lord Lao, sitting in seclusion, composed
the seven-character verses." In that Lord Lao is also referred to in the *Admonitions*
as the "Perfected" or the "Perfected Transcendent" (see p. 170), it seems most likely
that the "Wondrous Perfected" mentioned here is Lord Lao himself.
§ All of this refers to Zhang Lu's submission to Cao Cao, founder of the Wei
dynasty, in 215 C.E. (See the section "Historical Background" in the introduction to
this text.)

Great Peace, you must first experience chaos. Since the evil of humanity could not be rooted out, you must first pass through war, illness, flood, drought, and even death. Your life spans have been depleted, and so it is appropriate that you must come up against these things.* Though this is so, the favored will be without injury, since such persons have practiced the Dao in the past in order to prepare against such things as have come upon us today. Even if you die without reaching the age of Great Peace, your children and grandchildren will be blessed with Heaven's favor.

Those of these final generations are frivolous and lacking in substance. They are not resolute of heart. Both the prior and the new families [of Daoists], observing the people of this generation and perceiving the coming change, should be able to reform their hearts. If you perform good deeds, practicing humanity and duty, then all will be well with you. You will see Great Peace. You will pass through the catastrophes unscathed and become the seed people of the later age. Although there will be disasters of war, illness, and flood, you will confront them without injury. Thus you are named after the Dao.† If you keep your mind fixed on the Dao, the Dao will keep you in mind. If you do not, the Dao will not be mindful of you.

As to you men and women of the former populace [of Hanzhong] who held various offices, you should devote yourselves to solemnly refining your bodies, purifying yourselves, being mindful of your master, and revering the Dao. Although our lineages are short-lived [in these latter days], your families—husbands and wives, fathers and sons—should protect one another. In this way you may endure, but you will not be able to succeed one another [in office].‡ Your

15b

---

* As explained in the *Xiang'er* commentary, evil actions lead to a reduction in life span.

† That is, "you are called Daoists," or, more literally "people of the Dao."

‡ The author seems to be urging those who held parish positions in Hanzhong to continue their service despite the fact that they can no longer expect to pass their former titles on to members of their own families. This was certainly the case after the diaspora of the Hanzhong community and would further seem to indicate that, at least as of this writing, the parishes had not been reassigned on the basis of birth dates (as they were to be in later Celestial Master communities), but were still tied to their former locales in Hanzhong and Shu.

service has been pure. You have been chaste and filial, have followed the Dao and revered your master; [was all this] in homage to demons or in imitation of the spirits?

Henceforth, all people under Heaven will be harassed and in panic like sheep. War and pestilence presses on all sides; evil pneumas circulate. You should keep in mind the good of the day, revering Heaven and honoring the spirits. If you cherish life and practice the Dao with your thoughts on the True and Correct, the Dao will cherish you. If you do not remain mindful of the Dao, the Dao will distance itself from you. When you are suddenly confronted with disaster or injury, you should be careful not to regret [your service to the Dao], since this will cause suffering later.*

I have circulated day and night, traveling around within the four seas and journeying beyond the eight extremities, all from the desire to cause the ruler to be humane and his ministers loyal, fathers magnanimous and sons filial, husbands faithful and wives chaste, elder brothers respectful and the younger obedient—in short, to bring peace to all below Heaven.† You former people [of Hanzhong] have been muddled and benighted for a long time. Although you have heard the speech of the divine Transcendents and the words of long life, your hearts are confused and your thoughts led into deception, so that once again you do not preserve your faithfulness. Sometimes you perform good deeds, but still do not know the True and Correct. You teach one another in ignorance, transmitting all manner of deviance from one to the other. Not only do you not eradicate evil, you even go so far as to slander one another, so that lords and ministers struggle for influence, fathers and sons are not close to one another, husbands and wives envy one another, and divisions arise between brothers. In the name of public good, you practice self-

16a

---

* The sense might be either "on your descendants" or "on you in the afterlife." It is possible that both are meant, since according to the concept of "inherited burden" the sins of the ancestors, as well as their sufferings in the earth-prisons, were visited on their descendants.

† The "four seas" are those that mark the limits of the world. The "eight extremities" are the horizontal limits of the world in the four cardinal directions and their intermediate points.

ishness. Male and female lightly engage in erotic excess. You transgress both heaven and earth and destroy the five constants.* Outwardly you seem to be true, but inwardly you are not. You thus wreak havoc on the supporting tenets and mainstays of the Dao.

By now the Three Heavens are infuriated, and killing pneumas criss and cross throughout the world.† The five planets have lost their measured movement, and Grand White shines forth.‡ There are perverse winds, thunders in winter, and aphelial and parhelial comets that dip and rise.§ In these ways, Heaven suspends images in the sky to inform people that if they do not keep faith with the Dao, the Dao will become enraged. Those who die will find their pneumas resting in the dark valley.‖

The *Seven-Character Verses on the Three Numina and the Yellow Court,* which the Wondrous Perfected composed through me, is a gloss on and explanation of the basic scriptures.# It is the shining efflorescence of the Dao. As for the Dao, you should not point to any shape and call it the Dao, but the wise, having seen one part, will know it in all its multiplicity.** They are just like one who

---

* The "five constants" are the Confucian virtues of humanity, duty, ritual propriety, knowledge, and trust.

† On the concept of the three heavens, see the introduction to the *Inner Explanations of the Three Heavens.*

‡ "Grand White" is the planet Venus. White is associated with metal, thus weapons, and with autumn, the season of death and executions. Not surprisingly, any deviation in the path or appearance of Grand White was thought to be a harbinger of war.

§ These two sorts of ominous stars, our comets, are literally called "bursting" and "sweeper" stars, respectively. For the identification given here and for many examples of the sorts of earthly catastrophe they were thought to portend, see Schafer, *Pacing the Void,* pp. 105–16. The same sorts of celestial omens are listed in the *Xiang'er,* lines 546–48.

‖ The "dark valley" mentioned here is most likely an underworld like the earthprisons.

This seems to be a a variant title for the text mentioned on p. 14b of this text. The name of the scripture, the *Yellow Court,* is presented in the opening passages of the text as a palace in the spleen. When a spirit embryo is nurtured within this palace, long life results.

** The injunction that one "not point to any shape and call it the Dao" is number six of the *Xiang'er* precepts. See also *Xiang'er,* lines 111–12, 176–80, and 211–15.

understands another through his music.* The Dao is to be found
in your whole body.† Why seek to find it in others?

But you, in your study of the Good, have missed the basis. You
16b   do not accept the words of the scriptures, but rather instruct one
another in deviant views, drawing near to the false and discarding
the true.

A long time ago, I recorded all of this in a short paper containing
miscellaneous remarks on deviant texts, ordering that all such texts
be eradicated.‡ But the Libationers were ineffectual and their under-
lings hid the [deviant] texts away so that today they not only survive
but are frequently put into practice. At present those with little
learning delight in frivolous talk. They point to the false, calling it
true.§ This is all a transgression of celestial prohibitions. Such people
will come to harm and will never attain to good fortune. [Such
teachings as are found in these texts] are only a waste of your energies. Laboring assiduously on something that is without substance is
not even so good as giving free rein to your will and just being
happy.‖ You should not open yourself to celestial punishment or
take lightly the law of the [spiritual] officials.

You should convert people by means of Great Peace. People must

---

* The reference is to a famous pair of friends, Bo Ya and Zhong Ziqi. No matter
what Bo Ya was thinking of when he played his lute, Zhong Ziqi would always
know by the tone. The implication is that the wise and sagely are "attuned" to the
Dao. For Han-period representations of the pair and their Daoist connections, see
Suzanne E. Cahill, "Po Ya Plays the Zither: Taoism and the Literati Ideal in Two
Types of Bronze Mirrors in the Collection of Donald H. Graham," *TR* 5.1 (1994),
pp. 25–40.
† This wording recalls that of the *Xiang'er*, lines 105–8, on the movement of the
pneumas of the Dao within the human body, where it is stated that "the Dao is
everywhere within your skin."
‡ This may refer to the *Xiang'er* commentary, which certainly could be so characterized. The fact that this writing is here described as "short" and the remarks
"miscellaneous" are standard displays of humility when one is discussing one's own
writings and should not be taken as seriously characterizing the work.
§ This passage parallels the *Xiang'er*, lines 221–22: "Those mortals who continually practice the false arts do not know the significance of the constant. They
blindly point to their writings, and thus all is disaster for them."
‖ In the context of Chinese society as a whole, the individualism implied in this
latter phrase was always seen as leading to disaster. Here the pejorative force of the
phrase "to give free rein to one's will" (*renxin ziyi*) is heightened by the following
statement that all such willful activity, although joyous in this world, will be severely
punished in the next.

aid Heaven in bringing about Great Peace through their actions. Heaven's understanding proceeds from the understanding of our people. When within them the five are correct, then the three and the five[5] will be settled, since they also respond to humanity.*

All you people and families [of the faithful], both those who were formerly members and those newly joined—male and female, old and young—if from today, the seventh day of the first month, second year of the Corrected Prime reign period [1 February 255 C.E.], you are able to devote yourselves solemnly to embracing good deeds; if you are able to act in accordance with the essential teachings—so that ministers are loyal, children filial, husbands trustworthy, wives chaste, elder brothers respectful, younger brothers obedient—and you are not inwardly of two hearts, then all may go   17a
well for you and you may achieve the status of seed people. It is difficult to enter the ranks of the seed people, and it cannot be done without help. If, whether old or young, you cherish life and delight in the Dao, you should make upright your heart and rectify your thoughts, aiding the kingdom and supporting its destiny, for the spirit luminaries know all of your good and evil deeds. You must not continue to harbor wild fantasies. If you should happen to speak with the false and deviant, say to them, "I know the Dao," and instruct them by means of the Dao.†

Of all male and female officers of the various ranks granted previously, not very many are still with us. Ever since the fifth year of the Grand Harmony reign period [231 C.E.], each of the holders of parish positions has been self-appointed.[6] Their selection and pro-

---

* The "five" are the five viscera and the spirits that inhabit them. The "three and the five" I take to mean primarily the three pneumas and the five phases. The cosmologies associated with these two numbers are complex, though the various elements are interrelated. For "three" we might also read the three offices and the triad heaven-earth-humanity. The "five" include, spatially, the four directions and the center or the five naked-eye planets and their areas of control, and temporally, the four seasons and their governing nodes. Whatever the specific referent—and the author is likely to have had all the above in mind—the context makes it clear that the powers of Heaven will not be settled until humanity has turned to correctness, a concept emphasized as well in the Xiang'er.

† This injunction echoes lines 414–16 of the Xiang'er commentary, which state: "Ever performing good deeds, the Sage, seeing evil persons, does not forsake them but approaches to instruct them by means of the precepts of the Dao. If those persons will not be converted, there is nothing more that the Sage can do."

motion no longer emanates from my pneumas or from the True
Pneuma Controllers of Spirits.* Instead you sometimes obey voices
that break through the pneumas, placing your faith in shadows and
dreams apprehended by your wives; sometimes you present petitions, but at other times, not knowing what else to do, you do not
follow the old rites at all, but accept faith offerings and make all
sorts of "special explanations."† Sometimes one parish has redundant officers, while in other parishes offices remain empty.

Those who receive office are to carefully watch for signs among
the pneumas of heaven and earth and to put in order the documents
to be submitted to the Three Offices.‡ [But those self-appointed
officials?] who serve only themselves and eat lavishly ... [lacuna⁷]
... as well as all the "idle" officials, those who occupy their posi-
17b   tion without proper documentation, may at any time have their
name brought up for criminal investigation before the Officers of
Heaven.§ They will then ever sit in the judgment of the spirit luminaries, all for the sake of wanting to lord it over the vulgar folks of
this world.

* The wording of this phrase is somewhat unclear. The "Controller of Spirits"
was a parish official in charge of "selecting the worthy and demoting transgressors,
so as to redirect and merge the pneumas, controlling all that deviate" (Chen Guofu,
Daozang yuanliu kao, p. 349). Following the suggestion of Terry Kleeman, I take
the term "True Pneuma Controller of Spirits" to be an expanded form of this title.
Kleeman (Great Perfection) also corrects wu ("my") to wu ("five") and suggests that
the "Five Pneumas" and the "True Pneumas," like the "Controller of Spirits," are
official titles.
† Each step in the advancement of an adept into the ranks of the parish hierarchy
was to be accompanied by the formal bestowal of spirit registers, lists of protective
deities that were to be visualized and retained within the body or sent forth in ritual
to communicate with heaven. Though numerous, these deities were not separate and
individual entities but hypostases of the Dao. Nonetheless, Daoist texts often speak
of them as individual spirits, actors in the celestial hierarchy. The bestowal of spirit
registers thus depended both on an individual's merit and on the acceptance of the
deities with whom the covenant was to be made. In the Celestial Master organization, the issuance of registers, containing the various "pneumas" of the Dao, was
controlled by the Celestial Master. All of the abuses listed here are transgressions of
this order. The claim that it is "wives" who improperly act as mediums accords with
the shamanic traditions of Chinese popular religion. The "petitions" mentioned here
include the types discussed by Nickerson in his introduction to the Great Petition
elsewhere in this volume.
‡ The Three Offices are the administrations of heaven, earth, and water, to whom
memorials and petitions were to be addressed.
§ The Officers of Heaven, the first of the three offices, are charged with the keeping of celestial records of merit and demerit. (See p. 54.)

[Such officials] denigrate the Dao of the loyal minister and filial child. Having never experienced it, they all say that when disaster occurs, they will blame themselves. But if they should happen to actually meet with disaster, it is as if they reverse the grievance, wildly claiming that there is no benefit in revering the Dao.* All of these transgressions are of the three thousand class.† Those who follow such people will receive the same punishment they receive.

For a long time I have labored with concern to save your lives, desiring only that you see Great Peace. Do you still seek Great Peace?

Formerly, during the latter generations of the Han house, strong men began to carve up the empire. The mighty encroached upon the weak, and the people became deceitful and shrewd. Male and female lightly engaged in erotic excess. The government could not relieve the situation and families did not impose prohibitions. Cities were plundered and the common people were victims of injustice, even to the extent of being made slaves. The people were being devoured just as mulberry leaves are consumed by silkworms, and because of their grievances they began to consider revolt.‡

The pneumas [emanating from] their resistance blocked the heavens. This caused the five planets to depart from their measured movements, aphelial and parhelial comets to sweep the skies, and the fire star to depart from its position as adjunct.§ Then powerful ministers began to fight among themselves and hosts of treacherous people led one another [in rebellion].

---

* The concept that an official was responsible for everything that happened under his or her jurisdiction was a Confucian concern, predicated on the notion that the relation of ruler to ruled was that of father to son.

† This refers to the belief that counts of life were subtracted by the officials of heaven for all transgressions. The *Xiang'er* commentary (lines 271–72) also remarks that those who slander the Dao or say that it does not exist are subject to the deduction of the "full three thousand" counts.

‡ Anyone who has observed the voracious appetites of silkworms just before they spin their cocoons will recognize the horrific nature of this simile. Certainly, for those who practiced sericulture and had to gather and transport pounds of mulberry leaves, staying up day and night to do so, this image of gradual and inexorable destruction would have been clear.

§ The "fire star" is Mars, which was associated in China, as in the West, with war and rebellion. On the sorts of comets mentioned here, see footnote § on p. 175 above.

After more than a hundred years, the Wei house received the
18a   mandate of Heaven and eradicated all of these evils. Calendrical
signs showed that this was so. Their ascension was recorded in the
River [Chart] and the *Luo [River Writings]* and in other portents
suspended in the heavens.* Conforming to the celestial dispensation
and the propitious times, I received the mandate to be Master of the
Kingdom. The Martial Thearch [Cao Cao] launched the empire.

At that time, the bodies of the dead filled the ditches, but with the
glorious establishment of our kingdom, our children no longer suf-
fered injury. Instead, they were weighted with gold [insignia] and
wrapped in purple [sashes].† Far from perishing, they achieved
longevity. Of [my] seven sons, five were made lords and became
the luster of the kingdom.‡ The sons of others were made ministers,
generals, or given other official ranks, and not a few were also enfeoffed as lords. Silver and bronze [insignia] were numbered in the
thousands. When the father died, his sons inherited the position.
When a younger brother perished, his elder brother was ennobled.[8]
We bathed in the beneficence of the Sage-Ruler.

Who among you now is noted for virtue? Do you know the history of our Truth? In the past I opened my gates and taught those
who entered the practice of goodness, but now you do not listen.
From today, I will hide from the world. I entrust you to the pure
administration and the Daoist government of the Wei, [under whose
rule] one can travel alone for one thousand miles because tigers
and wolves are tamed, and one can sleep without fastening one's
door.

Yet evil ministers and their minions still do not know what it is

---

* The *River Chart,* the *Luo River Writings,* and the portents suspended in the
heavens (stellar signs) are also mentioned as foretelling sagely rule in the *Xiang'er*
(lines 266–67 and 446–49).
† Ōfuchi (*Shoki no dōkyō,* pp. 265–66) has collected evidence that the various
insignia of office mentioned in this passage were in fact employed under the Wei
kingdom.
‡ The *Chronicle of the Three Kingdoms* mentions only six of Lu's sons (*Sanguo
zhi,* 8:263–65), one of whom was murdered by Liu Zhang, while the five remaining
were enfeoffed upon Zhang Lu's surrender to Cao Cao. One late Daoist source provides various traditions concerning the names of Lu's sons (*HY* 296, 19:3b), but the
fact remains that little is known of them or their eventual fates. The whole question
has been analyzed by Fukui Kōjun (*Dōkyō no kisoteki kenkyū* [Tokyo: Rishosha,
1957], pp. 17 ff.).

to follow and what it is to transgress the mandate of Heaven. They compel others with trickery and lies. That which they fabricate is entirely inauspicious, and [the blame for their lies] will reach to their children and grandchildren. Will you know the source [of their descendants' suffering]?

In recent years, there have been plagues in the four quarters that have swept away all of the inauspicious. This was merely the slaughter of evil persons. Those who clung to the Dao and delighted in goodness were personally protected by Heaven as babes would be guarded from harm. Confronted by danger, they pass through it as easily as the tongue avoids the teeth. Do you all know now what I mean?

18b

From this time on, it is impermissible for you to recklessly establish anyone in any official parish position. If you disobey me again, you will incur injury. Do not blame me [when this happens].

When Libationers cure the ill, they should do so at the onset of the illness. But, once the illness is cured, if it returns again, that person is evil. Do not again treat or cure them.

All of our households should transform one another through loyalty and filiality, so that fathers are magnanimous and sons filial, husbands faithful and wives chaste, elder brothers respectful and the younger obedient. Mornings and evenings you should practice "clarity and stillness."* Root out all covetousness, abandon the pursuit of personal profit, and rid yourself of desire. Reform your evil cravings. Pity the poor and cherish the old. Be liberal in supplying others and in giving way to them. Drive from your heart excesses of jealousy, joy, and anger so that your emotions are constantly harmonious and your eyes and belly in accord. Aid the kingdom in strengthening its mandate. Abandon all of your past evil pursuits. Those who, from today on, practice good actions will find that disaster and disease melt away from them, and will become seed people of the later age.

The people should not complain of their poverty and suffering

---

* On the practice of "clarity and stillness," the meditation for eating pneumas and stilling the heart mentioned several times in the *Xiang'er* commentary, see the section "Meditation and Perfection of the Body" in my introduction to that text.

19a   or covet riches, happiness, and high position.* You have seen with
       your own eyes and heard with your own ears: From ancient times,
       have the rich and honored ever endured? Their possessions are
       abandoned on the ground and their bodies perish in the market-
       place. Looked at in this way, the old proverb is correct: "A dead
       prince is not worth a live rat." What you achieve will be life, and
       the Dao is where you should seek it.

          You should remember that the Dao conceals itself and is name-
       less. Name is an axe that hacks at the body.† "Good actions leave no
       trace." If they wish to make it so that others do not see their
       "traces," those who practice the Dao should regulate their bodies
       and nurture their lives to seek blessing.‡ Instead of which you teach
       others to give free rein to the self. If the self is given free rein, people
       will see its traces and the axe will be keen.§ If the axe that hews
       down the body is keen, good fortune departs and bad arrives.‖
       Should you not be cautious? Should you not be fearful? "The reason
       heaven and earth endure" is because they lack willfulness. And that
       which "does not act falsely, leaves nothing left undone."# Only
       when one does not allow others to see one's traces can one truly
       accomplish wonders.

          You vulgar people are truly comical: When you do some small
       good deed, you always want others to know of it, and when you

       * This is number nineteen of the *Xiang'er* precepts.
       † The phrase "X is the axe that hacks away at the body" occurs in the *Xiang'er* at
       line 350, where it is applied to evil in general.
       ‡ This follows the *Xiang'er* explanation of the *Laozi* passage given earlier that
       "traces" are left only by evil actions. Good deeds that leave no traces and go unre-
       marked upon in this world are rewarded in the next.
       § The truth of this depends on a pun: *zong*, "footsteps, traces," is a homophone
       with *zong*, "to give free rein to"; thus to indulge the self through evil deeds "makes
       tracks" of the self's passing.
       ‖ This is another pun. *Li* means both "profit" and "sharp, keen."
       # The citation in the preceding line is a rewording of *Laozi* 7: "The reason heaven
       and earth are able to long endure is because they give birth to themselves." Neither
       the *Laozi* nor the *Xiang'er* commentary mentions "*wu wei*" at this point. The com-
       mentary merely states that heaven and earth endure because they "model themselves
       on the Dao" (lines 65–66). The Dao itself "never acts falsely [or willfully (*wu wei*)],"
       in that, as the commentary tells us, "it does not perform evil deeds" (line 573). Since
       only evil deeds leave traces, people are naturally unable to see its traces. In short, this
       entire passage, a pastiche of extracts from the *Laozi*, depends for its logic on the
       Xiang'er commentary.

differ by so much as a grain of rice from others, you expect to be   19b
considered worthy.* These are the sorts of benefit derived from
what is not the Dao. In all cases, such behavior is a violation of the
proscriptions of the Dao.

Now I transmit my teachings so that you people [of the Dao],
both those who joined previously and new members, shall know my
heart. Do not forsake it.

NOTES TO ADMONITIONS: TRANSLATION

1. *Zhouyi zhengyi,* 9:96a, translated in Richard Wilhelm, *The I Ching or Book of Changes,* trans. Cary F. Baynes (Princeton, N.J.: Princeton University Press, 1950), p. 540.

2. According to Gong Xuchun (*Sichuan junxian zhi* [Chengdu: Guji shudian, 1983], p. 50), Lin'ang 臨邛 County was a Han-period place name corresponding to present-day Dayi and Pujiang Counties. It appears, then, that "Red-Stone Wall" 赤石城 is another name for Mount Crane-Call.

3. Ōfuchi (*Shoki no dōkyō,* pp. 268–69), following Chen Shixiang ("*Xiang'er* Laozi," p. 56), takes the break following *xiang er* 想爾 (line 14b7) to indicate four missing graphs. This is unlikely, evidenced by the fact that there is a genuine lacuna in the *Admonitions,* marked—as is common with texts copied in the Ming edition of the *Daozang*—with a large circle (17a10). What has been taken for a gap, then, proves to be merely a paragraph break inserted by a copyist at some point during the transmission of the manuscript. A similar paragraph break appears, for instance, at the end of line 17a4. Thus I have translated this line in accord with the hypothesis, presented more fully in "The Authorship and Date of the *Xiang'er* Commentary," that the meaning of *xiang er* was "thinking of you." Although the *Admonitions* generally uses the colloquial expression *ruzao bei* 汝曹輩 for the second-person plural pronoun and occasionally *zi* 子 for the second-person singular, it does employ *er* 爾 for "you" [as a second-person singular object?] at 15b1 and at 17b4.

As for the sentence following, it seems to me a plausible topic-comment sentence with the understood subject omitted. See the sentence at 15a1–2 for an exact parallel, with the subject *huo* 或 supplied to distinguish the two parts of the topic.

---

* These two criticisms paraphrase *Xiang'er* precepts numbers eleven and twenty-six, respectively. Though these are common themes of the *Xiang'er,* the following passage is closest in expression to that found here: "Today, though ministers and children might be loyal or filial, they all do it in order to barter their acts with the lords and fathers for merit and fame. If, having performed some deed, that deed is not particularly remarked, they become privately angry about it and say, 'No one even noticed!'" (lines 262–64).

4. An alternative reading, proposed by Ōfuchi (*Shoki no dōkyō*, pp. 268–69), Yang Liansheng, and others, takes the last four characters of line 14b7 to the penultimate graph of line 14b8 as one sentence, reading, "Why do you take the *Xiang'er,* the XXXX, the *Miao zhen [jing],* and the *Seven-Character [text] on the Three Numina* to be untrue and, on this basis, say that the Dao deceives people?" The lack of evidence for a lacuna here is discussed in the preceding endnote. The term *miao zhen* appears again in line 16a7, where Ōfuchi reads, "The *Miao zhen [jing],* which I composed, and the *Seven-Character [text] on the Three Numina of the Yellow Court* both...." There is, in fact, a scripture, now lost, named the *Miao zhen jing* 妙真經. Surviving fragments, the most numerous of which are found in the *Wushang biyao* (HY 1130; see John Lagerwey, *Wu-shang pi-yao: Somme taoïste du VIe siècle* [Paris, 1981], p. 266) and copied by later collectanea, indicate that it was a book revealed by Laozi and largely devoted to explicating concepts found in the *Daode jing.* (The Buddhist citation of a *Miao zhen jie* 偈 [*gātha*], discussed by Kobayashi Masayoshi [*Rikuchō Dōkyōshi kenkyū,* pp. 347 ff.], is, as the sources claim, a lost fragment of the Lingbao scriptures. None of the *Miao zhen jing* fragments shows more than the slightest of Buddhist influences.) One citation of the scripture (HY 1130, 42:7a–8a), in fact, discusses the importance of Daoist morality for governance, using words that sometimes match those of the *Admonitions.* On the other hand, the *Miao zhen jing* fragments differ from the *Xiang'er* commentary in numerous ways, whereas the *Admonitions* is much closer to the *Xiang'er* in outlook. This leads me to the preliminary conclusion—since I have not thoroughly studied the fragments—that the *Miao zhen* scripture's infrequent terminological overlap with the *Admonitions* is fortuitous. There are other reasons, more related to this text, why the term *miao zhen* should not here be taken as a scripture title. First, given the way texts were produced in Daoist circles, it seems strange, to say the least, that an author would obligingly claim authorship of a "wondrous" text, particularly one pronounced by Laozi. When such a claim is made, the verb used is *shou* 受, "received" (through revelation), and not *zuo* 作, "made, composed." Compare also line 16a.1, where the author clearly claims authorship of another text in these words: "A long time ago, I recorded all of this in a short paper of miscellaneous remarks on deviant texts." Here the adjectives *duan* 短, "short," and *za* 雜, "miscellaneous," function as terms of polite self-effacement. "That I *myself* composed" is just not something Chinese authors normally stated so baldly. Second, given the fact that Lord Lao is described as a *zhenren* 真人 or *zhen xian* 真仙 at lines 13b6–10, on the occasion of his appearance before the barbarians of the western regions, it seems more likely that *miao zhen* (the Wondrous Perfected) is, for this text, an appellation of Lord Lao. To be sure, the received version of the outer *Scripture of the Yellow Court* begins: "Lord Lao, in ritual reclusion, composed these seven-character verses" (HY 1026, 12:28b). Thus I have translated this occurrence as the "*Seven-Character Verses of the Wondrous Perfected*" and

the occurrence below as the "*Yellow Court,* which the Wondrous Perfected composed through me [*zi wu* 自吾]."

5. The text has "two fives" [*er wu* 二五], probably a scribal error for *san wu* 三五, "three and five."

6. On the authority of the three Celestial Masters being invoked in the ritual practices of the sect, see Cedzich, "Das Ritual der Himmelsmeister." It is not clear why the year 231 was believed to mark a significant date in the decline of the church organization. Tang Changru proposes that the implementation of earlier prohibitions against the private practice of mediumism may have taken effect about this time. This may be part of the answer, yet we possess no record that would indicate why this particular year was important. For the speculation that this was the date of Zhang Lu's death, see the section "Historical Background" in the introduction to this text.

7. It appears that this lacuna is only one graph in length.

8. Yang Liansheng, following Hu Shi, suggests that this refers specifically to the death of Zhang Lu's youngest son and the ennoblement of his elder son Zhang Fu 張富 as his successor (personal communication reported in Rao, *Laozi xiang'er zhu jiaojian* [1991], pp. 163–65). Although the phrase is strange, the context seems a general one, separated by several sentences from the specific references to Zhang Lu's family. I would suggest, then, that the nouns were inverted by a copyist and that it should read, as we would expect, "When elder brothers perish, their younger brothers are ennobled [to succeed them in office]."

Scripture of the Inner Explanations of the Three Heavens

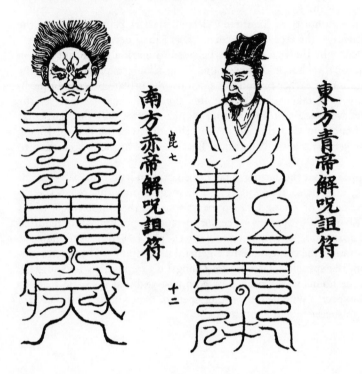

INTRODUCTION

The following translation represents the first chapter of the *Santian neijie jing* (*Scripture of the Inner Explanations of the Three Heavens*, HY 1196; hereafter *Inner Explanations*), a history of Daoism composed under the Liu-Song dynasty (420–79) of southern China.[1] The *Inner Explanations* was written both to support the mandate of the reigning emperor and as propaganda for the Celestial Masters, whose preeminence had recently been challenged by two new scriptural lineages. These two new Daoist traditions, both centered near the Liu-Song capital, presented themselves as superseding the old doctrines of the Celestial Masters with new information that

186

originated in heavens higher than those known by the Celestial Masters and that came from ages earlier in the history of the cosmos, when the Dao was more pure. The fact that the *Inner Explanations* has often been excerpted in modern Daoist studies as an early example of Celestial Master beliefs has tended to obscure what might seem the obvious conclusions to be drawn from the above facts: that the text represents a *redefinition* of Celestial Master Daoism, penned both to win the support of the emperor for the religion and to dispute the claims made against it by rival Daoist traditions and by Buddhism, in an effort to restore the Celestial Master tradition to its rightful place within Daoism.

It is not easy to disentangle the various strands that went into the fashioning of this message. Traditional accounts of the origins of the Daoist religion are here inextricably woven with imaginative embellishments of history meant to flatter the emperors of the Song dynasty (420–477), who claimed to be descended from the ruling Liu house of the Han. This feature makes the *Inner Explanations* less valuable as a veritable record of early Celestial Master Daoism or of early Daoist history, but quite interesting as a partisan account of the school in the mid–fifth century, when the survival of Celestial Master teachings was ensured by just such efforts as this to accommodate them to the evolving religious scene.

Translation of the entire text clarifies several points of great significance to the history of Daoism. Here I will mention only a few of these points.

Historical Background

The Liu-Song dynasty was founded by the general Liu Yu (356–422) in 420, when he forced the last Jin emperor to abdicate and took the throne himself in an elaborate succession ceremony conducted on the southern outskirts of the capital, Jiankang (modern Nanjing). A general who had distinguished himself through his role in overthrowing the Daoist rebellion of Sun En (for which see the discussion later in this introduction), Liu Yu was regarded as fit to rule because, of all the generals who had attempted to regain the northern lands lost by the Jin to the Xiongnu during the years 311–17, he had been the most successful. In 417, he had retaken

Chang'an and returned south to seize power. Further, he proclaimed himself a direct descendant, in the thirty-second generation, of the founder of the Han, Liu Bang (r. 206–195 B.C.E.). It was thus hoped that this successor to the Han ruling house could once again reunify the Central Kingdom.

The *Inner Explanations* provides an early proof of both Liu Yu's claim of descent from the Han house and of his aspirations.[2] Echoing assertions, already expressed—though rather less forcefully—in the *Admonitions,* that the Dao was directly responsible for the rise of the Han, and embellishing these with stories of a contract entered into by the Han dynastic house with Zhang Daoling, the text proceeds to detail portentous signs signifying heaven's approval of the Liu clan as proof that the Han has risen again to reunify China. But even more important for the author is the fact that this political reunification is to be based on a religious unity, accomplished by the abandonment of various "deviant ways" and a return to the "correct unity" of Celestial Master Daoism. As we will see, Buddhism is chief among these deviant ways.

The Three Heavens

None of the Celestial Master texts we have read so far has dealt systematically with the subject of cosmogony—the birth and makeup of the universe. We cannot conclude from this that the early Celestial Masters lacked their own distinctive cosmogonic myths. It is just that the overriding concern of both the *Xiang'er* commentary and the *Admonitions* was the present state of humanity and its relation to the Dao rather than the origins and structure of the universe. Where these texts use the word *heaven,* it has thus most often proved sufficient to translate the word in the singular.[3] The *Inner Explanations,* though not the earliest text to give an account of the cosmological notions of the Celestial Masters, certainly contains the fullest explanation. Just how much of this was new to the religion has been a matter of intense debate among scholars, a debate that often centers on the dating of texts not presented in this volume. The account I present here takes a conservative view, in that I suggest ways in which the cosmology of the Celestial Masters may have been profoundly changed by the new Daoist revelations that immediately preceded the composition of this text, and confine evidence of historical continuity to the texts presented earlier.

In the *Admonitions,* we saw that the Dao bestows on living beings three sorts of pneuma—"the mystic, the primal, and the inaugural"—which are further described there as follows:

> The mystic is azure and formed heaven. The inaugural is yellow and formed earth. The primal is white and formed the Dao. Within the three pneumas, the Dao controls all above and below and is the father and mother of the myriad things.[4]

That these are sequential rather than spatially arrayed arrangements of pneuma is already implicit in the fact that the triad presented in these phrases parallels in various details the lines of *Laozi* 42 that were taken as a formulaic statement of the arising of the "myriad things" of this world from the undifferentiated Dao. The phrases in question read as follows:

> The Dao gave birth to one. The one gave birth to two. The two gave birth to three. The three gave birth to the myriad things.

The "one" was usually taken as the Dao in its still undifferentiated, fecund fullness; the "two" as yin and yang; and the "three" as yin, yang, and a harmonious mixture of the two.[5] Unfortunately, the Dunhuang manuscript containing the *Xiang'er* commentary does not include *Laozi* 42, where it would likely have dealt with this question. But, adding in the *Admonitions* account and the traditional Chinese understanding that the heavens are yang to the earth's yin, we can easily see that the early Celestial Masters held to a fairly standard Han-period view of the arising of the myriad things of the universe from the Dao.

It might seem that the "three heavens," also first mentioned in the *Admonitions,* could be simply equated with these three pneumas. That the Celestial Master view might have been somewhat more complicated is fully revealed for the first time in the *Inner Explanations.* Unfortunately, the precise outlines of the early Celestial Master view are obscured by Shangqing and Lingbao innovations that clearly influenced the way this text presents its information. In order to understand this influence, we need then first to examine in a general way the cosmologies expressed in these two groups of scriptures. More detail on these matters will be found in the introductions to the *Purple Texts* and the *Scripture of Salvation.*

As Isabelle Robinet has noted, the Shangqing scriptures of Yang Xi do not mention the three pneumas of the Celestial Masters.[6] They do contain, however, a bewildering variety of celestial locales, among which the "three clear regions" are mentioned with particular frequency.[7] The lowest, the heaven of Grand Clarity, was the origin of the practices of alchemists, the Celestial Masters, and other Daoists.[8] The deities who appeared to Yang Xi all descended from the higher heavens of Upper Clarity. Above that were the gods of Jade Clarity, so impossibly exalted that they could not communicate with humans. These heavens were regarded as contemporaneous, but the gods of Jade Clarity all emanated from the "prior heavens," which existed before the creation of this heaven and earth.

In Daoist polemics, both against other religions and within Daoism itself, doctrinal struggle often played itself out as a battle of cosmologies. The Lingbao scriptures, which borrowed heavily from the Shangqing texts, asserted their priority over these latter by insisting that they themselves were originally composed of spirit characters that appeared at the first division of the Dao, not just in the prior world age, but many, many world ages ago. Above the heaven of Jade Clarity, then, they placed another, the Grand Veil heaven. Further, the Lingbao scriptures do speak of the mystic, primal, and inaugural pneumas, associating them with the first three world ages and with their central deity.[9] The subsequent divisions of these pneumas are responsible, we are told, for the formation of the three clear regions.

Thus, through the modifications and elaborations of the Shangqing and Lingbao texts, issues of textual worth quickly centered about questions of what we might call "cosmological priority."[10] The *Inner Explanations* represents an attempt to enter this ideological struggle with a new formulation. After a brief introduction, the *Inner Explanations* begins with the primordial Dao, describing it in words drawn from the *Huainan zi* as "dark and attenuated, vaporous and opaque," without any prior cause. From it is born the Elder of the Way and Its Power—clearly a hypostasis of the cosmic Laozi, in that the name echoes the title of his text. In this being (if we may call him such), the text asserts, the illimitable "Way of Grand

Clarity" finds its basis, before even the appearance of primal pneuma in the dark void. Here, then, Grand Clarity is once more elevated to a position of priority, against the assertions of the Shangqing and Lingbao texts. In fact, all of the deities addressed in the memorials of the Celestial Masters find their source in the primal Dao.

Significantly, the three pneumas are mentioned here as well, though in a variant form. The full phrase is "the Illimitable Great Way of Grand Clarity—the Mystic and Primal [pneumas] and the Highest Three Heavens." From this phrase, found in early Celestial Master memorials in the same form, it appears that the three heavens are not to be equated with the three pneumas, but associated with the third, the inaugural pneuma.[11] That is to say, the inaugural pneuma, the name of which (*shi*) suggests parturition, may have been thought to be the germinal form of the three pneumas that are active in the world—designated simply yang, yin, and "centrally harmonious" in the *Xiang'er* commentary.[12]

Whatever may have been the original Celestial Master view of these things, in the *Inner Explanations* we are, at this point in the exposition, still within the "Utter Blackness" of the undifferentiated Dao. All of the "birthing" we have witnessed so far is within that unity, though the potentialities for what is to follow have already taken shape. From the blackness comes the "Vacuous Grotto," which produces "Grand Nullity"—all without bursting the oneness of the Dao.[13] Finally, from Grand Nullity, the three pneumas— mystic, primal, and inaugural—issue forth, still mixed, to produce the Dark and Wondrous Jade Maiden, who will transform into Lord Lao. Lord Lao divides the three pneumas—mystic, inaugural, and primal—to form heaven, earth, and, in a unique addition to the triad to which we shall return momentarily, water. This is, at last, the moment of creation. Later, these three pneumas are seen to be productive of three religions in the human world—the Great Way of Inaction, Buddhism, and the Way of the Pure Contract, respectively.

Though all of this seems at first sight chaotic and unnecessary as an account of the origin of the universe, it serves to underscore two very important points. First, Grand Clarity of the Celestial Masters existed in utero—from the very first stirrings of the Dao before creation. Second, the concept of the three pneumas is shown to be cen-

TABLE 4.   COSMOGONIC DEVELOPMENT
OF THE THREE HEAVENS

UNITY. . . . .

1. Utter Blackness >	2. Vacuous Grotto >	3. Grand Nullity >
Dao >	Elder of the Way >	Way of
	and Its Power	Grand Clarity
		(a) Mystic
		(b) Primal
		(c) Highest Three
		Heavens

UNITY (continued) . . . .

4. three pneumas (merged) >	5. mother >	6. Lord Lao >
Mystic	Dark and	
Primal >	Wondrous Jade >	Laozi >
Inaugural	Maiden	

DIVISION . . . .

7. three pneumas (distributed)	> 8. the three ways
Mystic > heaven	> Great Way of Inaction
Primal > water	> Way of the Pure Contract
Inaugural > earth	> Buddhism

Note: Numbers 1–8 are the names of each of the stages in the movement of the Dao from unity to division. Under each of these names are listed the pneumas and deities that first made their appearance during that stage.

tral to the process. The Dao becomes potentially three and, in unity, passes through three stages, after which the three pneumas, still undivided, create the mother of Laozi, who is, we are told, actually Lord Lao in the process of creating himself. This movement from one to three-in-one to three ones back to three-in-one and to the One who will disperse the three is perhaps best visualized as in table 4.[14]

This process of evolution recalls the loops and spirals described by Robinet that lie at the heart of Shangqing practice.[15] But, although both the Shangqing and the Lingbao scriptures describe their texts as emanating from the Dao as glimmerings when it first divides, the *Inner Explanations* description finds warrant for its message one step further back in time. The full Celestial Master pantheon is present before the Dao even thinks of division.

Involved in these seemingly innocent cosmological speculations was the truly vital matter of assessing the cycles of time whereby new heavenly dispensations of rule—dynasties—seemed to rise and fall in regular succession. During the era of division and chaos that followed the fall of the Han, when all were looking for the appearance of a heavenly mandated dynasty, Daoist texts, with their concern for world ages and the achievement of an era of Great Peace, played a decisive role in this intellectual (and ultimately political) pursuit.[16] We have already seen in the *Admonitions* how the Dao would, as the current age ended in violent paroxysms, rescue its "seed people" for life in the era of Great Peace.[17] The failure of Great Peace to appear in the third century did not end people's dreams. Millennial expectations, based on the belief that a new cycle was surely about to begin, figure in literally all of the scriptural traditions of this period. In the Shangqing scriptures, practices emanating from the heaven of Jade Clarity, residence of the gods who had weathered such universal cataclysm, were to be the salvation of its seed people.[18] Similar claims are made in the Lingbao scriptures.[19]

This concern finds expression in the *Inner Explanations* in a slightly different form. This scripture offers the reappearance of the Liu dynasty, heritors of the Han, as proof that the new age is now to begin. What remains is the process of reunification under the "correct unity" of the Dao. The "stale" and "deviant" pneumas of the old age are described as being washed away by the Dao, but the participation of the heavenly appointed ruling house is required to complete the process.

The phrase used to describe these deviant ways, which we shall examine more fully later, is "the stale pneumas of the Six Heavens." In the Shangqing scriptures, the Six Heavens are described as the "six celestial palaces of Fengdu," located in the far north, where the souls of the unsanctified dead, those who have not transcended but who have performed deeds of virtue in the world, are confined.[20] In the *Inner Explanations,* the six heavens are shown to be something more than an isolated demonic realm. As the term "stale pneumas" implies, the six heavens are presented as a legitimate period of rule, instituted by the Dao, that has now reached the end of its cycle and must be replaced.[21] In fact, the "three ways" originally instituted by Lord Lao from the mystic, primal, and inaugural pneumas were representative of the six heavens. At the end of the Warring States period and again during the Han, the Dao manifested itself in human form in an attempt to correct the three ways of the six heavens, which were promiscuously mingling and becoming corrupt.[22] When the cycle of the Six Heavens reached its apex, the Dao formally declared its end:

> [The Most High] forthwith honored Zhang as the "Master of Three Heavens of the Correct and Unified Pneumas of the Grand Mystic Metropolis" and entrusted to him the Way of the Covenanted Authority of Correct Unity, to govern in the name of the Newly Emerged Lord Lao. In doing so, Lord Lao abrogated all authority of the age of the Six Heavens with its Three Ways.
>
> Zhang was to stabilize and correct the Three Heavens, eradicating the frivolous and returning the people to simplicity and truth.[23]

Unfortunately for contemporary mortals, despite the fact that the Dao, through its appointment of Zhang Daoling, had abrogated their authority, these "old pneumas" persisted in the form of deviant and dangerous practices. It is to a description of these that we now turn.

The Deviant Ways

Buddhism figures prominently among the deviant ways criticized in the *Inner Explanations*. Although it originally arose as one of the "three ways" of the old six heavens and thus has a respectable antiquity, Buddhism is but a foreign branch of Daoism, begun when Laozi went west to "convert the barbarians." This is the same story found in the *Admonitions,* though related here with more vigor and with much greater attention to detail, showing that by this time Daoists were better acquainted with the rival religion.

Following what was still perceived as the humiliation of the Han peoples at the hands of those other base barbarians from the west, the Huns, the attack on Buddhism is carried out with vehement ethnocentrism. Doctrinally, Buddhism is yin in nature, to match the perceived deficiencies of the ungovernable barbarians, whose need for the elaborate precepts and prohibitions supplied by Buddhism was consequently seen as greater than that of the Chinese. The religion is thus presented as necessary and proper for those outside of the Central Kingdom, whose natures require strict control, but useless for Chinese. The text goes on to complain that even though an enlightened family sits on the throne, the way of the Buddha still flourishes in the Central Kingdom. Worse yet, it was actually a Han emperor, Liu Zhuang (r. 57–75), who, having dreamed of a golden giant—which, he was told, was the Buddha—actually invited the foreign religion into China! Since that time there has been mixing of the two faiths and even intermarriage between the true descendants of the Han peoples and barbarians, described in this text as *fei lei* ("outside of categories," a term I am tempted to translate as "outside the species," given the animal names traditionally used to designate foreign peoples). The present rulers of the Liu family should certainly try to rectify *that* mistake.

Another ethnic slur leveled at Buddhism, its foreign missionaries, and Han devotees, shows that the author of the *Inner Explanations* was to some extent aware of recent developments in Buddhist scholarly circles. Toward the end of the first chapter, the following distinction between Buddhism and Daoism is given:

> Laozi is the lord of living transformation; Śakyāmuni is the lord of transformation by death. As a result, Laozi was born from his mother's left armpit and is lord of the left. The left is the side of the yang pneumas that govern the Azure Palace with its Registers of Life. Śakyāmuni was born from his mother's right armpit and is lord of the right. The right is the side of yin pneumas and the black records of the Registers of Death. In this respect the differences between the teachings of Laozi and Śakyāmuni are those between the laws of left and right. The transforming influences of the left accord with the palace of the left, so that the pneumas of life cause the adept's entire body to rise and fly off in transcendence. The transforming influences of the right accord with the palace of the right, so that the pneumas of death cause the adept to pass through oblivion and be reborn. Buddhist dharma robes are entirely black. [Buddhists] are made to wear these black garments in order to model themselves on yin pneumas and to represent the fact that their names are entered in the black records.
>
> ... One only makes it difficult for oneself when one repeatedly passes through destruction, undergoes transformation in the dark realms, and cycles through birth and death. Even though the transformation of the right is not so quick and easy as that of the palace of the left, is it not also good that they return to perfection through cycles of life and death? Yet it is said that "the right is not so good as the left."[24]

The author here implies that, rather than describing the cycle of rebirth and seeking to end it, the goal of Buddhists is in fact to be reborn.[25] His comments reflect knowledge of a debate going on within the Buddhist religion that was instigated in the capital of Jiankang by Zhu Daosheng (360–434) after Zhu had returned to the south from studying with the great translator Kumārajīva. Zhu held that one could attain enlightenment at once, instantaneously, rather than by the gradual accretion of good deeds, exercises, and study. This set off a debate in Chinese Buddhism that was to lead to the creation of the Zen sect. Of more interest here, however, is how some Chinese Buddhists responded to the prospect of an easy path to enlightenment. The Buddhist layman and poet Xie Lingyun (385–433) expressed, at about the same time that our text was written, the opinion that suddenness and gradualness in attaining the way are due to ethnic and geographical differences. Xie argued that Chinese have a predisposition for the direct path, whereas foreigners must "receive instruction."[26] This is precisely the position taken here, though the debating point is turned against the Buddhist religion as a whole. The methods of the Dao are described as "quick and easy," as opposed to the "difficult" ways of the foreign religion. Why should any Chinese, endowed with a natural disposition fully addressed in the teachings of the Dao, want to commit to an arduous cycle of rebirths?[27]

Whereas human rebirth is not to be desired, the repeated appearances of Laozi as the "Master to the Kingdom" are. In the course of presenting its own account of the epiphanies of the Sage, the *Inner Explanations* reveals its knowledge and disapproval of another Daoist sect that, thanks to the fortuitous survival of one of its scriptures, is known to us. This group, whose ideas are expressed in the *Scripture of the Transformations of Laozi*, held that the Sage had revealed himself repeatedly throughout Chinese history, but that he also underwent a series of regular esoteric transformations, during the course of which he could be perceived through meditation inside the body of adepts.[28] The *Inner Explanations* contains lists of both exoteric and esoteric transformations of Laozi that are almost identical to those found in the *Transformations*, but accounts for them in a way that signals its disagreement with one of the major tenets of the group: that Laozi might be discernible within the body through meditation.[29]

The remaining "deviant ways" described in the *Inner Explana-*

tions are not so well documented. They seem to represent popular movements that have disappeared from the pages of the history books.[30] Even the third of the "three ways," the Way of the Pure Contract instituted by the Dao in the kingdoms of Chu and Yue, is not entirely clear. The kingdoms of Chu and Yue comprise the homeland of the ancient Chu kingdom, whose ecstatic, shamanic religion is known from the *Chuci.*[31] But, as we have seen, while placing the origins of these "three ways" in high antiquity, the *Inner Explanations* is not really concerned with history. There must, then, have been some contemporary manifestation of the Way of the Pure Contract that would merit this treatment. One plausible suggestion is that the term represents the shamanic popular religion of the south, with which northerners, some of them Celestial Master faithful, came into shocked contact when the north fell to the Huns in 317. A more specific suggestion has been made by Miyakawa Hisayuki in his studies of the Sun En rebellion.[32] Miyakawa shows that the rebellion was inspired by a group of Celestial Master Daoists who had made great missionary inroads in the coastal provinces of the south, in the process picking up elements of the indigenous religion. The rebellion was thus a conflict between conservative and accommodationist followers of the Way of the Celestial Masters. Significantly, Liu Yu was instrumental in putting down the accommodationist rebellion. Unfortunately, the *Inner Explanations* does not provide enough detail concerning the Way of the Pure Contract to make this more than a suggestion.

The "Way of Clear Water" may have been another contemporary manifestation of what the *Inner Explanations* calls the primordial Way of the Pure Contract. It is described there as a heterodox form of Celestial Master Daoism, in that it was reportedly begun by an illiterate "slave" of the first Celestial Master, Zhang Daoling. I have found only one other reference to the cult, in a Buddhist text, which attests to the fact that the "Way of Clear Water" had adherents in the imperial family as late as 372.[33] The fullest description of the practices and beliefs of this sect is provided in the *Inner Explanations,* though we cannot call it an unbiased source. The "Way of Banners and Flowers" is even more obscure. Our text calls it "merely Buddhism," so it must be one of the many sinicized sects of the Buddhist religion.

It is extremely significant, I think, that the *Inner Explanations* does not criticize as "deviant" other major schools of Daoism that were beginning to flourish at about this time. Though it is whole-hearted propaganda for the Way of the Celestial Masters, it mentions with approval both the Shangqing and the Lingbao schools. The three Mao brothers are listed as officers of the new dispensation right after the three Celestial Masters and their ladies, with a version of the titles they are given in the Shangqing scriptures, where they play a central role.[34] The *Inner Explanations* also provides a plot summary of the *Inner Traditions of the Martial Thearch of the Han*, a propagandistic tale penned by a follower of the Shangqing movement that was intended to show that the Martial Thearch had been indoctrinated in Shangqing practices but had failed to follow them fully.[35] The appearance of the Lingbao scriptures is listed among the augural signs that greeted the ascent to the throne of Liu Yu. Thus, although both the Shangqing and the Lingbao scriptures portray the Way of the Celestial Masters as one of the "lesser practices" of the Dao, we find no overt response in the *Inner Explanations*.[36]

The way in which the *Inner Explanations* incorporates the refinements of these new Daoist scriptural lineages into its own central message marks, I think, a turning point in the history of Daoism.[37] Though there were to be doctrinal disputes, even "protestant" movements, such as that of Kou Qianzhi in the north, Daoism remained throughout its subsequent history remarkably unified. That the Celestial Master movement was able, so soon after these challenges to its supreme command of the Dao, to incorporate elements of these rival schools under the all-encompassing Way of the Covenanted Authority of Correct Unity marks perhaps the earliest example of the lack of sectarian strife that was to characterize the religion as a whole.

NOTES TO INNER EXPLANATIONS: INTRODUCTION

1. The author of the text, given as "Xu 徐, Disciple of the Three Heavens," has not been further identified.

2. The *Inner Explanations* is not the only Daoist text to have proclaimed the approbation of the Dao at Liu Yu's endeavor. See Anna K. Seidel, "The Image of the Perfect Ruler in Early Taoist Messianism," *HR* 9 (1970), pp. 237–40; and Mollier, "Messianisme taoïste," pp. 82–87.

3. The one exception to this is the references to the "Three Heavens" in the *Admonitions* (see the section "Lord Lao and the Dao" in the introduction to that text).

4. *HY* 788, 12a.

5. See Chan, *Two Visions of the Way*, pp. 125–26. We have already seen the importance of this third pneuma, the "centrally harmonious"—which the *Xiang'er* and the *Scripture of Great Peace* share—to the nurturance of long life in humans.

6. Robinet, *La révélation du Shangqing,* vol. 2, p. 90.

7. On these, see Strickmann, "T'ao Hung-ching," p. 180; and Robinet, *La révélation du Shangqing,* vol. 1, pp. 130–33.

8. "Grand Clarity" was one of the terms used to describe the undifferentiated state of the Dao, recoverable through the mystical meditations of the Sage, as early as the former Han. See the *Huainan zi,* 2:22–23; 7:104, 107; 8:113; and A. C. Graham, *Chuang-tzu: The Seven Inner Chapters and Other Writings* (London: Allen & Unwin, 1981), p. 164, where the term is translated "Ultimate Clarity." It is unclear how early the term entered the vocabulary of the Celestial Masters. (See endnote 11 below.)

9. See Bokenkamp, "Sources," p. 475 n. 145, for references.

10. Both the Shangqing and the Lingbao scriptures contain elaborate accounts of the origins of their texts in the earliest stages of the differentiation of yin and yang. For the most representative examples of this oft-repeated claim, see Robinet, *La révélation du Shangqing,* vol. 1, pp. 112–16; Campany, "Buddhist Revelation," pp. 21–25; and *HY* 1010, 1:8a–10a, and *HY* 22, 1:1a–2b.

11. This formulation is found, for instance, in *HY* 789, 2:1a; *HY* 421, 3:8b; *HY* 794, 9a, 12a, 14a; *HY* 797, 1a; *HY* 798, 1a; and in many of the memorials collected in *HY* 615. For further examples, see Chen Guofu, *Daozang yuanliu kao,* pp. 364–65. Robinet (*La révélation du Shangqing,* vol. 1, pp. 71–73) has suggested that the appearance of the term "Grand Clarity" (*Taiqing* 太清) in Daoist texts signals the fact that the alchemical Taiqing sect had co-opted certain elements of the Celestial Masters. Though it is difficult to prove, there may be merit to this idea. We can with assurance trace association of the term "Grand Clarity" with the Celestial Masters no earlier than the *Huayang guozhi,* which was written south of the Yangtze River in the second half of the fourth century.

12. See especially lines 409–11 of the *Xiang'er.* The Lingbao scriptures speak of each of the three pneumas (mystic, primal, and inaugural) as divided into three, creating nine heavens. (See *HY* 318.) This may be another, elaborated version of the older Celestial Master idea we are discussing here.

13. Already during the Han period there was speculation on the stages through which the undifferentiated Dao passed before division. The terminology employed here by the *Inner Explanations* is similar to that of some of these speculations. The *Yiwei qianzao du* 易緯乾鑿度, for instance, names

the stages of undifferentiated chaos as Grand Change (before the appearance of pneuma), Grand Incipience (the first appearance of pneuma), Grand Inauguration (the birth of form), and Grand Simplicity (the birth of substance). (See Yasui Kōsan and Nakamura Shōhachi, eds., *Isho shūsei* [Tokyo: Meitoku, 1971–1978], 1.1:24; and *DKW* 1:119b.) On the notion that the primordial Dao was undifferentiated chaos, likened to a sack or an egg, see especially N. J. Girardot, *Myth and Meaning in Early Taoism* (Berkeley: University of California Press, 1983).

14. It is this aspect of the text that has sometimes led to the conclusion that it is "complex" and even "confused" (Stein, "Religious Taoism," pp. 63–4) or that it is a "conflation of ... different traditions" (Erik Zürcher, "Buddhist Influence on Early Taoism," *TP* 66 [1980], p. 93). In fact, the cosmology the author forwards to counter those of the Shangqing and Lingbao scriptures is complex, but logical. He is not attempting to account historically for the origins of Buddhism and Daoism, but to associate them, in good Daoist fashion, with the primordial Dao. Of particular importance in the accompanying chart is the number of nascent divisions that appear within the primeval unity and how these come into fullness after the Dao's division.

15. Robinet (*Taoist Meditation,* pp. 103–17) describes the way the adept is, by means of meditation, to move back through these spirals to the original unity of the Dao.

16. On how Han thought influenced Daoist accounts in this regard, see Bokenkamp, "Time after Time."

17. See the section "Morality and Governance" in the introduction to the *Admonitions.*

18. See the section "Apocalyptic Predictions" in the introduction to the *Purple Texts.*

19. See, for example, *HY* 22, chap. 1, and *HY* 318, 5b–7a.

20. See Michel Strickmann, "The Mao-shan Revelations: Taoism and the Aristocracy," *TP* 63 (1977), pp. 12–13; and Robinet, *La révélation du Shangqing,* vol. 1, pp. 137–38. This account of the "six celestial palaces" is based on the fact that, by the numerology of the magic square, six is the number of the north, associated with death and winter. The six celestial palaces of Fengdu are located in the northeast by the diviner's compass. (*HY* 1010, 15:1a.)

21. There is controversy over just when the concept of the six heavens entered Celestial Master Daoism. See especially Kobayashi Masayoshi, *Rikuchō dōkyōshi kenkyū,* pp. 482–510. It should be recognized, however, that the Celestial Master concept of the six heavens, as presented here, is not to be simply equated with the localized "six celestial palaces of Fengdu" as they appear in the Shangqing scriptures. As was the case with many earlier Daoist concepts, Yang Xi seems to have provided his own unique elaborations. Further, given the dearth of textual data that have survived, the dating of texts on the assumed first appearance of a word or

concept is simply not a reliable procedure. Though Kobayashi denies that this could have been an influence, the term "six heavens" is also one that predates the Celestial Masters. According to the influential Han-period Confucian cosmologist Zheng Xuan (127–200), the "six heavens" were represented by the Five Thearchs and Grand Unity, the objects of state ritual (Gu Jiegang and Yang Xiangui, "Sanhuang kao," *Yenching Journal of Chinese Studies,* Monograph Series, no. 8. [1936]; and Howard J. Wechsler, *Offerings of Jade and Silk: Ritual and Symbol in the Legitimation of the T'ang Dynasty* [New Haven, Conn.: Yale University Press, 1985], p. 111). This system was fully explicated in the "weft texts," of which Zheng was a devoted partisan, and which had a wide influence, as yet not fully explored, on the development of Daoism (Seidel, "Imperial Treasures"). In that the demonic generals of the six heavens are described in Celestial Master accounts as worshiped with meat sacrifices, as were the six heavens of the state cult, it is not impossible that, in addition to popular sacrifice, elements of the state cult were also targeted for replacement by the pure sacrifices of Daoism. (For the prohibition of meat sacrifices in the early Celestial Master texts presented here, see the *Xiang'er,* lines 373–77.)

22. These attempts at reformation included the revelation of the *Scripture of Great Peace* to Gan Ji 干吉 and the appearance of the Perfect Wang Fangping 王方平 and Dongfang Shuo 東方朔. *HY* 1196, 1:4b–5a.

23. See *HY* 1196, 1:6a.

24. See *HY* 1196, 1:9b–10a.

25. The passage depends on an uninformed understanding of the term *miedu* 滅度 (nirvana). Early translators of Buddhist scripture fashioned the term to mean something like "destruction [of the cycle of rebirth] and crossing [the sea of suffering into nonexistence]"—in other words, the longed-for end of the samsaric cycle of death and rebirth. Here it is understood as an adverb-verb construction meaning "the passage through oblivion." "Oblivion" is in this case understood in its usual connotation of death, not as a "cessation" of the cycle of rebirth. This Daoist explanation of the term is not original to the author of the *Inner Explanations* but finds its source in the Lingbao scriptures. See Bokenkamp, "Stages of Transcendence."

26. See Xie's *Bianzong lun* 辨宗論 [Disputing the Heritage], in the *Guanghong mingji* (*T* 2103, 52.224c ff.); and, for the terms of the "sudden-gradual" debate, Paul Demiéville, "The Mirror of the Mind," and Rolf A. Stein, "Sudden Illumination or Simultaneous Comprehension," both in Peter N. Gregory, ed., *Sudden and Gradual: Approaches to Enlightenment in Chinese Thought* (Honolulu: University of Hawaii Press, 1987), pp. 13–40 and 41–66, resp.

27. For more on the ramifications of this view, see Bokenkamp, "Stages of Transcendence."

28. This sect has been fully studied by Seidel (*La divinisation de Laotseu*). According to the evidence of the *Transformations,* the sect was active

in Sichuan from 130 to 155, but the diffusion of its teachings must have been wide indeed, given that the text was found at Dunhuang (S 2295).

29. See footnote ‡ on p. 209 to the *Inner Explanations* translation.

30. For an analysis of the Daoist attitude to popular religion during this period, see Stein, "Religious Taoism."

31. The *Chuci* is a reworked collection of Chu rituals and folklore. For a translation and analysis, see David Hawkes, *The Songs of the South: An Anthology of Ancient Chinese Poems by Qu Yuan and Other Poets* (Harmondsworth: Penguin Books, 1985).

32. Miyakawa Hisayuki, "Son On, Ro Jun no ran ni tsuite" [On the rebellion of Sun En and Lu Hsün], *Tōyōshi kenkyū* 30.2–3 (1971), pp. 1–30; Miyakawa Hisayuki, "Son, Ro Jun no ran hokō" [Supplementary studies on the rebellion of Sun En and Lu Hsün], in *Suzuki hakushi koki kinen Tōyōgaku ronsō* (Tokyo: Meisō, 1972), pp. 533–48; Miyakawa Hisayuki, "Local Cults around Mount Lu at the Time of Sun En's Rebellion," in Homes Welch and Anna Seidel, eds., *Facets of Taoism: Essays in Chinese Religion* (New Haven, Conn.: Yale University Press, 1979), pp. 83–102.

33. See *T* 2063, 50.936b.15 ff.

34. According to legend, the three Mao brothers, borne on the backs of cranes, each alighted on one of the three peaks of what was thenceforth known as Mount Mao (approximately seventy kilometers southeast of modern Nanjing). They figure among the highest Perfected of Shangqing Daoism and are charged with keeping the registers of destiny of those pursuing transcendence. In the Shangqing scriptures they are assigned titles as follows: Mao Ying 茅盈, the Director of Destinies; Mao Gu 固, the Certifier of Registers; and Mao Zhong 衷, the Guarantor of Destinies. They are also known as the elder, middle, and younger Lords Mao, respectively. See Edward H. Schafer, *Mao Shan in T'ang Times* (Boulder, Colo.: Society for the Study of Chinese Religions, 1980), and Strickmann, "Mao-shan Revelations." Yang Xi received through revelation a biography of the three brothers, which included the practices they had followed to achieve Perfection. See Robinet, *La révélation du Shangqing*, vol. 2, pp. 389–98.

35. The text is to be found at *HY* 292 and was first translated and studied by Kristofer M. Schipper (*L'empereur Wou des Han dans la légende taoïste* [Paris, 1965]). Robinet (*La révélation du Shangqing*, vol. 1, pp. 229–31), after a study of the reliance of this text on the Shangqing scriptures, provides the conclusions presented here.

36. In the second and final chapter of the text, not translated here, there is, however, a distinction drawn between the "Greater Vehicle" (reformed Celestial Master) practices and those of the "Lesser Vehicle." This latter, judging by the practices listed, includes both Buddhists and other Daoists, including those who wish to "leave the world and fly off to Upper Clarity [*Shangqing*]." (*HY* 1196, 2:3b5–5a3.) Still, the Shangqing and Lingbao schools are not mentioned by name, as they tend to mention the Celestial

Masters in their orderings of practice, so that though the strategy of attempting to subsume other traditions is the same, the conflict is ameliorated.

37. It is at about this time, we should note, that Daoists began to organize their scriptures into the "Three Caverns" that were to form the basis of the Daoist canon. In 437, about fifteen years after the *Inner Explanations* was composed, Lu Xiujing (406–477) signed his catalog of the Lingbao scriptures with the title "Disciple of the Three Caverns." See Ōfuchi, "Formation," for an account of this process. It should be noted that, whereas Ōfuchi holds that "it is highly unlikely that any spontaneous pressure from within could have conferred on the separate schools [of Daoism] a sense of unity or common identity" (p. 259), a dynasty as sympathetic toward Daoism as the Liu-Song and the concomitant need to present to the throne an ordered account of the faith (such as that of the *Inner Explanations*) would have likely provided just such an impetus.

Translation

*Scripture of the Inner Explanations
of the Three Heavens*

[PREFACE]

1a   The body with which humans are born receives endowments from heaven above and models itself on earth below.* Just as sun and moon mark the division of light and dark, as cold and heat contain pneumas that wither and provide growth, as thunder and lightning have appointed times for emerging, as wind and rain have seasons in which they are active or still, so human beings possess the quality of wisdom or ignorance, natures that are good or evil, vivifying pneumas that are rigid or pliant, a long or short allotment of life, an exalted or humble position, a rank of honor or humility, good fate or ill, and seasons wherein they either reach or fall short of their goals.

  Without humanity, heaven and earth would not stand; without

---

* The term translated as "models itself on" is *xiang*, "to image." As the passage that follows makes clear, this phrase does not mean that humans were created by heaven in imitation of earth, but that there is a strict correlation between the universe as macrocosm and the human being as microcosm so that each influences the other. Classical statements of this idea usually begin with the observation that the human head is round like the revolving heavens, while the feet are square like the four-cornered earth. See Graham, *Disputers of the Tao,* pp. 338–40. The same formulation occurs in Daoist texts, but generally more emphasis is given to the fact that the potentially divine aspects of the human being are endowments of celestial pneumas.

heaven and earth, human beings would not be born. A heaven and earth without humans would be like a person lacking spirits inside, an empty form that could not stand.* [Humans beings without the material basis heaven and earth provide would be like a person who] possessed internal spirits but lacked a form: the spirits would have nothing to control.†

That which establishes human life is heaven; what gives it mobility is the Dao. In the Dao, human beings' natures, endowments, and spirits are fused to become one. In the same way, the three basic   1b
constituents of the universe—heaven, earth, and humanity—in fulfilling their intrinsic potential are the progenitors of the myriad things. Heaven cannot but nurture life; earth cannot but provide growth to things; and human beings cannot but nourish their own lives through the intake of breath. When heaven turns away from its status as the Mystic and Primal, the result is catastrophic change through the swelling and erosion[1] of yin and yang energies.‡ When earth shrugs off its original yellow mantle, the disasters of violent winds and earthquakes occur.§ When people turn their backs on the ultimate Dao, they suffer wasting away and death.

Essence and pneuma float above, and myriad forms of essence flow below.[2] Those above and below are interconnected, proceeding from one another "as shadow and echo follow their sources." When human affairs become confused, disasters respond below and allotments of life are annulled, while above there are flarings and eclipses of the sun and moon and the starry timekeepers slip from their places.‖ All of these catastrophic changes proceed from lack of regulation in human affairs.

* The term *shen* ("spirit" or "spirits") needs to be rendered in the plural here to accord with classical Chinese notions of the spiritual constituents of the body. For more on how the Daoists of this time viewed the corporeal spirits, see especially the *Purple Texts*, translated later in this book.
† With the bracketed interpolations, I have attempted to maintain the parallelism in this passage that is clear in the Chinese original but tends to get lost in English.
‡ For the "Mystic and Primal" as a description of the original state of heaven, see endnote 4 to this translation.
§ "Yellow mantle"—or, more exactly, "yellow skirts"—is a term for the earth that is already found in the *kun* ("earth") hexagram of the oldest stratum of the *Yijing*.
‖ The term here translated as "flarings and eclipses" (of the sun and moon) is the same phrase rendered as "swelling and erosion" above, where it refers more gen-

Now, in the age of lower antiquity, people's lives have been cut short so that corpses and bones are scattered about and no one enjoys a full span of life.* All of this is because their practice has lost its source. They marry outside of their type, mingling their pneumas with those chaotic and turbid.† They place their faith in the deviant and discard the true, perverting the original Dao. All sorts of ignorance abound, so that no one knows whence their misfortune arises. Some even slaughter and cook the six sorts of domestic animal to supplicate empty nothingness.‡ They chant, drum, and dance, making their entreaties with liquors and meats! Seeking life, they gain only death. The deviant ways that they practice ensure it. Their actions are as inconsistent as if they were to scratch their feet when it was their head that itched. Through calculating and excessive prayer, they actually bring about the destruction of their own bodies. The shortness of their life spans is truly lamentable.

Now I have collected and written out these essential explanations of the Three Heavens to instruct the unenlightened. You should be careful to keep these explanations secret. Do not recklessly or lightly transmit them to others. If you transmit them to the wrong persons, calamity will flow down even to your sons and grandsons.§

2a

---

erally to the pneumas of yin and yang. Since the moon was regarded as a concentration of yin and the sun of yang, the Chinese usage is exact.

* For the three ages of antiquity, see line 243 of the *Xiang'er* commentary.

† In Celestial Master Daoism, the marriage rite was known as the "joining of the pneumas" and was conceived of as a merger of corporeal spirits rather than a joining of bodies. As this passage makes clear, though, unsanctified marriage was also viewed as a "mingling of pneumas," though one could hope for little benefit from joining with someone "outside of one's type." As we will see, the reference here is not to the social distinctions within China, but to marriages between Chinese and non-Chinese.

‡ That is, they perform sacrificial offerings to the spirits. The Dao, at least in terms of mundane existence essentially a "void nothingness," does not require such sustenance. Further references to the fact that the powers of the Dao do not require offerings appear on pp. 7b–8a of this text.

§ That is to say, this text should be treated as if it were revealed scripture. This is why the title proclaims it an "inner" or "esoteric" explanation of the three heavens. An exoteric explanation would be one available to all without rites of transmission. As Robinet (*La révélation du Shangqing*, vol. 1, p. 120) has noted, the Celestial Masters seem to have lacked elaborate rites of scriptural transmission such as those practiced in the Shangqing school. (See the *Purple Texts*, translated later in this book.) The paragraph here is further evidence that this text was influenced by Shangqing and Lingbao scriptures, where passages such as this are pro forma.

[THE EXPLANATIONS]

The Dao originally arose with nothing prior to it. Dark and attenuated, vaporous and opaque, it had no cause.[3] It was born in the
Void through self-actualization. Transforming, it gave birth to the
Elder of the Way and Its Power, who appeared before there were
primal pneumas. Since he is the venerated one within the Dao, he
serves as the Elder of the Way and Its Power.* Based on this, there is
the Illimitable Great Way of Grand Clarity—the Mystic and Primal
[pneumas] and the Highest Three Heavens—[and from it] the Most
High Lord Lao, the Most High Elders, the Thearchs of the Heavens,
the Nine Ancient Lords of the Transcendent Metropolises, the Elders
of the Nine Pneumas, and so forth—in sum, a billion pneumas of
the Dao, twelve hundred official lords, all below the throne of Grand
Clarity.[4] When mortals of the present day send up written memori-   2b
als to Grand Clarity, it is these Perfected of the heavens whom they
address.

After this, the Vacuous Grotto was born in Utter Blackness. Then
from the Vacuous Grotto, Grand Nullity was born. Grand Nullity
transformed itself into the three pneumas: the Mystic, the Primal,
and the Inaugural.† Joined alike in undifferentiated Chaos, these
three pneumas transformed to give birth to the Dark and Wondrous
Jade Maiden.‡ Once the Jade Maiden had been born, the undiffer-

* He is, in short, the Dao in anthropomorphized form. Through his title, we recognize not only the name of Laozi's text but the fact that this deity represents Laozi
himself in his cosmogonic form. This is why the author later states that Laozi was
born by "cyclically transforming himself."

† This modifies earlier Celestial Master accounts of the "three pneumas," which
give them the colors azure, yellow, and white and state simply that they are the
breaths that separated to form heaven, earth, and the Dao. There is also no clear
indication in earlier texts that the "three pneumas" were believed to precede the creation. Rather, they are described as divided out of an original, singular pneuma. (See
the *Admonitions, HY* 788, 12a.) The reasons for these modifications in the *Inner
Explanations* are clear from the terminology employed. The term "vacuous grotto"
(*kong dong*) is important in the cosmogonic accounts of the Lingbao scriptures,
which portray themselves as products of a Vacuous Grotto—the womb of the Dao—
that came into existence with the first breath, the Mystic Pneuma. (*HY* 22, 1:1a10–
1b2.) In the *Inner Explanations*, by contrast, the three pneumas are seen to issue
after the Celestial Master deities of Grand Clarity are already in place, thus giving
temporal priority to Celestial Master teachings.

‡ See Livia Kohn, "The Mother of the Tao," *TR* 1.2 (1989), pp. 37–109, for a
discussion of the various myths concerning the mother of Laozi. The reason our text

entiated pneumas coalesced in her to give birth to Laozi. Laozi was born from the left side of the Dark and Wondrous Jade Maiden. Born with white hair, he was styled Laozi ["the Elder Master"].

Now, Laozi is Lord Lao. Lord Lao transformed and the pneumas took shape as the heavens, earth, humanity, and all beings. This was the result of Lord Lao cyclically transforming himself, refining his form and pneumas. Lord Lao spread out the Mystic, Primal, and Inaugural pneumas. Still, the clear and the turbid pneumas were not divided from one another, but remained undifferentiated, in shape like the yolk of a chicken egg.*

Thereupon he divided and distributed the pneumas. The Mystic pneumas were clear and pure, so they ascended to become the heavens. The Inaugural pneumas were thick and turbid, so they congealed below to form earth. The Primal pneumas were light and subtle, so they flowed throughout as water.† With this, the sun, moon, and stars were arrayed.

3a   Lord Lao then mixed together the pneumas and, transforming them, made nine kingdoms, placing in them nine sorts of human beings, three male and six female.‡ During the time of Fu Xi and Nü

---

recounts two births of Laozi is that the first occurs in the "prior heavens," before the differentiation of pneumas. The highest gods worshiped in Daoism are all "prior heaven" deities.

* The likening of heaven and earth to an egg is a feature of the "Enveloping Sky" theory of Han cosmologists, who pictured the earth as floating within a spherical envelope of sky. On this theory, see Schafer, *Pacing the Void*, pp. 35–36. Here, though, the analogy is used to express the original undifferentiation of primordial Chaos. In placing the genesis of the three pneumas within the prior heavens, in the stage of undifferentiated Chaos, the author of this text further accedes to the claims of the Lingbao scriptures, while still giving priority to the Celestial Master gods and Lord Lao in particular.

† The *Admonitions* states that primal pneuma is white in color and associated with the Dao. In the *Xiang'er* commentary, on the other hand, white primal pneumas are compared with essence in the human body, which in that context can refer only to the visible essence—semen. It is likely, then, that primal pneuma is associated both with water, or liquid, and with the Dao as it is made available to humanity, in that humans receive their initial apportionment of primal pneuma as essence. Primal pneuma is thus the active, life-giving manifestation of the Dao in the world. We see in the introduction to the *Inner Explanations*, for instance, that essence was regarded as liquid in nature in that "myriad forms of essence flow" in the world below.

‡ The division of the earth into nine parts occurs earliest in the "Canons of Yao" chapter of the *Shang shu*. Zou Yan (ca. 305–240 B.C.E.) is said to be responsible for the idea that there were in fact eighty-one (nine times nine) habitable lands.

Wa, each made for themselves names and surnames.* At this time, Lord Lao issued the three ways to instruct the people of heaven. In the Central Kingdom the yang pneumas are pure and upright, so he caused them to serve the Great Way of Inaction. Outside [of the nine-part Central Kingdom], in the eighty-one regions of barbarian kingdoms, yin pneumas are strong and flourishing, so he caused them to adhere to the Way of the Buddha. The prohibitions and precepts of this religion are extremely strict, so as to suppress the yin pneumas. In Chu and Yue, the pneumas of yin and yang are thin, so he caused them to serve the Way of the Pure Contract. At that time, the rule of the Six Heavens flourished and the Three Ways were put into practice.[5]

During the reigns of one thearch after another, Laozi emerged as Master to the Kingdom, instructor of the thearchs:[†]

During the reign of Fu Xi, he was styled Yuhua zi.
During the reign of Ju Rong, he was styled Guangshou zi.
During the reign of Shen Nong, he was styled Dacheng zi.
During the reign of Huang Di, he was styled Kuangcheng zi.
During the reign of Zhuan Xu, he was styled Chijing zi.
During the reign of Thearch Ku, he was styled Lutu zi.
During the reign of Thearch Yao, he was styled Wucheng zi.
During the reign of Thearch Shun, he was styled Yinshou zi.
During the reign of Yu of Xia, he was styled Zhenxing zi.
During the reign of Tang of Yin, he was styled Xize zi.[6]   3b

But his transformations are not regular.[‡] At times he was sur-named Li with

---

* The mythical rulers Fu Xi and Nü Wa were depicted as having intertwined ser-pent tails. Together, they form the first of the mythical rulers of antiquity known as the Three Sovereigns. See Girardot, *Myth and Meaning,* pp. 202–7, for the mythol-ogy of this "primordial couple."
    † The title here translated as "Master to the Kingdom" might also be translated as "teacher" or "precentor" to the kingdom. In short, it is not the title of a ruler, but of a sagely adviser.
    ‡ The following list is a truncated version of the "nine esoteric transformations of Laozi," which figures in the late-second-century *Scripture of the Transformations of Laozi,* studied by Seidel (*La divinisation de Lao-tseu,* pp. 65, 95–110). The *Trans-formations* differentiates clearly between this list of names and that which appears above with the words: "[W]hen he withdraws, he nourishes his vital principle; when

1. the name Hong and the appellation Jiuyang;
2. the name Dan and the appellation Boyang;
3. the name Zhong and the appellation Boguang;
4. the name Zhong and the appellation Ziwen;
5. the name Zhai and the appellation Bochang;
6. the name Yuan and the appellation Boshi;
7. the name Xian and the appellation Yuansheng;
8. the name De and the appellation Bowen.

Sometimes he transforms himself nine times in a single day; sometimes twenty-four times. Through a thousand changes and ten thousand transformations, he rises up and sinks out of sight through the generations—so many times that they cannot all be recorded.

Coming to the time of King Wu Ding of the Yin dynasty, he returned to the womb of Mother Li.* Within her womb he chanted scriptures for eighty-one years. Then, breaking through her left side, he was born with white hair and again called Laozi. The *Scripture of the Three Terraces* possessed by people of our times is none other than the scripture that Laozi recited in the womb.†

---

he emerges, he is the master to Thearchs and Kings." The "nine transformations" are thus representative of the hidden forms of Laozi, of which the *Transformations* says: "Confess your sins and observe your body.... I am in your pneumas and [internal] spirits." Seidel shows that this mythology of nine transformations of the body of Laozi (or Pan'gu in another tradition) is in itself part of an ancient cosmogonic myth concerning the formation of the nine regions of the world. There are Daoist meditations, spaced over the period of a month, that invite the adept to participate in this autogenesis. Given this, the phrases with which the *Inner Explanations* precedes and concludes this truncated list are significant: his transformations are "not regular ... sometimes he transforms himself nine times in a single day; sometimes twenty-four times." Clearly, the practice of meditating on the nine transformations of the divine body of Laozi is not endorsed in the *Inner Explanations*.

* The traditional reign dates of King Wu Ding of the Yin [Shang] dynasty are 1339–1281 B.C.E. Later texts specify the year of Laozi's birth as 1331 B.C.E. Kusuyama (*Rōshi densetsu*, pp. 373–81) shows how the various dates given for Laozi's birth and departure from China are related to the theory that he transformed into the Buddha Śakyāmuni and are therefore keyed to theories regarding the date of the Buddha's birth.

† Only a brief summary of this text survives. The "Three Terraces" are a constellation formed of three pairs of stars in Ursa Major, also known as the "three steps." As part of the potent circumpolar constellations, these six stars were closely watched to determine the fate of the empire and its rulers. A Han-period text, known as the *Scripture of the Six Tallies of the Great Steps* and attributed to the Yellow Thearch, asserts that the two stars known as the Upper Step represented the emperor

Now, this "return to the womb of Mother Li" means that he himself transformed his void and insubstantial body into the form of Mother Li. In this way, he made a womb for himself. There was in fact no Mother Li. People of these times, unaware of this, say that Laozi entrusted himself to the womb of Mother Li, but this is not so.   4a

Coming to the time of King You of the Zhou [r. 781–770 B.C.E.], Laozi perceived that the Zhou dynasty's divine authorization was to expire, so he disheveled his hair to feign madness and, taking leave of the Zhou kingdom, departed.* When he reached the pass, riding his cart pulled by a blue ox, he met [the pass guardian] Yin Xi.† He bestowed on Yin Xi the *Upper, Lower, and Central Scripture* in one scroll and the *Five-Thousand Character Text* in two scrolls, a total of three scrolls.⁷ When Yin Xi received these scriptures, he achieved the Dao.

The Dao saw that the barbarians of the west were extremely stubborn and difficult to convert, so, together with Yin Xi, Laozi traveled west to Kashmir. There, he spiritually transformed himself into the Elder Mijia, so that he might convert the barbarian king and bring about his submission.⁸ He made for the king Buddhist scriptures of six hundred forty thousand words.⁹ The king and his whole country came to revere and practice these scriptures. This kingdom is forty thousand *li* from the Han kingdom.

Once those of the kingdom of Kashmir had all come to be obedi-

---

and his consort; the two known as the Middle Step, the various classes of officials; and the two known as the Lower Step, the nobility and commoners. Changes in these areas of the sky portended changes among the corresponding groups of people on earth. See the *Han shu*, 65:2851, and, for examples of prognostications based on these asterisms, Schafer, *Pacing the Void*, pp. 115, 151. Laozi's association with this asterism seems to originate with Daoism. The *Scripture of Laozi's Transformations* contains the following lines in a verse from Laozi himself: "I wear the constellation Three Terraces on my head [as a crown], / I clothe myself in the formless." (Seidel, *La divinisation de Lao-tseu*, p. 69.)

* King You was the last of the Zhou kings to rule over a unified kingdom. His reign ended with "barbarian" invasions that pushed the capital eastward and allowed the lords of former dependent fiefdoms to assert more independent control of their kingdoms. The detail that Laozi disarranged his hair and feigned madness places him in the tradition of "holy fools" who appear in the capital city to utter mysterious political prophecies.

† The tradition recounted here is an extremely old one, appearing first in the biography of Laozi in the *Shiji* and elaborated in various texts. The most complete study to date is Kusuyama, *Rōshi densetsu* (see especially pp. 273–472).

ent to the Great Law, Laozi went farther west to the kingdom of India, another forty thousand *li* from Kashmir. The consort of the king of India, named Qingmiao [Māyā], was taking a nap. Yin Xi was riding a white elephant, and Laozi caused it to transform into a titmouse and fly [with Yin Xi] into Māyā's mouth. As they [flew], their shape was like that of a comet.

4b

In the following year, on the eighth day of the fourth month, Māyā's right side split open and she gave birth. The child fell to the ground, walked seven steps, and, raising his right hand, pointed to heaven, intoning: "In heaven above and in the world below heaven, I alone am the honored one. In these three realms all is suffering. How could one delight in anything here?" As soon as he was born, he devoted himself to religious austerities. This was the Buddha in body. At this, the Way of the Buddha flourished once more.*

Coming to the age of lower antiquity, the pneumas of the Dao thinned, so that perversity and evil arose in their turn. [People] failed to distinguish between the true and the false, pouring out libations for mediums and making offerings to the spirits of the dead.

Then the Most High bestowed the *Scripture of the Way of Great Peace* on Gan Ji in Langye. Li Wei in the Commandery of Shu and others were ordered to aid the Six Heavens by correcting its deviant pneumas.† But Wei and the rest were not able to rectify the pneumas of the Six Heavens.

---

* The version of the myth of Laozi's "Conversion of the Barbarians" (*hua hu*) given here is part of the early controversies between Buddhism and Daoism over which religion deserved priority. The debate was carried on in polemic treatises and in "authentic" scripture, Buddhist and Daoist, with both sides arguing that deities of the other were mere "transformations" or copies of their own. It is a fascinating story, which, unfortunately, must be reconstructed from textual fragments, since the original scriptures were suppressed and scattered. For an excellent account of this controversy, see Zürcher, *Buddhist Conquest*, pp. 288–300, and, for an enlightening discussion of this passage, Zürcher, "Buddhist Influence," pp. 94–96. The account given here belongs to the tradition that Laozi transformed once more into a teacher to instruct the king of Kashmir, a violent and cruel monarch. As part of his proofs for the recalcitrant monarch, Laozi foretells the birth of the Buddha and claims that he will convert India as well. Then he causes the guardian of the pass, Yin Xi, who has by this time "achieved the Dao" through his study of Laozi's texts, to transform himself into Śakyāmuni.

† Gan Ji of Langye (in modern Shandong Province) is generally presented as the recipient of the *Scripture of Great Peace*. This particular account of his receipt of the scripture belongs to the Celestial Master tradition that holds that he received it from

On the contrary, under the rule of the Han house all sorts of deviant forces flourished and the pneumas of the Six Heavens flared up. The Three Ways mingled and disease vapors ran amok. Physicians and mediums then gained prominence, but they all abandoned the true Way in order to follow the false. Singing and dancing to the music of drums and strings, they slaughtered and cooked the six domestic animals, then made oblations and sacrifices to the deviant forces and the unholy dead. The lives of heaven's people were thus cut short, and corpses of those who died suddenly were scattered about.

The Most High then sent Perfected persons, including Wang   5a
Fangping and Dongfang Shuo, desiring that they assist the Han house.* He had them roam throughout the Han kingdom, gauging the sentiments of the people. But the Han thearchs did not believe this, taking these envoys to be deceivers. This is why the Han house weakened and was destroyed, so that Wang Mang came to rule over the Liu family.†

Laozi during the latter days of the Zhou dynasty. Li Wei of Shu (the western portions of modern Sichuan Province) is unknown outside of this text. The *Han shu* (82:3376) contains, in a memorial, a reference to a musician by the name of Li Wei, but this memorial was presented in the capital of Chang'an during the Han period, and so the musician is probably not the same person.

* Dongfang Shuo (154? [161?]–193 B.C.E.) was a counselor of Liu Che, the Martial Thearch of the Han, and was particularly renowned for his eloquence. Like the emperor he served, he became the subject of Daoist hagiography, which held that he was secretly a descended celestial being. Several texts of cosmology and fantastic geography are attributed to him. Interestingly, he is the one who presented to the emperor the Yellow Thearch scripture on the Three Terraces (discussed in footnote † on pp. 210–11 above). The identity of Wang Fangping is much harder to trace. This is because Fangping is commonly given as the byname of Wang Yuan, the Perfected of the Western Citadel, one of the prominent deities of the Shangqing scriptures. As a result, hagiographical references to Wang Yuan seem to have become inextricably confused with those to Wang Fangping. According to the most reliable evidence, Wang Yuan lived during the Latter Han, c. 150 C.E., whereas the Wang Fangping mentioned here is said to be a contemporary of Dongfang Shuo and so must have lived during the Former Han. We have only a few references, all in Celestial Master texts, that relate unquestionably to this Wang Fangping. Accounts of the original twenty-four parishes of the Celestial Masters relate that he received a revelation from Laozi (HY 599, 12b; HY 1026, 4:12a and 28:8a), while the *Scripture of the Transformations of Laozi* lists him as one of the transformations of Laozi (Seidel, *La divinisation de Lao-tseu*, p. 66). Myths concerning him seem to center on Mount Pingdu (in modern Fengdu County, Sichuan), where a temple still marks the spot of his ascent into the heavens.

† This is the Wang Mang interregnum, 8–25 C.E.

Now, the Han thearchs were children of dragon seed. The body
bequeathed to them from the Great Sage was to pass on through
twenty-four lords over a span of four hundred and more years.* It
was not proper that this line of thearchical descendants be broken,
and so the Shining and Martial Thearch was caused to renew the
Han house.† That their rule was interrupted was entirely due to the
fact that they did not keep faith with the True and Correct and thus
lacked divine support. Then all sorts of evil and disorder arose, and
they were destroyed by demon officers.‡

Ever since the separation of heaven and earth, there have always
been on the borders the Yi, the Qiang, the Man, the Rong, and the
Di peoples to act as a hedge around the Central Kingdom.§ In marriage, each people correctly adhered to their type. In worshiping the
ultimate Dao, each stuck to their own truth. Never was there inter-
mingling. But after the time of the Shining and Martial Thearch,
customs gradually deteriorated. People and demons began to have
intercourse with one another.

The son of the Shining and Martial, [posthumously styled] the
Luminous Thearch of the Han, said that he dreamed of a giant over
ten feet in height whose body was of a golden color.‖ His officials

5b

* That is to say, the Han rulers were of divine descent. Liu Ao, the mother of the
Han founder, Liu Bang (r. 206–195 B.C.E.), was said to have given birth to him as a
result of having been impregnated by a spirit in the form of a dragon. Thereafter, the
dragon was seen to hover protectively over the future emperor. (Shiji, 8:341–43.)
There were in fact twenty-eight recognized rulers in the Han line. The number
twenty-four is symbolic, based on the twenty-four divisions of the year.

† This was Liu Xiu (r. 25–57 C.E.).

‡ As the following passage makes clear, the designation "demon" (gui) refers in
this text primarily to foreigners. The author exaggerates the contributions of foreigners, many of whom were brought in as mercenaries in the struggles that brought
down the Han. The events of more recent history (the fall of the Jin capital to the
Xiongnu in 317 and the partition of northern China by foreign "barbarians") most
likely color his account. Buddhism will bear much of the blame for all of this.

§ These are not the names of ethnic groups that existed at the time the author was
writing, but generic designations for the "barbarians" on the peripheries of the Central Kingdom. Though these names may once have referred to specific peoples, the
graphs adopted to write them are derogatory.

‖ The Luminous Thearch is Liu Zhuang (r. 57–75 C.E.). His "dream of the golden
giant" is part of the legend of the introduction of Buddhism into China. See Zürcher,
Buddhist Conquest, pp. 22–23. As can be seen here, the notion that the Han
emperor had actually "invited" Buddhism into China served not only early Buddhist
propagandists, but Daoist polemicists as well.

interpreted this dream to mean that this was the Perfected form of the Buddha, so they sent envoys into the Western Kingdoms to copy and bring back Buddhist scriptures. Then they built Buddhist stupas and temples. Buddhist teachings were thus disseminated throughout the Central Kingdom, and the Three Ways became intermingled.

As a result, the Han people became disorderly, mingling promiscuously with outsiders, and each person had his or her own particular object of veneration. Some placed their faith in the deviant and discarded the True; others offered supplication to demonic [i.e., foreign] spirits.

When human worship is excessive and misguided here below, the pneumas of heaven flare up and become disorderly above. This causes the pneumas of heaven to become turbid and the people to lose their original perfection. As a result, during the time of the Conforming Thearch of the Han [r. 125–44], the Most High selected Celestial Court Commissioners to subdue the rule of the Six Heavens, to distinguish the true from the false, and to make manifest the pneumas of the higher Three Heavens. On the first day of the fifth month in the *renwu* year, the first year of the Han peace reign period [11 June 142 C.E.], Lord Lao met with the Daoist Zhang Daoling in a stone chamber on Mount Quting in the Commandery of Shu.[10] Lord Lao, in his role as the Newly Emerged Most High, brought Zhang to visit him at the Great Parish on Mount Kunlun.*

The Most High announced to him: "The people of this generation do not hold in awe the True and the Correct, but fear [only] the deviant and demonic. Thus I have proclaimed myself the Newly Emerged Lord Lao."†

---

* The mythical Mount Kunlun was held since early times to be the paradisial residence of the goddess Queen Mother of the West, located in the far western reaches of the world. In the *Xiang'er* commentary (lines 105–13) we saw that Mount Kunlun was where the Dao concentrated its pneumas as the Most High Lord Lao. The "parish" (or "administrative seat") created there by Lord Lao was the model for the twenty-four parishes that Zhang Daoling was to establish in Sichuan. An alternate name for this exalted parish is the "Grand Mystic Metropolis," a phrase that appears later in the text.

† The *Admonitions* quotes Lord Lao's words of investiture similarly: "Thus did the Dao cause heaven to bestow its pneuma, called the 'newly emerged Lord Lao,' to rule the people, saying, 'What are demons that the people should only fear them and not place faith in the Dao?'" *HY* 788, 14a.

6a   He forthwith honored Zhang as the "Master of Three Heavens of the Correct and Unified Pneumas of the Grand Mystic Metropolis" and entrusted to him the Way of the Covenanted Authority of Correct Unity, to govern in the name of the Newly Emerged Lord Lao. In doing so, Lord Lao abrogated all authority of the age of the Six Heavens with its Three Ways.

Zhang was to stabilize and correct the Three Heavens, eradicating the frivolous and returning the people to simplicity and truth. [For this purpose,] he received the true scriptures of the Most High and established regulations and ordinances.

After sixteen years had elapsed, in the *dingyou* year, the third year of the Eternal Longevity reign period [157], Zhang went to the court of the Han thearch as subject and made a covenant with the thearch sealed with the blood of a white horse and with an iron tally inscribed in cinnabar as verification.* This covenant was made by the two together before the Three Offices of Heaven, Earth, and Water and before the General of the Year Star [Jupiter]. Both vowed that they would eternally employ the correct law of the Three Heavens and not proscribe the people of heaven. The people were not to wantonly carry out improper sacrifice to the demons or spirits belonging to other groups. This was to deprive demons of sacrificial sustenance.

[Further, according to the covenant,] Masters are not to accept money or in any other way illicitly steal from the people. They are to cure the ill and may not drink alcohol or eat meat. The faithful among the people are to sacrifice only on the five propitious *la* days of the year to the primogenitor and ancestors, male and female, of their own family and in the second and the eighth months to the god

6b   of the soil and the god of the stove.† Everything not emanating from the correct law of the Three Heavens—that is, the true way of the various heavens—is [a manifestation of] stale pneumas.

Those afflicted with illness who are above the age of seven—that is, the age of cognition—are to personally seek forgiveness for their transgressions and to employ all proper offerings, protocols, peti-

---

* This event is not recorded in the histories and is almost certainly fabrication.
† On the five *la* days and the other authorized sacrifices, see Stein, "Religious Taoism," pp. 68–71.

tions, and talismans.[11] For even long-standing diseases or difficult maladies that physicians cannot cure, one need only take refuge in the law and confess in order to be immediately cured.

Zhang Daoling established twenty-four parishes, placing male and female officers called Libationers to head them and to take charge of the converted populace of the true law of the Three Heavens. They were to receive families into the faith by means of a pledge of five pecks of rice. The converted numbered ten thousand families in a hundred days. The people came in masses, like clouds.

Zhang made statutory articles and petitions in ten thousand copies. He entrusted these to his son and grandson, who succeeded him as masters to the kingdom. Once the affairs of the law were settled and the division between humans and demons safely delineated, Zhang rose up in broad daylight to take up the position of Celestial Master in the heavens.* The Celestial Master's son, Zhang Heng, as well as his grandson, Zhang Lu, together with their wives, achieved liberation from the corpse and ascended into heaven. Thus there are three Masters and three Ladies.†

After the three Masters ascended, the techniques of the Way were transmitted by the Libationers of the various parishes.‡

Those who received transmission were to kneel to accept the   7a
scriptural writings and [having copied them] do obeisance as they returned the originals. They were to make certain that these were indeed the true laws of the Three Heavens. But most people did not act in this fashion. If they happened to obtain a single scroll of scripture, they immediately said that it was "the scripture of the Dao" and then transmitted it to others. Sometimes the book contained stale matters of the old Six Heavens. In this way, things

---

* To "rise up to heaven in broad daylight," without dying, is a stock phrase of Daoist hagiographies.

† Only the names of the first two of the Celestial Masters' spouses are known: Lady Sun and Lady Lu, respectively. See Chen Guofu, *Daozang yuanliu kao*, p. 100. Cedzich ("Das Ritual der Himmelsmeister") has found that the three Ladies were invoked together with the three Masters in early Celestial Master ritual.

‡ It is significant that Daoists of this time regarded succession to the title "Celestial Master" to have been intended only for the three Zhangs. As we have seen in the case of the *Admonitions*, this may not have been the original intent. By Tang times, a continuous lineage of Celestial Masters had been reconstructed.

became confused, and, since these texts have been employed for a long time now, it is difficult to distinguish them from the scriptures of the three Masters.

The Celestial Master received the true law of the Three Heavens, the way of the Covenant of Correct Unity of the Most High. This he entrusted to his son and grandson, who [both] inherited the title Master to the Kingdom, saying that this [teaching] should endure forever.* How is it right that this way should become intermingled and confused? But not much time has passed, and already old matters of the Six Heavens have become gradually intermingled. The descendants of the Masters have faded into powerless obscurity, the populace mix up their parishes, and Libationers support one another in revering deviant ways, in each case calling it "true and correct." What absurdity!

Today, though there are some who revere the "Way of Five Pecks of Rice," there are yet others who uphold the "Way of Banners and Flowers," which is merely Buddhism. All of these [deviant ways] are old matters of the Six Heavens. All have been abolished!

In addition, there are those who practice the "Way of Clear Water."† This is also not a correct way. They say that the Celestial Master had a slave who was illiterate and thus could not be converted by means of texts. When the Celestial Master was just about to ascend to heaven, he took pity on him for his reverence. So he ordered the issue of a well of water for him to use in healing illness and contagious disease. The water of this well was not to be used for

7b

---

* "Master to the Kingdom" is in fact the title claimed by the pseudo–Zhang Lu in the *Admonitions*. (See HY 788, 18a.) It is given added force here by the preceding description of the way in which Laozi himself repeatedly appeared as "Master to the Kingdom." The appearance of the Dao in human form was thus continued in the persons of the Celestial Masters.

† The "Way of Clear Water," which this text associates with the popular festival Qingming (the festival of "Clarity and Light," held in the middle of the second month, 105 days after the winter solstice), seems to have been a rather influential cult during this period in southeastern China, for it found adherents even in the imperial household. The *Biqiuni zhuan* [Biographies of Buddhist Nuns], composed early in the sixth century by Baochang, contains an account of a confrontation in 371 or 372 between a nun and a master of this sect who had followers among the emperor's family. (See T 2063, 50.936b.15 ff., and T 2122, 53.616b.5 ff., where the story is repeated.) The description given in the *Inner Explanations* seems to be the most complete surviving account of the practices of this sect.

any other purpose, such as bathing, drinking, or in food preparation. Thanks to the curative powers of this well of water, none who
touched it went unhealed. Its effects were instantaneous.

Then the slave returned bodily to Grand Darkness, and the water
in the well dried up.* The Celestial Master provided the water only
for his slave personally. Later people did not understand this and so
passed down a method of worship that they call the "Way of Clear
Water." On their day of vows and supplication, the festival of
Clarity and Light, they have no chambers of the Dao, no booths
for feasts of consecration, no petitions, no talismans, no rites of
offering—only a single urn of clear water, which they worship by
burning incense. They say that the Dao is in the water. This is all
false.

Those who revere the Dao without employing the five pecks of
rice cannot be considered adherents of the Way of the Covenanted
Authority of Correct Unity of the Three Heavens. The purpose of
the five pecks of rice is precisely to be offered to the Five Thearchs,
that the Thearchs might know the extent of the peoples' desire to
worship the Dao. The sagely join with the pneumas completely,
from beginning to end; thus they do not die.† The destinies of the
common people are joined to rice. Without rice and grain, people
would starve to death, so they take that which they value most and
offer it up to the mysterious and hidden. It is not that [the Five
Thearchs] actually desire this rice!

The High Thearch of the Han was a child of dragon seed.‡ He
entered officialdom as a functionary of the Sishui Neighborhood
office but straightaway began his rise to the position of thearch.
During the reign of the Cultured Thearch [180–157 B.C.E.], Laozi
descended to a spot on the banks of the Yellow River and so was
called the "Sire on the River." The Cultured Thearch sent riders to
inquire of him concerning the Way. Laozi bestowed upon them the
five-thousand character text on the Way and Its Power [i.e., the

8a

---

* On the Palace of Grand Darkness, see lines 227–30 of the *Xiang'er*.
† That is to say, sages "eat" the pneumas of the Dao, not grain.
‡ This is Liu Bang, usually referred to in historical texts as "the High Ancestor."
On his miraculous birth, see footnote * on p. 214.

Daode jing or *Laozi*] in two scrolls, an upper and a lower, and then departed.*

The Martial Thearch of the Han [r. 141–87 B.C.E.] desired to study the higher Dao and the methods of becoming a flying transcendent. As a result, the Most High dispatched Dongfang Shuo to assist the Han rule. Still, the Martial Thearch was unaware that Dongfang Shuo was a perfected person and so made him a minor official, treating him no differently than a mortal. The Queen Mother of the West and the Lady of the Upper Prime both descended in carriages to the Martial Thearch in hopes of completing his practice of the Dao, but the Martial Thearch could not be enlightened.† He was able to raise his gaze and thereby incite the beneficence of the spirits, to free himself of filth and impurity, but still he coveted the glories of this world. He continued to murder and to conduct military campaigns, with the result that there were bloody transgressions entangling him in the courts of the Three Offices. With disheveled hair [the aggrieved shades] proclaimed their innocence, stating their accusations to the ghostly tribunal. Further, [the thearch] was never able to still his sexual desires. As a result of all this, he never achieved the Dao and his physical form was returned to the Palace of Grand Darkness.‡

8b

When the Shining and Martial Thearch struggled with Wang Mang to achieve the rule, there was a disastrous flood of the Yellow River. The thearch's fate hung by a thread. At that time, the Most High worked wondrous transformations to aid him. In the sixth month, at the height of summer's heat, the Most High caused the

---

* This is the foundation legend of the Heshang Gong commentary to the *Laozi*. See Chan, *Two Visions of the Way*, pp. 90–95.

† The Martial Thearch's meeting with the Queen Mother is recounted in the *Han Wudi neizhuan* (HY 292), a Shangqing-inspired Daoist account of the emperor's meeting with the Perfected. For a translation and study of this text, see Schipper, *L'empereur Wou*, and, for a complete analysis of its debt to the Shangqing scriptures, Robinet, *La révélation du Shangqing*, vol. 1, pp. 229–31.

‡ This is the first clear indication we have seen of the Palace of Grand Darkness as an undesirable postmortem destination, contrasted with immediate ascent into the heavens. The Shangqing and Lingbao scriptures had largely replaced Grand Darkness, as a place where the bodies and souls of the dead were refined for extended life, with the Southern Palace. See Robinet, *La révélation du Shangqing*, vol. 1, p. 132; and Stephen R. Bokenkamp, "Death and Ascent in Ling-pao Taoism," *TR* 1.2 (1989), pp. 1–20.

waters of the Yellow River to turn to ice so that foot soldiers and cavalry might cross to aid the thearch in his distress.*

At the renewal of the Han dispensation, heaven bestowed the Charts of Response [to his virtue] and sweet dew fell in the courtyard. Perfected beings, mounted on phoenixes, appeared at the rites. The sun was circled with a nimbus; the three-legged [sun-] crow again appeared within its orb. Such numinous portents as the nine-tailed fox appeared in blazing glory.[12] Crowds of the sagely supported the thearch, and the Correct Dao aided him.

But after the time of the Shining and Martial Thearch, the Han house gradually declined. The Most High pitied them. That is why he drew to himself the great-great-grandchild of Zhang Liang, Daoling, to manifest the pneumas of the Dao and thereby aid the Han house.[†] The Most High caused Daoling to establish the great Way on Mount Mang, just north of Luoyang.[13] The thearch, as well as his princes, ministers, and officials, all pledged their allegiance to the Dao at this spot.

At that time, the correct pneumas were widely spread. Of all the years of the Han house, a total of 425 years, this was the time when the greatest number of people and citizens achieved the Dao.[14] But members of the Han ruling house were haughty and remiss and so were unable to ascend to the ineffable.[‡] As a result, the people obtained the Way from the Celestial Masters. Three generations— both husbands and wives, six persons in all—filled the position of the Three Masters. The three brothers, the Lords Mao, held the rank of Directors of Destinies.[§] Their unranked Transcendent disciples, from Wang Chang and Zhao Sheng on, were numbered in the hundreds—so numerous that I cannot name them one by one.[15]

Now the descendants of the Liu house embody the Dao. Although

9a

---

* This incident is reported in the *Song shu* (27:770) as a celestial sign that Liu Xiu was destined to gain the throne. In the official report of the miracle, however, there is no mention of any participation by Lord Lao.

† On Zhang Liang, see the *Admonitions*, HY 788, 14a.

‡ This likely refers primarily to Liu Che, the Martial Thearch of the Han, the emperor commonly mentioned in Daoist texts for his failure to heed the teachings of the Dao. (See pp. 8a–b of this text.)

§ On the three Lords Mao, patron saints of the Shangqing tradition, see endnote 34 to the introduction to this translation.

their link with the Way was interrupted, it now continues again. Heaven has bestowed upon them the Charts of Response, the thirty-two jade rings, and the ingot of gold—holy and auspicious signs from the Central Mountain [Mount Song]—in order to confirm their original surname.[16] The nine-tailed fox has approached. The Numinous Treasures [i.e., the Lingbao scriptures] have appeared in the world.[17] Sweet dews have fallen in the central courtyard. A three-horned ox was brought to court. The six bells revealed themselves.[18] The great beast and the paired elephants that appeared in the human world in response to ritual summons have devoured the terrestrial spirits of unofficial shrines.[19] In one stroke, heaven totally eradicates the useless and regulates the correct, sweeping away the stale pneumas [of the Six Heavens] by means of the Dao. Is this not a pledge of good faith from the Most High?

9b   The Song Thearch, as a member of the Liu clan, is a descendent of the Han house. This is a family whose fate is constantly linked with the Dao. That is why many persons within the kingdom of Song possess the Dao. During the Han, there was already a model for these events. Scholars cannot but exert themselves [to collect and analyze these precedents].

Now the three ways are but different branches extending from the same root. The Great Way of Inaction, the Great Way of the Pure Contract, and the Way of the Buddha—all three are equally methods of the Most High Lord Lao, though their teachings differ. All three find their source in the True Way.

Laozi is the lord of living transformation; Śakyāmuni is the lord of transformation by death. As a result, Laozi was born from his mother's left armpit and is lord of the left. The left is the side of yang breaths that govern the Azure Palace with its Registers of Life. Śakyāmuni was born from his mother's right armpit and is lord of the right.* The right is the side of yin breaths and the black records of the Registers of Death. In this respect the differences between the

---

* The story of the Buddha's birth from his mother's right side figures in one of the earliest Chinese biographies of the Buddha, translated by Zhi Qian between 222 and 229 C.E. (*T* 185, 3.473c.1–2.).

teachings of Laozi and Śakyāmuni are those between the laws of left and right.* The transforming influences of the left accord with the palace of the left, so that the pneumas of life cause the adept's body to rise and fly off in transcendence.† The transforming influences of the right accord with the palace of the right, so that the pneumas of death cause the adept to pass through oblivion and be reborn.‡ Buddhist dharma robes are entirely black. [Buddhists] are made to wear these black garments in order to model themselves on the breaths of yin and to represent the fact that their names are entered in the black records.

The Most High created these three Ways. Although their teach-   10a
ings and methods of transformation are distinct, each path in the end returns without distinction to the True Way. But, as I have stated, humans achieve their form through receipt of primal pneumas. One only makes it difficult for oneself when one repeatedly passes through destruction, undergoes transformation in the dark realms, and cycles through birth and death. Even though the transformation of the right is not so quick and easy as that of the palace of the left, is it not also good that they return to perfection through cycles of life and death?[20] Yet it is said that "the right is not so good

---

* The force of this statement depends on long-standing Chinese notions concerning the priority of left over right. As this passage makes clear, left is the side of yang, associated with light, life, and growth, whereas right is the side of yin, representing darkness, death, and decline. In court functions, for example, those officials standing to the left of the emperor outranked those to his right. On the Celestial Master concept of the tallies (or registers) of the books of life and death—left and right, respectively—see the *Xiang'er*, especially lines 325–28 and 519–21.

† That is to say, the body of the Daoist adept does not dissolve into its constituent parts at death. Whereas Indian Buddhism denies the existence of a permanent ego, Chinese Buddhists, at least through the fifth century C.E., invariably argued that it was the soul that separated from the body at death to be reborn in another form. On this issue, see Zürcher, *Buddhist Conquest*, pp. 11–12; and Walter Liebenthal, "The Immortality of the Soul in Chinese Thought," *Monumenta Nipponica* 8.1/2 (1952), pp. 327–97. Daoists, on the other hand, held to the traditional Chinese idea that life beyond the grave would be impossible if the constituents, both physical and material, of the self were permanently scattered. For more on the importance of this concept, see Bokenkamp, "Death and Ascent."

‡ "Pass through oblivion" translates *miedu*, an early Chinese Buddhist translation of the Sanskrit *nirvana*. Buddhist translators undoubtedly meant by the term something like "to be obliterated and pass [into nonexistence]," but Daoist writers of this period invariably take it as referring to rebirth.

as the left," and the scriptures state: "The true Way delights in life and abhors destruction."* That which pertains to long life is the Dao; that which pertains to death and destruction is not the Dao. "A dead prince is not worth a live rat."† As a result, the transformative teachings of the Sage cause people to have compassion toward all forms of life. Life is valuable. Those with hearts to hold this truth should memorize the *Five-Thousand Character Text*. This scripture leads one to maintain the Dao and to achieve a lengthy existence beyond both life and death. The ultimate source of the Dao resides in this scripture.

NOTES TO INNER EXPLANATIONS: TRANSLATION

1. The term "swelling and erosion" 勃蝕 generally describes the reciprocal actions of yin and yang in the cosmic cycle. When one increases, the other decreases proportionately. Here, though, the term refers specifically to the catastrophic end points in the cycle when one or the other is at its apex. A method of computing these cycles and the associated disaster years was developed during the Han and figures in a number of apocalyptic Daoist texts of the fourth and fifth centuries. See the *Han shu,* 21A: 980–86; and Bokenkamp, "Time after Time." The terminology used here seems to have been drawn from the Shangqing scripture known as the *Santian zhengfa jing* 三天正法經 [Scripture of the Correct Law of the Three Heavens], which has descriptions of both "swollen yang and eroded yin" (the small kalpa cycle) and its reverse, "eroded yang and swollen yin" (the large kalpa cycle). According to this text, the end of a small kalpa cycle occurs, for instance, when "the pneumas of heaven reach a culmination in grand yin and the pneumas of earth are depleted in grand yang. Yang is thus excited and swells, while yin is obstructed and so erodes. When yin and yang swell and erode like this, the pneumas of heaven and earth are overturned. . . . The ten thousand thearchs shift positions, the nine pneumas shift their cycles, sun and moon contract their orbits, and the dry land is inundated by the nine subterranean springs. . . . When this happens, calamities eradicate the seeds of life and only the good people survive." (Cited in *HY* 1026, 2:4b–5b, and *HY* 1130, 6:3b–4b.)

2. On the relation of essence and pneuma in Celestial Master ideology, see the section "Meditation and Perfection of the Body" in the introduction

---

* Many Daoist texts contain similar statements, but I have not been able to locate the source of this precise wording.

† For a reference to this proverb in an identical context, see the Admonitions, HY 788, 19a.

to the *Xiang'er*. For more on these terms, especially in medicine, see Harper, *Early Chinese Medical Literature*, and Shibata Kiyotsugu, "*Kanshi shihen ni okeru shin to dō*," *Nihon Chūgoku gakkai hō* 36 (1984), pp. 12–24.

3. "Dark and attenuated" 溟涬 and "vaporous and opaque" 鴻濛 render a pair of rhyming binoms with a rich history in Chinese cosmogonic speculation. The best description of the former is found in Zhang Heng's 張衡 (78–139) treatise "The Spiritual Charter" 靈憲: "Before the age of Grand Simplicity, it was dark and clear, mysterious and still. In this vast emptiness and profound tenebrosity, no images could be formed. There was only void. There was only nothingness. It was this way for a long time. This was called the 'dark and attenuated'" (*QSGSD*, 1:776). My translation of the term is drawn from a comparison of such occurrences with noncosmological uses of the term such as that found in *Huainan zi* (8:118), where it is descriptive of the seas and is glossed "boundless; without banks."

The term "vaporous and opaque" occurs earliest in an account in the *Huainan zi* (12:205) of a mysterious traveler who goes so far beyond the boundaries of the known world that "above there is no heaven and below no earth; nothing to hear, nothing to see." Compare the occurrence here with Wang Chong's 王充 (27–91) use of the two terms to describe the universe "before the pneumas had divided" in the "Discussing Heaven" chapter of his *Lunheng* (*LHJS*, 31:105).

4. The term "Grand Clarity" 太清 is found in the *Huainan zi* (see 2:22, 7:104, 7:107, and 8:113), where it refers to the unsullied condition of the nascent universe and states that it may be apprehended by the sage. In cosmological writings of the Han, the term "dark primordial" was already a way of describing the embryonic movements of the refined pneumas that would form the heavens (*Huainan zi*, 8:113), but here we need to distinguish two separate stages. In this text, the "mystic and the primal" denotes the first two stages in the movement of the Dao before it divides at creation. Through the mid-fourth-century history the *Huayang guozhi* (2:114–115), we know that the early Celestial Masters held that the revelations bestowed on Zhang Daoling originated in "Mystic and Primal [pneumas] of Grand Clarity." The deities named in the appended list, then, arise from these as yet undivided pneumas, hypostases of the pneumas that will be made available to humanity by the actions of the cosmic Laozi at creation. As the *Inner Explanations* states, this list of deities is commonly addressed in Celestial Master memorials to the celestial powers. Precisely the same formula occurs in a memorial discussed by Tao Hongjing (456–536) in *HY* 421, 3:8b. For further examples, see Chen Guofu, *Daozang yuanliu kao*, pp. 364–65; and endnote 11 to the introduction to this translation.

5. As this phrasing indicates, the "Six Heavens" here represent a world age and should not simply be equated with the six northern palaces of Fengdu found in the Shangqing scriptures. Rather, the six palaces of Fengdu are the headquarters of the Six Heavens, whose control over the cosmos

has now come to an end. This is confirmed in the Shangqing and Lingbao scriptures, both of which seem to have adopted—and perhaps embellished—this Celestial Master idea. The *Shangqing Santian zhengfa jing* (cited in *HY* 1130, 6:2b–4b, and *HY* 1026, 2:4b–8a) states that at the end of the large kalpa cycle, the "cycle of the Six Heavens will come to an end." Similar phrasing occurs in the Lingbao *Chishu yupian* (*HY* 22, 1:6b.6–7). As Robinet (*La révélation du Shangqing*, vol. 2, pp. 87–91) has noted, the Celestial Master conception of the Six Heavens was influenced by the method of calculating disaster years, known as *yangjiu bailiu* 陽九百六, associated with Liu Xin's 劉歆 *Santong* 三統 calendar. (See *Han shu*, 21A: 983–88; and Bokenkamp, "Time after Time.")

6. Kusuyama (*Rōshi densetsu*, pp. 349–72) and Seidel (*La divinisation de Lao-tseu*, pp. 65–67, 102–5) discuss these transformations of Laozi, providing variant forms of the names found in seven other texts. Our list approximates most closely that found in the *Shenxian zhuan*, attributed to Ge Hong 葛洪 (283–343). Compare these transformations of Laozi with the list of epiphanies of the Dao provided in the *Admonitions* (listed in the section "Lord Lao and the Dao" in the introduction to the *Admonitions*).

7. The *"Upper, Lower, and Central Scripture* in one scroll" survives in the Daoist canon as a two-chapter work listing the deities of the macrocosm and microcosm, titled simply *The Central Scripture of the Most High Lord Lao* (*HY* 1026, chaps. 18–19; *HY* 1160). The title given here apparently stems from the fact that the text was originally divided into three rolls (*pian*). The *HY* 1026 version of the text contains in its final section the injunction of Laozi to those receiving the text, which includes the words: "From time to time I myself come to inspect these three rolls"—to which a note has been added: "[T]he three rolls are the upper, lower, and central scripture" (*HY* 1026, 19:21a). The *HY* 1160 version of this passage has been amended to "these two rolls, the upper and lower [parts of] the Central Scripture" (*HY* 1160, 2:21a). That the *HY* 1026 passage should be given priority is indicated by *HY* 1228, which states: "Of old, Yinzi first received [this scripture from Laozi]. The *Central Scripture* in three rolls in large characters is found in the Taiqing division of the canon. It is an appendage to the two scrolls, an upper and a lower [of the *Daode jing*, found in the Taixuan section]." Kusuyama (*Rōshi densetsu*, p. 141) punctuates this passage somewhat differently, but, taken in the context in which it appears, the passage clearly deals with an original division of the *Central Scripture* into three parts.

8. The name "Mijia" 彌加, which Laozi assumes in Kashmir, is puzzling. I have been unable to find it in any of the *hua hu* ("conversion of the Barbarian") fragments that have come down to us. The term normally transliterates the Sanskrit *megha* (cloud), which is the name of a bodhisattva, but not one who is normally associated with the Buddha's birth. The scripture featuring this bodhisattva, *T* 388, translated by Zhu Fonian 竺佛念 c. 375, has not survived intact, but there is no reason to believe that it was involved

in the *hua hu* debates. One is tempted to read "the Mahāsattva [大人＝大士] Mahākāśyapa [彌加＝摩訶迦葉]," since this venerable elder and disciple of the Buddha figures as a transformation of Laozi in several Daoist and Buddhist versions of the story. This speculation, though, seems unlikely, since (1) we have no other examples of the idea that Laozi became the *previous incarnation* of Mahākāśyapa, which would have to be the case here; and (2) the process of textual corruption by which one name could become the other is nigh inconceivable.

9. Reading *shi* 十 for *qian* 千 (a common copyist's error). The correct number is given in citations of the *Huahu jing,* on one of the versions of which this passage is undoubtedly based. (See *HY* 1131, 9:7b.3.)

10. The name of the mountain upon which Laozi appeared to Zhang is usually given as Heming ("Crane-Call"), although other texts do give the name Quting 渠亭 ("Moated Pavilion"). Though later gazetteers do not equate the two mountains, they do give the same location—present-day Dayi County of Sichuan Province. In fact, Crane-Call Mountain is formed of two summits with a rounded hill between them. According to popular legend, the two summits are the wings of the crane, and the rounded hill, the crane's head. The first temple one would reach upon arriving at the mountain was the rounded hill, which is encircled by two streams. This prominent terrain feature may account for the name "Moated Pavilion."

11. On the various initiation rites of the Celestial Masters, see Schipper, "The Taoist Body"; and Schipper, *The Taoist Body,* pp. 63–67. For a Celestial Master petition, see Peter Nickerson's translation of the *Great Petition for Sepulchral Plaints* elsewhere in this volume.

12. Some of these auspicious signs, though of course not attributed to the assistance of the Dao, are mentioned in the "Treatise on Portents" of the *Song shu*—the phoenixes (riderless) at 27:770 and 28:794, and the sweet dew at 28:813-4. The "Charts of Response" refers to the "Tally of Red's Conquest" 赤伏符 that was presented to the emperor (27:770). The rest seem to be fabricated or derived from sources now lost, but they are commonplace signs of celestial approbation.

13. Although Mount Mang, site of imperial graves since the Han period, is listed among the twenty-four parishes in the earliest accounts that have come down to us, it is unlikely to have been one of the original parishes of Zhang Daoling. It is probable that it was added after the diaspora of the Hanzhong community. (For references, see *HY* 1130, 23a ff.; *HY* 1131, 7:1a–15a; and *HY* 599, 11a–15a.)

14. The dates traditionally given for the Han are 206 B.C.E. to 220 C.E., but since the last Han emperor was forced to abdicate in 220, that year is counted as the first of the Wei Kingdom rather than the last year of the Han in Chinese histories. The count given here is thus precise.

15. Wang Chang 王長 and Zhao Sheng 趙昇 were early disciples of the first Celestial Master, Zhang Daoling. The surviving fragments of hagiography concerning these two figures seem all to stem from the *Shenxian*

zhuan. (The relevant passages are cited in *HY* 596, 2:14a, and *HY* 1026, 109:19b–21a.) There is also an extant scripture that claims to contain the "oral instructions" bestowed on Zhao Sheng by Zhang Daoling (*HY* 1263).

16. The text reads "twenty-two jade rings," but since this number is to "confirm the original surname" of the Liu clan, and since the founder of the Liu-Song dynasty, Liu Yu, was held to be a descendant in the thirty-second generation of the founder of the Han, thirty-two (reported in the texts listed below) is undoubtedly the correct number. The story of the discovery of the jade rings and ingots of gold from beneath a stone ritual platform in the temple of Mount Song (in modern Henan Province) is recounted in the "Treatise on Portents" of the *Song shu* (27:784), where it is followed by a decipherment of the portent, and in the *Gaoseng zhuan* (*T* 2059, 50.7:368c.2 ff.). The location of the treasure was said to have been pointed out to an elderly monk by the spirit of Mount Song. Before this monk died, he informed a disciple, who passed the information on to the monk Huiyi 慧義 (or Fayi 法義; 372–444). Huiyi, sent to find the portents, discovered the rings and the gold below the altar to the god of Mount Song in 417. The inclusion of this portent provides a *terminus a quo* of 417 for the composition of this text.

17. This seems to refer not to the general category of spiritual treasures, since all of these prophecies are quite specific, but to the publication of the Lingbao ("Numinous Treasure") scriptures. These scriptures give the date of their release in the human world as a *gengzi* year, when their timely appearance will help to settle the natural and manmade disasters of a time of immense turmoil. The year in question seems to be 400 C.E. See Bokenkamp, "Sources," pp. 438–448, and, on the concept of celestially bestowed imperial treasures and the ways in which Daoist texts came to be regarded as such, Max Kaltenmark, "*Ling-pao*—note sur un terme du taoïsme religieux," in *Mélanges publiés par l'Institut des Hautes Études Chinoises* (Paris: Collège de France, 1968), vol. 2, pp. 559–88; and Seidel, "Imperial Treasures," pp. 291–371.

18. The text reads 靈形, "holy forms," but the parallel syntax of these phrases requires that the first graph be a verb. I thus take *ling* 靈 to be a scribal error for the similar graph *lu* 露, "to reveal." The six bells, inscribed with 160 "archaic graphs," were discovered on Mount Huo (near present-day Nan'an County, Fujian Province). See the *Song shu*, 27:784, and, for the location of Mount Huo, Strickmann, "T'ao Hung-ching," p. 152 n. 85. The sweet dew that fell, auguring the birth of Liu Yu, is also mentioned in the *Song shu* (27:783). I have been unable to locate contemporary references to the miraculous appearances of the "three-horned ox" or the "nine-tailed fox."

19. R. A. Stein ("Religious Taoism," p. 64), complaining that this section of the text is "confused," has explicated the phrase 食房廟之祇 as meaning "who feed on the offerings of the little temples (of the popular cults)." Given the goals of his article—analysis of the Daoist-inspired

repression of local cults to deities who "feed" on bloody sacrifice—it is not difficult to see how he arrived at this reading. In addition to reading the verb *shi* 食, "to devour," in line with other passages he analyzed, his understanding hinges on the word *chi* 祇, which means "chthonian deities" and, by extension, sacrifices to such deities. Still, coming at the end of a list of auspicious signs, it is difficult to see how this passage might "contrast ... the Three Zhangs and the Three Mao brothers on the side of Good with the divinities on the side of Evil." Rather, the Zhangs and the Maos are clearly examples of how the Dao was upheld by commoners during the Han, whereas *this* passage somehow relates events surrounding the Dao's reestablishment of imperial rule. I think it makes better sense to accept the passage as it stands. I would suggest that the "great beast and paired elephants," whatever they might have been in reality, correspond to that class of demons who, converted to the service of the Dao, are regularly employed as the most potent defense against pernicious forces. (See, for example, *HY* 335, chap. 1, which dates to the beginning of the Song period.) They are here clearly an auspicious omen, since the words used to portray their arrival—*lai yi* 來儀, "to arrive during ritual" (or "in auspicious response"; see David R. Knechtges, *Wen Xuan—or—Selections of Refined Literature, by Xiao Tong* [Princeton, N.J.: Princeton University Press, 1982–1987], vol. 1, p. 460, line 554)—are used in the passage preceding this one to describe the advent of the spirit-phoenix, a portent attending the founding of the Han. This reading has the advantage of providing for a smooth transition between the preceding list of portents and the following description of the rectifying force of the Dao. These beasts (or beast, since the term might be construed "that great beast, the doubled [i.e., two-headed?] elephant"), then, provide one of the ways in which the "stale pneumas are swept away."

20. For a discussion of this passage in the context of Buddhist and Daoist views of the stages of transcendence, see Bokenkamp, "Stages of Transcendence."

The Great Petition
for Sepulchral Plaints

Peter Nickerson

INTRODUCTION

As indicated at the outset by its title, the *Great Petition for Sepulchral Plaints* [*Da zhong song zhang;* hereafter *Great Petition*) brings together two elements that were central to the early Daoist religion.[1] First, our text is a "petition" (*zhang*); this immediately identifies it as part of the larger trend toward the bureaucratization of ritual practice that was the essence of the Celestial Master tradition (at least as that tradition was understood by its proponents in the early medieval period, like Lu Xiujing [406–477] and the author of the *Inner Explanations*). Petitions were documents, in form based on state officials' communications to the monarch, that were ritually dispatched by Daoist priests on behalf of their parishioners to celestial officials, especially for purposes of healing illness. Our text is a model petition, one that—with appropriate names, dates, and other particulars inserted—would have been used by priests in their day-to-day operations.

Second, the title refers to "sepulchral plaints," lawsuits initiated by aggrieved spirits of the dead in the courts of the underworld, which could also implicate the living (especially the living kin of the accused) and punish them with illness. This of course brings even closer to the fore the influence of bureaucratic styles of organization on religious ideology and practice: morality, judgment, and illness—all (on one level at least; we will see that the situation is somewhat more complicated) are understood in terms of the Chinese state's legal codes and judicial and penal systems. More surprisingly, perhaps, given that Daoism is often portrayed as a religion whose primary concern is the attainment of immortality, the "sepulchral" component of the title has especially great import: the Great Petition was to be used to combat the ill effects on the living of sepulchral plaints and constitutes just one of many examples of the use of Daoist ritual documents to handle the dangers posed by death. The tomb itself was a locus of intense anxiety about the dead, and the bureaucratization of Chinese religion, of which Daoism is perhaps the most developed example, went hand in hand with an increase in the intensity of the attention that was paid to the tomb.

Before dealing with these larger issues, something should be said about the ritual in which the Great Petition was employed and about the beliefs that provided the basis for the attribution of disease and other misfortunes to sepulchral plaints. Then follows a brief account of the date and provenance of our text and of Master Red-pine's Almanac of Petitions (Chisong zi zhang li [HY 615]), where the Great Petition may be found. Finally, this introduction concludes with an examination of the complex of ideas about death and the tomb that underlies the Great Petition and the multiple strands of historical influence that contributed to that complex. This will allow us better to assess what the text says about the place of early Daoism in the history of Chinese mortuary ideology and practice. We will find that when the bureaucratic exterior of Daoist ritual and ideology is removed, the roots of Daoism in popular traditions, especially

those of exorcistic ritual performances at the grave, become strikingly visible. Revealing the popular roots of the Daoist religion will
also make it possible to show how early Daoism embodied fundamentally new ideas about the tomb, death, and salvation.

Sending Up Petitions

The ritual of sending documents to the gods was essential to the
Way of the Celestial Masters. According to an early commentary on
the *Record of the Three Kingdoms,* the lowest-ranking members of
the Celestial Master priestly hierarchy

> were responsible for praying for the sick. The ritual of prayer was that
> the sick person's name was written down, along with a statement of
> confession of his or her sins. Three sets were made: one was sent up to
> heaven and was placed on a mountain; one was buried in the earth; and
> one was sunk in the water. These were called "handwritten documents
> of the Three Offices" [the three offices being those of Heaven, Earth, and
> Water].[2]

By the time the *Great Petition* had reached something like its
present form, perhaps the sixth century, this rite had become greatly
elaborated. Medieval texts give instructions of some precision for
carrying it out.[3]

Petitions were always to be dispatched from the priest's *jingshe*
(also known as *jingshi* or *qingshe*), the "cottage of quiescence," or
oratory, which was a small, detached wooden hut.[4] "Entering the
oratory," or the "audience in the oratory," was a rite preliminary to
the sending up of the petition and consisted primarily of prayers—
aloud with accompanying visualizations—to each of the four quarters and their resident deities. After each prayer the priest kowtowed
and slapped his own face several times, the standard Daoist gesture
of penitence. Tao Hongjing (456–536), who compiled a set of instructions on the petitioning ritual as part of his editorial work on
the Shangqing scriptures, adds that, if the situation was serious
enough, one might tear off one's turban and weep.[5]

The priest next proceeded to the writing of the petition, for which
procedure the ritual texts set out meticulous rules.[6] The content of
the petition should, according to Tao, be limited to three subjects:
first, one describes the supplicant's malady and its assumed cause;

then the supplicant repents of his or her sins; finally, the relevant celestial officials are requested to render aid. The priest could select the appropriate celestial functionaries by consulting the Celestial Masters' liturgical guide called the *Protocols of the Twelve Hundred Officials*.[7] Once the petition had been written, the priest was to check it over once silently, then send it off. This "sending" was in fact a multifaceted procedure, involving several distinct means of ensuring the arrival of the petition at the Celestial Bureaux (*tiancao*, the courts and offices of the celestial officials). First, the priest simply read the text aloud, sotto voce. Second, by means of visualization, the priest materialized several messenger spirits out of his own body—for example, the Envoy of the Merit Bureau—and called on them to deliver the petition to the proper celestial address.

Finally, following an additional rite, the Sealing of the Petition, the priest himself undertook through visualization the journey to the Celestial Bureaux. After paying respects to the Celestial Master, Zhang Daoling, the priest was conducted into the presence of the Grand Monad (*Tai yi*, the northern polar astral deity, also known as the Thearch, *Di*) and the Most High (the god Laozi) himself. When the written assent of the Most High had been appended to the petition, the messenger spirits were sent off to deliver the petition to the appropriate subordinate office. The priest again paid his respects to the Most High and the Celestial Master and then visualized his return to the oratory, now accompanied by the spirits of his own body that he had previously materialized. This completed the ritual of petitioning; following the ceremonies that brought the audience to an end, such as the Covering of the Incense Burner, the priest could leave the oratory.

Two additional aspects of the petitioning process deserve mention: the offerings (*gui*; elsewhere "pledges" [*xin*], or "pledge offerings" [*guixin*]) and the ceremony of thanksgiving, or Statement of Merit (*yan gong*). Early Daoists prohibited both sacrifices to the gods and payments to masters, but "pure" (i.e., vegetarian) offerings were permitted, and the ritual codes give long lists of the offerings to accompany each type of petition. In addition to grain, these might include oil, silk, and other objects useful to priests, such as brushes, ink, and paper, as well as more valuable items like gold rings and coins (normally in small numbers).[8] These offerings were tallied, and presumably displayed, when the initial petition was dispatched, but they were actually "offered" only subsequently, if the petition proved to be efficacious.[9] If the petition was successful, a Statement of Merit ceremony would be held, in which the celestial authorities would be asked to give promotions in the otherworldly hierarchy to the assisting divine officials, with the number of grades of promotion determined in accordance with the severity of the situation remedied.

As was noted earlier, from a certain perspective the bureaucratic aspects of early Daoism constituted merely a visible exterior that sometimes concealed Daoism's roots in popular, exorcistic ritual traditions. One might say as well, though, that bureaucratic forms acted as a kind of exoskeleton, providing structure for those more inchoate elements. Thus, although we will later try to peel back that bureaucratic veneer, it will be useful initially to mention the most juridical aspects of the petitioning ritual and of sepulchral plaints and the cosmology that underlay them.

Even through this brief description, one can sense the very strongly bureaucratic nature of the ritual. Some acts of purely religious inspiration (like the penitential face slapping) are involved, but in the main the priest acts much like a state official communicating in writing with his superiors. A standard term for petitioning is "to memorialize in a petition" (*zou zhang*), using the same verb, *zou*, as was used to refer to sending a memorial to an emperor; the word *zhang* itself was employed from Han times onward for written communications sent by officials to the monarch. Tao Hongjing explicitly identified the use of vermilion writing in Daoist petitions with its use in emergency communications dispatched by state officials. The priest even carries a *hu*, the same type of tablet as was borne by an official when he presented himself before his ruler.[10]

Sepulchral Plaints

This thoroughgoing bureaucratism did not end with ritual form, nor, cosmologically speaking, did it encompass merely the Celestial Bureaux, with their system of step-by-step promotions for their graded hierarchy of invisible functionaries. Chinese religion bureaucratized its subterrestrial regions at least as early as it had bureaucratized the celestial spheres. The germs of the mature Daoist cosmology of the other world are already present in the accounts and texts of the Celestial Masters. The Three Offices of Heaven, Earth, and Water have already been mentioned as destinations for the penitential healing documents dispatched by the early Libationers. The *Xiang'er* commentary's "Earth Offices"—to which ordinary people of limited merit became subject after they died—appear in the same passages as does the Grand Darkness (Taiyin), the "palace where those who have accumulated the Dao refine their forms," avoiding real death.[11]

In the cosmology of the Shangqing Daoists, all of these elements were further systematized and developed. Grand Darkness—also known as Mount Luofeng or Fengdu—itself became the realm of the chthonian administration of the Six Heavens, whose demon officials were deceased rulers and members of the official class. Fengdu was the seat of the Three Offices, the place where the dead were judged, and an archive for registers that recorded individuals' behavior and fates. As Buddhist influence was increasingly absorbed, the underworld offices came to be known as "earth-prisons" (*diyu*) or hells (and the punishments inflicted there became increasingly severe and gory).

In the *Great Petition*, reference is made to the "Twenty-four Prisons of Mount Tai," incorporating yet another strand of religious folklore: the belief that Mount Tai, the sacred mountain of the northeast, was the seat of the administration of the shades. As time progressed, the number and variety of Daoist underworld offices and prisons multiplied. For example, in another petition from *Master Redpine's Almanac,* one that is probably later than the *Great Petition,* release is sought for the soul of an ancestor from (among other places and powers) "the Twenty-four Prisons of Mount Tai, the Great Prison of the Central Capital, the Northern Prison of the Celestial Monad, the Prison of the Nine Pacifications of August Heaven, [and] the Three Officials of Heaven, Earth, and Water."[12]

The subterrestrial realm was more than a passive repository for priestly cosmological speculations. To the medieval Chinese, it was a real, working administration that wielded great influence over the world of the living. The sepulchral plaint, or "lawsuit of the tomb," is the clearest example of this mode of thinking. It was in the Three Offices or other such netherworld tribunals that the dead could place accusations against those, living or dead, who had injured them. Illness was commonly conceived as the product of these suits. Though the plaints arose in the world of the dead, they could implicate the living descendants of the accused (or the accuser), often owing to the application in the Administration of the Shades of the legal principle of the collective responsibility of close kin.[13] The word *kao*, "examination" or "investigation," as used in the context of sepulchral plaints inevitably connotes something like "inquisition"; it meant the simultaneous questioning and judicial torture common to many legal traditions. Once the ancestor was in the dock, the descendants began to suffer from demonic harassment and noxious vapors, or "demonic infusions" (*guizhu*).[14] The sepulchral plaint became the chief explanation of misfortune in Daoism. As Tao Hongjing stated: "Depletion, disaster, and misfortune in people's households always come from sepulchral plaints."[15]

In order to illustrate the way in which the notion of the sepulchral plaint influenced peoples' lives, we may turn to the Shangqing revelations. These esoteric, celestially dictated scriptures were transmitted to mortals through the mediation of the shadowy Yang Xi, who seems to have been a kind of house medium and spiritual adviser for the Xu family, in particular for Xu Mi and his son Hui. In addition to providing them with the latest in celestial revelation, Yang transmitted to his patrons advice on more mundane, and even inframundane, affairs.

Sometime during the years 363–365, Tao Kedou, the wife of Xu Mi, died. Her fate in the afterworld was a matter of great concern for Xu, Yang Xi, and his contacts in the other world. Not long after Kedou's death, Xu began suffering from both illness and nightmares, and other members of his family may have been affected as well. Xu's sufferings were explained by Yang Xi's informants as the product of a sepulchral plaint involving Xu's deceased uncle, Xu Chao (c. 268—c. 322).[16] During the night of the sixteenth day of the sixth month, probably of 366, Lord Mao the Youngest, the most junior of the three transcendent Mao brothers for whom Mao Shan was named, made the following declaration:[17]

> Xu Chao violently murdered Zhang Huanzhi of the Merit Bureau of Xinye Commandery. He also unjustly killed Qiu Longma. These men have both been waiting for an opportunity and recently have placed an

accusation before the Water Official [*Shuiguan,* the judge in the most feared of the Three Offices]. The Water Official has compelled Xu Dou [i.e., Tao Kedou] to return to her tomb, there to keep watch for a child in her household who is due to weaken.[18]

The Xus were suffering, according to Lord Mao, as a result of otherworldly retribution in response to murderous acts committed by a deceased member of the Xu clan: Xu Chao had killed two men, and these two had filed a sepulchral plaint before the Water Official. The punishment for the murders was to be exacted through the deceased wife, who, forced to return to her tomb, was from that location to select a child of the Xu family whose illness and death might requite the murders of the two plaintiffs. (One might speculate from this that a young Xu had already fallen ill.)

As Tao Hongjing commented, the Xu family had been so blessed as to have been vouchsafed the revelations of Shangqing, and yet had been continually troubled by sepulchral plaints; just imagine the need of ordinary folk to cope with troubles emanating from tombs and the magistracies of the dead! "Given this, to gain the heart of the principles of sending up petitions ought to be greatly advantageous," Tao writes.[19]

The sepulchral plaint, then, was an explanation for misfortune on which early Daoist priests and their clients relied with utmost frequency.[20] All the ills to which flesh was heir could be attributed to events in the courts of the dead. If oneself or a family member was ill, doubtless this was because a deceased ancestor had been dragged before the underworld magistrates. Naturally, the Daoist priest not only proffered this diagnosis, but also was able and willing to provide a cure. The sending up of petitions to the Celestial Bureaux was chief among these remedies. Thus one can appreciate the practical value that must have been ascribed to ritual texts such as our *Great Petition.*

The Text

Master Redpine's Almanac of Petitions, where the *Great Petition for Sepulchral Plaints* appears, contains in total some four scrolls (*juan* 3–6) of petitions; they represent models of the documents actually used by medieval Daoist priests during petitioning rituals: names and other particulars are left as "so-and-so" or "such-and-such," to be filled in appropriately on each ritual occasion. The petitions in the *Almanac* cover a variety of topics, from ending drought to taking up office, but the primary issue is death and demonic infestation.[21]

The *Almanac* in fact contains two petitions entitled *Great Petition for Sepulchral Plaints* (the title of the second is prefaced by the word *another* [*you*]), and these are the most extensive documents in that compilation. Both of the petitions make specific reference to and borrow extensively from Tao Hongjing's *Concealed Instructions for Ascent to Perfection*, making them products of the sixth century at the earliest. It is likely that the shorter *Great Petition*, translated here, dates from the sixth century, or not much later, and that the longer one dates from around the time of the final or near-final redaction of the almanac in the late Tang.[22]

Tao Hongjing had prescribed three essential matters for petitions to cover—description of the problem, repentance, and invocation of celestial aid—and our text conforms, roughly, to these prescriptions. The priest identifies himself, then describes, on behalf of the supplicant, his client, the miserable condition of the supplicant's household: its members' enterprises meet with no success, "their dwelling is unquiet" (perhaps a reference to nightmares or spectral phenomena), and, above all, they "have been burdened with successive illnesses." The passing of infectious diseases from one household member to another is of course a not unfamiliar phenomenon, but here the cause is assumed to be a sepulchral plaint—an infestation by demonic vapors, shared on the basis of common descent:

> One must suspect that, among [the supplicant's] ancestors to the seventh generation, or his forebears to the ninth, among his close relatives or his near kin, [there was someone who,] since when alive his or her trespasses were excessive, after death became subject to all manner of inquisitions and punishments.

The petition then goes on at length about the possible causes of the suit, an issue that will be explored in greater depth later on in this introduction.[23] Next, following the invocation of the authority of the teachings of the first Celestial Master, Zhang Daoling, a wide-ranging attack is made on the sources of demonic affliction, as the petition moves on to the third major section, the "Invitation of Officials" (Qing guan), which makes up the bulk of the text.

The petition purports to call upon a cadre of twenty-four celestial officials (although only twenty-three are named), giving the title of each, usually stating the number of civil and military subordinates attached to the particular official, and sometimes additionally naming the celestial mansion governed by the same.[24] The officials are requested to rectify any and all problems that might have resulted from the plaint, with each individual or group of functionaries assigned a more or less specific task—from dispelling the demons of tombs, to correcting problems caused by the failure of tomb construction to accord with the principles of geomancy or other mantic arts, to putting an end to the infernal lawsuit itself.

Finally, the petition alludes to the subsequent ceremony of the Statement of Merit, which would be held to recommend the promotion of the assisting celestial functionaries if they had carried out their tasks as requested. Then the promised pledge offerings are listed and the purpose of the petition is summarized, with the "etc., etc." indicating that the remainder of the petition is to follow the standard closing form, in which the priest's name and titles are given, the petition is addressed, and so forth.

Exorcism, Astro-Geomancy, and Bureaucracy: The Petition and Its Antecedents

Exorcism of the Tomb and the Stabilization of the Soul

The sepulchral plaint was an all-purpose explanation of misfortune, but how did it explain? Superficially, the issue would appear to be quite clear-cut: the suits were the products of the legal machinery of the underworld, set in motion by the complaints of the aggrieved dead. However, further examination of the *Great Petition* makes clear that the etiology of disease and other calamities assumed by the text is highly multivalent. The religious bureaucratization evident in the conception of the sepulchral plaint and its remedy through petitioning did not represent the abandonment of older learned and popular traditions connected with geomancy, exorcism, tomb construction, and funeral rites. Instead it provided an overarching, structuring framework that actually facilitated the perpetuation within early Daoism of pre-Daoist magico-religious practices. Thus both the meaning of the *Great Petition* and the significance of the sepulchral plaint as an explanatory device are closely tied to the issue of the relationship between early Daoism and certain antecedent religious traditions.

Graves in China (and of course elsewhere as well) have long been considered dangerous places. One of the earliest literary traces of the fears that surrounded death and burial is the description in the *Rites of Zhou* (*Zhou li*) of the *fangxiang shi,* or "exorcist":

> The duty of the *fangxiang shi* is to cover himself with a bearskin, [a mask having] four eyes of gold, a black upper garment, and a vermilion lower garment; grasping his halberd and brandishing his shield, he leads the hundred functionaries in the seasonal *Nuo* [the "Great Exorcism" held on the eve of the *La,* or New Year] in order to search through the rooms and drive out pestilences.[25]

In the Great Exorcism the *fangxiang* was assisted by 120 (or 240, 60, or 24) youths and 12 dancers in animal masks and costumes, and he invoked in an incantation 12 demon-animal servants to devour the specters due to be exorcised. But what is of greatest importance here is that the *fangxiang* also was said to have had duties during royal funerals. The *Rites of Zhou* continues:

> In great funerals he goes before the coffin. When the grave has been reached he enters the pit and with his halberd strikes the four sides in order to drive out the *fangliang* [demon].[26]

Elaborating on this, Ying Shao (c. 140–c. 206), in his *Critique of Customs,* explains: "[According to] the *Rites of Zhou,* the *fangxiang shi* enters the pit to drive away the *wangxiang.* The *wangxiang* likes to eat the liver and brain of the deceased."[27]

Both the *Rites of Zhou* and the *Critique of Customs* describe funeral rites that emphasize the danger to the corpse posed by demonic attack. The *fangliang* and the *wangxiang* are demons of earth and water (and in essence the same creature) that must be repelled by the exorcistic actions of the *fangxiang* and so prevented from consuming the deceased's remains. Anxiety over the corruption of the corpse was expressed in terms of the fear of hungry demons; thus exorcistic ritual became an appropriate remedy.

As implied by the multiplicity of regional designations that early authors equate with the *fangxiang,* such as *qitou*—the "griffin head" spirit-mask or the practitioner who wore it—there must have been many local traditions of exorcistic funeral performances. These involved masked players who danced, perhaps in a state of ecstatic possession—the animal masks and dancing certainly suggest shamanism—in order to drive away the demons that would eat the corpse. Moreover, at least by the time of the Latter Han, when Ying Shao wrote, the functions of the exorcist seem to have broadened to include the protection of the soul:

> The cloudsoul vapor of the deceased floats about. Therefore one makes a griffin head [mask] to preserve it.... Sometimes the griffin head is called "striking-the-pit." This is a special local term.[28]

Indeed, against this background, speculations that the famous "Summons of the Soul" ("Zhao hun") is a poetic reflection of a shamanic rite intended primarily to direct the soul of the dead into the tomb (rather than to revive the sick) would appear to make a great deal of sense.[29] The ministrations of the *qitou* and his colleagues might constitute a widely diffused form of shamanistic ritual aimed at protecting the potentially wandering spirit of the deceased by providing it with safe lodgings.

At the outset, there would seem to be very little to connect the ecstatic, oral performance of the *fangxiang,* who himself leaps into the tomb, with the reserved, clerical operations of the medieval Daoist priest, who accomplished his task by means of a written petition. However, the *fangxiang* provides a basic paradigm for exorcistic death ritual that was built upon by nearly all subsequent types of death ritual in the Chinese tradition, especially the Daoist ones. The literary form aside, the *Great Petition* implies a ritual dynamic that is none too different from the *fangxiang*'s descent into the grave pit. The major part of the *Great Petition* is made up of the "Invitation of Officials": just as the *fangxiang* in the Great Exorcism invoked his spirit assistants to drive away the noxious influences, just as he drove off the demons that lurked in the grave, so the priest who used the *Great Petition* called down invisible, allied powers in order to disperse all manner of demons connected with the tomb. Such requests for assistance inevitably end with exorcistic commands along the lines of "Annihilate them all!"[30] And just as the *qitou* sought to stabilize the soul and keep it from wandering, so the priest (as we will see in detail in the final section of this introduction) attempted to establish the soul peacefully in the next world, so that it would not want, or be able, to trouble the living.

Thus there was much continuity between the funeral exorcisms of archaic ritualists like the *fangxiang* and *qitou* and the mortuary and therapeutic practices of medieval Daoist priests. Other elements, though, were not present in the archaic rites. Chief among these is, first, the incorporation within the Daoist petitions of much of the language and concepts of astro-geomancy and astro-hemerology— the divinatory sciences of, respectively, the positioning of houses and tombs and the choosing of days and times for various activities, as governed by the movements of the stars and the directional grid of the earth's energies. And second, there is the issue of morality: the dead might encounter difficulties in the beyond, not simply from corpse-eating demons or the perils of wandering without a home, but also owing to punishments for misdeeds committed while living. Finally, there is the thoroughgoing bureaucratization of ritual, discussed earlier. All of these features had been germinally, and in some cases substantially, developed in Chinese religion prior to the Way of the Celestial Masters.

"Prohibitions and Taboos"

Worries about death that are expressed through the astro-geomantic aspects of burial are especially pronounced in the *Great Petition*. These anxieties are in turn rooted in a more basic fear: the act of digging deep into the earth, as required for the construction of tombs, was thought to disturb the spirits of the earth and bring their anger down upon the living. The operative phrase was *fan tu,* "offending the soil," or *fan tu jin,* "offending the prohibitions of the soil." Wang Chong (27–91), recording the customs of the southeast China of his own day, notes:

> When the people of today have completed the work of repairing dwellings, or of [otherwise] piercing the earth and digging into the soil, they disperse and propitiate the spirits of the soil.[31] This is called "dispersing the soil." They make a human figurine to represent a demonic being, and have a shaman [*wu,* "spirit-medium"] make an invocation. After an offering has been made, their hearts rejoice and their thoughts are happy,

and they say that the spirits have been exorcised and propitiated, and that the misfortune has been gotten rid of.[32]

According to a Jin work, *Family Records of the Jiang Clan,* there was a taboo on digging into the soil more than three feet, but the taboo applied only "in [certain] sectors in accordance with the four seasons."[33] Thus, beyond the basic worry about disturbing the earth by digging, astro-geomancy (determination of the "sectors" in which digging would or would not be appropriate), as further influenced by hemerology and calendrics (since such calculations would vary in each of "the four seasons," or even from day to day), played a central role in early beliefs about the earth and its violation. All these notions came under the more general category of "prohibitions and taboos" (*jin ji*). Besides construction, these governed travel, marriage, sacrifice, and funerals—all kinds of disruptive or transitional events. For instance, if one held a funeral on the wrong day, or if the funeral procession proceeded in the wrong direction, one might "strike" or be "eaten" by Jupiter, also known as Great Year (Taisui), the most terrible of the baleful stars, and this could result in illness or even death in one's household.[34]

The *Great Petition* makes clear the substantial points in common between rituals aimed at appeasing or dispersing spirits offended by construction and rituals intended to ameliorate the condition of the dead in the afterlife (following the construction of the tomb). The *Great Petition* worries that an ancestor "in his or her burial has offended the establishing, breaking, ruling, or impoverishing influences of the twelve months, or the Eight Generals and the Six Opposites [all spirits representing astro-geomantic forces], thus violating the prohibitions and taboos." The *Great Petition* thus subsumed within itself the ritual purposes of the shamanistic exorcism for "dispersing the soil" that Wang Chong had described in the first century. In each case the aim of the ritual was to remove the offended spirits of the soil, the stars, and abstract concepts of space and time like the symbols of the sexagesimal cycle. The *Great Petition* covered worries relating to less technical geomantic faults as well:

Perhaps it is a plaint over burial on a spring, or over a funeral's having encroached on a god's temple. Perhaps it is a plaint over a grave having been dug into a cavern, or over a coffin having been damaged. Perhaps it is a plaint over old sepulchers lying atop one another, or over new sepulchers striking against one another.

Bureaucratization and Grave-Securing Writs

Parallel with the centralization and routinization of political administration that began during the Warring States period (i.e., around the fifth century B.C.E.), both the cosmology of the afterlife and the rites for dealing with it came increasingly to rest on bureaucratic premises. Tombs resembled more and more the houses of the living (or, in the case of rulers, palaces), and at the same time the afterworld domain in which the tomb was situated similarly began to be conceived along the lines of the newly emerging centrally administered state. The chthonian realm was overseen by a cadre of officials and thus was most appropriately communicated with through documents in bureaucratic format. It is for this reason that texts excavated from Warring States and Han tombs include memoranda transferring the deceased into the care of the underworld regime and grave-goods lists that do the same for the deceased's possessions.[35]

Religious bureaucratization reached perhaps its highest point before the Celestial Masters with the use in Latter Han funerary ritual of "grave-securing writs" (*zhen mu wen*). The texts were usually written on pottery jars, which may have contained some kind of medicinal substance (e.g., the "medicine for exemption from forced labor" in the writ discussed just below). They are phrased as orders from a supreme thearch, the Celestial Monarch, or the Yellow God, (Ruler) of the Northern Dipper[36]—or from the high god's representative, the Envoy of the Celestial Monarch—and they command the god's underworld subordinates: spirits of the tomb and the chthonian administration. The grave-securing writs announce the death and burial, and their greatest concern is to enforce a separation between the living and the dead, ensuring that the living will not be vexed by their ancestors or implicated in the crimes for which the deceased might come to be accused in the otherworldly tribunal.[37]

A typical example, from the year 174 C.E., was written on the occasion of the death and burial of one Zhang Shujing.[38] The writ is phrased as an announcement of the Envoy of the Celestial Monarch to an extensive chthonian pantheon, including "the Assistant of the Sepulcher, the Director of the Sepulcher, the Director of the Office that Rules Sepulchers, the Hostel Chief of the Gate of the Cloudsoul, ... the Assistant of the Mound, the Sire of the Tomb, the Subterrestrial Two Thousand Bushel Officials ... and the Squad Chiefs of Haoli." After the addressees are named, the Envoy states that the writ is to be issued "because the deceased, Zhang Shujing, had a barren fate and died young, and is due to return below and [enter] the mound and tomb." Then, after the invocation of the power of the Celestial Monarch, or "Yellow God"—who "rules over the registers of the living,[39] summons the cloudsouls and whitesouls, and rules over the records of the dead"[40]—the offerings dispatched to the underworld realm during the burial are listed: "medicine for exemption from forced labor, with the desire that there will be no dead among those of later generations; nine roots of ginseng from Shangdang,[41] with the desire that they be taken in replacement of the living; lead men, to be taken in replacement of the dead; and yellow beans and melon seeds, for the dead to take to pay the subterrestrial levies." Then the Envoy relays his final commands:

> Let the odium of the soil be driven off, with the desire that evil be kept from propagating. Once these orders have been transmitted, the civil servants of the earth shall be bound and are not to trouble the Zhang household again. Quickly, quickly, in accordance with the statutes and ordinances!

In this grave-securing writ, the bureaucratic features that had been developing in mortuary religion for centuries stand out in full relief. The underworld administration—the existence of which had been implied by some texts from Warring States and Former Han tombs—has become greatly developed, with many titles being drawn from state nomenclature ("Assistant" [cheng], "Director" [ling]), and some being closely based on Qin and especially Han government ("Two Thousand Bushel Officials" [er qian shi], a classification of officials based on the amount of their salary, which was calculated in grain; "Hostel Chief" [ting zhang], a minor, nonofficial local functionary). The underworld is administered in the same manner as the world of the living, with population registers, taxes, and corvée labor requirements (hence the desire to provide human figurines that can perform the labor in place of the deceased, as well as medicine that seems to have been intended somehow to prevent the survivors also from being called to serve in the underworld realm). The closing formula, "in accordance with the statutes and ordinances," is a standard phrase in Han official communications that indicates that the matter under discussion is subject to the provisions of the legal code and should be dealt with as prescribed therein. This may imply that some kind of actual written formulary served as the basis for the religion of the grave-securing writs; it is in any event a clear indication of the assimilation of ritual practice to state bureaucratic practice.[42]

Nonetheless, the ritual paradigm implied by the grave-securing writs remains closely linked to the popular, oral, and by all appearances nonbureaucratic rite of "dispersing the soil" that was described by Wang Chong. This is clear from the reference to the "odium of the soil" (*tu jiu*), which means principally the offense caused to the earth by the construction of the grave and the interment of the polluting corpse. Standing in the same tradition of mortuary exorcism as the *fangxiang,* the writ seeks to neutralize potentially hostile spirits of the tomb, though now they have become "civil servants of the earth" who are best controlled through written documents rather than oral spells and violent, exorcistic action (like the *fangxiang*'s striking of the sides of the grave pit).

The *Great Petition* in Historical Context

It is against this historical background that the *Great Petition* may be most profitably understood. Consider the passage from the "Invitation of Officials" section in which the spirit bureaucracy of the tomb is made subject to the command of the General of Assistance and Protection. Just like the grave-securing writ, the *Great Petition* names as recipients of celestial commands the "subterrestrial Two Thousand Bushel Officials," the "Assistant of the Mound," the "Sire of the Tomb," and so forth. These are charged with checking the noxious influences of the sepulcher, the agents of the illness stemming from the plaint. The petition has moved far from its initial emphasis on ancestral sin and collective punishment. The tomb and its geomancy are the focus of interest, and special attention is given to the various spirits of astro-geomancy, like the astral Eight Generals (whose number includes Great Year), that might have been disturbed by a geomantically incorrect burial. Sepulchral plaints have more to do with sepulchers than one might initially have thought: the siting and construction of the tombs themselves, and the astrological correlations thereof, are as much a source of worry as is the moral behavior of their occupants.[43]

Finally, the passage ends on a theme typical of pre-Daoist exorcism and especially of the grave-securing writs: the separation of living and dead. The religious world of the late-Han grave-securing writs—orders issued in the format of official state communications by a celestial monarch to an underworld pantheon commanding the "release" (*jie*) of the deceased, and the dispersion (also *jie*) of the demons of the tomb—lived on in the mortuary and therapeutic rituals of medieval Daoism.[44] The core procedure remained the same: the invocation of the power of a heavenly ruler in order to effect the installation of the deceased securely in the afterlife, free from punishment or demonic harassment. The accomplishment of this goal would in turn prevent the return of the wandering spirit to vex the living. "Let living and dead take separate paths, a myriad *li* apart from one another," stated a grave-securing writ of 133 C.E. "Turn calamities into blessings, so that life and death, dark and light, do not interfere with one another," requests our *Great Petition,* while the longer version echoes the grave-securing writs even more closely: "[L]et men and demons take separate paths, and living and dead be kept apart."[45] To the famous dictum of classical mortuary ritual— "O Soul, come back!"—must be added another and perhaps more urgent cry: "O Soul, *do not* come back!"[46]

The development of the notion of the sepulchral plaint was in many ways simply an elaboration of the very ancient theme of the postmortem settlement of scores by the aggrieved dead.[47] Instead of returning in person to gain vengeance, the wronged party relied on the legal institutions of the afterworld. Still, as was the case in the story of Xu Mi's wife, Tao Kedou, who had been forced to reenter her tomb as the result of a sepulchral plaint, as described earlier, the impact on the living of underworld judicial proceedings might ultimately remain the return of the dangerous dead. Prior to Daoism, the indigenous solution to this problem had been (outside, perhaps, of the sacrificial cult of ancestors) rites of exorcism. Daoists transformed these into rites of salvation.[48]

Soteriology and the Transformation of the Tomb

As we have seen, the early Daoist religion did in some very significant ways represent a departure from the conception of death represented by the Han grave-securing writs (and by the older exorcistic
rites that preceded them). The *fangxiang*'s securing of the tomb, as
well as the use of grave-securing writs, implied that the tomb was to
be the final destination and dwelling place for the deceased. According to the ideas of some early Daoists, on the other hand, if the
deceased remained entirely present in the tomb, that meant that the
mortuary rites of transition had not been successful. For example,
Xu Mi's problems that had ensued after the death of Tao Kedou
began when she had been "compelled ... to return to her tomb."
Her salvation was declared by one of Yang Xi's invisible informants
to lie in unblocking the passage that led out of the tomb:

> Yesterday [I, Yang Xi] asked Marksman [of the Center] Xun all about
> the matter of the tomb. He said, "When extreme yin accumulates to the
> point of blockage, at length it passes into the grave, and then it causes
> the Officials of Earth to give rise to infusions and the spirit of the tomb
> [i.e., of the deceased] to become bogged down. Evil winds always arise
> and strike following upon these [causes]. Still, the clashing vapors are on
> the point of dispersing, and the sources of the inquisition are gradually
> subsiding. Securing and stopping up [the path of entry for the hostile
> forces—i.e., the tomb] is not yet urgent. It would be better to unblock
> the well of the wife's tomb so as to smooth the path to Yiqian.[49]

In this passage, Kedou remains "bogged down" in her tomb; her
presence there is simply another component of the complex that
includes pathogenic dampness, wind, and demonic infusions. Kedou
herself has become an unwilling agent of disease, as from the tomb
she "keeps watch for a child in her household who is due to
weaken."

Here Marksman Xun suggests a remedy based on the knowledge
that the plaint and its effects have already begun to subside, rendering more forceful apotropaic techniques—"securing and blocking"—unnecessary. "Securing" (*zhen*) is the same function as is fulfilled by the grave-securing writs of the Han; the reference is no
doubt to apotropaic measures of some kind, perhaps even to the
use of a petition for sepulchral plaints. Precisely what is meant by

"unblocking the well of the wife's tomb" is less clear. The "well" almost certainly refers to the "celestial well" (*tian jing*): the depictions of the constellations of the heavens on the ceiling of the tomb.[50] The means by which the celestial well was to be unblocked are not specified; one could speculate that some ritual action, or perhaps even a simple, customary sweeping of the grave, was indicated. In any event, the goal of the unblocking is quite unambiguous within the context of Shangqing cosmology. The Yiqian guan, the "Hostel of Mutation and Promotion," was one of four conservatories in the cavern-heavens beneath Mount Mao where virtuous Daoists who were not yet prepared for immediate transcendence could, following their departures from this world, begin a gradual progression toward that goal, reconstituting and refining their bodies in stages over the course of years. Thus, however Kedou's path was to be unblocked and "smoothed" (literally, "lubricated"), the desired end was her liberation from the tomb and, ultimately, transcendence. The final goal of the process was not only the resolution of the sepulchral plaint, but also the salvation of the person implicated in the plaint.

For the morally, mystically, and physiologically cultivated, the tomb became merely an empty symbol of a superficial spectacle, the appearance of coming-into-being and dying for one who in fact is destined for life everlasting. This might require further cycles of death and reincarnation, and in that case the tomb might be useful as "a place to which the refined form can return" to retrieve whatever bodily components might be necessary before it emerged again in life.[51] Nonetheless, essentially the tomb did not function as a dwelling place for the future transcendent, and thus it could not serve, as did tombs for ordinary people, to mark a true death.

For the non-immortals, too, "those 99.9 per cent of men who did die," as Anna Seidel put it, the tomb, and the earth in general, similarly became an undesirable residence. Although the Celestial Master petitions in the *Almanac* show some influence of the elaborate Shangqing and Lingbao soterio-physiologies and notions of selective reincarnation, the sentiments expressed in their petitions tend to be rather simple and direct: "Release the departed, forever away from the paths of darkness, in ascendant transfer to the Hall of Blessings, clothed and fed spontaneously, and unable to infuse and sue the living."[52]

Mortuary and therapeutic ritual continued to have at their core an awareness of the need for "release from the soil": for ensuring that the deceased and his or her survivors would not be held responsible for the intrusion of the polluting corpse (whether polluting by virtue of fleshly corruption or the corruption of sin) into the realm of the spirits of the soil, and that the dead would therefore be "unable to infuse and sue the living." That concept simply was broadened to fit new notions of morality and retribution. This was accomplished by means of the development of a soteriology that saw salvation as release from captivity in the tomb, or from punishment in the underworld—that is, release from harassment by the demons of the earth.

Salvation in early Daoism of course meant a number of other things as well. The transcendent exercises of Shangqing and the Buddhicized Lingbao notions of reincarnation, not to mention the Celestial Masters' own practice of sexual rites—all these very different "soteriological paradigms" contributed to the repertoire of ways in which salvation could be represented by early Daoists. Still, despite the process of the adaptation of liturgical documents to embrace new deities, new kinds of ritual, and new cosmologies, the overall soteriological conception remained an elaboration of the pre-Daoist rite of exorcising hostile earth spirits. And that conception continued to be embodied in the central ritual and healing texts of the Celestial Masters, whose ceremonies came to compose the core of the Daoist liturgical tradition. Ideas of pollution and exorcism did not disappear with the bureaucratization and moralization of death: instead, pollution and exorcism were themselves bureaucratized and moralized.

NOTES TO GREAT PETITION: INTRODUCTION

1. The text of the *Great Petition* appears in the *Chisong zi zhang li* 赤松子章曆 (*Master Redpine's Almanac of Petitions;* hereafter *Master Redpine's Almanac,* or simply the *Almanac*), HY 615, 5:19a–23b. The *Almanac* survives in a late recension, probably from the late Tang, but it contains much material that dates back to the early centuries of the Way of the Celestial Masters. See Cedzich, "Das Ritual," pp. 15–17; and Marc Kalinowski, "La littérature divinatoire dans le Daozang," *CEA* 5 (1989–1990), pp. 96–99. Seidel ("Post-Mortem Immortality, p. 233), though certainly aware

that the surviving redaction is late, believes the text to date from the third to fifth century. The petition treated here is followed in the *Almanac* by a longer petition, merely labeled "another" *Great Petition for Sepulchral Plaints* (HY 615, 5:23b–34b). In this introduction, *Great Petition*, unless otherwise noted, always refers to the shorter version. For the probable dates of these two petitions, see the section of the introduction titled "The Text."

2. *Sanguo zhi*, 8:265, commentary quoting the *Dian lüe*.

3. The petitioning ritual (referred to variously as *shang zhang* 上章, *bai* 拜 *zhang, zou* 奏 *zhang,* etc.) has been reconstructed in detail and analyzed in its historical context by Ursula-Angelika Cedzich ("Das Ritual"). Cedzich's chief source, and the principal source for the following outline of the petitioning ritual, is the greater part of the third *juan* (3:5b4–27a10) of the *Concealed Instructions for Ascent to Perfection* (HY 421). This text consists of fragments from the Shangqing revelations received by Yang Xi that later were collected, edited, and annotated by Tao Hongjing around the year 500. Only three scrolls of a much larger original *Concealed Instructions* survive today. The relevant portion of the third scroll of the extant *Concealed Instructions* is composed of part of the *Biography of Lady Wei* 魏夫人傳; this extract is presented as a revelation from the first Celestial Master, Zhang Daoling, to Lady Wei Huacun 魏華存 (251–334) during the period when she served as a Libationer of the Way of the Celestial Masters, and hence prior to her "liberation from the corpse" (*shijie* 尸解) and service as Yang Xi's transcendent instructor. (The *Biography* came to Yang Xi as a further revelation from another transcendent, one Fan Miao 范邈, or "Watch Officer Fan" 范中侯.)

4. Some instructions dictated that the oratory should be built with the doorway facing southeast and one small window opening to the south (HY 1010, 18:6b–7a). Lu Xiujing's directions regarding the oratory emphasize its sacred character: the oratory had to be kept entirely apart from profane things and activities. It was to be an independent structure, not linked to other rooms, and could contain only four items: an incense burner, an incense lamp, a petition table, and a scholar's knife. Lu criticizes the laxness of some Daoists of his day who, he says, even if they have an oratory, allow their domestic animals to wander through it, or use it for storing household items (HY 1119, 4b3–5a2). Those who had encountered any sort of pollution (from contiguity to death, childbirth, etc.) similarly were to stay away (HY 188, 19b4–5; HY 615, 2.23a–b).

5. HY 421, 3:9b9–10. Concerning Tao's instructions and their place in the Shangqing corpus, see the earlier note to this introduction concerning the *Concealed Instructions for Ascent to Perfection*.

6. First, incense was to be burned. The brush and ink used were to be reserved only for petitions (and perhaps the copying of scriptures); they certainly were not to be employed for worldly tasks (HY 421, 3:12b3–8). The text of the petition had to be treated with great care: it was to touch neither the surface of the petition table (a cloth was placed over the table), nor

one's own clothing, nor the ground. During the writing, the brush was not to be dipped in water or placed in one's mouth. Elaborate rules specified the size and spacing of characters on the page—words like *demon* and *death,* for instance, could not appear at the top of a line—and limits were placed on the number of corrections that could be made in the text: three characters only in the case of a short petition (*HY* 615, 2.3b–4a).

7. Much of the Celestial Master's revelation to Lady Wei is in effect an "improved" version of the *Protocols.* Tao Hongjing's commentary further reproduces extensive quotations from a manuscript copy Tao had of the *Protocols.* Tao's version is believed to date back to the early days of the Celestial Masters (Cedzich, "Das Ritual," pp. 35 ff.; Anna K. Seidel, "Early Taoist Ritual," *CEA* 4 [1988], p. 199). A *Scripture of the Law of Correct Unity, Section on Petitions and [Celestial] Officials* 正一法文章官品, which exists as an independent scripture in the Daoist Canon (*HY* 1208), is also based on the *Protocols.* Its date of compilation is very late, however (at least as late as the Song, as indicated by the observance of certain Song imperial name taboos [Cedzich, personal communication]), and the redaction is uncritical, repetitive, and generally sloppy.

8. It is clear from other scriptures, though, that priests and scriptural authors could and did inflate the requirements for pledge offerings to a much higher, and for the priests more profitable, level. This was especially the case with offerings required in connection with the transmission of scriptures and their registers. See Strickmann, "Mao-shan Revelations," pp. 15–30.

9. The pledge offerings ostensibly were provided to requite the clerks, soldiers, and other subordinate members of the invisible hierarchy who had rendered the supernatural assistance requested in the petition (see, e.g., *HY* 1010, 7:6b10–7a3). Daoist masters could take for their own use only three-tenths of the offerings, and they were to distribute the rest to recluses or the poor; they were threatened with serious otherworldly sanctions, reaching even to ancestors nine generations back, for taking more than their due (*HY* 463, 11.9b8–10a1; *HY* 421, 3:21a1–4).

10. *HY* 421, 3:7b10–8a1.

11. See the *Xiang'er,* lines 227–30.

12. *HY* 615, 6:11a–12b.

13. The family relationships involved in sepulchral plaints could be very complicated. In addition to the basic scenario in which deceased ancestors were called to account for wrongs they actually had committed during life, ancestors could be victims of malicious, baseless suits filed by others among the dead (in which case the descendants would suffer unjustly as well). On the other hand, living kin could be the objects of plaints (justified or unjustified) initiated by hostile ancestors. That ancestors could be innocent victims, guilty sinners, or malicious aggressors no doubt reflected ambiguous attitudes—products of medieval family life—toward one's senior kin, dead and living.

14. The word *zhu* means literally "to pour in." Demonically induced illness is also sometimes described using metaphors closer to the gaseous than the liquid (e.g., *gui qi* 鬼氣—demonic vapors or pneumas; *gui chui* 吹—demonic blowing), though still the connotation of the induction or pouring in of some noxious, flowing substance is retained. In his commentary on the *Zhen'gao* [*Declarations of the Perfected*], Tao Hongjing relates this anecdote: "Formerly, there was someone who became ill and lay on the ground. In his illness he saw a demon boring a hole through the wall and then using his hand as a tube and blowing through it. This is precisely a matter of 'demonic blowing'" (*HY* 1010, 15:9b4–5). On all matters related to sepulchral plaints and demonically induced illness, the work of Michel Strickmann (especially *Le taoïsme du Mao chan: Chronique d'une révélation* [Paris: Collège de France, Institut des Hautes Études Chinoises, 1981], pp. 144–69) should be consulted.

15. *HY* 421, 3:14b5.

16. See *HY* 1010, 20:7b4–7, for a brief biography of Xu Chao.

17. On the Mao brothers, see endnote 34 to the introduction to chapter 3.

18. *HY* 1010, 7:6a9–b1.

19. *HY* 421, 3:13a3–7.

20. Secular sources removed from the Daoist tradition likewise record instances in which members of the medieval upper classes—we are simply less well informed about what commoners were doing—resorted to Daoist priests to dispatch penitential healing petitions for them. Wang Xianzhi 王獻之 (344–388), son of the renowned calligrapher-aristocrat Wang Xizhi 羲之, was dangerously ill and had a petition sent in an attempt at a cure. It is reported that he had experienced difficulty with the penitential aspect of the rite, being unable to recall any grievous sins: he could think only of his divorce from his wife, Chi Daomao 郗道茂, as cause for regret. In another case, in the year 513 Shen Yue 沈約, author of the official history of the Liu-Song dynasty and then vice president of the Imperial Secretariat, believed himself to be ill owing to the vengeful spirit of the last emperor of the preceding dynasty (Emperor He 和 of the Southern Qi), whose forced suicide had occurred in response to Shen's counsel. Shen employed a Daoist priest to send up a "vermilion petition" on his behalf, in which he claimed (falsely, it would appear) "that the idea for the abdication and succession had not come from him." See Peter Nickerson, "Taoism, Death, and Bureaucracy in Early Medieval China" (Ph.D. diss., University of California at Berkeley, 1996), pp. 485–86, 525. A related anecdote, though one involving Daoist medicinal talismans rather than petitions, concerns Chi Yin 郗愔 (313–384), the uncle of Chi Daomao and an ardent follower of the Daoists. While suffering from a digestive disorder that doctors had been unable to cure, he called on the renowned Buddhist monk Yu Fakai 于法開 (c. 310–370). Yu took his pulse and told him straight off that his ailment was due to an excess of pious zeal. Yu gave him some medicine, and Chi immediately

evacuated several large wads of paper that, when inspected, turned out to be Daoist talismans he previously had swallowed (*Shishuo xin yu jiaojian*, 20:383, no. 10; cf. Richard B. Mather, *Shih-shuo Hsin-yü: A New Account of Tales of the World* [Minneapolis: University of Minnesota Press, 1976], p. 361).

21. The *Almanac* is replete with remedies for problems of this nature, including petitions for "propitiating the five tombs" (*HY* 615, 4.7a–9b), "dispersing the five tombs" (4.9b–11a), "propitiating ancestors" (4.11a–12a), "eliminating the registers of death at Mount Tai" (5.5a–b), and "on behalf of the departed confessing repentance, redeeming sins, and gaining release from punishment" (6.11a–12b). As even this small sampling indicates, the ritual of petitioning soon became primarily a rite for the settling of the dead and the expulsion of the baneful influences of death and tombs.

22. The close relationship between the shorter *Great Petition* and the *Concealed Instructions* is apparent not merely from the direct reference to the latter in the text of the former (19b8–10), but from the many parallel passages in the "Invitation of Officials" (Qing guan 請官) section of the *Concealed Instructions* as well. The *Great Petition* and the *Concealed Instructions* both begin the Invitation of Officials with the Lord of Celestial Glory and his yellow-attired troops 天昌君黃衣兵 and use the same words to describe the demonic afflictions he is charged with destroying (cf. *HY* 615, 19b10 ff., and *HY* 421, 3:14b1 ff.). The Celestial Masters' *Protocols of the Twelve Hundred Officials*, as quoted by Tao in the *Concealed Instructions*, contains identical language in its depiction of the Lord of Celestial Glory, but other parallel passages show that the *Great Petition* draws on the *Concealed Instructions*, not on the *Protocols* directly. For example, the petition (*HY* 615, 20b8, 21a1) invokes two celestial officials that are identified in the *Concealed Instructions* (in what seems as if it is actually part of Tao's commentary, although it is printed in large characters as part of the main text) as "newly revealed" by the Celestial Master, and hence not in the received version of the *Protocols* transmitted from Hanzhong (*HY* 421, 3:22a5–b2). It would seem unlikely that the "revealed" version would have been in circulation prior to Tao's compilation in such a way that it could have been incorporated into a ritual document of the Celestial Masters like the *Great Petition*. This confirms that our petition dates from the sixth century at the very earliest (subsequent to Tao Hongjing's compilation of the *Concealed Instructions*).

I am likewise not inclined to believe that it was written much after the sixth century, in that it does not contain the features typical of mid- or late-Tang religious developments—for instance, mentions of city gods (*cheng huang* 城隍) in connection with village soil-god altars (*li she* 里社), or more elaborate cosmologies of hell—that are present in some of the other petitions in *Master Redpine's Almanac*. It is at least manifestly earlier than the second and longer *Great Petition for Sepulchral Plaints* (*HY* 615, 5:23b–34b) that follows it in the *Almanac*: the latter includes innovations like the ritual burning of paper clothes and money for the departed, as well as the construction of bathhouses for the bathing of the soul of the deceased, all of which are absent in the shorter version. The construction of visible bath-houses for the washing and salvation of invisible spirits closely resembles the bathing rituals used in the Buddhist "Water and Land" (*Shui lu* 水陸) rite for universal salvation, which appears to have been performed initially in the first half of the tenth century (Michel Strickmann, *Mantras et mandarins: Le bouddhisme tantrique en Chine* [manuscript, 1991], chap. 8). This suggests a roughly contemporary development of a common Buddho-Daoist ritual paradigm and tends to confirm my suspicions that the longer *Great Petition for Sepulchral Plaints* is a relatively late text.

23. The suggestion that the plaint is due to the sins of an ancestor and the lengthy speculations on possible causes for the plaint are the closest the *Great Petition* comes to penitence. Unlike much of the anecdotal literature (cf. the earlier discussion of the sepulchral plaint involving Tao Kedou, Xu Mi's wife, as well as endnote 20 to this introduction), which emphasizes the recognition of specific misdeeds, either on the part of an ancestor or on the part of the supplicant himself or herself, the ritual documents, like the *Great Petition*, tend to take a kitchen-sink approach in which all possible causes for the plaint are covered. The reasons for this—in particular the ramifications of Daoist priests' relations with competing practitioners such as spirit-mediums and diviners, who specialized in identifying the specific spectral sources of maladies—are explored in Nickerson, "Taoism, Death, and Bureaucracy," especially chap. 7.

24. The text refers to the invitation of twenty-four celestial officials at HY 615, 5:22b8–9. That only twenty-three are named implies that some textual corruption has taken place. The text at 5:21b3–4, in which the governance of the Mansion of Grand Clarity is attributed first to one official, then another, indicates similarly that the text is somewhat corrupt, whether owing simply to transmission via successive manuscript copies or to difficulties in reconciling variant textual traditions during the process of redaction.

25. *Zhou li zhushu*, 31:851a. The *Zhou li* 周禮 [Rites of Zhou] was probably compiled during the Warring States period (fifth century to 221 B.C.E.). On the *fangxiang* and the *Nuo*, see Marcel Granet, *Danses et légendes de la Chine ancienne* (Paris: Félix Alcan, 1926), vol. 1, pp. 298–337; Kobayashi Taiichirō, "Hōsōshi kueki-kō," *Shinagaku* 11 (1946), pp. 401–47; Derk Bodde, *Festivals in Classical China* (Princeton, N.J.: Princeton University Press, 1975), chap. 4; and William G. Boltz, "Philological Footnotes to the Han New Year Rites," *JAOS* 99.3 (1979), pp. 423–39.

26. *Zhou li zhushu*, 31:851b.

27. *Fengsu tongyi*, 88; *Taiping yulan*, 954:4a8–10; cf. Donald Harper, "A Chinese Demonography of the Third Century B.C.," *HJAS* 45.2 (1985), p. 482.

28. *Fengsu tongyi*, 88; *Taiping yulan*, 552:10a3–4. See also Duan

Chengshi's 段成式 (c. 800–863) *Youyang zazu* 酉陽雜俎 (13.69–70), which explicitly identifies the *qitou* and the *fangxiang:*

> When a person dies nowadays, there is someone who acts and plays music that is called "funeral music." The griffin head [*qitou*] is that by which the *cloudsoul* vapor of the deceased is secured. One name for [the performer] is Fright 蘇, because his clothing and coverings are frightening 蘇蘇. Others call him Crazed Suspicion 狂阻. [The *Zhou li zhushu,* "Xia guan," 28:831c, states that the *fangxiang shi* is assisted by four "madmen" 狂夫.] If he has four eyes he is called a *fangxiang;* if he has two eyes he is called a dervish 僷.

Cf. the translation of this passage in Kiang Chao-yuan, *Le voyage dans la Chine ancienne, considéré principalement sous son aspect magique et religieux* (Shanghai, 1937; reprint, Ventiane: Éditions Vithagna, 1975), pp. 92–93.

29. This poem is included in the *Chuci,* an anthology of songs from the southern state of Chu. The traditional interpretation is that it was written to call back the soul of the exiled Qu Yuan 屈原 (340?–278 B.C.E.), whereas David Hawkes (*Songs of the South,* pp. 221–23) believes it to have been written for King Xiang 襄 of Chu between 277 and 248 B.C.E. It is movingly translated in Hawkes, pp. 223–30. Cf. the "Great Summons" ("Da zhao" 大招), also in the *Chuci.* For the summoning of the soul as a mortuary rite, see Bokenkamp, "Death and Ascent," n. 21; and Nickerson, "Taoism, Death, and Bureaucracy," chap. 2, sec. 4, and app. 3.

30. In funeral rites proper, medieval Daoist priests might additionally place apotropaic documents in the tomb that were very similar to the late-Han grave-securing writs discussed later; see Nickerson, "Taoism, Death, and Bureaucracy," chap. 3. In a sense, one can see the lowering of the documents into the grave as a transformation of the *fangxiang*'s in-person descent.

Moreover, it is significant that in the Great Exorcism, at least, the number of the *fangxiang*'s youthful assistants was always a multiple of twelve, and that both the visible masked dancers and the spectral demon-servants invoked through his incantation also numbered twelve. The twelve animals can be understood as symbolically homologous transformations of the twelve zodiacal animals and hence of the twelve months and the twelve "terrestrial branches" or chronograms (*chen* 辰) (cf. Bodde, *Festivals in Classical China,* pp. 81–95). When viewed in this light, the frequent appearance of groups of twelve and multiples of twelve allows the roots of the petitioning ritual in ancient traditions of exorcism to begin to emerge. Not only are there twelve hundred officials in the early Celestial Master roster of celestial officials, but these officials also are most frequently accompanied by a retinue of a "hundred and twenty civil and military officials" or an "army of twelve thousand." Moreover, in the *Great Petition* the demonic enemies themselves likewise tend to come in twelves: "the hundred and twenty harmful anomalies," "the twelve punishing killers," "the hundred and twenty harmful inquisitors," and so forth.

The centrality of groups of twelve to exorcistic traditions is further confirmed by the presence of the "duodecimal determination" in both the form (twelve sections) and the content (twelve vows, twelve *yakṣa* commanders, etc.) of the roughly contemporaneous *Consecration Sūtra* (*Guanding jing* 灌頂經, *T* 1331), an apocryphal Chinese Buddhist scripture of the mid–fifth century largely devoted to protective rituals that operated by employing converted demons to exorcise still-recalcitrant ones (Michel Strickmann, "The *Consecration Sūtra*: A Buddhist Book of Spells," in Robert E. Buswell, Jr., *Chinese Buddhist Apocrypha* [Honolulu: University of Hawaii Press, 1990], pp. 75–118, especially p. 84). Thus again one sees the combination of twelves and apotropaic rituals that employ demonifugic spirit protectors.

31. This passage appears to make no specific mention of tombs. However, the term "dwelling" (*zhai* 宅) had always been applied to both the houses of the living and those of the dead, and one should be able safely to assume that ceremonies of this type were carried out after the construction of tombs (which, in any case, similarly involved extensive digging).

32. *LHJS*, 4.25.1044.

33. *Taiping yulan*, 735:5b8–12.

34. Technically speaking, Great Year is Jupiter's opposite, or "shadow." In early astronomy, the position of Great Year (Tai sui) was determined in accordance with the position of Jupiter (Sui xing 歲星) in its twelve-year cycle, but Tai sui progressed in the opposite direction from Jupiter and the other planets. In the popular conception, both today and most likely in early times, too, Great Year and the visible planet Jupiter were identical (Needham, *Science and Civilisation in China*, vol. 3 [1959], pp. 402–6; Hou Ching-lang, "The Chinese Belief in Baleful Stars," in Holmes Welch and Anna Seidel, eds., *Facets of Taoism: Essays in Chinese Religion* [New Haven, Conn.: Yale University Press, 1979], pp. 200–209).

The importance of "prohibitions and taboos" substantially predated Daoism and even Wang Chong. The title *Book of Days* (*Rishu* 日書) has been applied to two very similar manuscripts on mantic topics recently excavated from a tomb in Shuihudi 睡虎地, Hubei, that has been dated to 217 B.C.E. (Only the so-called B version is explicitly so titled.) For the texts and a transcription, see *SHDCMCJ*, pp. 89–140, 177–255; for studies, see Harper, "Demonography," and Marc Kalinowski, "Les traités de Shuihudi et l'hémérologie chinoise à la fin des Royaumes-combattants," *TP* 72 (1986), pp. 175–228. The manuscripts contain sections such as "Taboos on Houses" (Shi ji 室忌; *SHDCMCJ*, p. 196), listing days of the year on which it is dangerous to put up new buildings, and "Taboos on the Soil" (Tu ji 土忌; *SHDCMCJ*, pp. 196, 225–26), which enumerates the days on which one should not undertake any "achievements of the soil" (*tu gong* 土攻 [功])—for example, putting up buildings or destroying walls. These days were determined through various hemerological calculations involving seasons, months, days, and the sexagesimal cycle (Kalinowski, "Les traités de Shuihudi," p. 195). One recalls Wang Chong's account of "dispersing the soil," which was carried out after someone had "completed the work [*gong*]" of construction or repairs that included excavation. For an early reference to the general category of "prohibitions and taboos" in the received literature (in which they are described as a debased application of the science of yin and yang), see *Han shu*, 30:1734-35.

35. On these points, see Lothar von Falkenhausen, "Sources of Taoism: Reflections on Archaeological Indicators of Religious Change in Eastern Zhou China," *TR* 5.2 (1994), pp. 1-12; and Harper, "Resurrection."

36. The title depends on whether one takes the word *zhu*—"ruler," or "to rule," "to be in charge of"—as part of the title or the beginning of the next phrase. Terry F. Kleeman ("Land Contracts and Related Documents," in *Chūgoku no shūkyō, shisō to kagaku: Festschrift in Honour of Makio Ryōkai* [Tokyo: Kokusho kankōkai, 1984], p. 22) chooses the former punctuation, whereas Seidel ("Post-Mortem Immortality," p. 28) and Ikeda On ("Chūgoku rekidai boken ryakkō," *Tōyō-bunka kenkyūjo kiyō* 86 [1981], p. 275, nos. 10 and 11) punctuate after *dou* (Dipper).

37. Kleeman, "Land Contracts," pp. 4-6; Seidel, "Traces," especially pp. 31-34, 42-44.

38. Ikeda, "Chūgoku rekidai boken ryakkō," p. 273, no. 6.

39. Reading 錄, "registers," following Seidel ("Traces," p. 30) and Guo Moruo ("You Wang Xie muzhi de chutu lundao 'Lanting xu' de zhenwei," *Wenwu* 6 [1965], p. 22), rather than Ikeda's 祿.

40. Cf. Sarah Allan's speculations (*The Shape of the Turtle: Myth, Art, and Cosmos in Early China* [Binghamton, N.Y.: SUNY, 1991], pp. 64-67, 162) concerning the dominion of the Yellow Thearch (Huang Di) over the underworld and the dead.

41. On Shangdang ginseng 上黨人參, or *dang shen*, see G. A. Stewart, *Chinese Materia Medica: Vegetable Kingdom* (Taipei: Southern Materials Center, 1987), pp. 16-17.

42. Seidel, "Traces," pp. 39-41. In a later, more ambitious formulation, Seidel has further speculated that the grave-securing writs are representative of "the religion of a literate class outside of officialdom—village elders, exorcists and specialists in funerary rites—[which existed] since at least the first century CE" (Anna K. Seidel, "Chronicle of Taoist Studies in the West, 1950-1990," *CEA* 5 [1989-1990], p. 237).

43. That moral faults and wrong behavior did not differ in essential quality from geomantic error or inauspicious horoscopic conjunctions in their capacity to cause misfortune for humans is confirmed, from another angle, by a Daoist scripture with links to the Celestial Masters, the *Demon Statutes of Nüqing* 女青鬼律 (*HY* 789), from c. 400 C.E. On this text, see Mollier, "Messianisme," p. 24; Michel Strickmann, "Demonology and Epidemiology," in *Magical Medicine: Therapeutic Rituals in Mediaeval China* (manuscript, 1987), pp. 32-44; and Kobayashi Masayoshi, *Rikuchō dōkyōshi kenkyū*, especially pp. 376-78 and 415-19. As is usual with early Celestial Master texts, the *Demon Statutes* likely contains much older

material, with portions perhaps even dating back to the second century and the very beginnings of the Way of the Celestial Masters, but these early strata are difficult to isolate. The *Demon Statutes* heads its third scroll "Prohibitions and Taboos in the Daoist Statutes" (*Daolü jinji* 道律禁忌). That section lists a number of proscriptions governing the behavior of Daoist parishioners, from expected prohibitions of general misdeeds (e.g., duplicitous speech, disrespect for the aged, and insufficient filiality) to injunctions against participation in spirit-medium cults and a number of types of sexual behavior (e.g., copulating in the open air, which offends the the sun, moon, and stars [presumably depending on the time of day], and especially the misuse of the Celestial Master ritual of "uniting pneumas" [*he qi*]). What is of significance here is the fact that all of the rules are labeled "prohibitions and taboos," thus assimilating the realm of social morality to that of astro-geomancy and hemerology. Hence the addition of a moral dimension to the mortuary scenario was also effected by the subsumption of social and religious faults under the category of astro-geomantic and hemerological taboos.

It should also be noted that the word *jiu*, "odium"—which was encountered in the previous section of this introduction in connection with the "odium of the soil" that the grave-securing writs sought to avert—also seems to have begun taking on moral connotations, at least in some contexts, during the Latter Han. Portions of the *Scripture of Great Peace* (*Taiping jing*) that can be dated with some confidence to the Latter Han refer frequently to the concept: for example, if people "do not act in accordance with the teachings of heaven [*tian jiao*] they will inevitably experience [its] harmful odium" (*Taiping jing hejiao*, p. 571). (On the dating of various strata of the *Taiping jing*, see Jens Petersen, "The Early Traditions Relating to the Han Dynasty Transmission of the *Taiping jing*," parts 1 and 2, *Acta Orientalia* 50 [1989]: 133–71; 51 [1990]: 173–216.)

44. See Seidel, "Traces," pp. 42–46.

45. *HY* 615, 5.31a8–9.

46. For the classical formulation, see the *Li ji zhengyi*, 21:1415c, and the *Yi li zhushu*, 35:1128c.

47. See, for example, the story of Boyou 伯有 in the *Zuo zhuan zhengyi*, 40:2012c–2013a and 44:2049c–2050b; see also James Legge, *The Ch'un Ts'ew, with the Tso Chuen* (Hong Kong: Hong Kong University Press, 1960), pp. 557 and 618. The notion of "returning killers" (*gui sha* 歸煞/殺), another form of malevolent ancestral spirit, in practice and in texts like *Master Redpine's Almanac* similarly becomes intertwined with sepulchral plaints; in turn, the "killers" are a form of death pollution. See footnote ‡ on p. 262 and the first endnote to the translation, and Nickerson, "Taoism, Death and Bureaucracy," chap. 4.

48. Some preliminary observations concerning the relationship between the ancestral cult and Daoist mortuary practice are made in Nickerson, "Taoism, Death, and Bureaucracy," chap. 3.

49. *HY* 1010, 10:15b5–9.

50. The imagery of the celestial well is entirely appropriate. Just as one might reach heaven by climbing a sacred mountain, whose ascent would end in a journey through a narrow, tortuous passage that also was called a celestial well (Rolf A. Stein, *The World in Miniature: Container Gardens and Dwellings in Far Eastern Religious Thought* [Stanford, Calif.: Stanford University Press, 1990], pp. 217–19), so the soul's ascent to heaven (or, in Kedou's case, her descent into the cavern-heavens of Mao Shan) was accomplished by passage through the celestial well of the tomb. See also Stein, *The World in Miniature*, pp. 105 and 149 ff., especially figs. 45 and 64–69, which depict various types of celestial wells in East and Central Asian architecture.

51. *HY* 1010, 10:16a4–10. See also Strickmann, "T'ao Hung-ching," pp. 182–83; Bokenkamp, "Death and Ascent"; and Bokenkamp, "Stages of Transcendence."

52. *HY* 615, 6.2b.

Translation

The Great Petition for Sepulchral Plaints

Translated by Peter Nickerson

Complete religious title [of the priest]
We address our superiors:

Now (so-and-so), of (such-and-such) region, district, township, and village, has provided a full statement in which he has said that the auspices of his house are in disastrous decline, and the members of his household have been burdened with successive illnesses. Their activities are unprofitable; their dwelling is unquiet. Thus he has pleaded for a petition for the dispersal and elimination of a sepulchral plaint.

Now, judging by the appearance of the situation, one might seek out the [plaint's] roots in a rough fashion. One must suspect that, among his ancestors to the seventh generation, or his forebears to the ninth, among his close relatives or his near kin, [there was someone who,] since when alive his or her trespasses were excessive, after death became subject to all manner of inquisitions and punishments. His descendants having yet to redeem him, in the darkness he is crying out bitterly.

Perhaps it is a plaint over burial on a spring, or over a funeral's having encroached on a god's temple. Perhaps it is a plaint over a grave having been dug into a cavern, or over a coffin having been damaged. Perhaps it is a plaint over old sepulchers lying atop one another, or new sepulchers striking against one another. The months and years having passed long away, the heirs would be unaware [of the problem]. Perhaps it is a plaint over drowning in water, or being burned by fire, or wounding with vermin, or poisoning with drugs. Perhaps it is a plaint over weapons and imprisonment, or plague and ulcers. Perhaps there are paternal uncles or brothers, or paternal aunts, nieces, nephews, or sisters, infecting each other in succession and causing calamities and harm.

Once there is deception and calumny and [the culprit] is not called to account, the Mansions of Feng[du]* will make their indictment arbitrarily. However, the Mysterious Statutes may yet send down their beneficence, and [the issue of responsibility for] the trespass may still be pursued.

Your servant, relying completely on the *Protocols of the Twelve Hundred Officials* and the rituals for curing illness and extinguishing evil bestowed on the Southern Marchmount's Primal Suzeraine of the Purple Void [Wei Huacun] by the Perfected of Upright Unity, the Ritual Master of the Three Heavens [Zhang Daoling],† respectfully invites his superiors:

The Lord of Celestial Glory and his hundred thousand troops dressed in yellow to apprehend these demons in (so-and-so's) household—the hundred and twenty harmful anomalies, the violent harmers within and without, and the twelve punishing killers‡— and annihilate them all.[1]

20a

---

* Concerning Fengdu as the site of the magistracies of the dead, see the section "Sepulchral Plaints" in the introduction to this text.

† These instructions on petitioning were revealed by the first Celestial Master, Zhang Daoling (from his celestial see), to the Shangqing preceptress Wei Huacun (251–334), when she was a Libationer of the Celestial Masters. (See the section "Sending Up Petitions" in the introduction to this translation and endnotes 3 and 7 thereto.)

‡ "Harmers" (*yang*), as well as killers (*sha*), unite fears about wandering spirits of dead ancestors—the killer-demons are the spirits of the recently deceased who return to their old homes and attack their surviving kin—with worries relating to the spirits of astro-geomancy and taboos on burials and funerals. According to an explanation given in *Master Redpine's Almanac*, killer-demons, or "Harmers of the Soil" (*tuyang*), are released from the eyes of the dying. They represent the vital spirit, which becomes dangerous once it is freed from the body. The killer-spirits' hostility can be unleashed only under certain astro-geomantic and human conditions. Traveling over the world, following the warp and woof patterns that parallel the grid of the Nine Continents, these birdlike demons, when they collide with Great Year or other baleful stars, vent their ire by squirting deadly poison from their pinions and claws at any who conduct funerals in the wrong sector (*HY* 615, 6:18b–19a).

Also we invite the Supreme Lord of the High Storehouse and his ten thousand troops.* On behalf of (so-and-so's) household they are to apprehend and place under their control those demons of the five tombs that come and go, wounding and killing, attaching themselves to the descendants and causing harmful anomalies and calamitous injuries, making (so-and-so) ill to the point that his deadly wounds are unceasing.† Annihilate them all.

Also we invite the Lord Who Revolves Pneumas and Disperses Disasters and his army of ten thousand. On behalf of (so-and-so) they are to disperse and eliminate the contrary infusions in his household,‡ the twelve punishing killers in (so-and-so's) body that inflict distress, and the hundred and twenty harmful inquisitors. Let them all be dissipated, so that infusional obstructions may be brought under control, demons extinguished, and calamities brought to an end. Dispel the vapors of the Six Heavens.§

Also we invite the Great General Who Benefits Heaven and his great army of ten thousand, the five Lords of Ten Thousand Blessings and their hundred and twenty civil and military officials, the Lord of Lapideous Peace and his hundred and twenty civil and military officials, and the Lord of Shuoping and his hundred and twenty

---

* The Supreme Lord may be a deity associated with the planet Jupiter (see the discussion, in a later footnote, of the "Mansion of Luminous Jupiter," which is invoked on p. 22a of the *Petition*).

† Regarding the "five tombs," see footnote ‡ on p. 267.

‡ These "contrary infusions" (*ni zhu*) are pestilential vapors "infused" or poured (*zhu*) into the bodies of humans (on *zhu*, see "Sepulchral Plaints" in the introduction to this text). Their "contrary" nature may lie simply in their malevolence and disorderliness, common meanings of *ni*. More likely, *ni* may have a special medical meaning, referring to the movement of the pathogen upward from the earth into and through the body. As the *Declarations of the Perfected* explains: "When demonic pneumas encroach upon people, it is always by sticking close to the earth and then contrarily (*ni*) forcing their way upward" (*HY* 1010, 15:9b2–3). This is a direction contrary to the natural flow of the pneuma of the earth and of demons, which is yin and should sink downward. In more purely medical terms, *ni* may also refer to a rush of warm blood to the brain that leaves the feet cold (*Su wen*, 28:176). In any case, the concept of *ni* relies on the idea that if there is a deficiency of a certain vital pneuma within one of the organs, sickness may enter the body and fill that void. See Paul U. Unschuld, *Medicine in China: A History of Ideas* (Berkeley: University of California Press, 1985), pp. 207–8. It is the depletion of vital pneumas within the body that allows the demonic pneumas from sepulchral plaints, also conceived of medically as wind, to invade the body from below.

§ The Six Heavens are the headquarters of the demonic forces led by dead generals.

civil and military officials who govern the Mansion of Mysterious Beginnings.[2] Together on behalf of (so-and-so) they are to drive off
stale vapors and arrest the world's demon bandits that are lording it up, eating and drinking [i.e., receiving sacrifices], creating all kinds of spirit afflictions, and disturbing (so-and-so) and young and old in his household.[3] Let them all be apprehended and severed, immediately pulverized, and directly destroyed. Dispel death and send life; extinguish calamities and bring blessings.

Also we invite the Lord of Lapideous Transcendence and his hundred and twenty civil and military officials. On behalf of (so-and so's) household they are to dispel the demons of violent harm and suppress spirit afflictions so that they may do no injury.

Also we invite the five Lords of the Four Ministers and their hundred and twenty civil and military officials.* On behalf of (so-and-so) they are to dissipate the demonic afflictions of inquisitions and plaints in the household and all incorrect pneumas that disturb the dwelling, bringing disquiet. Directly apprehend and execute them all. Dissolve the plaint's inquisitions; separate the clear from the turbid.

Also we invite the Lord of the Vermilion Heaven Who Imbibes Pneumas and his hundred and twenty civil and military officials. On behalf of (so-and-so) they are to drive off the arrests resulting from plaints [instigated by] near and distant relatives and those of other surnames, as well as all manner of the malignant and rancorous accusations with which [souls] disturb one another, unwilling to
withdraw. Bring under control, sever, and annihilate all the affliction and injury thereby caused.

Also we invite the Lord of Highest Illumination Who Receives Divinity and his hundred and twenty civil and military officials. On behalf of (so-and-so) they are to disperse and eliminate derangements brought on by evil dreams, dispossessions of souls, and

---

* The "Four Ministers" likely are the four pairs of "celestial branches" that, according to the *wangxiang* system of divination, respectively during each of the four seasons have the capacity to assist certain activities, such as construction, planting, travel, and so forth (and hence to act as "ministers" for the "rulers" [*wang*] of the same time periods). On the *wangxiang* system as it was employed by the Celestial Masters, see the *Xiang'er*, lines 17–26.

departures of essence and spirit, making him at rest and well. Put infusions from previous generations to rest.

Also we invite the Lord of the Grand Mystery and his hundred and twenty civil and military officials who govern the Mansion without Moats. They are to take charge of any vapors of malignant infusions in (so-and-so's) household that cause the loss of essence and spirit, debilitating illnesses, and delirious fright and insensibility. Annihilate these criminal injurers so that they may never cause harm or trouble.

Also we invite the five Lords Who Control the Earth and their hundred and twenty civil and military officials, who [below] govern the Mansion of the Shady Springs.[4] On behalf of (so-and-so) as well as old and young in his household, they are to disperse all subordinate junior demons, whether high or low [in rank],[5] that have caused afflictions[6] and injury owing to blows or offenses against the Motion of the Year, the Original Destiny, Great Year, the Kings of the Soil, or the establishing or breaking influences of the chronograms of the tomb.* Annihilate them all.

Also we invite the Supreme Lord of Heavenly Birth and his army of ten thousand and the Supreme *Fangxiang* Lord and his army of ten thousand. Together on behalf of (so-and-so), they are to apprehend those of his recently or long-ago deceased kin who have seized him with infusions. Let them be annihilated.

21b

---

* All these terms are astro-geomantic or horoscopic in origin. The Motion of the Year (*xing nian*) is represented by one of the sixty binomial combinations of the ten celestial stems and twelve terrestrial branches, also called chronograms (*chen*), from the sexagesimal calendric cycle. Based on the moment of birth, the Motion of the Year changes from year to year. More easily calculated is the Original Destiny (*ben ming*), which is fixed and is identical with the sexagesimal signs of the year of birth (Kalinowski, "La littérature divinatoire," pp. 99–101). Great Year (Tai sui) is a baleful star—Jupiter (or its "shadow," which progresses at the same speed but in the opposite direction). Like the "spirits of the soil" (*tu shen*) addressed in the rites for "dispersing the soil" described by Wang Chong, the "Kings of the Soil" most likely are minor spirits of the earth. (On "dispersing [the spirits of] the soil" and the relationship of that rite to Tai sui and other astro-geomantic entities, see the section "Prohibitions and Taboos" in the introduction to this translation.) The "establishing or breaking influences of the chronograms of the tomb" (*mu chen jian po*) would have been determined with reference to the hemerological system known as "Establishment and Elimination" (*jian chu*), in which twelve mantic activities or qualities (in addition to establishment and elimination, also "breaking," "completion," "opening," "closing," etc.) were assigned to each day in the yearly cycle. See Kalinowski, "Les traités de Shuihudi," pp. 198–99.

Also we invite the Marksman* Lord of Distressed Districts and his hundred and twenty civil and military officials who govern the Mansion of Grand Clarity, and the Lord of Release by Petition and his hundred and twenty civil and military officials who govern the Mansion of Grand Clarity.[7]

Also we invite the General of Assistance and Protection and his clerks and soldiers to bestow on us a True Talisman of the Grand Mystery that will bring under control the Nüqing Edicts,[8] the sub-terrestrial Two Thousand Bushel Officials, and the Twenty-four Prisons of Mount Tai.[†] [Cause them] on behalf of (so-and-so) to arrest and disperse the tomb demons that seize and harm. They should subject to their orders the Officials and Chiefs in the Earth, the Assistant of the Mound and the Sire of the Tomb, the Lord of Canglin, the Lord of Wuyi, the Marksmen of the Sepulcher of Left and Right, the Director of Boundaries[9] in the Earth, the Grave Minister's Official of the Right, the Elders of Haoli, and the powers of all earth regions.[‡] Let them together cut off the vapors of injurious inquisitions and infectious infusions, totally annihilating them.

---

* *Hou,* "marksman," is often translated as "marquis."

† In the developing language of Celestial Master petitions and in other Daoist scriptures of the same time period, one frequently finds that written artifacts—for example, the True Talismans of the Grand Mystery and the Nüqing Edicts—are transformed into deities whose powers may be drawn upon through petitioning. In our petition, the Nüqing Edicts are simply another category of underworld entity, like the Assistant of the Mound and the Sire of the Tomb (both mentioned later), that might either detain or release the soul. In the *Great Petition,* the True Talisman of the Grand Mystery—which emanates from the god Laozi's administrative see, the Grand Mystic Metropolis—is the gift of a celestial official. But in a "Petition for Release from Punishment," also from *Master Redpine's Almanac* (HY 615, 6:1b–2b), the True Talisman seems additionally to have been deified. The petition asks "the True Talisman of the Grand Mystery" to "order the offices of the Officials of Heaven, Earth, and Water, the Nüqing Edicts, [and] the subterrestrial Two Thousand Bushel Officials ... to release the departed."

‡ The Assistant of the Mound (*Qiu cheng*) and the Sire of the Tomb (*Mu bo*) are ubiquitous in tomb ordinances and mortuary documents; they are addressed as minor spirit functionaries of the tomb at least as early as the grave-securing writs of the Latter Han. The Lord of Wuyi is the god of Wuyi Mountain in Fujian Province. He too is named in the Latter Han grave-securing writs and became well established in the mortuary tradition; he appears in numerous Daoist funeral texts as well. The Lord of Wuyi was receiving cult at the time of Emperor Wu of the Han (r. 140–187 B.C.E.; see *Shiji,* 28:1386), if not earlier. The Lord of Canglin also is invoked by more than one grave-securing writ. This deity is most likely a similar figure, but I have been unable to identify him. Could he be a forest deity—"Lord of the Green-

If in the family of (so-and-so), from the time of grandparents or
great-grandparents onward—whether departed earlier or dead later,
male or female, old or young—someone in his or her burial has
offended the establishing, breaking, ruling, or impoverishing influences of the twelve months,[10] or the Eight Generals* and the Six
Opposites,† thus violating the prohibitions and taboos; or the orientation [of the tomb] was not correct with respect to the tone;‡ or

22a

---

wood"? Alternatively, there may be some relationship with Clansman Canglin,
identified as a son of the Yellow Thearch (*Guoyu*, 10:356). The Elders of Haoli represent yet another group among the members of long standing in the pantheon of the
tomb and underworld that were assimilated into Daoist ritual documents. Haoli is a
hillock at the foot of Mount Tai. Beliefs concerning Haoli (or Gaoli), the "village of
the dead," developed over the course of the Han (see Edouard Chavannes, *Le T'ai
Chan—Essai de monographie d'un culte chinois* [Paris: Annales du Musée Guimet,
1910], pp. 104–8, 354–60). The Haoli tradition is also pervasively reflected in the
late-Han grave-securing writs, some of which invoke Haoli's "Elders," or, in the
case of the writ discussed in the introduction (see the section "Bureaucratization and
Grave-Securing Writs"), the "Squad Chiefs of Haoli."

* The "Eight Generals" (Ba jiang) are the baleful stars Great Year (Tai sui), the
Great General (Da jiangjun), Grand Yin (Tai yin), Yearly Punisher (Sui xing), Yearly
Breaker (Sui po), Yearly Killer (Sui sha), Yellow Banner (Huang fan), and Leopard's
Tail (Bao wei). See Hou Ching-lang, *Monnaies d'offrande et la notion de trésorerie
dans la religion chinoise*, MIHEC, no. 1 (Paris, 1975), p. 115; and his "Baleful
Stars," especially pp. 197–98.

† The "Six Opposites" (Liu dui) are perhaps the same as the Six Spirits (Liu shen)
identified in the *Wuxing dayi* (Nakamura Shōhachi, *Gogyō taigi* [Tokyo: Meitoku,
1973], pp. 187–88), which include the astral animals of the four directions—the
green dragon (east), the white tiger (west), the vermilion sparrow (south), and the
turtle-snake "murky warrior" (*xuan wu*; north)—plus the constellation Climbing
Snake (*teng she* 螣蛇), which rules over aquatic reptiles and other water creatures
(see *Jin shu*, 11:296, and Ho Peng Yoke, *The Astronomical Chapters of the Chin
Shu*, Le monde d'outre-mer passé et présent, ser. 2: documents, vol. 9 [Paris, 1966],
p. 88), and the Hooked Array (Gou chen), which denotes either the central, northern
polar region of the heavens generally, or a specific asterism corresponding to the
handle of the Little Dipper.

‡ This refers to the one of the five musical tones—*gong, shang, jue, zhi,* or *yu*—
that corresponds to the surname of the tomb's occupant. This conception reflects a
tradition that is already attested in the first century. According to Wang Chong, the
people of his time believed that both dwellings (including, no doubt, the dwellings
of the dead) and surnames should be classified according to the five tones, hence
also putting them in relation with the five phases. (The basis for the association of
surnames with tones was the movements made by the mouth—e.g., opening and
closing—when pronouncing each name.) If the dwelling and the name were not co-
ordinated, misfortune, illness, and death would result. For example: "The doorway
of a *shang* family should not face south; the doorway of a *zhi* family should not face
north" (*LHJS*, "Jie shu," 25:1027–28, 1032, 1038). That such principles could be
applied to tombs is clear from Tao Hongjing's comment in the *Concealed Instructions* that the phrase "the five tombs"—that is, tombs in the five directions, a meto-

the order of feeding* was not correct; or from left or right, above
or below, hidden corpses or old remains of those who died before
reaching adulthood[11] contravened the [separate?] positions of
male and female—as for all these things that cause punishment
and calamity and bring disquiet, causing illness among the descendants, let them be entirely dissolved and let harmony be restored.
Trace [the case] to its origins and repair the situation;[12] change
the inauspicious into the auspicious. Turn calamities into blessings,
so that life and death, dark and light, do not interfere with one
another.

We invite the Lord Who Dwells in the Stars and his hundred and
twenty civil and military officials who rule the Mansion of the Floriate Canopy,† the Lord Who Executes Harmers and his hundred
and twenty civil and military officials who rule the Mansion of
Luminous Jupiter,‡ and the Illuminated Lord of the Great White's
[i.e., Venus's] Central Phalanx and his hundred and twenty civil and
military officials. Together, on behalf of the seven generations of
deceased ancestors of (so-and-so's) household—departed earlier or
transformed later, male or female, old or young—they are to disperse the infectious ties of the Offices of the Stars, to apprehend the
lingering, contrary killers of the twelve periods of the day that bring
punishment and calamities, and to eliminate them all, together with
their deadly influences.[13] Cut off infectious infusions.

If stale vapors of subordinate officials assume form and lead
22b   demon troops, driving forth the demons of wounding infusions
among the previously departed, [forcing them to] come and go from
the family's gate to intimidate the living, seizing cloudsouls and

---

nym referring simply to all tombs—means "tombs of the five tones' surnames" (*HY*
421, 3:20b9–21a1).
    * "The order of feeding" translates *buci,* a term I suspect refers to the sequence of
offerings at the family's graves.
    † The Floriate Canopy (*hua gai,* the imperial umbrella) is formed by nine stars
that lie above the northern polar star called "Great Thearch, the Celestial Augustus"
(*Jin shu,* 11:289).
    ‡ *Cang,* "storehouse," is often written for *cang,* "green," and as such may also
indicate Jupiter—the "Wood Star" (Mu xing, also associated with the east and the
color green) or Year Star (Sui xing)—as in "*cangling,*" the spirit of Jupiter (*DKW,*
1:823b). These associations may also be relevant to the "Supreme Lord of the High
Storehouse" (i.e., the Supreme Lord of Lofty Jupiter?) invoked previously.

whitesouls and thereby causing illness, let them all be brought under the control of the Demon Statutes. Annihilate them all.[14]

Also we invite the Supreme Lord of the Celestial Mystery and his army of twelve thousand. On behalf of (so-and-so) they are to apprehend and place under their control all those—be they far or near, noble or base, male or female—who might have [given rise to] pneumas of plots involving dispute, slander, or curses and oaths. Make them hide themselves away and do no injury.

Also we invite the Lord of Vermilion Cinnabar and his hundred and twenty civil and military officials who govern the Mansion of Southern Glory. On behalf of the family of (so-and-so) they are to apprehend the Five Gu-Poisons, the Six Goblins, and the hundred and twenty demons of malignant disasters and impoverishment that are always causing decrement and loss in (so-and-so's) home.* Annihilate them all.

Let all the twenty-four Lords, civil and military officials, and clerks and soldiers who have been invited descend all together this very day. Let each in accordance with his own office on behalf of (so-and-so) dissipate the inquisition and punishment, destroy the harmful affliction, and pacify and dissolve all the infusion-vapors that have been thus cut off. If there are demons of those who [died by] violence or injustice or were exiled and buried away from home, or who [died] without descendants—be they departed earlier or dead later, agnates or affines—and whether the affair is one of those anticipated in the eighty-one plaints named above, or any one of a hundred myriad types of inquisitory infusions, let [those troubles] be altogether laid to rest, not allowed to stir, and entirely washed away.[15]

23a

---

* *Gu,* frequently referred to in medieval sources as *wugu,* "the gu-poison of spirit-mediums," narrowly speaking is a kind of fatal poisoning with gnawing worms (Wolfram Eberhard, *The Local Cultures of South and East China* [Leiden: E. J. Brill, 1968], pp. 149–53; Unschuld, *Medicine in China,* pp. 46–50), but the term is often used to denote a number of kinds of black magic. *Mei,* "goblin," is a common demonological term: the *Shan hai jing* (12:3b10–4a1) describes the *mei* as having "the body of a human, a black head, and slanting eyes," though that name too is frequently used more generically. Both the *chi mei,* likely a type of *mei,* and *gu* are named in Han sources as evil creatures driven off by the *fangxiang* during the Great Exorcism (Bodde, *Festivals in Classical China,* pp. 100, 102).

If there are still those who want to give vent to grudges and are lying in wait for openings whereby they can send down depletion and then stir up calamities and injury, let one and all be bound and pulverized, speedily destroyed, and so prevented from interfering with (so-and-so). Let present and departed have their separate realms, and calamities and blessings stand opposed to one another.

From now on, as for (so-and-so) and his family, let divine pneumas radiate all about them and celestial numina aid and protect them. Let their five organs be attuned and their six viscera be open and clear, replete with perfected essence, with the hundred illnesses put to rest. Let their enterprises be successful and their merit be renewed daily. Let all auspicious things descend and wickedness be dissipated. Let both their public and private affairs flourish, with the living and the departed [beneficially] relying on one another.

As for the Celestial Officials, Lords, Generals, Clerks, and Soldiers—both civil and military officers—who have been invited, if they diligently achieve results and drive off demonic injury, and in apprehending and executing [the malefactors] establish merit, then we beg directly to state their merit and reward them with promotion, adding to their offices and advancing their rank, in order of high and low in accordance with the constant codes of the Celestial Bureaux, so that they shall be without resentment.

23b

As for the pledges offered by (so-and-so)—forty feet of figured purple cloth, one bushel and two pecks of Destiny Rice,* twelve hundred cash, one set of pure clothes for wearing,† one hundred and twenty sheets of deposition paper,‡ two sticks of ink, two brushes, one ounce of cinnabar, one scholar's knife, a pure mat, and one pure

---

* On "Destiny Rice" (*ming mi*), see Hou, *Monnaies d'offrande*, pp. 106–26, especially p. 109.

† "Pure clothes" refers to special clothing worn during religious services and was a common term also in Buddhism, whose laypeople wore white. For Daoist uses of the various "pure" items the petition lists as offerings, see *HY* 1026, 33:7a8 (pure clothes), 41:6a4 (pure turban), and 61:25a7 and 80:22a8 (pure mat).

‡ The term "deposition paper" (*zhuang zhi*) appears in some contexts as paper used for making criminal accusations—standard, printed forms with blanks left for the particulars of the case—although this may be a somewhat modern usage (*DKW*, 7:675d). It is of course tempting to consider these as some type of form created to facilitate the writing of the texts of petitions or other ritual documents. Such forms, now printed, are used by Daoist priests today.

turban—they are for requiting the Officials, Lords, Generals, and Clerks for their efficacious diligence.

We pray to the Most High, etc., etc.... Because (so-and-so) is ill, and in order to disperse the inquisitory pneumas and seizing infusions of those departed earlier or dead later, your servant respectfully offers up this Great Petition for Sepulchral Plaints and presents himself on high, etc., etc.

NOTES TO GREAT PETITION: TRANSLATION

1. Tao Hongjing's comments regarding Tao Kedou's forced return to her tomb (cf. the section "Sepulchral Plaints" in the introduction to this translation) illustrate clearly the connections between killer-demons and sepulchral plaints. Since Kedou was sufficiently advanced in the Way to have been promised a place in the cavern-heaven of Mutation and Promotion (Yi qian guan), Tao admits to being somewhat puzzled that she could have been forced to return to the place of her burial. He concludes: "Dou was of transcendent rank [*xian pin* 仙品] and yet she still was subject to the compulsion of the Water Official; this is because the harmful pneumas of the mourning clothes still involved her" (HY 1010, 7:6b10). Thus Kedou was vulnerable to implication in a sepulchral plaint and forced return to the tomb because of the lingering pollution that was created by her recent death (pollution that was also absorbed by the mourners).

The merging of concerns about the pollution of the corpse with those relating to the hostile soul is also suggested by James L. Watson's analysis of that subject in contemporary rural Cantonese society. *Sat hei* (*sha qi* 殺氣)—"killing pneumas"—"emanates from the corpse at the moment of death.... There appear to be two aspects of death pollution: one associated with the release of the spirit and the other relating to the decay of the flesh. This distinction is not made in everyday speech; villagers use the Cantonese term *sat hei* ... to describe any adverse effect caused by exposure to death" (Watson, "Death Pollution in Cantonese Society," in Maurice Bloch and Jonathan Parry, eds., *Death and the Regeneration of Life* [Cambridge: Cambridge University Press, 1982], pp. 158–59). Like the killer-demons (*sha*), the *sha qi* leaves the body at death, and, in its active aspect, may attack the living. In its passive aspect, the threat comes from the inert, corrupting corpse. The indigenous use of the identical term suggests the underlying unity of both types of pollution: the corpse is threatening precisely because it has been vacated by the now disembodied, and hence dangerous, soul; when spirit and body are separated, each of the former partners becomes a threat.

2. The term "Shuoping" may refer to a contemporaneous place name. Shuoping was a district (*xian*) during the (Jurchen) Jin and a prefecture (*fu*)

under the Qing. The name appears to have derived from the combination of Shuo Province (a Tang unit) and nearby Pinglu (*DKW*, 5:1046c). See Tan Qixiang, *Zhongguo lishi ditu ji* (Shanghai: Ditu chubanshe, 1982), vol. 4, pp. 7–8, which locates both a Shuo zhou and a Gaoping on its map of Sixteen Kingdoms North China (in what is now the southernmost portion of the Ningxia Hui Autonomous Region); it would seem possible that Shuoping itself may date back to Northern and Southern Dynasties times.

3. *Sui* 祟, "affliction," is used frequently on the oracle bones of the Shang to denote ancestral curses that were responsible for illness (Unschuld, *Medicine in China*, p. 21). The *Shuowen jiezi* (1A.9A) defines *sui* simply as a "spirit calamity." In medieval and later uses the term often refers to spirit possession, but here it should probably not be limited to cases of possession.

4. 下治 The *xia* (meaning "below") is probably an extraneous interpolation; cf. the parallel passage in the *Dengzhen yinjue* (*HY* 421, 3:19b8–20a4), which also has "Suitable [宜] Springs" rather than "Shady [冥] Springs."

5. Perhaps "subordinate junior demons, whether high or low [in rank]" 高下卑幼之鬼 is a corruption of "the world's demons of higher and lower merit" 天下高功卑功之鬼, the parallel passage from the *Protocols of the Twelve Hundred Officials* as quoted by Tao Hongjing in the *Dengzhen yinjue* (*HY* 421, 3:19a3–4). On the acquisition of merit and rank by demons, see Cedzich, "Das Ritual," pp. 41–60; and Nickerson, "Taoism, Death, and Bureaucracy," chap. 8.

6. Reading 業害 as 祟害; cf. *HY* 615, 5:20b10.

7. The reduplication concerning jurisdiction over the Mansion of Grand Clarity and the failure to request any services of these two Lords would appear to indicate fairly substantial corruption of the text at this point.

8. The origins of *nüqing* 女青 as a term in Daoism remain (to this writer at least) somewhat of a puzzle. *Nüqing* might actually be read as *nü jing* 女精, "feminine essence." It is also the name of a malodorous medicinal plant and demonifuge that is listed in the Han materia medica (Strickmann, "Demonology," p. 33; cf. *nan qing* 男青; quotations concerning both are collected in the *Peiwen yunfu*, 1:1198B). In the *Demon Statutes of Nüqing* (*HY* 789, c. 400 C.E.), the term seems at one place (5:4a6) to refer to the revealer of a book of statutes, perhaps the *Demon Statutes* themselves, whereas elsewhere (2:5b8) it is associated with the star Tianyi 天一, the "Celestial Monad," which is identified by Tang writers as the "spirit of the Celestial Monarch" 天帝之神 and as another name for the "spirit of the Pole Star" (*bei ji shen* 北極神) (*Shiji*, 27:1290–91, 28:1386, commentaries). In the Lingbao scriptures (*HY* 456, passim), Nüqing is named as the one who has established the otherworldly offices that keep the records on good and evil behavior, the Three Primes (*san yuan* 三元), themselves transformations of the first Celestial Masters' Three Offices (San guan, concerning which see the section "Sending Up Petitions" of the introduction to this translation). Eventually, however, Nüqing became merely one of twenty-four prisons or "hells" for the souls of sinners. The earliest source of which I am aware that identifies Nüqing as a hell is the *Jade Monarch of the*

Grand Perfection's Scripture of the Illuminated Codes of the Four Culmens (HY 184, fifth or perhaps sixth century), where Nüqing is listed as one of the twenty-four hells of Mount Fengdu. In the *Illuminated Codes of the Four Culmens,* the trend away from the concrete understanding of the terminology referring to documents in favor of deification and cosmologization is continued: in addition to the hell of the Nüqing Prison (Nüqing yu 女青獄) there is also a "Green Edict Prison" (*Qing zhao* yu 青召獄); thus two hells are created out of the original term "Nüqing Edicts" (*Nüqing zhao shu*) (HY 184, 1:6a–b; cf. Xiao Dengfu, *Han Wei Liuchao Fo Dao liangjiao zhi tiantang diyu shuo* [Taipei: Xuesheng shuju, 1989], pp. 423 ff.). One suspects that the inclusion by the *Illuminated Codes of the Four Culmens* of a Nüqing Prison and these related hells within the group of twenty-four (along with, inter alia, a Prison of the Sire of the River—He Bo yu 河伯獄) could represent a relatively late attempt at rationalization and systematization. Like the better-documented Sire of the River, one suspects that Nüqing's origins are substantially older than are the hells of Daoism.

9. Reading 徼 for 激.

10. On "establishing" and "breaking," see footnote * on p. 265. "Impoverishing" (*hao* 耗) appears as if it might be an alternate member in the set of calendric functions that is sometimes enumerated as ruling (*wang*), ministerial (*xiang*), dying (*si* 死), imprisoning (*qiu* 囚), and resting (*hsiu* 休). See Jiao Xun's 焦循 extended commentary on the "celestial times" 天時 of Mencius (*Mengzi zheng yi,* 4:148–49). On the other hand, *hao* could simply have been mistakenly written for the *xiang* of the *wangxiang* system.

11. Reading 殤 for 傷, a common substitution. (See *DKW,* 1:910a.) Child burials presumably could pose a greater risk in this regard since they were normally less formal and thus might be unmarked.

12. This phrase reads, literally, "trace the springs/origins and repair and restore." See the longer *Great Petition for Sepulchral Plaints,* in which celestial officials are asked to descend into various hells and other underworld places of incarceration in order to "go to the origins of the case, investigate it, and straighten it out" (HY 615, 5:31b1–2).

13. 皆使除滅死亡 There are perhaps two verbal characters missing before *si wang,* "death" or "deadly influences."

14. This introduces yet another variation on the basic juridical scenario of the sepulchral plaint. One's ancestors could be victims, not of a malicious lawsuit, but instead of extralegal action by rebellious spirits of the dead and other demons. The petition has already taken aim at "demon bandits that are lording it up, eating and drinking, creating all kinds of spirit afflictions." These ideas about rebellious demons—caricatures of popular deities—creating havoc among the populace are the same as those that inspired Lu Xiujing's (406–477) polemic against popular cults, in which he describes the social disorder and religious decadence of late-Han and subsequent times in terms of the rise of cults to the spirits of the dead, the demon officials of the Six Heavens of Fengdu whom we have already encountered as the magistrates of the underworld tribunals.

The stale pneumas [*gu qi* 故氣] of the Six Heavens took on official titles and appellations and brought together the hundred sprites and the demons of the five kinds of wounding, dead generals of defeated armies, and dead troops of scattered armies. The men called themselves "Generals"; the women called themselves "Ladies." They led demon troops, marching as armies and camping as legions, roving over heaven and earth. They arrogated to themselves authority and [the power to dispense] blessings. They took over people's temples and sought their sacrificial offerings, thus upsetting the people. (*HY* 1119, 1a)

Lu Xiujing's popular gods clearly are the same type of beings as are referred to here in our petition. One additional element in the petition, however, is that these demons are said to be able to "drive forth the demons of wounding infusions among the previously departed," seemingly making the ancestral spirits return to their families to cause illness, or even to seize the souls of family members. If the language is somewhat vague in the shorter *Great Petition,* it is quite clear in the longer version, which refers to the same "stale vapors of subordinate officials" not only "leading demon troops" but also "forcing the departed to return to and seize family members" (*HY* 615, 5:33a10–b1).

There is a further point of resonance here with the story of Xu Mi's wife, Kedou, which was discussed in the introduction to the translation as a paradigm for the sepulchral plaint: as the result of a plaint against another member of the Xu family, she had been "compelled ... to return to her tomb, there to keep watch for a child in her household who is due to weaken." Again one sees a deceased family member forced by the powers of the underworld to return and cause family members to suffer. The only difference between Kedou's situation and that described by Lu Xiujing is that, in the former case, the "subordinate officials" in the underworld are acting in their official, judicial roles, whereas in the latter they are arrogating additional authority to themselves and taking up arms as rebels. The sepulchral-plaint petitions thus allow room for both scenarios, the judicial and the nonjudicial. Moreover, whatever the specific mechanism, one of the chief concerns of the sepulchral-plaint petition remained the return of the unquiet dead. Another aspect of that same concern is bound up with the notion of the returning dead as "killer-demons" (*sha;* see the endnote concerning the "twelve punishing killers" that are mentioned on p. 20a of the text).

15. As opposed to the longer *Great Petition for Sepulchral Plaints,* which enumerates at least roughly eighty-one possibilities (*HY* 615, 5:26a–27a), depending on how one counts, the version translated here mentions many fewer in its introductory statement speculating on possible causes for the plaint at hand. Either some text has been lost or the introductory speculations and this closing statement came initially from distinct textual families. Further possibilities are that the text is simply presuming a certain amount of arithmetic license, or that the method of counting employed is elusive.

The Upper Scripture
of Purple Texts Inscribed by the Spirits

INTRODUCTION

The *Upper Scripture of Purple Texts Inscribed by the Spirits* is one
of the texts revealed to the Daoist Yang Xi (330–386?) by deities
who appeared to him in visions between the years 364 and 370.[1]
During this time, Yang was employed as a spiritual adviser by a
southern gentry family in the county of Jurong, just southeast of
the Eastern Jin capital Jiankang (modern Nanjing). Yang's principle
patrons were Xu Mi (303–373), a minor official at the imperial
court, and his son Xu Hui (341–c. 370), but the contents of the revelations were passed through them to a small group of gentry families. Transmitted from person to person among this privileged group,

Yang's Shangqing (Upper Clarity) scriptures and revealed fragments of divine instruction eventually achieved a paramount status in medieval Daoism and came to be collected into the first of the tripartite divisions of the Daoist canon.[2]

The *Purple Texts* exemplifies some of the more compelling features of the Shangqing scriptures, features that led to the remarkable success of what began as a series of obscure revelations.

First of all, the texts emanated from the highest reaches of the heavens, realms that are carefully described in the revelations, and were from the hands of the highest gods. The Transcendents (*xian*) of earlier Daoist scripture, we now learn, occupy only lower positions in the celestial hierarchy. Above them are ranks of even more exalted and subtle beings, the Perfected (or "Realized Ones," *zhen-ren*)—a term originating in the *Zhuangzi* but here developed to a much greater extent.[3]

The iconography of the Perfected, who appeared directly to Yang Xi in his midnight visions, finds full description in the Shangqing scriptures so that adepts might recognize them in their own visions. The Perfected, male and female, are clothed in resplendent garb, described in terms of mists and auroras. They are decked out with tinkling gems, symbols of their high office. Their bodies are formed of the purest pneumas and glow with a celestial radiance as they move about the heavens in chariots of light.

The texts such beings brought were likewise exalted in that they described the practices the Perfected themselves employed to subtilize their bodies. In fact, one form the Shangqing scriptures take is that of a biography of one or another of the Perfected, replete with descriptions of the practices associated with that deity. Such is also the case with the *Purple Texts,* which is described as composed of practices transmitted orally by various high deities before it was compiled by them and transcribed in writing for transmission to a select few mortals. The scripture describes this process with some precision. Although the texts had to undergo further "translation" into the script of the mundane world, a celestial original was preserved in "gemmy bookcases of purple petals" in the highest heavens. This is the meaning of the text's title, the *Upper Scripture of Purple Texts Inscribed by the Spirits,* and accounts as well for its somewhat fragmented appearance. It is, in fact, a collection of discrete practices. The text also includes an example of Perfected biography—that of Li Hong, the Sage Lord of the Latter Age, composed by his disciple, the Perfected known as Azure Lad (both of whom are more fully described later).

Second, the Shangqing scriptures clearly earned their eventual popularity in large part through the compelling way in which they are written. There is a long tradition in Chinese literature of regarding poetry as somehow most closely connected to the secret patternings of the universe. Yang Xi, in responding to this tradition and attempting to convey the imagined perfection of celestial speech and verse in the mundane idiom, must be counted among the major innovators in the history of Chinese letters. The language of his texts—both poetry and prose—is abstruse, dense, and obscurely allusive. It seems to exemplify as much as express the mysterious qualities of the spirit world to which he had been granted privileged access as the result of his strivings.

Philosophically, there is an intensification of the homology of part and function between the human body and the cosmos, microcosm and macrocosm, that we have already seen in earlier texts. This leads to a multivalence of signification whereby literally whole passages refer, for instance, at once both to the placement of palaces in the heavens and to the arrangement of spirit residences in the viscera. Beyond that, however, Yang Xi employs willfully outlandish metaphor in his desire to express the ineffable. The appearance of the Sage Lord in the final days of the world-age is, for example, preceded by eerie manifestations: a light that is liquid and yet more of a scent, and musical notes of a palpable plasticity ("[E]ssences of the moon spurt forth as fragrances. Soaring tones ... enwrap the sun").

Words are employed in contradictory and shocking ways both to portray the ultimate otherness of what Yang wants to describe and to evoke in the reader a sense of the higher realms where such apparent contradictions collapse into one. This strategy, too, finds its model in early Daoist texts, but, since the age of the *Laozi* and the *Zhuangzi*, it had never been done so well. One measure of Yang Xi's status as a writer is the widespread and immediate influence of his texts on the works of other Daoist authors. Tao Hongjing (456–536), the Daoist scholar to whom we owe the collection and editing of many of Yang Xi's texts, found it extremely difficult to distinguish

Yang's writings from those of his imitators. He did so primarily on the basis of autograph manuscripts, relying on Yang's unique script. A number of Tang poets were also influenced by Yang Xi, though the impact of his style on secular writing remains to be fully assessed.

Finally, the Shangqing texts were prized for their message. In fact, the Shangqing texts do not represent a radical break with the past. All of the meditations and rituals found in them have analogs in earlier Daoist literature. Some, as we will see, are even conscious improvements on earlier Celestial Master techniques. What is really new is the way in which the constituent parts are modified to give preeminence to guiding the meditations and visualizations of the individual practitioner. Though it would be misleading to portray the Shangqing texts as individualistic in the modern Western sense, they do focus almost exclusively on solo practice.

The reasons for this are not far to seek. The disruption of Celestial Master communities in the third century has already been discussed. The dislocation of large numbers of emigrés into the south in the first quarter of the fourth century exacerbated the fragmentation of organized Daoism. At the same time, we begin to have evidence of the infiltration of Daoism into the higher strata of the gentry classes, folk who would not have looked with favor on communal practice that required them to mingle with the masses; who favored the private meditation chamber over the communal parish. All of this brought about a reemphasis on an older model whereby a religious figure would minister to the needs of only a few paying clients or disciples in exchange for their support. Thus, Yang Xi was writing for his patrons, the Xus, and their circle. The practices he promoted included those that they could undertake while still engaged in their official lives. Nonetheless, those who had withdrawn from the world to practice long purifications in the mountains and who could devote themselves single-mindedly to the pursuit of the Dao stand higher in the hierarchy of being, and the Perfected continuously urge upon the Xus this preferred option.

The Text and Its Sources

As Isabelle Robinet has shown in her monumental work on the Shangqing corpus of scriptures, the *Purple Texts* was at some point

divided into four separate scriptures.[4] The constituents of the original text are now to be found under the following titles in the Daoist
canon:

I. *HY 639, Huangtian shangqing jinque dijun lingshu ziwen shangjing.*

II. *HY 255, Taiwei lingshu ziwen langgan huadan shenzhen shangjing.*

III. *HY 442, Shangqing housheng daojun lieji.*

IV. *HY 179, Taiwei lingshu ziwen xianji zhenji shangjing.*

In the translation, these four parts of the text will be identified by
Roman numerals and abbreviated versions of their titles in English
translation.

The divisions are fairly coherent. *HY 639* introduces the text and
reveals meditation practices centering around the absorption of solar
and lunar pneumas. *HY 255* contains the recipe for an elixir. *HY
442* gives the biography of a high Shangqing deity and foretells his
coming to save the elect. It also contains the signs by which one
might know that one will figure among the elect. Only the final text,
HY 179, seems not to stand well on its own, since it contains the
misdeeds that will destroy the signs of election introduced in *HY 442*
without explaining what they are. As I will argue, this portion of the
text contains an interpolation from another scripture and has been
recast into the form of a Buddhist book of precepts.

As Robinet notes, the *Purple Texts* "is the Shangqing text of
which the authenticity is most certain."[5] The connections between
these various pieces of the original text are still evident in that they
refer to one another at several points and there is little reason to
believe that anything has been lost. Nonetheless, there are certain
minor differences between the received versions of these texts and
citations found in other sources. Only one of these proves to be of
any consequence. *HY 639* lacks two terms—"jade placenta" in the
name for the pneumas of the sun and "jade fetus" in the name for
the effluents of the moon—that appear in early citations of the text.
The significance of these terms, which highlight an aspect of the
meditation practices found here that might otherwise be missed, will
be discussed later.

Although I have found no evidence that passages were lost, certain material does seem to have been added when the text was di-

vided into four parts. For example, the final section of HY 255 (7b2–8b9) presents a recapitulation of information found in a more detailed form in HY 442. It also contains rites of transmission for each separate part of the scripture. For these reasons, I have not included this passage in the present translation.

A more troublesome textual problem involves HY 179, the text that describes the actions that destroy the marks of transcendence. In this text, under the tenth of the ten taboos listed, a series of interdictions tied to certain days, such as one finds in almanacs of the period, appears to have been added from another source.

Though a certain number of taboo days do occur in passages Tao Hongjing flags as authentically drawn from Yang's revelations, only one "almanac-type" list appears in the *Zhen'gao,* where Tao has collected fragments of the writing of Yang and the Xus. At the end of this list, Tao remarks, "I fear that this was not transmitted by the Perfected." Still, he does allow that such information might be useful and so has included it.[6] He applies the same principle of inclusion to lists of activities prohibited on specific days found elsewhere as well.[7] From this it seems that, at least in the view of Tao Hongjing, such "almanac-type" lists did not appear among the revealed Shangqing texts. On this basis, it seems probable that this paragraph of HY 179, cited in the *Yunji qiqian* under another title (*Precepts Noted by the Transcendents in Gold Writing*), has been inserted into the text together with other taboos for certain days of the sexagesimal cycle.[8]

We find further evidence of tampering in the fact that the prohibitions of this suspicious paragraph at some points directly contradict those of the first nine. For instance, number three of the taboos is "Do not get drunk on liquor," whereas the suspicious paragraph urges "Do not get drunk on *yimao* days." Even the opening of the passage in question—"Do not face to the north when squatting to relieve yourself or when you look up to observe the sun, moon, or stars"—conflicts with the advice of the *Purple Texts* as a whole in that the meditations specifically require one to face north when swallowing a talisman that will mix solar and lunar pneumas. Whereas breaking the other taboos listed in HY 179 leads to the dissolution of the body's internal spirits, no such reasons are given for the dangers of facing north. It appears likely, then, that this taboo, as well as the passage that follows it, were inserted to bring the number of taboos to ten on the model of the Buddhist "Ten Precepts." I have, in accord with Tao Hongjing's principle of inclusiveness, translated the passage where it appears in *HY* 179, setting it off from the rest of the text by rows of asterisks.

Structure of the Text

The *Purple Texts* opens with the story of its composition. We meet first with the "Grand Lord Azure Lad of the Eastern Seas, resident of the Eastern Palace of Fangzhu," as he ritually prepares for his journey in quest of the scripture. The image of this deity, associated with the color of vegetation, east, dawn, and new beginnings, has roots in the ancient legend of the lord of cosmic forces of the east and his counterpart in the west, usually figured as the goddess Queen Mother.[9] These paired deities were believed to be reunited once each year and were thus associated with the cycles of time and, hence, the life span of humans. In some versions of the myth, the eastern deity was replaced with a semidivine historical monarch, whose meeting with the Queen Mother of the West was the occasion for the transmission of celestial texts.[10]

Although this mythic complex has definite resonances in this text, the most important role of the Azure Lad in the Shangqing texts is that of mediator. In this function, he usurps the role other texts assign to the Queen Mother of the West. He approaches the impossibly august and remote deities of the highest heavens in search of scriptural knowledge and transmits it to select humans in the world below. The quest of the Azure Lad in this scripture, though it does include a minor role for the Queen Mother, directs itself toward a male deity, Li Hong, Sage Lord of the Latter Heavens. The term "Sage of the Latter (Heavens)" of Li's title refers to the fact that he is not one of the deities born in the "prior heavens"—that is, before the formation of the present world system.[11] In fact, according to the biography provided in the *Purple Texts*, he was born as a mortal during the time of the emperor Zhuan Xu, grandson of the Yellow Thearch. The scriptures that he possesses thus had already proved efficacious at the dawn of the present human era.

Like the semidivine monarchs from whom her son was descended, the Sage Lord's mother was impregnated by celestial emanations, and his surname, Li, derives from her. Li is also the surname of Laozi, who was likewise divinely engendered and took his name from his mother or, by some accounts, the tree under which he was born. This parallelism suggests that Li Hong was held to be an avatar of Laozi, who appeared in human form under a variety of names. But, though Li Hong undoubtedly played such a role for other Daoist traditions, there is nothing to suggest his doing so in the Shangqing texts. In the Shangqing texts Li Hong was not considered, as Laozi was, to be the Dao in human form. Instead, Li is here portrayed as a mortal who, after pursuing successfully the practices presented in the *Purple Texts* as well as others only alluded to here, gained the status of Perfected being.

Li Hong rules in the Golden Porte, a palace in the upper reaches of the Shangqing Heavens, where they join the even higher heavens of Yuqing [Jade Clarity], peopled by the gods of the prior heavens, who have no intercourse with humanity whatsoever.[12] Here, he reigns as the highest of four lords. Li Hong obtained this elevated rank through practicing the methods recorded in the *Purple Texts,* thus making him, for the Shangqing adept, an "exalted model extremely wondrous." It is in pursuit of these methods, both for his own practice and for eventual transmission to mortals, that the Azure Lad approaches Li Hong.

The Azure Lad first recounts his own history and expresses his need for the text, but Li Hong pays him no attention. After further entreaties, Li Hong finally agrees to help him. This he does by first intoning a verse while accompanying himself on a zither.[13] The verse recounts again the ascent of the Azure Lad to the Golden Porte, portraying it as a spiritual ascent on the model of the "Lisao" and "Far-roaming" poems of the *Chuci,* a Han-period anthology of songs associated with the southern state of Chu. In this retelling, the journey of the Azure Lad is a successful spiritual quest, rewarded by the acquisition of techniques detailed in the scripture. When Li Hong subsequently feasts the Azure Lad, the fruits and liquors he provides are likewise the products of the alchemical practices found in the scripture. With this the rites of investiture are complete. In short, in the spiritual economy of Daoism, the capping verse and the meal signify that the master has inducted the disciple into the arcane understandings of a text. The transmission of the scripture, as an actual object, is the final step.[14] The Azure Lad, his own needs met, then takes the scripture for the sole purpose of transmitting it to mortals.

There follows a description of the way in which the text was collated and copied, a listing of spirits that guard the text, and regulations concerning its proper use. The regulations, in particular, reflect Daoist attitudes toward scripture. Each text represents, in effect, a register of deities whose names may not be casually uttered, along with a description of their functions and powers. In addition to guarding the text and its possessor, spirits observe the conduct of those who come into ownership of the text and report infractions to the celestial bureaucracy.

This orderly opening to the scripture betrays certain stylistic influences from Buddhist scripture. First, the beginning lines, although they lack the stereotypical "Thus I have heard" opening, do parallel the *nidāna* opening of Buddhist texts in giving first a description of the marvelous location where the text is revealed before an audience of attending luminaries. Second, as in Buddhist texts, where the *gāthās* ("verses") often summarize doctrinal points, the song of Li Hong serves to restate the opening and alludes to elements of the text.[15] The main difference between this opening and that common to Buddhist scripture is that, although the *Purple Texts* does have an oral origin, the transaction described here is primarily textual rather than the report of a sermon.

What follows the orderly story of the opening betrays no immediately apparent structural coherence. It is, as claimed, a collection of methods, listed item by item, with minimal introduction.

Meditation Practices

The meditation exercises presented in the *Purple Texts* describe methods for ingesting the pneumas of the sun and moon, controlling the three "cloudsouls" and seven "whitesouls" of the body, and activating the spirit of the Gate of Destiny. Despite the apparent lack of coherence between these three sections of the text, they are linked by means of a summary included near the end of *HY 639*. This summary, which focuses on the structure of the body and the spirits that inhabit its various parts, indicates that the meditations do in fact deal with a single aspect of physical cultivation. In order to see this more clearly, we need to consider the summary first.

The body contains three groupings of palaces, known as the Palaces of the Three Primes. These are found in three regions of the human body, also called the three "Cinnabar Fields": the brain (known in this text as the "Muddy Pellet," an old transliteration for Sanskrit *nirvana*), the heart, and the region just below the navel. This latter region, not directly objectified in any single organ, is the most important for the practices described here.[16] Located three inches below the navel, the lower Cinnabar Field, or "Gate of Life," is associated with the reproductive organs and the kidneys. Thus it was of particular interest to those who practiced sexual techniques for recycling the essence to nourish the brain.[17]

As we have seen, the Celestial Masters espoused a method of *coitus reservatus* in order to form and nourish corporal spirits. It is this Celestial Master practice that the meditations found in the *Purple Texts* are meant to replace.

Within the Mystic Pass behind the navel—which, the text states, "joined the placenta to your viscera when you were first born"— is the Palace of Life, residence of the Grand Sovereign, or "Peach Child."[18] This is the same deity who is presented in the Celestial Master sexual rites as the product of the commingled pneumas of the male and female participants. In the Celestial Master rite, the term "Gate of Destiny" refers to the sexual organs; in this text, it is the navel.[19] Thus, the *Purple Texts* finds the deity Peach Child already in residence, clothed in vermilion and wearing a purple lotus crown. His function is to mix pneumas in order to "replenish the fetus and restore the placenta." In short, he is to reenact the process of gestation and birth, creating the germ of perfect life within the body. In the text, this new embryo is called the "Ruddy Infant."

Ruddy Infant is also the name of the deity resident in the upper Cinnabar Field, in the brain. The Peach Child's role, it seems, is to mix and circulate pneumas and essence, rejuvenating the embryo— which, as the fully developed corporal spirit Ruddy Infant, will find lodging in one of the palaces of the head. This suggests that the process of creating a perfected embryo also owes something to the ancient methods derided by the Celestial Masters known as "recycling essence to augment the brain." At the same time, the spirits of each of the Three Primes are described as having the appearance of infants. The practitioner is instructed to:

> [e]nvision the three spirits with jade coloration, golden emanations, and possessing the features of newborn babes. The spirits of the upper and middle primes are clothed entirely in vermilion and that of the lower prime in yellow. Their heads are shaped like those of newborn babies.[20]

The names given to each of these spirits further emphasize their extreme youth. The spirit of the Upper Prime is, as we have seen, Ruddy Infant; that of the Middle Prime, "Perfected One"—a name that suggests the primal unity of the newly emerged cosmos—and that of the Lower Prime, "Newborn."

In the *Purple Texts,* then, the Palace of the Lower Prime is involved in a "sexual practice" even more sublimated and ethereal than that of the Celestial Masters, one neither strictly physical nor entirely spiritual.[21] Instead of two human partners, it involves only the practitioner's own body, which is to be made fecund and nourished by the ingestion of cosmic pneuma.

In order to accomplish this, all three of the methods detailed in this text should be practiced. The ingestion of the pneumas of the sun and moon is meant to replace the exchange of grosser physical "essences" by men and women in mortal conception as well as the joining of even more subtle pneumas by the Celestial Masters in their sexual practice. Intercourse with a human partner for the purpose of attaining transcendence, even when what is exchanged is only pneuma, leads, in words borrowed from Celestial Master scriptures themselves, "to death and destruction more quickly than the slice of an axe."[22] The only sure method of creating and nourishing the inner embryo involves a merging of solar and lunar essences.

The terminology used for these practices makes this clear. Unfortunately, the picture is muddied somewhat by the fact that the canonical version of the text has been altered. Perhaps the most significant difference between the received version of this scripture, *HY* 639, and early citations is the absence in the received text of the terms "jade placenta" in the name for the pneumas of the sun and "jade fetus" in the name for the effluents of the moon.[23] Textual evidence indicates that these two terms were at some point dropped from the text. Since the sun is yang and masculine and the moon yin and feminine, the terms are in fact counterintuitive. We would not expect the male pneumas of the sun to form the "placenta" where the perfected child is to be born, nor the feminine moon to provide the spermatic essences to engender the child. But even without the evidence of early citations of this scripture there is enough evidence in the received text to indicate that this is precisely what was to occur. The effluent of the sun to be ingested is throughout described as "pneuma" or "auroras," whereas the moon contributes liquid "essence."

The notion of a yin element in the yang sun and a yang element in the yin moon is an old one, as ancient perhaps as the idea of the complementarity of yin and yang. In folklore, the sun was thought to be inhabited by a dark crow and the moon by a fecund hare.[24] In the meditation provided here, these nascent aspects of the two celestial bodies are taken as given. In fact, though, the common associations of the moon as white and watery might also have lent credence to the notion that it was of the same stuff as human sperm, whereas the purple retinal afterimage produced by staring at the sun might have suggested its role as purple placenta. To suggest such gross physical reasons for the *Purple Texts'* poetic metaphors is, however, to debase them. We are in the presence here of a religious mystery built from the arcane symbolism of earlier Daoist practice.

The providers of these subtle constituents of Perfection are the Five Ladies of the moon and the Five Thearchs of the sun, each to be called by their secret names.[25] There are complex procedures for envisioning the solar and lunar emanations, so potent that the sun or moon need not even be visible when they are undertaken. These include the proper incantations to be uttered and the talismans to be ingested by the practitioner.

The second visualization method presented in the text, that for "securing the three cloudsouls" and "controlling the seven whitesouls," is also closely tied to the effort to create and nourish a perfected embryo within the body. This is first of all because the souls already resident in the body are to be in effect augmented by the "cloudsouls" of the sun and the "whitesouls" of the moon through the practice just described. Then, when the spirit Peach Child is properly positioned in the body to mix pneumas and create the perfected embryo, the three cloudsouls are required to be stationed by his side in attendance. Further, the original seven whitesouls are inimical to the spiritualization of the physical body and must be strictly controlled so that they do not disrupt the practices described here.

This division of duties is based on the ancient Chinese conception that a human possesses two sorts of souls, the *hun* or "cloudsoul," a volatile sort of soul associated with heaven and its pneumas, and the *po* or "whitesoul," the heavier, liquid soul, of one substance with the earth.[26] Although the whitesouls are thus associated with the spiritual components of the body, it should not be imagined that Daoist transcendence ever involved the separation of the soul from the body, or even of the more ethereal souls from their more earth-bound counterparts. The goal for Daoists was always, as here, the maintenance of spiritual and physical unity in the face of forces of dissolution and corruption.[27]

The cloudsouls are to be "secured," for it is their nature to fly off freely, particularly in dream but also during moments of distraction, fear, or confusion. Once free of the body, they are subject to attack by demons or may become involved with the cloudsouls of others. All of this accounts for the substance of our dreams. Those dreams that deal with Transcendents and Perfected beings, indicating a healthy orientation on the part of the roaming cloudsouls, are to be encouraged. Thus we have, among the writings of Yang and the Xus, careful accounts of such dreams.[28]

The cloudsouls prove relatively easy to control. They may be held in place by the visualization of a restraining net of fiery pneumas, summoned from the heart and made to encircle the body. The in-cantation that accompanies this practice directs the cloudsouls to wholesome destinations: "If they wish to fly, they are permitted to visit only the Grand Bourne or Upper Clarity."

The whitesouls are a graver threat. Wishing to return to their proper environment in the earth, they "delight in [one's] death; their most ardent desire, to destroy [the body that now houses them]." When the whitesouls wander, they join in lascivious embrace with demons, sprites, and even corpses, providing the sexual content of dreams. These vagrants must be threatened and, indeed, incarcer-ated within the body through visualization of the four directional animals—the green dragon of the east, the white tiger of the west, the vermilion sparrow of the south, and the "Murky Warrior" (a tortoise with a snake head) of the north—and other spirits in the form of Jade Maidens, who station themselves at likely points of egress. The whitesouls are not to be allowed to leave the body at all. The directional animals and Jade Maidens are, in fact, the very figures inscribed on the walls of tombs to secure the bodily spirits of the tomb occupants. They thus seem particularly appropriate guardians for restraining the earthy impulses of the whitesouls.

The third and final visualization of this section of the *Purple Texts* is a rather simple practice designed to empower the Great Sovereign, Peach Child, to fulfill the duties of mixing solar and lunar pneumas, forming the placenta, and transporting essences within the body. As with the other practices, this one involves not only visualization of the deity, but also incantation and the ingestion of a talisman. Through these means, the practitioner asserts authority derived from celestial deities to command and control lesser deities, in this case those resident in the practitioner's own body, to accomplish the goals of the ritual. Unlike the Celestial Master ritual for the merging of pneumas, this exchange involves no outside human mediation, whether that of a ritual partner or that of a priestly facilitator. Instead, the agent of control resides in the body itself.

To empower the body's resident spiritual forces, the adept must activate both the spirits of the body and the fertilizing pneumas of their celestial counterparts. This is accomplished by a method of Daoist meditation brought to perfection in the Shangqing scriptures. Known as "retentive contemplation" (*cunsi*) or "retentive visualization" (*cunjian*), the method involves the creation and manipulation of images to achieve desired goals. Despite the omnipresent language of freedom and personal release found in the Shangqing texts, these are guided visualizations. The adept is not to let the mind wander freely, but is to follow the precise guidelines of the text.

Not all of the action of meditation takes place in thought, however. Concrete actions punctuate the visualizations. The adept is to knock the teeth together, swallow pneumas, gulp breath, mumble incantations, and perform prostrations. Each of these actions has symbolic meaning, but they are also described as accomplishing the goals of the ritual. Swallowing pneuma, as we might expect, is the means by which subtle stellar effluvia enter the body; but knocking the teeth together too has its effect: it alerts the spirits resident in the body to the fact that the ritual is about to begin.

The Langgan Elixir

Though based firmly in the more prosaic tradition of the *Divine Elixirs of the Nine Tripods,* the alchemical formulas of the *Purple Texts,* like their meditation practices, take the facts of physiology and chemistry of the day only as a starting point, moving directly into the realm of religious imagination. This approach to the subject of operative alchemy is already implicit in the name given the elixir. *Langgan* was a blue-green gemstone of lustrous appearance mentioned in a number of ancient texts. It was listed among authentic tribute products presented to the throne from outlying regions of the Central Kingdom, but also as the mineral substance of the fabulous trees of even more remote locales, Mount Kunlun and the fairy isles of the Eastern Seas. Edward Schafer has determined that some of the mundane references to langgan may refer to malachite, a green carbonate that seemed to "grow" from copper and that, polished and set, was a common gemstone in ancient times.[29] Nonetheless, the precise referent of the name was uncertain even in the fourth century. It is, finally, the slow, vegetative growth of the miraculous trees of Kunlun and the fairy isles that most informs the series of elixir transformations found in the *Purple Texts.*

The procedures presented here begin straightforwardly enough. We are given precise, detailed directions for constructing the closed clay crucible that will hold the elixir ingredients as they are fired, for sealing the crucible with luting material (a clay slip with admixtures of other ingredients), and for constructing the building in which the elixir will be fired. Even the ritual accompaniments to the process differ little from those found in manuals of operative alchemy. Strict rules of secrecy are to be maintained and proper sacrifices made to the local earth deities—in this case, through the agency of river gods.[30] The fourteen ingredients required for the elixir, though given exalted cover names, such as "Solar Cloudsoul of the Cinnabar Mountains" for realgar and "White-Silk Flying Dragon" for quartz, are those commonly found in other elixirs. Like that for the *Nine Tripods* elixir known to Ge Hong, the procedure given here, too, is divided into successive stages.[31] The products of each stage are as follows:

1. Elixir of Langgan Efflorescence
2. Lunar Efflorescence of the Yellow Solution
3. Jade Essence of the Swirling Solution
4. Fruit of the Tree of Ringed Adamant
5. Fruit of the Phoenix-Brain Polypore
6. White Fruit of the Red Tree
7. Blue Fruit of the Vermilion Tree
8. Liquid Blue Florets of Aqueous Yang
9. Silver and gold

Although the products of each stage but the last may be ingested, the more patient alchemist might also continue on to the next stage in the transformation of the elixir product with the promise of ever-increasing reward. Through ingesting the Langgan elixir, one achieves a "jadelike glow of metallic efflorescence" and rises immediately to the heaven of Upper Clarity. But again one may, we are told, refrain from opening the crucible and fire it for a further one hundred days to produce the Lunar Efflorescence of the Yellow Solution, which, when eaten, will transform the body into a glowing semblance of the moon and allow access to the Palace of Purple Tenuity. If the long-suffering alchemist refrains from opening the crucible at this stage as well, the product of the next stage will ensure an even more glorified body—one that will glow like the sun and rise to be exalted as Adjutant to Heaven.

From this point on, the description becomes increasingly fantastic. It is possible, we are told, to plant the products of the furnace so that the transformations may continue in the mineral-rich womb of the earth. The fruits of trees grown in this fashion will be, quite literally, the food of the gods. They are, in fact, the sustenance offered to the Azure Lad by the Sage Lord Li Hong in the opening pages of this scripture.

Michel Strickmann, in his insightful analysis of alchemy in the Shangqing texts, has shown that the Langgan elixir figures prominently in what he styles "astro-alchemy," a type of alchemy based on the analogical relationship between alchemical practice and meditation directed toward absorbing into the body astral effluence. The steps in the development of this art proceeded according to the same ideas concerning mutual resonance—codified in the doctrines of yin-yang and the Five Phases—that underlie all Daoist practice.

Alchemy, from the beginning, was a way of manipulating natural processes along these lines. Minerals were believed to undergo a vegetative growth in the earth from a less perfect to a more perfect state. Their ultimate perfection was to be seen in the firmament, in the crystalline nature of the stars to which they responded, just as did vegetable life, with its more rapid but less enduring growth. Through careful manipulation of the elements, the alchemist might then hope to accelerate and extend the process by which minerals mutated to produce higher substances. In an earthen crucible, subjected to precisely timed firings, metals would liquefy and eventually "grow" into a substance that would, it was believed, work the same magic on the humble manipulator, whose body was, after all, subject to the same elemental forces—earth, fire, metal, wood, and water.

There is ample evidence that alchemists were quite aware of the consequences of ingesting the metallic compounds produced in their furnaces, but they believed that the practitioner would suffer only an apparent death (often described in vivid terms) while in fact passing without dying into the heavens. Alchemical drugs were one method of achieving what Daoist texts call "release from the corpse." Strickmann cites the following passage describing the fates of historical figures who had eaten the Langgan elixir:

> Those who feigned construction of a tomb after swallowing Efflorescence of Langgan are Yan Menzi, Gao Qiuzi, and Master Hongyai. The residents of the three counties [in which their graves are found] all call them vacant tumuli of the dead of highest antiquity. They are unaware, though, that on one occasion Gao Qiuzi entered Mount Liujing through liberation by means of a corpse. He afterwards consumed a powder of Liquefied Gold, then ingested Efflorescence of Langgan at Zhongshan and feigned the appearance of still another death, whereupon he at last entered Xuanzhou.[32]

It should be noted, though, that the Transcendent positions achieved by these worthies through the ingestion of Langgan are *not* in the Shangqing heavens, as promised in the *Purple Texts,* but among the terrestrial paradises. Gao Qiuzi ended up on Xuanzhou, the Mystic Isle in the eastern seas, while Yan Menzi and Master Hongyai found positions in the cavern-heavens of, respectively, Mount Meng and Mount Qingcheng, both within the boundaries of the Central Kingdom. Alchemical practice, for all its promise, remained for the Shangqing Perfected one of the lower methods, fit only for attaining "earthbound transcendence."

How, then, are we to account for the more extravagant promises of the *Purple Texts?* Why do we find alchemical recipes here at all? Though it is impossible to know, on the basis of textual evidence, precisely what Daoists did with the instructions contained in their scriptures, we can hope to gain insight into what the authors of these texts proposed that they do. On the evidence of the *Purple Texts,* the Langgan elixir, despite the careful instructions given for at least the initial stages of its preparation, seems unlikely to have been meant for actual production and consumption. Instead, there is sufficient evidence in the *Purple Texts* to indicate that, for those aspiring to the Shangqing heavens, the elixir could, in a manner quite similar to those practices that would eventually be known as "internal alchemy"—methods whereby the transcendent drug could be fired in the furnace of the adept's body without recourse to laboratory procedures—be produced within through the proper ingestion of stellar pneuma.[33] The Langgan elixir recipe, it seems, stands as a symbolic demonstration, worked out in a related technology, of how the gradual perfection of the body through the ingestion of solar and lunar essences was believed to have worked.

The ingredients for the Langgan elixir number fourteen. This is precisely the number of corporal spirits featured in the text's meditation practices—Peach Child, the Lords of the Three Primes, the three cloudsouls, and the seven whitesouls. Although precise identification is not given in the text, we might speculate that the three principal ingredients of the elixir—the Red Infant (cinnabar), the Solar Cloudsoul (realgar), and the Lunar Efflorescence (orpiment)—represent the Lords of the Three Primes. On another level, the latter two cover names replicate the names given to solar and lunar pneumas in the *Purple Texts,* while the Red Infant stands for the perfected embryo that will result from mixing the two.[34] The three cloudsouls might find representation in the names given the next three ingredients, judging by the quantities listed—White-Silk Flying

Dragon (milky quartz), Mysterious Pearl of the Northern Thearch (saltpeter), and White Paste of Flowing Cinnabar (lead carbonate)—all of which have connotations of volatility and whiteness. Further identifications are suggested by the secret alchemical cover names given for other ingredients. In fact, suggesting such associations seems to be the only reason for the cover names at all. Unlike other alchemical texts, where the identity of drugs is hidden from the uninitiated by similar fanciful titles, in the *Purple Texts* the common names for the drugs are given throughout the text.

Alchemy was believed to work by means of the sympathetic resonances between diverse substances and the human body, so the fact that symbolic correspondences were ascribed to the elixir ingredients does not in itself indicate that the recipe is specious. More suggestive evidence that it was not meant to be followed, or at least that it is more of symbolic than of practical value, is to be found in the description of the elixir's products.

First, as if to underscore the pro forma nature of the alchemical procedures given here, the final paragraph of this section of the text describes a method for making gold and silver in vast quantities by boiling lead and mercury with Efflorescence of Langgan. A similar procedure is given in authentic alchemical treatises for testing the results of recipes, but no such reason is given here. Instead, the alchemist is instructed to present all one hundred pounds of the precious metals to the river gods, who were appeased with clear liquor at the opening of these proceedings. The alchemist should then "return immediately without looking back." With this stroke, the whole series of procedures in effect erases itself. The gods of the rivers are propitiated so that the alchemy might be successful, and when it is, a goodly share, if not all, of the product goes to propitiate them again.

Second, this is a recipe—containing passages of verisimilitude, to be sure—that could not be followed. To mention only the technical difficulties, one would have to begin the procedures all over again a second time to even plant the Tree of Ringed Adamant (since the crucible should not have been opened the first time and the planting requires Efflorescence of Langgan). The same applies to the remaining elixir products, in that each must be completed in an unopened crucible but requires admixture of an earlier product that could be obtained only by opening the crucible. By my calculations, one would have to begin making the elixir from the beginning eight times in order to accomplish all of the recipes given here, granting for the moment that such trees could grow, and at least twice for any one of them beyond the third product (Swirling Solution). Yet nothing is mentioned in the text about starting over.

Finally and, I think, more significantly, the initial products of the elixir, to be achieved within the alchemist's crucible, are described in terms analoguous to those denoting the substances that might be ingested by meditating on the moon and the sun. The first product of the Efflorescence of Langgan, which, like the Peach Child in the human body, mixes essences within the closed body of the crucible, proves to be the substance sipped from the rays of the moon—Lunar Efflorescence of the Yellow Solution. If eaten at this point, the elixir will cause one's eyes to glow like the moon. But the fertilizing properties of this yellow liquid, which turns semen-white within the unopened crucible, produce a second product that is egg shaped, like the spherical "pill" of sun pneuma in the visualizations.

At this point the "alchemist" is instructed to open the crucible to observe these transcendent embryos. They are three in number, one for each of the three primes of the body. Ingested, they make the whole body glow like the sun; planted, they grow into trees like those of Mount Kunlun. Once again we are in the presence of a refinement of the sexual rites of the Celestial Masters. It is the same refinement we observed earlier. This is the way of "the yellow [moon] and the red [sun]," superior in that it takes place in a hermetically sealed environment without the intervention of gross human seeds of reproduction.

The succeeding stages in the elixir's development are, it seems, no more than demonstrations of the power of alchemically worked lunar and solar effluents. Four different trees might be germinated with the elixir product as seed and the lunar Yellow Solution or the solar Swirling Solution as fertilizing agents. Finally, the two liquids might be mixed to form the "Liquid Blue Florets of Aqueous Yang." But who would need to go to all that trouble? Directions for producing the two potent solutions have already been given in the meditations, and the fruits of marvelous trees are promised the successful meditator in heaven.

For all these reasons, then, the recipes for the Langgan elixir seem more a product of religious imagination, drawing on the prestigious metaphors of the language of alchemy, than a laboratory manual drawing on the metaphors of meditation. Indeed, the alchemical metaphor does operate throughout the *Purple Texts*. The effluents of the sun to be absorbed by the practitioner to form the placenta for the embryos of perfection within the body are described as "cinnabar pneumas of the vermilion furnace," while the cloudsouls and whitesouls, whose reasons for wandering include their need to seek nourishment beyond the body, are enjoined to dine instead on the Yellow Solution and Swirling Solution produced internally.

The evidence of the *Purple Texts* does not prove that operative alchemy was never practiced by Yang Xi or members of the Xu clan. In fact, alchemical texts are mentioned often in Shangqing revealed literature and also figure prominently among the texts that seem to have been added later. Tao Hongjing himself, though doubting the authenticity of some of these later texts, apparently believed that certain of the recipes, including that for the Langgan elixir, were in earnest. Still, although the first stage of the procedures given here, that for Efflorescence of Langgan, might have been carried out, I have found no compelling evidence that it ever was.

Apocalyptic Predictions

To this point, we have dealt with the Sage Lord, Li Hong, only in his role as celestial overlord. He is seated both in space and time between the impossibly exalted deities of the prior heavens and those below, such as the Azure Lad, who might have dealings with humans. Having achieved perfection through the very practices revealed in the *Purple Texts,* he oversees all below him, from humans to deities residing in the depths of the cavern-heavens to Perfected Officials who occupy the palaces of the Shangqing heavens. Like the emperors of ancient China, he exercises his overlordship by conducting journeys of inspection throughout his realm. We are given an awe-inspiring description of what to watch for, should we wish to catch a glimpse of him as he passes. Suddenly, in the midst of this description, things grow ominous. The sun, moon, and stars, which shone forth simultaneously with the appearance of the

Sage Lord, now all go black. At this, we enter a darker scene, one that reminds us forcefully of the historical backdrop against which this scripture was written.

Although the outlook for individuals aided by the *Purple Texts* might appear rosy, that for the world they inhabit is bleak. Ever since the latter days of the Han dynasty, the conviction had grown that the cosmic cycle was reaching its nadir and that the world was about to end. Signs of this were everywhere. Since, by the doctrine of correspondences, humanity and heaven were linked, the eclipse of civil order by the forces of disorder and destruction meant that the end was at hand for the cosmos as a whole.[35]

We lack appropriate terminology to properly describe the eschatological visions of traditional China. The words *millennium, apocalypse, end times,* even *eschatology,* all imply a linear concept of history, whereas Chinese notions of time, based on revolving systems of markers (yin-yang and the five phases), were predominantly cyclical. Like the rotation of the seasons, though of impossibly greater magnitude, the cosmos passed through cycles of time, becoming ever more brittle, showing signs of weakness and decay, until it finally collapsed, only to be reborn with all in it fresh, like the new shoots of spring. Within this complex of ideas, the role of Li Hong proves to be at once that of millennial savior and of creator deity. At his arrival, the world will end in a final paroxysm of war and disaster, a chosen few will be saved, and a new world will begin.[36]

These events were thought to be near at hand, calculated to occur forty-six cycles of sixty years after the reign of the emperor Yao, the first of the "Five Thearchs." It was to inaugurate the reign of Yao, we are told, that the Sage Lord last appeared to set in motion the current world-age.

As the structure of this prediction already indicates, the Chinese calendar was well suited to writers of apocalyptic inclination. Dates are generally given in Chinese texts in terms of reign dates (e.g., "the twelfth year of Emperor X" or, when there was more than one reign title under a monarch, "the fourth year of Emperor Y's Grand Beginning"). The only way of marking time across reigns and dynasties was a repeating series of sixty-year designations. Predictions were generally phrased in terms of these designations—*jiazi, yichou, bingyin,* and so forth. The advantages of this procedure for the fortune-teller are obvious: if something failed to occur in the designated year, one could always claim that it was sure to happen in sixty years' time.

Predictably, then, we cannot tell from the *Purple Texts* which years Yang Xi regarded Yao's rule to have encompassed or what his calculations were regarding when the fatal final years would begin, but it is clear that he felt those years to be imminent. If, as is likely, he believed that he had already entered the forty-sixth sixty-year cycle, the cyclical dates referred to in the text would work out as follows: around 384 (the *jiashen* year), the destruction would begin; in 387 (the *dinghai* year), it would reach its apex; and in 392 (the *renchen* year), the Sage Lord would appear. Of course, the prophecy is phrased in such a way that the final days could be calculated in other ways. Tao Hongjing, for instance, determined that the first year of Yao's reign fell on the thirty-fifth year of a sixty-year cycle and 2,803 years before the year in which he wrote, 499. Since the *dinghai* year of Yao's reign, the twenty-fourth year of the cycle, would then occur forty-nine years into Yao's reign, the crucial *renchen* year would come about in 512, within Tao's own lifetime.[37]

Equally as important as knowing when the Sage Lord would come is knowing who might be saved. The metaphor employed in the *Purple Texts* is the same as that encountered in Celestial Master texts: those who will be saved are the "seed people," who will repopulate a new heaven and earth after the evil have been destroyed by fire and flood, war and disease. Those who have gained access to the *Purple Texts* need not fear; their inclusion among the seed people is ensured. Even those who do not follow its teachings, so long as they own the text, will be allowed access to the cavern-heavens so that they might study its contents. The simple procedure of wearing the text tied to one's belt as a talisman is enough to activate its protective powers, allowing one to pass unscathed through the calamitous birth pangs of the new age.

Further, all of the Shangqing texts provide protection of one sort or another. Twenty-four envoys have been sent down to instruct mortals in the practices that they will need to save their lives. At this point we get a veritable outpouring of Shangqing scriptures and practices. Many of these are unrevealed in the world below—or at least were so when the *Purple Texts* was written, for this listing provided material for Yang Xi's later imitators.

Despite such reassurances, the level of anxiety seems to have remained high. Was it possible to know just what ranking one would reach in the future world or in the heavens? An answer, of sorts, to this question, too, was forthcoming. After detailing the texts of Shangqing and the Perfected ranks to which one might aspire through following their practices, the *Purple Texts* goes on to list "marks of Transcendence"—bodily signs that one is destined for higher things. To the modern reader, these will seem bizarre. It should be remembered, though, that in a corporate society where individualistic expression tended to be discouraged in favor of ritualistic conformity, it was natural that various means of judging the true, but necessarily concealed, character of a person should have taken on importance. Prominent among these was the art of physiognomy: judging the character and "fate" of people through oddities of appearance, the shape and size of their features, the placement of moles, and so forth. During the Han period, when this art seems to have been much developed, handbooks of physiognomy were written, and the histories of the period spend at least a sentence or two in their biographies to describe the subject's appearance as it relates to inner character. Particularly marked were the physical oddities ascribed to ancient culture heroes and emperors. Yao was said to have had square eyes; the sage-king Yu, queller of the world flood, had hairless shins as the result of his labors and walked with a limp; and even Confucius was said to have had ponderous brows, like mounds on top of his head—a sign of sagacity.

The "marks of Transcendence" fit into this tradition. Apparent marks as well as those hidden signs that could be known only to the spirits are here related to moral character and to the condition of one's book of life in the various heavens. Some of these characteristics were ascribed to Shangqing Perfected of the recent past (Lady Wei was said to have possessed purple viscera and "phoenix bones," and Lord Pei had the mark of a constellation on his back), while others may have belonged to Yang and the Xus, if only we knew where to look.

The predictions of the *Purple Texts* were to play a role of extreme importance in the development of apocalyptic thought during the Six Dynasties period. Its description of Li Hong and the Azure Lad found echoes in a number of later texts, including Buddhist texts written in China. Just as the alchemical passages found in this scripture seem to have taken on various roles of their own, so the account of the Sage Lord's imminent arrival blossomed in other texts. The account given here, though, seems intended to introduce the other scriptures of Shangqing, together with their practices and requirements, as much as to warn of the coming disasters. The text betrays little sense of urgency concerning the nearness of the time, much more concerning the necessity of maintaining fidelity to the deities. The Sage Lord is less terrifying as harbinger of the apocalypse than as overseer of human deeds who warns: "From above the Grand Barrens or within the Mystic Void I observe you as closely as your eyes regard your own nose." It is to this moral aspect of the *Purple Texts* that we now turn.

Morality and Proper Conduct

The moral aspects of Shangqing Daoism have not been subjected to modern study, outshone as they are by the literary pyrotechnics devoted to visualization practice and the description of paradises. Nevertheless, there is a strong moral component to this scripture. Elements of this moral message are similar to the messages of Confucian and Buddhist scripture, but the mix is characteristically Daoist and of particular interest for that reason.

In general, the approach of the Shangqing texts to moral instruction seems identical to that found in the *Xiang'er* commentary: rather than instruct people in moral absolutes or give them lists of rules, one need only remind them of the spirits' oversight of their actions and they will act morally, even in the most secret recesses of their thoughts. Celestial supervision is carried out by spirits at every level of the hierarchy. The ultimate overseer, as evidenced in the passage cited earlier, is the Sage Lord, but the spirits of the body report on one's deeds as well. On the autumnal equinox, we are told in the closing pages of the scripture, the spirits report one's transgressions on high so that confession of sins is required on this day. In addition, the text of the scripture itself is guarded by Jade Maidens and Jade Lads, whose jobs include reporting transgressions related to the scripture such as revealing its contents to the unworthy or disobeying its injunctions.

A prominent feature of the Shangqing attitude toward morality, shared with other schools of Daoism, is that of corporate responsibility within the family. Family responsibility has, at least since Confucius, been taken as the matrix from which all other moral values derive. This gradually became part of Daoist doctrine as well. In the Shangqing scriptures, one's fate is particularly tied to that of one's ancestors, most often to the seventh or the ninth generation. Good or evil deeds reflect on them, and conversely, one's own progress toward transcendence is helped or hindered by their deeds (and even by their postmortem activities, though that does not play a role in this text).

Despite this emphasis on corporate responsibility, the taboos listed at the end of the text seem not to concern anyone beyond the individual. The emphasis is on actions that "negate the marks of transcendence" and so wreck the project of purifying the internal spirits and creating the perfected embryo. The first nine taboos (the tenth, along with its accompanying list of taboo days, is probably a later insertion, as discussed earlier) are:

1. sexual debauchery;
2. theft and violence;
3. drunkenness;
4. uncleanliness;
5. eating the flesh of the animal associated with the natal days of one's parents;
6. eating the flesh of the animal associated with one's own natal day;
7. eating the flesh of any of the six domestic animals;
8. eating any of the five bitter herbs;
9. taking life, even that of insects.

Although avoiding the flesh of animals associated with the natal days of one's parents might be justified under the rubric of filiality, one of the primary Confucian virtues, here it is not. Like the other taboos, this one is justified by the notion that the perfection of the corporal spirits would be frustrated thereby. Since one's flesh (the primal body) comes from one's parents, anything that would injure them injures their offspring as well.

This grounding of Confucian virtues in the project of self-perfection, something we associate most strongly with Song neo-Confucianism, appears as well in the description of the marks of transcendence. There we find that the signs created by the transfer of one's records of life to one of the heavens correspond to outward acts of humaneness, benevolence, reverence, compassion, and love—all good Confucian virtues. These are coupled with qualities more Daoist in nature, such as purity, quiescence, and zeal. But such virtues prove to be a prerequisite for, rather than a result of, practicing the Dao of Shangqing. We are reminded again that the *Purple Texts* were written for people of quality, not in their status as governor or official—roles in which they were responsible for moral suasion—but as aspiring celestial officials. Because of this difference in perspective, Confucian texts tend to address members of the gentry class as upholders of social order; the *Purple Texts* address them as potential contributors to a preexisting celestial order.

Confucian virtues, by themselves, qualify one only for the lower levels of the celestial bureaucracy, for the status of underworld overseer, or for residence in the cavern-heavens. Persons possessing only such virtues are urged to commence immediately their study of the practices found in the *Purple Texts* so that they might be numbered among the seed people:

> Some practice extensively secret virtues, aiding the poor, rescuing those in difficulty, spreading benevolence, befriending the destitute, and burying desiccated bones [i.e., those whose descendants, for one reason or another, have failed to do cult to them]. Their virtue surpasses that of the ancients. Chaste and pure, they are warmly reverent and generous with those below them. They are not lascivious; neither do they steal. Some have ancestors who bestow grace on them, having established merit for generation after generation with the Three Offices, so that they already have three hundred merits. All those with this advantage who study the Dao might achieve Transcendence. If their hearts are upright, nothing in heaven or on earth can subvert them. If their corporal spirits are strong,

then demons and spirits will not oppose them. If their cloudsouls are luminous, the myriad perversities cannot invade them.[38]

Something very much like what Confucian texts call "sagehood" is thus but the first step on the Daoist path.

The moral worldview of the *Purple Texts* also seems to be influenced to some extent by Buddhism and particularly by the image of the bodhisattva as presented in Mahāyāna scripture. Although containing very little in the way of terminological or stylistic borrowing from Buddhism, the *Purple Texts* does show the beginnings of the profound impression that the salvific figure of the bodhisattva, who had vowed to save all sentient beings within his world system before himself achieving Buddhahood, was to make on the religious worldview of China.[39] In this case, the influence is still slight but noticeable, and is particularly evident where the Confucian virtue of "benevolence" spreads in an unmediated fashion to include all suffering humanity and even all living things. The Sage Lord, Li Hong, stands as a model for the adept in this regard. In his biography, we find the following:

> When the appointed time came for the Lord's harmonious tones to be introduced on high and when even the slenderest attachments binding him to the mortal world had been obliterated, he looked down with kindness on his mortal companions to draft the traces of his spiritual endeavors in written form. Breaking through all their obstructions, he washed away their doubt.[40]

The text goes on to explain that, despite the bodhisattva-like intentions of the Sage Lord, humans were unable to grasp the subtleties of his message, so that now the text had to be released again by the Azure Youth. In line with this new model of compassion, we find, among the taboos listed earlier, the requirement that one not "take the life of any living thing, from insects on up" and that one not "turn weapons on the myriad forms of life." We are also told that those whose records are now kept in the Dipper possess a humaneness that "reaches even to birds and beasts." In later Daoist scripture and particularly in the Lingbao texts, represented by the *Scripture of Salvation*, translated later in this book, the image of the bodhisattva and the doctrine of universal salvation will play a much more central role. As here, though, it will be melded almost seamlessly to the Confucian virtues that informed the society as a whole.

NOTES TO PURPLE TEXTS: INTRODUCTION

1. On the Shangqing revelations of Yang Xi, see primarily Michel Strickmann ("Mao-shan Revelations," "T'ao Hung-ching," and *Le taoïsme du Mao chan*) and Isabelle Robinet ("Les randonées extatiques des Taoïstes dans les astres," *MS* 32 [1976], pp. 159–273; *Méditation taoïste* [Paris: Dervy-livres, 1979]; and *La révélation du Shangqing*). Both Strickmann and Robinet find that this is one of the earliest of the scriptures revealed to Yang. Strickmann concludes that it was transmitted to Xu Mi 許謐 by Yang "early in 365" ("T'ao Hung-ching," p. 171).

2. On the diffusion of the Shangqing texts, see Strickmann, "Mao-shan Revelations," and, on the formation of the earliest Daoist canon, Ōfuchi, "Formation."

3. The term *zhen* also means "true," and is sometimes so translated. It should be noted, however, that *zhen,* as used in Daoism, equates with English "true" more in the sense we see in the expressions "true vacuum" or "true jade" than as the antonym of *false*. It means, in short, "genuine." The *zhen* person's previous state was flawed and partial, not false or nonexistent. *Realized* encompasses some of this meaning, but I have chosen not to use this word because of the fact that uninformed readers might take it to refer only to mental or spiritual "realization" when in fact the state of *zhenren* is a physical *and* spiritual condition.

4. Robinet has proved this by reference to the numerous citations of the scripture in later texts and collectanea. For her proofs, see Robinet, *La révélation du Shangqing,* vol. 2, pp. 101–10.

5. Robinet, *La révélation du Shangqing,* vol. 2, p. 109.

6. *HY* 1010, 18:6a–b.

7. See especially *HY* 1010, 10:22b ff.

8. *HY* 1026, 40:11b–12a; this passage lacks most of the taboos assigned by sexagesimal day designations that are found in *HY* 179. Another passage collected in *HY* 1026 (33:6a) also lacks the taboos and is presented under the title "Ten Precepts of the Way of Transcendence." The passage as it appears in *HY* 179 is reproduced in a Tang work (*HY* 836, 5a–6a) and in another collection of uncertain date (*HY* 427, 22b–25a). *HY* 427, however, shows traces of Buddhist influence not normal to the original Shangqing scriptures. See my endnotes to the translation and, on *HY* 836 and *HY* 427, Robinet, *La révélation du Shangqing,* vol. 2, pp. 412 and 415. This portion of the scripture was clearly subject to substantial tampering by later writers. Unfortunately, though perhaps predictably, the section of the *Wushang biyao* where this text was cited has not survived (Lagerwey, *Wu-shang piyao,* p. 64). *P* 2751 (lines 179–80), which may possibly be a lost fragment of Tao Hongjing's *Dengzhen yinjue* (Cedzich, personal communication), is of no help in resolving this matter either. It makes reference to only a few of the ten precepts and does not assign them numbers. *P* 2751 (lines 182–195)

does, however, cite the closing portion of the text, which is thus likely to be original.

9. For early evidence of the paired spirits of the east and west, see Jeffrey K. Riegel, "Kou-mang and Ju-shou," *CEA* 5 (1990), pp. 55–84.

10. Schipper, *L'empereur Wou;* Suzanne E. Cahill, *Transcendence and Divine Passion: The Queen Mother of the West in Medieval China* (Stanford, Calif.: Stanford University Press, 1993), especially pp. 43–58.

11. Robinet, *La révélation du Shangqing,* vol. 2, p. 107.

12. See Paul W. Kroll, "Spreading Open the Barrier of Heaven," *Asiatische Studien/Études Asiatiques,* 40.1 (1986), pp. 22–39. In this article, Kroll translates a substantial portion of another Shangqing text that shares some of the terminology found in this scripture and, like it, was bestowed upon the Azure Lad by the Lord of Grand Tenuity. "Porte" translates the word *que* 闕, the twin gate towers that stood as entryway to any palatial dwelling or sacred building. As this is the entryway to higher heavens, Golden Porte is an appropriate synecdochical expression for Li Hong's palace.

13. This verse is also to be found in what appears to be a later scripture of the Shangqing corpus. See HY 1320, 6b7–7a5; and Robinet, *La révélation du Shangqing,* vol. 2, pp. 145–49.

14. One element missing from the rites of transmission as actually conducted by Daoist masters is the reciprocal *xin* 信 or "faith offering" that was to be presented by the disciple on receipt of the text. Apparently there is no need for such a thing among deities.

15. See Zürcher, "Buddhist Influence," pp. 99–101, for these stylistic features of Buddhist scripture.

16. Robinet has aptly characterized the region comprising the kidneys, reproductive organs, and the lower Cinnabar Field as the "fecund abyss of the body" (*Méditation taoïste,* p. 120).

17. As Douglas Wile cogently argues, early Western accounts of such practices that claim that it is the semen that is cycled to the brain fail to take into account the multivalence of the Chinese term *jing,* which I uniformly translate as "essence." For a general account of the practice, see Wile, *Art of the Bedchamber,* especially pp. 36–43, and, for his critique of previous scholarship, pp. 56–69.

18. In translating the name of this deity, I follow *P* 2751, line 123, which has 桃孩 rather than the 桃康 [Peach Vigor] of HY 639, 12a2. "Peach Vigor" is the form of the name used in Celestial Master and Lingbao scriptures. See HY 1284, 15a7, and the *Scripture of Salvation* translation in this volume.

19. See Robinet, *La révélation du Shangqing,* vol. 1, pp. 70–71 and 175–76; and HY 1284, 15a7.

20. HY 639, 11b.

21. Robinet, *La révélation du Shangqing,* vol. 1, pp. 176–80.

22. See HY 639, 13b.

23. The term "jade placenta" figures in the *Zhen'gao* citation of the portion of the *Purple Texts* dealing with the ingestion of solar pneumas (*HY* 1010, 9:24b), as well as in commentaries to the *Huangting jing* (*HY* 1026, 11:51a and 12:7a–b) and in various methods based on the *Purple Texts* (see *HY* 1312, 4a.4; *HY* 435, 6a; and Robinet, "Randonées extatiques," pp. 204–6). It is thus fairly certain that it appeared in the autograph text. Because the section on ingesting lunar pneumas is not as widely cited, the term "jade fetus" occurs in the same position only in the alternate name for the section on ingesting lunar pneumas as reported by *HY* 1312 (4b2–3). Nonetheless, the parallel structure of the passages on the sun and moon indicates that these titles too must be balanced. On this basis, I have restored both terms to the translation.

24. See Schafer, *Pacing the Void*, pp. 163–70 and 188–91; and Schafer, *Mirages*, p. 110.

25. It was Isabelle Robinet who first noticed, as with so much else regarding this text, the way in which the secret names of these deities are presented. (See footnotes ‡ and * on pp. 314 and 319.)

26. These ideas are of great antiquity, though the concept that the cloudsouls were three in number and the whitesouls seven can be traced back with certainty no earlier than Ge Hong (c. 283–343). See especially Needham, *Science and Civilisation in China*, vol. 5 pt. 2 (1974), pp. 85–93; the relevant passages are cited on pp. 88–90.

27. See Bokenkamp, "Death and Ascent."

28. See *HY* 1010, 17:5b–12a, and, for a translation of an account of one such dream, Michel Strickmann, "Dreamwork of Psycho-Sinologists: Doctors, Taoists, Monks," in Carolyn T. Brown, ed., *Psycho-Sinology: The Universe of Dreams in Chinese Culture* (Washington: Woodrow Wilson International Center for Scholars, 1988), pp. 31–33.

29. Edward H. Schafer, "The Transcendent Vitamin: Efflorescence of *Lang-kan*," *Chinese Science* 13 (1978), pp. 27–38.

30. Since the furnace was of necessity placed upon an earthen platform, alchemists believed it was necessary to repress undesirable earth pneumas that might leak in and spoil the process. As a result, texts of operative alchemy generally include a ritual for sacrifice to local earth gods. See Strickmann, "T'ao Hung-ching," p. 148 and n. 78.

31. Although the ninth product does not quite represent a successive stage in the transformation of the elixir, in that it requires not the product of the eighth stage but that of the first, the division of the text into nine procedures does parallel that of the formula for the *Nine Tripods* elixir.

32. Strickmann, "T'ao Hung-ching," p. 131, citing *HY* 1010, 14:16a.

33. On the role of the Shangqing texts in the development of inner alchemy, see Robinet, *La révélation du Shangqing*, vol. 1, pp. 176–80.

34. This has already been pointed out by Robinet (*La révélation du Shangqing*, vol. 1, p. 177).

35. My translation of the portion of the scripture dealing with apoc-

alyptic predictions is indebted to Michel Strickmann's French translation in his *Le taoïsme du Mao chan*, pp. 209–24.

36. I will speak of this as a "world cycle," but it should be remembered that everything in the cosmos—with one exception, which I mention later—participated in this cycle. The unavoidable terms "millennium" and "apocalypse" should be understood here to refer to stages in this cycle.

37. See Strickmann, "T'ao Hung-ching," pp. 153–55.

38. *HY* 442, 12a–b.

39. For an overview of the question of Buddhist influence on Daoism, see Zürcher, "Buddhist Influence."

40. *HY* 442, 2b.

Translation

The Upper Scripture
of Purple Texts Inscribed by the Spirits

I. THE UPPER SCRIPTURE
OF PURPLE TEXTS INSCRIBED BY THE SPIRITS

The Grand Lord Azure Lad of the Eastern Seas, resident of the 1a
Eastern Palace of Fangzhu, conducted a purification retreat for three
years within the yellow chambers and cinnabar-red gates of his holy
tower.* Then he mounted his cloudy chariot, composed of dark-
blue auroras and the flowing effulgences of his three spirit registers.[1]
He threw across his shoulders the halcyon-plumed dragon cloak of
flying azure and, leading a retinue of a thousand Perfected from the
Mulberry Groves, proceeded on high to visit the Golden Porte of
Upper Clarity.[2] There he requested the *Upper Scripture of Purple
Texts Inscribed by the Spirits*.

Within the Golden Porte there are four Thearchical Lords. Among
them, the Sage Lord of the Latter Age occupies the highest position,

---

* The Eastern Palace of Fangzhu is a paradisiacal continent in the hidden reaches
of the Eastern Seas. The name *Fangzhu,* for which Paul Kroll has proposed the
translation "Square Speculum," derives from the name of a bronze, mirrorlike basin
that was said to have been used in ancient times to collect the sweet dews emanating
from the full moon. See Kroll, "In the Halls of the Azure Lad," *JAOS* 105.1 (1985),
pp. 79–81. According to the *Li ji,* a *xie* (tower) was a chamber atop a pounded-earth
platform in which ritual implements were stored. Here, the term "holy *xie*" apparently refers to the Azure Lad's meditation chamber.

that of the left.* He resides in the Palace of the Grand Void, with
rose-gem estrades all constructed of cinnabar and malachite. Thirty-
thousand maids and Perfected beings attend him. Poison dragons,
thunder tigers, and heaven-clawing beasts guard his gates, wrapping
themselves about the portals. Krakens and serpents, thousands of
yards in length, twine themselves around the walls and cornices.[3]
Flying steeds, together with darting sparrows and other birds with
massive wingspans, pecking with their beaks and brandishing their
talons, are spread throughout the broad courtyard.

1b

    The Lord's celestial might flashes throughout, throwing off beams
of light that illumine in all directions. The wind beats at dark banners; oxtail-pennoned canopies swirl and dance. Gemmy trees are
shaken and sound out, blue-gem plants act as sounding hollows[4]—
all playing the songs of the clouds as phoenixes intone "Azure
Peace." The spirit consorts sing in harmony, while the great rocs
dance and simurghs step in unison.

    Once the Azure Lad had reached this place, he crawled into the
awesome presence. Then, raising his head and facing to the north,
he said:

> I, the minor official Fanmei, dare to present my request before the table
> of his bright majesty, the sage Thearch. Long ago, when order was
> plucked from the Grand Barrens, I was made an official among the flying
> Perfected. My charge was to inspect the vast border region of the five
> sacred realms, to oversee what fell beyond the purview of my mystic
> Master. Rising up, I bathed myself in clear and volatile yang pneumas,
> sounding my bells in the vacant fields.† I made bright and flourishing my
> three modes of perception,[5] intricate and complex my wondrous under-
> standings—[just as] within the vast fastnesses of the Numinous Park
> cleansing floods purge green valleys.
>
>   This accomplished, I withdrew in hesitation from the constant net to
> pace on high with the Mystic Elders. I joined nine simurghs in the barren

---

   * The biography of the Sage Lord figures later in this scripture. His status is that
of Thearchical Lord, superior to that of Perfected person.
   † The "clear and volatile" alludes to a description of the division of yin from
yang pneumas at creation found in the *Huainan zi:* "The clear and volatile scattered
abroad to make the heavens; the heavy and turgid coagulated to form the earth."
The Azure Lad here describes his origins in the very beginnings of the present world-
age, when "order was plucked from the Grand Barrens"—another name for the
undifferentiated chaos from which all things arose.

wastes of Lang precipice, shooting flowing beams out over the shrouded efflorescences beyond.* In a wavelike rush, I attained the paired mysteries, exhausting to its limits my spiritual perception.† Merging with the utter stillness of the dragon void, I then buried my impulse to split hairs⁶ deep within the cinnabar chambers of my heart and opened the spirit-gates of my consciousness that I might give myself over to transformation and release myself from entanglements through following the progress of my changing form.

2a

Just at this moment, my bonds and fetters fell away; my bodily spirits and breaths were subtilized. Reverently sloughing off my five bodily spirits, I entered into the flowing refinement of the hollow void, like a fish leaping through the shallows of a dark-blue ford, boldly and effortlessly.‡

Although I have now achieved self-sufficiency in my observations into the eight horizontal directions and there should in fact be no obstructions to my view of the glowing heights of heaven, still I am concerned that my perfected qualities have not yet been sufficiently opened and that my spiritual substance requires further honing. I wish to allow the winds to sprinkle dew over fragrant groves and to sound the heavenly pipes along the edges of the clouds. I want to eradicate the seven transgressors and solidify [human] understandings of the arcane.§ For these purposes, I wonder if the *Upper Scripture of Purple Texts Inscribed by the Spirits* might be taught to those below?

At this particular moment, the Sage Lord of the Latter Ages had clasped to him his writing table and had transformed himself outwardly [so as to be visible to those around him]. Collecting from on high his far-ranging thoughts, he was composing with his brush a commentary to the *Mysterious Scripture of the Grand Cavern* to

---

* *Lang* is short for *langfeng*, "wind on the fells," an archaic name for the loftiest peak of Mount Kunlun. (See Edward H. Schafer, "Wu Yün's Stanzas on Saunters in Sylphdom," *MS* 35 [1981–1983], p. 338, n. 126.) The "shrouded efflorescences" or "darkened flowerings"—a fine example of the sort of contradictory terminology beloved of Yang Xi—seem unique to this text.

† The "paired mysteries" are the sun and moon. See *HY* 1010, 10:21a.6, where they are described as the "paired phosphors, doubled in mystery."

‡ The five spirits inhabit the three registers of the human body. They are responsible for forming the embryo at birth and for keeping the registers of merit and demerit during the course of one's life. See Robinet, *La révélation du Shangqing*, vol. 1, p. 129, and vol. 2, p. 156; Robinet, *Taoist Meditation*, pp. 101–2; and *HY* 1319, 20a–27b. For more on these spirits, see the section "Bodily Deities of Salvation" in the introduction to the *Scripture of Salvation*. Having subtilized his physical form, the Azure Lad has no further need of these spirits.

§ The "seven transgressors" are presumably the seven whitesouls. See "The method for controlling the Seven Whitesouls" later in this text.

instruct the several hundreds of Higher Perfected, Exalted Chamber-
lains, holy lads, and Jade Maidens.* Not only did he not lend ear to
the words proffered by the Azure Lad; he did not cease for even an
instant his chanting to those who observed him.

Then the Azure Lad crawled farther forward on his knees and
implored him further, showing no signs of desisting. After a long
time, the Sage Lord pushed his writing desk away and stretched
out in an attitude of repose. Suddenly, heaving a long sigh, he said:
"Your bitter words are mysterious and exalted, and your quintes-
sential sincerity has awakened me. You have been extremely arduous in your pursuits."

At this, the Sage Lord pointed beyond to the barren regions. On
his face was an expression of compassion. Accordingly, he took up
his zither of the cloudy spheres. Strumming and plucking it, he produced a concatenation of cascading notes, which echoed forth clear
and numinous. Their gemlike brightness shook the nine barren
realms and penetrated clearly to the highest empyrean. With this
accompaniment, he sang the strophes of the *Spirit Isles of the
Grand Cavern,* to the tune of "Concentrated Cloudsouls." These
mystical verses of divine ornamentation contained heavenly harmonies vague and subtle. They reflected into the dashing pneumas
with persistent tones, both open-stringed and dampened. The lyrics
were as follows:†

In the dark barrens, breaths of Upper Clarity—
Colors of the Three Elementals rush into the mottled murk.[7] ‡
Toward the abyss, numinous portals open—
Seven gates swung wide by feathered lads—[8]
Allowing unobstructed descent[9] to a vision of the cinnabar empyrean,

---

* The *Mysterious Scripture of the Grand Cavern,* also called the *Perfected Scripture of the Grand Cavern,* is the most exalted of the Shangqing scriptures. The name
sometimes stands for the Shangqing scriptures as a whole. See Robinet, *La révélation
du Shangqing,* vol. 2, pp. 29–44.

† The song that follows describes in poetic terms the quest of the Azure Lad and
sings the praises of the techniques contained in this scripture. I leave unglossed those
terms and phrases that are explained more fully later.

‡ The term "three elementals," according to the Shangqing scripture *Secret
Words on the Eight Ways,* refers to tricolored clouds of various combinations of the
five direction-associated colors (green, red, white, black, and yellow), hues derived
from these, and purple, representing the highest heavens. (See *P* 2751, lines 421–78.)

So that, distant yet clear, the dark cycles are made manifest.
You achieve realization,[10] awakening to the mystic junctures;*
Perch on the brink, then fly into the Grand Void.
The Solar Estrade, in the wilds of the Grand Cavern,
Shrouded and fleeting, beams from a blossoming fungus.
In an abandoned realm, a canopied conveyance of the barrens:
Cut off from your dwelling, you communicate with the hidden,
For an exalted meeting within the gate towers of the mystic timekeepers.
Bareheaded, you attend morning audience with the Jade Monarchs.†
Your spirits blossom to the tones of the Ruddy Spirit,[11]   3a
While the rhythms of the Void sound forth from rose-gem chimes.
As your nine-harnessed cloud coach crosses the sky,
You roam among peaks wrapped in purple auroras.
Where cyan rooms open on the Cinnabar Mound,
Five chambers are arrayed within a green court.‡
The Golden Porte flashes ruggedly in the distance.
Shaded and vague are the palaces of Upper Clarity.
Savor the flowers of sun and moon;
Glimpse the contours of the formless realm!
Mystically bring about perception of your three spirit registers,
As you glide silently across kalpas and fathoms.
Why are you seated while still on the road?
The five difficulties will grow in your breast.§
Why not take control of the Ruddy Infant
And depend on your personal Sire of the Muddy Pellet?‖
Then you will not die, nor will you be born;
You will not begin, nor will you end.

---

* The "mystic junctures" are points in time when the celestial secrets might be made known to those below.
† The "Jade Monarchs" meant here are most likely the Celestial Thearch of Grand Tenuity and the Celestial Thearch of Purple Tenuity mentioned later.
‡ Presumably these are sights encountered along the celestial journey. The verses may contain oblique references to physical cultivation as well: Cinnabar Mound is an alternate name for the southern palace where the body is to be refined for trans-feral to the higher heavens. (For more on the Southern Palace, which is known in the Shangqing and Lingbao texts by a variety of names, see the introduction to *Scripture of Salvation*.) The "five chambers," here presented as part of the Cinnabar Mound, are likely the loci where different parts of the body are transformed.
§ The "five difficulties" are those inherent in: (1) giving to the poor when one is oneself poor, (2) studying the Dao when one is rich and powerful, (3) controlling one's destiny to achieve deathlessness, (4) being able to see the scriptures, and (5) being born at the time when the Sage of the Latter Age will appear. (See *HY* 1010, 6:8a.7–9.)
‖ The "Muddy Pellet," written with characters used in early Buddhist translations for the Sanskrit *nirvana,* is the palace of the Upper Prime, alternatively known as the "upper Cinnabar Field," and is located three inches beyond the midpoint between

When the Sage Lord had finished his singing, he beckoned to the
Azure Lad, urging him to be seated. He spread before him liquors
of flowing auroras, fruits of ringed adamant, white fruits of vermilion gem trees, and green kernels from scarlet gem trees.* Then he
ordered the upper Perfected Five Ancient Ones and the Higher Duke
of the Transcendent Metropolis to open the gemmy bookcases of
purple petals and the book bags of cloud brocade to extract the
Upper Scripture of Purple Texts Inscribed by the Spirits.[12] This he
entrusted to the Azure Lad, that the Azure Lad might bestow it
below to those whose names are written on jade in the Mystic Palace
3b   and who thus are destined to become Perfected.

The Azure Lad, retreating from his mat, knocked his head in
obeisance to receive it. Then, taking the text with him, he returned
to the Eastern Palace of Fangzhu.

The *Upper Scripture of Purple Texts Inscribed by the Spirits* is the
essential text that the Sage of the Latter Heavens, Lord Li, himself
received and practiced when he studied the Dao as a young man. It
contains methods of achieving Perfection transmitted orally by the
Celestial Thearch of Grand Tenuity and the Celestial Thearch of
Upper Perfection from Purple Tenuity, two Celestial Thearchs from
the heavens of Jade Clarity.† It represents the most vital practices
for salvation from the age of the Higher Luminaries, which they
extracted from heavenly scripture and compiled to compose this
work.‡ The methods of practice, incantations, and explanations

---

the eyebrows. See Rolf Homann, *Die wichtigsten Körpergottheiten im Huang-t'ing
ching* (Göppingen: Verlag Alfred Kummerle, 1971), p. 60 n. 2. The second word of
this line, *wo* [I, me, personal], is puzzling. Either the Sage Lord is speaking as the
Dao so that the Sire of the Muddy Pellet is regarded as his envoy in the human body,
or the word here means "personal," as I have translated it here.

* These are the mineral fruits of the Langgan elixir.

† These two exalted gods issue from the heaven of Jade Clarity, above that of
Higher Clarity. The gemlike glitter of their celestial residences is but faintly visible to
human eyes in the starry skies. The Palace of Purple Tenuity, a circumpolar constellation composed of stars in Draco, surrounded the star that in ancient times represented the Celestial Thearch (our Polaris). The Palace of Grand Tenuity was symbolically the southern residence of the Celestial Thearch, as it lay on the ecliptic in
our Virgo and Leo, a portion of the sky associated with the south. Both are described elegantly by Edward H. Schafer (*Pacing the Void*, pp. 44–52).

‡ The "age of the Higher Luminaries" is one of the imaginative reign titles of
previous world-ages of the "prior heavens." See Robinet, *La révélation du Shang-*

were graded, compared, and arranged item by item to form a single scroll. This text was then incised on jade slats bound together, and the graphs were colored in with green and gold.

Then the Tortoise Mother guided the brush [to recopy the scripture], Perfected lads arranged the mats, Celestial consorts watched over the incense, and Jade Lads tied the inscribed slips into scrolls.* The text was then given its name, the *Upper Scripture of Purple Texts Inscribed by the Spirits,* and copies were presented to the upper Perfected Five Ancient Ones and the Higher Duke of the Transcendent Metropolis, who secreted it in gemmy bookcases of purple petals, wrapping these in book bags of cloud brocade.

As guardians of the text, ten Jade Maidens were commanded to remain by it. Ten Jade Lads were commanded to guard the *Annals of the Sage Lord.* These spirits are also to oversee those Daoists who come into possession of the texts, reporting their merits and transgressions to the masters who have gone before and who now reside in mystery in Upper Clarity. Major oversights will be punished by the Three Offices; minor oversights will result in an expropriation of years and a shortening of the life span. Major transgressions will result in calamities reaching to the three degrees of ancestors; minor transgressions will be visited on the individual. If one treats the text slightingly, the spirits will depart. If one sullies the text, then the text will hide itself away.

4a

When those who study transcendence open these spirit texts, they should always rise to bow, wash their hands, and burn incense. Since celestial spirits guard it, one should be especially cautious and reverential. One should not carelessly speak of its contents to any of those to whom the text is not to be transmitted. Even uttering the names of the sections of this text is a violation of the regulations forbidding the disclosure of celestial writ.

---

qing, vol. 1, pp. 112–13. This one is likely to have originally referred to that of the first of the "Three Monarchs."

  * "Arranging the mats" is an important ritual function dating back to state ritual in which mats and writing tables were laid out for spirits. See, for instance, the *Zhou li zhushu* (20:774c) for a discussion of this function. The "Tortoise Mother" is the Queen Mother of the West, a deity important to the Shangqing scriptures. See Cahill, *Queen Mother.*

THE METHOD FOR COLLECTING AND INGESTING THE FLYING
ROOT AND SWALLOWING THE SOLAR PNEUMAS FROM THE
PURPLE TEXTS INSCRIBED BY THE SPIRITS OF THE PALACE
OF GOLDEN PORTE IN THE HEAVEN OF UPPER CLARITY

Of old, [I] received this method from the Celestial Thearch, Lord of
Grand Tenuity.* One name of this text is the *Scripture of Red Cin-
nabar, Essence of Metal, Mineral Phosphorescence, and the Jade
Placenta*[13] *of the Mother of Water.*[14]

4b

You should regularly observe the precise moment of the first
emergence of the sun at sunrise. Face the emerging sun in the east
and knock your teeth together nine times.† This complete, you
should in your mind secretly invoke the spirits, calling the names of
the cloudsouls of the sun and the bynames of the Five Thearchs of
the sun and saying:

> Cloudsouls of the Sun, Orbed[15] Phosphors,
> Envelope of Reflectivity, Green Glare,
> Red lads of the Revolving Auroras,
> Dark Blaze, Whirlwind Simulacra.‡

Having invoked the spirits in your mind, calling these sixteen

---

* Grand Tenuity, a constellation at the autumnal equinox, in our Virgo and Leo,
represents the administrative center of one of the more exalted gods of the Shangqing pantheon, the Celestial Thearch. On this asterism, see Schafer, *Pacing the Void*,
pp. 52–53. Earlier in this scripture, it was related that Li Hong, Lord of the Palace of
the Golden Porte, received this entire text together with oral instructions from the
Celestial Thearch. The first-person pronoun I have supplied represents the fact that
this scripture is in part a transcript of Li Hong's bestowal of the text on the Azure
Lad.

† Knocking the teeth and swallowing saliva are ancient practices associated with
various exercises meant to lead to longevity through the retention and circulation of
breath within the body. See Sakade Yoshinobu, "Chōsei jutsu," in Fukui Kōjun et
al., eds., *Dōkyō* (Tokyo: Hirakawa shuppansha, 1983), vol. 1, pp. 266–68.

‡ This verse, as Robinet has noted (see her "Randonées extatiques," p. 205),
seems to be a mnemonic device for remembering the bynames of the solar Thearchs.
Each byname is formed of three graphs, and the first and third of these figure in the
verse here. The relevant names, along with their colors according to the five-phase
alignment, are: green—"(Dragon) Envelope of Reflectivity" (*zhao long dao*); red—
"Green (Rainbow) Glare" (*lu hong ying*); white—"Revolving (Metallic) Auroras"
(*hui jin xia*); black—"Dark (Green) Blaze" (*xuan lu yan*); and yellow—"Whirlwind
(Shining) Simulacra" (*piao hui xiang*). Though translation of these secret names
accomplishes little more than to compound their original mystery, it does help us to
understand precisely which aspects of the sun—and of the afterimage it leaves on the
human retina—are emphasized in this visualization.

words, then close your eyes and seal your fists. Visualize the flowing auroras in five colors from within the sun all approaching to receive your body down to your feet.* Then envision these five pneumas rising to the top of your head. With this, the five-colored flowing auroras of sunlight will enter into your mouth. Moreover, within the sunlight auroras there will be also a purple pneuma, as large as the pupil of your eye, but wrapped in several tens of layers and flashing brilliantly within the five-colored rays of sun. This is called the flying root of solar efflorescence, the jade placenta, mother of water. Together with the five pneumas it will enter into your mouth.

Facing toward the sun, you should swallow these auroras, gulping breath forty-five times. Once you have completed this, swallow liquid [saliva] nine times, then knock your teeth together nine times   5a and incant softly:

Cinnabar pneumas of the vermilion furnace,
Nurturing germs of the orbed heavens:
The brittle accepts the pliant,†
Blazing liquids and shadowy blossoms.
The primal phosphors of the solar chronogram
Are called the Grandly Luminous.
Their ninefold yang coordinates transformation,
As the two smoky vapors issue forth,‡

---

* To "seal the fist" means to form a fist with the thumb locked inside the fingers like an infant. This action is meant to assist breath-recycling practices known as "womb breathing" and is partly based on interpretations of the *Laozi* no. 35 passage: "Its bones are weak and its sinews flexible, yet it is able to seal its fists." See Henri Maspero, *Le taoïsme et les religions chinoises* (Paris: Gallimard, 1971), pp. 497–503; and Sakade, "Chōsei jutsu," pp. 263–65. "Visualize" translates *cun jian*. As Schafer has noted, "the word [*cun*] means 'to make sensibly present,' 'to give existence to,' almost 'to materialize'" (Schafer, "The Transcendent Vitamin," p. 387).

† According to associations as ancient as the *Yijing*, the "brittle" is yang and the "pliant," yin. In Daoist symbology, beginning with the *Laozi*, pliancy and suppleness become qualities associated with the Dao and thus much to be sought. Here the "pliant" is associated with the heavenly pneumas, which enter into the "brittle" human body.

‡ The "two smoky vapors" seem to be the visible exhalations of the sun and moon as visualized in these meditations. Another instance in which these breaths are described as smoky occurs in the exercise recounted in the *Zhen'gao* for blocking the passages by which the seven whitesouls leave the body. This is accomplished by dotting the left cheekbone with a (red) cinnabar-impregnated brush and the right cheek with a brush dipped in (yellow) orpiment, accompanied by visualizations and incantations. According to the instructions, the procedure will not only block these vital

To congeal my cloudsouls, harmonize my whitesouls.
From within the germs of the five breaths,
The Five Thearchs emerge,
Riding on beams, controlling my bodily form.
I grasp the flying by means of its emptiness;
Pluck the root to achieve fullness.
Heads wrapped in dragon flowers,
Caped in vermilion, belted in green,
Reining on the raven-black, flowing darkness,
Their auroras reflect in Upper Clarity.
I will be presented a writ on jade slats;
The Golden Porte will inscribe my name.
Consuming the flowers of dawn,
I will join in spirit with the Perfected,
Will fly in transcendence to Grand Tenuity,
Will rise above to the Purple Court.

Having completed this incantation, face the sun and bow repeatedly.

Even among Transcendents and Perfected, not one in a million knows the names of the cloudsouls of the sun. This is a mystic and wondrous Way—not one of which those blood eaters with their rotting skeletons might have heard.*

When the day is overcast and without sun, you may perform this rite by retaining the sun in vision within a secret room where you lay yourself to rest, so long as the spot is clean. This is because those Daoists who practice in purity and whose essential natures move sympathetically the spirits on high are able to practice this method without even seeing the sun.

5b

Those Daoists who have renounced grain and live in the mountains and forests, who conduct lengthy purification rites on the Five Marchmounts, who have cut themselves off from the dust of the mortal world, or whose far-ranging meditations reside only in clarity and perfection, should daily swallow the auroras of solar root and swallow the essences of Grand Solarity. They will immediately notice

---

spots, but also "attract the vapors of the two phosphors"—that is, the sun and moon. (*HY* 1010, 10:22a.2–3).

* The "blood eaters with their rotting skeletons" are the unhallowed dead of popular cults and the humans who revere them.

their bodies exuding jade fluids and their faces emitting flowing light.

For those who are still involved in external human affairs, who have not yet achieved stillness of body, who float aimlessly along the byways of the world, or whose hearts are bound by ropes and fetters, it is essential that this practice be carried out as described above on the first, third, fifth, seventh, ninth, thirteenth, fifteenth, seventeenth, nineteenth, and twenty-fifth of each month.* Each month, you should practice ten times. These are the days on which the cloudsouls of the sun might descend to join with you, when the flying root is overflowing and full, and the Mother of Water might ward off [your] dreams.[16] If you practice this for eighteen years, Upper Clarity will refine [your form] to golden perfection, so that you reflect a gemmy light. Your rank will reach that of Jade Sovereign and you will fly through the Grand Void, mounted on the efflorescences of the Three Elementals, exalted over all below heaven.

6a

The talisman above [see fig. 2] is to be written in red on blue paper at midnight on the last night of each month.† Face east and swallow it to provide prior notification to the cloudsouls of the sun. Just before you swallow it, block your breath and, grasping the talisman in your left hand, incant silently:

> Cinnabar writ of Grand Tenuity,
> Entitled "Opening Luminescence,"
> Bring to me the cloudsouls of the sun on high,
> To come and transform (so-and-so's) shape.
> Just at dawn, carefully garbed,
> They issue from the Round Court:
> Mother of water as a flying efflorescence;
> The golden essence, solar root.
> Their purple reflections flow within its beams,
> Which are called the Five Numens.

6b

Having completed the incantation, swallow the talisman.

---

* The odd-numbered days are associated with yang.

† A note written under this talisman in the *HY 639* version of this text adds that, even if you are unable to practice this every month, it is essential that you do so in odd-numbered months.

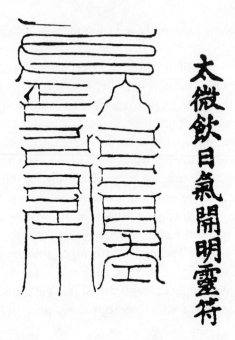

太微飲日氣開明靈符

Fig. 2.   The Numinous Talisman of Grand Tenuity for Swallowing the Pneumas of the Sun and Opening Its Luminescence

THE METHOD FOR COLLECTING AND SWALLOWING THE YIN FLOWER AND SWALLOWING LUNAR ESSENCE FROM THE PURPLE TEXTS INSCRIBED BY THE SPIRITS OF THE PALACE OF GOLDEN PORTE IN THE HEAVEN OF UPPER CLARITY

Of old, I received this method from the Celestial Thearch, Lord of Grand Tenuity. One name of this text is the *Scripture of Yellow Pneuma, Essence of Yang, and Fetal Germ Stored in Heaven and Hidden in the Moon.*

You should envision the moon, at the time when it is newly emerged. Then, facing the moon in the west, knock your teeth together ten times. This complete, secretly incant, calling the names of the whitesouls of the moon and the bynames of the five Ladies within the Moon, saying:

> Whitesouls of the moon, shadowed artemisia;
> Scented Loveliness, shrouded and scattered;
> Pliant Vacuity, holy orchid;

Mottled Flower, joined tail feathers;
Pure Gold, clear and glittering;
Glowing Visage, displayed atop the estrade.*

Having invoked the spirits in your mind, calling these twenty-four
words, then close your eyes and seal your fists, visualizing the flow-   7a
ing essences in five colors from within the moon all approaching to
receive your body down to your feet. Then envision these five pneumas rising to the top of your head. With this, the five-colored flowing essences of moonlight will enter into your mouth. Moreover,
within the moonlight essences there will also be a yellow pneuma, as
large as the pupil of your eye, wrapped about several tens of times
and arriving within the five-colored rays of lunar essence. This is
called the flying yellow of lunar efflorescence, the germ of the jade
fetus. Together with the five pneumas it will enter into your mouth.

Facing toward the moon, you should swallow these essences,
gulping breath fifty times. Once you have completed this, swallow
saliva ten times, then knock your teach together ten times and incant
softly:

Mystic gleam, yellow and clear,
Highest pneumas of primal yin,
Scatter in profusion your chill whirlwinds,
Ordering numinous spirits and gathering them in my stomach.
Empty waves swell over the strand,
Immediately cleansing and purifying the vessel.
Moon essences, phosphors of the night,
Exalted on high in the Dark Palace—
The Five Sovereign Ladies
Each maintain the position of mother.
May the fetus fly in;
May the newborn babe gradually emerge.
The circling yin joins thrice,
Its beams mystically darkening in all directions.   7b

---

* In the same fashion as in the incantation given earlier for the Five Thearchs of
the Sun, this incantation provides a mnemonic for the names and bynames of the five
ladies who reside in the moon. The bynames, along with their colors according
to the five-phase alignment, are: green—"Scented and lovely (newborn)" (*fen yan
ying*); red—"Pliant (and extended) vacuity" (*yuan yan xu*); white—"Mottled (and
linked) flowers" (*yu lian hua*); black—"Pure (and connected) gold" (*chun shu jin*);
and yellow—"Glowing (and fixed) visage" (*jiong ding rong*).

Pacify my cloudsouls, control the whitesouls;
May the five embryos circulate.
As flying essence mounted on auroras,
They depart the barrens in the east.
The hair of their heads knotted in numinous clouds,
Their glowing efflorescence summons the wind.
With dragon talismans belted on the left,
Tiger insignia tied on the right,
They wear vermilion cloaks of phoenix feathers,
Jade pendants, gold medallions.*
Soaring trees, roots knotted to the slope[17]—
These are called the Wood Kings.
The divine toad draws at their roots,
So that the moon now wanes, now waxes.†
The luminous essence glows within,
Then spurts forth as a bridge across dark waters.
Present me with writings and jade slips,
Inscribe my name in the cloudy chambers.
I now feed on the lunar efflorescences,
Joining thereby with the Perfected.
I will fly as a transcendent to Purple Tenuity,
There to pay court to the Grand Luminaries.

Having completed this incantation, face the moon and bow
repeatedly.

For retaining in vision the sun and the moon, you may either sit
or stand as is more convenient.

Among Transcendent officials, not one knows the bynames of the
whitesouls of the moon. Only those about to become Perfected
know them.

---

* "Jade pendants, gold medallions" (*yupei jindang*) here, as elsewhere in the
Shangqing texts, denotes the decorations of the Ladies within the Moon. However,
such items of apparel all have significance. The whole phrase is a part of the name
of a scripture (*HY* 56), which provides the information that "jade pendants" represents the cloudsouls and "gold medallions" the whitesouls of the deities of the Nine
Heavens. The souls—yang and yin, respectively—are themselves the object of visualization practices. See Robinet, "Randonées extatiques," pp. 170–218. The fact
that the ladies wear these emblems betokens their level of perfection. Robinet translates *jindang* as "anneau d'or." One of the denotations of the term is "golden ear
ornament," though there is no evidence that it was ring shaped. The chapter of the
Hou Han shu on habiliments (30:3668) describes a ceremonial military headgear
adorned with a *jindang* that is decorated with cicada patterns and dangles a sable
tail. The object imagined here might equally be some sort of circular belt ornament.

† In traditional belief, the moon was inhabited by a toad and by a grove of cin-
namon trees. On these images, see Schafer, *Pacing the Void*, pp. 185–95. These elements of popular folklore are here deified.

When the sky is overcast or there is no moon, you may perform this rite within doors. Carry out the essential instructions just as in the method for swallowing the beams of the sun. Those who daily practice this method will immediately notice their bodies exuding gleaming beams of light and their eyesight filled with flying essences.*

8a

In its most essential form, this practice should be carried out on the second, fourth, sixth, eighth, tenth, fourteenth, sixteenth, eighteenth, twentieth, twenty-second, and twenty-fourth of each month.† Each month, you should practice eleven times. This is enough to achieve transcendence. These are the nights on which the yin essences fly and merge,[18] when the three pneumas overflow, the lunar waters form efflorescences, and their yellow spirits might descend to join with you. If you practice this for eighteen years, Upper Clarity will refine your cloudsouls and change your whitesouls, so that you reflect a gemmy light. You will mount mystically reined phosphors to fly through the Grand Void.

The talisman above [see fig. 3] is to be written in yellow on blue paper at midnight on the last night of each month.[19] Face east and swallow it to provide prior notification to the whitesouls of the moon after first swallowing the Numinous Talisman for Opening Luminescence. Just before you swallow the lunar talisman, block your breath and, grasping the talisman in your right hand, incant silently:

8b

> Yellow writ of Purple Tenuity,
> Entitled "Grand Mystery,"
> Bring to me the waters of lunar efflorescence,
> To nurture my whitesouls, harmonize my cloudsouls.
> This austere practice of the secret prescriptions
> Issues from the Mystic Pass.‡
> Stored in heaven, concealed in the moon,
> The Five Numinous Ladies
> Let fly their beams of light in nine paths,
> To illumine my Muddy Pellet.

Having completed the incantation, swallow the talisman.

---

* This description seems to refer to the sort of afterimage discussed in footnote ‡ on p. 314.

† The even-numbered days are associated with yin.

‡ On the location of the Mystic Pass in the human body, see *HY* 639, 11b–12a, translated further on. This is the spot where spirit embryos are to be engendered in

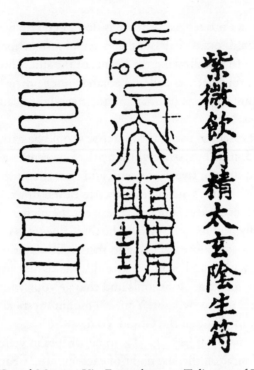

Fig. 3.   The Grand Mystery Yin-Engenderment Talisman of Purple
Tenuity for Swallowing the Essences of the Moon

THE METHOD FOR SECURING THE THREE CLOUDSOULS FROM THE PURPLE TEXTS INSCRIBED BY THE SPIRITS OF GRAND TENUITY

The nights of the third, thirteenth, and twenty-third days of the

9a   month are the time when the three cloudsouls are unstable. This is
when Bright Spirit floats off to roam; when Embryo Light releases
his shape; when Tenebrous Essence becomes agitated.

These three sovereigns—Bright Spirit, Embryo Light, and Tenebrous Essence—are the spirit names of the three cloudsouls. On
these nights they depart the body to roam afar, fleeing the chamber

---

the human body. In the macrocosm, the "Mystic Pass," also know as the "Barrier of
Heaven," stands for the triple passes through which one must proceed to reach the
Golden Porte. See Kroll, "Barrier of Heaven." In other words, this statement has a
double frame of reference. The practices described here issued from the highest
heavens through the gates of life and involve the creation of corporeal spirits within
the counterpart of the gates of life in the human body.

like whirlwinds. Sometimes they are forcibly detained by others' cloudsouls or by outside demons. Sometimes they are captured by sprites and enregistered as one of them. Sometimes they are unable to find their way back and are thenceforth separated from the body. Sometimes they are attacked by outside cloudsouls and the two pneumas engage in combat with one another. In all such cases, the Ruddy Infant will be driven by anxiety. Its concentration will be focused on other things and it will lack form as it moves about. Your heart will be grieved and your thoughts constricted.

Daoists should always secure their cloudsouls to keep them from roaming and getting lost. The method for detaining them is as follows:

Lie down to sleep facing upward with a pillow beneath your head, your feet extended, and your arms crossed over your heart. Close your eyes and block your breath for the space of three normal breaths, knocking your teeth three times. Envision a vermilion pneuma as large as a chicken's egg coming from within your heart and rising to emerge from between your eyes. After it emerges from between your eyes, this vermilion pneuma will become large enough   9b to cover your body and will flow over the body to the top of your head. Transforming, it will become fire that wraps all around your body.

Once the body is encircled, cause the fire to penetrate your body as if it were igniting charcoal. Once this is complete, you should feel slightly hot internally. When this happens, again knock your teeth three times and, envisioning them, call the three cloudsouls by name—Bright Spirit, Embryo Light, and Tenebrous Essence—telling the three spirits to stay put. Then quietly incant:

> Mysterious officers of Grand Tenuity,
> Central Yellow and Inaugural Green,*
> Refine within my three cloudsouls
> So that Embryo Light is at rest,
> A spirit treasure in the jade chamber.
> They should all live with me
> And not be permitted to move about blindly.

---

* The three elemental colors associated with the lord of Grand Tenuity are black, yellow, and green. Green is the color of spring and new growth, while yellow is the color of the center and earth.

Overseeing them is the Grand Spirit.
If they wish to fly,
They are permitted to visit only the Grand Bourne or Upper Clarity;*
If they become hungry or thirsty,
They are permitted to sup only on Jade Essence of Swirling Solution.†

THE METHOD FOR CONTROLLING
THE SEVEN WHITESOULS FROM THE PURPLE TEXTS
INSCRIBED BY THE SPIRITS OF GRAND TENUITY

10a   The nights when the moon is beginning its cycle, when the moon is
full, and when the moon is darkened are the times when the seven
whitesouls wander free, roaming into all sorts of corruption and
filth. Sometimes they have intercourse with blood eaters, those
demons and sprites who wander to and fro. Sometimes they enter
into sexual relations with corpses. Sometimes they corrupt and
delude the Ruddy Infant, joining together in lasciviousness to attack
their own residence. Sometimes they visit the Three Offices or the
River Sire to tell of your transgressions.‡ Sometimes they are transformed into Wangliang demons to bewitch you.§ Sometimes they
lead demons into the body or call perverse forces to destroy you. All
injuries and illnesses are caused by the transgressions of the whitesouls. The whitesouls' nature is to delight in your death; their most
ardent desire, to destroy you.

Daoists should always discipline them through control, transform
them through refining their natures, rectify them through sub-
jugation, and overpower them through strict regulation.

---

* The "Grand Bourne" or "Grand Culmination" (*taiji*) represents as much a
point in time as in space. In early cosmogonic accounts, it marked the differentiation
from primordial yin and yang of the "ten thousand things" of the sensible world.
(See Schafer, *Pacing the Void*, pp. 25–30.) This sense of the term was preserved in
Yang Xi's writings (see especially *HY* 1010, 5:1a), but, more and more, the Grand
Bourne came to be seen as a heavenly realm, replete with palaces and powers, accessible to the spirits who were able to travel back in time to the origins of the Dao. The
Palaces of the Grand Bourne are thus situated on the borders of the horizontally
arrayed celestial paradises, as if the Grand Culmination, like the "Big Bang," had
exploded outward so that its most ancient constituents now lay at the greatest distance. (See, e.g., *HY* 1010, 5:15a, where Yang Xi describes the Grand Bourne as the
highest of the nine palaces atop Mount Kunlun.)
    † This is one of the products of the Langgan elixir.
    ‡ The River Sire, god of the Yellow River, oversees the Yellow Springs, the
underworld home of the dead in traditional Chinese belief.
    § Wangliang demons are sprites that inhabit mountains and can take on human
form. (*Guoyu*, 5:7a)

The first whitesoul is named "Corpse Dog," the second "Subduing Arrow," the third "Sparrow Lunarity," the fourth "Gulping Thief," the fifth "Negating Poison," the sixth "Filth Expeller," and the seventh "Stinking Lungs."

These are the hidden names of the seven whitesouls, the demons   10b
of turbidity within the body. The method of controlling and overseeing them is as follows:

You should lie down with your head away from the pillow, your feet extended, and the centers of your two palms covering your ears. Your fingertips should just cross in the middle of the nape of your neck. Stop breathing for the space of seven normal breaths, knock your teeth seven times, and envision a white pneuma as big as a small bean on the tip of your nose. After a while, it will gradually enlarge to cover your body in nine layers, from above your head to below your feet.

Once this is complete, the white pneuma will suddenly change into the celestial beasts. Cause the two green dragons to position themselves in your eyes and the two white tigers to place themselves within your nostrils. These should be facing outward. The vermilion sparrow should be above your heart, facing your mouth. The gray-green tortoise should be below your left foot and the numinous snake below your right foot.* Within your two ears will be Jade Maidens, dressed in dark brocade and blocking the ear canals. They will hold torches in both of their hands. After a long time, when all of these are in place, swallow saliva seven times, knock your teeth seven times, and call the names of the seven whitesouls. When you   11a
are finished, softly incant:

> With elemental pneumas nine times wound,
> I control the perverse ferocity of the whitesouls.
> Celestial beasts guard the gates,
> Enchanting maidens hold the passes.
> They refine the whitesouls to passive compliance,
> Granting me peace and calm.

---

* These beasts are the traditional directional animals: the green dragon is east; the white tiger, west; the vermilion sparrow, south; tortoise and snake (the "murky warrior"), north. They have a long history as demon-quellers and are to be found, for instance, represented on the walls of tombs. The dragon and tiger have even been found, represented in shell, in a neolithic burial site. They are seen in this role, as guards and demon-quellers, throughout the Shangqing scriptures.

You are not to engage in reckless movement!
They keep watch over the source of your shapes.
If you hunger or thirst,
You are to obediently partake of Lunar Yellow and Solar Cinnabar.*

Once the preceding incantation is finished, the seven whitesouls will be shut inside, where they will accept your control and keep to their positions.

If you regularly practice this method, the turbidity of the white-souls will be eliminated and they will revert to goodness. Your whole body will then match the Three Palaces above and you will join in holiness with the Three Primes.†

♦   ♦   ♦   ♦

The body of a person contains the spirits of the Palaces of the Three Primes. Within the Gate of Destiny are the Grand Sovereign of the Mystic Pass and the spirits of the three cloudsouls.[20] Altogether there are seven spirits within the body who desire that the person live a long life. These are the greatly propitious sovereigns of kindness and benevolence. The seven whitesouls also are born within the same body, but they are thieves who attack the body. 11b This is why they must be controlled. If Daoists know only the methods of seeking transcendence and do not know the way to control their whitesouls, they can but labor in vain.

♦   ♦   ♦   ♦

As for the placement of the Palaces of the Three Primes, the Palace of the Upper Prime is in the Muddy Pellet. Its spirit is the Ruddy

---

* Lunar Yellow, under the name "Lunar Efflorescence of the Yellow Solution," is one of the products of the Langgan elixir. Solar Cinnabar may well refer to another product of the Langgan elixir, the "Jade Essence of the Swirling Solution," in that ingestion of this substance causes one's body to "become a sun." (See the following translation from HY 255, 5b.)

† The term "three primes" has a multiplicity of referents. The meaning of the term in the microcosm of the human body will be described later. In the macrocosm and at the most basic level, the three primes represent the first pneumas engendered by the Dao at creation, when it divided into yin, yang, and a third, which merged the two. Various triads are thus associated with the three primes: heaven-earth-humanity; heaven-earth-underworld; the essences of sun, moon, and stars; the three heavens of Celestial Master Daoism; and the three clear regions of Shangqing Daoism—to name but a few.

Infant, with the byname "Primal Priority" and the alternate name
"Thearch's Chamberlain." The Palace of the Central Prime resides
in the Scarlet Chamber—that is, the heart. Its spirit is "Perfected
One," with the byname "Thane Cinnabar" and the alternate name
"Shining Durability." The Lower Prime is the Palace of the Cinna-
bar Field, three inches below the navel. Its spirit is "Newborn,"
with the byname "Primal Yang" and the alternate name "Valley
Mystery."[21]

These are the spirits of the triple unity. Whenever you wish to
secure your cloudsouls and control your whitesouls, you should
always first secretly call the names of these spirits.

Envision the three spirits with jade coloration, golden emanations, and possessing the features of newborn babes. The spirits of
the upper and middle primes are clothed entirely in vermilion and
that of the lower prime in yellow. Their heads are shaped like those
of newborn babies. When you practice the Dao and swallow pneumas you should also call their names.

The "Gate of Destiny" is the navel. The "Mystic Pass" is the passageway which joined the placenta to your viscera when you were   12a
first born. Within this passageway is the Palace of Life. Residing
within this palace is the Grand Sovereign named "Peach Child,"
with the byname "Join and Extend." This spirit wears vermilion
clothing and head scarf and a purple lotus cap. He sits facing the
Gate of Destiny. The three cloudsouls stand at his side in attendance.
This Grand Sovereign constantly holds in his hand a talisman with
the image of the Celestial Sovereign, with which he mixes and pours
primal pneumas to replenish the fetus and restore the placenta.

When you lie down at night, first block your breath for a space
of twenty-four normal breaths and silently incant the names of the
Great Sovereign three times. Then swallow saliva fifty times, knock
your teeth together thrice, and softly incant:

Great spirit of fetal numinousness,
Celestial Lord of the Resplendent Mainstay,*

* Professor Robinet has called to my attention the fact that, according to another
account of this practice, "Fetal Numinosity," apparently another name for the Peach
Child, was to reside in the spleen, while the cloudsouls and whitesouls take up

Holds in his hands the placental talisman,
His head capped in purple.
He cycles the yellow and the red[22]
As he elevates essence through the Gate of Destiny,
Transforming my spirits and giving me life.*
The Bureau of the Six Courses relies on him.†
My skeletal frame gleams and glistens,
And Jade Maidens lodge in my body.[23]

If you are able to regularly practice this for eighteen years, the Great Sovereign will be enabled to incite the three Cinnabar Fields on his left and to control the three pneumas on his right. The Cinnabar Fields will be transformed into flying conveyances and the pneumas will form dark dragons. When he looks up, the twenty-four spirits will do his bidding.‡ When he looks down, he will dispatch the cloudsoul spirits and summon the yang officers of the six *jia* and the yin officers of the six *ding*.§ Then, with a thousand conveyances and ten thousand riders, you will ascend to heaven in broad daylight. This can all be brought about in response to the actions of Lord Peach.

♦   ♦   ♦   ♦

Above [see fig. 4] is the Talisman of the Image of the Celestial Sovereign, to be presented to Peach Child, byname "Join and Extend,"

---

positions in the liver and lungs, respectively. See *HY* 1026, 11:12b, and, for the role of the spleen as central organ, Robinet, "Le Ta-tung Chen-ching," pp. 75 ff. "Mainstay of Heaven" is an appellation of the Dipper, referring to its central role in linking the stars regulating the cyclical movements of the heavens. Here, the honorific "Resplendent Mainstay" probably evokes the Peach Child's central role among the spirits of the body.

* The cycling of the yellow and red refers to the practice of "merging pneumas" to perfect the essences, the sexual rite of the Celestial Masters. Here the whole procedure is accomplished immaculately within the body.

† The Bureau of the Six Courses is charged with control of vision. It rests in the temples, the "small indentation to the rear of the eyebrows" (*HY* 1010, 9:6b10–7a4). It is named the Bureau of the Six Courses because, once it is perfected, the Daoist is able to see in six directions (front and rear, to both sides, down and up) simultaneously. In the present instance, the Bureau most likely stands for the centers of all the senses.

‡ The twenty-four spirits, in three groups of eight, are the inhabitants of the Palaces of the Three Primes in the human body.

§ The "six *jia*" and the "six *ding*" are spirits derived from the diviner's cosmological compass (or a table derived from it) according to a method known as *dunjia*

12b

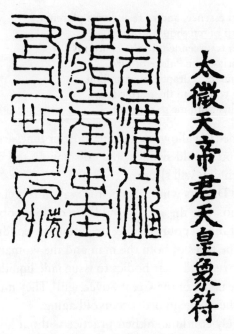

太微天帝君天皇象符

Fig. 4.   The Talisman of the Image of the Celestial Sovereign—the
Celestial Thearch, Lord of Grand Tenuity

the Great Sovereign of the Palace of Life, that he might mix the   13a
primal pneumas from on high, arrange the placenta, and transport
essence. This talisman is to be written in vermilion on green paper.
At midnight on the nights of the new moon and the full moon, you
should face north to swallow it. Holding the talisman in your left
hand, block your breath and silently incant:

> This dark writing of the Celestial Thearch,
> Numinous talisman of the Sovereign's image,
> Is to mix the primal pneumas,

(Kalinowski, "La littérature divinatoire," pp. 91–95). This method was based on
a sexagesimal system, computed by combining the ten "celestial stems" with the
twelve "terrestrial branches." The two celestial stems *jia* and *ding* came to hold particular importance through their positions in the cycle. *Jia,* being the first sign of
each ten-day "week," was designated yang, and *ding,* as the fourth day, was designated yin. These became the gendered *jia* and *ding* spirits of Daoism. For more on
these spirits, see Poul Andersen, "The Practice of Bugang," *CEA* 5 (1990), pp. 33–
34; and Schipper, *The Taoist Body,* pp. 142–44.

To transport essence, and to restore the placenta.
The newborn of ten thousand years
Shall fly as a transcendent to the Heavenly Pivot.*
O Great Spirit of the Palace of Life,
Robed in cinnabar, draped in vermilion,
Wearing on your head the purple lotus,
Work together with me to this end.

Once finished, swallow the talisman. After that, arise and bow repeatedly. You should swallow the talisman on top of the bed platform on which you will sleep.

If there are Daoists who practice the way of recycling the seminal essences—who cycle the yellow and the red, doing obeisance to the essence that it might pour out life, irrigating the conduits with fluid and causing the faces of both the man and the woman involved to turn cinnabar red and their bodies to issue jade liquids—they should also know the name of the Great Sovereign.† They must swallow the Talisman of the Image in order to avoid aging.

13b   If they merely continue in their practice without knowing the names of the spirits; if they recycle the essences and do not swallow this talisman, never see this incantation and explanation, never know who resides in their internal palaces and storehouses—though they live to be a thousand years old, their corpses will be returned to the Palace of Grand Darkness. They will have assembled a long span of life in vain and their bones must be returned to the Three Offices.

Those Daoists who regularly, when they lie down at night, envi-

---

* The "Heavenly Pivot" is the polestar, around which the sky seems to turn. With the precession of the equinoxes, the identification of the "central" star shifted. Whether because the reassignment of this label bothered some sky watchers or for other unknown reasons, the appellation Heavenly Pivot was also given to Dubhe, the brightest star of the Big Dipper, which at least continued to point to the center. See Schafer, *Pacing the Void*, pp. 44–45.

† "Cycling the yellow and the red" refers to the sexual rites of the Celestial Masters, also known as "merging pneumas." (See the *Xiang'er* commentary.) Feminine essence was regarded as yellow because of women's association with earth. Men are yang and thus associated with red. According to Yang Xi, the books of sexual practice were also written in yellow, on paper or silk with red borders (*HY* 1010, 2:1b.4). Notice that the description given here, though unapproving, does not accuse Daoists who employ this method of practicing sexual vampirism of the sort we have seen criticized in the *Xiang'er*. Still, the methods revealed in this text are presented as clearly superior to those of the Celestial Masters.

sion the Grand Sovereign and perform the incantations according to
this method and who swallow the talisman at the new and full moon
in order to foster the growth of the fetus and essences will achieve
transcendence in this fashion. There is no need to bother about techniques to be performed by man and woman together for cycling and
augmenting essences. Moreover, intercourse with a woman for the
purpose of rising up to the heavens and recycling pneumas in order
to become a Heavenly Transcendent are methods more treacherous
than fire and water. They lead to death and destruction more
quickly than the slice of an axe.* Those who do not with equanimity
hold to the One by nature will certainly not be able to avoid destruction through these methods. For those of middling attainments who
practice them, it is like "swallowing swords and hoping the throat is
not injured"; can this really be done?

The Great Spirit, Lord of the Palace of Life, prohibits humans   14a
from eating living, full-blooded creatures. He prohibits the cooking
of the six domestic animals, fur-bearing animals, the peels or leaves
of onion, or any of the strong-smelling herbs.† All of these attack
and disturb the fetal pneumas and injure the newborn spirits with
their stench. Be cautious about this.

II.   ELIXIR OF THE EFFLORESCENCE OF LANGGAN,   *HY 255*
FROM THE *PURPLE TEXTS INSCRIBED BY THE SPIRITS*

First conduct a purification of forty days in the mountain forests, not   1a
concerning yourself at all with outside affairs; then begin to make
the spirit lute. It will take a full hundred days from the beginning of
your purification rites to the luting and the sealing of the crucible.
Choose a heat-resistant crucible with an upper chamber that will
hold three gallons of liquid. It makes no difference if it is white or
red, so long as it can bear heat without cracking or breaking.

---

* This warning is phrased in terminology drawn from the Celestial Master texts
themselves. See line 350 of the *Xiang'er* and p. 19a of the *Admonitions,* where various practices are described as like "an axe that hacks away at the body."

† The "strong-smelling herbs" include garlic, leeks, ginger, coriander, and the
like. These plants were believed to possess vapors inimical to the pure breaths of
physiological practice.

Method for making the spirit lute

Ingredients:

shell of left-oriented oyster from Donghai*—6 parts
earthworm castings—3 parts
fine hairs shed by a horse—1 part
talc—3 parts
scarlet clay—2 parts
fine goat hair—2 parts
salt crystals—$\frac{1}{2}$ part

Mix the above seven substances and pound them in a mortar.
Strain them through a fine mesh and mix the powder with one-
hundred-day-old rice-wine vinegar.

Then pound this thirty thousand times more. If the lute is mushy,
add more scarlet clay; if it is too stiff, add more vinegar and continue
pounding until you have obtained a fine slip. Strain this mixture
through a mesh to remove all coarse particles.

You should extract only the white inner substance of the oyster
shells. Do not use the external layer. The horse and goat hair should
be first washed and carefully selected. The earthworm castings
should also be separately ground and cleansed of all roughage and
contaminants.

The "parts" noted above are not tenths of an ounce; the weights
should be determined proportionately on the basis of how much lute
will be needed for both halves of the crucible. The interior and exterior of the halves should be luted to a uniform thickness of seven-
tenths of an inch. This is done gradually. First apply a thin layer of
lute and allow it to dry in the shade. When this is dry, add successive
layers in the same fashion until the coating reaches seven-tenths of
an inch.

When the desired thickness is reached and the coated crucible has
been allowed to dry, mix Yellow Cinnabar with rice-wine vinegar,
pounding thirty thousand times to form a further lutelike substance.

1b

* According to Tao Hongjing's glosses to the *Bencao,* male oysters have a
pointed shell that hinges to the left and are always to be found oriented to the east. It
is thus important that only those oysters obtained from knowledgeable collectors be
used in the lute. (See Bernard Read, *Turtle and Shellfish Drugs,* vol. 3 of Bernard
Read, ed., *Chinese Materia Medica* [1937; reprint, Taipei: Southern Materials Center, 1977], p. 39.)

Lute the interior of both halves of the crucible with this to a thickness of three-tenths of an inch. If cracks appear, add more lute and then dry the crucible in the shade for ten days until the surface is perfectly free of cracks. "Yellow Cinnabar" is red oxide of lead. Do not use this mixture to lute the outside of the vessel.

Once the drugs are put into the vessel, you must lute the vessel to seal it firmly. Seal the joint carefully so that it is completely secure. Also, you must again lute the outside of the vessel, above and below as well as on the four sides, to a thickness of four-tenths of an inch. Then it must be placed in a clean spot and dried in the shade for seventeen days. If there are any hairline fractures, use a brush made from the beard of a goat to coat them, then allow the vessel to dry for seven more days. It is best if the external thickness is between one and four-tenths and one and a half inches. This is the final step in producing a spirit lute, luting the crucible, and inserting the drugs.

This luting method is simpler than that for the Golden Liquor Nine-Times Recycled Elixir vessel, but the lute must be finer and purer, the mixing and pounding must be more regulated, and overall more care must be taken. Be cautious so that the floriate essence does not leak away! If it leaks away there will be no benefit.

You should also be assiduous with regard to ritual purification. Start on the established day of that month and carry on for one hundred days. When you have finished your purification, take three barrels of clear wine and toss them into an east-flowing stream. Gazing down at the water, incant, saying:

> Azure flow of Great Mystery,
> Nine Rivers and Eight Seas;
> Mountain spirits, chthonian powers:
> From above I will obtain cinnabar essence—
> Now with fine wine, three full barrels,
> I respectfully sacrifice to the River Spirits.

When you have finished incanting, return without looking back and, on that day, place the drugs in the crucible.

For making the elixir you must locate a spot in the mountain forests that looks down on an east-flowing stream. It should be a spot where humans never pass and where chickens and dogs cannot be heard. Be careful about this.

The drugs for compounding the Elixir of Langgan Efflorescence
are as follows:[24]

Red Infant of the Scarlet Mound (cinnabar)	10 lbs.
Solar Cloudsoul of the Cinnabar Mountains (realgar)	5 lbs.
White-Silk Flying Dragon (milky quartz)	1 lb.
Blue-Waisted Middle Daughter (azurite)	5 oz.
Civil Lord of Purple Mound (amethyst)	5 oz.
Volatile Efflorescence of the Cyan Wall (graphite)	5 oz.
Mysterious Pearl of the Northern Thearch (saltpeter)	1 lb.
Yellow Lad of the Nine Numina (sulfur)	5 oz.
Golden Goat of the Five Essences (asbestos)[25]	5 oz.
Flying Blossoms of Rain Flowers (mica)	5 oz.
Dropped Teeth of the White Tiger (iron pyrite)[26]	5 oz.
White Paste of Flowing Cinnabar (lead carbonate)[27]	1 lb.
Inverted Spirit Bone (Turkestan salt)[28]	5 oz.
Lunar Efflorescence of the Dark Estrade (orpiment)	5 lbs.

3a

All together there are fourteen ingredients. Grind them in order,
beginning with the cinnabar granules, five thousand times each.

The person who grinds the drugs must be equable, cautious, and
of few words. Have him conduct purification rites for thirty days
before beginning the grinding. Also, when mixing the drugs, only
three or four people can be involved. It is difficult to find ideal
people, but if even one is not of like mind, it will ruin the matter for
the others. Once the floriate elixir is finished, one ounce constitutes a
"transcendent dose." If one wishes to remain in the mundane world,
half an ounce is sufficient.

Once the ingredients have been ground separately, they should
be placed in the crucible. First put in the Turkestan salt, scattering
it evenly about the bottom of the crucible. Then add, in order, sal
peter, mica, asbestos, iron pyrite, lead carbonate, azurite, sulfur,
milky quartz, graphite, amethyst, orpiment, realgar, and finally the
cinnabar granules on top. As each ingredient is placed in the crucible, spread them and press them down slightly so as to make sure
each layer is thin. Then take three pounds of liquid mercury and
pour it over all the drugs. When this is done, seal the top half of the
crucible to the bottom half with "Yellow Cinnabar" lute applied at

3b

the joints. Outside the joints use the oyster-shell lute. Once this has dried in the shade, lute the outside of the vessel, above and below and around the four sides, to a thickness of four-tenths of an inch.

For building the foundation of the furnace chamber, you should first dig to a depth of three feet, removing the contaminated soil and replacing it with clean loam. The foundation to be built on this level surface should be two feet five inches in height. Do not build your furnace on the site of an old grave mound or residence. The furnace chamber should be thirty feet long, sixteen feet wide, and sixteen feet tall. It must be pure, clean, and well constructed. Roof it with fragrant grasses, and plaster the walls both inside and out so that they are sturdy and secure. There should be two doors, four feet wide, covered with curtains, that face east and south. The head alchemist and those who watch the fires are to stay in this chamber.

4a

The furnace is to be placed in the center of the room. The mouth of the furnace should face east. The furnace is to be constructed of fine brick, mortared together. Then pound white clay and the hair of oxen, horse, and river deer into bitter liquor [wine vinegar?] and east-flowing stream water to make plaster for the furnace. Set the crucible on an iron stand that has been placed inside the furnace. The crucible should be set in the center of the furnace, with all four sides three and a half inches from the sides of the furnace. The furnace should rise two feet above the top of the crucible, with the bottom of the crucible one and eight-tenths feet off the floor.

The fine chaff that will be ignited beneath the crucible should initially be one foot below the bottom. Take turns keeping close watch over the fire so that it does not become too intense. After twenty days, allow the fire to reach within six inches of the crucible for twenty days, within four inches for another twenty days, within one inch for ten days, touching the crucible for ten days, and finally let the flames reach halfway up the crucible for twenty days. After one hundred days of firing, the drug will be completed.

4b

The crucible should be cooled for three days before being opened. The volatile efflorescence is light and will have adhered to the roof of the upper half of the crucible. Brush this off with the feather of a three-year-old rooster. The efflorescence should have thirty-seven hues. It is a volatile liquid both brilliant and mottled, a purple aurora darkly flashing. This is called the Elixir of Langgan Efflorescence.

If, just at dawn on the first day of the eleventh, fourth, or eighth month, you bow repeatedly and ingest one ounce of this elixir with the water from an east-flowing stream, seven-colored pneumas will rise from your head and your face will have the jadelike glow of metallic efflorescence.[29] If you hold your breath, immediately a chariot from the eight shrouded extents of the universe will arrive. When you spit on the ground, your saliva will transform into a flying dragon. When you whistle to your left, divine Transcendents will pay court to you; when you point to the right, the vapors of Three Elementals will join with the wind.* Then, in thousands of conveyances, with myriad outriders, you will fly up to Upper Clarity.

5a

If the efflorescence has not all risen to the upper half of the crucible, you may reseal the halves, luting their joints as before, and fire the crucible up to the center for forty-nine days. After this, there will be no chance that it is not finished.

Lunar Efflorescence of the Yellow Solution

After having fired the crucible for one hundred days to produce the Elixir of Langgan Efflorescence, do not open it but begin firing again just as before, gradually decreasing the distance between the fire and the crucible, for an additional one hundred days.

Cool the crucible for six nights, open it, and observe it. The essences will have risen to the upper chamber, forming a curtain. Within the curtain will be a yellow liquid. This liquid will contain yellow efflorescences like a lotus flower. This is called the Lunar Efflorescence of the Yellow Solution. The curtain that has risen to the upper chamber of the crucible will have the shape of a black gallbladder. Pluck it out. By ingesting the efflorescence together with one pint of the Yellow Solution, you will change forms ten thousand times, your eyes will become luminous moons, and you will float above in the Grand Void to fly off to the Palace of Purple Tenuity.

5b

◆   ◆   ◆   ◆

* For the pneumas of the three elemental colors, see footnote ‡ on p. 310.

Jade Essence of the Swirling Solution

After having fired the drugs for two hundred days to form the Lunar
Efflorescence of the Yellow Solution, do not open the crucible, but
again begin the phased firing as before for another one hundred
days. Cool the crucible for nine nights and open it. The essences will
have formed bubbles that will have risen to the top of the upper
chamber. Within the bubbles will be a white liquid, like jade paste.
This liquid will be swirling by itself to the left within the bubbles.
Within the white liquid will be three pearls as large as chicken eggs.
These are called the Jade Essences of the Swirling Solution.

The pearls will have an extremely pleasing sweetness, succulent
and soft like malt syrup. If you ingest just one pearl, you will become
an adjutant to heaven. Your body will immediately give off liquid
and fire. If you spit out breath, it will form gems. Your body will
become a sun, and the Thearchs of Heaven will descend to greet   6a
you. You will rise as a glowing orb to Upper Clarity.

♦   ♦   ♦   ♦

Dig a pit, seven feet square and seven feet deep. Then take the Elixir
of Langgan Efflorescence, mixed with the egg-shaped Essences of the
Swirling Solution, and plant these in the pit. Cover them with earth
and tamp it firmly down.

After three years, a tree red like the jujube will grow, three to four
feet tall. The fruit of this tree will be ring shaped. Its name is the Tree
of Ringed Adamant. Eating its fruit causes you to be born together
with the heavens and rise up to the Grand Bourne, your form transformed into clouds.* One name of this tree is the Hidden Polypore
of the Grand Bourne.

♦   ♦   ♦   ♦

Dig a pit six feet square and six feet deep, and plant one of these
ringed fruits, watering it with five drams of Yellow Solution and
tamping down the earth over it. In three year's time a plant will

---

* To be "born together with the heavens" represents the closest thing in Daoism
to immortality. Such a Transcendent would live as long as heaven itself and, presumably, be born again with the heavens after the destruction concluding each
world-cycle.

grow like a calabash, with seed like five-colored peaches. This is
called the Phoenix-Brain Polypore. If you eat this fruit you will rise
above to the Grand Bourne. When you spit on the ground, your
saliva will turn into cock and hen phoenixes. You may mount these
to soar up.

◆   ◆   ◆   ◆

6b   Dig a pit ten feet square and ten feet deep, and plant one phoenix-
brain fruit, watering it with four drams of Yellow Solution. Cover it
with earth and tamp it down. In three year's time a red tree, like a
pine, five or six feet in height, will grow. Its fruit is like a pear and
white as jade. Eating this fruit, you will ascend to Grand Tenuity. If
you spit on the ground, your saliva will form green jade.

◆   ◆   ◆   ◆

Dig a pit eight feet square and eight feet deep and plant the seed of
the red tree, watering it with five drams of Swirling Solution. Tamp
down the earth over it and in three years a vermilion tree like a
plum, six or seven feet in height, will grow. Its halycon-blue fruit
will be like the jujube. By eating its fruit you will ascend to Purple
Tenuity. When you spit on the ground, your saliva will become gold.
You may then travel, riding the dark clouds.

◆   ◆   ◆   ◆

Liquid Blue Florets of Aqueous Yang

Take one and a half pints each of the Yellow Solution and the
Swirling Solution and boil them separately in iron pots seven times.
Then, when mixed, they will transform into a blue liquid called the
7a   Blue Florets of Aqueous Yang. If you drink this all just at dawn,
your body will issue a blue and gemmy light, your mouth will spew
forth purple vapors, and you will rise above to Upper Clarity. When
you spit on the ground, your saliva will form cinnabar and the eight
minerals.

◆   ◆   ◆   ◆

In an iron pot, liquefy one pound of lead together with two ounces of mercury. Once this is boiling rapidly add one scruple of the Elixir of Langgan Efflorescence and this will transform into pure silver.

In an iron pot, liquefy one pound of lead together with five ounces of mercury. Once this is boiling rapidly, throw in three scruples of the Elixir of Langgan Efflorescence and this will transform into purple gold. Once you have made one hundred pounds of this gold and silver, form ingots of fifty pounds each and throw them into an east-flowing stream. Looking down on the water, incant and say:

> Weaver Maid of the Celestial River,
> Water Uncle of the rivers of earth:*
> The grand elixir has effloresced.
> My cloudsouls transcendent, my whitesouls refined,
> I now depart from the earth,
> Ascending to be a guest of the Thearch.
> I present to you these two treasures
> To pacify the water source.

Once you have finished incanting, return immediately without looking back.

If you wish to plant the spirit trees, you should dig the pit on the north side of a mountain of renown. Clear away all four sides   7b of the pit and do not allow humans or animals to walk across the spot.

III.   ANNALS OF THE LORD OF THE DAO,   HY 442
SAGE OF THE LATTER (HEAVENS) OF SHANGQING

Lord Li, Sage of the Latter Age of the Golden Porte of Upper   1a
Clarity, has the taboo name Hongyuan, with the alternate taboo name[30] Xuanshui.[31] His byname is Ziguang and his alternate byname is Shanyuan. A descendant of the Earth Sovereign, he was

---

* The "Celestial River" is our Milky Way, and the "Weaver Maid" the star Vega. See Schafer, *Pacing the Void*, pp. 144–48, for a number of legends concerning the Weaver Maid and her lover, from whom she was separated by the Celestial River. The Water Uncle is apparently the Sire of the [Yellow] River, foremost of the river gods of China. Here, then, the two most important river deities, one for the river of heaven and one for the rivers of earth, are invoked.

a man of the time of the Dark Thearch.* He was first engendered
below Celestial-Admantine Mountain in the northern kingdom on
the apposite day of the third month in the seventh year of the Upper
1b   Harmony reign period, when Jupiter was in *bingzi*.† His mother of
the Li clan had previously dreamt herself among dark clouds, with
the sun and moon enwrapping her body.‡ In this manner, her womb
was quickened and she bore him. When she bathed him, there were
also dragons that spouted water into the washbasin as a sign.

At the age of five, Lord Li came to delight in the Dao and in the
Perfected and could elegantly discourse on the Dao. Often would he
raise his head to the sun, laughing in joy, or face the moon, sighing,
for he observed the flashing glare of the yang pneumas and detected
the deficiencies of yin in its path.§ At this, he collected his cloudsouls,
trained his whitesouls, maintained his embryos, and treasured his
internal spirits. He enregistered his spermatic essences, took control of his blood, closely supervised his bodily fluids, and firmed his
sinews.‖ Then he studied the art of swallowing light and drinking
auroras, sipping from the Flying Root.# Having practiced this to
the age of twenty, he obtained a golden form and a visage of white
jade.

Thereafter, he left home and family, transcended the world of

* The Earth Sovereign is the second of the Three Sovereigns of highest antiquity. They are associated respectively with heaven, earth, and humanity. The Dark
Thearch is the fifth of the Five Thearchs, whose age followed that of the Three Sovereigns. The identification of these figures with various culture heroes varies in early
texts. According to the system followed by Yang Xi, the Dark Thearch was Zhuan
Xu, grandson of the Yellow Thearch. (See HY 1010, 12:2a.5 ff.)

† "Upper Harmony" is yet another fictitious reign title.

‡ Strickmann, *Le taoïsme du Mao chan*, p. 272 n. 355, notes that, like Laozi, of
whom he is an avatar of sorts, the Sage Lord, engendered of heaven, takes the name
of his mother.

§ That is to say, he derived his knowledge of the principles underlying existence merely through watching the yang sun and yin moon in their circuits. By
extrapolating these principles he is able to control his own yang cloudsouls and yin
whitesouls. The procedure he employed is presumably that provided in this text.

‖ To "enregister" means to control strictly through keeping close account of
something. It is a term that Yang Xi sometimes uses with respect to potentially dangerous spiritual entities, such as the whitesouls. It is possible that this usage of the
term is related to the Celestial Masters' registers, containing the names of protective
deities. See Schipper, "The Taoist Body"; and Schipper, *The Taoist Body*, pp. 64–
67.

On the Flying Root, see HY 639, 4b–5a, in this translation.

wind and dust, and hid himself away in a chamber for a long purification. He roamed the famous mountains, grasping only the Talisman of the Spirit Estrade, which illumined the orderly process of
transformation.* Enlightened concerning the three pneumas, he was
able to internalize change, and, by occluding his spiritual nexus, he
was able to match the Perfected. Through overcoming his will, he
came to place emptiness above all things. Through controlling his
devotion, he became profoundly subtle. In response to his respectful
purity, the numinous spirits arrived, their mystic intent grand and
secret. The hidden principles were granted him by special dispensation. In solitude, he was imbued with the most profound and exalted   2a
truths.

Setting his heart on what lay beyond the glittering orbs in the firmament, he gathered his cloudsouls, returning them to the Scarlet
Courtyard, and controlled his whitesouls, causing the green and
the black to guard them.† Then he nurtured the pneumas within
the cinnabar and white chambers.‡ This done, his corporal spirits
were not prone to diminution, nor could his numinous forces be
scattered. His inner power was complete and his external attachments cut off. Shielding himself from those nets that tie Transcendents to earth, he sought the upper reaches of Perfection in the
Purple Hostels.§

Thus, his seminal essences resonating with the Grand Void, his
heart open to the spiritual dawn, he prepared the way for the Celes-

---

* "Spirit Estrade" is one of the several metaphors for the heart. (See *HY* 1026,
11:40b ff.) I have found no further reference to the Talisman of the Spirit Estrade.
The claim that he "grasped only the Talisman of the Spirit Estrade" may be a poetic
way of emphasizing, as has been done throughout this passage, that the Sage Lord
was to this point self-taught and that his connection with the Dao was fixed with
only his heart/mind as a talisman.

† The "Scarlet Courtyard" most likely refers to the envelope of red pneumas
emanating from the "Scarlet Chamber" (the heart) and used to enwrap the body in
the meditation for securing the cloudsouls (see *HY* 639, 8b–9b, in this translation).
The "green and the black" refers specifically to the green dragon and the black tortoise, but the words stand as synecdoche for all of the celestial beasts visualized in
the meditation for controlling the whitesouls.

‡ The "cinnabar and white chambers" are the three Cinnabar Fields and the
spotless residences of the remaining spirits of the body. Their description appears at
HY 639, 11b–12b, in this translation.

§ The term "Purple Hostels" refers specifically to residences within the complex
of Purple Tenuity (for which see footnote † on p. 312 above).

tial Thearchs to send down their teachings in the form of flowing beams of extraordinary brilliance.* They bestowed on him the great chapters of the *Shadowed Regalia* and the *Perfected Scripture of the Grand Cavern.*† They gave him the Flying Canopy of Sinuous Dawn for sustenance, provided drink for him using the Jade Essence of the Swirling Solution, and presented him with the *White Wings and Dark Pinions*—all so that he might rise above to the eight directions of space.‡ With this, he received the command and withdrew for purification so that he might put the scriptures into practice and recite their contents—a total of twenty-four practices.§

Ardent in his desire to join with those above, he did not tire either emotionally or mentally. Sometimes, as he was leisurely mulling over the hidden and abstruse contents of the texts, he would suddenly be transported, forgetting to return. Extrapolating on the motive forces, he traced them to their cause and found happiness in it. He then devoted himself solely to rehearsing the scriptures and singing their

---

* I have found no further reference to the term "spiritual dawn." The passage, however, clearly describes the Sage Lord's openness to spiritual forces: his "essences"—concretions of primal pneuma in his body—are in harmony with the celestial void, while his heart, here representing the more ethereal of corporal spirits, communicates with the distant dawnings of spiritual power in the macrocosm. Interestingly, precisely the same parallelism of essence and heart appears in Lu Ji's (261–303) "Rhapsody on Literature" to describe how the poet's inner meditation opens to awareness of the cosmos: "His essence gallops out to the eight poles, while his heart roams to a height of ten thousand fathoms" (*Wenxuan,* 17:350).

† On the *Shadowed Regalia,* see endnote 35 to this translation. The *Scripture of the Grand Cavern* is the paramount celestial text of Shangqing Daoism. In a general sense, the name of this scripture can stand for the Shangqing texts as a whole. For an account of the names of this text, the surviving versions, and their authenticity, see Robinet, *La révélation du Shangqing,* vol. 2, pp. 29–44.

‡ The Flying Canopy of Sinuous Dawn is the name of a potent elixir from the now-lost *Sword Scripture.* See Strickmann, "T'ao Hung-ching," p. 134. The Jade Essence of the Swirling Solution is a product of the Langgan elixir. The *White Wings and Dark Pinions,* Professor Robinet suggests (personal communication; see Robinet, *La révélation du Shangqing,* vol. 2, pp. 193 and 199–200), is an alternate name for the text entitled the *Talisman of White Wings and Black Pinions for Dragon Flight* (HY 83 and HY 1315).

§ These "twenty-four practices" are not identified. Presumably, the number is somehow related to the eight effulgences of the three regions of the Sage Lord's body. At least this is the conclusion we might draw from the Lingbao scripture known as the *Twenty-four Life-Bestowing Charts* (HY 1396), which discusses both talismanic texts and the Sage Lord's envoys (mentioned at HY 442, 7b–8a, in this translation), describing them as having issued forth from his body. See Bokenkamp, "Sources," pp. 458–59.

mysteries, clearing away all external objects and lodging his spirits   2b
in the nine remote heavens, so that he might achieve contemplation
through complete inaction and forgetfulness.*

When the appointed time came for the Lord's harmonious tones
to be introduced on high and when even the slenderest attachments
binding him to the mortal world had been obliterated, he looked
down with kindness on his mortal companions to draft the traces of
his spiritual endeavors in written form.[32] Breaking through all their
obstructions, he washed away their doubt. Yet his mystic principles
were so beyond the common experience that even when his contemporaries daily drank from the clear waves of his understandings,
they still could not discern the fountainhead of his celestial depths,
so completely had he comprehended vacuity and explored the holy
primordial.

At this, the Higher Perfected of Purple Tenuity, Celestial Thearch
and Lord of Jade Clarity, sent a rose-gem chariot of eight phosphors
to greet the Sage Lord and ascend with him to Upper Clarity. He
bestowed upon the Sage Lord the cinnabar-red jade phoenix seal of
stamen adamant, and the Jade Beams of Golden Perfection. He provided him with the Tiger talisman, the *Wings of Flight,* as well as
a dragon skirt of scarlet brocade, a cyan cape and tiger sash—all
flashing with beams of rosy sunlight.† He capped the Sage Lord
with a round and full spirit crown and provided him with certifica-
tion as Lord Thearch, Sage of the Latter Age of the Golden Porte of
Upper Clarity. Above he might rise to the heavens of Upper Clarity;
in the center he could roam the palaces of the Grand Bourne. Below
he governs the ten heavens and has charge over mortals, as well as
all the rivers, seas, spirits, Transcendents, lands, and water sources

---

* The text reads, literally, "nine remotenesses"—a reference to the vertical ar-
rangement of nine heavens and, by extension, the highest reaches of the empyrean.
"Forgetting" has to do with fully surrendering one's being to the Dao, merging with
it effortlessly by releasing all personal inclinations and concerns. (See Livia Kohn,
Seven Steps to the Tao: Sima Chengzhen's "Zuowang lun," MS Monographs, no. 20
[Nettetal: Steyler Verlag, 1987].)

† *Wings of Flight* most likely refers to a text of the Shangqing corpus and not to
actual wings. See Robinet, *La révélation du Shangqing,* vol. 2, pp. 190–206, for the
surviving versions of this scripture. The Perfected, at any rate, have no use for wings,
in that they travel the heavens borne in resplendent carriages formed of the glowing
spirits of their own bodies.

of those various heavens.* In secret he inspects the inner roots of
earth, extending from the Cavern Estrade of Yujue.† He orders the
mysteries, spreads the pneumas, arrays the clouds, and shakes the
watercourses. Soaring to spy on the Xiaoyou Cavern-Heaven, or
dropping his reins on Tortoise Mount, he plumbs the darkness and
brings to light the hidden, involving himself in the most minuscule
of details.‡

If you wish to observe the Sage Lord in his travels, you must
watch for rose-gem wheels on a *langgan* chassis, cyan shafts
tethered to dark dragons. There will be flowing auroras of the three
elemental colors, while the essences of the moon spurt forth as fragrances. Soaring tones will enwrap the sun, with its flowing light-
nings raised forth in barbs. Darting serpents strike with their
swords—their long teeth sounding out like gongs. Efflorescences
mix and flash, as the three candles of the heavens merge their brilliance.§ Piping before, the nine phoenixes sing in unison; trumpeting
behind, the eight simurghs call out as one. Spirit tigers rear up and
snarl; flying dragons crouch and roar. The spheres of heaven sound
their pennoned canopies in a hundred tones that issue from their
vacant halls. The holy consorts jointly praise him, while his Tran-

---

* The term "ten heavens" refers not to celestial realms, but to the ten cavern-
heavens situated within earthly mountains. Each of the cavern-heavens was a miniature cosmos, with its own sun, moon, and stars, palaces and temples. They housed
those who were still advancing on the Transcendent path and were not ready yet to
ascend to the heavens. The first of the cavern-heavens was Xiaoyou, underneath
Mount Wangwu.

† The Cavern Estrade of Yujue is a celestial region described fully in the *Biography of Lord Pei*. See HY 1026, 105:10a–b; and Robinet, *La révélation du
Shangqing*, vol. 2, p. 379.

‡ Xiaoyou is the cavern-heaven lying underneath Mount Wangwu in present-day
Yangcheng County, Shanxi Province. It houses the Palace of Clear Vacuity, where
those who have just achieved the Dao go to perfect their practice. (See HY 1010,
5:14b.5–8.) "Tortoise Mount" is one name of Mount Kunlun, residence of the
exalted Queen Mother of the West. See Strickmann, *Le taoïsme du Mao chan*, p. 274
n. 385, for more on these paradises. Since Kunlun is the most exalted of the sub-
lunary paradises and Wangwu the most humble, the former in the far west and the
latter in the east, the movement of the Sage Lord to these locales seems calculated to
express the completeness of his oversight rather than any direct connection with
these places. That he "soars" to the most lowly of the two and "releases his reins" at
the highest is yet another example of the contradictions in which Yang Xi delighted.

§ The "three candles" are the sun, moon, and stars.

scendent retainers clear the road. Spirit maidens wave purple incense to enliven the air. Jade Lads gesture with flowers of the sun to drive off the dusk. There is unending song among the ranks of clouds. Day and night are no more.

Just at this moment, the light of heaven will grow dark and distant, the flowing beams streaming off to the eight extremities. This in truth is a majestic vision of the Grand Bourne, a glimpse of the highest Thearch of Upper Clarity. They sing out loudly in Upper Clarity because he is spiritually exalted in the holy Void. He travels   3b
to the Grand Bourne to assemble the masses of Transcendents and provide audience to the flying Transcendents. He regulates all below the ten heavens because he has ultimate control of mortals. He secretly inspects the cavern-heavens because there is nothing below him with which he is not concerned.

Now, the two pneumas both separate and join. According to the principles, all things have their appointed times. The three paths[33] have times of growth and of depletion.* Emergence and withdrawal are in complete accord with the fated cycles. When he thus approaches, the end of the cycle draws near. It was during the years of the succession of Tang that the Sage Lord last came to set the cycle in motion.[34] According to the calculations the end should fall within the space of forty-six *dinghai* years. Sooner or later, within this space of time, it will be an age of birds and beasts, when the kingdom's blessing begins to evaporate. To the east and west there will be those who declare themselves hegemon to support a weak ruler. That ruler will have the given name, vertical and horizontal, "nine" and "one." He will be bestowed the style name "Light Traces, Flourishing Prime."†

Later, both before and after the *jiashen* year of his rule, the good

---

* Contrary to the explanation given by Strickmann (*Le taoïsme du Mao chan*, pp. 274–75 n. 389), the term "three paths" here is not to be associated with religious doctrines. Instead, in the context of cosmic change, it refers to the paths of the three celestial luminaries: sun, moon, and stars.

† These predictions are likely to have had a specific referent, at least in Yang Xi's mind. They probably referred to a specific ruler's name, formed in a mystical manner from the graphs, or parts of the graphs, I have attempted to translate here. For more on the form of such Daoist prophecies, see Bokenkamp, "Time after Time."

will be planted as seed people and the remaining mortals will be eradicated.* Pestilence and flood will wash over them; weapons and fire will circle below them. All the evil will be eradicated at once; all the violent will be destroyed. Those who delight in the Dao will hide away in the land; the good people will ascend mountains. The flowing filth will be shaken off, driven into the vast abyss. In this way all mortals will be divided, the good from the evil.

Coming to the sixth day of the third month in the *renchen* year, the Sage Lord will descend and appear to mortals in all his glory. At this time, the Sage Lord will set out from the western peak of Green Citadel Mountain, issuing from the clouds south of Long.† To the north, he will inspect the land beyond Dragon Candle. To the west, he will circle the passes of the Nine Currents. To the east, he will proceed to the dawn precincts of the Fusang Grove. To the south, he will be seen in the clouds above the Scarlet Mountains.‡ Riding his flying chariot of the three elemental colors, followed by void-traversing carts and myriad dragons, he will inspect the three celestial timekeepers as the lights of heaven all shine forth.

At this time, the evil persons will all have been destroyed by flood and fire; all the good and the benevolent will have been preserved as seed people. Those whose studies have just begun will be

---

* On the concept of "seed people," the elect of Daoist eschatalogy, see the section "Morality and Governance" in the introduction to the *Admonitions*.

† "Long" is an ancient name for the area around what is now Long County in Shaanxi Province. The land south of Long is the Sichuan Basin. Green Citadel Mountain is some fifty kilometers to the west of Chengdu, near Crane-Call Mountain, where Lord Lao was reported to have descended to Zhang Daoling.

‡ These are all mythical place names. According to the *Scripture of Mountains and Seas* (HY 1025, 8:1a; also see David R. Knechtges, *Wen xuan—or—Selections of Refined Literature, by Xiao Tong* [Princeton, N.J.: Princeton University Press, 1982], vol. 1, p. 426 n. 772), "Dragon Candle" (also rendered "Dragon Torch," "Torch Dragon," or "Torch in the Darkness") is the name of the human-headed, snake-bodied spirit of Mount Zhong, so far to the north that the sun never shines there. Instead, day and night occur whenever Dragon Candle opens and shuts her eyes. The "Nine Currents" refers to the wastes of flowing sands to the far west of China, while the Fusang was, according to ancient legend, the tree in the far east where the nine suns were hung to dry after having made their journey through the waters of the underworld from where they had set in the west. The Scarlet Mountains border China in the extreme south. These imaginative boundaries set the limits of the world.

Transcendent functionaries; those who have achieved the Dao will be Transcendent officers.

If you have been able to make essential the Cavern Chamber in your Upper Prime, have cultivated the Nine Perfected to widely exert their control, have paced according to the secret writings on the seven holy stars, and have assiduously completed the Eight Simplicities, then you will be able to pass through the three plagues without injury.* You will also certainly be born again in the age of Great Peace and will receive documents as a Transcendent officer or as a Perfected spirit endowed with long life.

Since these mystic writings and holy practices are hidden in the palaces of Upper Clarity, inside the Golden Porte, few are those who have even seen their titles. When the spiritual Perfected descend to instruct mortals, they are transmitted but three times every seven hundred years. Those who receive them by transmission need to have no particular level of intelligence; all who practice them wholeheartedly will achieve the status of flying Transcendent. But only those listed in the mystic records of Fangzhu as having the bones of a Transcendent and a jade name will receive them. Those without these signs will never see these texts. If, by a one-in-a-million chance, an unqualified person should happen to obtain the texts, it will probably be because that person has a relationship with someone to whom the transmission officers wish to entrust the texts and so might act as a spirit envoy. In this way, one who merely obtains the text to pass it on to another will possess it without practicing its abstruse teachings.

4b

* Proceeding into the skull from a point directly between and above the eyebrows, the Cavern Chamber is the second palace of the brain that one encounters; there are nine such palaces in all. The deities that inhabit this palace are Nonpareil and White Prime. See Homann, *Huang-t'ing ching*, pp. 72–73; Robinet, *Méditation taoïste*, pp. 195–201; and, on the role of the palaces in assuring life, the section "Bodily Deities of Salvation" in the introduction to the *Scripture of Salvation*. The "seven holy stars" are the Dipper. The "Eight Simplicities" refers specifically to the carriages of colored clouds and mists that bear eight goddesses, the feminine counterparts of the spirits of the Eight Phosphors, and refers, by extension, to the meditation practice during which the goddesses are visualized. See Robinet, *La révélation du Shangqing*, vol. 2, pp. 51–57, and, for a description of this meditation, Robinet, "Randonées extatiques."

Those who study transcendence should widely travel the famous mountains, kneeling to invoke the celestial spirits in search of instructions from the unseen. Do not those who obtain the precious secrets in this way find themselves ranked among the Perfected or Transcendent officials?

5a   Thereafter, the Sage Lord will again consider their merits and award them ranks in the bureaucracy, some as Transcendent earls, some among the assembled marquises, so that they might assist him in instructing the people, regulating the pneumas, and spreading virtue. Some will control a city; others will be entrusted with the governance of a kingdom.

All those who revere the *Shadowed Regalia* for the purpose of summoning the rays of the sun, who practice the *Knotted Spangles* for absorbing moonbeams, who chant the *Upper Scripture of the Grand Cavern* and the *Revolving Writing of Seven Transformations,* who base their practice on the *Perfected Writings of the Golden Porte,* or who may wear at their sash the grand talisman Spirit Tiger;* all those who employ the Eight Ways to retain their corporeal spirits, who open the *Purple Texts* to startle floating sprites, who chant the *Golden Root* to achieve longevity, or who display the *Nine Vermilion* to seal their fate in the mountains; all those who, by means of the *Sinuous Simplicity,* command demons or employ the *Purple Measures* to illumine primal pneumas; those who drink the talismans of the *Five Phases* to call their whitesouls or ingest the Langgan elixir that they might endure; who, passing trials among the peaks, have no doubts; who, walking through war and fire, have no fear†—all such as these will be ranked Perfected Dukes of the

---

* This paragraph lists texts and practices of the Shangqing canon. Not all of them were "revealed" in the world when this text was written; their very mention in this text led later Daoists to construct scriptures around practices only hinted at in the scriptures of Yang Xi. For further information on these texts, I can do no better than to refer the reader to the magisterial study of the Shangqing scriptures by Isabelle Robinet. Specific references to her work are given in the endnotes that follow.

† The "spiritual trial" by which an adept's resolve is tested is well known in the folklore of Daoism. Generally, such trials take the form of demons or spirits changing shape to try the spiritual insight of the adept. See, for example, the trial of Aqiu Zeng (Bokenkamp, "Sources," pp. 474–75) and the trials set for the disciple of Tao Hongjing, Zhou Ziyang (Stephen R. Bokenkamp, "Answering a Summons," in Donald Lopez, Jr., ed., *Chinese Religions in Practice* [Princeton, N.J.: Princeton University Press, 1996], pp. 108–202).

Left and Right or Grandees of the Left and Right.[35] Some will hold the office of Grand Chamberlain or Transcendent Lord of the Higher Kingdoms.

The Sage Lord travels followed by tiger palanquins and myriads of dragons so that he might observe all Transcendents and reward them according to their abilities. That the Sage Lord might control the mortals and oversee the myriad forms of life, he

> Leisurely roams the Golden Porte,
> Making his palace and offices in Upper Clarity;
> Lodges his shape in the Great Void
> Or travels to the five citadels,*
> To inspect the ten heavens
> So that the hundred regions know Great Peace.

Those who will see the era of Great Peace include:

Those mortals who are humane and benevolent—that is, those who cling only to goodness;

Those who study the Dao and keep faith with the Transcendents and may be instructed;

Those who are holy and have received the writings, who preserve their seminal essences and treasure the embryo;

Those zealous individuals who have achieved the Dao and obtained Transcendence;

Those who are marked for Transcendence by the fact that their name is registered in the mystic slips and whose seven generations of ancestors have acquired merit that reaches their descendants;

Those born with azure bones, who therefore are possessed with supernatural powers and may join with the Perfected;

Those who are by nature of exceptional quietude and whose purity allows them to surpass their celestial allotment of years.

Several hundred greater and lesser ranks are accorded those who will become Transcendent. The Sage Lord will in each case rank them as officials on the basis of their abilities, giving them rank that

---

* The "five citadels" were, according to a tradition derided by Ge Hong (*Baopu zi neipian*, 20:101), part of the palace complex of the Queen Mother atop Mount Kunlun. (See also *Shiji*, 28:1403.)

they might be lords over the seed people. These assembled lords will ascend to Upper Clarity once each year to pay homage to the Sage Lord and to receive their instructions. Once every five years the Sage Lord will descend to visit his officers, to inspect the seed people, and to judge matters pertaining to Transcendence.

As for the Sage Lord's own study of the Dao, it was replete with all manner of difficulty. He received the instruction of his master in the world of mud and ashes, where he experienced the pangs of hunger and cold and the grinding assault of flood and fire. He rid himself of all personal emotional ties to his relatives and repeatedly underwent the great trials set for him by the Celestial Thearchs. Through all of this, his heart was firm and fixed on his responsibilities, in the knowledge that the hours of life and death are fixed. The myriad evil influences were unable to encroach upon his internal spirits; the spectral malignities were unable to delude him. Instead he was sincere and open to the mysteries so that the numinous spirits responded to him and filled him. This is why the Higher Sovereign announced to him the secret instructions and the Celestial Worthies bestowed upon him the Dao.

This is called total awareness of the distant harmonies, an opening of the mystic portals. He represents an exalted model extremely wondrous, his vision into the essentials unparalleled. Through the hidden joints and myriad channels of his body, the celestial order flows. His greatness is such that we lack paper and ink to record it fully. I have described only one part in a thousand, merely a rough outline of his outstanding qualities to transmit to those who have the bones and marks of Transcendence. Those who are able to see this have their names inscribed in the mystic records that are presented in Upper Clarity, where their rank is Transcendent Chamberlain. If such as these are able to practice the perfected matters of the Golden Porte, they will be exalted as Grandees in the celestial courts.*

* The title of grandee was, during the time this text was written, an honorific appellation given to various officers and those granted high ranks of nobility. The exact denotations of this and other titles Yang uses are not entirely clear. Clearly, the celestial bureaucracy was ordered in much the same fashion as that of the mundane world—at least this is the assumption of Tao Hongjing in his notes to the *Zhen'gao*, where he frequently wonders at the the discrepancies between various persons' mor-

Attendant on this book are ten Jade Lads. Attendant on the *Purple Texts* of the Golden Porte are ten Jade Maidens. Each time you chant this scripture or put its contents to use, you should bow respectfully to them. Wash your hands and burn incense to the left and right of the writing. Those who sully this holy record will be bodily demoted to the status of lower specter and their three generations of ancestors will undergo infernal interrogation. This is because the Jade Lads and Maidens will report above each transgression and will make known who is sincere of heart. Each good or evil deed, no matter how insignificant, will be recorded.

The Lord Azure Lad of the Eastern Palace of Fangzhu composed this, the *Annals of the Lord of the Dao, Sage of the Latter [Heavens]*, to be presented on high to the Sage Lord and for transmission to his disciple, Wang Yuan.* Wang was instructed to show it below to those with the bones and marks of Transcendence. He might transmit it again within the space of one hundred years, but no more than three times every seven hundred years, to those who study the Dao and are fated to achieve Transcendence.

The Sage Lord said:

> Those who obtain my *Annals* are all those secretly known to possess
> the stuff of Transcendence and whose mystical records are in order or,
> in some cases, those who will become Transcendents and whose names
> have been submitted, written in jade on slips of gold. Those who have   7a
> obtained these *Annals* should revere them and protect their secrecy,
> practicing no other discipline. All who do so will be granted deliverance
> from the corpse in full daylight. Those who have obtained it but do not
> revere the Way and its power, who leak its truths to the profane, whose
> natures are perverse, and who abandon their goals are but persons of
> lower ability without fragrant bones, whose fate it is to wander about

---

tal and celestial rankings. For specifics on the history of the title "grandee," see Charles O. Hucker, *A Dictionary of Official Titles in Imperial China* (Stanford, Calif.: Stanford University Press, 1985), p. 465.

* The received text has Wang Yuanyou, but the final graph is almost certainly a copyist's error. (The phrase *yuanyou*, "distant traveling," is a common one in Daoist writings.) Wang Yuan, byname Fangping, is also known as Lord Wang of the Western Citadel, the "Upper Steward" mentioned later in the text. A person of the former Han period, he has a rich history in Daoist hagiographical literature. (See HY 1026, 109:10a–11a; HY 1131, 8:4b; and HY 1238, 16:20a, for biographies of Wang drawn from the *Shenxian zhuan*.) In the Shangqing scriptures, he is revered as the teacher of Mao Ying and is associated with the practices found in this scripture.

aimlessly. Still, by virtue of the fact that they have obtained my *Annals,* they will be granted the rank of Underworld Lord in order that they might dissolve their turgid forms and cleanse their sullied whitesouls.* From this status they will be allowed to advance slowly up the ranks, as they awaken from their delusive dreams. All of you should be diligent and cautious concerning this.

Do not reveal the existence of this text to the untrustworthy corpses. By wearing my *Annals* at your sash, you may pass unscathed through calamity and pestilence, flood, fire, and warfare. None of the myriad sprites of the mountains and forests or the multiple forms of perversity and disaster will dare stand against you. When others see you, they will be filled with joy. This is because the writing is attended by Jade Lads that might protect your person. If evil persons malevolently drive you off 7b or curse you, I will send the holy spirits of the mountains and streams to take their lives. Do not imagine that, since the Dao is distant, such spiritual oversight is impossible. From above the Grand Barrens or within the Mystic Void I observe you as closely as your eyes regard your own nose. If you do not believe, you are welcome to try it once by breaking my prohibitions or your oaths to me. See if I do not plumb the wordless depths of your heart to respond to such indiscretions with the proper punishment! Those who receive this text should make an oath, guaranteeing that they will not divulge it.

Now I have sent certain individuals below to instruct those whose bones reveal their destiny and who are sincere in their zealous study of Transcendence. I have sent Ma Ming, Zhang Ling, Yin Sheng, Wang Bao, Mo Di, Sima Jizhu, as well as, from the Heaven of the Clear Barrens of the Grotto Estrades, the Seven Perfected and the Eight Elders.† There are twenty-four envoys in all, some whose names are

---

* The Underworld Lords were fated to rule in the realms of the unholy dead, the six palaces of Fengdu, or in the cavern-heavens. Their rate of advance in the transcendent hierarchy was painfully slow. See Bokenkamp, "Death and Ascent," pp. 3–7; and Yoshikawa Tadao, "Nitchū muei: Shikaisen-kō" [Throwing No Shadows at Noon: Immortals Delivered from the Corpse], in Yoshikawa Tadao, ed., *Chūgoku kodōkyōshi kenkyū* (Kyoto: Dōbōsha, 1992), pp. 196–204.

† These figures are all well known from other sources. Zhang Ling is Zhang Daoling, revered as the founder of Celestial Master Daoism. Ma Ming and Yin Sheng, better known as Ma Mingsheng and Yin Changsheng, are two persons reported to have lived during the Latter Han and to have achieved transcendence through alchemical practices. See Fukui Kōjun, *Shinsenden* (Tokyo: Meitoku, 1983), pp. 158 ff.; Robinet, *La révélation du Shangqing,* vol. 1, p. 11; and, for an earlier version of the Yin Sheng legend, Kaltenmark, *Le Lie-sien Tchouan,* p. 158. On Wang Bao, the teacher of Wei Huacun (Yang Xi's own master), we have a biography said to have been written by Wei herself. (HY 1026, 106:1a–8a; Robinet [*La révélation du Shangqing,* vol. 2, pp. 369–73] contests the authenticity of the received text). Mo Di is the Warring States–period philosopher Mozi. He became an important figure in alchemical writings. Already in the *Baopu zi,* alchemical texts are

hidden and others whose names are manifest. As they have changed their patronymics and given names, they are in fact difficult to distinguish from others. You have only to maintain the zealous purity of your heart day and night without slacking and they will certainly appear to you. Once they have appeared to you, they will tell you their true names.

The Sage Lord ordered Lord Wang to oversee the twenty-four 8a
Perfected in their meritorious action of descending to provide instruction. All twenty-four received the materials they are to transmit from the Azure Lad of Fangzhu and are assigned disciples by Lord Wang. Lord Wang also told them in advance who might succeed in the study, so that the twenty-four Perfected might receive the appropriate materials to instruct them. The *Annals of the Sage Lord* were bestowed on Lord Wang alone. He was charged with selecting those to whom it could be transmitted; not all of the Perfected were allowed to transmit it.* If you wish to know the names of the twenty-four Perfected, they are listed at the end of my *Scripture of the Azure Essentials from the Multiple Documents.*† A catalog of the texts, talismans, and spiritual instructions assigned for each to teach is also given in the scripture.

All those who receive the *Shadowed Regalia* and the *Knotted Spangles,* the *Mysterious Scripture of the Grand Cavern,* the *Purple Texts Inscribed by the Spirits* of the Golden Porte of Upper Clarity, the *Perfected Scripture of the Eight Simplicities,* the *Hidden Writings of the Most High,* the *Central Scripture of the Nine Perfected,* the *Secret Words of the Yellow Lord Lao on the Eight Ways,* and the *Ten Instructions on the Grand Elixirs in Jade Graphs* will be

---

attributed to him, and his techniques are further discussed in Yang Xi's revelations. See Ware, *Alchemy, Medicine and Religion,* pp. 316–17; and Strickmann, "T'ao Hung-ching," pp. 131–32. Sima Jizhu (d. c. 170 B.C.E.) was a Han-period diviner whose biography is found in the *Shiji.* See *Shiji,* 127:3215–20, and Strickmann, "T'ao Hung-ching," pp. 131–32, for his place in Yang Xi's writings.

* The reason for this claim is not far to seek: Wang Yuan was the teacher of Mao Ying, who was among the deities regularly appearing to Yang Xi. Yang was thus in line to receive the text through the orthodox line of transmission. For a fragment of Wang Yuan's instructions concerning the text in Yang Xi's hand, see HY 1010, 9:22b–23a.

† A Shangqing text by this title does survive, but it does not list the Perfected or the scriptures they have been mandated to teach. See Robinet, *La révélation du Shangqing,* vol. 2, pp. 119–25, and, for a translation of materials from the text, Kroll, "Barrier of Heaven."

8b   awarded the rank of Transcendent Duke of the Left or Right, Grandee of the Left or Right, or will hold the office of Grand Chamberlain or Transcendent Lord of the Higher Kingdoms.[36]

Those who receive the *Transformations of the Nine-Times-Recycled Elixir*, the *Upper Scriptures of Grand Clarity*, the *Essences of the Dao in Yellow and White*, or the *Celestial Barrier Recorded in Azure* will attain the rank of Perfected and will be given oversight of a Perfected Palace or enfeoffed as lord or earl of a Transcendent kingdom.[37] The order and distinctions of these various ranks are all recorded in the azure records on white slips in the Palace of Fangzhu.

The Sage of the Latter Heavens, Lord Peng, has the name Guangyuan and the alternate name Xuanxu, the byname Dachun and the alternate byname Zhengyang.* Peng is also surnamed Li, though some call him Peng. He studied the Dao earlier than did Lord Li. He was born during the time of the Sovereign of Humanity.† His rank is Lord Protector of the Left Ranks of the Perfected of Grand Tenuity. In addition he will receive the mandate to regulate mortals as the Grand Master of Lord Li. His administrative center is at the Estrade of Spirit-Transcending Light of the Palaces of the Northern Ramparts in Grand Tenuity. Every twenty-five hundred years, Lord Peng changes his name and circles the Grand Barrens, traveling in

9a   turn to the eight dark regions—above to the ultimate heights, below to the ultimate depths. Rare are the Perfected officials who are able to see his glowing visage. Nonetheless, his experiences and names since he began the study, as well as his fixing of Perfection, are all recorded on the white slips of the azure records.

The four assistant Grand Ministers are:

The Upper Minister of Lord Li, Sage of the Latter Age, the Lord Azure Lad of the Fangzhu Palace;

The Upper Guardian of Lord Li, Sage of the Latter Age, the Primal Lord of the Southern Bourne of the Palace of Grand Cinnabar;

---

* This is the only biographical information we have on the powerful Lord Peng. For another mention of him in the Shangqing scriptures, see Robinet, *La révélation du Shangqing*, vol. 2, p. 107.

† The "Sovereign of Humanity" is the third of the mythical Three Sovereigns, Shennong, the "Divine Farmer."

The Upper Precentor of Lord Li, Sage of the Latter Age, the Perfected Lord of Grand Simplicity of the White Mountain Palace;

The Upper Steward of Lord Li, Sage of the Latter Age, Lord Wang, overseer of the Perfected of the Western Citadel Palace.

In addition, there are Grand Ministers, Transcendent Dukes, and Grandees for a total of 360 officers. All of these are listed in the catalogs of the azure records on white slips, so I will not here list their names.

The Lord Azure Lad said: Those whose fate is inscribed on their   9b
bones delight in Transcendence. Those who delight in Transcendence all aspire to Transcendence. But those who aspire to Transcendence are sometimes blocked, sometimes urged on. Those who are blocked lack a sufficiency of merit from previous generations. Those who are urged on are predestined in the mystic records. [In some cases, people delight in Transcendence but are not single-minded. This is also because they lack a sufficiency of generational virtue.]³⁸ If one's celestial records in the Great Metropolis are manifest in one of the Mystic Palaces, the pneuma-induced indications of this might be observed on one's physical body in the following fashion:

If one's record is blazoned forth in the Grand Bourne, the spirits of one's heart are well ordered in their Cinnabar Chamber.

If a mortal has a jade name in the Golden Porte, that person's eyes will flash with the light of the sun, the teeth will be azure, and the blood white. Such a person is benevolent, delighting in Transcendence; luminous; and of outstanding talent.

Those who have a jade record in the golden books of Upper Clarity have the River Kui constellation marked on their backs and a flat breastbone in their chest.* They are respectful and unassuming, manifesting virtue even toward insects.

Those who have azure documents on the cinnabar slips of the

---

* "River Kui" refers not to the bowl of the Dipper, but to a six-star, C-shaped constellation in Ursa Major a little to the side of the Dipper's bowl, also named "Literary Glory." See Schafer, *Pacing the Void,* pp. 121–25; and Schlegel, *Uranographie chinoise,* p. 530. Lord Pei is said to have had such a marking on his back. See the surviving version of his biography in *HY* 1027, 105:2a.2.

Grand Bourne Palace have in the lines of their palms interlocked
ren ("person") graphs and an inverted *da* ("great") graph. They are
cautious of the secrets and delight in Perfection. Of clear vacuity,
they are magnanimous even toward the deluded.

Those who have purple names on the mystic plain silk texts of
Fangzhu have square eyes that emit purple beams of light so that
they can inspect within their own bodies.[39] They are extremely
skilled in the practice and, being extremely pure, avoid con-
tamination.

[Those who have an inner record on the jade weft texts in the
cloud chambers have round eyes and a square forehead, a dragon
mouth with a slender tongue. Such people are expansive and
embody perfection. They are discriminating and decisive.

Those who have purple names in cinnabar-red graphs in the Vermilion Palace walk like simurghs and leap like phoenixes. Their Palace of the Navel is luminous and moist.* Such people are respectful
and controlled in their actions, yet they are happy and active.][40]

Those who have a scarlet name in the Jade Records of Grand
Clarity have a jade timbre or a bronze resonance to their voice.
Their mouth is square and their eyes round. Such people give mag-
nanimously and love without distinction, regarding harm to others
as if it were they themselves who were injured.

Those who have a golden name on the rose-gem slips of Grand
Simplicity have a white sign on their belly and a mouth that issues
purple breath. They are full of the power of compassion and supernatural abilities; yet, hiding their humaneness, they seem inferior to
the masses.

Those who have purple records on the cinnabar texts of the
Southern Bourne have five-color pneumas issuing from their head to
form a multistoried cloud above them. They are kind and cherish the
poor, always helping those in difficulty.

Those who have green records in the mystic jades of the Dipper
have nine orifices in their hearts and brocade markings on the exte-

---

* The "Palace of the Navel" may also refer to the Palace of Life, the "womb"
behind the navel where the Peach Child is born. (See *HY* 639, 11b–12a, in this
translation.)

rior of their lungs. On their cheek is a jade "nine."* Within their   10b
eyes are green tendons, and at the corners of their eyebrows there
should be thousands of paired striations, perfectly even, like layered
walls. Their temples lack hair, revealing their neck—a "Luminous
Hall"—flat and white. The thousand striations are streams that join
them to the Perfected; their broad neck is a residence for the reception of spirits. They are benevolent to the poor and lowly. Their
humaneness reaches even to birds and beasts.

Those who have red writing on the azure gold of the Upper Prime
of the Mystic Palaces have purple orifices in their cinnabar heart and
yellow efflorescences encircling their stomach. Their breath is fragrant, and jade liquors flow abundantly between their teeth. Such as
these, when yet young, enjoy observing the flowing auroras of the
sun and moon and delight in the glowing images of the constellations. Their bodies unblemished and their bones strong, they revere
the deep secrets.

Those who have golden graphs on the white jades of the Cinnabar Estrade of the Mystic Metropolis have azure livers with purple
veins, gray-green kidneys with figured patterns, and black breast-
bones replete with seminal fluids. Spotlessly pure in form and in the
spirits that inhabit them, their bodies are fragrant and supple. Their
blood is clear and their breath moist. As for their personality, they
can envision the mysterious at a distance and apprehend the phosphors that spiritualize their form. Amicable and forgiving, they
humble themselves, aiding those in trouble or want.

Those with azure writing on the green-gem billets of the Three
Primes Palace have purple brains and brocade-patterned tongues.   11a
There is a dark mark at the apex of their temples. Their viscera are
green and their marrow scarlet. The top of their head is square and
their forehead round. There is a hidden bone in their pubis. Their
hair is soft—purple and glistening. There are three orifices in their
nether regions, and their evacuation has a tangy odor. An azure light
flows from their eyes—an azure essence, a congealed liquid. The

---

* The number of stars in the Daoist Dipper is not seven but nine, including the
two invisible stars "Sustainer" and "Straightener." (Schafer, *Pacing the Void*, pp.
49–51, passim.) Presumably, then, the "nine" on such a person's cheek would be a
replica of the Dipper and not the graph *jiu* (nine).

striations of their hands reach to all four sides of their palms, and their incisors are triple-pronged. They are holy in thought and of humane vacuity. Their benevolence moves the spirits, and they delight in the subtle with respectful trustworthiness. They find joy in the spring growth of forests and cherish the clear flow of water. Their emotions respond in harmony to the mountains and rivers, and they willingly cast offerings from the banks. Safeguarding their whitesouls and nurturing their cloudsouls, their aspirations reaching to the regions of "Azure Peace," they taste at a distance the joys of the heavenly Transcendents.*

Those who possess the above signs are certainly higher Transcendents. They may achieve Transcendence whether they study or not; it is essential only that they delight in the Dao. If they delight in the Dao and study the subtleties, though, they will sooner ascend, transformed.

Next are those who have a "dark mountain" on their nose. The "dark mountain" is a black mark on the nose. Such as these should also have a dark mound on their belly to match the dark mountain. This "dark mound" is also a black mark. If one of these is missing, the other alone is not a sign of Transcendence. If one's breath is foul and one is by nature accustomed to the unclean, this will destroy the black mountain and the black mound marks.

Next is the mark of azure bones. One with azure bones delights in smelling the scents of "five fragrances" and enjoys studying matters pertaining to the spirits.†

Next are the goose walk, the dragon leap, the jade pillow growing from the nape of the neck, the hidden dawn behind the ear, the azure mark below the crotch, the striated patterns on the body, the

11b

---

* "Azure Peace" is the name of the song that flows throughout the palace of the Sage Lord in the opening passages of this scripture.

† Although the term "five fragrances" is noted in the *Bencao gangmu* as a name for *Saussurea costus* or costusroot (see Akira Akahori, "Drug Taking and Immortality," in Livia Kohn, ed., *Taoist Meditation and Longevity Techniques* [Ann Arbor, Mich.: Center for Chinese Studies, 1985], p. 85 n. 7), in Daoist texts it refers to an incense or aromatic bath composed of five distinct herbs. The specific constituents differ, but one text, citing the *Scripture of the Three Sovereigns*, lists sweet basil, cherry blossoms, melilot, costusroot, and sandalwood (*HY* 1026, 41:3b). For another recipe, see *HY* 1026, 41:4a.

perfected heart and stilled gallbladder, and the hardened ears and expansive breath; these are all marks of the Lower Transcendent.

The Mystic Isle also has records where names are carved in gold.* Those listed may achieve release from the corpse without study. Those who study may become Transcendent through casting aside their corpse in broad daylight.†

Next are the bureaus of the Three Offices in Mount Tai. This is a realm of life yet separated from the lands of deathlessness.‡ The cloudsouls of the people here have not perished, and so they float about endlessly in death. Through studying the Dao of Transcendence, they might become landlocked Transcendents, no more. They must, every thirty years, relocate to a new residence, changing their name. They have no fixed date of death. This is because there is no date of death entered for them in the white annals of the Mystic Records kept in the Three Offices. It is not the case that the Three Offices ever mistakenly inscribed anyone's name in the records of death.§

12a

For registering the living and dead, Grand Darkness has black

---

* With the Mystic Isle, we have moved from the celestial heavens to those situated on earth, albeit remote from the lands of human habitation. The Mystic Isle is a Transcendent paradise located in the northwest quadrant of the North Sea, according to the *Shizhou ji*, attributed to Dongfang Shuo (154–93 B.C.E.). For a translation of the relevant passage, see Thomas E. Smith, "Record of the Ten Continents," *TR* 2.2 (1990), p. 92.

† The distinction being made here is between different levels of physical transformation. Those who achieve "release from the corpse" disappear either before burial or after it, leaving some trace—hair, a sword, sandals, a staff, or a weightless corpse like the sloughed-off husk of a cicada—behind as a substitute for the body. Those who rise in "broad daylight," however, simply disappear into the heavens. For much more on these means of corporal transformation, see Robinet, *Méditation taoïste*, pp. 57–66; and Needham, *Science and Civilisation in China*, vol. 5, pt. 2 (1974), pp. 301 ff.

‡ Mount Tai, in present-day Shandong Province, is the traditional locus of the lord of the underworld. Here it is regarded as housing the "Three Offices" of Celestial Master Daoism. One may proceed to all of the previously mentioned paradises without dying. In order to enter Mount Tai, one must first die.

§ This statement is meant to contradict popular stories regarding the structure and inhabitants of the underworld. Many such stories center around the motif of the "untimely summons." A person is taken to the earth-prisons only to find that there has been a bureaucratic error and more years of life are indicated. Upon being returned to the mortal world, the traveler is able to recount what he or she has seen. See Robert F. Campany, "Return-from-Death Narratives in Early Medieval China," *Journal of Chinese Religions* 18 (1990), pp. 91–125.

records and white registers, and rolls of slips in cinnabar and vermilion. These receive the records of the living, in proper order from
beginning to end, as well as the records of the dead from first to last
to compare with them. In total there are six thousand slips, all recording the fate of a single person. If there is no record for death,
most people will live a long life, as it is difficult for them to die. Their
years often exceed one hundred, and when they do die, it is quickly,
without sickness or pain. If people of this sort also study Transcendence, they are near enough to achieving it that they may be instructed. Moreover, the natures of such people are often respectful
and amicable. They frequently delight in service to the subtle and
wondrous. These are all marks of Transcendence.

Next are those who keep their will fixed on the ultimate Dao,
their zealous intent firm and correct. Some practice extensively secret
virtues, aiding the poor, rescuing those in difficulty, spreading benevolence, befriending the destitute, and burying desiccated bones.
Their virtue surpasses that of the ancients. Chaste and pure, they are
warmly reverent and generous with those below them. They are not
12b   lascivious; neither do they steal. Some have ancestors who bestow
grace on them, having established merit for generation after generation with the Three Offices, so that they already have three hundred
merits.* All those with this advantage who study the Dao might
achieve Transcendence. If their hearts are upright, nothing in heaven
or on earth can subvert them. If their corporal spirits are strong,
then demons and spirits will not oppose them. If their cloudsouls are
luminous, the myriad perversities cannot invade them. If their whitesouls are unsullied, the myriad specters will not oppose them. If their
seminal essence is clear, then lascivious corpses may not couple with
them. If their bodily fluids are pure, the three worms may not wreak
havoc on them.† If their blood is congealed, then the turgid pneumas
may not scatter it.

---

* This describes the positive results of the system of *chengfu* [inherited burden]
whereby one's fate was thought to be closely connected to the moral achievements
and failures of one's ancestors, particularly those in the seventh generation. See
Zürcher, "Buddhist Influence," pp. 46–49.

† The "three worms" (sometimes, as later in the text, called the "three corpses")
are maleficent, grain-eating parasites that seek the early destruction of the body that

In this way, those who study the Dao perfect their hearts and strengthen their internal spirits, strictly controlling their whitesouls and embracing their cloudsouls. They confine the myriad perversities in the prison houses of the eight wilds and lock the masses of bewitching sprites at the outer limits of the nine directions. They are zealously sincere in holding to perfection, one with the unflagging energy of the primal age of Grand Incipience.* Their constant desire is to fly away to Transcendence on darting pinions. Their ruddy spirit is at peace in its scarlet residence and their five treasures secure in the clear mystery of their bodies. Encountering trial, they observe but do not topple; glory and dishonor do not move   13a them. Summoned by the South-Facing Monarch, they pay him no heed.† They can discard ten thousand in gold with no expression of regret. They are content in the face of grinding cold and suffering, delighting in still fasts in the mountains. Maintaining their determination without flagging, they may live as long as heaven and earth.

Only those who are like this may we begin to call students of the Dao. If one lacks these signs and these actions, though he be a renowned hero whose aspiration is to swallow the Four Seas, or one of vast energy and boundless might whose influence overtops the clouds; though he be one of profound knowledge with flying brush and disputatious speech or one of exceptionally elegant action who might impose order on the unseen and clear away doubt, whose mouth speaks of Nothingness and whose eyes flash to the eight directions—still he does not have the qualities of a Transcendent.‡ When we say that "one labors in vain for a lifetime, never knowing

---

they might be free to roam within the earth. See Maspero, *Taoism and Chinese Religion,* pp. 331–39.

* On this age in the creation of the world, see endnote 13 to the introduction to the *Inner Explanations.*

† This phrase echoes the skull's reply to Zhuangzi when Zhuangzi offered it the means to return to life: "Why should I give up the happiness of the south-facing monarch for the sufferings of the living?" (Graham, *Chuang-tzu,* pp. 124–25).

‡ Yang Xi is here speaking, no doubt, of the practitioners of "Mystic Learning," who were, even as he wrote, in vogue in the high society of the southern capital of the Jin. For examples of the style of discourse and comportment derided here, see Mather, *Shih-shuo Hsin-yü;* and Zürcher, *Buddhist Conquest,* pp. 87–92 and 124–26, passim.

what one fails to achieve," it is this sort of person of whom we speak.

IV.   TABOOS FOR TRANSCENDENTS
RECORDED BY THE PERFECTED,
FROM THE *PURPLE TEXTS INSCRIBED
BY THE SPIRITS*

1a   The Lord Azure Lad said: There is more than one thing that renders
the study of Transcendence difficult. This difficulty is not the sort of
difficulty known among mortals. Transcendence is so difficult that it
cannot be encompassed in writing. Though a person have the visage
of a Transcendent and be thereby marked for ascendancy, there are
1b   ten items that negate the marks of Transcendence. If one depends
on the marks of Transcendence and still transgresses these items,
the marks will be negated and one will not become a Transcendent.
Now I will secretly inform those with the marks of Transcendence.
You should adhere to these things:

1.   Do not delight in sexual debauchery. When you engage
in debauchery, your cloudsouls and bodily fluids flow away, your
glowing essences wither and dry up. Your spirits are scorched,
your whitesouls scatter. Your bones become thin, your marrow
sullied. Then your cloudsouls will call out to the numinous Bureaus,
notifying the celestial offices. The palaces in the three registers of
your body will fall into contention. Your embryonic flowering will
become mixed and confused. This is the first of the ways to destroy
the marks of Transcendence.*

2.   Do not steal or act violently. If you are violent, your Yellow
Court will be sunk in wild contention and the three corpses will
delight in killing you.† Your cloudsouls and corporeal spirits will
observe the lasciviousness as your whitesouls have intercourse with
demons, blocking your inner chambers. Thereafter, your eyesight
will become unfocused and injurious vapors will issue from your
mouth.

---

* Each of the following items, with the exception of the tenth, ends with this formula. I have deleted it for the remaining items.

† The Yellow Court is one of the nine palaces of the brain. See Robinet, *Taoist
Meditation,* pp. 127–31.

3. Do not get drunk on liquor. When drunk, your physical form deteriorates and your internal spirits become confused. Your cloudsouls forget their proper chambers and your whitesouls roam off to perverse dwellings. Then the Ruddy Infant will fly away on the whirlwind while your throat and brains are scorched by fire.

4. Do not become sullied and impure. Filth and impurity lead to the clear spirits' loss of perfection. Your essences and cloudsouls will not then remain, and the worms will be produced in the Three Palaces. While the Ruddy Infant floats off or flies away, your blood will thicken and your marrow rot. The spiritual luminescences will depart their lodgings and your whitesouls will flee to the gates of evil to seek your book of death. 2a

5. Do not eat the flesh of the animal associated with the natal days of your father and mother.* If you do so, your primal body will lose its originator and your source will be unreachable. Your embryonic spirits will scream in agony and the Vermilion Lord will wail with longing.† Your three cloudsouls will be brutally poisoned and your whitesouls will search out your grave. Once such meat enters your mouth, your fate is to descend to the eternal darkness.

6. Do not eat the flesh of the animal associated with your own natal day. When you do so, both the body and its spirits depart from perfection, the Muddy Pellet gradually sinks into decrepitude, and the Three Palaces are deserted. Then the newborn is encroached upon, the cloudsouls flee, and the whitesouls seek out your coffin.

7. Do not eat the flesh of the six domestic animals. To do this leads the body and its pneumas to be beclouded with stench, their essences blocked and muddied. Your brain will yellow, your teeth turn brittle, and your spleen will nourish pneumas of death. Your cloudsouls cannot, under these conditions, be perfected, while your 2b

---

* Chinese practice is to mark each year by a combination of one of the ten celestial stems and one of the twelve earth branches. Each celestial stem combines with only six of the earth branches, resulting in a cycle of sixty. Twelve animals are associated with the earth branches, and the reference here is to the two that correspond to the years of one's father's and mother's birth. The twelve animals are rat, ox, tiger, hare, dragon, snake, horse, sheep, monkey, chicken, dog, and pig.

† The "Vermilion Lord" seems to be a variant name for the ruler of the heart known as the Lad of the Cinnabar Prime.

whitesouls will swell with perverse energy. Then your body will sink into the eternal chasm and your bones will long to be buried in the earth.[41]

8.   Do not eat the five bitter herbs. If you do so your five viscera will develop an evil stench, the three floriate palaces will collapse in disorder, and the spirits will be unable to properly reach them.* The essential embryos will sink in the mire and your souls will depart. The Ruddy Infant will be beset with trouble, since the flying spirits will fail to guard it. Your vision will wander distractedly.

9.   Do not take the life of any living thing, from insects on up. To turn weapons on the myriad forms of life is to bind your body in blood-debt. You will become physically violent: your whitesouls will turn vicious and your cloudsouls will war against one another. The embryonic spirits will be caught in indecision and the perfected child will flee. The Muddy Pellet will become duplicitous and crazed, the Ruddy Infant will turn on you in rebellion, and your body will be boiled in a pot, where it will be poached until it disintegrates.†

*   *   *   *

3a   10.   Do not face to the north when squatting to relieve yourself or when you look up to observe the sun, moon, or stars. Do not face north to arrange your hair or to remove your clothing. Do not face north to spit or curse. Do not encroach upon the "destroyer" or obliterate the "ruler."‡ The "destroyer" is the asterism marked by

---

* The "three floriate palaces" are the palaces of the Three Primes. See HY 639, 11a–b, in this translation.
† This seems to refer to the punishment awaiting the dead in the earth-prisons. In fact, however, the concept of corporal suffering in the earth-prisons seems to enter Daoism only with the Lingbao scriptures, which were much more heavily influenced by Buddhism (see Robinet, La révélation du Shangqing, vol. 1, p. 186). The punishment of boiling in oil, usually for the crime of treason, was also practiced in China before the arrival of Buddhism (see A. F. P. Hulsewé, Remnants of Han Law [Leiden: E. J. Brill, 1985], pp. 122–24). Nonetheless, in this context, where it is a fitting retribution for those who have broiled the carcasses of animals, the punishment can hardly be explained as that of mundane officials. The reference to "myriad forms of life" also has a Buddhist ring to it. If these are not embellishments added by a later scribe, however, they certainly constitute one of the few Shangqing references to the earth-prisons as places of torture.
‡ These terms refer to the wangxiang system. See the Xiang'er, lines 20–26.

Jupiter. The "ruler" is the direction of the preeminent pneuma. Do not express anger to the sun, moon, or stars.* Do not carry out corporal punishments on the days of the eight nodes.† Do not become angry or vexatious on the first day of the lunar month. Do not consume the flesh of turtles, dragons, or shell creatures on any of the six *jia* days.‡ Do not eat the flesh of fowl on *bingwu* days or black animals on *bingzi* days. Do not have sex or sleep on the same bed with a woman on *gengshen* days. Do not become greatly drunk⁴² on *yimao* days. Do not face north and take life on the fourth day of the first month, eat fish on the ninth day of the second month, eat visceral flesh or the hearts of vegetables on the third of the third month, cut plants or chop trees on the eighth of the fourth month, look at blood on the fifth of the fifth month, turn the earth on the sixth of the sixth month, think of evil matters on the seventh of the seventh month, buy or sell shoes or any manner of foot covering on the fourth of the eighth month, lift bedclothes or curtains on the ninth of the ninth month, penalize or accuse anyone on the fifth of the tenth month, fail to bathe on the eleventh of the eleventh month, or fail to purify yourself, burn incense, and contemplate the Transcendents on the three days of lunar darkness in the twelfth month.

3b

These taboos are the great prohibitions of the celestials. When the Three Offices order investigations, these are counted as major transgressions. Some of them cause one's three cloudsouls to become ill and the seven whitesouls to roam and contend. Some are times detested by the spirits of the placenta, when the three palaces might be infected with evil. This is because evil dreams encroach on the heart and weird *mei* sprites mount its scarlet gate towers. The essen-

---

* This seems to refer to cursing others with the celestial bodies as witness or as the agents by which the curse is to be put into effect.

† This refers to the "eight seasonal nodes," the solstices, equinoxes, and the first days of each of the four seasons by the Chinese lunar calendar. A passage that Tao marks as an authentic part of the Yang Xi revelations, stipulating that one should "avoid conflict, joy, and anger and not carry out corporal punishments" on these days devoted to retreat and meditation, is found at HY 1010, 19b. On these days in Lingbao practice, see footnote * on p. 413 to the *Scripture of Salvation*.

‡ The graph *jia* means "shell" or "carapace."

tial liquid then becomes infected, and the spiritual Perfected become dazed and confused. When this happens, one begins to transgress the interdictions with no regard at all for the taboos.

If you are able to observe the celestial interdictions, you indeed possess the stuff of Transcendence; if not, you will meet with destruction.

◆   ◆   ◆   ◆

4a   At the autumnal equinox, those who study the Dao should envision the Perfected and conduct purification rituals. They should fix their minds not on evil but on their desire to fly up in Transcendence. As an ancient divinity said:[43] "If you wish to rise into the heavens, be cautious on the autumnal equinox. On that day transgressions, no matter how small, are all reported on high. It is extremely difficult to seek Transcendence with transgressions to one's name. Therefore one should study the Dao with fear and trepidation."

This is the heart of the matter. Those Daoists engaged in long retreats should, on the autumnal equinox, repent of their transgressions as well as those of their fathers and mothers for seven generations. They should take an oath to reform themselves. If you are not one whose nature is already otherworldly in its perfection, you should repent on this day. Be attentive to this.

The Lord Azure Lad said: It is not vital that you know the signs of Transcendence, but you should know how these signs are destroyed. This is an essential secret. Those sunk in the mire of the world possess in vain their physical forms and their bones; which of them knows the path to preserving their signs? Those who study the Dao should first widely practice secret virtue, with benevolence to the myriad forms of life. Aid and rescue those in trouble or distress. Value the Dao rather than material goods, giving generously to 4b   others that you might spread virtue. Do not be parsimonious with your wealth, but spread it among the poor. Make an oath to the Perfected pneumas, kneeling to beg their assistance with an empty heart.

As the ancient saying has it, "Plant fields of goodness that you might harvest Transcendence."

NOTES TO PURPLE TEXTS: TRANSLATION

1. The term *sanling* 三靈 (three spirits) most likely here refers to the Azure Lad's corporeal spirits in three registers, which he projects out of his body as mists to form his conveyance. (See *HY* 1026, 80:10.7 and 81:14a.) The three registers are explained later in this scripture. Bai Lü-zhong (fl. 722), however, regards the occurrences of *sanling* in the *Huangting jing* as referring to the three cloudsouls. (See *HY* 1026, 11:50a.5–6.)

2. On this garment, fashioned of the glistening wing feathers of the halcyon kingfisher, see Kroll, "Azure Lad," p. 77.

3. "Cornices" is conjectural for *xi* 析, which means "to split" or "split wood." It might here refer to the short rafters along the tops of the walls or perhaps to barricades of brushwood.

4. This image is taken from the "Qiwu lun" chapter of the *Zhuangzi*. See Graham, *Chuang-tzu* (1986), pp. 48–49.

5. I have found no further reference in the Shangqing scriptures to *san guan* 三觀, the term I have translated here as "three modes of perception." In the Buddhist *Lotus sutra*, the term refers to perception of emptiness, of falseness, and perception of the middle way. This tripartite system influenced later Daoist texts (see, for instance, *HY* 1121, 5:3b–5b), but it is unlikely to have been more than a terminological borrowing in the writings of Yang Xi. Later, the Sage Lord is described as observing: above, the heavens of Upper Clarity; in the middle, the palaces of the Grand Bournes; and below, the cavern-heavens. It is possible that the term refers to this sort of spatial division.

6. The term I have translated "to split hairs," *haomang* 毫芒 (literally, "hair tips") has a long history in mystical writings, where it generally refers to someone who indulges in an overly refined analysis of a vast problem. The following, from chapter 2 of the *Huainan zi*, is typical: "[In apprehending the nothingness before things began:] though you think of the infinitely deep or vastly large, you cannot move beyond it; though you split hairs and dissect their tips, you cannot go inside it" (2:19).

7. *HY* 1320 reproduces the first two-thirds of this hymn on pp. 6b–7a. Significant variants found in this text are given in the following notes. Instead of *huameng* 華濛, "mottled murk," *HY* 1320 reads *huamang* 芒, "mottled beams (of light)."

8. *HY* 1320 reads *yuzhang* 玉章, "feathered stanzas," for the graphically similar *yutong* 玉童, "feathered lads."

9. On the term *huoluo* 豁落, see Edward H. Schafer, "Li Po's Star Power," *Bulletin of the Society for the Study of Chinese Religions* 6 (1978), pp. 5–15.

10. For *you jue* 有覺, "to realize," *HY* 1320 has *liu jue* 六覺, "six realizations"—a term about which I have no information.

11. I have found no further reference in the Shangqing scriptures to the "Ruddy Spirit." Given the concerns of this text, the term might refer to the

perfected form of the embryonic "Ruddy Infant" referred to later. *HY* 1320 has the graphically similar, but equally enigmatic, *muling* 木靈, "wood spirit," in place of *zhuling* 朱靈, "ruddy spirit."

12. According to a surviving fragment from the *Central Scripture of the Nine Perfected*, a text that collects Shangqing methods (Robinet, *La révélation du Shangqing*, vol. 2, pp. 67–80), the Five Ancient Ones were the spirits of the five naked-eye planets. (See *HY* 1366, 3a–b; I would like to thank Professor Robinet for bringing this passage to my attention.) These deities are already described in the Han-period weft texts, where they are recorded to have appeared to the sage-king Shun (Yasui and Nakamura, *Isho shūsei*, vol. 2, pp. 107–8; and Bokenkamp, "Sources," p. 453, where the monarch is incorrectly identified as Yao).

13. On my restoration of the term "jade placenta," which does not figure in *HY* 639, both here and directly below, see endnote 23 to the introduction.

14. The name "mother of water" has another meaning in the Shangqing texts, apparently distinct from its use here. The Water Mother, an asterism perhaps to be identified with the four stars elsewhere called the Water Throne (Gustav Schlegel, *Uranographie chinoise* [Taipei: Chengwen, 1875], vol. 1, pp. 419–20), augurs the cataclysmic world floods of the apocalypse. This goddess rules the world's rivers. The *Santian zhengfa jing* describes her as follows: "The Great Bird will sweep the filth from the sacred peaks as the Water Mother receives her charge over the rivers of the nine [continents]" (*HY* 1026, 2:5a; see also *HY* 1026, 24:6a, for a description of the asterism; and Robinet, *La révélation du Shangqing*, vol. 1, p. 140 n. 1). Though such a vision of the oncoming apocalypse may be connected to the references in this text, I have found no indications that such was the case. I thank Professor Robinet for calling this role of the Water Mother to my attention.

15. This verse, which serves as a mnemonic device, is reproduced in a number of texts, with only one significant variation: The graph *zhu* 朱, "vermilion" (given in *HY* 639; *HY* 1393, 11a; and *HY* 435, 6a), appears with the jade radical as *zhu* 珠, "pearl, round jewel, orb," in *HY* 1130, 94:1a; *HY* 1026, 12:7a; *HY* 140, 1:6a; and *HY* 219, 23:1a. This seems to be a free variation, as the textual lineage that appears closest to the autograph text (represented by the citations in *HY* 1130 and *HY* 435, and the citation in *HY* 1026) falls on both sides of the question.

16. For *pi meng* 辟夢, "to ward off dreams," both *HY* 1393, 12b, and *HY* 435, 6a–b, have *qun meng* 群夢, "to crowd? dreams," which seems like an attempt to rationalize what is after all a very obscure passage. *HY* 1130, 94:2b, simply replaces the offending clause with "jade placenta," which followed the term "mother of water" twice earlier. Given the text's warnings about dreams in subsequent sections and the importance of all the souls' participation in this meditation, it seems to me that the *HY* 639 passage should, barring other discoveries, be the preferred reading.

17. "Soaring trees" (*qianshu* 騫樹, reading *qian* 騫 as a loan for *xian* 鶱)

are miraculous trees that appear in celestial locales throughout the Shang-qing and Lingbao scriptures. In Lingbao texts, they are described as composed of the seven gemstones with leaves that are celestial texts, while in Shangqing texts they appear most often on the moon. See *HY* 614, 11b, and *HY* 87, 2:13b, for glosses on their appearance in the Lingbao scriptures, and Robinet, *Taoist Meditation,* p. 190, for their association with the cinnabar trees of the moon.

18. *HY* 639 reads, "[These are the times when] yin and yang merge" 是陰陽之合, whereas all other witnesses read, "[These are the times when] yin essences fly and merge" 是陰精飛合 (*HY* 435, 16a; *HY* 1393, 14b; *HY* 219, 23:4b; *S* 4314, line 2).

19. Underneath the talisman in the *HY* 639 version of this text it is noted that if you cannot practice every month, it is most essential that this talisman be swallowed in the even-numbered months.

20. On the Gate of Destiny and the Mystic Pass, as well as the gods that inhabit them, see Robinet, *Méditation taoïste,* pp. 120–29.

21. The names and bynames of the spirits of the Three Primes derive, as Robinet has shown, from distinct textual traditions. See Robinet, *La révélation du Shangqing,* vol. 2, pp. 30–32 and 80–82.

22. The term translated here as "to cycle," *huizhuan* 迴轉, implies transformation. See Robinet, *Méditation taoïste,* pp. 42–45; and Robinet, *Taoist Meditation,* pp. 60–63.

23. The Dunhuang manuscript *P* 2751, line 136, has the variant "the Jade Maiden becomes my wife." The commentator goes to great length to explain that there is really no question of an actual marriage here and that this practice can be accomplished by both men and women. The role of the Jade Maiden, by this account, is to "regulate" the vital forces.

24. All fourteen of the following ingredients figure, under the same cover names (with one exception—graphite is known as "Cultured Watchlord of the Cyan Mound" instead of "Volatile Efflorescence of the Cyan Wall") in the recipe for another Shangqing elixir, the "Fourfold Floriate." See *HY* 1365, 2:9b–11a; Robinet, *La révélation du Shangqing,* vol. 2, p. 106; and Strickmann, "T'ao Hung-ching," pp. 171–73. For an analysis of the possible chemical composition of this elixir, see Schafer, "The Transcendent Vitamin," pp. 35–36, from which the parenthetical alternative identifications are taken.

25. Perhaps to be identified as actinolite asbestos or tremolite. See Schafer, "The Transcendent Vitamin," n. 31, for a full discussion.

26. Also identified as lead oxide, litharge, or massicot.

27. Also identified as ceruse.

28. The precipitate of desert lakes, containing gypsum, anhydrite, and halite.

29. The *Wushang biyao* citation of this passage specifies that this procedure is to be carried out in the tenth, fourth, or eighth month (*HY* 1130, 92:8a).

30. Reading, with Strickmann (*Le taoïsme du Mao chan,* p. 272 n. 352), *hui* 諱, "taboo name," for *zhu* 諸.

31. My translation of this portion of the scripture (down to the names of the four ministers listed at *HY* 442, 9a) is much indebted to the French translation of Michel Strickmann (*Le taoïsme du Mao chan,* pp. 209–24). Where my translation differs from his, I note it in the footnotes. It is not possible to list individually all of the points at which my translation has benefited from his work.

32. My reconstruction of this passage is conjectural. Strickmann (*Le taoïsme du Mao chan,* p. 212) translates " . . . il condescendit à soulager la foule de ses frères humains, en faisant souffler sur eux la manifestation de son esprit, comme sur l'herbe qui ploie souffle le vent." This latter phrase is a common metaphor for moral suasion in Chinese texts, but there is no mention of the wind, or of *bending* grasses, here. I take *shenji* 神迹, "spirit traces," to refer to a written account of spiritual action. This is a common meaning of "traces" in this period, and the word *ts'ao* 草 ("grasses") may well function verbally, meaning "to draft" a document. However, *xin* 釁 is not a common adjective. I take it as a loan for *xin* 釁 in the sense of "in his leisure moments (before his ascent)." If this interpretation is accepted, the document the Sage Lord drafts most likely refers to the *Mysterious Scripture of the Grand Cavern,* the text he is found to be expounding in the opening passages of this scripture. See *HY* 639, 2a.

33. The transcription of this passage found in *HY* 769, 49b, reads *er dao* 二道 for *san dao* 三道.

34. "Tang" refers to the sage-king Yao. The *Santian zhengfa jing* version of this prediction reads, instead of *Tang cheng* 唐承, *cheng Tang* 承唐 (*HY* 1026, 2:7a). The same phrase is found in other Shangqing texts as well (*HY* 1304, 1:16b; *HY* 1010, 8:14a). Whatever the order, I assume that the word *cheng* refers to Yao's receipt of the mandate as primogenitor of the new era. This wording is apparently unique to Daoist texts, as Yao is more commonly known as *Tao Tang* 陶唐, an appellation that refers to his place of origin.

35. "Shadowed Regalia" and "Knotted Spangles" are secret names for the transcendents who pilot the sun and moon in their courses. The meditations known by these names involve envisioning the movements of the sun and moon and traversing the sky together with them. For the later scriptures that expand on this practice, see Robinet, *La révélation du Shangqing,* vol. 2, pp. 67 ff. The full name of the *Revolving Writing* is the *Scripture of Seven Revolutions for the Spiritual Technique of Seven Transformations.* It is an unrevealed set of seven texts based on the seven transformations undergone each day by the three mountains of the Spirit Isle. (See *HY* 1010, 5:3a.3 and 5:14b–15a.) The name *Perfected Writings of the Golden Porte* refers to the present account. The talisman Spirit Tiger is one of the more potent of Shangqing talismans, often worn by the Perfected who appeared to Yang Xi. See, for example, *HY* 1010, 1:12a. On the sur-

viving example of this talisman, see Robinet, *La révélation du Shangqing*, vol. 2, p. 249; and *HY* 1374, 1:4a–8b. The technique of the "Secret Words on the Eight Ways" allows the adept to envision stellar deities, particularly those of the Dipper, as they enter into and vivify the body. See Robinet, *La révélation du Shangqing*, vol. 2, p. 72; and *HY* 1365, 1:11b–15b. The *Purple Texts* is the present text, especially that part devoted to controlling the cloudsouls and whitesouls. The *Golden Root* is, in the Shangqing scriptures, another way of referring to the "Flying Root"—that is, solar essences to be ingested during meditation. The incantation to be intoned in the method given earlier in this text contains mention of "the golden essence, solar root" (see *HY* 639, 6b) and may very well be that meant here. There is in addition a (possibly later?) Shangqing text containing a variant meditation practice that insists that the *Scripture of the Yellow Court* should be intoned. See Robinet, *La révélation du Shangqing*, vol. 2, p. 122. *Nine Vermilion* refers to the *Spotted Talismans of the Nine Vermilion*, which was designed to erase the adept's name from the registers of death and inscribe it in the books of life held in the Five Marchmounts. See Robinet, *La révélation du Shangqing*, vol. 2, pp. 175–78; and *HY* 1318, 6a–31a. *Sinuous Simplicity* refers to talismans employed to command the demon kings and avoid the disasters accompanying the end of the kalpa cycle. See Robinet, *La révélation du Shangqing*, vol. 2, pp. 187–90; and *HY* 1361. The *Purple Measures* refers to texts written on purple tablets that were said to contain a method of "inner observation" for illumining the deities of the body and nourishing them with pneumas. See Robinet, *La révélation du Shangqing*, vol. 2, pp. 111–16. The *Secret Talismans of the Five Phases* for controlling the cloudsouls and whitesouls is mentioned in Yang's writings (see *HY* 1010, 5:3a.10). A version of the talismans is to be found in *HY* 1361 (15b ff; see Robinet, *La révélation du Shangqing*, vol. 2, p. 189). Such talismans were ingested by burning them and mixing their ashes with water. The procedures for making and ingesting the Langgan elixir are to be found in the main text.

36. The scripture titles given here in many instances contain the practices mentioned at *HY* 442, 5a ff. For the *Shadowed Regalia* and *Knotted Spangles*, see the previous endnote; for the *Scripture of the Grand Cavern*, see footnote * on p. 310 to the translation. On the remaining texts, see Robinet, *La révélation du Shangqing*, vol. 2, at the page numbers noted after each title: *Perfected Scripture of the Eight Simplicities* (51–57), *Hidden Writings of the Most High* (151–61), *Central Scripture of the Nine Perfected* (67–76), *Secret Words of the Yellow Lord Lao on the Eight Ways* (72–73), *Ten Instructions on the Grand Elixirs in Jade Graphs* (151–61).

37. The identification of these lesser texts and practices is less sure. Most seem to be early alchemical texts that played some role in the formation of Shangqing doctrine. The title *Transformations of the Nine-Times-Recycled Elixir* may well refer to the text known to Ge Hong as the *Scripture of the Divine Elixirs of the Nine Tripods of the Yellow Thearch*. (See Fabrizio

Pregadio, "The Book of the Nine Elixirs and Its Tradition," in Yamada Keiji and Tanaka Tan, eds., *Chūgoku kodai kagakushi ron* [Kyoto: Kyoto daigaku jinbun kagaku kenkyūjo, 1991], vol. 2, pp. 543–639.) The *Upper Scriptures of Grand Clarity* may refer to the Grand Clarity scriptures as a whole, particularly those associated with alchemical practice and "retaining the one." See Robinet, *La révélation du Shangqing*, vol. 1, pp. 10–11 and 40–43. The *Essences of the Dao in Yellow and White* seems to be the same text mentioned under the name *Scripture of the Dao in Yellow and White* in the *Zhen'gao* (*HY* 1010, 5:9b.8; Robinet, *La révélation du Shangqing*, vol. 2, pp. 56–57), which is transmitted by a specialist in alchemy. The title *Celestial Barrier Recorded in Azure* may refer to the text known as the *Three Charts of the Celestial Barrier,* which Tao Hongjing records as a "text from the catalogs of the lower Perfected." (See *HY* 1010, 9:5b.7–9 and 5:3a.6.)

38. The bracketed phrases do not appear in the *HY* 1131 transcription of this portion of the text. Indeed, they read like a gloss that may have inadvertently become part of the text.

39. On *kui* 規 as "eye socket," see *HY* 1010, 5:13b.7–10, where it is explained that, when tested by a demonic apparition, one should closely examine its eyes. If they are lusterless, it is is a demon; if they are luminous and square, it is a Transcendent.

40. The bracketed paragraphs are restored from the transcription of the text found in *HY* 1131, 8:16a.1–4.

41. *HY* 427, 22b–25a, contains a Buddhist-inspired revision of precepts five, six and seven. These read as follows:

5. Do not eat the flesh of any living beast....
6. Do not eat the flesh of any aquatic being....
7. Do not eat the flesh of any bird....

42. *HY* 427, the same text that contains the Buddhist-inspired revisions mentioned in note 41 above, replaces "become greatly drunk" (*da zui* 大醉) with "drink liquor" (*yin jiu* 飲酒), adding "you should conduct a purification rite and rectify your heart." All other witnesses (*HY* 1026, 40:12a; *HY* 836, 6a) agree with *HY* 179.

43. According to the *Inner Traditions of the Lord of Ziyang,* the name of this divinity was Gong Zhongyang, who received the *Transcendent Interdictions* directly from the Azure Lad himself. (See *HY* 1026, 106:13b.10, and *HY* 1130, 84:14b.2.)

The Wondrous Scripture
of the Upper Chapters
on Limitless Salvation

INTRODUCTION

The scripture translated here is, without a doubt, the most influential
and widely known of the original Lingbao corpus of scriptures.[1] The
Scripture of Salvation, to use the shortened version of its title, was
the first Daoist scripture—if we exclude the *Laozi*—to be annotated
and to have its abstruse language explained.[2] Early in the Tang period, the *Scripture of Salvation* was taken as one of the three scriptures to be studied by Daoists for the official exam leading to Daoist
investiture. At about the same time, some of the "celestial language"
of the text, though incomprehensible outside of scriptural exegesis,
entered the literary language and was used widely in secular poetry,

attesting to the popularity of the scripture.[3] During the Northern Song, the scripture was expanded from its original one chapter, translated here, to the magnificent length of sixty-one chapters.[4] Despite the fact that, as a Lingbao scripture, it should belong to the second of the three major divisions of the canon, the *Scripture of Salvation* was placed first in the Ming-period canon.[5] The scripture is still recited in liturgy wherever Daoists practice.

The popularity of the *Scripture of Salvation* represents but one example of the success of the Lingbao scriptures themselves. The Lingbao scriptures were, according to the earliest records, revealed to the world around 400 C.E. by Ge Chaofu, the grandnephew of Ge Hong (283–343). As these records make clear, Ge Chaofu did not claim to have received the scriptures from spirits directly, but through a line of transmission extending back to the great-uncle of Ge Hong, Ge Xuan. The scriptures contain references to at least part of this line of transmission, which included members of the Ge clan already well known in Daoist circles. And, as we will see, these references gave the Lingbao scriptures the added advantage of placing their original revelation years earlier than the bestowal on Yang Xi of the Shangqing scriptures, from which these texts borrowed heavily.

The earliest references to the release of the Lingbao scriptures uniformly describe them as wildly popular and as having already prompted unscrupulous persons to forge imitations. The reasons for this immediate popularity are evident. The Lingbao scriptures are the first Daoist scriptures to wholeheartedly embrace the Buddhist conception of rebirth, though in a modified form that takes into account the importance of one's ancestors in the face of the perceived Buddhist threat to the stability of Chinese family altars. Among traditional Chinese beliefs threatened by the Buddhist doctrine of rebirth, the most vital were those linking individuals to their family, for rebirth meant that one's ancestors had in effect joined other clans—a sort of postmortem betrayal by those one was duty-bound to respect. But filiality and reverence for one's ancestors represent only one aspect of the complex of beliefs that made the notion of rebirth difficult to accept. Throughout Chinese history, the prosperity of a family was believed to be directly influenced by the merit of its ancestors, including their postmortem merit. According to the form this took in Daoism, known as "inherited burden," the fates of succeeding generations were influenced by the deeds of their ancestors, particularly those of the seventh generation. Rebirth thus represented a potential loss of spiritual capital.

The Shangqing scriptures of Yang Xi were perhaps the earliest Daoist texts to deal with the idea of rebirth. They describe rebirth as a method available to the lowest class of transcendents, those resident in the cavern-heavens, who need a second chance at life that they might continue their sluggish pursuit of perfection. Still, those who are reborn must leave a foot bone in the Three Offices to show that their fates are still causally connected to their original ancestors.[6] For Yang Xi, then, rebirth still represented an option and not the predestined fate of all mortals.

The Lingbao texts, on the other hand, accepted the increasingly popular concept of rebirth but subtly modified it in ways that were seen as more agreeable to the Chinese worldview. Through Lingbao rites of salvation, such as the recitation of the *Scripture of Salvation,* one might rescue one's ancestors, wherever they might be, for favorable rebirth, thereby reaffirming familial ties by debts of reciprocal obligation and ensuring that the family remained intact, despite the rebirth of its members into other clans. Of course, the most favorable outcome would be that, having benefited from the rites performed on their behalf, the ancestors might move directly into the heavens, from which vantage point they might, in their turn, work favorably for the salvation of all (their heirs foremost). This is the option on which the Lingbao texts tend to focus.[7]

Because of this focus and of other ways in which they adapted Buddhist doctrines to accommodate Chinese beliefs, the Lingbao scriptures were seen as Daoism's best response to the foreign threat of Buddhism, from whose scriptures the Lingbao texts borrow heavily, always redefining concepts to fit their own ideological structures. To take but the most immediate example, the highest deity of the Lingbao scriptures, the Celestial Worthy of Primordial Commencement, is a Daoist version of the Buddha in his cosmic form. The "Celestial Worthy" of his title derives from the first words reportedly pronounced by the Buddha at his birth—"Above the *heavens* and below the heavens, I alone am *revered*"—so that we might also translate "the one revered in all the heavens." There is evidence that, as a result of the popularity of this Daoist divinity, Chinese Buddhist translators eventually dropped the epithet "Celestial Worthy" as a translation of Sanskrit *bhagavat* (blessed one) in favor of *shizun* (world-honored one).[8]

"Primordial Commencement" refers to the second and third of the "three pneumas," the primal and the inaugural, and signifies that the Celestial Worthy was born in the earliest differentiation of pneumas when the Dao first divided. He is thus, we are to understand, inconceivably more ancient than the Buddha. In that he is the pure product of Chinese cosmology, his ability to manipulate the cycles of birth and destruction, life and death, according to the accepted principles of yin, yang, and the five phases, is likewise greater.

A second feature that assured the popularity of the Lingbao scriptures is that, like that of the *Xiang'er* commentary, their message of salvation is meant for all, rich and poor alike. Unlike Celestial Master doctrine, though, the Lingbao scriptures allow for varying degrees of fidelity to their precepts and practices on the part of the faithful.[9] Borrowing elements of the Buddhist bodhisattva ideal, the Lingbao scriptures hold that salvation can be achieved on behalf of others, through the conduct of appropriate rites. This idea would lead to the establishment of professional Daoist priests and a flourishing marketplace of ritual services. Those who sought to forge their own scriptures were, as we will see, quite aware of the economic benefits of owning (or even composing their own) Lingbao scriptures.

Although the *Scripture of Salvation* in itself calls for a book-length study, that is not feasible here. In the sections that follow, we will explore briefly: (1) the historical background of the Lingbao scriptures as a whole, including information concerning the dating of the *Scripture of Salvation*; (2) the cosmology expressed in the text and the deities it contains; (3) the celestial language presented in the text; and (4) the ritual innovations of the text, with its new approach to rescuing humanity from the terrors of death.

Historical Background

Beyond his association with the Lingbao scriptures, we know next to nothing about Ge Chaofu. During the course of Tao Hongjing's account of the diffusion of the Shangqing scriptures, he mentions that one forger of both Shangqing and Lingbao scriptures was motivated by the fact that the Lingbao texts of Chaofu were "flourishing as if the teaching was borne on the wind." Other Daoist records relate that Chaofu was the grandnephew of Ge Hong and in line for the master-disciple transmission of the texts that had to that point been kept largely within the Ge family. Then, "at the end of the Long'an reign period [397–401]" he transmitted them to two disciples, Ren Yanqing and Xu Lingqi (d. 473? 474?), and they were thenceforth "transmitted down through the generations."[10] These references, coupled with the fact that the scriptures mention the *gengzi* year (400) as the year the Lingbao doctrine would emerge to replace all others, lead to the conclusion that it was Ge Chaofu himself who was responsible for their composition.

There is ample circumstantial evidence to support this conclusion as well. The Ge family resided in Jurong, the home of the Xu family, original beneficiaries of Yang Xi's revelations, and were related by marriage to the Xus through Chaofu's generation. Members of the Ge family, and evidently Chaofu himself, thus had access to the Shangqing revelations at a time when they were not widely circulating. This goes some way to explaining the attitude toward the Shangqing scriptures expressed in the Lingbao texts. They are portrayed as authentic and valuable, but emanating from heavens lower than those in which the Lingbao texts are to be found and, worse yet, as having in some cases been transmitted to the world by female divinities![11] Further, there is the fact that the scriptures, devoted to ancestral salvation, stress so strongly the role of the Ge family. Ge family notables, particularly Ge Xuan and Ge Hong, are constantly singled out as suitable recipients of this most holy of revelations. Even the contents of Ge Hong's library, as recounted in a book he actually did compose, the *Baopu zi,* is shown to have been derived from the oral instructions of the Celestial Worthy himself.[12]

Despite all of this it is unlikely that the Lingbao texts, as they have come down to us, remain in the form in which they were originally written. This is due in part to the fact that they were so widely imitated. Already by 437, when the Daoist Lu Xiujing, "disciple of the Three Caverns," came to compile a catalog of the Lingbao scriptures, it was difficult for him to separate the "true from the imitation." We do not know Lu's source for his catalog, though there was certainly such a list, because imitators used it to title their own productions. From this list, Lu was able to derive a catalog of the "ten parts" of the celestial scriptures in thirty-six chapters, incised in gold on slats of jade and stored in the heavens. This first part of the catalog included even the names of texts not yet revealed in the world. The second part of his catalog comprised oral instructions and teachings conveyed by Ge Xuan, as well as accounts of Ge's own activities.[13]

From the preface to this catalog, which survives in a Song-period source, we can gain some idea of the popularity of the Lingbao scriptures in the 430s, as well as of the confusion caused by their many imitators. Since this preface provides nearly all the information we have on the diffusion of the Lingbao scriptures, I will in the course of this discussion cite a good portion of the text.

Lu begins by recounting the origins of the Lingbao scriptures from creation on, describing their original appearance in high antiquity and how they were taken back to heaven during the time of the six heavens. Then, after mentioning a series of revelations, including Laozi's appearance to the first Celestial Master, that serve to prove that the Celestial Worthy has not forgotten humanity, he continues, selectively citing a Shangqing apocalyptic text to show that, with the accession of Liu Yu, the time was right for the texts to be revealed in the world:

> The scripture states: "Forty-six *dinghai* years after the time of the flourishing of Tang, sooner or later within this period of time ... In the *gengzi* year ... the short-lived ones will continue to form gangs at Yu's Mouth; the rebellious hordes will fill with their corpses the streams of Yue[14] ... A strong minister will declare himself hegemon; a weak lord will spread out toward the west ... The descendant of dragon seed, the lord who will continue the mandate ... "[15] This lord is to eradicate the false ruler, cut down and drive off the rebellious people. At this the strength of the myriad ways will come to an end and these scriptures will circulate.[16] Figuring by the fated numbers and considering what actually happened, all of [these predictions] have proved trustworthy. Since the foretold cycle has arrived, the Grand Law [of Lingbao] has risen to prominence.
>
> But the scriptures have only begun to flourish and have not yet been entirely revealed or put into practice. Of the ten sections of the old catalog, only three parts are out.[17] Though the mystic storehouse has not yet poured forth, still the wheel of the law reaches to the eight directions. Were it not for the coincidence of the fated cycles, how would this overflowing success be possible?

Recently, the scriptures have been scattered, so that the counterfeit has become mixed with the true. Some [of the titles] are recorded in the old catalog, others are seen within the sections [of the scriptures], so that there are [now] fifty-five scrolls of new and old scriptures.[18] Students [of the Dao] respectfully receive them.[19] Rarely does anyone bother to distinguish among them. I was formerly not aware of this and single-handedly set about searching among [these texts], thus becoming aware of how intermixed [was the true with the false]. Sometimes [references to] the Shangqing [scriptures] were excised or muddled; sometimes they borrowed [passages] from other scriptures. Sometimes there were fabricated prefaces and explanations; in others chapters were reversed, sentences and sections added, and [new] charts and talismans created. Sometimes [these scriptures were written] to complete the old canon, but in other cases separate covenants and precepts [of transmission] were posited. The writing was heterodox and the rhymes were not correct. The expressions were vulgar and the meaning shallow and coarse. [The scriptures were] confused and unsystematic; matters were expressed without any regard for order. Comparing these false [texts] with the excellence [of the true texts], it seemed as if they were written by madmen—persons lacking the inner qualities to reach the mysterious and without any desire to seek out the Perfected—who had written [these texts based on] what they were able to spy out [of the original scriptures], falsely taking on the name of "Daoist" in their greedy search for income.[20]

Lu goes on to relate the celestial censure such persons have incurred in causing legitimate students of the Dao to waste both energy and wealth in pursuit of such falsehoods. After humbly expressing his own qualifications for the job, he concludes: "Now I list the scriptures of the old catalog, [marking those] already issued, together with those matters transmitted by the Duke Transcendent [Ge Xuan], with annotations. I will leave out [my own?] ideas and doubts." If this last phrase means that Lu will refrain from expressing completely which scriptures he had found to be "counterfeit" and who was responsible for them, as Tao Hongjing did in the case of the Shangqing revelations, we have good reason to wish that he had not been so reticent. He nowhere mentions the line of transmission through Ge Hong and Ge Chaofu, much less the roles of Chaofu's disciples Ren Yanqing and Xu Lingqi. Barring future discoveries (always possible given the textual wealth Chinese archaeology has already produced), we are in no position to assess properly Lu's role in the final form and the diffusion of the Lingbao scriptures.

In the case of the *Scripture of Salvation,* then, we can be sure only
that it is listed in Lu's catalog and that it has come down to us in the
same form as that in which it was annotated by Yan Dong around
485.[21] There are numerous manuscript copies of the scripture from
Dunhuang, more than of any other Daoist text, and, although many
of these are fragmentary, they preserve very few character variants.[22]
The transmission of this scripture, then, was remarkably accurate,
attesting to the care copyists seem to have taken, as indeed the scriptures enjoin them, in transcribing it.

Given what we know (and what we cannot know) of the origins
of the Lingbao scriptures, it is safe to describe the *Scripture of Salvation* as a text of the original Lingbao scriptures probably issuing
from the hand of Ge Chaofu. Compiled and edited by Lu Xiujing, it
was put into its final form by 485 at the latest.

Cosmology and Pantheon

The cosmology and pantheon of the Lingbao scriptures, adapted
from earlier Daoist traditions and from popular Buddhism, seem to
us today bewilderingly complex. Yet this complexity dissolves once
we begin to see how both are organized according to the basic principles of early Chinese science—the division of the Dao from one to
two to three of ancient cosmology, the five phases, and the eight trigrams of the *Yijing.* Here I will simplify as much as possible and deal
only with those deities and celestial locales that appear in the pages
of the *Scripture of Salvation.* For this purpose, we can divide the
deities into three groups that correspond fairly closely to the order
of the three pneumas that produced them: (1) the higher, primordial
deities; (2) heaven's people, the inhabitants of world systems formed
in previous ages who have already become Perfected through the
salvific action of the scriptures; and (3) the gods of the human body.

Primordial Deities

At the apex of the pantheon is the Celestial Worthy of Primordial
Commencement.[23] This deity plays the same role in the Lingbao
scriptures that the Dao or the deified Laozi played in the Celestial
Master scriptures. His emergence in the heart of the primeval Dao is

traced through a series of lengthy kalpa cycles that are given reign names in the manner of human dynasties.[24] The Celestial Worthy first appeared during the *Longhan* (Draconic Magnificence) era. Lacking shape, he also lacked a name, and was indistinguishable from the "Brahmā pneumas" that would bring forth future transformations. During the *Yankang* (Extended Vigor) era, the primal pneumas appeared, though the Dao was as yet undifferentiated and the Celestial Worthy still lacked a true form. Finally, with the *Chiming* (Vermilion Brilliance) period, the primal and inaugural pneumas appeared, heaven and earth were divided, and the Celestial Worthy took form as the "Nameless Lord." The Lingbao scriptures first appeared at the beginning of this period as well, in the form of mysterious graphs that flickered forth within the Dao at the first division of pneumas. These graphs were refined into legibility by the Celestial Worthy in the Halls of Flowing Fire, organized in texts in five parts associated with the five phases, and named the *Perfected Script in Five Tablets, Written in Red.*[25]

The Celestial Worthy took his present name at the very beginning of the *Kaihuang* [Opening Monarch] period, when the celestial scriptures were revealed in parallel world systems, the thirty-two heavens.[26] This celestial revelation forms the subject of the *Scripture of Salvation.*

The scripture is related by the Most High Lord of the Dao, a deity who serves as the disciple of the Celestial Worthy and interlocutor in many Lingbao scriptures.[27] The story he recounts in the opening pages is that of the salvation of the people of the thirty-two heavens, who had strayed from the Dao, and of his own initiation into the text. The word *du* (salvation) means, literally, "to ferry across." It is used in Daoist texts both for the initiation of disciples and for the concept of salvation in general.[28] In the Lingbao texts, then, proper initiation into the scriptures in itself brings salvation.

The Most High Lord of the Dao also invites those who recite the scripture for their own salvation and that of their ancestors to first perform a simple visualization accompanied by an incantation in which he is the first deity invoked. Through the title by which he is addressed in this incantation, we understand him to be a deity originally formed together with the mystic and primal pneumas, the first two of the "three pneumas."

Below these two deities in the celestial hierarchy are those associated with the Southern Palace, the place where the corporal spirits
of the deceased were refined for rebirth or postmortem existence in
one of the heavens.[29] The head of this cohort is the Perfected of the
Southern Extremities. Under his direction come the Director of the
Equerry, in charge of the life records of those whose souls are refined
in the Halls of Flowing Fire, and Lord Han, who rules over Fengdu
and controls the records of death kept there. The roles of these latter
two deities, one in charge of the records of life and the other of the
records of death, echo the concerns of the *Xiang'er* commentary. At
the same time, their duties reflect the goal of Lingbao salvation—
physical existence beyond the grave. The Palace of Darkness in the
Lingbao texts is no longer simply the place where the dead are
refined, but the place where the *physical body* is readied for future
existence. The souls have their own destination, the Southern Palace.
After this dual refinement, the two constituents of the whole person
are rejoined, either for rebirth in a favored family or for continued
existence in the heavens.[30]

Finally, below the Grand Veil Heaven, where the Celestial Worthy
holds court, lie the "three clear regions," the Shangqing heavens of
Jade Clarity, Upper Clarity, and Grand Clarity. All of the deities described in the Shangqing scriptures reside here, but only a few of
them make brief appearances in this scripture.

Heaven's People

Beyond the specifically named higher deities just presented are vast
multitudes of similar gods, beings known by generic labels such as
"the Great Spirits of Heavenly Perfection," "the Most Honored of
the Exalted Sages," and "the Perfected of Wondrous Deeds." Lacking all specificity, they are reminiscent of the caparisoned courtiers
of Shakespeare's histories or the crowds of adoring angels in medieval religious art. They shout huzzahs and hosannas at the appropriate times, but have little other function in this scripture.[31] These
are the deities of the former world systems, the thirty-two heavens.

The thirty-two heavens are based on the twenty-seven (or twenty-
eight) heavens ringing the cosmic mountain, Mount Sumeru, of
Buddhist scripture.[32] Like the Buddhist heavens, the thirty-two are

divided into the realms of desire, form, and formlessness.[33] Unlike the Buddhist realms, though, those in the Lingbao version circle a mountain that towers above them, the Jade Capitoline, which stands in the Grand Veil Heaven, the residence of the Celestial Worthy high above all other celestial realms. Further, the thirty-two heavens are divided into four groups of eight, one in each of the four directions. The thirty-two heavens are each ruled over by a thearch and populated by the "heavenly people" of the *Chiming* era.

The opening passages of our scripture take place in the Inaugural Azure Heaven, the sixth heaven of the north, and thus, by five-phases thought, the heaven associated with the earliest stirrings of yang within the midnight of yin. Once the heavenly people of this realm and of the other realms of the thirty-two heavens hear the Celestial Worthy's recitation of the *Scripture of Salvation* they are saved and their worlds perfected.

Also at this level in the hierarchy are the Demon Kings of the Three Realms.[34] These beings are not provided with biographies, but from their terrible names, such as "Mountain-Toppler Six-Eyes," and from the verses they recite near the end of the text, we can conclude that they are demons converted to the Dao. Most likely we are meant to regard them as the demons that plagued the outlying world systems of the thirty-two heavens before the appearance of the scriptures. They are ambiguous creatures, showing profound reverence for the Dao and ensuring that the hordes of lesser demons and sprites remain under their charge, but assigned the task of testing the merit of the departed, who must pass through their realms to reach the higher heavens. The "Song of the Demon King of the Realm of Form," for instance, ends:

Transforming, I fly through the void
In order to provide physical trials for you.
Some succeed, some fail, some are negligent, some flee—
Only a few pass through.
I scoff at you who do not pass,
And so make this song.[35]

Such trials, usually involving a demon taking the form of a deity or an ancestor to tempt an adept, already play a role in the Shangqing scriptures.[36] The Lingbao texts contain such lively tales as well. Particularly interesting is the story, adapted from a translated Buddhist scripture, of the young woman Aqiu Zeng, whose devotion to the doctrine a Demon King tried to shake with the horrifying news that her father was to be reborn as a woman.[37] Daunting as the prospect of postmortem trials may be, we are assured that, through chanting the scripture, the Demon Kings can be summoned to greet us in the three realms and to safely escort us through.

Bodily Deities of Salvation

The gods resident in the human body are, in the Lingbao scriptures, primarily those we have already met in the pages of the *Purple Texts*. Those emphasized in the *Scripture of Salvation*, however, are but five in number. These spirits, first introduced in the Shangqing *Scripture of Great Profundity*, are:[38]

   1.   Grand Unity, essence of the embryo of perfection, who lives in the palace of the head known as the "Muddy Pellet";[39]
   2. and 3.   Nonpareil, with the byname "Lordling," and White Prime, with the byname "Penetrating Yang"—two spirits who inhabit the Cavern Chamber palace of the head and also descend into, respectively, the liver and the lungs.[40]
   4.   the Director of Destinies, whose residence is in the heart and the sexual organs;
   5.   Peach Vigor, the deity we have already encountered in the *Purple Texts* under the name "Peach Child," who resides in the lower Cinnabar Field.[41]

These deities are responsible for forming the embryo of perfection at birth, guarding the registers of life, overseeing the functioning of the five viscera, and regulating the souls during one's lifetime. We encounter them in the *Scripture of Salvation* within the perfected bodies of the people of heaven:

> Grasping tallies and clutching registers,
> They ensure the fate and the root of life.
> Roaming on high in Upper Clarity,
> They come and go from the floriate chambers.
> From the eight reaches of outer darkness,
> To within the smallest interstices,
> They descend to secure the human body.[42]

The "floriate chambers" are the human viscera into which these gods descend, but the gods also roam freely into the higher heavens. One with the deities of the macrocosm, they are responsible for seeing the various constituents of the body through the cycles of refinement that result in ultimate perfection.[43]

In the Lingbao scriptures, these vivifying spirits are activated not through visualization, but through recitation of the scripture. This aspect of Lingbao soteriology is made particularly clear in the visualization and incantation that is to precede recitations of the scripture. Having entered the meditation chamber, the adept is to alert the gods of the body through knocking the teeth and then visualize the three pneumas. Following this, the adept is to visualize a total darkness, both within and without his body, in which appear the directional animals of the five phases and two additional animals, above and below, to guard the adept's bodily spirits. Then the sun and moon shine brightly into the dark chamber, illuminating the adept and creating a halo, like those depicted on Buddhist statuary of the period. The incantation that follows these visualizations, known in ritual as "issuing the officers," is designed to send the gods of the body up to the highest heavens.[44]

The purpose of all this is not, as in the *Purple Texts,* to empower the interior deities with draughts of celestial pneuma, but "to inform those on high of what is said" during the recitation of the text. The prostrations, incantations, and visualizations, then, serve one purpose only—to ensure that all of the gods, both of the macrocosm and of the microcosm, are present and listening.

The Hidden Language of the Great Brahmā

The *Scripture of Salvation* is a text meant for recitation. That those meant to hear it are not mortals, but the deities of the highest heavens, is shown by the fact that its most potent words are totally incomprehensible to humans. The core of the scripture, comprising the secret names of deities and demons, is not in any human language, but is transcribed from the language of the thirty-two heavens. Quite beyond the translation problems faced here of rendering classical Chinese into acceptable English, this celestial language requires a two-step process of translation and interpretation before its meaning can even begin to be expressed in Chinese. The scripture for this purpose is over four times as long as the *Scripture of Salvation.* Needless to say, I will not here attempt a retranslation of this "Hidden Language."[45]

As it forms the very heart of the scripture, though, we cannot leave the Hidden Language of the Great Brahmā unexplained. The term *fan,* translated "Brahmā" here, transliterates two Sanskrit terms: the creator god Brahmā and the prefix *brahma-,* which might be affixed to anything regarded as Indic or Buddhist, especially the written languages from which Buddhist texts were translated, known in Chinese simply as "Brahmic script." Both aspects are important here, for the Lingbao scriptures regularly use the term *fanqi,* "Brahmā-pneuma," to represent the primordial Dao in its creative aspect. "Brahmā-script" (to coin a term that may make some Indologists shudder), in that it is formed of these primordial pneumas, is the stuff of which the highest heavens are made as well as a language that perfectly represents the powers of these heavens. As the *Scripture of Salvation* puts it, the Hidden Language

> speaks the inner names of the thearchs and the sounds of the secret rhymes of all the heavens, as well as of the taboo names of the demon kings and the secret names of the myriad spirits. These are not common words of the world. Only the highest sages, those who have already become Perfected beings, who communicate with the mysterious and comprehend the subtle, will be able to completely comprehend these stanzas.[46]

Elsewhere, the actions of "Brahmā-pneuma" at creation are depicted as follows:

> In the midst of undifferentiated chaos,
> Above, there was no other color,
> Below, there was no deeper depth—
> Only a windblown moisture, penetrating and vacant;
> A diamond riding the Heavens.
> . . . .
> Dark and attenuated, the Grand Brahmā;
> Extending into the distance, void of light.[47]

Examples of the Hidden Language in the text include the names of the thirty-two heavens and their thearchs and a longer passage of

256 characters found at the end of the scripture. All of these passages are transcribed into the characters of the human world for ease of memorization and recitation.[48] The celestial forms of the graphs, eight for each of the thirty-two heavens, used as talismans in ritual, appear in another scripture. Upon close examination, we find that this script is but an elaborate version of written Chinese, perhaps modeled on barely recognizable, archaic forms of the written language such as those found on bronze tripods from the Shang or Zhou periods.[49]

As Erik Zürcher has shown, the Hidden Language is a "pseudo-Sanskrit," transcribed, as were the languages from which Buddhist texts were translated, into infrequently used Chinese characters employed primarily for their sound value.[50] This translated "celestial" language in fact contains bits of recognizable Buddhist terminology. Like the mantras of Buddhist scripture, each syllable of the Hidden Language represents the longer names of deities, celestial locales, and forces of the heavens. The explanations of the graphs' celestial significance are meant to underscore the power invoked by means of their recitation. More important, these explanations highlight a feature that made Buddhism attractive in the eyes of its Chinese audience—the fact that its scriptures were translated from the potent languages of the exotic lands, so enticingly described in Buddhist scripture, where the historical Buddha lived and taught.

A brief comparison of the *Scripture of Salvation* with one of the translated Buddhist sutras that might have served as a model will show more clearly the depth of Buddhist influence on the *Scripture of Salvation*. The *Scripture of Salvation* opens with the miracles attending the Celestial Worthy's recitations of the scripture in the kingdom of Fuli. When, "suspended in air, floating above a pentachromatic lion," he pronounced the scriptures ten times, all of the celestial beings of the realm assembled, the lights of heaven stopped in their courses, and all became gemlike as the world system was bathed in perfect light. Though this opening is perhaps reminiscent of the cosmic Buddha as portrayed in any number of Mahāyāna sutras, the details of this opening scene match fairly closely those of the *Prajñāpāramitā* in twenty-five thousand lines, translated into Chinese as the *Scripture of Radiant Prajñā* (*T* 221) by Mokṣala in

291.[51] In the *Scripture of Radiant Prajñā*, the Buddha, before expounding the sutra from atop his lion throne, flashes light from various parts of his body that serve to illuminate the world systems in the "ten directions." At this, in the translation of Mokṣala:

> The blind achieved sight, the deaf hearing, and the mute speech. Those with withered limbs could extend them, and the crippled regained use of their arms and legs. The crazed achieved normality and the wild, mindfulness. The sick were healed and the hungry and thirsty, filled. The weak achieved strength and the aged, youth.[52]

Precisely the same miracles, in almost the same order, occur when the Celestial Worthy recites the *Scripture of Salvation*.[53] Other minor details also serve to show that the opening chapter of the *Scripture of Radiant Prajñā* may have had an influence on the author of the *Scripture of Salvation*.

More interesting for our present purposes, though, is the "mystical alphabet" *arapacana*, based on the Gāndhārī language and written in the Kharoṣṭhī script, explained in the twentieth chapter of the *Scripture of Radiant Prajñā*. The forty-two syllables of *arapacana* serve as mnemonics to aid the memorization of points of doctrine and, at the same time, function as charms that magically augment the abilities of those who recite them.[54] For example, in the translation of Edward Conze:

> The syllable *A* is a door to the insight that all dharmas are unproduced from the very beginning (*ādy-anutpannatvād*); *RA* is a door to the insight that all dharmas are without dirt (*rajas*).[55]

Although the Sanskrit words enclosed in parentheses appear only as translations, not transliterations, in Mokṣala's text, the fact that such a mnemonic was known in China is of great significance to an understanding of the Hidden Language of the Great Brahmā, for it functions in a similar fashion. Each of the syllables of the Hidden Language is shown to be part of longer words that have meaning and protective value as mantras.[56] Like the mnemonics of *arapacana*, they point beyond common Chinese words to the celestial language in which the scripture was first pronounced.

The sorts of Buddhist borrowings found in the *Scripture of Salvation* are legion, but the sources of such elements and the means by which they found their way into the Lingbao scriptures are obscured by the fact that it regularly transfigures any borrowed doctrine to fit its own systems. Such, as we will see directly, occurred with the concept of wisdom (*prajñā*) itself, which means something substantially different here than it does in the *Prajñāpāramitā-sūtra*.

Ritual and Recitation

The success of the liturgies of the Lingbao scriptures resulted in the ritual texts of the canon being expanded and modified. This was, in fact, one of Lu Xiujing's primary contributions to the development of the Lingbao school. Lu pieced together passages from the original scriptures to fashion communal rituals. As more temples were built and the numbers of professional priests grew, it was ritual manuals such as those of Lu Xiujing, rather than the accounts of the original Lingbao rituals, that came to be valued and transmitted.[57] One result of this development is that entire scriptures from the original canon containing directions for ritual performance survive only in the great ritual compendia of later Daoist writers and not as separate works. We are thus, despite remarkable advances, far from having an accurate picture of early Lingbao ritual.[58] Nonetheless, it is possible to gain some idea of the structure and goals of early Lingbao ritual from the *Scripture of Salvation* and from other texts of the canon.

It seems that most of the early Lingbao rituals were meant for individual practice, to be conducted either in the meditation chamber or in the courtyard of the house.[59] The practitioners of these rites are described as "students of the Dao" and not as professional priests.[60] These particular features perhaps mark the early days of the Lingbao movement, when there was not yet a widely established priesthood or temples to house its members.

The ritual chanting of the *Scripture of Salvation* fits into this stage in the development of the Lingbao liturgies. It is to be performed by the individual practitioner in the ritual space of his or her own meditation chamber, which, according to the commentators, may even be a sleeping chamber, so long as rules of proper cleanliness are observed.[61] The term *zhai* (retreat) in this text is not to be equated, then, with the elaborate communal rituals, involving numbers of priests, that were known by the same name. Borrowed from Confucian ritual practice, where it denoted a period of solitary withdrawal from everyday affairs accompanied by the consumption of "pure" foods, the term here describes a ritual that involves bathing, fasting, and visualizations—all to be accomplished by a lone practitioner.[62]

The Lingbao scriptures contain instructions for how the *Scripture of Salvation* is to be chanted, particularly the Hidden Language of the Great Brahmā, the most potent portion of the text. We are told that the assembled sages on Mount Kunlun, whom we should certainly emulate, read the text "in controlled tones, neither mournful nor anguished, neither slow nor fast ... in a steady, rustling murmur that reaches clearly to a distance ... causing those who hear to become lost in thought."[63] Further, it is to be read in the refined pronunciations of the Central Kingdom—presumably the correct northern dialect of the time, at least as it was spoken in the southern court—and not the debased argot of outlying regions.[64] After every five hundred graphs, practitioners are to stop chanting, knock their teeth together, run their tongues over their lips, and swallow saliva—not to awaken the corporal deities or to ingest pneuma as in the *Purple Texts,* but to allow the practitioners to continue reading in a clear voice.[65]

Foremost among the days prescribed for recitation of the *Scripture of Salvation* are the days of the "Three Primes," associated with the Three Offices—heaven, earth, and water.[66] These are the fifteenth days of the first month, the seventh month, and the tenth month—the days when the assemblies of gods in the Three Offices meet to assess the life and death records of all humans, the living and the dead.[67] According to the Lingbao scriptures, the other days when the scripture should be recited—the eight seasonal nodes and the days of one's "natal destiny"—are the occasion of similar assemblies of the high deities and the inspection of one's records of life.[68] Thus, we should expect that the *Scripture of Salvation* would include bureaucratic memorials to the officials of heaven, charging them to rectify the records, as was done in Celestial Master petition rituals.[69] This does not prove to be the case. There are references to the celestial chains of command and even to the orders, authenticated by a talisman, that the Celestial Worthy issues to ensure that the souls of the departed are transferred to the Southern Palace, but the *Scripture of Salvation* is not itself a bureaucratic document.[70] Instead, it is what Daoist texts of this period themselves refer to as a "wisdom" scripture.

In Buddhist translations, *zhihui* (wisdom) was one rendering of Sanskrit *prajñā*, "transcendent insight into the illusory nature of all phenomena."[71] For Daoism as well—a religion that, though it did not regard the phenomenal world as "empty" in the Buddhist sense, did hold that it was ultimately grounded in the nothingness of the Dao—wisdom constituted the ability to see beyond the surfaces of things. In the Shangqing scriptures, the term "wisdom" was applied to divinely bestowed knowledge of drugs and charms of sufficient power to destroy demons.[72] In a related fashion, the Lingbao scriptures entitled "wisdom" texts provide knowledge of the earth-prisons, of the methods that might be employed to release those suffering there, and of the precepts and practices enjoined on the living to ensure their own postmortem status.

All of this stems as much from ancient therapeutic rituals by which disease demons could be cast out through accurate knowledge of their names and appearances as it does from Buddhist wisdom literature.[73] The *Scripture of Salvation* turns this demon-quelling weapon of gnosis against the celestial bureaucracy, which had by this time (and thanks in large part to the contributions of the Lingbao scriptures themselves) swollen in size and complexity to the point where there seemed almost no way to negotiate with it. This anxiety finds expression, for instance, in contemporary stories of the "untimely summons," in which people are mistakenly brought to the realms of the dead due to some bureaucratic foul-up.[74] Rather than face such eventualities, it is better, as anyone who has dealt with bureaucracies knows, to have a friend high up in the chain of command. This is precisely what the *Scripture of Salvation* provides. Through knowledge of the origins of the universe, the names and locations of the celestial bureaucracy, and its orderly workings, the practitioner might hope, if not to make it do his or her bidding, at least to ensure its proper functioning.[75]

This is expressed quite plainly by the Most High Lord of the Dao in the final postface to the scripture, which serves to "announce the merit" of the ritual of reciting the text:[76]

> The various heavens will send down spirit kings who fly through the heavens to keep watch over the bodies and record the meritorious strivings of all those who know these pronunciations and are able to chant them during retreats. These things will be reported back to the heavens.

The myriad spirits will reverentially honor such persons; chthonic spirits will guard their households. The Demon Kings who render service to the Dao will ensure their elevation to the status of higher Transcendent. When the Dao of such persons is complete, they may roam freely throughout the Three Realms, rising to enter the golden portals.[77]

Individual salvation, the rescue of one's ancestors from the earth-prisons, even the salvation of the kingdom—all are possible through the proper recitation of this scripture with its precise accounts of the Daoist pantheon, from the beginnings of time to the present, from "the eight reaches of outer darkness, to within the smallest interstices." Even the looming destruction of the present world-age can be avoided, not through the expedient of becoming a "seed person," but through dissolving the threatening disaster.

What cannot be conquered through recitation of the *Scripture of Salvation* is finally but one thing—death itself. The text states the matter commonsensically enough:

> The cyclical movements of heaven and earth have their depletion and end. The sun, moon, and five planets have their times of fullness and eclipse. The highest sages and spirit beings, in like fashion, have their times of growth and decay, and those who come late to the Study have their time of illness and injury.[78]

We are so used to thinking of Daoism as the "religion of immortality" that such words seem almost not to belong. Yet even the highest of deities, residing where disaster cannot reach them, merge back into the Dao at the end of each kalpa cycle. The pangs of earthly death might be bypassed or death might be reduced to passing "like a sleep," but the cycles of the Dao include it still. The message of the *Scripture of Salvation,* then, is not that death can be eradicated, but that it can be understood and, once understood, smoothly traversed (*du*).

On the Translation

The following translation is based on the scripture as it appears in *HY* 87, which is nearly identical to the transcription of the text in *HY* 1, chapter 1.[79] There are three sorts of witness to the original version of the *Scripture of Salvation:* (1) Dunhuang manuscript copies; (2) annotated versions of the scripture in the Ming canon; and (3) citations from other works in the Ming canon. Variant readings found in these sources are remarkably few in number and inconsequential—except in the case of the Hidden Language, which is not translated here. The overwhelming majority of variant readings from the remainder of the text prove to be alternate character forms, homophones, and, in one or two cases, transpositions—only one of which has any impact on the translation of the text.[80]

The care taken in reproducing the *Scripture of Salvation* is in part due to the strictures expressed in the Lingbao corpus regarding transmission. Copied scriptures were to be checked against the original, character by character, "three times"—a locution that may mean "repeatedly." This is important because "a year of life will be deducted for each wrong character ... and also for each missed or added character."[81] Then, too, the *Scripture of Salvation* is a fairly short text meant for memorization, which may account for the fact that the majority of errors are homophones of similar meaning.

Those who would memorize and recite the text have further been aided by the fact that much of it is in rhymed verse of various meters. Although I have not indicated the rhymes followed—though they are interesting themselves in that they represent the Jiangnan dialect of the fifth century—the rhymed portions of the scripture are indicated in the translation through indentation and line breaks.

The translation is divided according to the "Explanation of the Scripture" found at the end of *HY 87*. Although this division is not original, it does coincide nicely with the internal logic of the text and thus seems useful for modern readers who might otherwise be confused by the seeming shifts in viewpoint. The translation is divided into sections as follows:

Preface: The Most High Lord of the Dao relates his receipt of the scripture and ordination into its mysteries, the benefits of reciting the scripture, and the methods for doing so.

Section 1: The scripture proper begins here. This section relates the origins of the scripture in the primal void and the bases of its salvific efficacy, listing the higher gods who might be moved by its recitation.

Section 2: After repeating the story of the scripture's origins, this section goes into some detail concerning the lesser gods who work for human salvation and relates the songs of the Demon Kings, who test those passing through the three realms.

Postface 1: The Most High Lord of the Dao relates information on the transmission and efficacy of the scripture, as well as the full text of the Hidden Language of the Great Brahmā, necessary to understanding the names of the deities given in the previous sections.

Postface 2: In this brief conclusion, the Most High Lord of the Dao explains the origin of the Hidden Language of the Great Brahmā and provides a final verse on the benefits of chanting the scripture.

All of these, including the preface and postfaces (*xu*), are equally part of the scripture. The decision to call some parts of the text *xu* seems to be based on the fact that these three sections are explanatory, spoken by the Most High Lord of the Dao. The remainder is the central portion of the text, where first-person pronouns refer to anyone who chants the scripture. Seen in this light, the *Scripture of Salvation* is at once a description of the "ordination/salvation" of the Lord of the Dao and of those who follow his strictures in chanting the text. This function is made plain in *HY* 97, the Lingbao text that explains fully the Hidden Language, in that it begins with a simple rite of ordination investing the body of the text's recipient with the gods to be called out in recitations of the *Scripture of Salvation*.[82]

NOTES TO SCRIPTURE OF SALVATION: INTRODUCTION

1. The Lingbao scriptures are not, like the Shangqing scriptures, named after the heaven of their origin. The name means "Numinous Treasure" and is derived from an ancient term for mediums, regarded as the locus into which the spirits might descend. Within Daoism, the name had earlier been used by the author of the *Five Talismans of Lingbao,* a scripture said to have been recovered as a "holy treasure" within a mountain. (See Kaltenmark, "*Ling-pao*"; Max Kaltenmark, "Quelques remarques sur le "T'ai-chang Ling-pao wou-fou siu," *Zinbun* 18 [1982], pp. 1–10.; Bokenkamp, "The Peach Flower Font and the Grotto Passage," *JAOS* 106.1 [1986], pp. 65–77; Yamada Toshiaki, "Longevity Techniques and the Compilation of the *Lingbao wufuxu*," in L. Kohn and Y. Sakade, eds., *Taoist Meditation and Longevity Teachings* [Ann Arbor, Mich., 1989], pp. 99–124; and, for

the concept of the celestially endowed treasure, Anna K. Seidel, "Kokuhō: Note à propos du terme 'trésor national' en Chine et au Japon," *BEFEO* 69 [1981], pp. 229–61.) Within the Lingbao tradition, the scriptures themselves are the "Numinous Treasure." For a listing of the surviving scriptures of this corpus, see Bokenkamp, "Sources," pp. 479–85.

2. The title as it is translated here is that used in the Dunhuang catalog of Lingbao scriptures (Ōfuchi Ninji, "On *Ku Ling-pao ching*," *Acta Asiatica* 27 [1974], pp. 34–56). To it may be added, as prefixes, a number of tags indicating the provenance of the scripture. Chiefly the following prefixes are used: *taishang dongxuan*, indicating that the text belongs to the "cavern mystery" section of the canon; *lingbao*, the sectarian affiliation of the scripture; and *yuanshi* (primordial commencement), indicating that it was spoken by the Celestial Worthy. The *Scripture of Salvation* now appears as the first chapter of HY 1 (1:1a–18a9). The commentary of Yan Dong, composed c. 485, is to be found in the "Four Commentaries" version of the *Scripture of Salvation*, HY 87. This collection of commentaries was compiled by Chen Jingyuan (1025–1094) and includes, besides Yan's commentary, the commentaries of Cheng Xuanying (fl. 631–650), Xue Youxi (fl. 740–754), and Li Shaowei, also of the Tang period. On the compilation of this collection, see Judith M. Boltz, *A Survey of Taoist Literature: Tenth to Seventeenth Centuries* (Berkeley: University of California Press, 1987), p. 205. The canon also contains a brief analysis of the scripture (HY 95) by Zhang Wanfu (fl. 710). All five of these commentaries have been consulted in the preparation of the translation, though, as will become apparent in the notes, the Tang-period commentators in some cases forward a novel interpretation of the text, based on the great scriptural productions of the sixth and early seventh centuries. Wherever possible, then, I follow the interpretations of Yan Dong and the information found in other early Lingbao texts.

3. See Stephen R. Bokenkamp, "Taoism and Literature: The *Pi-lo* Question," *TR* 3.1 (1991), pp. 57–72.

4. Strickmann, in his "Mao-shan Revelations," chronicles the story of this development.

5. On the early history of the canon, see Ōfuchi, "Formation," and, for the Ming canon, Judith M. Boltz, *Survey of Taoist Literature*.

6. A fuller account of this development is given in Bokenkamp, "Stages of Transcendence."

7. Zürcher, "Buddhist Influence," pp. 135–41.

8. Anna K. Seidel, "Le sūtra merveilleux du Ling-pao Suprême, traitant de Lao-tseu qui convertit les barbes (le manuscrit TH S.2081)—Contribution à l'étude du Bouddho-taoïsme des Six Dynasties," in M. Soymié, ed., *Contributions aux études de Touen-houang* (Paris, 1984), vol. 3, p. 330; and Seidel, "Taoist Studies in the West," p. 288.

9. The concept of *upāya* (expedient means), if not the term itself, is everywhere in evidence in the Lingbao texts. On the various stages of disciplehood, see Bokenkamp, "Stages of Transcendence"; and Kusuyama

Haruki, "Seishin deshi kō," in *Chūgoku no shūkyō, shisō to kagaku: Festschrift in honour of Makio Ryōkai* (Tokyo: Kokusho kankōkai, 1984), pp. 139–55.

10. *HY* 1121, 2:6b; *HY* 1026, 3:12a. An account that leaves out Chaofu and seems to credit the release of the scriptures to Ge Hong, who by 400 would have been dead for more than fifty years, is to be found at *HY* 1026, 6:9b. The garbled grammar at line 6:9b3 of this latter account indicates that characters are missing just before the phrase "the end of the Long'an reign period." Thus, the passage may once have contained a more accurate history of the scriptures.

11. See Bokenkamp, "Sources," pp. 442–46, and, for more on the misogyny of the Lingbao texts, pp. 473–75.

12. Bokenkamp, "Sources," pp. 449–60.

13. This catalog, as copied by Song Wenming (fl. c. 549–551), was found among the Dunhuang texts (*P* 2256). It has been translated and compared with other surviving lists of the Lingbao scriptures by Ōfuchi Ninji ("On *Ku Ling-pao ching*").

14. This locution may refer to the Sun En rebellion of 399–402.

15. Lu is here selectively quoting the *Santian zhengfa jing*, a Shangqing scripture that was probably not composed by Yang Xi (Robinet, *La révélation du Shangqing*, vol. 2, pp. 87–91). This scripture no longer survives as a separate work, but the passages cited here are to be found in *HY* 1026, 2:7a–7b, and *HY* 1131, 9:3b–4a, with only minor variations. The ellipses in my translation represent portions of the text Lu has chosen not to cite. The passages Lu does cite were clearly chosen to underscore the notion that Liu Yu, here as in the *Inner Explanations* a descendent of "dragon seed," continues the mandate of the Han, and to tie the release of the Lingbao scriptures to this auspicious event. Significantly, Lu skips two other sexagesimal year designations to highlight the *gengzi* year (400), "predicted" in the scriptures as the year the Lingbao texts will appear. In fact, the *Santian zhengfa jing* states that the *gengzi* year is to be that in which "both propitious and unpropitious signs will appear" and goes on to list these. Lu cites only the inauspicious signs, connecting these to the rectifying appearance of Liu Yu and thereby leaving the impression that the *gengzi* year is singled out in the scripture he cites, when it clearly is not.

16. This line paraphrases the first of the Lingbao scriptures, *HY* 22, 1:6b8–9. This text also mentions the *gengzi* year as that in which the Lingbao scriptures are to flourish.

17. Kobayashi Masayoshi (*Rikucho dōkyōshi kenkyū*, pp. 144 ff.) selectively cites this passage as evidence that only three-tenths (or ten to eleven *juan*) of the "ten-part scriptures in thirty-six *juan*" had at this time been revealed in the world. Thus, he reasons, the catalog found in *P* 2256, which lists twenty-one *juan* in this section, must represent the Lingbao section of the *Catalog of Scriptures and Writings of the Three Caverns* that Lu presented to the throne in 471 and not Lu's Lingbao catalog of 437. Between

437 and 471, he concludes, Lu and the Daoists around him must have con-
cocted another ten to eleven *juan* of scriptures. Several objections might be
raised to this proposal. First, this seems like a slender bit of evidence on
which to hang such weighty conclusions regarding the dating of the scriptures. There are several copyist's errors in this late transcript of Lu's preface. It is possible, though there is of course no evidence, that a *wei* 未 might
have been left out at this point so that the text should read "three parts are
not yet issued" or that the *san* 三 is a misreading of *liu* 六 (a possible error if
the original preface had been written in *bafang* script), so that it should
read "six parts have been issued." Second, Lu is obviously not discussing
the precise number of scriptures at this point, but the miracle that they have
spread so widely when they have "not yet been entirely revealed or put into
practice [or circulated]." The expression "three parts" fits this context. It is
a general expression that should be taken to mean "less than half." Third,
Kobayashi has provided no speculations as to why Lu would have wanted
to fill out the catalog, something he here roundly criticizes others for doing.
Had Lu included Lingbao texts in his second catalog that were not in the
first, he would have had to explain the increase and, further, was in a perfect position to claim that he had received them by revelation, both things
we know he did not do. (Tao Hongjing, for one, would not have remained
silent had there been such discrepancies.) From the rest of this passage, we
learn that Lu had a good deal to do with putting the texts in order and may
well have himself composed passages and even reshaped whole scriptures to
fit his notion of their internal coherence. It is dangerous, however, to try to
gauge the extent of this well-intentioned tampering on the basis of the single
expression "three parts."

18. "New and old" refers here to, respectively, the scriptures associated
with Ge Xuan and the "ten-part scriptures in thirty-six *juan*." Kobayashi
(*Rikucho dōkyōshi kenkyū,* p. 168) takes this phrase to mean that the two
parts of the catalog at this time equaled fifty-five scrolls of *authentic* scriptures, of which many were not yet revealed. He derives from this the theory
that some scriptures were moved from one part to another by the time of
the second Lu Xiujing catalog, released in 471. But this catalog, as reported
in *P* 2256 and elsewhere, whether written in 437 or 471, totals only fifty
juan of texts, revealed and unrevealed, even when all of the later divisions
of texts into greater numbers of *juan* are taken into account. Kobayashi
thus presents us with the rather inexplicable vision of Lu Xiujing, between
437 and 471, writing new texts, while at the same time decreasing the total
number of *juan* in the catalog and moving some titles from one section to
another, all without inciting the comment of Tao Hongjing and other Daoists. In fact, as the context here makes clear, this was the total number of
scriptures from which Lu had to distinguish the "counterfeit from the true."
The Lingbao canon at this time, then, equaled fifty-five *juan* of texts, from
which Lu culled a "total of thirty-five *juan*" that he believed to be authentic
(*HY* 528, 1b).

19. Kobayashi (*Rikucho dōkyōshi kenkyū*, p. 182 n. 15) has provided evidence that the *jing* 竟 here is a mistake for *bing* 稟.

20. *HY* 1026, 4:5a1–5b7.

21. For the date of Yan Dong's annotation, see *HY* 1238, 16:14a. It appears in *HY* 87, the "Four Commentaries" edition of the *Scripture of Salvation*. (See endnote 2 above.) Ōfuchi ("On *Ku Ling-pao ching*," p. 51) noted that Yan Dong's commentary is not listed for the opening section of the scripture (pp. 1a–5b of *HY* 1) and so concluded that it might have been added later, a finding I duly reported in my early work on the Lingbao texts (Bokenkamp, "Sources," p. 482). In fact, though, Yan Dong does make reference to the opening passages of the scripture (*HY* 87, passim; see especially 2:58a–b). Yan appears to have annotated only portions of the text. Witness, for instance, the section on the "Hidden Language" (*HY* 87, 4:4a–26a), where none of Yan Dong's glosses are recorded, though he does gloss the opening words of the section. From this, it appears that Yan likely did see the opening section but began his annotation only with what he regarded as the scripture proper.

22. See Ōfuchi, *Tonkō dōkyō mokurokuhen,* for collation notes on the Dunhuang manuscripts.

23. See the beginning of this introduction for the ways in which this deity was modeled on the figure of the Buddha. Though his name derives from the primal and inaugural pneumas, I will here translate it "Primordial Commencement" in order to distinguish the title of this deity from the names of the two pneumas.

24. The term "kalpa" is Buddhist in origin, denoting a world-age of unfathomable length. It was one of the earliest of Buddhist terms to appear in the texts of Daoism. The series of kalpa cycles is explained in *HY* 457, 2a ff., and in *HY* 23, 11b ff. Also see *HY* 87, 2:7a, in the present translation.

25. Transcripts of the celestial forms of these graphs are given in *HY* 22, 1:7b–29b, and translated into mortal script in *HY* 352, 1:8b–16a. The refinement of the primordial graphs in the Halls of Flowing Fire seems to be the origin of the practice of burning texts at the conclusion of ritual. The celestial scriptures return to the highest heavens at the end of each kalpa cycle, to be refined by fire and born again to inaugurate the new age. In ritual, this enormous span of time is collapsed into the space of a day or two. See Schipper, *The Taoist Body,* pp. 89–91. Schipper notes that today only the *Scripture of Salvation* is burned after its recitation.

26. Like Buddhist scriptures, the Lingbao texts tell of countless world systems beyond our own. Those figuring in this text are thirty-two in number and lie like a ring around the Grand Veil Heaven.

27. His journey to obtain the *Perfected Script in Five Tablets* for revelation to suffering humanity is recounted in a fashion that recalls the similar quest of the Azure Lad in the opening passages of the *Purple Texts.* (*HY* 22, 1:5a–7a.)

28. The word *du* 度 finds its earliest appearance in this latter sense in the

expression *dushi* 度世 (to cross generations—i.e., "to live a longer than normal lifespan"), already attested in Han texts. It was this sense of the word that was in the minds of Buddhist translators when they rendered the term *nirvana* as *miedu.* The Daoist understanding of *miedu* 滅度, discussed earlier in connection with the *Inner Explanations,* finds its source in the Lingbao scriptures.

29. For the various names by which the Southern Palace is known, see footnote * on p. 411 to the translation.

30. For more on this concept, which plays a relatively minor role in this scripture, see Bokenkamp, "Death and Ascent" and "Stages of Transcendence." We should note as well that the Halls of Flowing Fire in the Hall of Penetrating Yang is the spot where the Celestial Worthy first refined the graphs of the *Perfected Script in Five Tablets* in order to make them legible (*HY* 22, 1:1b). This is why the *Perfected Script* is said to be "written in red." The process by which the Perfected texts were formed is thus the same as that by which the bodies of mortals might be perfected.

31. This is not the case for other Lingbao texts. In *HY* 97, we find lists of these deities and learn that the Hidden Language of the Great Brahma (briefly discussed later in the introduction) is in fact a recitation of their secret names.

32. For the concept of the "heavens" of Mount Sumeru in Buddhist scripture, see Randy Kloetzli, *Buddhist Cosmology* (Delhi: Motilal Banarsidass, 1983), pp. 29–34; Zürcher, "Buddhist Influence," pp. 121–22; and Stein, *The World in Miniature,* pp. 246–59. Another aspect of the mountain— that it was the residence of the thirty-three gods, chief of whom was Indra— may have influenced this Lingbao account, in that the term *deva* (god) is regularly translated as *tian* 天 (heaven) in Chinese Buddhist scripture.

33. At least this is what the commentators, beginning with Yan Dong, tell us. They divide the thirty-two heavens into the Three Realms, beginning in the east, as follows. The first six heavens are the realm of desire. The twelve heavens from number seven of the east through the eight heavens of the south to number two of the west are the realm of form. The next ten heavens are the realm of formlessness. The last four heavens of the north he describes simply as being "above the realm of formlessness." (See *HY* 87, 3:24b, 3:29b, and 3:35a for Yan's glosses.) I have not found any source for this division in the extant scriptures. (See, though, the explanation of the "gates to the three realms" in *HY* 97, 3:26a.) Ge Chaofu leaves many borrowed Buddhist terms undefined, and this may have been one of them.

34. The term here translated as "demon," *mo* 魔, seems to have been a coinage developed to transliterate the name of the Buddhist tempter Māra, lord of the six heavens of desire. The term was adopted in Daoist texts very early, used in a generic way to refer to demons in general. (Zürcher, "Buddhist Influence," p. 127.) The author of the Lingbao scriptures, in his portrayal of the Demon Kings as tempters, betrays a greater knowledge of

the way Māra functions in Buddhist texts than do the authors of earlier Daoist scriptures.

35. *HY* 87, 3:34a–b.

36. See Bokenkamp, "Master Zhou's Records."

37. Bokenkamp, "Sources," pp. 474–75.

38. On the *Scripture of Great Profundity*, see Robinet, *La révélation du Shangqing*, vol. 2, pp. 29–49; and Robinet, *Taoist Meditation*, pp. 97–117. The importance of this scripture to the Lingbao canon is particularly apparent in *HY* 425, but it is mentioned and cited throughout the scriptures.

39. On the "Muddy Pellet," see footnote ‖ on p. 311 to the *Purple Texts*.

40. The Cavern Chamber is located between the eyebrows and two inches into the head, just in front of the Muddy Pellet (Homann, *Huang-t'ing ching*, pp. 72–73).

41. See *HY* 639, 11a–12a, translated in the previous chapter.

42. *HY* 87, 3:18b–19b.

43. It is likely that these five spirits are to be identified with the "five transcendents" described in the Lingbao mortuary rite found in the *Wondrous Scripture on Salvation through Extinction: Refinement of the Five [Spirits] for Revivifying the Corpse* (*HY* 369). (See Bokenkamp, "Death and Ascent.")

44. For the more elaborate forms these procedures would take in later Lingbao liturgy, see Judith M. Boltz, "Opening the Gates of Purgatory: A Twelfth Century Technique for the Salvation of Lost Souls," in Michel Strickmann, ed., *Tantric and Taoist Studies in Honour of R. A. Stein,* (Brussels, 1983), vol. 2, pp. 488–510.

45. For those interested in what such a translation might entail, in endnote 1 to the *Scripture of Salvation* I have explicated one phrase of the "Hidden Language" that appears in the opening lines of the scripture.

46. *HY* 87, 1:19a–b.

47. *HY* 87, 3:2b–5a.

48. Strickmann has noted the curious fact that Daoist accounts of the devolution of language from its primal purity stress that it is the written language that fragments and changes over time, whereas the spoken language, it is held, is unchanging. This is exactly the opposite of what actually occurred in China in that, while dialects bifurcated, the written language remained relatively constant. See Strickmann, *Le taoïsme du Mao chan;* for a general analysis of the role of such scripts in Daoism, see Seidel, "Taoist Studies in the West," pp. 250–54.

49. Bokenkamp, "Sources," pp. 461–65.

50. Zürcher, "Buddhist Influence," pp. 110–12.

51. At about the same time, another translation, the *Scripture Praising the Radiance* (*T* 222), was undertaken by Dharmarakṣa (fl. 266–308). See Zürcher, *Buddhist Conquest*, pp. 63–65, for the importance of these trans-

lations, of which that of Mokṣala seems to have been the most widely known.

52. T 221, 8.1c.9–12.

53. See HY 87, 1:6b–8a, translated in this chapter. When we compare the order of the miracles given in the Sanskrit text (Edward Conze, trans., *The Large Sutra on Perfect Wisdom* [London: Luzac, 1961], p. 4), it does not so closely match that of the *Scripture of Salvation* as does the T. 221 passage. There is in the Sanskrit text no mention of mutes or of the aged becoming young again, and the sick and crippled are mentioned below those suffering from hunger and thirst (who do not appear in the *Scripture of Salvation* at all). Further, Dharmarakṣa's translation of the passage is identical to the Sanskrit version of Conze. Mokṣala's translation thus is the most likely source for the *Scripture of Salvation*.

54. For the origins of *arapacana* and an account of previous scholarship on the question, see Richard Salomon, "New Evidence for a Gāndhārī Origin of the Arapacana Syllabary," *JAOS* 110.2 (1990), pp. 255–73. The syllabary appears at T 221, 8.26b–27a. The account ends with a list of the "twenty meritorious powers" to be gained by memorizing and reciting the syllables. These include wisdom, memory, persuasiveness, the ability to know at once the karmic consequences of other's thoughts, and so forth.

55. Conze, *The Large Sutra*, pp. 148–50; see also xxxvi ff.)

56. As Zürcher has remarked in his survey of Buddhist borrowings in Daoist scripture, influences seem to come mostly from lay Buddhism (Zürcher, "Buddhist Influence," p. 143). Yet, given the widespread popularity of the *Prajñāpāramitā-sūtra*, we might well expect that instruction in such mnemonics was regularly afforded Chinese laity—at least those of the gentry class.

57. The best surviving example of Lu's work on Daoist ritual is his initiation rite (HY 528), which he pieced together primarily from the *Golden* and *Yellow Registers* (lost), the *Jade Instructions of the Luminous Perfected* (HY 1400), and the instructions of the *Self-Generated Scripture of Perfect Unity* (P 2356). Lu conducted a twenty-day-long Three Primes Retreat for the ailing emperor and the welfare of the state in 471 (Chen Guofu, *Dao-zang yuanliu kao*, p. 468). We also have from Lu's hand a list of nine Lingbao retreat rituals (HY 1268, 4b ff.), only three of which seem to have been detailed in the original revelations: the Luminous Perfected (HY 1400), the Golden Registers, and perhaps the Three Primes (if the latter two issued from the now-lost *Awesome Rites of the Three Primes according to the Bamboo Slips of the Golden Registers*). Something of Lu's creative process might be gauged from the sixth-century compendium the *Wushang biyao*, where many of the rituals Lu describes are given, together with references to the original scriptures from which they were taken (HY 1130, chaps. 48–54). Particularly interesting in this regard is the Retreat of Mud and Ashes, a Celestial Master ritual listed by Lu as a Lingbao rite. It is largely pieced together from the Lingbao Retreat of the Luminous Perfected (HY 1130,

chap. 50); the Celestial Master source, if there was one, is lost. Lu Xiujing's role in the formulation of liturgies and the evolution of priestly communities is further described in Catherine Bell, "Ritualization of Texts and Textualization of Ritual in the Codification of Taoist Liturgy," *HR* 27.4 (1988), pp. 366–92; and Charles D. Benn, *The Cavern-Mystery Transmission: A Taoist Ordination Rite of A.D. 711* (Honolulu: University of Hawaii Press, 1991).

58. For an account of the work that has been done in this area, see Seidel, "Taoist Studies in the West," pp. 265–69. For general descriptions of Daoist ritual, consult Schipper, *The Taoist Body*, pp. 72–99; and John Lagerwey, *Taoist Ritual in Chinese Society and History* (New York: Macmillan, 1987).

59. One notable exception is the ritual found in *HY* 22, which seems to be the earliest of the communal practices. See Schipper, "Reihō kagi no tenkai," in Yamada Toshiaki, trans., *Nihon, Chūgoku no shūkyō bunka no kenkyū* (Tokyo: Hirakawa, 1991).

60. See, for instance, the Retreat of the Luminous Perfected (*HY* 1400). Source of many of the communal rituals of the *Wushang biyao*, the retreat is still described in *HY* 1130 (51:2b) as performed in the courtyard of the house, and Lu Xiujing notes that it is to be performed by the "students" of the Dao, rather than by priests (*HY* 1268, 5b).

61. Xue Youxi states that the "chamber" may be a meditation chamber especially reserved for the purpose or one's normal sleeping chamber so long as the rules for cleanliness and ritual purity are upheld (*HY* 87, 1:30a–b). This is yet another indication that the ritual was not originally written for performance by professional priests.

62. The Lingbao scriptures prescribe the retreat as preparation for all sorts of ritual activities. Specifically mentioned are "reciting, collating, and copying scriptures, writing talismans, mixing drugs, performing alchemy, meditating, visiting a Master for instruction, performing ritual obeisances, receiving scriptures, curing illness, driving off calamities, and summoning the Perfected." *HY* 425, 15b; see also Schipper, "Reihō kagi," p. 227.

63. *HY* 425, 9a.

64. Bokenkamp, "Sources," pp. 463–4.

65. *HY* 425, 7a. A note by an unnamed "Perfected Person" suggests that one might, while chanting, sip boiled water in which bamboo leaves have been steeped. This suggestion may have been prompted by observation of Buddhist monks drinking tea as they chanted their scriptures.

66. The term "prime" (*yüan* 元) connotes that the triad heaven-earth-water was formed from the divisions of primal pneuma. As we have seen, this triad, based on the common view of Han cosmologists that at creation the light pneumas rose up to form heaven and the heavier pneumas congealed to form earth, was worked out in various ways in Daoist texts, with only the first two members—heaven and earth—remaining constant. The *Xiang'er* commentary spoke of yang (celestial), yin (terrestrial), and cen-

trally harmonious pneumas (lines 328–29 and 409–11), the *Admonitions* of heaven-earth-Dao (*HY* 788, 12a), and the *Inner Explanations* of heaven-earth-water (*HY* 1196, 2b). It is this latter explanation that gave rise to the concept of the Three Primes and to the new dates of the year (differing from the dates of the Celestial Masters' "three assemblies") associated with them.

67. *HY* 456, 31a. The Three Primes were to become the occasion of communal ritual, to some extent replacing the three assemblies of the Celestial Masters (Stein, "Religious Taoism," pp. 69–71), but this is not yet the case for the *Scripture of Salvation*. In the Shangqing scriptures, as we have seen in the case of the *Purple Texts* (*HY* 639, 11b–12a), the term "three primes" refers above all to the three registers of the human body, and not to the Three Offices (Robinet, *La révélation du Shangqing,* vol. 1, pp. 66 and 126).

68. *HY* 22, 3:8a–9b.

69. See the *Great Petition,* translated herewith.

70. This is not to say that the Lingbao scriptures did not include petitions and other forms of bureaucratic documents. See especially Bokenkamp, "Death and Ascent," and Schipper, "Reihō kagi."

71. Zürcher, "Buddhist Influence," p. 27.

72. Robinet, *La révélation du Shangqing,* vol. 2, pp. 179–86.

73. See Harper, *Early Chinese Medical Literature,* sec. 5.

74. See Campany, "Return-from-Death Narratives," and, for an expression of this same fear in the texts translated here, *HY* 442, 12a, in the *Purple Texts.*

75. The *Scripture of Salvation* is not the first to employ this tactic. Recitation of the *Scripture of the Yellow Court* was believed to ensure the stability of the deities residing within the body and the proper functioning of the internal organs (Robinet, *Taoist Meditation,* p. 58). Here, though, the recitation is directed to the gods of the macrocosm, not the microcosm, and to highest spirits, not to demons or chthonic spirits.

76. The act of "announcing the merit" came at the end of Celestial Master rituals. It served to enunciate the benefits accrued by the performance of the ritual as a whole and to reward the deities who had participated in the rite (Lagerwey, *Taoist Ritual*).

77. *HY* 87, 4:27b–28a.

78. *HY* 87, 3:44b–46b.

79. On *HY* 87, see endnote 2 above. The original text, as attested in *HY* 87 and in the Dunhuang manuscripts, extends from the beginning of *HY* 1, chap. 1, to *HY* 1, 1:18a9.

80. I had originally planned to do a critical edition of the *Scripture of Salvation,* but, after laying out for myself all of the witnesses, I had to conclude that such a procedure would yield no new information on the early history of the text. The best one might do is to trace the parentage of nearly identical canonical versions dating from the Song on. Readers interested in the manuscript copies of the *Scripture of Salvation* should consult Ōfuchi,

Tonkō dōkyō, pp. 52–59, and especially his conclusions on p. 59. Although I have found a few omissions in Ōfuchi's work, the only variants worth recording here are those that influence the translation. These are mentioned in the endnotes. They are:

1. A brief phrase that was excised from the *HY* 1 copy of the scripture, presumably when it was adapted for communal liturgies;

2. A paragraph, dealing with the third of the days of the Three Primes, that is omitted from two of the Dunhuang manuscripts (this passage can be confidently restored on the basis of other witnesses and because, even in the two Dunhuang manuscripts, the first two days *are* mentioned, implying the third);

3. A Buddhist-inspired term that is written in a variant, but homophonous, form in *HY* 1 and in several of the post-Tang versions of the scripture.

In sum, *HY* 1 differs significantly from *HY* 87 and the Dunhuang texts at only two points, whereas two of the Dunhuang witnesses contain a significant lacuna. From these findings, we can conclude no more than that *HY* 1 seems to have been slightly altered—a fact already apparent from its concluding section. In terms of textual transmission, the omission found in the two Dunhuang manuscripts (one perhaps copied from the other?) seems to represent no more than a regional lapse, as I have found no other witness that contains this lacuna. (For further details, see endnotes 3, 5, and 11 to the translation.)

81. *HY* 425, 10b.
82. *HY* 97, 1:14a–15b.

Translation

The Wondrous Scripture
of the Upper Chapters on Limitless Salvation

PREFACE

The Dao* said:

Of old, in the *Biluo kongge dafuli* land in the midst of the Inaugural Azure Heavens, I received the *Boundless Upper Chapters of the Scripture of Salvation of Primordial Commencement.*[1] When the Celestial Worthy of Primordial Commencement pronounced this scripture, he made ten complete recitations to summon in the ten directions the Great Spirits of Heavenly Perfection, the Most Honored of the Exalted Sages, and the Perfected of Wondrous Deeds in all their countless multitudes who might attend his throne. These beings came, mounted on air. They arrived in flying clouds and cinnabar-red cirrus wisps, in green chariots with rose-gem wheels.[†] Their feathered canopies shrouded the land, while their streaming essences glittered with gemmy light, so that the five colors billowed forth, flashing penetratingly throughout the Grand Void.[‡]

For the space of seven days and seven nights, the suns and moons,

---

* This is a shortened form of the title "Most High Lord of the Dao."

† "Cirrus wisps" translates *xiao,* a word denoting the heights of the visible sky as well as the sorts of vapors found there. Li Shaowei and Cheng Xuanying suggest that these red-tinged clouds form the clothing of the celestial beings (*HY* 87, 1:4b–5a).

‡ The "streaming essences" are the glowing pentachromatic emanations of the spirits' bodies.

stars and lodgings, even to the Cogs, Armils, and Jade Transverses
of all the Dippers of all the heavens, stopped at once in their rota-
tions.* The spirit-driven winds were still and silent. The mountains
and seas hid away their cloudy emanations. The heavens lacked even
floating haze; the air was perfectly clear in all directions. Throughout the whole kingdom, the earth—all mountains and rivers, forests
and groves—became uniform and flat, so that there were no longer
high and low places. All became as cyan jade; there were no other
colors. As the multitude of Perfected attended his throne, the Celestial Worthy of Primordial Commencement sat suspended in the air,
floating above a pentachromatic lion. When he spoke the scripture
through for the first time, all of the assembled great Sages voiced
their approval. At once all those in the kingdom afflicted with deaf-
1:7a   ness, both male and female, were able to hear again. When he expounded the scripture a second time, the eyes of the blind were
opened to the light. When he expounded the scripture for the third
time, the mute were able to speak. When he expounded the scripture
for the fourth time, those long lame or paralytic were able to arise
and walk. When he expounded the scripture for the fifth time, those
with chronic illnesses or diseases were immediately made whole.
When he expounded the scripture for the sixth time, white hair
turned black again and lost teeth were regrown. When he expounded
the scripture for the seventh time, the aged were restored to youth
and the young were made strong. When he expounded the scripture
for the eighth time, wives became pregnant, while birds and beasts'
wombs were quickened. Not only were those already born made
whole, but the unborn as well came whole into life. When he expounded the scripture for the ninth time, the stores of earth were
1:9a   leaked forth; gold and jade lay revealed. When he expounded the
scripture for the tenth time, desiccated bones were revivified; all rose

---

* "All the heavens" refers to the thirty-two heavens listed later in the text. The
"lodgings" are the twenty-eight lunar lodgings. The "Cog and Armil" refers to the
four stars of the bowl of the Dipper, while "Jade Transverse" refers to the three stars
of its handle. On these asterisms and their role in marking time, see Needham,
Science and Civilisation in China, vol. 3 (1959), pp. 232–52; and Schafer, *Pacing the
Void*, pp. 47–53 and 79–84. To say that these celestial timekeepers stood still is to
say that time stopped.

up to become human beings again.* At once the whole kingdom, both male and female, inclined their hearts to the Dao. All received protection and salvation. All achieved long life.

The Dao said:

At that time, when the Celestial Worthy of Primordial Commencement spoke the scripture for the first time, the innumerable grades of completely perfected Great Spirits in countless numbers from the limitless realms of the east arrived, mounted on air. When he spoke   1:11b
the scripture for the second time, the innumerable grades of the completely perfected Great Spirits in countless numbers from the limitless realms of the south arrived, mounted on air. When he spoke the scripture for the third through the tenth times, the Great Spirits of the west, the north, the northeast, the southeast, the southwest, the northwest, the zenith, and the nadir all arrived in their turn, mounted on air.†

When the ten recitations were completed, the Celestial Perfected   1:13a
and Great Gods of the illimitable realms of all ten directions had assembled as one. The entire kingdom, male and female, inclined their hearts and took refuge in the Dao. Those assembled were like droplets of mist or dense fog, countless in their multitudes. They crowded

---

* The doctrinal significance of the miracles attending the Celestial Worthy's ten recitations of the scripture is explained by the commentators as follows:

1. All are made able to hear the Daoist dharma.
2. All are then able to see the Celestial Worthy.
3. Through seeing the Celestial Worthy, they are able to speak the truths of the Dao.
4. All are thus able to walk the path of the Dao.
5. Through practicing the Dao, their bodies are perfected.
6. Since their bodies are perfected, they are made young again.
7. In this way, they are strengthened.
8. The beneficent influence extends even to animals and the unborn.
9. Even the earth is made to yield up its treasures.
10. In the same fashion, those who have formerly returned to earth are brought back to life.

† The full formulation, given here only for the first two directions, is repeated for each of the ten directions—the eight points of the compass on the horizontal plane plus the two general directions above and below. I have abbreviated it here. Also, it is worth noting that this is not a new set of ten recitations of the scripture. The first description of the ten recitations tells of the effects on earth, in this case the kingdom of Fuli, whereas the second description records the effect in the heavens.

into one-half of the area of the kingdom, so that it tipped to the side,
but still they would not be stopped.*

At this, the Celestial Worthy of Primordial Commencement suspended a precious pearl, as big as a grain of millet, in the empty
darkness fifty feet above the ground.† Then he rose to lead the
countless assembly of the celestially perfected Great Gods, the Highest Sages, and the Most Honoured Perfected of Wondrous Deeds of
all the innumerable realms in the ten directions into the middle of
the precious pearl. When the celestial citizens of the kingdom raised
their eyes to look, they saw only the swelling multitudes following

1:15a   into the opening of the precious pearl. Once these had entered the
pearl, they disappeared. The inhabitants of the kingdom then dis-
persed and the land returned to level, so that it no longer tipped to
one side.

Straightaway the Celestial Worthy of Primordial Commencement,
within the precious pearl, expounded this scripture to the end and,
with the host of Perfected overseeing the ordination, transmitted
the scripture to me. At this, my rejoicing was beyond description.
Once the ceremony was over, all of the heavens returned to their
normal positions. With a rush of wind, all was still and without
reverberation.

1:17a   The inhabitants of this heaven, having encountered this scripture
and its ritual practice, at once universally achieved salvation and
lived out their originally allotted spans of life. None of them died
before their time from any injury. Those of the entire land were inclined to the Way and practiced only goodness. They neither killed
nor harmed. They were neither envious nor jealous. They were neither lascivious nor thieving. They did not covet or desire. They did
not hate or act selfishly. Their words were not frivolously ornate,
nor did evil sounds emerge from their mouths. They were benevolent
and loving to all equally, so that they treated as family even those

* To "incline [*qing*] to the Way" is a common metaphor. Here it becomes quite
literal.

† The word translated "darkness" here means also mystery. Among the meta-
phorical lessons the commentators draw from this scene is the interesting observation that, since the precious (or "treasure") pearl is where the Lingbao (spirit treasure) scripture will be spoken, we might call it a "treasure within a treasure" or,
echoing *Laozi* 1, a mystery within a mystery, darkness within darkness.

not of their own blood.* The kingdom was harmonious and the people flourished, in joy and Great Peace.

When this scripture first emerged, it instructed an entire kingdom by means of the Dao. Those with the intention of wholeheartedly revering it as the source of their practice will without fail transcend their generation.†

The Dao said:

The scripture that the Celestial Worthy of Primordial Commencement pronounced speaks the inner names of the Thearchs and the sounds of the secret rhymes of all the heavens, as well as of the taboo names of the Demon Kings and the secret names of the myriad spirits. These are not common words of the world. Only the highest sages, those who have already become Perfected beings, who communicate with the mysterious and comprehend the subtle, will be able to completely comprehend these stanzas. When they intone it ten times, the ten heavens will sound forth in the distance, the ten thousand Thearchs will all do obeisance. The rivers and seas will become still and silent; the mountains and marchmounts will hide their clouds. The sun and moon will hold back their refulgence and the Cog and Armil will stop moving. The myriad demons will be physically restrained and spectral essences will be destroyed. Corpses will return to life and the dead will be raised, their white bones forming again into human beings.

When those mortals who have mastered the study recite this

1:19a

1:20a

---

* These virtues approximate the ten precepts of the Lingbao scriptures, which are, in the most common formulation:

1. Do not hate or be overcome with jealousy;
2. Do not kill;
3. Do not act lasciviously;
4. Do not covet;
5. Do not lie or speak evil;
6. Do not drink;
7. Do not envy others;
8. Do not slander the scriptures;
9. Do not cause discord;
10. Act with equanimity.

See HY 177, 1b–2b; HY 352, 1:2b–3a; and HY 457, 1:6a–b.

† To "transcend one's generation" means to live beyond one's allotted lifespan and implies that one will ascend to heaven without having to pass through death.

scripture, the Five Thearchs will stand guard over them and those in the three realms will bow their heads.* Demonic sprites will lose their sight; spectral incursions will be destroyed. Salvation will extend even to the dead, and though they be cut off, they will achieve life. The reason for this is that the polluted pneumas of those still engaged in study are not yet completely dispelled, so that their bodies have not yet become completely Perfected. When they summon spirits of the ten directions, their might is not yet such as to control the celestial governors.† Yet they may overcome and control chthonic powers, binding both demons and spirits. Such as these may fend off death, but they are not yet able to revivify the dead.

1:21a

> Disrespectful chanting of these stanzas
> Brings disaster for the individual.
> Respectfully carrying out the revered rites
> Causes one's family to prosper.
> Generation after generation, these latter will flourish—
> Granted good karmic causes.
> The myriad calamities will not block them;
> Spirit luminaries will guard their gates.
>
> This scripture, venerable and wondrous,
> Alone allows one to walk the Jade Capitoline.‡
> It provides salvation limitlessly—
> Primogenitor of the myriad ways!
> Lofty and towering, this grand model—§
> Its potencies are not to be excelled.

---

* Those who have mastered the study are, according to Xue Youxi, those with hearts more firmly fixed on the Dao than iron or stone, more ardent than the fire, who are not deceived by demons and are able to accomplish what other mortals cannot accomplish. More importantly, their names are already inscribed high in the heavens. (*HY* 87, 1:20a.)

† That is to say, they cannot control the movements of the celestial bodies, as the Perfected mentioned earlier are able to do, and thus cannot make time stand still or the dead return to life.

‡ "Jade Capitoline" is the name of the celestial mountain in the midst of the Grand Veil Heaven of Lingbao cosmology, often referred to as the Jade Capitoline of the Mystic Metropolis. Its most prominent palace is the Upper Palace of Purple Tenuity, not to be confused with the lower, visible constellation. See *HY* 1427, 1a ff.; *HY* 1130, 4:8b; and Stephen R. Bokenkamp, "The *Pacing the Void Stanzas* of the Ling-pao Scriptures" (master's thesis, University of California at Berkeley, 1981), pp. 100–101.

§ *Fan*, the word translated as "model" here, has an ancient pedigree. It is the same word used in the earliest Confucian classic of history, the *Shangshu*, as part of a chapter title (the "*Hongfan*"). In the Confucian case, the "grand plan," as this title

The Dao said:

Whenever anyone chants this scripture ten times, it reaches alike all the various heavens. The myriad generations of ancestors, those souls suffering in darkness as well as those bitterly departed—all alike will be saved and ascend on high to the Vermilion Palace.* After the regulation nine years' detainment, they will receive rebirth as honored personages who delight in studying the highest scriptures.² Once their achievements and virtues on earth are accomplished, they will all attain the rank of divine Transcendent. Flying up, they will ascend through the Golden Porte to roam and feast in the Jade Capitoline.†

1:23a

When those with higher attainments in the Learning recite and practice this scripture, they will immediately fly up to the Southern Palace on high. When ordinary mortals receive and recite it, they will extend their years and live long lives. At the end of their lives, they will achieve the way of release from the corpse.‡ Their cloud-

---

is usually translated, delineates the political and religious principles of rule. The *Scripture of Salvation*, we are to understand, is the vehicle of an even more exalted cosmological model.

* The "souls suffering in darkness" are those ancestors whose souls are still in the earth-prisons and whose ancestral tablets are still kept in the family temple. Those "bitterly departed" are no longer represented by a tablet in the family shrine, but have not yet been reborn. (See the gloss of Xue Youxi, HY 87, 1:22b.) The Vermilion Palace, also called the Vermilion Mound, the Southern Palace, and Southern Glory in this text, was the locale where the corporal spirits of the dead were refined for rebirth. See Robinet, *La révélation du Shangqing*, vol. 2, pp. 209 ff. Originally, the Vermilion Palace seems to have been associated with the seven southern lunar lodgings—Well, Ghost, Willow, Star, Spread, Wing, and Axletree. On these translations of the star names, their identifications, and much else pertaining to the lunar lodgings, see Schafer, *Pacing the Void*, pp. 75–84, and especially the chart on pp. 76–77. For the Lingbao identification of the Vermilion Palace with them, see HY 352, 1:10a–11a, and HY 22, 1:31b–32a. The Lingbao scriptures contain yet another name for the hall not mentioned in Robinet's list—the Southern Palace of Penetrating Yang. They describe the Hall of Flowing Fire within this palace, where the body is refined for a certain length of time under the direction of the two deities, the Perfected Lord of the Southern Culmen and the Director of the Equerry. (See HY 87, 2:15a–18b, later in this translation.)

† On the Golden Porte, see endnote 12 to the introduction to the *Purple Texts*.

‡ On "release from the corpse," an ancient method of transcendence already mentioned in Han texts, by which a person might "in broad daylight" leave the corpse behind as a cicada sheds its husk, see HY 442, 11b, in the translation of the *Purple Texts*. Although there are many methods for accomplishing this release, the one at issue here clearly envisions the reuniting of the body with its spiritual components.

souls and bodily spirits will be obliterated for only an instant and
will not pass through the earth-prisons, but will be immediately
returned to the body so that they might roam the Grand Void.

1:25a   Subtle and wondrous is this scripture. It provides universal,
unending salvation. All those of heaven receive its benefits. Its blessings are without count, its grace bestowed on the living and the dead
alike. Treasured in the highest heavens, it was not transmitted to the
world below. Now, when those of highest attainment proffer gold
and valuables, binding their hearts in a covenant with heaven, it is
to be transmitted to them. If they treat it lightly, leak its contents, or
are dilatory with respect to its injunctions, disaster will reach even to
their nine generations of ancestors and they will all do hard labor
with the demon officers.

Attendant on this scripture are twenty-four Jade Lads and twenty-
four Jade Maidens of the Five Thearchs. They guard the spirit text
and protect the persons of those who have received it.

The Dao said:
If in the first month you conduct a long retreat and chant this
scripture, it will end the detention within the earth of the departed
cloudsouls of those of previous generations, transferring them above
to the Southern Palace.

1:27a   If in the seventh month you conduct a long retreat and chant this
scripture, you will attain the status of divine Transcendent. Where
your name is inscribed in all the various heavens on the white slips
of the Yellow Registers, "death" will be scratched out and "life"
written over it.

If in the tenth month you conduct a long retreat and chant this
scripture on behalf of your thearchs and princes, rulers of the kingdom, your lords and ministers, fathers and sons, then the mandate
of the kingdom will be secure. Preserved by heaven, it will long
endure, not dying out for generation after generation. For the lords
of humanity, it will secure their region; for the citizens it will ensure
Great Peace.[3]*

---

* The fifteenth days of the first, seventh, and tenth months are the festivals of the
Three Primes, associated with heaven, earth, and humanity. These major liturgical

If on the days of the eight seasonal nodes you chant this scripture, you will become a Perfected being in the Nine Palaces.*

If on the days of your natal destiny you chant this scripture, your cloudsouls and bodily spirits will be purified, and the myriad pneumas will preserve you.† You will not encounter vexations, and your body will become luminous. The Three Realms will stand guard   1:29b
over you and the envoys of the Five Thearchs will be sent to receive you.‡ With the myriad spirits in ritual attendance, your name will be written in the highest heavens so that, once your merit making is complete, your virtues fulfilled, you may fly above to Upper Clarity.

The Dao said:

On the days on which you practice this Dao, you should bathe in perfumed water. Then, having purified and observed the prohibitions, enter your chamber. Facing east, knock your teeth thirty-two times to alert the thirty-two heavens on high. Then mentally bow thirty-two times.§ Shutting your eyes, in stillness imagine your   1:31a
body seated in the midst of tricolored clouds of green, yellow, and

---

festivals seem to have developed from the three assemblies of the Celestial Masters. See Stein, "Religious Taoism," pp. 69–71, and, for the Lingbao celestial bureaucracy that is associated with the Three Primes, HY 456, especially 31a.

   * The eight seasonal nodes are the equinoxes, the solstices, and the first days of the four seasons by the Chinese lunar calendar. The Lingbao Retreat of the Eight Seasonal Nodes is described by Lu Xiujing in HY 1268, 5b ff. The Nine Palaces are arrayed horizontally, in the disposition associated with the Luoshu. (See Kalinowski, "La transmission du Dispositif.") Through this arrangement, they have a number of associations, including three triads associated with heaven, earth, and water. The Lingbao names of these palaces and their associated minions are listed in HY 456, 1a–19b.

   † The day of natal destiny is that day bearing the cyclical designation of the year of one's birth. On these days, which occur six times a year, the Director of Destinies was believed to check one's deeds and enter them in the books of life. (See HY 87, 1:29a.8–10.)

   ‡ The Five Thearchs of the Lingbao texts are the lords of the four cardinal directions and the center. The names given these deities derive from the Han-period weft texts and the imperial rites of the Han dynasty. The names, seasons, and numerical associations of the Five Thearchs in the Lingbao scriptures are to be found in HY 388, 1:14b.10 ff.; HY 22, 1:31a ff.; and HY 352, 1:29b ff. See Bokenkamp, "Sources," pp. 451–54.

   § Li Shaowei specifies that each of these prostrations should be performed facing the direction of the heaven to which the obeisance is directed and accompanied by visualizations of the thirty-two thearchs (HY 87, 1:30b–31a).

white.* Both within and without it is obscure and dark. To the left
and the right, arrayed closely beside you, are the green dragon, the
white tiger, the vermilion sparrow, the murky warrior, the lion, and
the white crane.† The sun and moon, in full luminescence, shine
penetratingly into the chamber. From the back of your neck emerges
a round image that, with its beams, shines into the ten directions.‡

When all of this appears clearly before you as described, secretly
incant as follows:§

1:32a   Most High Lord of the Dao of the ultimate Mysterious and Primordial
               pneumas, summon from this servant's body the official envoys of the left
               and right from the three and the five Merit Sections, the thirty-two Jade
               Lads who attend the incense, the thirty-two Jade Maidens who transmit
               messages, and the thirty-two incense officers, talisman bearers of the Five
               Thearchs who correspond to this day.⁴ They are to inform those on high
               of what I say. Today is a day of blessings. I now hold a long retreat in
               the pure hall to practice the ultimate scripture for limitless salvation.
               Your servant, for the sake of (so-and-so), recites the scripture repeatedly
               to receive life.⁵ I vow that my entreaties should penetrate above to the
               daises of the most revered High Thearchs of Primordial Commencement
               who control the highest thirty-two heavens.‖

* These are the colors of the three pneumas: the mysterious pneuma is green, the
primal pneuma yellow, and the inaugural pneuma white.

† The green dragon, white tiger, vermilion sparrow, and "murky warrior" are the
directional animals of the east, west, south, and north, respectively. Beginning in the
Han period, these animals are commonly depicted on the walls of tombs as guardians in the four directions. The "murky warrior" is usually depicted as a turtle
wrapped about with a snake or sometimes a turtle with the head of a snake. The lion
and the white crane seem here to be symbols of the center, below and above.

‡ This "round image" is in fact like the halo that appears on Buddhist and Daoist
images of deities in this period. The "ten directions" are the eight points of the compass, up, and down.

§ The following incantation is a Lingbao version of the Celestial Master procedure for summoning forth the gods (chu guan) inhabiting the body of the adept to
merge with their celestial counterparts for the accomplishment of some ritual action.
The names of these deities were listed in the registers bestowed on each initiate. See
Cedzich, "Das Ritual," pp. 65–77, for a full account of the development of this
practice, and HY 352, 3:30a–32a, for the portion of the Lingbao investiture in which
the gods first are charged to descend into the initiate. As the Lingbao text Jade Instructions on the Red Writings puts it: "Whenever those who study the Dao make a
request or conduct one of the higher rituals, they will be thwarted by demons if they
do not first announce it on high. For if their practice does not reach those above, it
will not move the spirit luminaries to observe, and they will labor in vain" (HY 352,
1:16b.7–9).

‖ Just as the Lord of the Dao was held to be generated from the first two of the
three pneumas of creation, so the thirty-two thearchs are associated with the latter

Once you have completed this, draw the pneumas into your body thirty-two times.* Then face east and chant the scripture:

SECTION I

The Wondrous Scripture of the Upper Chapters   2:1a
on the Limitless Salvation of Primordial Commencement

The original stanzas of the Numinous Gem of Primordial Commencement that comprehend the Mysterious are

> Wondrous verses from the upper chapters;†
> With ten turnings, they provide salvation.
> The one hundred demons, the secret rhymes,   2:5a
> Join and separate within the Self-Actualizing.‡
> The red script that penetrated the turbulent void
> Represents Highest Perfection from when Nothingness was yet not.§
> In the ancestral kalpas‖ of Primordial Commencement,
> It transformed to shape all of the heavens.
> Opening to illumine the Three Phosphors,#
> It was the root of heaven and earth.
> Above it there is no further parent;
> Only the Dao constituted its body.

---

two of the three. In this fashion, the adept's body becomes the locus where the highest god communicates with those lower in the pantheon.

* Although this seems to refer simply to breathing practice, what the adept is enjoined to ingest are the tricolored primal pneumas envisioned earlier in this practice.

† The term "upper chapters" refers to the fact that the Lingbao scriptures, formed of primordial pneumas at creation, are the ancestors of all later scriptures and writings. (See Yan Dong's lengthy explanation in *HY* 87, 2:3a–4b.)

‡ This implies that the demons, the chief of which are named later on, as well as the deities, palaces, and powers mentioned in the Hidden Language, are one with the self-actualizing Dao so that they emerged with its differentiation and will merge with it again when it folds in its pneumas at the end of the cosmic cycle.

§ The "red script" is the *Perfected Script in Five Tablets, Written in Red,* which appeared in the heavens at the differentiation of pneuma at creation and was further refined by fire in the Palace of Penetrating Solarity. (See *HY* 22, 1:1a–2b.) It was regarded as the ancestor of all Lingbao scriptures and other Daoist texts. This entire passage extols the virtues of the Lingbao texts.

‖ Kalpas are the immensely long periods of time that came into Daoism from Buddhist translations. Yan Dong gives the following metaphor: were there a city wall four hundred miles in length and width and four hundred miles high, filled with mustard seeds, and were celestial beings to take one mustard seed every hundred years, a kalpa would equal the length of time it takes to empty the city of mustard seeds.

The "Three Phosphors" are the sun, moon, and stars.

The Five-Part Script spread abroad,
Planting everywhere its spiritual power.
2:9a   Without the script there would be no light;
Without the script there would be no brilliance.
Without the script nothing would be established;
Without the script nothing would have been formed.
Without the script there would be no salvation;
Without the script there would be no life.

At this, it created the Great Brahmā—
Most celestial among the heavens.
Murky and veiled, the remote tower—
The higher capitol atop Jade Mountain.*
At the highest limits, with nothing above,
Stands Jade Clarity of the Grand Veil;
2:11b   Faint in the distance, the Tower of Kalpas and Rods,†
As if vanishing, as if enduring;
The Triply Floriate, separated off by the Gates of Ease,⁶
In the wondrous courts of Grand Existence.‡
The gemmy chambers of the Golden Porte—
All arrayed in veiled profusion, pure and purged.⁷
There greatly circulates Brahmā pneumas,
Circling through the ten directions of space.

Within dwell the saviors of humanity,
The spirits of deathlessness:
Within is the Perfected of the Southern Extremities,
Lord of long life;§

---

* The terminology used here explicates for us the name "Grand Veil Heaven." It hangs like a veil over all of the lower heavens and is itself veiled in mists.

† In contradistinction to kalpas, the immense periods of time of Indian thought, "rods" are a more mundane Chinese measurement of length, equal to eight Chinese feet. The Tower of Kalpas and Rods is one of the features of Jade Capitoline mentioned in the "Hymn for Pacing the Void." The term expresses at once the incalculable longevity of the tower and its height. See HY 87, 2:11b–12a; Bokenkamp, "Pacing the Void," pp. 91–92; and HY 1427, 4b.1–3.

‡ "Grand Existence" is another name for the Dao.

§ The Perfected of the Southern Extremities rules over the Three Palaces and Nine Bureaus of the middle prime palaces associated with earth. These three palaces and their functions are as follows: (1) Clear Spirituality, in charge of the Five March-mounts and earthbound Transcendents; (2) Penetrating Yang, in charge of earth gods and the righteous dead who serve as officials in the earth; and (3) Northern Feng, which oversees the death records of those with merit. The Palace of Penetrating Yang is another name for the Southern Palace. See HY 87, 2:15a–16a; HY 97, 3:18a.3–4; and HY 456, 7b–12a. The two deities listed immediately afterward—the Director of the Equerry and Lord Han—are under the direction of the Perfected of the Southern Extremities. For a list of these deities in another ritual context, see the Lingbao text HY 22, 3:3a.3–4.

Within is the Deliverer of the Generations,
The Great Spirit, Director of the Equerry;[8]
Within is the Lord of Life,
The Elder, Lord Han.[9]
Within dwell these Southern Highnesses,   2:17a
Directors of Destinies and Directors of Registers;
Extending life, adding to the count of years,
These venerable gods save us from perversity.
Returning the physical frame, raising the dead,
They limitlessly provide salvation.

Today, as they collate the registers,
The gods of all the heavens appear before the Celestial Worthy:

The heaven-soaring spirit kings and great sages of long life of the
illimitable heavens of the eastern regions who provide countless
mortals salvation;

The heaven-soaring spirit kings and great sages of long life of the
illimitable heavens of the southern regions who provide countless
mortals salvation; . . . *

The completely Perfected heaven-soaring spirit kings and all of   2:22a
the countless greater deities who provide long life and salvation in
the ten directions are all alike borne by carriages with cinnabar-red
compartments, green shafts, feather canopies, and red-gem wheels,
all formed of soaring clouds. To these are harnessed vermilion
phoenixes and pentachromatic mystic dragons. Held aloft are bla-
zons of nine colors and spirit banners of ten striations.† Before, nine
whistling phoenixes sing out in unison. Behind, eight trumpeting
simurghs sound at once. Lions and white cranes whistle and sing in
austere harmony. The Five Ancient Ones clear the road ahead, while
the masses of Transcendents flank the carriage shafts.‡ In myriad
conveyances, on thousands of mounts, the procession arrives, float-

* This formula is repeated for all of the ten directions.
† The "nine colors" are azure, red, white, yellow, black, green, red, purple, and
maroon. The banners have ten stripes across them to symbolize the unity of the ten
directions.
‡ The Five Ancient Ones are the Five Ancient Thearchs listed in the introduction.
"Clearing the road" is not a janitorial function, but a ritual and apotropaic one. In
ancient times, the way to be traversed by the emperor on his way to ritual locales
was swept clean of evil spirits in this manner. In some cases, this purification was
accomplished by the "Eight Potencies," deities associated with the eight phosphors.
See Edward H. Schafer, *The Eight Daunters,* Schafer Sinological Papers, no. 21

2:27a   ing through the void. Then, on slanting beams of light, they ride
          back to oversee the perfection and salvation of mortals.*
              In the various heavens, the Chief Councillors, together with
          Director Han of the upper palace Southern Glory, control the
          records.† The great spirits who inspect the ledgers of life carry the
          registers and assemble before the Thearchs. The records of those
          who are to be saved in each place are strictly collated in the various
          heavens. Then a universal announcement is made throughout the
          illimitable spirit lands of the Three Realms, down to the Bureau of
          Spring-Bend and Luofeng of the Northern Metropolis, addressed to
          the Three Offices, the Nine Agencies, and the Twelve River
          Sources:[10]

2:37a   Above we have released the primogenitors,
          Together with their seed and descendants for millions of kalpas.
          Forthwith withdraw their ledgers of transgressions
          And eradicate the roots of evil within them.
          Do not shackle or detain them;
          Do not compel them to join the ghostly hordes.
          The talismanic command of Primordial Commencement
          Ensures that they be immediately transferred above.
          The Cold Pool of the Northern Metropolis
          With its cohorts to guard their forms and cloudsouls,
          Controls all demons to ensure their ascent,
          Transferring their documents of salvation to the Southern Palace,
          Where the cloudsouls of the deceased are refined
          And, through transcendent mutation, become human;
          Where the body is vivified and receives salvation,
          To endure for kalpa after kalpa.‡
          With the turning of kalpa cycles,
          They will enjoy a longevity equal to that of heaven,
          Forever free of the three kinds of servitude,[11]
          The five sufferings, and the eight difficulties.[12]

(Berkeley, Calif., 1985); and *HY* 87, 2:67b, in this translation. Here the chore goes
to some of the highest of Lingbao gods.

   * After having attended the throne of the Celestial Worthy and received his
charges, the deities return to their own heavens to oversee the salvation of those in
their realm.

   † On the Director of Registers Han, see *HY* 87, 2:16b, in the present translation.
"Southern Glory" is an alternate name for the Southern Palace.

   ‡ The ancestors who undergo this process are readied for rebirth in blessed families. The phrasing here also indicates that those reborn will be reborn again and
again throughout the length of the kalpa. Presumably, they will each time improve
their transcendent status.

Skimming beyond the Three Realms,   2:41a
They will roam unhindered in Upper Clarity.

The Celestial Thearch of the Upper Clarity heaven, named the
Jade Perfected, travels the Brahmā-pneumas throughout the glowing
scenes of the formless regions.[13]
[The list of the thirty-two heavens and their thearchs appears in
the text at this point. These names are given in the Hidden Language
of the Great Brahmā and are thus untranslatable.]
Above are the hidden taboo names and given names of the thirty-   2:54b
two heavens and the thirty-two thearchs. The self-actualizing numinous stanzas of the Vacuous Grotto within each of the heavens represent the secret rhymes of the heaven in the sounds of that heaven.*
They represent the venerated of these heavens, the spirits of these
heavens, the great demons of these heavens, and the numinous
[powers] of these heavens—those who, with nine mergings and ten
joinings, have transformed themselves to enter Upper Clarity.† The
innumerable profundities of these stanzas are deep and unfathomable. Spread abroad, they descend as the spiritual Perfected to universally save the people of heaven.‡
Today, there is rejoicing at my ordination. All the heavens are   2:58a
informed:§

You are requested to eradicate the three evils
And chop away the earthen roots.[14]
Flying, I cross above the five portals,

---

* The Vacuous Grotto is one of the stages of creation in the Daoist texts of this
period. See HY 1196, 2b, in the translation of the *Inner Explanations*. The stanzas
of the thirty-two heavens, given in the Hidden Language of the Great Brahmā in
this text, thus partake of the pneumas of this pristine period in the formation of the
cosmos.
† The stanzas extolled here are given at HY 87, 4:2b–25a. (As explained in the
introduction, these celestial verses require a lengthy scripture [HY 97] to be compre-
hensible even in Chinese and will thus not be translated here. See figure 5 for an
example of the celestial forms of Chinese characters in which the verses appeared at
creation.) The deities mentioned have passed through the nine agencies of corporal
refinement to be transformed ten times and enter the heaven of Upper Clarity. See
HY 87, 2:56b.7–57a.4. On the notion of ten cycles of corporal transformation in the
Lingbao scriptures, see Bokenkamp, "Stages of Transcendence."
‡ The deity names presented in the stanzas are inseparable from the deities
named. This sentence speaks at once of both.
§ This is written in the persona of the Lord of the Dao, whose ordination is described in the opening of the scripture, but the stanzas that follow refer as well to the
salvation of the individual who adheres to the practices described in this text.

And my name is listed in Grand Mystery.*
Demon kings oversee my elevation;
I am not detained outside the Gates of Heaven.

2:60a   The Eastern Dipper controls my span of life.
The Western Dipper inscribes my name.
The Northern Dipper drops my record of death.
The Southern Dipper adds my notation of life.
The Central Dipper, the Great Head,
Commands overall the hordes of numinous powers.[15]

The Green Thearch protects my cloudsouls;
The White Thearch attends to my whitesouls.
The Red Thearch nurtures the vivifying pneumas;
The Black Thearch circulates my blood.
The Yellow Thearch controls the center,
That the myriad spirits stay within bounds.

The Demon King of the Green Heavens is Serpent-Primordial Evil
    Earl.
The Demon King of the Red Heavens is Heaven-Supporting Stone-
    Porter.
The Demon King of the White Heavens is Mountain-Toppler Six-
    Eyes.
The Demon King of the Black Heavens is Evil Overseer Vivid-Scent.
The Demon King of the Yellow Heavens is Heaven-Crosser Power-
    Bearer.[16]

2:65a   The Five Thearchs and Five Demon Kings[17]
Are the ancestors of the myriad spirits.
Their flying processions attended by drumming,
They have overall command of the demon soldiers.
With banners, streamers, drums, and insignia,†
They roam on tours of inspection throughout the Grand Void.
They proclaim themselves "resplendent,"
And their achievements are foremost in the various heavens.
In the highest heavens they provide salvation for the people
Through strict regulation of the Northern Feng.‡
The Spirit Dukes obey their commands
And sweep away all that is infelicitous.

---

* The "five portals" are the entranceways to the five sufferings in the earth prisons (see endnote 12 to this translation). "Grand Mystery" refers to the Mystic Metropolis on Jade Capitoline Mountain, residence of the Celestial Worthy.
    † These various flags and drums are not merely decorative. Such devices were
used to command the movements of armies in the field.
    ‡ "Northern Feng" is another name for the Palace of Luofeng. See endnote 10 to
this translation.

The Eight Potencies spit poison;
Like fierce chargers they race through the four quarters.*
Celestial stalwarts charge before;
Grand generals plant their pennons.
Casting fire over ten thousand *li,*
The sound of their folly bells flows to the eight directions.[18]
Who dares to stand against them or try them?
Who dares to resist the Higher Perfected?
Golden halberds slaughter all before them;
Massive celestials carve up all behind,†

Butchering the demonic departed   2:69a
With incessant wind and fire.
By the thousands they are decapitated!
By the millions their forms are cut into pieces!
Demons dare not oppose them;
The dead do not become perverse sprites.
The Three Offices and the Palace of Northern Feng
Thoroughly oversee the demon armies,
So that they may not hide away.
The Golden Steed rides up with reports.
It is announced throughout the limitless realms
That the myriad deities are all to be obeyed.
Those of the Three Realms and under the Five Thearchs
Spread the news throughout Upper Clarity.

SECTION 2

According to the precious calendar of the Primal Caverns,   3:1a
From the era *Longhan* to the era *Yankang*—
During the vastly extended trillions of kalpas—
In the midst of undifferentiated chaos,
Above, there was no other color,
Below, there was no deeper depth—
Only a windblown moisture, penetrating and vacant;
A diamond riding the heavens.‡
In the heavens, above and below,

---

* Yan Dong identifies the "Eight Potencies" as dragon, phoenix, tiger, leopard, lion, red snake (cobra?), celestial horse, and fierce beast (?). For him, the "fierce charger" is one of the eight. (*HY* 87, 67b.)

† The term "massive celestial" is another appellation of the "Celestial Stalwarts"—mighty warrior heroes in the service of the Dao.

‡ The "windblown moisture," insubstantial yet adamantine in its durability, describes the Brahmā-breath that will form the Celestial Worthy.

There was no obscurity, no darkness,
No form, no shadow,
No limit, no end.
3:5a   Dark and attenuated, the Grand Brahmā;
Extending into the distance, void of light.
Then, when the era *Chiming* unfolded,
Through the self-actualization of cyclical progression,
Primordial Commencement, to provide stability,
Caused to descend the Five Tablets.
These jade graphs in red writing,
Along with the dragon script of the Eight Potencies,*
Protect and regulate the cycles of kalpas
So that heaven might long endure.
The Brahmā-pneumas covered all
And the myriad patterns were spread abroad.
The primordial net flowed throughout
All of the thirty-two heavens,
3:9a   Turning about in the Formless,
Cycling in all of the ten directions.
Turning through the Dipper, passing Winnower,
Pneumas cycled in the orderly fashion of the five regularities.†
The thirty-five celestial divisions
Are controlled by one pneuma of the highest primordial.‡
The Eight Phosphors darkly joined,
Their pneumas entered the mystery of mysteries.
Within the Mysterious, the Most Resplendent Ones,
The Higher Thearchs, the Elevated Perfected—
Their phosphors floated in the Grand Auroras

---

* Both the red writing and the Dragon Script of the Eight Potencies are given in
the first of the Lingbao scriptures, the *Perfected Script in Five Tablets, Written in
Red* (HY 22). The red writing in which the five tablets are inscribed is a celestial language like the Hidden Language, whereas the Dragon Script consists of the direc-
tionally aligned talismans associated with the five tablets. The division is reminiscent
of the Shangqing division of celestial writing into the "writing of the three primes
and eight conjunctions" and the "cloud-seal script of the Eight Dragons" (HY 1010,
1:8b–9a).

† Dipper and Winnower are two of the twenty-eight lunar lodgings, situated in
the northeast quadrant of the sky. See Schafer, *Pacing the Void,* pp. 76–77. The
"five regularities" are the five phases.

‡ Yan Dong and Cheng Xuanying hold that the "thirty-five celestial divisions"
include the thirty-two heavens and the three clear regions, the heavens of Grand
Clarity, Upper Clarity, and Jade Clarity. A variant explanation is provided by Xue
Youxi, who holds that the term refers to the twenty-eight lunar lodgings plus the
sun, the moon, and the five naked-eye planets. These latter, however, roam the sky
and so were not generally held to occupy "divisions" (*fen*) of the sky. (HY 87,
3:10b–12b.)

As they whistled and chanted the Cavern Stanzas.*
The golden perfection of the texts, clear and full,
Flowed in echo throughout the cloudy assemblies.
The jade tones control the pneumas;
Numinous winds gather the vapors.
The Purple Barrens, thronging and flourishing,
Have as adjutants the myriads of Transcendents.†
Through a thousand harmonies, ten thousand joinings,   3:17a
They became Perfected through natural completion.
Among the Perfected are Spirits,
The Grand Lords of Long Life:
The lordling Nonpareil,
The revered spirit White Prime,
Grand Unity, the Director of Destinies,
And Peach Vigor, named "Join and Extend."‡
Grasping tallies and clutching registers,
They ensure the fate and the root of life.
Roaming on high in Upper Clarity,
They come and go from the floriate chambers.
From the eight reaches of outer darkness
To within the smallest interstices,
They descend to secure the human body—
The Muddy Pellet and the Scarlet Palace.
From within, they order the five pneumas
And merge in undifferentiation the hundred spirits.
With ten cycles, they return [all] to holiness,   3:21b
So that the myriad pneumas at once transcend.§

The Way of Transcendence values life,

---

* The thirty-two Cavern Stanzas, one for each of the heavens, are generated from the Hidden Language of the Great Brahmā given in this scripture. See Bokenkamp, "Sources," pp. 461–65; and *HY* 97, 3:7a–4:20b. There are also hymns of praise associated with the thirty-two heavens that were recorded in the *Numinous Stanzas of the Cavern-Heavens*. Chap. 29 of *HY* 1130 contains a copy of all but two of the stanzas. Given the fragmentary nature of this latter text, it is difficult to assess the relationship between the two sets of songs. Either or both might be meant here.

† According to Yan Dong and Li Shaowei, the term "Purple Barrens" refers to the precincts of the Palace of Purple Tenuity in the Heaven of Jade Clarity. On this palace, see footnote † on p. 312 to the *Purple Texts*. Xue Youxi holds that it refers to the Heaven of Jade Clarity as a whole by reference to its alternate name, Purple Clarity. (*HY* 87, 3:16a–b.)

‡ On the five corporal spirits listed here, see the section "Bodily Deities of Salvation" in the introduction to this scripture.

§ "Ten cycles" is explained by the commentators as meaning ten recitations of the scripture in the Muddy Pellet of the head, salvation in the ten directions, or ten revolutions of the Barrier of Heaven around the polestar. (See *HY* 87, 3:21b–22a.) In fact, the early Lingbao scriptures explain that ten life cycles (nine deaths and rebirths

Providing limitless salvation for humanity.
Above, it opens the Eight Gates—
The Wheel of the Law to the soaring heavens.*
The prohibitive precepts of blame and blessing,
The inherent fate of causation—
All alike are revealed and transcended
As the departed cloudsouls revivify the body.
When the body receives life,
It is announced above in all the heavens.

In all of the heavens above, there are Gates of Life. Within each
are the chanted verses of the Vacant Caverns.† The following lyrics
from the holy tablets of the Demon Kings merge with those of the
Highest Perfected.

I. *Song for Flying through the Void
    in the Realms of Desire*

3:25a   The Way of humanity is petty and insignificant;
         The Way of the Transcendents is complex and vast.
         The Way of demons delights
         In blocking people's gate of life.
         The Way of Transcendence values life;
         The Way of demons values death.
         The Way of Transcendence ever brings good fortune;
         The Way of demons ever brings disaster.
         The Elevated Ones, with numinous inner clarity,
         Sing mournful songs that penetrate the Grand Void.
         Their only desire is that the Way of Transcendence be complete;
         They do not wish the Way of humanity to end.
         Within the Spring-Bend Bureau of the Northern Metropolis
         Reside the myriad hordes of demons—‡

---

from a convert's first acceptance of the doctrine) were necessary to be reborn into
the heavens. See Bokenkamp, "Stages of Transcendence," for traces of this short-
lived belief.

* This refers to the eight gates leading from the earth-prisons, the routes to salvation for the suffering souls incarcerated there. (See HY 455, once part of the Lingbao scripture *Blame and Blessings of the Wheel of the Law*.)

† On the two sorts of "cavern verses," see footnote * on p. 423 above. It is
undoubtedly the verses in the Hidden Language of the Great Brahmā that are meant
here.

‡ On the Bureau of Spring-Bend, see endnote 10 to the translation.

Their only desire, to subtract from people's count of life,
To block people's gate of destiny.
We sing the Cavern Stanzas[19]
To control Luofeng in the north;
To send off bound the weird and devilish sprites;
To raze the six demon peaks.*
In all the heavens the pneumas are purged and cleansed—   3:29a
As our Dao daily strengthens and prospers.

II. Song of the Demon King of the Realm of Form

Spread on high, vast and endless,
Luminous pneumas arch into the four quarters.
The Brahmā-pneumas move through the heavens,
Circling the ten directions.
The innumerable grand deities
All issue from my body.
I possess the Cavern Stanzas—
Through ten thousand recitations I have become transcendent!
The Way of Transcendence values salvation;
The Way of demons, only its own continuance.
Heaven and earth fade away
In swirling pneumas of filth.
The Three Realms are joyous;
Those who traverse them achieve longevity.
Those who bodily pass into my realm
Physically enter into self-actualization.
Then there is rejoicing,
As they are invested through my grace.
The era of Draconic Magnificence, vast and vibrant—   3:33a
Who might perceive its perfection?
My realm is difficult to traverse;
As a result, the cavern texts were composed.
Transforming, I fly through the void
In order to provide physical trials for you.
Some succeed, some fail, some are negligent, some flee—
Only a few pass through.
I scoff at you who do not pass,
And so make this song.

* The "six demon peaks" refer to the Six Heavens. Here the term is metonymic.
It is the demons of the Six Heavens that are to be decapitated.

III.   Song of the Demon King of the Realm of Formlessness

3:35a   High above the Three Realms,
            Dim and distant, the Grand Veil Heaven.
            Overtopping its formless roots,
            In lofty layers of clouds,
            There is only [the Celestial Worthy of] Primordial Commencement,
            At home there for countless kalpas.
            His minions regulate my realm;
            He rules from the Mystic Metropolis.
            Those who pass through my realm
            Enter bodily into the Jade Barrens.*
            My position is that of higher prince,
            In command of legions of demons.
            In the Void, myriad transformations,
            Defiled pneumas, confusing and alluring—
            Few are those who maintain their perfection;
            Many are those who, beguiled, lose their way.
            The Way of Transcendence is hard to fix;
            The Way of demons finds it easy to pervert.
            The Way of humanity resides in the heart—
            In truth it arises from nothing else.
3:39a   The Way of Transcendence values substance;
            The Way of humanity values ornate appearance.
            If you do not delight in the Way of Transcendence,
            How will you traverse the Three Realms?
            For those who wish to return along the five paths,
            What further can I do?†

                        ◆   ◆   ◆   ◆

            From above in the Three Realms,
            In the midst of the flying void,
            These are the songs of the Demon Kings,
            The tones of which merge with the Cavern Stanzas.
            If you chant them one hundred times,
            Your name will be passed to the Southern Palace.
            If you chant them a thousand times,

---

* The Jade Barrens are the vast reaches surrounding the Mystic Metropolis.

† The "five paths" are to be identified with the "five sufferings" mentioned earlier. (See endnote 12 to the translation.) Interestingly, the Demon King's sigh of
exasperation, *nai he* ("What further can I do?"), entered the popular imagination as
"the River Nai" (*Naihe*), in later Daoist and Buddhist texts the punning name of the
river of blood and corruption over which the dead must cross as they pass into the
earth-prisons.

The Demon Kings will come to greet and protect you.
Ten thousand times and your Dao is complete;
You will ascend flying into the Grand Void.
Passing through the Three Realms,
Your rank will be that of Duke Transcendent.

Upon hearing these numinous tones,   3:41a
The Demon Kings adopt postures of reverence.
They command the chthonic powers
To stand in attendance and to act as escort.
Plucking open the gates of earth,
Eradicating the five sufferings and eight difficulties,
They transfer the seven generations above,
Where they are forever separated from the officers of the dead.
Their cloudsouls pass through the Vermilion Mound,
Where they are refined for rebirth.*
This is called Illimitable,
Universal Salvation without End.

One who is able to keep secret this text of the higher heavens
Will be honored in all of the heavens alike.
Those who leak it or are remiss will fall into the earth-prisons
And disaster will reach even to the heads of their seven generations of
    ancestors.

POSTFACE I

The Dao said:

The above two sections contain the secret intonations of the
Highest Thearchs of the various heavens and the most holy Demon
Kings. They contain the words of the Grand Brahmā, which are not   3:43a
the ordinary terms of this world. This language lacks resonance and
ornamentation; its melodies lack artful fluidity.† Thus it is said that
the deepest mysteries are difficult to understand.

These words are treasures of the highest heavens, hidden in the
upper palaces of Purple Tenuity in the Mystic Metropolis. According to the Mystic Statutes, they are to be transmitted only once in
every forty thousand kalpas.‡ One of higher attainments who con-

---

* The Vermilion Mound is another name for the Southern Palace.
† That is to say, it is not written through human artifice.
‡ According to Yan Dong, the limitation of forty thousand kalpas applies only to
the higher heavens. In human terms, this translates to one transmission of the text

tributes gold and valuables as a token of belief and who, in accord
with the old statutes, makes a covenant with the ten heavens may
then be granted this text.

3:44b   The Dao said:
         The cyclical movements of heaven and earth have their depletion
and end. The sun, moon, and five planets have their times of fullness
and eclipse. The highest sages and spirit beings, in like fashion, have
their times of growth and decay, and those who come late to the
Study have their time of illness and injury. Whenever such calamities
occur, you should in the same fashion purge your heart and practice
the retreats. When you conduct a retreat, you should offer incense
and recite the entire scripture ten times at six points during the day.*
Then fortune-giving power will immediately descend to you, dissolving all unpropitiousness. The boundless script provides universal
salvation without end.

3:47a   The Dao said:
         Those who come to the Study late and whose grasp of the Dao is
shallow in some cases do not possess Transcendent rank sufficient
to have overcome the cycles of rebirth.† Such as these must pass
through oblivion, passing bodily through Grand Darkness. As they
are about to pass through, their fellow adepts and persons of attainment may offer incense and recite the scripture ten times for the salvation of their physical forms in accordance with the law.‡ Their

---

every forty years. For Xue Youxi, a "thousand springs" in the heavens is equal to the
space of a single morning on earth. He further points to the fact that there is no limit
placed on transmission of the text to those of higher attainments. (HY 87, 3:43b–
44a.)
     * These are the six two-hour periods of daylight.
     † The soteriological rituals of the Lingbao scriptures are predicated on the notion,
already apparent in the Shangqing scriptures, that each individual has a "ranking"
in the unseen world. For the Lingbao texts, though, this ranking depends on the
merit accumulated in previous lives. See Bokenkamp, "Stages of Transcendence," for
the development of these ideas.
     ‡ Yan Dong and Xue Youxi both seem to take the term lin guo ("on the verge of
passing over") as a reference to physical death, rather than to passing through the
Palace of Grand Darkness. Though this scripture was certainly recited at the death-

cloudsouls and spirits will then ascend directly to the Southern Palace, where a date will be fixed in accord with their studies and merit so that they might receive rebirth. Through cycles of birth and death they will not perish and will eventually attain the state of divine Transcendence.

The Dao said:

Whenever the cycles of heaven and earth come to their end, you should practice retreats, presenting incense and reciting this scripture. When the stars and lunar lodgings depart from their paths or the sun and moon are darkened by eclipse, you should also practice retreats, presenting incense and reciting this scripture. When the four seasons lose their measure or yin and yang are inharmonious you should also practice retreats, presenting incense and reciting this scripture. When the ruler of the kingdom meets with disaster and the rebellious take up arms in the four quarters you should also practice retreats, presenting incense and reciting this scripture. When pestilential disease spreads and mortals die or fall ill you should also practice retreats, presenting incense and reciting this scripture. When master or companion come to the ends of their lives you should also practice retreats, presenting incense and reciting this scripture. The merit of practicing retreats, keeping the precepts, and reciting this scripture is indeed great. Above, it dissolves celestial disasters and provides surety for the thearchs and kings who rule on earth; below, it drives off pestilential injuries and provides salvation for the masses. It provides a security in both life and death; its propitiousness is unequaled. This is why it is said to provide universal and limitless salvation for the people of heaven.

3:49a

---

bed (see the passages that follow), here it is more likely that "passing through" refers to the occasion of the postmortem ritual contained in the *Scripture for the Revivification of the Corpse*. This scripture calls for the inscription on a stone of that section of the *Perfected Script in Five Tablets* appropriate to the natal day of the deceased; the stone is to be interred with the body, along with ritual invocations. These invocations specifically request the postmortem fate outlined here: the corporal spirits and cloudsouls will be remanded to the Southern Palace and, after refinement, are to be returned to the body, which has meanwhile been remade in the Palace of Grand Darkness. See Bokenkamp, "Death and Ascent."

4:1a   The Dao said:

Whoever possesses this scripture is able to mobilize its powerful merit on behalf of heaven and earth, the thearchical rulers, and the masses of people. When, in times of calamity, you arouse your faith and practice retreats, burning incense and reciting this scripture ten times, your name will in all cases be recorded in the various heavens and the myriad spirits will guard you. In contradistinction to the aforementioned whose grasp of the Dao is shallow, those who excel in its study will serve as ministers of the Sage Lord in the Golden Porte.*

In recording peoples' merits and transgressions, the various heavens do not miss even the slightest event. The Demon Kings of the various heavens will also protect your body and cause you to ascend. Those who are to achieve the Dao in this way must have penetrating insight into the ultimate teachings.

[The Hidden Language of the Great Brahmā appears in the text at this point. See figure 5.]

POSTFACE 2

4:25b   The Dao said:

Above are the Illimitable Tones of the Hidden Language of the Grand Brahmā of All the Heavens. The ancient graphs were all one *zhang* square. Of old, the Heavenly Perfected Sovereign wrote out this script in earthly graphs in order to reveal the correct pronunciations. The various heavens will send down spirit kings who fly through the heavens to keep watch over the bodies and record the meritorious strivings of all those who know these pronunciations and are able to chant them during retreats.† These things will be reported back to the heavens. The myriad spirits will reverentially

---

* The Sage Lord is Lord Li, Sage of the Latter Age of the Golden Porte of Upper Clarity. (For his biography, see *HY* 442, 1a ff., in the *Purple Texts,* translated in the previous chapter.) Those who "excel in the study" have by definition achieved such merit that they will not be reborn as mortals.

† The "spirit kings who fly through the heavens" are sometimes referred to in the Lingbao texts as simply *feitian,* a common translation of *apsara,* the celestial spirits of Buddhism best known from the enchanting depictions of them found on the walls of the Dunhuang grottoes.

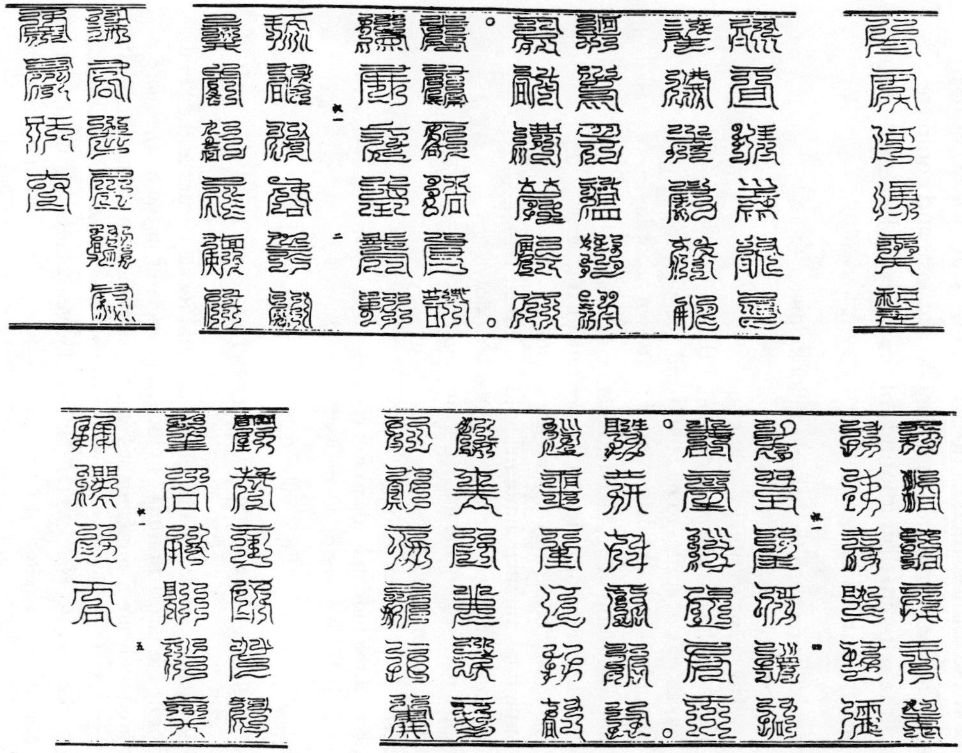

Fig. 5. The Illimitable Tones of the Hidden Language of the Grand Brahmā of All the Heavens —Composed by the Lord of the Dao: The Central Chapter of the Numinous Writings of Primordial Commencement [the first sixty-four graphs]

honor such persons; chthonic spirits will guard their households. The Demon Kings who render service to the Dao will ensure their elevation to the status of higher Transcendent. When their Dao is complete, they may roam freely throughout the Three Realms, rising to enter the golden portals.

As for these sounds, there is no evil that they do not expel and cleanse; there are no mortals that they do not save and complete. They are the self-actualizing sounds of the Celestial Perfected. As a result, chanting them causes:

4.29a

> Those who fly through the heavens to look down;
> The highest thearchs to sing afar;
> The myriad spirits to ritually honor one;
> The Three Realms to assemble on one's behalf;
> The masses of evil sprites to be bound and decapitated;
> The demonic essences to disappear of their own accord.
>
> Chiming and resounding, its reverberating echoes
> Cause all in the ten directions to be reverential and clear.
> Rivers and seas cease moving and are silent;
> The mountains and marchmounts hold back their mists.
> The myriad numinous spirits, trembling, bow down
> As it calls to assembly the massed Transcendents.
> In heaven, no miasmic vapors;
> On earth, no ill-omened dust.
> Wisdom of the hidden leads to full clarity,
> Illimitable, the mystery of mysteries!*

NOTES TO SCRIPTURE OF SALVATION: TRANSLATION

1. The pseudo-Sanskrit name of this celestial locale occurs in the "Hidden Script of the Great Brahmā" (which appears later in the text), where it is associated with the *Dengsheng* heaven, the sixth heaven of the northeast. In another text of the Lingbao canon, the *Inner Sounds and Self-Generating Graphs of the Various Heavens* (HY 97), the heavenly language of the *Scripture of Salvation* is explicated by a celestial being, the Heavenly Perfected Illustrious One. The Illustrious One explains the phrase as follows:

> Azure [*bi* 碧] auroral clouds are constantly produced in the *Dengsheng* heaven and serve to shade it. *Luo* 落 is the airborne spirit who eternally rides a chariot of

---

* "Mystery of mysteries" recalls the line "made more mysterious than the mysterious" of *Laozi* 1.

azure auroras, roaming the *Dengsheng* heaven. Three times each day he leads the assembled sages of this heaven to audience in the Palace of the Seven Treasures. *Fuli* 浮黎 is the secret name of the king of this heaven.... *Kong* 空 is the name of the attendant official whose whistle summons the spirit wind and collects the vapors. This spirit wind arrives with the sound that forms the cavernous strophes of that heaven. (*HY* 97, 4:18a)

Based on this gloss, we might roughly render the opening phrase of the *Scripture of Salvation* as follows:

The Dao said:
Of old, in the land of the Great King Fuli, realm of the Azure cloud-borne spirit *Luo* and of the songs of the spirit wind, in the midst of the Inaugural Azure Heavens, I received the *Boundless Upper Chapters of the Scripture of Salvation of Primordial Commencement.*

The term "Azure *Luo*," which lies at the heart of the phrase in question, was, however, treated somewhat differently by the Tang commentators, who rendered it "Azure Precincts." This term has a curious history of its own in Tang literature, for which see Bokenkamp, "Taoism and Literature."

2. Xue Youxi associates the nine-year period of purification in the Vermilion Palace with the fact that the number associated with the south is three and thrice three equals nine. Li Shaowei points to the fact that one of the Lingbao scriptures mentions three periods of purification before rebirth: for the greatly blessed, three years; for those with middling blessings, nine; and for those with lesser blessings, twenty-four. (See *HY* 87, 1:23a–b, and *HY* 456, 9b.4–5).

3. This paragraph does not appear in *P* 2606 or *P* 2355, the only two Dunhuang manuscripts to reproduce this passage. See Ōfuchi, *Tonkō dōkyō*, p. 53. It does, however, appear in *HY* 1 (4b–5a), *HY* 87 (1:28a), *HY* 88 (1:26a), *HY* 89 (1:28b–29a), *HY* 90 (2:25a), *HY* 91 (1:31b), and *HY* 92 (1:15a). Although Yan Dong's commentary is not reproduced in *HY* 87 for this portion of the scripture, he does cite extensively the *Sanyuan pinjie* (*HY* 456; see *HY* 87, 3a–4b), the original Lingbao scripture explanation of the days of the Three Primes. Thus it seems that this passage concerning the tenth month was original to the scripture. Indeed, it would be odd for the scripture to have mandated recitations on the first two of the Three Primes had the system not been in place when the scripture was written.

4. The Most High Lord of the Dao is identified with the Mysterious and Primordial because he appeared with the earliest formation of pneumas at creation. During the Han dynasty, the "Merit Section" was an agency of local government charged with forming labor gangs and monitoring their work. In this connection, members of this agency frequently submitted reports on the accomplishments and failures of those within their jurisdiction. (Hucker, *Dictionary of Official Titles*, p. 296.) It is likely that the Celestial Master adoption of this title for deities who oversaw the deeds of humans was based on these various functions of the government agency.

The officers of the Merit Sections within the adept's body here are associated with the Three Pneumas and the five phases. The "talisman bearers of the Five Thearchs" are those deities who attend the talismans of the Five Thearchs revealed in the Lingbao scriptures (*HY* 22, 1:35b ff.). Apparently, only those associated with the day on which the reading is to be held are summoned. The list of interior gods summoned here does differ slightly from that found in other Lingbao texts. The number of Jade Lads, Jade Maidens, and officers summoned is here thirty-two, in accord with the number of heavens visualized, rather than the thirty-six invoked in other rituals. (Compare *HY* 352, 1:16b, and *HY* 1400, 17a, as well as the even more impressive list given by Lu Xiujing in *HY* 528, 13b ff.)

5. This sentence does not appear in the *HY* 1 version of the scripture, but does appear in line 79 of *P* 2606 and *P* 2355, the only Dunhuang texts to reproduce this part of the scripture, and in *HY* 87, 1:32a. This blank is to be filled in with the names of the beneficiaries of the reading depending on the day upon which the reading is conducted. The list of appropriate days appears at *HY* 87, 1:26b–28b. The term I am translating as " to recite repeatedly" is *zhuan* 轉, a word that literally means "to turn" and that came to be used for a student's repetitions of a text.

6. The commentators agree that the three "Gates of Ease" are the gates that lead from the three realms into the highest heavens, but they differ on the identity of the "Triply Floriate" found above them. (*HY* 87, 2:12a–b.) Yan Dong, turning naturally to the Lingbao gloss of the Hidden Language, finds that there is only one mention of a celestial place name with "floriate" in the title—the Azure Floriate Gate above the Palace of the Grand Ultimate (*HY* 97, 3:11a.8–9). This, he concludes, must be the "Triply Floriate" mentioned here. Xue Youxi, apparently following the Shangqing *Scripture in Forty-nine Sections,* holds that "Triply Floriate" is another name for the Palace of the Three Primes in the heaven of Jade Clarity (*HY* 1029, 8:4b–5b). Neither of these glosses is convincing, but I have no further information that would allow us to decide between them.

7. I have not found the rhyming binom *******heng-dz'jeng* 淨霝 (pure and purged?) in other sources. Both Xue Youxi and Cheng Xuanying gloss it as "pure and cleansed." Yan Dong cites the only occurrence of the graph 霝 in the Hidden Language, where it is given as the "inner name of the spirit who oversees the heavens" (*HY* 97, 3:25b.7). See *HY* 87, 2:13a–13b, for these various glosses.

8. "Director of the Equerry" is an ancient title that once referred to the officer in charge of the empire's cavalry units and later came to be applied to various sorts of military commanders. (See Hucker, *Dictionary of Official Titles,* p. 452.) Here, the Director of the Equerry is an official of the Southern Palace under the Perfected Lord of the Southern Extremities and is charged with the life records of those who are to be refined in the Hall of Flowing Fire.

9. Lord Han has the secret name You and is the Director of Registers

of the Fengdu Palace under the Southern Palace. See *HY* 97, 3:13b.8 and 4:1b.9–10; and *HY* 369, 6a.10 ff.

10. The *Graded Precepts of the Three Primes* contains the Lingbao account of the Three Offices. Each office is divided into three palaces, with three bureaus subordinate to each palace. The "Bureau of Spring-Bend" is the lowest bureau of the Palace of Luofeng of the Northern Metropolis and thus the bottom of the hierarchy. (See *HY* 456, 18a.4–6.) The "Nine Agencies," the commentators inform us, represent the nine palaces of this system. According to Li Shaowei and Cheng Xuanying, the "Twelve River Sources" refers not to twelve separate places, but to the constellation Eastern Well (eight stars in Gemini). This is the lunar lodging that was regarded as the source of the waters of the Sky River (our Milky Way) as well as of earthly waters. The moon releases these waters twelve times a year when it passes through this constellation; hence the name. (See *HY* 87, 2:32b.8– 33a.2 and 2:36b7–37a.2; and Schafer, *Pacing the Void*, pp. 76–77.) This elaborate explanation is probably unnecessary. More likely this locution refers simply to the lower reaches of the Water Office, which in the *Graded Precepts* is referred to as controlling the "three rivers and nine torrents" (*HY* 456, 19a.8).

11. *HY* 1 gives the variant *santu* 三途, which accords with the Buddhist notion of the "three paths" of unfortunate rebirth (see endnote 12 below). Both *HY* 87, 2:39b, and *P* 2606, line 118 (missing from Ōfuchi's collated edition), give the reading *santu* 三徒. This latter reading is also found in *HY* 90, 3:28a, and *HY* 92, 2:9a, though the other canonical editions (*HY* 88, 2:17a; *HY* 89, 15b; and *HY* 91, 2:14a) accord with *HY* 1. As the reading *santu* 三徒 is the one glossed by all the pre-Tang commentators, it is likely to be the original one.

12. These terms are all adapted from Buddhism. The standard Buddhist explanations are as follows. The three paths of unfortunate rebirth (*trayo durgatayah*) are: (1) in the hells, (2) as a hungry ghost, and (3) as an animal. Buddhist notions of the "five sufferings" reflect the doctrine that all forms of existence lead to suffering (*duḥkha*). Thus the term *pañca-gati* (five karmic destinations; in Chinese, *wu dao* 五道) is also translated *wu ku* 五苦 (five sufferings). A standard list gives the five sufferings as those: (1) of the hells, (2) of hungry ghosts, (3) of animals, (4) of the demons, and (5) of humans. The "eight sorts of unfortunate rebirths" (*asāv akṣaṇāḥ*), those conditions under which it is difficult to see a Buddha or to learn the Buddhist law, are: (1) in the hells, (2) as a hungry ghost, (3) as an animal, (4) in a frontier region, (5) as a long-lived god, (6) as one born deaf, blind, or dumb, (7) as a worldly philosopher who adheres to heretical views, and (8) in the intermediate period between a Buddha and his successor. See Zürcher, "Buddhist Influence," pp. 117–18. These lists clearly overlap. Nevertheless, we do find them used together, as they are here, in translated Buddhist scripture in such formulations as "the three destinations and eight misfortunes" or "the three destinations and five sufferings." (For sources, see Mochizuki

Shinkō, *Bukkyō daijiten* [Tokyo: Sekai seiten kankō kyōkai, 1933–1936], pp. 1620c and 4222b.)

All of these elements present in Buddhist texts are found in the Lingbao texts as well, with the exception of "rebirth as a god," this being, in Daoism, an indisputably favorable outcome. Specific explanations of these terms, though difficult to locate in the Lingbao scriptures as they have come down to us, seem all to present Daoist understandings only loosely based on the Buddhist terms. The *ba nan* 八難 (Eight Difficulties or, more accurately, "difficult things"), are listed in the Lingbao *Instructions from the Self-Generated Scripture* as (1) to be reborn human and male; (2) to be reborn with wisdom, health, and wholeness; (3) to be reborn in a kingdom possessed of the Dao; (4) to be reborn poor, yet able to give to others; (5) to be reborn rich and honored, yet able to revere the Dao; (6) to be reborn able to help others to reach transcendence; (7) to be reborn with the opportunity to encounter the three caverns of scriptures; and (8) to be reborn able to receive the direct teachings of transcendents, sages, and the Perfected. See *HY* 1130, 7:4b–5b, and *P* 2356, lines 40–52; also, for a Shangqing list of "nine difficulties" that varies slightly from this one, see *HY* 1010, 6:6b.6–7a.2.

For the other two terms, we must now rely on the commentaries to the *Scripture of Salvation*. For instance, the *Major Precepts from the Upper Chapters of Wisdom* contains the following passage: "[T]hey die and enter the earth-prisons ... where they are made to [1] embrace (red-hot) bronze pillars, [2] tread mountains of swords, [3] step on trees of knives, [4] enter boiling cauldrons, or [5] swallow fire and coals, so that the five sufferings are all complete" (*HY* 457, 1:7b). Although it is not made explicit that this was meant to be a list of the "five sufferings" (*wu ku* 五苦), both Pan Shizheng 潘師正 (585–684) and Li Shaowei take it as such. Yan Dong presents another list, equally based on specific sufferings in the earth-prisons. (See *HY* 87, 1:7b.4–9 and 2:40a–41b). The *san tu* 三徒 (three kinds of servitude) are given equally Daoist explanations. (See endnote 14 below.) The Buddhist term "three evil paths [of rebirth]" 三途 does appear in the writings of Yang Xi, where Tao Hongjing glosses it as meaning rebirth among birds, beasts, or domestic animals, leaving out rebirth as a hungry ghost or in the hells (*HY* 1010, 6:6b).

13. The commentators are divided on how this passage fits in with the rest of the text. Since it rhymes with the preceding passage but lacks the four-four prosody, it appears that two graphs might be missing before 天帝. But, as all of the exemplars that contain this portion of the text record it in the same fashion, this must remain a hypothesis.

14. The "three evils" (*san e* 三惡) refer to the "three kinds of servitude" introduced earlier. Yan Dong associates them with the "three worms" or "three cadavers" that were held to inhabit the human body, desiring only the death of their host. These manifest their presence in the desires for "form" (*se* 色, "sex"?), "love," and "greed" (*HY* 87, 2:40a and 2:58b). As

the three evils are associated here with the "earthen roots," those transgressions from this and previous lives that cause one to end up in the earth-prisons, this seems the best explanation. Both Xue Youxi and Li Shaowei think that the three evils are types of service in the earth-prisons, but differ on the details. For Xue, they consist of: (1) laboring in eternal darkness, (2) laboring in the cold [earth-prisons], and (3) transporting stones; whereas Li holds that they consist of: (1) managing lightning and thunder for the heavenly offices, (2) moving mountains and carrying stones for the earth offices, and (3) producing tides and waves for the water offices (*HY* 87, 2:41b).

15. The five dippers mentioned here are not separate asterisms, but five stars of the Big Dipper, with the following Daoist names: Eastern Dipper, Dubhe (no. 1 Yang Luminosity); Southern Dipper, Merak (no. 2 Yin Embryo); Western Dipper, Alioth (no. 5 Cinnabar Prime); Northern Dipper, Mizar (no. 6 Northern Extremity); and Central Dipper, Alkaid (no. 7 Heaven's Bar). On these names and identifications, see Schafer, *Pacing the Void*, pp. 50–51. Heaven's Bar, the star at the end of the Dipper "handle," is here referred to as *da kui* 大魁, the "Great Head," a term that usually refers to the first four stars of the Dipper "bowl." The "Five Dippers" figured as well in Shangqing meditation practice. (See Robinet, *Méditation taoïste*, pp. 194–95; and Robinet, *La révélation du Shangqing*, vol. 2, pp. 300–301.) It does not seem to be the case, though, that the identification of five important stars in the Dipper began with the Shangqing texts. The *Nüqing guilü*, an early Celestial Master demonography, also contains a list of the "killing demons" associated with the Five Dippers. (See *HY* 789, 1:2a.) Although the demon names given in *HY* 789 differ from those provided in this text, the contexts are similar enough to lead us to suspect a Celestial Master origin for this concept. Later commentators tended to reject this early belief. Li Shaowei, for instance, regards the "dippers" of the four cardinal directions as the seven lunar lodgings of each direction, with the Big Dipper as the "Central Dipper." I have found no support for Li's identification in the early Lingbao texts.

16. The translation of these names is based on Yan Dong's description of their appearance and powers, where these elucidate the secret names. For instance, Yan reveals that the Serpent-Primordial Evil Earl was born in the same era as the Celestial Worthy of Primordial Commencement and is in charge of all the demons of the Three Realms. Yan also gives alternate names for each of the Demon Kings. (*HY* 87, 2:63b–64b.)

17. Strangely, Yan Dong takes this as yet another category of demon king—the Demon Kings of the Five Thearchs. Here I follow Xue Youxi's gloss (*HY* 87, 2:65a–b).

18. On "fiery folly bells of flowing metal" see Robinet, *La révélation du Shangqing*, vol. 1, p. 235.

19. The term here translated "we" is *a ren* 阿人, which I have not found attested in any other source. Yan Dong provides the explanation that *a ren*

is a term by which the Demon Kings refer to themselves collectively. Presumably this parallels the southern usage of the Jin period by which *a* became a familiar prefix attached to familial terms. See, for instance, the terms *a nu* and *a weng* used to refer to the younger members of one's family and one's grandfather, respectively. (Xu Zhen'e, *Shishuo xinyu jiaojian* (Beijing: Zhonghua shuju, 1984), vol. 2, pp. 502–3.)

Abbreviations

Huang Hui et al. 4 vols. Rev. ed. Beijing: Zhonghua shuju, 1990.

MIHEC   Mémoires de l'Institut des Hautes Études Chinoises, Collège de France

MS   *Monumenta Serica*

P   Pelliot Collection, Dunhuang manuscripts housed in the Bibliothéque Nationale, reproduced in Ōfuchi 1978 and Ōfuchi 1979

PEFEO   Publications de l'Ecole Française d'Extrême-Orient, Paris

QSGSD   *Quan shanggu sandai Qin Han San guo liu chao wen.* Edited by Yan Kejun (1762–1843). 5 vols. Taipei: Hongye, 1975.

S   Stein Collection, Dunhuang manuscripts housed in the British Museum, reproduced in Ōfuchi 1978 and Ōfuchi 1979

SBBY   *Sibu beiyao.* Shanghai: Zhonghua shuju, 1927–1935.

SHDQMZJ *Shuihudi Qin mu zhujian*

SSJZS   *Shisan jing zhushu.* Edited by Ruan Yuan (1764–1849). 2 vols. Beijing: Zhonghua shuju, 1980.

T   *Taishō shinshū daizōkyō.* Edited by Takakusa Junjirō and Watanabe Kaikyoku. Tokyo: Daizōkyōkai, 1924–1935.

TP   *T'oung Pao*

TR   *Taoist Resources*

ZZJC   *Zhuzi jicheng.* Beijing: Shijie shuju, 1954. Reprint, Beijing: Zhonghua shuju, 1957.

Glossary of Chinese Characters

Aqiu Zeng 阿丘曾
bafang 八方
Bai Luzhong 白履忠
bajiang 八將
Bao Chang 寶唱
Baowei 豹尾
baoyi 抱一
Bencao gangmu 本草綱目
benming 本命
Biluo kongge dafuli 碧落空歌大
   福黎
Biqiuni zhuan 比丘尼傳
Bo Ya 伯牙
buci 哺次
cang (green) 蒼
cang (storehouse) 倉
Canglin 蒼林
cangling 倉靈
Cao Cao 曹澡
Cao Fang 曹芳
Cao Huan 曹奐
Cao Mao 曹髦
Cao Rui 曹叡
Cao Shuang 曹爽
Cao Yu 曹宇
Chan 禪
Chang'an 長安

chen 辰
Chen Jingyuan 陳景元
cheng 丞
Cheng Xuanying 成玄英
chengfu 承負
Chijing zi 赤精子
chimei 螭魅
Chiming 赤明
Chiyou 蚩尤
chizi 赤子
chu guan 出官
Chu 楚
Chuci 楚辭
chun shu jin 淳屬金
Chunqiu 春秋
cunjian 存見
cunsi 存思
da (great) 大
Da zhong song zhang 大塚訟章
Dacheng zi 大成子
Dachun 大椿
Dadao jialingjie 大道家令戒
Dan, Boyang (names of Laozi)
   聃，伯陽
Dao 道
Daode jing 道德經
daojiao 道教

de 德
De, Bowen (names of Laozi)
　德，伯文
Dengsheng 騰勝
Di (peoples) 氐
Di (Thearch) 帝
Dianlüe 典略
ding 丁
Diwang shiji 帝王世紀
diyu 地獄
dong 洞
Dongfang Shuo 東方朔
Donghai 東海
du (salvation) 度
Dunhuang 敦煌
dunjia 遁甲
e (repellant) 惡
er 爾
er qian shi 二千石
fan (Brahmā) 梵
fan (model) 範
fan tu jin 犯土禁
Fan Li 范蠡
fangliang 方良
fangshi 方士
fangxiang (shi) 方相 [士]
Fangzhu 方諸
Fanmei 梵湄
fanqi 梵氣
fei lei 非類
feitian 飛天
fen (divisions) 分
fen yan ying 芬豔嬰
Feng Hou 風后
Fengdu 酆都
Fu Xi 伏羲
Fuli 福黎
Fusang 扶桑
Gan Ji (var: Yu Ji) 干吉，于吉
Gao Qiuzi 高丘子
Ge Chaofu 葛巢甫
Ge Hong 葛洪
Ge Xuan 葛玄
Gong Chong 宮崇
gongcao shizhe 功曹使者

Gongzi 龔子
gu (valley) 谷
Guangcheng zi 廣成子
Guangshou zi 廣壽子
gui (faith offering) 脆
gui (revenant, demon) 鬼
Guigu zi 鬼谷子
guizhu 鬼注
guizu 鬼卒
Guoyu 國語
Han (Divine Lord) 韓
Han (dynasty) 漢
Han shu 漢書
Han Wu Di neizhuan 漢武帝內傳
Hanzhong 漢中
Haoli 蒿里
heqi 合氣
Heshang Gong 河上公
Hong, Jiuyang (names of Laozi)
　弘，九陽
Hong (yuan) 弘
Hongfan 鴻範
Hongyai 洪涯
hou sheng 後聖
Hou (Marksman) 侯
Hou Han shu 後漢書
hu (tablet) 笏
Hu (peoples) 胡
hua gai 華蓋
huahu 化胡
Huainan zi 淮南子
Huang Di 黃帝
Huang fan 黃幡
Huangjin 黃巾
Huangting jing 黃庭經
Huayang guozhi 華陽國志
hui jin xia 迴金霞
hun 魂
huo you wei 貨有為
ji (initiatory mechanism) 機
ji (marks) 紀
jia 甲
jianchu 建除
Jiankang 建康
jie (admonish, admonishment) 誡

jie (precepts) 戒
jie (release, dispersion) 解
jin (prohibitions) 禁
Jin (dynasty) 晉
jing (essence) 精
jing (reverence) 敬
jing (scripture) 經
Jingdian shiwen 經典釋文
jingshe 靜舍
jingshi 靜室／靖室
jinji 禁忌
jiong ding rong 炅定容
jiu (nine) 九
Ju Rong 祝融
juan (chapters, scrolls) 卷
jueqi 決氣
Jurong (county) 句容
Kaihuang 開皇
kao 考
Kong 孔
kongdong 空洞
Kou Qianzhi 寇謙之
Ku 嚳
kui 魁
kun (earth hexagram) 昆
Kunlun 崑崙
la 臘
lai yi 來儀
langfeng 閬風
langgan 琅玕
Langye 琅邪
Langzhong 閬中
Laozi 老子
Laozi Xiang'er zhu 老子想爾注
li 里
li (profit/keen) 利
Li (surname) 李
Li Hong 李弘
Li Shaowei 李少微
Li Wei 李微
Liexian zhuan 列仙傳
lin guo 臨過
ling 令
Lingbao 靈寶
lingjue 領決

Lingshu ziwen 靈書紫文
Lisao 離騷
Liu Ao 劉媼
Liu Bang 劉邦
Liu Che 劉徹
Liu Xiu 劉秀
Liu Yu 劉裕
Liu Zhang 劉璋
Liu Zhuang 劉莊
Liu-Song (dynasty) 劉宋
liudui 六對
Liujing Shan 六景山
liutian guqi 六天故氣
Long (county) 隴
Long'an (reign period) 隆安
Longhan 龍漢
Lu 魯
lu hong ying 綠虹映
Lu Ji 陸機
Lu Xiujing 陸修靜
Lu Yun 陸雲
Lü Wang [Shang] 呂望 [尚]
Lun Heng 論衡
Luo (River) 洛
Luofeng Shan 羅酆山
Luoshu 洛書
Luoyang 洛陽
Lutu zi 錄圖子
Ma Mingsheng 馬明生
Mang Shan 邙山
Mao (brothers) 茅
Mao Ying 茅盈
Mawangdui 馬王堆
mei (beauty) 美
mei (goblin) 魅
Meng Shan 蒙山
miedu 滅度
Mijia 彌加
mingmi 命米
mingtang sandao 明堂三道
Mo Di 墨翟
Mu bo 墓伯
mu chen jian po 墓辰建破
nai he 奈何
Naihe (River Nai) 奈河

ni zhu 逆注
niwan 泥丸
Nü Wa 女娃
Nuo 儺
Nüqing 女青
Pan'gu 盤古
Pei (Divine Lord) 裴
Pei (placename) 沛
Peng (Divine Lord) 彭
pian 篇
piao hui xiang 飆暉象
Pingdu 平都
piqi 被氣
po 魄
qi (implement, vessel) 器
qi (pneuma) 氣
Qi 齊
Qiang (peoples) 羌
Qin (dynasty) 秦
qing (lightness) 輕
qing (to incline) 傾
qing guan 請官
Qingcheng Shan 青城山
qingjing 清靜
Qingmiao 清妙
Qingming 清明
qingshe 清舍
qitou 魁頭
Qiu cheng 丘丞
Qiu Longma 求龍馬
Quting 渠亭
ren (benevolence) 仁
ren (person) 人
Ren Yanqing 任廷慶
renxin ziyi 任心恣意
Rong (peoples) 戎
Rongcheng 容成
ruo 若
Sanguo zhi 三國志
Sanhuang 三皇
Sanhuang wen 三皇文
Santian neijie jing 三天內解經
Santian zhengfa jing 三天正法經
sha (killers) 殺
shan 善

Shang (dynasty) 商
Shang shu 尚書
Shangdang 上黨
Shangqing 上清
shanxing 善行
Shanyuan 山淵
shen (spirit) 神
shen (urogenital vesicle) 腎
Shen Nong 神農
Shenxian zhuan 神仙傳
shi (corpses) 尸
shi (inaugural) 始
Shi 詩
Shiji 史記
Shizhou ji 十洲記
shouyi 守一
Shu 書
shuiguan 水官
Shun 舜
Sichuan 四川
Sima Jizhu 司馬季主
Sima Shi 司馬師
Sima Yi 司馬懿
Sishui 泗水
Song (dynasty) 宋
Song shu 宋書
suan (count) 算
Sui po 歲破
Sui sha 歲殺
Sui xing 歲星
Sun 孫
Sun En 孫恩
Sunü jing 素女經
Suwen 素文
Tai Shan 泰山
Tai yi 太一
Tai Yin 太陰
taiji 太極
Taiping dao 太平道
Taiping jing 太平經
Taiping qingling shu 太平清領書
Taiqing 太清
taishang dongxuan 太上洞玄
Taishang 太上
Taisui 太歲

Taixuan 太玄
Tang 唐
Tao Hongjing 陶弘景
Tao Kedou 陶科斗
tiancao 天曹
Tianshi dao 天師道
Tianzhu 天竺
ting zhang 亭長
tu jiu 土咎
tu shen 土神
tuyang 土殃
waishuo 外說
Wang Bao 王褒
Wang Bi 王弼
Wang Chang 王長
Wang Chong 王充
Wang Fangping 王方平
Wang Mang 王莽
Wang Yuan [Fangping] 王遠
wangliang 魍魎
Wangwu Shan 王屋山
wangxiang (demon) 魍象
wangxiang (divination system) 王相
wei (artificial, fabricated) 偽
wei (fear, awe) 畏
wei (to act) 為
Wei (kingdom) 魏
Wei Huacun 魏華存
wen 文
wo (I, me) 我
wu (five) 五
wu (me, my) 吾
wu (shaman, medium) 巫
Wu Ding (king) 武丁
Wu Zhao 武曌
Wucheng zi 務成子
wugu 巫蠱
Wuliang duren shangpin miaojing 無量度人上品妙經
wuwei 無為
Wuyi 武夷
Xi Zhong 奚仲
Xia (dynasty) 夏
xian (transcendent) 仙

Xian, Yuansheng (names of Laozi) 顯，元生
xiang (images) 象
xiang'er 想爾
xianshi 仙士
xiao 霄
Xiaoyou 小有
xie 邪
xie (tower) 榭
Xie Lingyun 謝靈運
xin 信
xing 行
xingnian 行年
Xinye (commandary) 新野
Xiongnu 匈奴
Xiuruo 脩柔
Xize zi 錫則子
xu (preface/postface) 序
Xu Chao 許朝
Xu Hui 許翽
Xu Lingqi 徐靈期
Xu Mi 許謐
xuan lu yan 玄綠炎
xuan nü 玄女
xuan wu 玄武
Xuanshui 玄水
Xuanxu 玄虛
Xuanzhou 玄洲
Xue Youxi 薛幽棲
Xun Zhonghou 荀中侯
xungu 訓詁
yan gong 言功
Yan Dong 嚴東
Yan Menzi 衍門子
yang 陽
yang (harmers) 殃
Yang Xi 楊羲
Yankang 延康
Yao 堯
yayin 雅音
Ye 鄴
yi (responsibility) 義
Yi (peoples) 夷
Yijing 易經
yin 陰

Yin 殷
Yin Changsheng 尹長生
Yin Xi 尹喜
Ying Shao 應邵
Ying Zheng 嬴政
Yinshou zi 尹壽子
Yiqian guan 易遷館
yishe 義舍
you 有
You (king) 幽
yu (desire) 欲
Yu 禹
yu lian hua 鬱連華
yuan yan xu 宛廷虛
Yuan, Boshi (names of Laozi)
  元，伯始
yuanqi 元氣
Yuanshi 元始
yuanyou 遠遊
Yue 越
Yuhua zi 鬱華子
yupei jindang 玉珮金璫
Yuqing 玉清
zhai 齋
Zhai, Bochang (names of Laozi)
  宅，伯長
zhang (chapters) 章
Zhang Daoling 張道陵
Zhang Heng 張衡
Zhang Huanzhi 張煥之
Zhang Jue 張角
Zhang Liang 張良
Zhang Ling 張陵
Zhang Lu 張魯
Zhang Shujing 張叔敬
Zhang Wanfu 張萬福
Zhang Xiu 張脩
zhao long dao 照龍韜

Zhao hun 招魂
Zhao Sheng 趙生
zhen mu wen 鎮墓文
zheng 正
Zheng Xuan 鄭玄
zhengfa 正法
Zhengyang 正陽
Zhengyi 正一
zhenren 真人
Zhenxing zi 真行子
zhi 治
Zhi Qian 支謙
zhihui 智慧
zhiyi 執一
zhong (weightiness) 重
Zhong, Boguang (names of Laozi)
  中，伯光
Zhong Shan 中山
Zhong Ziqi 鍾子期
Zhong, Ziwen (names of Laozi)
  重，子文
zhonghe zhi qi 中和之氣
zhongmin 種民
Zhou (dynasty) 周
Zhou (last ruler of Shang dynasty)
  紂
Zhou Ziyang 周紫陽
Zhu Daosheng 竺道生
zhuan 轉
zhuangzhi 狀紙
Zhuangzi 莊子
Zhuanxu 顓頊
Ziguang 子光
ziran 自然
zong (footsteps) 蹤
zong (give free rein to) 縱
zou zhang 奏章
Zou Yan 騶衍

Works Cited

WORKS IN THE DAOIST CANON
(LISTED BY *HY* NUMBER)

1   *Lingbao wuliang duren shangpin miaojing* 靈寶無量度人上品妙經
    [Wondrous Scripture of the Upper Chapters on the Limitless
    Salvation of Lingbao], *LB* 15.

22 *Yuanshi wulao chishu yu* [=*wu*] *pian zhenwen* 元始五老赤書玉(＝
    五)篇真文天書經 [Perfected Script of the Five Ancients of Pri-
    mordial Commencement in Five Tablets, Written in Red],
    LB 1.

23 *Taishang zhutian lingshu duming miaojing* 太上諸天靈書度命妙經
    [Wondrous Scripture of Salvation in the Numinous Writing
    of the Various Heavens], *LB* 16.

56 *Taishang yupei jindang taiji jinshu shangjing* 太上玉珮金璫太極金書
    上經.

83 *Baiyu heihe ling* [var. *long*] *fei yufu* 白羽黑翮靈(龍)飛玉符 [Talisman
    of White Wings and Black Pinions for Dragon Flight].

87 *Yuanshi wuliang duren shangpin miaojing sizhu* 元始無量度人上品
    妙經四註 [Four Commentaries on the Scripture of Salvation],
    compiled by Chen Jingyuan 陳景元 (1025–1094).

88 *Yuanshi wuliang duren shangpin miaojing zhu* 元始無量度人上品妙
    經註 [Commentary on the Scripture of Salvation], composed
    c. 1204?

89 *Yuanshi wuliang duren shangpin miaojing tongyi* 元始無量度人上
    品妙經通義 [Comprehensive Significance of the Scripture of
    Salvation].

90 *Yuanshi wuliang duren shangpin miaojing neiyi* 元始無量度人上品

妙經內義 [Inner Signifigance of the Scripture of Salvation], early thirteenth century.

91 *Taishang dongxuan lingbao wuliang duren shangpin miaojing zhu* 太上洞玄靈寶無量度人上品妙經註 [Commentary on the Scripture of Salvation], by Chen Zhixu 陳致虛 (fl. 1329–1336).

92 *Yuanshi wuliang duren shangpin miaojing zhu* 元始無量度人上品妙經註 [Commentary on the Scripture of Salvation], by Xue Jizhao 薛季昭 (fl. 1304–1316).

95 *Dongxuan lingbao wuliang duren jing jue yin yi* 洞玄靈寶無量度人經訣音義 [Instructions, Sound Glosses, and Meanings for the Scripture of Salvation], by Zhang Wanfu 張萬福 (fl. 710).

97 *Taishang lingbao zhutian neiyin ziran yuzi* 太上靈寶諸天內音自然玉字 [Inner Sounds and Self-Generating Graphs of the Various Heavens], *LB* 7.

140 *Shangqing wozhong jue* 上清握中訣 [Shangqing Instructions for Grasping It in One's Palm].

177 *Taishang dongzhen zhihui shangpin dajie* 太上洞真智慧上品大誡 [Great Precepts from the Upper Chapters of Wisdom], *LB* 9.

179 *Taiwei lingshu ziwen xianji zhenji shangjing* 太微靈書紫文仙忌真記上經 [Supreme Scripture on Taboos for Transcendents Recorded by the Perfected, from the Purple Texts Inscribed by the Spirits of Grand Tenuity].

184 *Taizhen yudi siji mingzhen ke* 太真玉帝四極明真料.

188 *Xuandu lwen* 玄都律文.

219 *Lingbao wuliang duren jing shangfa* 靈寶無量度人經大法 [Great Rites of the Lingbao Scripture of Limitless Salvation].

255 *Taiwei lingshu ziwen langgan huadan shenzhen shangjing* 太微靈書紫文琅玕華丹神真上經 [Supreme Scripture on the Elixir of Langgan Efflorescence, from the Purple Texts Inscribed by the Spirits of Grand Tenuity].

263 *Xiuzhen shishu* 修真十書 [Ten Writings on Cultivating Perfection], a late-thirteenth-century compilation?

292 *Han Wudi neizhuan* 漢武帝內傳 [Inner Traditions of the Martial Thearch of the Han].

296 *Lishi zhen xian tidao tongjian* 歷世真仙體道通鑑 [A Comprehensive Mirror on Successive Generations of Perfected, Transcendents, and Those Who Embody the Dao], by Zhao Daoyi 趙道一 (fl. 1294–1307).

300 *Huayang Tao yinju neizhuan* 華陽陶隱居內傳 [Intimate Biography of Tao Hongjing, the Retired Master of Huayang, the Cavern-Heaven of Mao Shan], by Jia Song 賈嵩 (Tang period).

303 *Ziyang zhenren neizhuan* 紫陽真人內傳 [Intimate Biography of the Perfected of Purple Yang], fourth century.

318 *Dongxuan lingbao ziran jiutian shengshen zhang jing* 洞玄靈寶自然

九天生神玉章經 [Stanzas of the Vitalizing Spirits of the Nine Heavens], *LB* 5.

335 *Taishang dongyuan shenzhou jing* 太上洞淵神咒經 [Scripture of Spiritual Spells for Penetrating the Abyss].

352 *Taishang dongxuan lingbao chishu yujue miaojing* 太上洞玄靈寶赤書玉訣妙經 [Jade Instructions on the Red Writings], *LB* 2.

369 *Taishang dongxuan lingbao miedu wulian shengshi miaojing* 太上洞玄靈寶滅度五鍊生尸妙經 [Salvation through Extinction: Refinement of the Five (Spirits) for Revivifying the Corpse], *LB* 17.

388 *Taishang lingbao wufu xu* 太上靈寶五符序 [Five Talismans of Lingbao, with Preface], early third century.

421 *Dengzhen yinjue* 登真隱訣 [Concealed Instructions for the Ascent to Perfection], compiled and annotated by Tao Hongjing.

425 *Shangqing taiji yinzhu yujing baojue* 上清太極隱注玉經寶訣 [Concealed Commentary and Treasured Instructions of the (Perfected) of the Grand Bourne], *LB* 21.

427 *Shangqing xiuxing jingjue* 上清修行經訣 [Shangqing Scriptures and Instructions on Practice].

435 *Taishang yuchen yuyi jielin benriyue tu* 太上玉晨鬱儀結璘奔日月圖.

442 *Shangqing housheng daojun lieji* 上清後聖道君列紀 [Annals of the Lord of the Dao, Sage of the Latter (Heavens) of Shangqing].

455 *Taishang xuanyi zhenren shuo santu wuku quanjie jing* 太上玄一真人説三途五苦勸誡經 [Admonitory Scripture on the Three Paths and the Five Sufferings Pronounced by the Most High Perfected of Mysterious Unity], part of *LB* 14.

456 *Taishang dongxuan lingbao sanyuan pinjie gongde qingzhong jing* 太上洞玄靈寶三元品誡功德輕重經 [Lingbao Scripture on the Assessed Merit of the Graded Precepts of the Three Primes], *LB* 18.

457 *Taishang dongxuan lingbao zhihui zuigen shangpin dajie jing* 太上洞玄靈寶智慧罪根上品大誡經 [Major Precepts from the Upper Chapters of Wisdom], *LB* 8.

463 *Yaoxiu keyi jielü chao* 要修科儀戒律鈔 [Transcribed Codes, Practices, Precepts, and Rules Vital for Practice].

524 *Dongxuan lingbao zhaishuo guangzhu jiefa dengzhou yuan yi* 洞玄靈寶齋説光燭戒罰燈祝願儀 [Explanation of Lingbao Retreats: Dharma Lamps, Regulations, Penalties, and Vows], by Lu Xiujing.

528 *Taishang dongxuan lingbao shoudu yi* 太上洞玄靈寶授度儀 [Initiation Rites of Lingbao], compiled by Lu Xiujing 陸修靜.

596 *Xianyuan bianzhu* 仙苑編珠 [Strung Pearls from the Garden of Transcendence], by Wang Songnian 王松年 (fl. 920).

599 *Dongtian fudi yuedu mingshan ji* 洞天福地嶽瀆名山記 [Record of Cavern-Heavens, Holy Spots, Marchmounts, Rivers, and

Famous Mountains], compiled by Du Guangting 杜光庭 (850–933).

614 *Dongxuan lingbao shengxuan buxu zhang xushu* 洞玄靈寶昇玄步虛章序疏 [Preface and Explanations on the Lingbao Stanzas on Ascending to the Mysterious and Pacing the Void].

615 *Chisong zi zhang li* 赤松子章歷 [Master Redpine's Almanac of Petitions].

639 *Huangtian shangqing jinque dijun lingshu ziwen shangjing* 皇天上清金闕帝君靈書紫文上經 [Upper Scripture of Purple Texts Inscribed by the Spirits of the Thearch, Lord of the Golden Porte, of Shangqing].

679 *Tang Xuanzong yuchi daode zhenjing shu* 唐玄宗御製道德真經疏 [Glosses on the Scripture of the Dao and Its Potencies, Ordered by Li Longji, the Xuanzong Emperor of the Tang].

682 *Daode zhenjing zhu* 道德真經註.

725 *Daode zhenjing guangsheng yi* 道德真經廣聖義.

769 *Hunyuan shengji* 混元聖紀 [A Chronicle of the Sage from Primordial Chaos], compiled by Xie Shouhao 謝守灝 (1134–1212).

773 *Youlong zhuan* 猶龍傳 [Traditions Concerning "He Who Is Like a Dragon" (i.e., Laozi)], by Jia Shanxiang 賈善翔 (fl. 1086).

785 *Taishang Laojun jinglü* 太上老君經律 [Scriptures and Rules of the Most High Lord Lao].

786 *Taishang jingjie* 太上經戒 [Precepts from the Scriptures of the Most High].

788 *Zhengyi fawen tianshi jiao jie ke jing* 正一法文天師教戒科經 [Scripture of Precepts and Codes Taught by the Celestial Master, from the Texts of the Law of Correct Unity].

789 *Nüqing guilü* 女青鬼律 [Demon Statutes of Nüqing].

794 *Zhengyi chuguan zhang yi* 正一出官章儀 [Correct Unity Rites and Petitions for "Issuing the Officers"].

797 *Zhengyi zhijiao zhai yi* 正一指教齋儀 [Correct Unity Ritual of the Instructional Retreat].

798 *Zhengyi zhijiao zhai qingdan xingdao yi* 正一指教齋清旦行道儀 [Dawn Practices for the Instructional Retreat of Correct Unity].

807 *Taishang sandong chuanshou daode jing zixu lu baibiao yi* 太上三洞傳授道德經紫虛籙拜表儀, compiled by Du Guangting.

836 *Zhenzhong ji* 枕中記 [A Pillow Book].

879 *Taiqing jinye shendan jing* 太清金液神丹經 [Taiqing Scripture of the Divine Elixir of the Golden Liquor].

880 *Taiqing shibi ji* 太清石壁記 [Records from the Stone Wall on Great Purity].

882 *Taiqing jing tianshi koujue* 太清經天師口訣 [Oral Instructions of the Celestial Master on the Scripture of Great Purity].

900   *Shiyao erya* 石藥爾雅 [Synonymic Dictionary of Materia Medica], by Mei Biao 梅彪, preface dated 806.

1010   *Zhen'gao* 真誥 [Declarations of the Perfected], compiled and annotated by Tao Hongjing 陶弘景.

1025   *Shan hai jing* 山海經 [Scripture of Mountains and Seas].

1026   *Yunji qiqian* 雲笈七籤 [Seven Slips from the Bookcases in the Clouds], by Zhang Junfang 張君房 et al., completed c. 1030.

1027   *Zhiyan zong* 至言總.

1029   *Daoti lun* 道體論 [Treatise on the Body of the Dao], by Sima Chengzhen 司馬承禎 (647–735).

1119   *Lu xiansheng Daomen kelue* 陸先生道門科略 [Prior-Born Lu's Codes for Initiates, Abridged], from a work by Lu Xiujing.

1121   *Daojiao yishu* 道教義樞 [Pivot of Meaning for Teachings of the Dao], compiled by Meng Anpai 孟安排 (fl. c. 700).

1122   *Daodian lun* 道典論 [Treatise on Daoist Institutes], early Tang.

1130   *Wushang biyao* 無上秘要 [Supreme Secret Essentials], completed c. 580.

1131   *Sandong zhunang* 三洞珠囊 [Pearl Book Bags of the Three Caverns], compiled by Wang Xuanhe 王懸河 (fl. 666–683).

1160   *Taishang laojun zhong jing* 太上老君中經 [Central Scripture of the Most High Lord Lao].

1177   *Baopu zi neipian* 抱朴子內篇 [Inner Chapters of the Book of the Master Who Embraces Simplicity]; see under "Asian-Language Sources" below.

1196   *Santian neijie jing* 三天內解經 [Scripture of the Inner Explanations of the Three Heavens].

1208   *Zhengyi fawen jing zhang guan pin* 正一法文經章官品 [Scripture of the Law of Correct Unity: Section on Petitions and (Celestial) Officials].

1228   *Chuanshou jingjie yi zhujue* 傳授經戒儀注訣 [Rites for the Transmission of Scriptures and Precepts, Annotated].

1238   *Sandong qunxian lu* 三洞羣仙錄 [Records of the Hosts of Transcendents from the Three Caverns], compiled by Chen Baoguang 陳寶光 in 1154.

1263   *Zhengyi tianshi gao Zhao Sheng koujue* 正一天師告趙昇口訣 [Oral Instructions to Zhao Sheng from the Celestial Master of Correct Unity].

1268   *Dongxuan lingbao wu gan wen* 洞玄靈寶五感文 [Five Confessionals], by Lu Xiujing 陸修靜.

1284   *Shangqing huangshu guodu yi* 上清黃書過渡儀 [Ritual for Initiation from the Yellow Writings].

1304   *Dongzhen shangqing qingyao zishu jingen zhongjing* 洞真上清青要紫書金根眾經.

1312   *Dongzhen taishang basu zhenjing fushi riyue huanghua jue* 洞真太上八素真經服食日月皇華訣.

1315 *Dongzhen shangqing longfei jiudao chisu yinjue* 洞真上清龍飛九道尺素隱訣.

1318 *Taishang jiuchi banfu wudi neizhen jing* 太上九赤班符五帝內真經.

1319 *Dongzhen taiyi dijun taidan yinshu dongzhen xuanjing* 洞真太乙帝君太丹隱書洞真玄經.

1320 *Dongzhen shangqing shenzhou qizhuan qibian wutian jing* 洞真上清神州七轉七變舞天經.

1341 *Dongzhen taishang taoxiao langshu* 洞真太上太霄琅書.

1361 *Shangqing gaoshang yuchen fengtai qusu shangjing* 上清高上玉晨鳳臺曲素上經.

1365 *Shangqing taishang dijun jiuzhen zhong jing* 上清太上帝君九真中經 [Central Scripture of the Nine Perfected of the Most High Lord of Shangqing].

1366 *Shangqing taishang jiuzhen zhongjing xiangsheng shendan jue* 上清太上九真中經降生神丹訣.

1374 *Shangqing dongzhen tianbao dadong sanjing baolu* 上清洞真天寶大洞三景寶籙.

1393 *Shangqing taiji zhenren shenxian jing* 上清太極真人神仙經.

1396 *Dongxuan lingbao ershisi shengtu jing* 洞玄靈寶二十四生圖經 [Twenty-Four Life-Bestowing Charts], *LB* 19.

1400 *Dongxuan lingbao changye zhi fu jiuyou yugui mingzhen ke* 洞玄靈寶長夜之府九幽玉匱明真科 [Ordinances of the Luminous Perfected on the Bureaus of Enduring Night and the Nine Tenebrous Regions from the Jade Caskets], *LB* 11.

1427 *Dongxuan lingbao yujing shan buxu zhang* 洞玄靈寶玉京山步虛經 [Stanzas on Pacing the Void around Jade Capitoline Mountain], *LB* 4.

ASIAN-LANGUAGE SOURCES

Baopu zi neipian. By Ge Hong (283–343). Completed c. 317. In ZZJC.

CHEN Guofu

1963 *Daozang yuanliu kao.* Peking: Zhonghua shuju.

1983 *Daozang yuanliu xu kao.* Taipei: Mingwen shuju.

CHEN Shixiang

1957 "*Xiang'er* Laozi daojing Dunhuang canjuan lunzheng." *Ts'ing Hua Journal of Chinese Studies,* n.s., 1.2:41–62.

CHEN Yinke

1974 "Tianshi dao yu binhai diyu zhi guanxi." In *Chen Yinke xiansheng lunwen ji,* vol. 1, pp. 1–40. Beijing: Sanrenxing chubanshe.

DUAN Chengshi (c. 800–863)

Youyang zazu. In *Zhongguo shixue congshu,* vol. 35. Reprint of edition with 1608 preface. Taipei: Xuesheng shuju, 1975.

Fengsu tongyi jiaozhu. By Ying Shao (c. 140–c. 206). Annotated by Wang Liji. 2 vols. Beijing: Zhonghua shuju, 1981.

FUKUI Fumimasa
1983   "Dōkyō to Bukkyō." In Fukui Kōjun et al., eds., *Dōkyō,* vol. 2, pp. 95–134. Tokyo: Hirakawa shuppansha.

FUKUI Kōjun
1957   *Dōkyō no kisoteki kenkyū.* Tokyo: Risosha.
1983   *Shinsenden.* Tokyo: Meitoku.

FUKUI Kōjun, Yamazawa Hiroshi, Kimura Eīchi, and Sakai Tadao, eds.
1983   *Dōkyō.* 3 vols. Tokyo: Hirakawa shuppansha.

FUKUNAGA Mitsuji
1958   "Sha Reun no shisō ni tsuite." *Tōhō shūkyō* 13/14:25–48.

GONG Xuchun
1983   *Sichuan junxian zhi.* Chengdu: Guji shudian.

GU Jiegang and YANG Xiangui
1936   "Sanhuang kao." *Yenching Journal of Chinese Studies,* Monograph Series, no. 8. Beijing: Harvard-Yenching Institute.

GUO Moruo
1965   "You Wang Xie muzhi de chutu lundao 'Lanting xu' de zhenwei." *Wenwu* 6:1–25.

Guoyu. Shanghai: Guji chubanshe, 1978.

Han shu. By Ban Gu (32–92). Beijing: Zhonghua shuju, 1962.

Hou Han shu. By Fan Ye (398–445). Beijing: Zhonghua shuju, 1963.

HU Wenhe and ZENG Deren
1991–1992 "Sichuan daojiao shiku zaoxiang." Parts 1 and 2. *Sichuan wenwu* 1:31–39; 2:39–47.

Huainan zi. By Liu An (c. 120 B.C.E.). In Liu Wendian, ed. *Huainan honglie jijie.* Shanghai: Shangwu yinshuguan, 1923. Reprint, Kyoto: Chūbun shuppansha, 1980.

HUANG Shilin
1991   "Feitian zang di mudiao renxiang." *Sichuan wenwu* 5:31–34.

Huayang guozhi. By Chang Qu (mid–fourth century). Edited and annotated by Liu Lin. Chengdu: Bashu shushe, 1984.

IKEDA On
1981   "Chūgoku rekidai boken ryakkō." *Tōyō-bunka kenkyūjo kiyō* 86:193–278.

ISHII Masako
1980   *Dōkyōgaku no kenkyū.* Tokyo: Kokusho kankokai.
1987   "Shinko ni toku seishitsu ni tsuite." In Akizuki Kan'ei, ed., *Dōkyō to shukyō bunka,* pp. 136–53. Tokyo: Hirakawa.

Jinshi cuipian. Compiled by Wang Chang (1724–1806). Beijing: Zhongguo shudian, 1985.

Jin shu. By Fang Xuanling (578–648) et al. Peking: Zhonghua shuju, 1974.

KALTENMARK, Max
1969 "Ching yü pa-ching." In *Fukui hakase shōju kinen tōyō bunka ronshū*, pp. 1,147–54. Tokyo: Hirakawa.

KAMITSUKA Yoshiko
1982 "Reiho shisho gohen shimbun no shisō to seiritsu." *Tōhō shūkyō* 60:23–48.

KOBAYASHI Masayoshi
1990 *Rikuchō dōkyōshi kenkyū*. Tokyo: Sōbunsha.

KOBAYASHI Taiichirō
1946 "Hōsōshi kueki-kō." *Shinagaku* 11:401–47.

KUSUYAMA Haruki
1979 *Rōshi densetsu no kenkyū*. Tokyo: Sōbunsha.
1983 "Dōtokukyōrui." In *Kōza: Tonkō to Chūgoku Dōkyō*, vol. 4, pp. 3–58. Tokyo: Daitō.
1984 "Seishin deshi kō." In *Chūgoku no shūkyō, shisō to kagaku: Festschrift in Honour of Makio Ryōkai*, pp. 139–55. Tokyo: Kokusho kankōkai.

Laozi. In *SBBY*.

LI Fengmao
1983 "Liuchao daojiao yu yoxian shi di fazhan." *Zhonghua xue yuan* 28:97–118.

Liexian zhuan. Critical edition in Kaltenmark 1953.

Li ji zhengyi. In *SSJZS*.

Lunyu. Text in *Lun-yü yin-te*. Beijing: Harvard-Yenching Institute, 1940.

MAEDA Shigeki
1985 "Rikuchō jidai ni okeru Kan Kichi den no hensen." *Tōhō shūkyō* 65:44–62.

MARUYAMA Hiroshi
1986 "Shōitsu dōkyō no jōshō girei ni tsuite." *Tōhō shūkyō* 68:44–64.
1987 "Jōshō girei yori mitaru shōitsu dōkyō no tokushoku." *Bukkyō shigaku kenkyū* 30.2:56–84.

Mengzi zheng yi. Annotated by Jiao Xun (1763–1820). In *ZZJC*.

MIYAKAWA Hisayuki
1964 *Rikuchōshi kenkyū: Shūkyō hen*. Kyoto: Heirakuji shoten.
1971 "Son On, Ro Jun no ran ni tsuite." *Tōyōshi kenkyū* 30.2–3:1–30.
1972 "Son, Ro Jun no ran hokō." In *Suzuki hakushi koki kinen Tōyōgaku ronshū*, pp. 533–48. Tokyo: Meisō.
1983 *Chūgoku shūkyōshi kenkyū*. Kyoto: Tohosha.

MOCHIZUKI Shinkō
1933–1936 *Bukkyō daijiten*. 10 vols. Tokyo: Sekai seiten kankō kyōkai.

MUGITANI Kunio
1985 "Rōshi sōjichū ni tsuite." *Tōyō gakuhō* 57:75–107.
1985 *Rōshi sōjichū sakuin*. Tokyo: Hōyū shoten.

MURAKAMI Yoshimi
1956   *Chūgoku no sennin.* Kyoto: Heirakuji shoten.
NAKAMURA Shōhachi
1973   *Gogyō taigi.* Tokyo: Meitoku.
ŌFUCHI Ninji
1964   *Dōkyōshi no kenkyū.* Okayama: Okayama daigaku kyōzai-kai shoseki.
1978   *Tonkō dōkyō mokurokuhen.* Tokyo: Fukubu shoten.
1985   "Gokan matsu gotō beidō no soshiki ni tsuite." *Tōhō shū-kyō* 65:1–19.
1991   *Shoki no dōkyō.* Tokyo: Sōbunsha.
Peiwen yunfu. Compiled by Zhang Yushu (1642–1711) et al. 4 vols., including an index vol. Reprint of the 1711 and 1720 block-print editions. Taipei: Shangwu, 1966.
RAO Zongyi
1956   *Laozi xiang'er zhu jiaojian.* Hong Kong: Tong Nam.
1969   "*Laozi xiang'er* zhu xulun." In *Fukui hakase shōju kinen tōyō bunka ronshū,* pp. 1159–71. Tokyo: Hirakawa.
1991   *Laozi xiang'er zhu jiaojian.* Reissue of 1956 edition (q.v.), with new material added. Shanghai: Guji chubanshe.
REN Jiyu, ed.
1990   *Zhongguo daojiao shi.* Shanghai: Renmin chubanshe.
SAKADE Yoshinobu
1983   "Chōsei jutsu." In Fukui Kōjun et al. 1983, vol. 1, pp. 263–65.
1988   *Chūgoku kodai yōsei shisō no sōgōteki kenkyū.* Tokyo: Hirakawa.
Sanguo zhi. By Chen Shou (233–297). Annotated by Pei Songzhi (360–439). Beijing: Zhonghua shuju, 1959.
SASO, Michael R.
1977   "Dōkyō kenkyū no itchi hōhō—Reihō shinbun o rei to shite." *Tōhō shūkyō* 50:22–40.
SCHIPPER, Kristofer M.
1991   "Reihō kagi no tenkai." In Yamada Toshiaki, Sakai Tadao, Fukui Fumimasa, and Yamada Toshiaki, eds., *Nihon, Chū-goku no shūkyō bunka no kenkyū,* pp. 219–32. Tokyo: Hirakawa.
Shangshu (full title: *Shangshu zhengyi*). In *SSJZS.*
Shan hai jing jian shu. Annotated by Hao Yixing (1757–1825). Reprint of the 1886 Huandu lou edition. Shanghai: Zhonghua shuju, 1985.
SHIBATA Kiyotsugu
1984   "*Kanshi* shihen ni okeru shin to dō." *Nihon Chūgoku gak-kai hō* 36:12–24.
Shiji. By Sima Qian (c. 145–c. 85 B.C.E.) and Sima Tan (d. c. 112 B.C.E.). Beijing: Zhonghua shuju, 1959.

Shijing (full title: *Mao shi zhengyi*). In *SSJZS*.

Shishuo xinyu jiaojian. Edited by Xu Zhen'e. Beijing: Zhonghua shuju, 1984.

Shuihudi Qin mu zhu jian. Beijing: Wenwu, 1990.

Shuowen jiezi Duan Zhu. By Xu Shen (30–124). Annotated by Duan Yucai (1735–1815). 2 vols. Reprint of edition with 1808 preface. Chengdu: Guji shudian, 1981.

Song shu. By Shen Yue (441–513). Beijing: Zhonghua shuju, 1974.

SUN Kekuan
   1977   *Hanyuan daolun*. Taipei: Lianjing chuban shiye gongsi.

Su wen (full title: *Huangdi neijing Su wen jiaozhu yu yi*). Edited by Guo Aichun. Tianjin: Kexue jixu chubanshe, 1981.

Taiping guangji. By Li Fang (925–996) et al. Beijing: Zhonghua shuju, 1961.

Taiping jing hejiao. Edited by Wang Ming. Beijing: Zhonghua shuju, 1979.

Taiping yulan. Compiled by Li Fang (925–996) et al. Beijing: Zhonghua shuju, 1960.

TAN Qixiang
   1982   *Zhongguo lishi ditu ji*. Vol. 4. Shanghai: Ditu chubanshe.

TANG Changru
   1983   *Wei Jin Nanbeichao shilun shiyi*. Beijing: Zhonghua shuju.

TANG Yongtong
   1974   *Han Wei liang Jin nanbei chao fojiao shi*. 1938. Reprint, Taipei: Shixue.

WANG Ming
   1984   *Daojia he daojiao sixiang yanjiu*. Beijing: Shehui kexue yuan.

Wenxuan. Hong Kong: Shangwu, 1974.

XIAO Dengfu
   1989   *Han Wei Liuchao Fo Dao liangjiao zhi tiantang diyu shuo*. Taipei: Xuesheng shuju.

XU Zhen'e
   1984   *Shishuo xinyu jiaojian*. Vol. 2. Beijing: Zhonghua shuju.

YANG Liansheng
   1956   "Laojun yinsong jiejing jiaoshi." *Bulletin of the Institute of History and Philology of Academia Sinica* 28:17–54.

YASUI Kōzan and NAKAMURA Shōhachi, eds.
   1971–1978   *Isho shūsei*. 6 vols. Tokyo: Meitoku.

Yijing. Text in *Chou-i yin-te: A Concordance to Yi Ching*. Peking: Harvard Yenching Institute, 1935. Reprint, Taipei: Chinese Materials and Research Aids Center, 1966.

Yi li zhushu. In *SSJZS*.

YOSHIKAWA Tadao
   1992   "Nichichū muei: Shikaisen-kō." In Yoshikawa Tadao, ed.,

Chūgoku kodōkyōshi kenkyū, pp. 175–216. Kyoto: Dōhōsha.

YOSHIOKA Yoshitoyo

1958–1976   *Dōkyō to Bukkyō*. 3 vols. Vol. 1, Tokyo: Nihon gakujutsu shinkyōkai, 1958. Vol. 2, Tokyo: Nihon gakujutsu shinkyōkai, 1959. Vol. 3, Tokyo: Kokushō kankokai, 1976.

1976   "Rikuchō dōkyō no shumin shisō." In *Dōkyō to Bukkyō*, vol. 3, pp. 221–84. Tokyo: Kokushō kankokai.

ZHANG Jiyu

1990   *Tianshi dao shi*. Beijing: Huawen.

Zhou li zhushu. In *SSJZS*.

Zhou yi (full title: *Zhou yi zhengyi*). In *SSJZS*.

ZHU Weizheng

1987   "Zhongguo jingxue yu zhongguo wenhua." In *Zhongguo chuantong wenhua di zai guji*, pp. 109–20. Shanghai: Renmin chubanshe.

Zhuangzi. Text in *Chuang-tzu yin-te: A Concordance to Chuang-tzu*. Peking: Harvard-Yenching Institute, 1947. Reprint, Cambridge: Harvard University Press, 1956.

Zizhi tongjian. By Sima Guang (1019–1086). Beijing: Zhonghua shuju, 1957.

Zuo zhuan zhengyi (full title: *Chunqiu Zuo zhuan zhengyi*). In *SSJZS*.

WESTERN-LANGUAGE SOURCES

AKAHORI, Akira

1989   "Drug Taking and Immortality." In Livia Kohn and Yoshinobu Sakade, eds., *Taoist Meditation and Longevity Techniques*, pp. 73–98. Ann Arbor: Center for Chinese Studies, University of Michigan.

ALLEN, Sarah

1991   *The Shape of the Turtle: Myth, Art, and Cosmos in Early China*. Binghamton, N.Y.: SUNY.

AMES, Roger T.

1981   "Taoism and the Androgenous Ideal." *Historical Reflections: Women in China* 8.3:21–46.

ANDERSEN, Poul

1980   *The Method of Holding the Three Ones: A Taoist Manual of Meditation of the Fourth Century A.D.* London and Malmö: Curzon Press.

1990   "The Practice of Bugang." *CEA* 5:15–53.

1994   "Talking to the Gods: Visionary Divination in Early Taoism (The Sanhuang Tradition)." *TR* 5.1:1–24.

BAUER, Wolfgang

1956   "Der Herr vom Gelben Stein." *Oriens Extremus* 3:137–52.

BELL, Catherine
1988 "Ritualization of Texts and Textualization of Ritual in the Codification of Taoist Liturgy." *HR* 27.4:366–92.
BENN, Charles D.
1991 *The Cavern-Mystery Transmission: A Taoist Ordination Rite of A.D. 711.* Honolulu: University of Hawaii Press.
BODDE, Derk
1975 *Festivals in Classical China.* Princeton, N.J.: Princeton University Press.
BOKENKAMP, Stephen R.
1981 "The *Pacing the Void Stanzas* of the Ling-pao Scriptures." Master's thesis, University of California at Berkeley.
1983 "Sources of the *Ling-pao* Scriptures." In Strickmann 1983, pp. 434–85.
1986 "Ko Ch'ao-fu" and "Ko Hung." In William H. Nienhauser, Jr., ed., *The Indiana Companion to Traditional Chinese Literature,* pp. 479–82. Bloomington: Indiana University Press.
1986 "The Peach Flower Font and the Grotto Passage." *JAOS* 106.1:65–77.
1986 "Taoist Literature through the T'ang Dynasty." In William H. Nienhauser, Jr., ed., *The Indiana Companion to Traditional Chinese Literature,* pp. 138–52. Bloomington: Indiana University Press.
1989 "Death and Ascent in Ling-pao Taoism." *TR* 1.2:1–20.
1990 "Stages of Transcendence: The *Bhūmi* Concept in Taoist Scripture." In Buswell 1990, pp. 119–47.
1991 "Taoism and Literature: The *Pi-lo* Question." *TR* 3.1:57–72.
1993 "Traces of Early Celestial Master Physiological Practice in the *Xiang'er* Commentary." *TR* 4.2:37–51.
1994 "Time after Time: Taoist Apocalyptic History and the Founding of the T'ang Dynasty," *Asia Major,* 3d ser., 7.1: 59–88.
1996 "Answering a Summons." In Donald Lopez, Jr., ed., *Chinese Religions in Practice,* pp. 108–202. Princeton, N.J.: Princeton University Press.
BOLTZ, Judith M.
1983 "Opening the Gates of Purgatory: A Twelfth Century Technique for the Salvation of Lost Souls." In Strickmann 1983, pp. 488–510.
1987 *A Survey of Taoist Literature: Tenth to Seventeenth Centuries.* China Research Monograph no. 32. Berkeley: University of California Press.
BOLTZ, William G.
1979 "Philological Footnotes to the Han New Year Rites" (review of Bodde 1975). *JAOS* 99.3:423–39.

1982 "The Religious and Philosophical Significance of the 'Hsiang Erh' Lao-tzu in Light of the Ma-wang-tui Silk Manuscripts." *BSOAS* 45:95–117.

BRADBURY, Steve

1992 "The American Conquest of Philosophical Taoism." In Cornelia N. Moore and Lucy Lower, eds., *Translation East and West: A Cross-Cultural Approach,* pp. 29–41. Honolulu: University of Hawaii Press.

BUSWELL, Robert E., Jr., ed.

1990 *Chinese Buddhist Apocrypha.* Honolulu: University of Hawaii Press.

CAHILL, Suzanne E.

1993 *Transcendence and Divine Passion: The Queen Mother of the West in Medieval China.* Stanford, Calif.: Stanford University Press.

1994 "Po Ya Plays the Zither: Taoism and the Literati Ideal in Two Types of Bronze Mirrors in the Collection of Donald H. Graham." *TR* 5.1:25–40.

CAMPANY, Robert F.

1990 "Return-from-Death Narratives in Early Medieval China." *Journal of Chinese Religions* 18:91–125.

1993 "Buddhist Revelation and Taoist Translation in Early Medieval China." *TR* 4.1:1–30.

CEDZICH, Ursula-Angelika

1987 "Das Ritual der Himmelsmeister im Spiegel früher Quellen: Übersetzung und Untersuchung des liturgischen Materials im dritten chüan des Teng-chen yin-chüeh." Ph.D. diss., Julius-Maximilians-Universität, Würzburg. Reviewed in Seidel 1988.

CHAN, Alan K. L.

1991 *Two Visions of the Way: A Study of the Wang Pi and the Ho-shang-kung Commentaries on the Lao-tzu.* Albany: State University of New York Press.

CHAVANNES, Edouard

1895–1905 *Les mémoires historiques de Se-ma Ts'ien.* 5 vols. Paris: Leroux.

1910 *Le T'ai Chan—Essai de monographie d'un culte chinois.* Annales du Musée Guimet, vol. 21. Paris: Musée Guimet.

CHEN Shixiang

1953 *Biography of Ku K'ai-chih.* Chinese Dynastic Histories Translations, no. 2. Berkeley: University of California Press.

CONZE, Edward, trans.

1961 *The Large Sutra on Perfect Wisdom.* London: Luzac.

COHN, Norman
1993   *Cosmos, Chaos and the World to Come: The Ancient Roots
              of Apocalyptic Faith.* New Haven, Conn.: Yale University
              Press.
DEMIÉVILLE, Paul
1987   "The Mirror of the Mind." Translated by Neil Donner. In
              Peter N. Gregory, ed., *Sudden and Gradual: Approaches to
              Enlightenment in Chinese Thought,* pp. 13–40. Honolulu:
              University of Hawaii Press.
DESPEUX, Catherine
1989   "Gymnastics: The Ancient Tradition." In Livia Kohn and
              Yoshinobu Sakade, eds., *Taoist Meditation and Longevity
              Techniques,* pp. 225–61. Ann Arbor: Center for Chinese
              Studies, University of Michigan.
EBERHARD, Wolfram
1968   *The Local Cultures of South and East China.* Translated by
              Alide Eberhard. Leiden: E. J. Brill.
1971   *A History of China.* Berkeley: University of California Press.
EICHHORN, Werner
1954   "Description of the Rebellion of Sun En and Earlier Taoist
              Rebellions." *Mitteilungen des Instituts für Orientforschung*
              2.2:25–53 and 2.3:463–76.
1955   "Bemerkungen zum Aufstand des Chang Chio und zum
              Staate des Chang Lu." *Mitteilungen des Instituts für Ori-
              entforschung* 3:291–327.
1957   "T'ai-p'ing und T'ai-p'ing Religion." *Mitteilungen des Insti-
              tuts für Orientforschung* 5:113–40.
ENO, Robert
1990   *The Confucian Creation of Heaven: Philosophy and the
              Defense of Ritual Mastery.* Albany: State University of New
              York Press.
FALKENHAUSEN, Lothar von
1994   "Sources of Taoism: Reflections on Archaeological Indi-
              cators of Religious Change in Eastern Zhou China." *TR* 5.2:
              1–12.
GAUCHET, L.
1949   "Recherches sur la triade taoïque." *Bulletin de l'Université
              Aurore,* ser. 3, no. 10, pp. 326–66.
GIRARDOT, Norman J.
1983   *Myth and Meaning in Early Taoism.* Berkeley: University of
              California Press.
GRAHAM, A. C.
1981   *Chuang-tzu: The Seven Inner Chapters and Other Writings.*
              London: Allen & Unwin.
1986   *Chuang-tzu: The Inner Chapters.* London: Unwin Paper-
              backs.

1989   *Disputers of the Tao: Philosophical Argument in Ancient China.* La Salle, Ill.: Open Court.

GRANET, Marcel
1926   *Danses et légendes de la Chine ancienne.* 2 vols. Paris: Flix Alcan. Reprint, Paris: Presses Universitaires de France, 1959.

HARPER, Donald
1985   "A Chinese Demonography of the Third Century B.C." *HJAS* 45.2:459–98.
1987   "The Sexual Arts of Ancient China As Described in a Manuscript of the Second Century B.C." *HJAS* 47.2:539–93.
1987   "Wang Yen-shou's Nightmare Poem." *HJAS* 47.1:239–83.
1988   "A Note on Nightmare Magic in Ancient and Medieval China." *T'ang Studies* 6:69–76.
1994   "Resurrection in Warring States Popular Religion." *TR* 5.2:13–29.
1996   *Early Chinese Medical Literature: The Mawangdui Medical Manuscripts.* London: Royal Asiatic Society.
forthcoming "Warring States, Qin, and Han Manuscripts Related to Natural Philosophy and the Occult." In Edward L. Shaughnessy, ed., *New Sources of Early Chinese History: An Introduction to Reading Inscriptions and Manuscripts.* Berkeley: Society for the Study of Early China.

HAWKES, David
1985   *The Songs of the South: An Anthology of Ancient Chinese Poems by Qu Yuan and Other Poets.* Harmondsworth: Penguin Books.

HENRICKS, Robert G.
1979   "Examining the Ma-wang-tui Silk Texts of the Lao-tzu: With Special Note of Their Differences from the Wang Pi Text." *TP* 65:166–99.
1989   *Lao-tzu Te-tao ching: A New Translation Based on the Recently Discovered Ma-wang-tui Texts.* New York: Ballantine Books.

HO Peng Yoke
1966   *The Astronomical Chapters of the Chin Shu.* Le Monde d'outre-mer passé et présent, ser. 2: documents, vol. 9. Paris.

HOMANN, Rolf
1971   *Die wichtigsten Körpergottheiten im Huang-t'ing ching.* Göppingen: Verlag Alfred Kummerle.

HOU Ching-lang
1975   *Monnaies d'offrande et la notion de trésorerie dans la religion chinoise.* MIHEC, no. 1. Paris.
1979   "The Chinese Belief in Baleful Stars." In Welch and Seidel 1979, pp. 193–228.

HUCKER, Charles O.
1985   A Dictionary of Official Titles in Imperial China. Stanford,
          Calif.: Stanford University Press.
HULSEWÉ, A. F. P.
1985   Remnants of Han Law. Leiden: E. J. Brill.
JAN Yün-hua
1978   "The Silk Manuscripts on Taoism." TP 63.1:65–84.
JOHNSON, David
1985   "The City-God Cults of T'ang and Sung China." HJAS 45.2:
          363–457.
KALINOWSKI, Marc
1985   "La transmission du Dispositif des Neuf Palais sous les Six
          Dynasties." In Strickmann 1985a, pp. 773–811.
1986   "Les traités de Shuihudi et l'hémérologie chinoise à la fin des
          Royaumes-combattants." TP 72:175–228.
1989–1990 "La littérature divinatoire dans le Daozang." CEA 5:85–
          114.
KALTENMARK, Max
1953   Le Lie-sien Tchouan (Biographies légendaires des immortels
          taoïstes de l'antiquité). Pékin: Université de Paris, Publica-
          tions du Centre d'Études Sinologiques de Pékin. Reprint,
          Paris: Collège de France, 1987.
1968   "Ling-pao—note sur un terme du taoïsme religieux." In
          Mélanges publiés par l'Institut des Hautes Études Chinoises,
          vol. 2, pp. 559–88. Paris: Collège de France.
1969   Lao-tzu and Taoism. Translated by Roger Greaves. Stan-
          ford, Calif.: Stanford University Press.
1979   "The Ideology of the T'ai-p'ing ching." In Welch and Seidel
          1979, pp. 19–52.
1982   "Quelques remarques sur le 'T'ai-chang Ling-pao wou-fou
          siu.'" Zinbun 18:1–10.
KANDEL, Barbara
1979   Taiping Jing: The Origin and Transmission of the 'Scripture
          on General Welfare'—The History of an Unofficial Text.
          Hamburg: Deutsche Gesellschaft für die Natur- und Völker-
          kunde Ostasiens.
KIANG Chao-yuan
1937   Le voyage dans la Chine ancienne, considéré principalement
          sous son aspect magique et religieux. Translated by Fan Jen.
          Shanghai: Commission Mixte des Oeuvres Franco-chinoises.
          Reprint, Ventiane: Éditions Vithagna, 1975.
KIRKLAND, J. Russell
1986   "The Roots of Altruism in the Taoist Tradition." Journal of
          the American Academy of Religion 54.1:61–77.
KLEEMAN, Terry F.
1984   "Land Contracts and Related Documents." In Chūgoku no

shūkyō, shisō to kagaku: Festschrift in Honour of Makio Ryōkai, pp. 1–34. Tokyo: Kokusho kankōkai.

forthcoming   *Great Perfection: Religion and Ethnicity in a Chinese Millennial Kingdom.* Honolulu: University of Hawaii Press.

KLOETZLI, Randy

1983   *Buddhist Cosmology.* Delhi: Motilal Banarsidass.

KNECHTGES, David R.

1982   "Journey to Morality: Chang Heng's 'The Rhapsody on Pondering the Mystery.'" In Chan Ping-leung, chief ed., *Essays in Commemoration of the Golden Jubilee of the Fung Ping Shan Library (1932–1982),* pp. 162–82. Hong Kong: Fung Ping Shan Library.

————, trans.

1982–1987   *Wen xuan—or—Selections of Refined Literature, by Xiao Tong.* 2 vols. Princeton, N.J.: Princeton University Press.

KNOBLOCK, John

1988   *Xunzi: A Translation and Study of the Complete Works.* Vol. 1. Stanford, Calif.: Stanford University Press.

KOHN, Livia

1987   *Seven Steps to the Tao: Sima Chengzhen's "Zuowang lun."* MS Monographs, no. 20. Nettetal: Steyler Verlag.

1989   "The Mother of the Tao." *TR* 1.2:37–109.

KROLL, Paul W.

1985   "In the Halls of the Azure Lad." *JAOS* 105.1:75–94.

1986   "Spreading Open the Barrier of Heaven." *Asiatische Studien/ Études Asiatiques* 40.1:22–39.

LAGERWEY, John

1981   *Wu-shang pi-yao: Somme taoïste du VIe siècle.* PEFEO, no. 124. Paris.

1987   *Taoist Ritual in Chinese Society and History.* New York: Macmillan Publishing Company.

LEGGE, James

1960   *The Ch'un Ts'ew, with the Tso Chuen.* The Chinese Classics, vol. 5. Reprint of 1935 edition, with corrections. Hong Kong: Hong Kong University Press.

1967   *Li Chi: The Book of Rites.* Vol. 2. Reprint. New York: University Books.

LEVY, Howard S.

1956   "Yellow Turban Religion and Rebellion at the End of the Han." *JAOS* 76.1:214–26.

LIEBENTHAL, Walter

1952   "The Immortality of the Soul in Chinese Thought." *Monumenta Nipponica* 8.1/2:327–97.

LINCOLN, Bruce

1983   " 'The Earth Becomes Flat'—A Study of Apocalyptic Imagery." *Comparative Studies in Society and History* 25:136–53.

LOEWE, Michael
   1982   *Chinese Ideas of Life and Death*. London: Allen & Unwin.
MANSVELT-BECK, B. J.
   1980   "The Date of the Taiping Jing." *TP* 66.4–5:149–82.
MASPERO, Henri
   1971   *Le taoïsme et les religions chinoises*. Paris: Gallimard.
   1981   *Taoism and Chinese Religion*. Translated by Frank A. Kierman, Jr. Amherst: University of Massachusetts Press.
MATHER, Richard B.
   1958   "The Landscape Buddhism of the Fifth Century Poet Hsieh Ling-yün." *JAS* 18:67–81.
   1976   *Shih-shuo Hsin-yü: A New Account of Tales of the World*. Minneapolis: University of Minnesota Press.
   1979   "K'ou Ch'ien-chih and the Taoist Theocracy at the Northern Wei Court 425–451." In Welch and Seidel 1979, pp. 103–22.
   1987   "The Life of the Buddha and the Buddhist Life: Wang Jung's (468–93) 'Songs of Religious Joy' (Fa-le Tz'u)." *JAOS* 107.1:31–38.
MICHAUD, Paul
   1958   "The Yellow Turbans." *MS* 17:47–127.
MIYAKAWA Hisayuki
   1979   "Local Cults around Mount Lu at the Time of Sun En's Rebellion." In Welch and Seidel 1979, pp. 83–102.
MOLLIER, Christine
   1986   "Messianisme taoïste de la Chine mdivale: Étude du Dong-yuan shenzhou jing." Ph.D. diss., Université de Paris.
NAKAMURA Hajime
   1980   *Indian Buddhism: A Survey with Bibliographic Notes*. Ogura: Kansai University of Foreign Studies.
NEEDHAM, Joseph
   1956   *Science and Civilisation in China*. Vol. 2, *History of Scientific Thought*. Cambridge: Cambridge University Press.
   1959   *Science and Civilisation in China*. Vol. 3, *Mathematics and the Sciences of the Heavens and the Earth*. Cambridge: Cambridge University Press.
   1962   *Science and Civilisation in China*. Vol. 4, *Physics and Physical Technology*. Pt. 1, *Physics*. Cambridge: Cambridge University Press.
   1974   *Science and Civilisation in China*. Vol. 5, *Chemistry and Chemical Technology*. Pt. 2, *Spagyrical Discovery and Invention: Magisteries of Gold and Immortality*. With the collaboration of Lu Gwei-Djen. Cambridge: Cambridge University Press.
   1976   *Science and Civilisation in China*. Vol. 5, *Chemistry and*

Chemical Technology. Pt. 3, *Spagyrical Discovery and Invention: Historical Survey, from Cinnabar Elixirs to Synthetic Insulin*. Cambridge: Cambridge University Press.

NGO Van Xuyet

1976   *Divination, magie et politique dans la Chine ancienne. Essai suivi de la traduction des "Biographie des Magiciens" tirées de l'"Histoire des Han Postérieurs."* Paris: Presses Universitaires de France.

NICKERSON, Peter

1994   "Shamans, Demons, Diviners, and Taoists: Conflict and Assimilation in Medieval Chinese Ritual Practice (c. A.D. 100–1000)." *TR* 5.1:41–66.

1996   "Taoism, Death, and Bureaucracy in Early Medieval China." Ph.D. diss., University of California at Berkeley.

ŌFUCHI Ninji

1974   "On *Ku Ling-pao ching*." *Acta Asiatica* 27:34–56.

1979   "The Formation of the Taoist Canon." In Welch and Seidel 1979, pp. 253–68.

OVERMYER, Daniel L.

1988   "Buddhism in the Trenches: Attitudes toward Popular Religion in Indigenous Scriptures from Tun-huang." Paper presented at the panel "Rethinking Syncretism," at the annual meeting of the Association of Asian Studies, San Francisco.

OWEN, Stephen

1992   *Readings in Chinese Literary Thought*. Cambridge: Harvard University Press.

OZAKI, Masaharu

1984   "The Taoist Priesthood: From Tsai-chia to Ch'u-chia." In G. Devos and T. Sofue, eds., *Religion and Family in East Asia*, pp. 97–109. Osaka: National Museum of Ethnology.

PETERSEN, Jens

1989–1990 "The Early Traditions Relating to the Han Dynasty Transmission of the *Taiping jing*." Parts 1 and 2. *Acta Orientalia* 50:133–71; 51:173–216.

POKORA, Timoteus

1985   " 'Living Corpses' in Early Mediaeval China—Sources and Opinions." In G. Naundorf, K. H. Pohl, and H. H. Schmidt, eds., *Religion und Philosophie in Ostasien: Festschrift für Hans Steininger*, pp. 343–57. Würzburg: Königshausen und Neumann.

PREGADIO, Fabrizio

1991   "The Book of the Nine Elixirs and Its Tradition." In Yamada Keiji and Tanaka Tan, eds., *Chūgoku kodai kagakushi ron*, vol. 2, pp. 543–639. Kyoto: Kyoto daigaku jinbun kagaku kenkyūjo.

READ, Bernard
1977   *Turtle and Shellfish Drugs.* Vol. 3 of Bernard Read, ed.,
            Chinese Materia Medica. Reprint of 1937 edition. Taipei:
            Southern Materials Center.
RIEGEL, Jeffrey K.
1990   "Kou-mang and Ju-shou." *CEA* 5:55–84.
ROBINET, Isabelle
1976   "Les randonées extatiques des Taoïstes dans les astres." *MS*
            32:159–273.
1977   *Les commentaires du Tao To King jusqu'au VIIe siècle.*
            MIHEC, no. 5. Paris.
1979   *Méditation taoïste.* Paris: Dervy-livres.
1979   "Metamorphosis and Deliverance from the Corpse in Tao-
            ism." *HR* 19.1:57–70.
1983   "Le Ta-tung Chen-ching." In Strickmann 1983, pp. 394–
            433.
1984   *La révélation du Shangqing dans l'histoire du taoïsme.*
            PEFEO, no. 137. 2 vols. Paris.
1991   *Histoire du taoïsme: Des origines au XIVe siècle.* Paris: Cerf.
1993   *Taoist Meditation: The Mao-Shan Tradition of Great Purity.*
            Translated by Julian F. Pas and Norman J. Girardot. Albany:
            State University of New York Press.
ROTH, Harold D.
1990   "The Early Taoist Concept of *Shen:* A Ghost in the Ma-
            chine?" In Kidder Smith, Jr., ed., *Sagehood and Systematiz-
            ing Thought in Warring States and Han China,* pp. 11–32.
            Brunswick, Maine: Bowdoin College Asian Studies Center.
RUMP, Ariane, and CHAN Wing-tsit
1979   *Commentary on the Lao-tzu by Wang-pi.* Honolulu: Univer-
            sity of Hawaii Press.
RUSSELL, Terence C.
1985   "Songs of the Immortals: The Poetry of the Chen-kao."
            Ph.D. diss., Australian National University.
SAILEY, Jay
1978   *The Master Who Embraces Simplicity: A Study of the Phi-
            losophy of Ko Hung (A.D. 283–343).* San Francisco: Chi-
            nese Materials Center.
SALOMON, Richard
1990   "New Evidence for a Gāndhārī Origin of the Arapacana Syl-
            labary." *JAOS* 110.2:255–73.
SASO, Michael R.
1972   *Taoism and the Rite of Cosmic Renewal.* Seattle: University
            of Washington Press.
SCHAFER, Edward H.
1962   *The Golden Peaches of Samarkand: A Study of T'ang Exot-
            ics.* Berkeley: University of California Press.

1967   *The Vermilion Bird: T'ang Images of the South*. Berkeley: University of California Press.

1977   *Pacing the Void: T'ang Approaches to the Stars*. Berkeley: University of California Press.

1978   "The Jade Woman of Greatest Mystery." *HR* 17:387–98.

1978   "Li Po's Star Power." *Bulletin of the Society for the Study of Chinese Religions* 6:5–15.

1978   "The Transcendent Vitamin: Efflorescence of *Lang-kan*." *Chinese Science* 13:27–38.

1980   *Mao Shan in T'ang Times*. Boulder, Colo.: Society for the Study of Chinese Religions.

1981   "Two Taoist Bagatelles." *Bulletin of the Society for the Study of Chinese Religions* 9:1–18.

1981–1983   "Wu Yün's Stanzas on Saunters in Sylphdom." *MS* 35: 309–45.

1985   *The Eight Daunters*. Schafer Sinological Papers, no. 21. Berkeley, Calif.

1985   *Mirages on the Sea of Time: The Taoist Poetry of Ts'ao T'ang*. Berkeley: University of California Press.

SCHIPPER, Kristofer M.

1965   *L'empereur Wou des Han dans la légende taoïste*. PEFEO, no. 58. Paris.

1975   *Concordance du Houang-t'ing King*. PEFEO, no. 104. Paris.

1978   "The Taoist Body." *HR* 17:355–86.

1979   "Le Calendrier de Jade: Note sur le Laozi zhongjing." *Nachrichten der Gesellschaft für die Natur- un Völkerkunde Ostasiens* 125:75–80.

1982   *Le corps taoïste*. Paris: Fayard.

1985   "Vernacular and Classical Ritual in Taoism." *JAS* 45:21–57.

1993   *The Taoist Body*. Translated by Karen C. Duval. Berkeley: University of California Press.

SCHLEGEL, Gustav

1875   *Uranographie chinoise*. 2 vols. Reprint, Taipei: Chengwen, 1967.

SCHMIDT, Hans-Hermann

1985   "Die hundertachtzig Vorschriften von Lao-chün." In G. Naundorf, K. H. Pohl, and H. H. Schmidt, eds., *Religion und Philosophie in Ostasien: Festschrift für Hans Steininger*, pp. 151–59. Würzburg: Königshausen und Neumann.

SCHWARTZ, Benjamin L.

1985   *The World of Thought in Ancient China*. Cambridge: Harvard University Press.

SEIDEL, Anna K.

1969   *La divinisation de Lao-tseu dans le taoïsme des Han*. PEFEO, no. 71. Paris.

468 Works Cited

1970 "The Image of the Perfect Ruler in Early Taoist Messianism." *HR* 9:216–47.

1978 "Das neue Testament des Tao—Lao tzu und die Entstehung der taoistischen Religion am Ende der Han-Zeit." *Saeculum* 29:147–72.

1978 "Der Kaiser und sein Ratgeber—Lao Tzu und der Taoismus der Han-Zeit." *Saeculum* 29:18–50.

1981 "Kokuhō: Note à propos du terme 'trésor national' en Chine et au Japon." *BEFEO* 69:229–61.

1982 "Tokens of Immortality in Han Graves." *Numen* 29.1:79–114.

1983 "Imperial Treasures and Taoist Sacraments: Taoist Roots in the Apocrypha." In Strickmann 1983, pp. 291–371.

1984 "Le sūtra merveilleux du Ling-pao Suprême, traitant de Laotseu qui convertit les barbes (le manuscrit TH S.2081)—Contribution a l'étude du Bouddho-taoïsme des Six Dynasties." In M. Soymié, ed., *Contributions aux études de Touenhouang*, vol. 3 (PEFEO, no. 135), pp. 305–52. Paris.

1985 "Geleitbrief an die Unterwelt—Jenseitvorstellungen in den Graburkunden der späteren Han-Zeit." In G. Naundorf, K. H. Pohl, and H. H. Schmidt, eds., *Religion und Philosophie in Ostasien: Festschrift für Hans Steininger*, pp. 161–83. Würzburg: Königshausen und Neumann.

1987 "Afterlife: Chinese Concepts." In *The Encyclopedia of Religion* 1:124–27.

1987 "Post-Mortem Immortality, or: The Taoist Resurrection of the Body." In *GILGUL: Essays on Transformation, Revolution and Permanence in the History of Religions*, pp. 223–37. Leiden: E. J. Brill.

1987 "Traces of Han Religion in Funeral Texts Found in Tombs." In Akizuki Kan'ei, ed., *Dōkyō to shūkyō bunka*, pp. 21–57. Tokyo: Hirakawa.

1988 "Early Taoist Ritual" (review of Cedzich 1987). *CEA* 4:199–204.

1989–1990 "Chronicle of Taoist Studies in the West, 1950–1990." *CEA* 5:223–347.

1990 *Taoismus: Die inoffizielle Hochreligion Chinas*. Tokyo: Deutsche Gesellschaft für die Natur- und Völkerkunde Ostasiens.

SIVIN, Nathan
1966 "Chinese Conceptions of Time." *Earlham Review* 1:82–92.

1969 *Cosmos and Computation in Early Chinese Mathematical Astromony*. Leiden: E. J. Brill.

1969 "On the *Pao-p'u-tzu nei-p'ien* and the Life of Ko Hung." *Isis* 40:388–91.

1980 "The Theoretical Background of Elixir Alchemy." In Joseph

Needham, *Science and Civilisation in China*, vol. 5 (*Chemistry and Chemical Technology*), pt. 4 (*Spagyrical Discovery and Invention: Apparatus, Theories, and Gifts*), pp. 210–305. Cambridge: Cambridge University Press.

SMITH, Thomas E.

1990   "Record of the Ten Continents." *TR* 2.2:87–119.

STEIN, Rolf A.

1942   "Jardins en miniature d'Extrême-Orient." *BEFEO* 42:1–104.

1963   "Remarques sur les mouvements du taoïsme politico-religieux au IIe siècle ap. J.C." *TP* 50:1–78.

1979   "Religious Taoism and Popular Religion from the Second to the Seventh Centuries." In Welch and Seidel 1979, pp. 53–81.

1987   "Sudden Illumination or Simultaneous Comprehension: Remarks on Chinese and Tibetan Terminology." Translated by Neil Donner. In Peter N. Gregory, ed., *Sudden and Gradual: Approaches to Enlightenment in Chinese Thought*, pp. 41–66. Honolulu: University of Hawaii Press

1990   *The World in Miniature: Container Gardens and Dwellings in Far Eastern Religious Thought*. Translated by Phyllis Brooks. Stanford, Calif.: Stanford University Press.

STEWART, G. A.

1987   *Chinese Materia Medica: Vegetable Kingdom*. Reprint of 1911 edition. Taipei: Southern Materials Center.

STRICKMANN, Michel

1977   "The Mao-shan Revelations: Taoism and the Aristocracy." *TP* 63:1–64.

1979   "On the Alchemy of T'ao Hung-ching." In Welch and Seidel 1979, pp. 123–92.

1981   *Le taoïsme du Mao chan: Chronique d'une révélation*. Paris: Collège de France, Institut des Hautes Études Chinoises.

1985   "Therapeutische Rituale und das Problem des Bösen im frühen Taoismus." In G. Naundorf, K. H. Pohl, and H. H. Schmidt, eds., *Religion und Philosophie in Ostasien: Festschrift für Hans Steininger*, pp. 185–200. Würzburg: Königshausen und Neumann.

1987   "Demonology and Epidemiology." In *Magical Medicine: Therapeutic Rituals in Mediaeval China*. Manuscript.

1988   "Dreamwork of Psycho-Sinologists: Doctors, Taoists, Monks." In Carolyn T. Brown, ed. *Psycho-Sinology: The Universe of Dreams in Chinese Culture*, pp. 25–46. Washington: Woodrow Wilson International Center for Scholars.

1990   "The *Consecration Sūtra*: A Buddhist Book of Spells." In Buswell 1990, pp. 75–118.

1991   *Mantras et mandarins: Le bouddhisme tantrique en Chine.*
            Manuscript.

————, ed.
1983   *Tantric and Taoist Studies in Honour of R. A. Stein.* Vol. 2.
            MéLanges chinoises et bouddhiques, no. 21. Brussels: Insti-
            tut Belge des Hautes Études Chinoises.
1985a   *Tantric and Taoist Studies in Honour of R. A. Stein.* Vol. 3.
            Mélanges chinoises et bouddhiques, no. 22. Brussels: Institut
            Belge des Hautes Études Chinoises.

THOMPSON, Laurence
1985   "Taoism: Classic and Canon." In M. Denny and R. L. Tay-
            lor, eds., *The Holy Book in Comparative Perspective,* pp.
            204–23. Columbia: University of South Carolina Press.
1989   "On the Prehistory of Hell in China." *Journal of Chinese
            Religions* 17:27–41.

TOKUNO, Kyoko
1990   "The Evaluation of Indigenous Scriptures in Chinese Bud-
            dhist Bibliographical Catalogues." In Buswell 1990, pp. 31–
            74.

TS'AO T'ien-ch'in, HO Ping-Yü, and NEEDHAM, Joseph
1959   "An Early Mediaeval Chinese Alchemical Text on Aqueous
            Solutions." *Ambix* 7:122–58.

TSUKAMOTO Zenryū
1985   *A History of Early Chinese Buddhism.* Translated by Leon
            Hurvitz. 2 vols. Tokyo: Kodansha.

UNSCHULD, Paul U.
1985   *Medicine in China: A History of Ideas.* Berkeley: University
            of California Press.

VANDERMEERSCH, Léon
1965   *La formation du Légisme.* PEFEO, no. 56. Paris.

VERELLEN, Franciscus
1985   *Du Guangting (850–933)—un taoïste de cour à la fin de la
            Chine médiévale.* Mémoires de l'IHEC, no. 30. Paris: De
            Boccard.
n.d.   "La Liturgie de Tu Kuang-t'ing." Manuscript.

WARE, James R.
1966   *Alchemy, Medicine and Religion in the China of A.D. 320:
            The Nei P'ien of Ko Hung.* Reprint, New York: Dover Pub-
            lications, 1981.

WATSON, James L.
1982   "Death Pollution in Cantonese Society." In Maurice Bloch
            and Jonathan Parry, eds., *Death and the Regeneration of
            Life,* pp. 155–86. Cambridge: Cambridge University Press.

WECHSLER, Howard J.
1985   *Offerings of Jade and Silk: Ritual and Symbol in the Legit-*

imation of the T'ang Dynasty. New Haven, Conn.: Yale University Press.

WELCH, Holmes, and SEIDEL, Anna, eds.

1979   *Facets of Taoism: Essays in Chinese Religion.* New Haven, Conn.: Yale University Press.

WILE, Douglas

1991   *Art of the Bedchamber: The Chinese Sexology Classics.* Albany: State University of New York Press.

WILHELM, Richard

1920   *Dschuang Dsi—Das wahre Buch vom südlichen Blütenland.* Preface dated "Tsingtao, 1912." Jena: Eugen Diederichs.

1950   *The I Ching or Book of Changes.* Translated by Cary F. Baynes. Bollingen Series, no. 19. Princeton, N.J.: Princeton University Press.

WOLF, Arthur P.

1974   *Religion and Ritual in Chinese Society.* Stanford, Calif.: Stanford University Press.

WU Hung

1986   "Buddhist Elements in Early Chinese Art." *Artibus Asiae* 47:263–376.

YAMADA Toshiaki

1989   "Longevity Techniques and the Compilation of the *Lingbao wufuxu.*" In Livia Kohn and Yoshinobu Sakade, eds., *Taoist Meditation and Longevity Teachings,* pp. 99–124. Ann Arbor: Center for Chinese Studies, University of Michigan.

YÜ Ying-shih

1964   "Life and Immortality in the Mind of Han China." *HJAS* 25:80–122.

ZÜRCHER, Erik

1959   *The Buddhist Conquest of China.* 2 vols. Leiden: E. J. Brill.

1977   "Late Han Vernacular Elements in the Earliest Buddhist Translations." *Journal of the Chinese Language Teacher's Association* 12.3:177–203.

1980   "Buddhist Influence on Early Taoism." *TP* 66:84–147.

1982   "Prince Moonlight." *TP* 68.1–3:1–75.

Index

Compositor: Asco Trade Typesetting Ltd.
       Text: 10.5/13.5 Sabon
    Display: Sabon
    Printer: Edwards Brothers, Inc.
    Binder: Edwards Brothers, Inc.